INDUSTRIAL RELATIONS AND LABOUR MANAGEMENT OF BANGLADESH

IQBAL AHMAD

Professor

Institute of business administration

Order this book online at **www.trafford.com**
or email orders@trafford.com

Most Trafford titles are also available at major online book retailers.

Printed in the United States of America.

ISBN: 978-1-4269-9651-1 (sc)
ISBN: 978-1-4269-9652-8 (e)

Trafford rev. 04/04/2013

 www.trafford.com

North America & International
toll-free: 1 888 232 4444 (USA & Canada)
phone: 250 383 6864 ♦ fax: 812 355 4082

To my Parents : Zahanara Ahmad and Alauddin Ahmad

ABOUT THE AUTHOR

IQBAL AHMAD is a Professor of Human Resource Management in the Institute of Business Administration of University of Dhaka.

He did his B. Sc (Hons) and M.Sc from University of Dhaka. After completing his education he joined in a public limited company and during liberation war of Bangladesh he participated in the war as a freedom fighter. After independence he joined in Bangladesh Jute Mills Association and got his practical experience of running jute mills. Before joining liberation war he completed his post graduate degree in Personnel Management in the first batch on Personnel Management. This helped him run the mills. He observed that labor relations in practical and knowledge he gathered from the post graduate degree is far away due to prominent local conditions. To rather more in depth analysis and better understanding he went to Institute of Social Studies, The Hague, Netherlands, to study Industrial Relations. After obtaining his post graduate degree he worked as a research associate of a project on Labor Relations of Ghana for two years. To have better understanding on total management of business he went to Aston University, Birmingham, UK to study M.Sc in Industrial Administration in the year 1976.During his stay in Netherlands and UK he attended many international seminars and workshops including working in the then Yoguslavakia. After completing his degree Prof Iqbal Ahmad came to Bangladesh and joined the Institute of Business Administration as Assistant Professor on September 1978.

His present position he has to teach, research and provide professional services to different national and international organizations. He was the director of Sadharan Bima Corporation (General Insurance Company owned by the Government) which is one the largest insurance companies of Bangladesh. As a fellow of UNDP and World Bank he worked with George Washington University, Washington DC and Institute of Social Studies in Manila, Philippines. He was the fellow of National Productivity Organization and made several research works on supporting industry and small industry. Still he is the board member of Institute of Small Cottage Industry of Bangladesh. As fellow of ARIES, he went to Harvard University to attend workshop on "Teaching and Writing Case Study" in the year 1994.

He has also served as consultant to Asian Development Bank and Word Bank, Ministry of Youth and Sports and Ministry of Women Affairs. He worked as economist in Flood Action Plan for two years. He has been Chairman and Managing Committee Members of many educational institutions. He works with many private organizations including Non Government Organization as a professional member.

Prof Iqbal has been working as neutral member of Minimum Wages Board, of the Government of the Peoples" Republic of Bangladesh since 2002. He is also the Director of Bangladesh Biman National Airless. He has published book on Human Resource Management, Organizational Behavior and Application Labor Laws of Bangladesh. Besides that one case study book on micro credit was published by PRIP. He is active member of Rotary Club of Dhaka Downtown of Rotary International District 3280 and this club has published a book on adult literacy named, "Dishari" (means to provide guide and right direction).

PREFACE

The purpose of this book is to provide a general introduction of Industrial Relations with a critical analysis of Cox model of Industrial Relations and Trade Union Movement of Bangladesh. Now days in Bangladesh both public and private universities are teaching Industrial Relations as one of the major subjects of MBA and BBA program. This book will serve the academic purpose as well as to appeal to the largest possible readership and professional In Bangladesh mangers, supervisor and trade unionists confronting each other every day without understanding the process they are engaged. This book should also be useful to the public and specialist groups like teachers.

My experience as an administrator of a mill as well as teachers over a number of years in the class room and also as trainer in executive development programs of different professional institutions has made me aware that there is a need for a text book like this. I try not only to explain the Bangladesh industrial relations practices and to put them into their social perspectives. To have deeper and better understanding of industrial relations and trade union movement in Bangladesh one has to understand socio-economic-political, legal and psychological behavior of three actors namely Owner-professional, Worker-Trade Union Leaders and ideology of the government who govern the country.

The variety of industrial relations changes after independent of Bangladesh in 1972 with nationalizing all industries and denationalizing and emerging of new generation of entrepreneur as an industrialist has contributed to look at or to examine the industrial relations in more descriptive, analytical and conceptual frameworks. Further I like to state that in understanding this task of writing book, my complementary academic and teaching backgrounds and with the experience of working with Minimum Wage Board as a neutral member, my previous and present industrial experiences have given me some degree of balance to study and write this book.

One of the main objectives of this book is to make it informative and thought-provoking and to show the uniqueness of Bangladesh industrial relations and encourages its readers to understand the industrial relations phenomena, complexity and behavior.

In developing this book, I am indebted to many institutions and individuals—my graduate students of Institute of Business Administration and my colleagues of Dhaka University, human resource and labor relations managers and national and local union representatives and who have provided me with insights and background information. I am grateful to Sanjida Yeasmin Meer who helped me to complied the all works and Khondaker Sayeedul Haque who has gone through the first draft of the book. My special thanks to A.K.Roy who is currently Chairman of Minimum Wage Board former session judge for his valuable suggestions on couple of chapters. I am also grateful to ABM Nasiruddin who always encourage me to write this book. I do also acknowledge the service of Parthasharothi Mujumdar who renders his service for designing the pages of this book in computer.

Finally, I owe to my wife, Ferdous Iqbal, Tuhin for providing me support to undertake an academic career and to my son Ejaj Ahmad who is Harvard graduate, has grown up and succeeded despite his father's failings.

Iqbal Ahmad
IBA, Dhaka University
Bangladesh
April 2013

CHAPTER I

Bangladeshi Workers'

CONTENTS

1.0 Labor Conditions of Bangladesh

Bangladesh is a developing country in South Asian region with 130 million[1] of people. According to Labor Force Survey 2000 of the Bangladesh Bureau of Statistics (BBS), the total estimated civilian labor forces of the country is 60.3 million and among them 37.81% are female.

In Bangladesh, the active labor force is estimated to be 53.5 million. Of the total workforce, 38% are women. Unemployment rate is 3.3% and underemployment is estimated to be around 32%.

Among the workers, agricultural workers constitute 62.3%, industrial workers 7.6% and others 30.1%. As for sector-wise contribution to GDP: Agriculture 23.46%, Manufacturing 27.17%, service and other sectors 49.83%. It is notable that agriculture produces a medium-sized share of the GDP but it generates huge employment. In a country where unemployment and underemployment are prevalent problems, this is very significant.

1.1 Workers Defined

Literally worker means a person who works in an organization. But in The Bangladesh Labor Code, 2006 'worker' is defined more specifically. The exact definition of worker is given in labor act 2006. The labor act 2006 defines, in section 2(65), "worker" as 'any person including an apprentice employed in any establishment or industry, either directly or through a contractor, to do any skilled, unskilled, manual, technical, trade promotional or clerical work on hire or reward, whether the terms of employment be expressed or implied.

The law excludes employees of certain government organizations, educational or research institutions, charity organizations, and interestingly: workers of agricultural farm that employs less than ten workers.

An important question is regarding the status of migrant workers who are drawing the economy forward by sending remittances. They are not included under the labor law, but their significance is undeniable.

From a macroeconomic perspective or for preparing national accounting statements, the migrant workers can be properly excluded from the description. But if some on wants' to understand workers of Bangladesh from a more sociologically-oriented point of view, i.e. as a historically created dynamic social class, then the migrant workers must be included in exploration or description.

On the other hand, the term "Industrial Workers" refers to a very broad category of laborers that comprises factory workers, assemblers and mechanics, custodial and maintenance staff and many other semi-professional and non-professional workers. By definition industrial plants are factories where products are made in mass quantities, often using automated methods to increase productivity.

Industrial workers may perform any number of tasks related to chemical or mechanical construction of products, from unpacking materials to cutting and assembly to packaging of finished products.[2]

1.2 Classification of Bangladeshi Workers

The Labor Law 2006 classifies workers according to the type and nature of work:

1. Trainee: A worker who is employed in the organization for learning, and receives an allowance during training
2. Badli: If the worker is employed as a replacement for some permanent or apprentice worker.
3. Temporary: If the appointment is temporary.
4. Part-time: If the worker is employed for some work which is essentially part-time and which can be performed within a limited time.
5. Apprentice: If the worker is employed in some permanent post on adhoc and if his/her apprenticeship is not over yet.
6. Permanent: If the worker is employed permanently, or has finished the apprenticeship satisfactorily.

1.3 Working Condition in Bangladesh

According to the EIU Country Profile, 2008[3] the Bangladeshi labor force almost doubled in a matter of a decade, growing from 30.9 million people in 1985-86 to 56.0 million people in 1995-96. Although all sectors of the national economy experienced significant growth, they were far below the speed of the labor force growth. According to Bangladesh national statistics, in 1995-96 only 12.4 percent of the labor force had formal employment, while 40 percent were considered "employed in family-based" businesses, 29.6 percent were considered "self-employed," and 17.9 percent had their jobs on a "daily basis."

1.4 Wage and Productivity Conditions

In general, Bangladesh is known for cheap labor. Bangladeshi workers receive one of the lowest levels of wage in the world. Workers of the export industries, such as workers in factories involved in leather processing, shoe making, jute yarn manufacturing, shrimp processing and production of medicine; receive world's lowest wages. The average monthly wages of Bangladeshi garments factories are even less than one-third of the global average, despite the high-quality stitching by the female workers of Bangladesh. A recent global survey of the world's garment industries by the US-based consulting house, the Jassin-O'Rourke Group, shows that a Bangladeshi garment worker gets only 22 US cents per hour. A garment worker receives 33 cents in Cambodia, 38 cents in Vietnam, 37 cents in Pakistan, 43 cents in Sri Lanka, 44 cents in Indonesia, 51 cents in India, 86 cents in China, $1.07 in the Philippines and $1.18 in Malaysia.

There is no National minimum wage. The pay, allowances and other remunerations of the non-industrial public sector employees are determined by the National Pay Commission. The National Wage and Productivity Commission fix the wage and fringe benefits of public sector industrial workers at an average interval of five to seven years. These commissions are appointed by the government. The Minimum Wage Board fixes the wages of only individual private enterprises if demanded.

At the same time, due to low level of education and lack of training and expertise, the productivity level of the workers is also generally low. The low productivity may also be attributable to lack of research and development as well as insufficient technological progress. Bangladesh lags behind as productivity here is only 42 per cent compared to more than 70 per cent in China and around 60 per cent in India.

But productivity may not be only due to the fault of workers; management and marketing skills of managers is also very important.

1.5 Demographics of Bangladeshi Workers

The World Bank (1996), however, indicates that it is possible for Bangladesh to meet this challenge but this will require increasing GDP growth rate by seven to eight percent and finding employment for over 50 million people in the next 25 years. To do this, the World Bank argues, will require a shift away from subsistence agriculture to the introduction of high-yielding cash crops and a growth of employment in manufacturing industries such as garments and the like. Although Bangladeshi workers are praised as hard-working, flexible and loyal, there will be the need for huge investment in productive sector. Emphasis should be given on the reform of education as well as on health services. National and local governance will also need to be reformed and made more effective and there needs to be encouragement of private rather than state-owned enterprises. Added to this, the need to preserve environmental sustainability and improvement of the transport and power infrastructure are 'challenges' involving huge cost. However, the demographic trend through reducing the dependent young population may work to make this feasible.

1.6 Living Conditions of Workers

A problem faced by workers, especially in urban areas, is the lack of proper accommodation. This problem is severe in case of women workers in Bangladesh. Khan (1993:77) notes that it is terribly expensive for a single person to rent an accommodation on her own. It is also difficult to find a landlord who would let out his place to a single woman. 73.4% female workers live in a house with family and only 1.5% lives alone.

   a. **Bostee:** A "bostee" is equivalent to a squatter settlement. In Bangladesh a bostee comprises of a group of thatched or tin-roofed one-room houses that stand next to each other with inadequate shared sanitation facilities. An interview with the inhabitants of different bostees reveals that usually the rent is between Tk.800 to Tk.1800 per month. Sometimes there is electricity and stove with private bath facilities. Sometimes all of these facilities are absent and residents depend on polluted lake water for a bath, cook with fuel wood and burn kerosene lamp or hurricane as a substitute of electricity. Those living in bostees are subject to unhealthy living environment. It is also insecure in the sense that sometimes bostees are uprooted by the law enforcing agencies because most of the time they are built on others land without permission and proper papers.

b. **Factory Accommodation:** In some factories, especially in the EPZ areas, the company provides workers with accommodation facilities.

c. **Group Housing or Mess:** Many property owners are now interested in building 'mess' for garment workers and the demand for these mess are on the rise. However, living in the 'mess' is quite insecure for women as these are owned by 'mastans' or local touts. Women staying there are often easy prey because of its motel-oriented atmosphere where anyone can stay overnight and disappear the following day. No one ensures security for the residents either. These messes are very crammed and there are no recreation facilities.

1.7 Industrialization in Bangladesh

During the 20th century, Bangladesh like neighboring Burma (Myanmar) and Nepal largely missed the industrialization wave that changed the economies of many countries in the Asian region, such as Malaysia, Singapore, and Taiwan. At the beginning of 2001, manufacturing contributed about 24.3 percent of the GDP, providing employment to 6.2 million people or 11 percent of the workforce. Between 1989 and 1999, the manufacturing sector in Bangladesh grew at an average annual rate of around 7.2 percent, albeit from a very low base. The cheap, reliable, and abundant labor available in Bangladesh is attractive to the world's leading transnational corporations, but they have been very slow to move into the country, as they face regular industrial unrest led by radical trade unions, poorly developed infrastructure, red tape, and a very small local market. As in neighboring India, the Bangladeshi government promoted the idea of state-led industrialization combined with heavy state involvement in and state control of enterprise activities.

1.7.1 Industrial Policy of Bangladesh

The role of the industry sector, specially manufacturing, is indispensable for enhancing economic growth. The Fifth Five Year industrial policy plan of Bangladesh envisages that Bangladesh will have a sizable industrial sector competitive in both the deregulated domestic and international market. The vision of industrialization is to ensure that the manufacturing sector contributes 25% of GDP by 2010 which was 15.91% in 2002-2003[4] and at least 20 per cent of the employed workforce in place of present 7.7 percent. A vibrant and dynamic private sector will be the principal actor in Bangladesh's industrial arena. The goals of export orientation and external competitiveness imply the pursuit of industrialization in accordance with the dynamic comparative advantage of the economy. Given Bangladesh's resource endowment, the principle of dynamic comparative advantage means production of labor intensive manufactures with skill up-gradation and productivity growth as its cutting edge. Decentralized small and medium industries will constitute important elements in the industrial scene of Bangladesh. Industrial Policy, 1999 aims at addressing these concerns and builds on earlier efforts and gains towards industrialization of Bangladesh economy.

1.7.2 Main Targets of the Industrial Policy

Liberalization of industrial policy in Bangladesh started with the announcement of Industrial Policy, 1982 of Peoples' Republic of Bangladesh. This was followed by successive and progressive liberalization in 1991, 1992 and 1999 to make it compatible with globalization and competitive market economy. The targets of the policy are to:

1. Develop the industrial sector in order to increase its contribution to GDP, income, employment and poverty alleviation
2. Expand industries by the private sector and make role of Government 'promotional' rather than 'regulatory'
3. Encourage domestic and foreign investment in overall industrial and infrastructure development
4. Promote private sector—led export—oriented growth
5. Develop export-oriented, export-linkage and efficient import-substitute industries
6. Expedite development of labor intensive industries through acquisition and improvement of appropriate technology
7. Encourage the development of agro-based and agro-supportive industries and
8. Motivate investment in the intermediate and basic industries.

1.7.3 Impact of Government's Industrial Policy

The impact of government policies on various industrial sectors of Bangladesh has been considerable. In cases of main industrial segments like Readymade Garment agro-based, oil and gas etc, the government reforms and strategies have brought about many advantages.

Basically all the first three five year plans had focused on poverty alleviation. The country's fourth five year plan (1990-95) was the first plan that paid special attention to the gender issue in development and aimed to lessen gender discrimination in all socio-economic activities. Since the launch of the Millennium Development Goals (MDGs) at the Millennium Summit in New York in September 2000, the MDGs have become the most widely accepted yardstick of development efforts by governments, donors, and NGOs (United Nations 2000). Almost all the countries in the world including Bangladesh, have committed themselves in attaining the targets embodied in the Millennium Declaration by 2015.

Since the year 2000, government has liberalized the industrial and investment policies in recent years by reducing bureaucratic control over private investment and opening up many areas. Tax reduction has been a major strategy implemented by the government of Bangladesh in this regard.

Following are some financial incentives provided to various industries in Bangladesh.

1.7.4 Major incentives are as follows[5]:

- **Tax Exemptions:** Generally 5 to 7 years. However, for power generation exemption is allowed for 15 years.

  1. Dhaka and Chittagong Divisions (excluding 3 Hill Tract Districts of Chittagong Division) (5 years)
  2. Khulna, Sylhet, Barisal and Rajshahi Divisions And 3 Chittagong Hill Tract Districts (7 years)

- **Duty:** No import duty for export oriented industry. For other industry, it is @ 5%.
- **Tax Law:**

  1. Double taxation can be avoided in case of foreign investors on the basis of bilateral agreements.
  2. Exemption of income tax up to 3 years for the expatriate employees in industries specified in the relevant schedule of Income Tax ordinance.

- **Remittance:** Facilities for full repatriation of invested capital, profit and dividend.
- **Exit:** An investor can wind up on investment either through a decision of the AGM or EGM. Once a foreign investor completes the formalities to exit the country, he or she can repatriate the sales proceeds after securing proper authorization from the Central Bank.
- **Ownership:** Foreign investor can set up ventures either wholly owned or in joint collaboration with local partner.

The industrial enterprises of Bangladesh concentrate mainly on the production of jute goods, ready-made garments, foodstuff processing, and chemical production. Most of Bangladeshi jute goods are produced in large state-controlled enterprises for export to the United States, Europe, and other markets, contributing Tk. 13.3 billion in 1997-98 to the country's export earnings and Tk. 11.7 billion in 1998-99.

According to the EIU Country Profile, Bangladesh accounts for 90 percent of world jute fiber exports. The jute processing enterprises are vulnerable to downturns in the regional and international market and experienced some recession in 1998-99. Additionally, during the last few years the demand for jute in the international market has been in decline due to increasing use of synthetic materials in the areas where jute was previously used. However, these jute processing businesses still have plenty of the cheap local supply of raw materials and, if they continue to improve the quality of their products, with efficient management and marketing they may expand their export potential.

During the last 2 decades i.e. after 1990s, Bangladesh has found a strong niche in ready-made garments (RMG), becoming one of the world's leading exporters of these products. BGMEA, a conglomerate of 3600 Garment Manufacturers and Exporters directly employs over 1.8 million workers, 80 per cent of which are women and most of them are from the downtrodden rural households who would otherwise have been the net burden to the society. RMG has turned them into income generating members of their families on one hand and critical parts of the engine-of-growth of Bangladesh on the other.[6]

With the growth of RMG industry, linkage industries supplying fabrics, yarns, accessories, packaging materials, etc. have also expanded. In addition, demand for services like transportation, banking, shipping and insurance has increased. All these have created additional employment. More than 0.8 million workers are engaged in accessory industries related to the garment industries. Moreover, total indirect employment created by the RMG industry in Bangladesh is estimated to be some 10 million workers.[7]

Access to cheap and reliable local labor makes Bangladeshi RMG manufacturers very competitive in the international market, although most of the fabrics and machinery must be imported (in 2000 Bangladesh imported 160,000 metric tons of cotton from the United States). According to the U.S. Department of State, total clothing exports reached about US$5 billion in 1999-2000, mainly to the United States, Europe, and Canada. Bangladesh especially benefited from the multi-fiber arrangement with the United States and the generalized system of preferences with the European Union, which set special quotas for the RMG imports from Bangladesh. Though the RMG sector experienced rapid growth since 2000, with the rise of free trade and elimination of the quota system at the end of 2004, Bangladesh was supposed to face very tough competition from other Asian countries such as China, India, Indonesia, Thailand, and Vietnam. But the fact is not the same. Bangladesh is doing quite well in the RMG sector by leading the South Asian countries.

Bangladesh has a well-established food processing sector, which relies on domestic agricultural production and is oriented mainly to domestic needs. It includes sugar refining and milling, production of edible oils, processing and preserving of fruits and fruit juices as well as fish processing, especially shrimp and prawns. As a tropical country Bangladesh has a plentiful domestic supply of exotic fruits and sea species.

In the 1990s two major changes affected the development of the industrial sector in Bangladesh. First, the end of the numerous military coups and the establishment of civil government brought in political stabilization, which attracted direct international investments and encouraged the inflow of foreign aid. Secondly, the policy of economic liberalization, structural adjustment, and privatization helped to increase the competitiveness of the local industries and encouraged them to search for new overseas markets. In order to promote the attractiveness of the Bangladesh economy, the government established special export-processing zones (EPZs).

The eight EPZs are Chitagong, Dhaka, Karnaphuli, Ishwardi, Adamjee, Comilla, Mongla and Nilphamari's Uttara EPZs, where investors are given access to well-developed infrastructure and enjoy tax breaks and other privileges. Generally there are 3 types of investors who invest in Bangladesh EPZs. These are:

Type-A

100% foreign owned including Bangladesh nationals ordinarily resident abroad.

Type-B

Join venture between foreign and Bangladesh entrepreneur's resident in Bangladesh.

Type-C

100% Bangladeshi entrepreneurs who resides in Bangladesh.

The cumulative investments of over 500 companies in the eight EPZs are $1.53 billion and the companies' employ 0.23 million people.[8] As of July 2008, by the FY 2008-2009, the EPZs had attracted around US$ 1451.65 million worth of foreign investments. Companies from 33 countries invested in the EPZs with South Korea being the number one investor. South Korean companies invested $357 million and the next biggest foreign investor is Japan with $171 million. Most of the companies have invested in garments, textiles, terry towel, knit and other textiles while seven companies produce agro-products.[9]

The companies supply products to globally famous companies including Nike, Adidas, Wal Mart, K Mart, Sony, Mitsubishi, Nissan, Hino, Reebok, Gap, JC Penny, Fuji, Konika, Wrangler and Minolta.

1.8 Industry

Industry, in a general sense, refers to the production of goods and services in an economy. The term industry also refers to a group of enterprises (private businesses or government-operated corporations) that produce a specific type of good or service-for example, the beverage industry, the gold industry, or the music industry.

Some industries produce physical goods, such as lumber, steel, or textiles. Other industries-such as the airline, railroad, and trucking industries-provide services by transporting people or products from one place to another. Still other industries, such as the banking and restaurant industries, provide services such as lending money and serving food, respectively. Industry can be divided in three major parts. These are

1. **Primary Industry:** This includes fishery, pottery, agro based industries etc
2. **Secondary industry:** This includes textiles industry, glass factories, electronic and light industry etc.
3. **Tertiary industry:** This includes services like banking industries, restaurants etc.

The main industries of Bangladesh are readymade garments, Textiles, Jute, Chemical fertilizers, Pharmaceuticals, Tea processing, Paper & newsprint, Cement, Light engineering, Sugar, Leather goods. Whereas principal exports are readymade garments and knitwear, Frozen fish, Jute and jute goods, Pharmaceutical products, Tea, Leather products, Handicrafts, Chemicals.

The Industry and Labor Wing has separated sectors that are not related to agricultural activities. Those sectors are: (i) Small Manufacturing (ii) Wholesale & Retail Trade (iii) Hotel & Restaurant (iv) Service and (v) Household based economic activities.

These sectors have been divided into two groups, namely, small establishments and large establishments. In the manufacturing sector the small establishments are those that employ 1-9 people, and those that employ 10 or more people have been classed as large establishments. In the wholesale and retail trade, hotel and restaurant and service sectors the establishments that employ 1-19 people are called small establishments and those employing 20 or more people are large establishments. The household sector has been placed only in the small group irrespective of the number of persons engaged.

According to the report 'BANGLADESH CENSUS OF MANUFACTURING INDUSTRIES (CMI), 2001-2002[10] published by Bangladesh Bureau of Statistics in 2001-2002 FY the number of total establishments were 28065 when in 1999-2000 FY the number were 29573.

Number of Establishment		1995-96	1996-97	2002-03
Small Manufacturing Sector (AEIS)	**Total**	15,002	1,62,789	2,11,401
	By Ownership			
	Government	-	-	-
	Semi Government	-	-	-
	Private	15,002	1,62,789	2,11,401
	Joint Venture	-	-	-
	Others	-	-	-
	Number of Employees	593936	597608	590459
Wholesale and Retail Trade Sector (AEIS)	**Total**	10,93,977	10,99,296	15,74,334
	By Ownership			
	Government	15	125	179
	Semi Government	10,93,442	10,98415	15,67,204
	Private	401	754	143
	Joint Venture	119	2	6808
	Others			
	Number of Employees	1,59,3826	16,64,272	21,04,310
Hotel & Restaurant Sector (AEIS)	**Total**			2,15,103
	By Ownership			
	Government			713
	Semi Government			0
	Private			2,14,159
	Joint Venture			231
	Others			-
	Number of Employees			2,15,103
Service Sector (AEIS)	**Total**	5,98,169	5,05,412	9,46,413
	By Ownership			
	Government	36,694	27,117	19,004
	Semi Government	4,88,415	3,92,854	5,54,667
	Private	453	464	10,910
	Joint Venture	72,606	84,978	61,832
	Others			
	Number of Employees	14,78,166	13,33,496	17,36,767

Table 1 : Key Findings of Annual Establishment & Institution Survey[11]

1.9 Bangladesh: Labor Force

Occupationally, 75 percent of the civilian labor force, which is currently estimated at 56 million, is directly or indirectly engaged in agriculture. Only 12 percent is engaged in industry. Unemployment is estimated at around 18.5 percent.

Composition of the total, Employed and Unemployed labor force of Bangladesh (In Millions)										
	1961	1974	1981	1983-84	1984-85	1985-86	1989-90	1999-2000	2002-03	2005-06
Total Civilian Labor Force	16.9	21.9	25.9	28.5	29.5	30.9	50.7	40.7	46.3	49.5
Employed Labor Force	16.8	21.4	25.3	28.0	29.0	30.6	50.1	39.0	44.3	47.4
Unemployed Labor Force	0.8	0.5	0.6	0.5	0.5	0.3	0.6	1.7	2.0	2.1

Table 2 : Composition of the total, Employed and Unemployed Labor Force of Bangladesh (in millions)[12]

The above table shows the composition of the total labor force of Bangladesh from different past years—employed and unemployed. The percentage of the unemployed labor force to the total labor force indicates that the number of jobs is not increasing as fast as the size of the labor force increasing.

1.9.1 Size and Structure of the Labor Force

	Labor Force Survey (15+ Population)		
	1999-2000	2002-2003	2005-2006
Employment by Major Occupation (Million)			
Total	39	44.3	47.4
Professional, Technical	1.6	1.7	2.2
Administrative, Managerial	0.2	0.1	0.2
Clerical Workers	1.2	1.5	1.0
Sales Workers	5.8	6.5	6.7
Service Workers	2.2	2.0	2.8
Agriculture, Forestry and Fisheries	19.3	22.8	23.0
Production and Transport Labors and others	8.1	9.7	11.5
Employment by Major Industry (Million)			
Total	39	44.3	47.4
Agriculture, Forestry and Fisheries	19.8	22.9	22.8
Mining and Quarrying	0.2	0.1	0.1
Manufacturing	3.7	4.3	5.2
Electricity, Gas and Water	0.1	0.1	0.1
Construction	1.1	1.5	1.5
Trade, Hotel and Restaurant	6.1	6.7	7.8
Transport, Storage and Communication	2.5	3.0	4.0
Finance and Business Service and Real Estate	0.4	0.3	0.7
Health, Education, Public Administration and Defense	-	2.5	2.6
Community and Personal Services	5.1	2.7	2.6

Table 3 : Employment by Major Occupation and Industry

Table 3 presents statistics of employment from two aspects—Employment by major occupations and employment by major industry. The total number of labor force has increased to 47.4 millions in 2005-06 FY from 39 million in 1999-00 FY. In case of major occupations Administrative, Managerial job participation has remained same. On the other hand in case of major industry participation has increased except in Community and personal services and mining and quarrying.

	Labor Force Survey (15+ Population)		
	1999-2000	2002-2003	2005-2006
Employment by Broad Economic Sector (%)			
Total	100	100	100
Agriculture	51.3	51.7	48.1
Non-Agriculture	48.7	48.3	51.9

Table 4 : Employment by Broad Economic Sector (%)[13]

Table 4 gives percent wise change in distribution of labor force in agriculture and non-agriculture sectors from 1999-00 FY to 2005-06 FY. The above table shows that labor force participation in agriculture sector has decreased and moved to non-agriculture sector by 3.2% in 5 years.

	Labor Force Survey (15+ Population)		
	1999-2000	2002-2003	2005-2006
Employment by Sector (Millions)			
Formal Sector			
Total	9.6	9.2	10.2
Male	8.4	7.3	8.6
Female	1.2	2.0	1.6
Informal Sector			
Total	29.3	35.1	37.2
Male	22.7	27.2	27.5
Female	6.6	7.9	9.7

Table 5 : Employment by Sector[14]

The above table shows that more people are employed in the informal sector than formal sector which are 29.3% and 9.6% respectively.

The survey shows that in 2005-06 highest 23% labor force was engaged in agriculture, forestry and fisheries sector. Production and transport is the second highest (11.5%) employment occupation. But among the non-agro based workers most workers are involved in sales. Whereas in case of industry based employment, after agriculture comes the trade, hotel and restaurant industry which is 7.8%. But for both the cases, it is seen that the labor force participation trend moved upwards from 1999 to 2006.

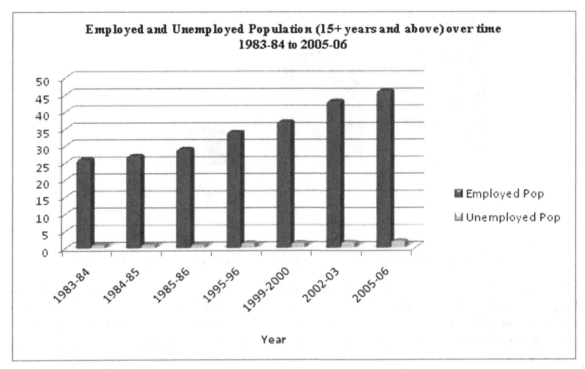

Figure 1 : Employed and Unemployed Population (15+ years and above) over time

In table 6 employed and unemployed populations over time is presented. It shows that from 1983 to 2006 in 23 years employed population has increased by 19.5 million as the total labor force also increased in a significant number. It is also a matter of fact that as the number of jobs is limited, unemployed labor force has also increased by 1.6 million in these 23 years.

Figure 1 is the graphical presentation of table 6 which clearly shows the increasing number of the employed as well as unemployed labor force.

Year	Total	Male	Female
2005-06	49.5	37.4	12.1
2002-03	46.3	36.0	10.3

Table 6 : Economically Active Population (15+ years and above) by Sex 2002-2003 and 2005-2006

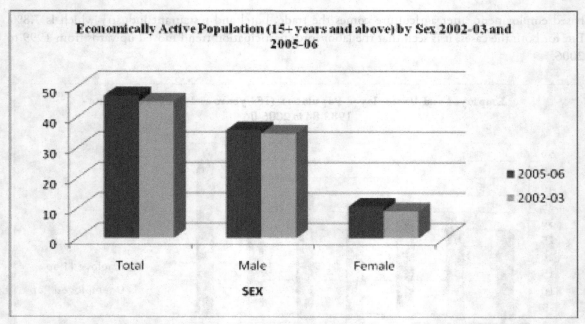

Figure 2 : Employed and Unemployed Population (15+ years and above) Over Time

Table 7 is about the number of economically active population (by sex). It compares the number change in year 2005-06 and 2002-03. It is observed from the table that the number of female labor force is almost 1/3rd of male labor force. The change in the number of male and female labor force separately from 2003 to 2006 is very insignificant which is clearly visible in figure 2 that graphically presents table 7.

	Number (in million) of Labors Engaged in Agro and Non-agro Based Sectors		
	1999-2000	2002-2003	2005-2006
Agriculture Workers (in percent)	19.3 49.5%	22.8 51.5%	23.0 48.5%
Non-agriculture Workers (in percent)	19.7 50.5%	21.5 48.5%	24.4 51.5%

Table 7 : Number (in million) of Labors Engaged in Agro and Non-agro Based Sectors

The above table shows that the number of agro-based labors has been decreased in past decades. In 1999-2000 periods when it was 49.5%, in 2005-2006 periods it becomes only 48.5%.

On the other hand the number of non-agro based workers has been increased in past decades. In 1999-2000 periods when the labor force was 50.5%, in 2005-2006 periods it has become 51.5%.

2.0 Industry Overview: Current Scenario

2.1 Garments Industry

The Ready-made Garments (RMG) industry is the flagship of Bangladesh. Since the late 1970s, the RMG industry started developing in Bangladesh primarily as an export-oriented industry.

The sector rapidly attained high importance in terms of employment, foreign exchange earnings and its contribution to GDP. The apparel industry employs directly more than 1.5 million workers of different skills, about 90.5% of who are female. The total indirect employment created by the RMG industry in Bangladesh is estimated to be some 200,000 workers.

The hundred percent export-oriented RMG industry experienced phenomenal growth during the last 15 or so years. In 1978, there were only 9 export-oriented garment manufacturing units, which generated export earnings of hardly one million dollar. Till the end of 1982, there were only 47 garment manufacturing units. The breakthrough occurred in 1984-85, when the number of garment factories increased to 587. The number of garment manufacturing units shot up to 3127 by March 2000.[15] Bangladesh is now the 12th largest apparel exporters of the world, the sixth largest supplier in the US market, (largest supplier among the South Asian countries) and the fifth largest supplier of T-shirts in the EU market. The industry has grown during the 1990s roughly at the rate of 22%. In the past, until 1980, margin and jute goods topped the list of merchandises exported from Bangladesh and contributed more than 50% of the total export earnings. By late 1980s, RMG exports replaced jute and jute goods and became the number one in terms of exports.

2.2 Condition of Garments Workers in Bangladesh: Different Social Issues

In reality, the condition of garments workers in Bangladesh is very bad. There are some changes due to the labor unrest, trade union movements and social pressure and for the pressure of developed countries consumers. But till now living standard of workers is unacceptable.

It is observed that many garment factories do not follow the labor laws and ILO conventions. Most of the cases the workers cannot enjoy the weekly holiday. There is no job security, social security, gratuity or provident fund for the garment workers. In most of the cases, the management does not provide appointment letters/ contract letters, identity cards and service books.

2.3 Working Hours

According to section 102 of labor code 2006 any adult worker could perform overtime-duty 8 hours per day including extra 2 hours. S/He would neither let nor allow working more than 48 hours per week. The total working hour of an adult worker would not exceed 10 hours per day and 60 hours per week or 56 hours on average per week in a year. But in most of the cases workers are forced to work 14 to 16 hours per day. Sometimes, they work whole night. Overtime work is often made compulsory and forceful but wages are withheld. According to subsection (1) (b) of section 65 of The Factories Act, 1965 (E.P. Act no. IV of 1965), no women would let to work other then the time between 7:00 am—8:00 pm. But most of the time women workers are deprived from Equal wage, Equal dignity, Equal rights and Equal promotions. Physical and sexual abuse in the workplace is common where most are girls as young as 12 years old.

2.4 Housing

There are no housing facilities for garments workers from the owners. Maternity leaves are not excused and even transportation facilities are not available. Lack of doctors, first aid, adequate light and ventilation are not present either. In some cases, there are no sufficient and pure drinking water and toilets for the workers. Health-safety and security condition are not sufficient.

2.5 Trade Unions

Management does not allow the workers to join the trade union or formation of trade union though the workers have the trade union rights according to the labor law and ILO conventions. Management fires the workers if he/she joins the trade union. Workers who try to set up a union are not protected before its registration and so are often subjected to harassment from their employers, which sometimes assume a violent form with police support.

2.6 Wages for the Garments Workers

The International Textile, Garment, and Leather Workers' Federation (TGLW) reports that an average garment worker makes less than tk. 75 (US $1) a day in Bangladesh, a paycheck stretched even thinner by the 33% rise in rice prices since last year. The ITGLW was urging the government of Bangladesh to restore full union rights and raise wages for garment workers, who drive the country's most lucrative industry.

There was no law for the national minimum wage. In 1994, the minimum wage for the unskilled garment workers was fixed at Tk. 930/ per month for the unskilled workers and Tk. 2300/ for skilled workers. This minimum wage was not revised for a very long time. But at last on October 5th, 2006 the Minimum Wage Board announced a pay structure for the workers in the readymade garment (RMG) sector fixing Tk. 1,662.50 as the minimum monthly wage including basic salary, house rent and other allowances for the entry-level workers.[16]

2.7 Ship Breaking Industry

The ship breaking industry has started its operation in 1960's and it was widely spread after 1980's in Sitakundu, Chittagong. There are 79 ship-recycling yards located on the beach of the Bay of Bengal in Sitakundu upazila of Chittagong, which is about 8-10 kilometers from the Chittagong city. At present only 19 ship-recycling yards are operating though not on regular basis. On an average 10 to 20 ships are recycled annually in those yards. It is found that there are only two shipyards that are able to build ocean going ships: one is called Karnafuli Shipbuilders and other one is called Anand Ship Builders.[17]

Since the government has not declared the sector as industry there are different types of commercial arrangements. With the Inspectorate of Factories and Establishments only 8 (eight) ship recycling yards are registered under the Factories Act 1965 and the rest are registered as commercial enterprises under the Companies Act 1913.

It's a very-big and profitable industry for Bangladesh. The activities contributed in many ways; those are:

1. **Production of steel:** The scrapping of ships provides the country's main source of steel and in doing so saves substantial amount of money in foreign exchange by reducing the need to import steel materials. Bangladesh needs 8 million tons of building materials per year, of which iron is a major component. The iron from recycled ships supplies around 90% of iron materials in the country. This does mean however, that the owners have more power and control over the amount of steel that is sold and the price it is sold at.
2. **Supply Raw Materials:** Almost everything on the ship and the ship itself is recycled, reused and resold. The scrapping of ships supplies raw materials to steel mills, steel plate re-manufacturing, as well as providing furniture, paint, electrical equipment and lubricants, oil to the number of businesses that have sprouted up specifically as a result.
3. **Generates Revenue:** It generates large amounts of revenue for various Government authorities through the payment of taxes. Every year the Government collects almost 9000 million taka in revenue from the ship breaking industry.
4. **Employment:** Despite the conditions that the workers are employed under, this is an industry that employs more than 30,000 people directly and 250, 000 more indirectly. It provides employment for some of the poorest people from the north of Bangladesh who would otherwise have no employment.

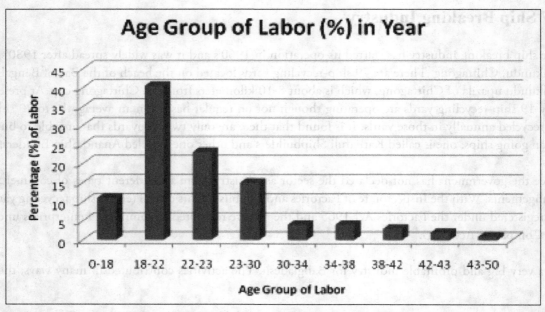

Figure 3 : Major Districts of Labor (%) in Yards

The above figure shows that 24.15% labors are from Bogra. But it is clear from the figure that most of the labors are coming from north Bengal. Poverty, lack of employment and education forces them to work in this sector. The working labors bring their relatives frequently.

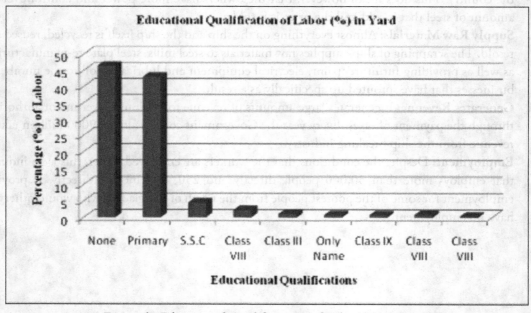

Figure 4 : Educational Qualifications of Labor (%) in Yards

It is observed from the figure that a huge number of labors (46.42%) are illiterate and 43.02% labors are educated up to primary education. The huge uneducated labor force has less scope for better professional jobs within and outside the sector. Less accessibility to different opportunities including information for exercising rights as they are less exposed to education and information etc.

2.8 Labor outside the Yard

There are many forward and backward linkage industries, which depend on ship breaking. Many labors engage in these industries bearing earlier bitter experiences of hard working in ship breaking industries. The labor inside and outside the yard, stay together in some places. The outside labor realize the problems of labor in the yard, they feel the pain honestly as because they are also deprived from their rights in many aspect. But labors outside the yard are in better position than the labor inside the yard.

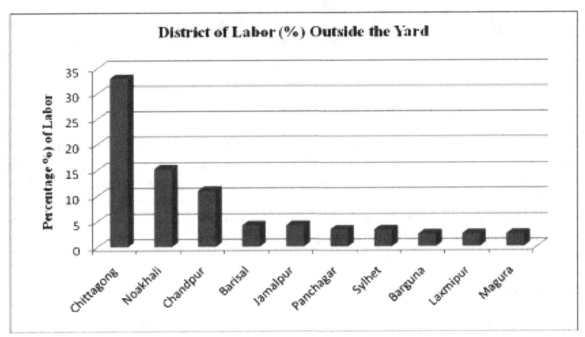

Figure 5 : Age Group of Labor (%) Outside the Yard

From the figure it is observed that 10.17% labor are child, 27.12% labor are between age 18-22 year, 27.97% labor are between the age 22-26 year and 22.03% labor are between age 26-30 year. These are the major age groups of the labor outside the yard. Marital status of labor: Married-39.83%, Unmarried-59.32%, Divorced-0.85% Child and adult: Child 9.32%, Adult Male-82.20%, Adult Female-8.47% Districts of labor: Labor outside the yard is from 24 different districts.

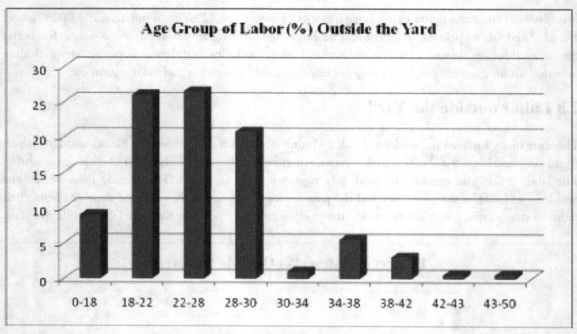

Figure 6 : Districts of Labor (%) Outside the Yard

33.05% labors are from Chittagong; this is because the local labors are not interested to the hard work of the yard. Some of them think, working inside the yard is an inferior job and they are also not too needy to engage in hard working job of the yard. The labor from Noakhali and Chandpur are 15.25% and 11.02% respectively. Most of the labor from Noakhali and Chandpur work in furniture shops. Another thing is that outside the yard the labor from the north Bengal are not dominated. 35.59% labors are illiterate, 42.37% labor have only primary education and 6.78% labor are S.S.C passed which is the most important finding.

2.9 Status of Social Security[18]

There is no kind of social security schemes for the workers in the ship breaking yards. If any worker is seriously injured, disabled and loses life at workplace, the labor contractor/shipyard owner provides some nominal amount of compensation to victimized worker or his family.

3.0 Status of Occupational Training of Workers[19]

The study found that the workers in the ship breaking yards do not have any professional training on ship scraping work. The workers first join in the job as helper and then gradually become skill labor.

3.1 Status of Occupational Health and Safety in the Ship Breaking Yards[20]

The health and safety facility in the visited ship breaking yards at the Sitakundu are far below from the expected minimum general standard. From inside and outside it looks like a scrap mountain. Various sizes of metal objects, working tools, small LP gas cylinders, unguarded house machine, metal chains and ropes, oxygen cylinders are left in the ground in unsafe condition. The ground workplaces inside the yards are most of the muddy.

Frequent movement of the groups of labors inside the yard area with noise is a common characteristic of the scrap yards at Sitakundu. The occupational accidents, injury and deaths are very frequent and normal event among employers and workers. Due to geographical isolation from the main city, very often little news comes outside the scrap yards, to the press or the public eye.

3.2 Causes of the Accidents[21]

The following are some reasons for causing accidents in the shipyards:

1. Purchase of unclean ships by the owners.
2. Lack of proper knowledge, technical ability of the ship-scraping yards to scrap the ship by applying the scientific low cost methods.
3. Absence of training of occupational safety, health and environment among the workers and management personnel in the ship scraping-yards.
4. Lack of personal safety equipment and necessary facilities inside the every ship-breaking yard.
5. Weak application of safety laws by concerned government agencies at the ship breaking yards.
6. Lack of positive discussion among the workers and employers regarding work place hazards and risks of accidents.
7. Lack of labor inspection facility and monitoring facility inside the yards on regular basis.

3.3 Use of Child Labor in the Ship Breaking Yards[22]

The use of child labor in the ship breaking yards with hazardous job is visible in every yard. There are around 2000 child labor (10-14+) engaged in different types of jobs in the ship scrap yards at Sitakundu. Most of them work as helper under various groups. Some of them work for very long hours and some work for fixed work hrs (8 hrs). From eight hours of labor, the child gets Tk.50-60 on average.

The owners and labor contractors mainly use the child labor to collect the small metal objects falling and hiding inside the mud during cutting work. Some of the child worker works as the helper of the cutter man. The children who work in the ship breaking industry are from the poverty stricken family.

3.4 Current Scenario

Bangladesh's ship building industry has entered to a new age after two ship builders grabbed order worth over $250 million in 2007 as said by ship builders on February 3, 2008[23].

Meghnaghat-based Ananda Shipyards has signed agreements worth around $180 million while Chittagong-based Western Marine put its total orders to more than $70 million. Ananda Shipyard has so far received orders to build 14 ships worth US$200 million, company officials told in a briefing in Dhaka on February 18, 2008. The ships will be delivered to German, Danish and Mozambique buyers by 2010. On March 14, 2008, another Bangladesh shipbuilding company, Highspeed Shipbuilding & Engineering Co Ltd, signed a memorandum of understanding with a Dutch firm to supply eight sea-going ships worth US$87 million[24].

Shakhawat Hossain, managing director of Western Marine expects that if Bangladesh can grab one per cent of the global order for small ships, the amount will be worth $4.0 billion. The global market for small ships is now about $400 billion. Experts said it was only a matter of time before Bangladesh emerges as a major hub for building small ocean-going ships.

3.5 Textile Industry

Bangladesh's textile industry, which includes knitwear and woven garments along with specialized textile products, is the nation's number one export earner. The sector, which employs 2.2 million workers, exports mainly to Europe and North America. Job creation in the sector has been particularly strong for women in poor countries, who previously had no income opportunities other than the household or the informal sector. It accounts for 75 per cent of Bangladesh's total exports of US$10.53 billion in FY 2005-06, in the process logging a record growth rate of 24.44 per cent. However, since May of 2006 the industry has been plagued by on-going industrial unrest, as textile workers, who are among some of the most lowly paid in the world, have staged regular violent demonstrations in a bid to achieve a higher minimum wage, regular rest days and safer working conditions.

3.6 Wage Disputes

Textile workers in Bangladesh get paid as little as five pence (Tk 6.9/=)[25] an hour to make cheap clothes for UK companies Tesco, Asda and Primark. The mainly female workers regularly spend 80 hours per week in "potential death trap" factories. Starting wages at the factories were as little as £8 (BDT 909.09)[26] a month, barely one third of the living wage. Wages rose to £16 (BDT 1818.2) per month for better-paid sewing machine operators, but that some workers spent up to 96 hours per week in the factories without even a day a week off.

Following the worst of the 'unrest' in late May, 2008 which saw at least one worker killed as police shot live rounds at protesters the government formed a Wage Board, ordering it to report on a suitable new minimum wage in three months.

The Commission, which included business and worker representatives, finally released its conclusions on October 9, recommending the wage be set at Tk 1,662.50, up from the current level of Tk. 950, but far below initial worker demands for Tk. 3,000.

Prior to the Minimum Wage Board's announcement of its recommended minimum wage, the rate had remained unchanged at Tk. 950 for more than 12 years. Although the government may allow up to three years for the new wage to be implemented, and inevitably there will be compliance issues as manufacturers drag their feet, it seems politically untenable for wages to remain at their current levels given the unprecedented industrial unrest.

3.7 Safety Concerns

The estimated 3,600 garment factories in Bangladesh have appalling safety conditions. Most factories are overcrowded and do not have functioning fire extinguishers and fire blankets. Factory owners commonly lock fire exits and use them for storage, practices that are illegal under Bangladesh's labor regulations. Factories rarely train staff in fire safety, do not have heat and smoke detectors and lack emergency lights and public announcement systems. They are also notorious for faulty electrical wires and switchboards and often do not have enough water to douse fires.

According to fire service officials, there have been 62 known fire incidents in garment and textile factories since 1990, costing over 350 lives. Hundreds more lives have been lost in textile factory building collapses. Factory fires can dent international confidence in the Bangladesh garment industry.

Although major foreign buyers like Primark, Tesco and Asda had all signed up to a set of principles to provide 'decent'[27] working conditions and wages for workers in their supply chain, some of their suppliers were "regularly violating" such rules.

Buyers are highly interested to work closely with the Bangladesh government to ensure that their labor standards are taken seriously.

Labor Abuse

Sewing operators are paid around a measly sum of BDT 6.9 to BDT 9.7 an hour and forced to work 10 ½ to 14 hours a day, seven days a week. They were routinely at the factory 74 to over 90 hours a week.

Workers report being slapped and hit, denied maternity leave, and docked a day's wages for arriving late, needing permission to use the toilet, only having access to unsafe drinking water, total denial of freedom of association and right to organize.

Workers have never heard of, let alone seen, any U.S. companies' codes of conduct.

Late payment of wages is common. As a result, workers often live in squalid conditions. Physical and sexual harassment is widespread.

Workers commonly work longer than the 72-hour week and are often forced to work on Friday, the weekly rest day.

Safety standards are virtually non-existent in Textile industries. In February 2007, more than 50 workers were killed and another 150 badly burned in the country's worst industrial fire. About 500 workers were trapped inside when fire broke out and many had to jump as one of the two exits was locked. Factories rarely have elementary safety measures such as fire alarms and extinguishers. More than 400 garment workers died since 1990 in factory fires but the figure is certainly much higher, as most are not officially recorded.

3.8 Tea Industry[28]

Tea Industry was pioneered in the 19th century by the British planters. Later, some Indian entrepreneurs purchased tea gardens from their European owners. Indian entrepreneurs also came forward to develop new plantations.

After the Partition of Bengal in 1947, East Pakistan inherited 133 tea estates covering 30,350 hectare and their annual production was 18.80 million kg of tea. Tea production rose to 25.17 million kg in 1964, but the rate of growth of production in the province was lower than that in major tea producing countries. Annual domestic consumption rose sharply from 13.15 million kg in 1949 to 22.59 million kg in 1962-63. During this period, export of tea declined because of increased consumption at home, especially in West Pakistan.

The war of liberation in 1971 caused severe damage to the tea industry of Bangladesh. Then the new government of Bangladesh appointed a committee in 1972 to make detailed study of the problems faced by the industry. The committee suggested measures to raise productivity and to reduce cost of production and marketing. Requirements identified by the committee included more intensive cultivation, replacement of old and uneconomic tea plants, use of improved seeds and clones, growth of subsidiary crops, modernization of factories, and grant of financial incentives for establishing co-operative factories for the benefit of small gardens.

In Bangladesh there are three kinds of ownership of tea gardens: foreign owned sterling companies, Bangladeshi Joint Stock Companies and privately owned proprietary tea estates. In early 1990s, a total of 12 sterling companies were in tea business. They owned 26 gardens; all located in Maulvibazar and Habigang districts. Fifty Bangladeshi companies owned and operated 73 gardens, of these the National Tea Company owned 12 and 57 were under proprietorship management.

3.9 Tea Workers

Most of the tea estates are located in the northeast region of Bangladesh. The first tea garden was established by the Duncan Brothers. Since then all the tea gardens have been established by clearing jungles. Those who did the jungle clearing were non-locals brought by Duncan from Assam, Bihar, Madras, Orissa and other places in India.

The tea workers with different ethnic identities are people who are less-talked-of and forgotten. They are not well aware of their origins. Their lives in Bangladesh are confined to the tea gardens and they do not interact much with people of other ethnic identities. They do not speak their language perfectly and most of them are illiterate.

As they are a socially excluded group, they are a very easy target for exploitation by the profiteers from the tea industry.

4.0 Size of household and number of school-going children[29]

In Bangladesh, the big size of a family is a negative factor affecting the productivity of female pluckers since the domestic demands of big household is very high on them. The average size of the tea workers' household has been found to be 5.6 persons.[30] Among the family members, 32 per cent are adult male, 30 per cent are adult female and the remaining 38 per cent are children. At the national level also, male outnumbered female (Census of 2001).

4.1 Living Conditions

The tea industry management provides each permanent worker with a house. But husband and wife do not get two houses even if they are permanently employed in the tea plantation. Workers, both male and female, have a right by tradition or convention to live in this house as a family unit and use the surrounding courtyards as a perk of their employment. Their children inherit this house after their death. Living conditions in these houses were found to very subhuman. More than five people live in a room of only 222 square feet. Cooking and living are done in the same room. In many cases, cows and goats are reared in a corner of the same room by building a partition. Not only is the room small, but its windows and doors are also very small. Most of the rooms have mud walls and straw roof.

It is very disappointing to know that in this age of technological development, about 68 per cent of the tea workers use open space as their toilet. More men than women use open space. Only about 19 per cent of the workers use sanitary toilet.

Very few households (a little more than 10 per cent) use electricity even though there is no supply of electricity in the labor line.

4.2 Wage Rate, Incentives and Fringe Benefits

Properly designed wage structure and incentive systems encourage workers to produce more. Wage rate for the tea plantation workers is fixed by an agreement between the Bangladesiyo Cha Sangsad (employers' association) and Bangladesh Cha Sramik Union (workers' association). This agreement is revised every two years. Wages are divided into two parts—basic and dearness allowance. Basic wages account for about 48 per cent of total wages.

Production target has also been set for the workers. Size of this target varies according to seasons and category of tea estate. For the peak season, production target per day has been set at 23 kg of green leaf for each worker employed.

In all gardens, wages are paid on a weekly basis. The amount of weekly wages varies widely according to the category of tea estate. On an average a male worker earned Tk.180 whereas his female counterpart earned Tk.150. Male workers earn more than female workers mainly because their efficiency is comparatively more than that of female workers. Absenteeism among male workers is also less than among female workers.

Every week, a large amount of money is cut from the worker's wages. Workers' contribution to provident fund, membership fees for trade union, workers' subscription for various festivals, etc are included in this wage cut. Physical Conditions at the Work Place and Occupational Hazards

In the plantation industry no machine is used. The workplace is a vast tract of land under the sky. Hence, it is believed that occupational hazards are minimal in this industry. There are a number of hazards that affect workers' productivity quite adversely. Among these, hazards arising from scorching sun, rain, snake biting, mosquito and other insect bites are important. Hazards arising from spraying insecticides and using chemical fertilizer in the tea garden are also widespread. May add Bank, Biman & other industries.

Female Workers in Bangladesh

"Because I am a woman, I must make unusual efforts to succeed. If I fail, no one will say, "She doesn't have what it takes." They will say, "Women don't have what it takes.""—Clare Boothe Luce

In 1980, UNESCO issued a report which stated that "women make up half of the world's population, work two thirds of the total working hours, and yet receive only one tenths of the income and own only one hundredth of the world's property." Later in 1993, UN reports that women on average earn 30-40% less than men even in industrialized countries.

'A woman's workplace is at home'. Traditionally this was the view of woman work role in Bangladesh. The negative image of woman, although very pervasive, depicts women as subservient and submissive; a creature dependent on male throughout her life cycle—on father when a child, on husband in the middle age or on the son at the later stage in life.

A woman is claimed as a deviant, if she claims space and identity for herself. A common approach to her economic worth is to view her as an unproductive person which is in fact perpetuation of a myth—for a woman performs very crucial productive and reproductive roles. It was only with advent of the revolution that woman have turned to gainful employment outside the household for wages. Now a large number of women participate in employment outside the home both in fully industrialized, developed and developing countries like Bangladesh.

4.3 Scenario of Women Employment—Bangladesh Perspective

According to the Bangladesh statistical Yearbook, 2006, the male and female ratio in Bangladesh is about 51 and 49 percent. However, in the urban areas this ratio is almost same while in the rural areas it has increased to some extent. Among the age groups, 30-64 years is comprised of more than 50% of the total population while 15-29 years group had the share of more than 40% of the labor force. In both urban and rural areas the female labor force of age group 15-29 outweigh their counterpart which is very significant for a country like Bangladesh.

Percentage of working age population by broad age group (as first April 2006)

Broad Age Group	Bangladesh			Urban			Rural		
	Total	M	F	Total	M	F	Total	M	F
Total Population (million)	137.3	70.0	67.3	32.4	16.4	16.0	105.0	53.7	51.3
Working Age Pop (15+)	100.0	100.0	100.0	100.0	100.0	100.0	100.0	100.0	100.0
15-29	40.6	39.3	41.9	42.1	39.1	45.2	40.1	39.4	40.8
30-64	53.0	53.9	52.0	53.4	56.2	50.4	52.8	53.1	52.6
65+	6.4	6.8	6.1	4.5	4.7	4.4	7.1	7.5	6.6

Table 8 : Percentage of Working Age Population by Broad Age Group[31]

But in case of the economically active population in Bangladesh male still dominates. Female here plays a very minor role and both male and female participation has not increased significantly.

In Bangladesh, as the population is increasing the labor force is also increasing. From the table underneath it is found that in 1995-96 the size of the labor force was 36.1 million while in 2005-06 it climbed to 49.5 million. The increase among male workforce was steady but female workforce in the same span of time increased rapidly which has become more than double of the 1995-96 labor force survey and this change in particular is easily visible among the female labor force in the rural area.

Comparison of Labor Force Aged 15 Years and Above by Sex (million)

Period	Bangladesh			Urban			Rural		
	Total	M	F	Total	M	F	Total	M	F
1995-96 LFS	36.1	30.7	5.4	8.3	6.8	1.6	27.7	23.9	3.8
1999-2000 LFS	40.7	32.2	8.6	9.2	7.1	2.1	31.5	25.1	6.4
2002-03 LFS	46.3	36.0	10.3	11.3	8.6	2.7	35.0	27.4	7.7
2005-06 LFS	49.5	37.4	12.1	11.7	8.9	2.8	37.8	28.5	9.3

Table 9 : Comparison of Labor Force Aged 15 Years and Above by Sex[32]

Moreover in the case of labor force participation rate the female ratio is again very significant. In 1983-84 survey they had 8.0 percent participation rate which in 2005-06 has became 29.2 percent. This is particularly because many new jobs—mostly for women—have been created by the country's dynamic private ready-made garment industry, which grew at double-digit rates through most of the 1990s. By the late 1990s, about 1.5 million people, mostly women, were employed in the garments sector.

Labor Force Participation Rate by Sex over Time, 1983-84 to 2005-06

	1983-84		1984-85		1985-86		1995-96		1999-2000		2002-03		2005-06	
	M	F	M	F	M	F	M	F	M	F	M	F	M	F
Labor Force Participation Rate	78.5	8.0	78.2	8.2	81.4	9.9	87.0	15.8	84.0	23.9	87.4	26.1	86.8	29.2

Table 10 : Labor Force Participation Rate by Sex Over Time, 1983-84 to 2005-2006[33]

There exists a variation between male and female population employed by occupation. It is observed from the table No. 11 given below that in the year 2005-2006, among the male workers, the highest 42.2% were engaged in agriculture, forest and related works followed by 26.8% in production, transport laborers and others, and 18% in service workforce. On the other hand, among the female workers, the highest 68.3% were engaged in agriculture and related works followed by production & transport laborers and others.

Population Aged 15 Years and Above by Major Occupation 2005-06

Major Occupation	1999-2000			2002-03			2005-06		
	Both Sex	Male	Female	Both Sex	Male	Female	Both Sex	Male	Female
Thousand									
Total	38979	31087	7891	44322	34478	9844	47357	36080	11277
Professional, Technical	1567	1192	374	1723	1319	403	2231	1737	494
Administrative, Managerial	188	173	15	96	92	4	223	201	22
Clerical Workers	1211	1081	130	1521	1336	185	1016	872	144
Sales Workers	5762	5321	441	6547	6261	286	6711	6476	235
Service Workers	2237	998	1239	1979	1027	951	2757	1892	865
Agriculture, Forestry & Fisheries	19343	15577	3767	22764	16992	5772	22926	15221	7705
Others	8671	6744	1926	9693	7450	2243	11493	9681	1812
Percentage									
Total	100.0	100.0	100.0	100.0	100.0	100.0	100.0	100.0	100.0
Professional, Technical	4.0	3.8	4.7	3.9	3.8	4.1	4.7	4.8	4.4
Administrative, Managerial	0.5	0.6	0.2	0.2	0.3	0.0	0.5	0.6	0.2
Clerical Workers	3.1	3.5	1.7	3.4	3.9	1.9	2.1	2.4	1.3
Sales Workers	14.8	17.1	5.6	14.8	18.2	2.9	5.8	5.2	7.7
Service Workers	5.7	3.2	15.7	4.5	3.0	9.7	14.2	18.0	2.1
Agriculture, Forestry & Fisheries	49.6	50.1	47.7	51.4	49.3	58.6	48.4	42.2	68.3
Production & Transport Labors and others	22.3	21.7	24.4	21.9	21.6	22.8	24.3	26.8	16.0

Table 11 : Population Aged 15 Years and Above by Major Occupation 2005-2006[34]

In case of female participation in industries, the trend is very significant for agriculture. As in the year 1999-2000, female has the percentage participation of 47.7 in agriculture which rocketed to 68.3 percent in 2005-06 whereas at the same time male participation in agriculture decreased to 42.2 percent from 50.1 percent. In transportation & transport laborers and others category female workforce decreased gradually and male participation increased slightly.

The numerical and percentage distribution of employed population (15 years and over) has been presented in the table next page.

Population Aged 15 Years and Above by Major Occupation 2005-06

Major Occupation	1999-2000			2002-03			2005-06		
	Both Sex	Male	Female	Both Sex	Male	Female	Both Sex	Male	Female
Thousand									
Total	38979	31087	7891	44322	34478	9844	47357	36080	11277
Agriculture, Forestry & Fisheries	19785	16136	3649	22931	17159	5771	22767	15084	7683
Mining and quarrying	174	95	79	82	80	1	51	44	7
Manufacturing	3721	2330	1391	4343	2637	1706	5224	3926	1298
Electricity, Gas and Water	134	116	18	98	90	8	76	73	3
Construction	1095	999	96	1541	1445	97	1525	1421	104
Trade, Hotel and Restaurant	6153	5633	500	6671	6424	247	7820	7366	454
Transport, Storage & Communication	2471	2425	46	3015	2989	25	3976	3910	66
Finance & Business services and real estate	403	357	46	417	390	26	745	619	126
Health, education, public administration & defense	2124	1743	382	2677	2127	549	2550	1982	568
Community and personal services	2919	1234	1686	2549	1136	1413	2622	1654	968
Percentage									
Total	100.0	100.0	100.0	100.0	100.0	100.0	100.0	100.0	100.0
Agriculture, Forestry & Fisheries	50.8	51.9	46.2	51.8	49.8	58.7	48.1	41.8	68.1
Mining and quarrying	0.4	0.3	1.0	0.2	0.2	0.0	0.1	0.1	0.1
Manufacturing	9.5	7.5	17.6	9.8	7.6	17.3	11.0	10.9	11.5
Electricity, Gas and Water	0.3	0.4	0.2	0.2	0.3	0.1	0.2	0.2	0.0
Construction	2.8	3.2	1.2	3.5	4.2	1.0	3.2	4.0	0.9
Trade, Hotel and Restaurant	15.8	18.1	6.3	15.1	18.6	2.5	16.5	20.4	4.0
Transport, Storage & Communication	6.3	7.8	0.6	6.8	8.7	0.3	8.4	10.8	0.6
Finance & Business services and real estate	1.0	1.1	0.6	0.9	1.1	0.3	1.6	1.7	1.1
Health, education, public administration & defense	5.4	5.6	4.8	6.0	6.1	5.6	5.4	5.5	5.1
Community and personal services	7.5	4.0	21.4	5.8	3.3	14.4	5.6	4.6	8.6

Table 12 : Population Aged 15 Years and Above by Major Industry 2005-2006[35]

It is observed from the table No. 13 that of the total employed population, as high as 48.1 % is engaged in agriculture, forestry and related workers, followed by trade, hotel and restaurant (16.5%) and manufacturing (11.0%). The trend is almost similar in the shown period though in case of agriculture, forestry and fisheries, and mining and quarrying the percentage decreased slightly and for the rest of the other categories the percentage increased slightly which does not show any significant impact on the total scenario.

4.4 Gender Discrimination at Workplace

In an age where we talk about equal rights for men and women, there are still instances of people being discriminated against because of their gender. People should realize that gender discrimination at workplace is a serious form of employment discrimination, which should not be dismissed. Gender based discrimination is defined as adverse action or differential treatment against a person that would not have occurred if the person had been of another sex. Gender discrimination is considered as a serious form of prejudice and is illegal in certain circumstances in most of the countries around the world.

There are four ways in which gender discrimination can take place worldwide:

4.4.1 Direct Discrimination

At times there are instances where men treat women differently at workplace. Direct discrimination includes acts like difference in salary based on gender although both are doing the same job, or promoting someone because they are men instead of an equally qualified women.

4.4.2 Indirect Discrimination

Instances where people are indirectly discriminated include for example a certain set of rules or laws which indirectly imply that people of a certain gender cannot qualify those laws or rules.

4.4.3 Harassment at Work

This type of discrimination is perhaps the worst of the lot since it not only discriminates but causes emotional as well as psychological trauma for the employee who is discriminated against. Sexual or verbal harassment or inferior treatment owing to gender is included under this category.

4.4.4 Victimization

Unfair or biased treatment based on the employee's gender translates into victimization at work. This is also a form of employee discrimination based on gender.

The level of discrimination against women in a society indicates the kind of approach it has towards the identity of womanhood. Violence and discrimination against women in workplace takes many forms in Bangladesh: sexual harassment, sexual division of work, temporary nature of job, lack of opportunity for promotion, nightshift danger, wage discrimination, child care problems, training bias for women etc.

It was found from a study that among the high—posts supervisor, production manager, quality controller etc. in garment industry, only 17 percent are women.[36]

Because of temporary service and lack of promotion, in many cases, women leave their job. About 14 percent of female workers in garment left their first job because of lack of promotion. In case of high profile jobholders like doctors or engineers, the circumstances is not so direly unfair in case of entry level and mid level jobs, but the discrimination becomes prominent when it comes to positioning the women at the helm, despite of having the essential qualifications. Furthermore as employers are usually male, they are skeptical about women holding a position of responsibility with administrative authority. Even highly educated women do not get administrative or policy—making jobs which are a male monopoly.

"Dr. Fatema Ashraf, the former head of gynecology department of Rajshahi Medical College says, "This profession has given me a lot, in terms of respect from colleagues and people. But sometimes I do feel that being a female has its own repercussions, like if I feel there is any step from the authorities that is unfair for female doctors, and gather enough courage to speak up against it, there is almost none on my side, because, being a woman I simply don't have that of social network and support that a male doctor in my position has. Apart from this, though having the same experience level and expertise (maybe even better in some cases) there is a glass ceiling for us which does not allow us to go the topmost administrative level of this medical college."

Now what Dr. Fatema said is the most common view in Bangladesh. Women though being able than men just cannot move up because of some social norms. Traditionally women are considered as lower and feeble than men. It is believed by many people that girls/women are not able to do physically stressful jobs or carrying out decision making roles.

4.5 Sexual Harassment

I'm willing to work for just one Taka, but with my honor intact"[37]

"It feels terrible when someone screams and abuses you this way. I can't put it out of my mind; I replay the incident over and over in my mind until my head begins to throb. It makes it difficult to concentrate on what I'm doing. My whole history comes back to me then. My life flashes before my eyes. I have to ask myself why on earth I even entered this line of work. Why am I working? I feel like crying, I get so depressed."

The general consensus among workers is that a woman's honor is her most valuable asset. Any incidence of harassment, sexual or otherwise, strikes at the very heart of that honor. Some women have the option of leaving but many others have no choice but to continue to work. They are undoubtedly in the worst of all positions. As a woman in the EPZ says about her counterparts,

"Whether it's cursing or sexual harassment, those who must, continue to work. If they talk back, they might lose their jobs. Tai koshto holeyo, kajer khoti holeyo, buke pathor bedhe kamrey dhore kaj kore. (That's why even if they are suffering intensely, even if their work suffers, they grit their teeth, turn their hearts into stone and keep on working.)."[38]

Sexual harassment means unwanted conduct of a sexual nature, or other conduct based on sex, affecting the dignity of men and women at work. This includes unwelcome physical, verbal or non-verbal conduct. Sexual harassment need not be limited to potential or actual conduct of a sexual nature, but can include conduct based on a person's social identity as a woman (or man, for that matter). Some commentators would call this gender role harassment—acts precipitated by a person's perceived transgression of socially sanctioned gender roles and spaces. This broader definition of sexual harassment accommodates the experiences of those women who are verbally or physically accosted without being threatened with sexual violence. The definition also stresses an individual's right to dignity—rather than the violation of her modesty. It thereby avoids engagement with culturally sanctioned—and highly masculinist—notions of female propriety. Finally, while it acknowledges the existence of workplace harassment, the definition is not limited to any specific context or location. The language of sexual harassment is relatively new, although the various behaviors it encompasses are not. American feminists in the 1970 have first made available a socially recognized vocabulary to describe specific gendered experiences as sexual harassment. Legally, the concept emerged through the development of civil rights legislation in the United States. Feminist legal scholar Catherine MacKinnon was foremost in naming sexual harassment as an expression of male dominance and as a form of sexual discrimination. The ILO recognizes sexual harassment as a violation of the fundamental rights of workers, one that constitutes a problem of safety and health, a problem of discrimination, an unacceptable working condition and a form of violence.

The Nari O Shishu Nirjaton Domon Ain (2000) for the first time made sexual harassment a criminal offence punishable by law in Bangladesh. Section 10(2) of the Act states:

Any man who, in order to satisfy his lust in an improper manner, outrages the modesty of a woman, or makes obscene gestures, will have engaged in sexual harassment, and for this, the above mentioned male will be sentenced to rigorous imprisonment of not more than seven years and not less than two years and beyond this will be subjected to monetary fines as well.

Women's work environment in Bangladesh doesn't begin and end at the workplace. In all the public spaces they inhabit—inside the factory and on the streets—they must negotiate culturally embedded and highly gendered codes of spatial use and respectability. Consequently, working women face a double jeopardy with respect to sexual harassment. Not only are they vulnerable to physical, verbal and sexual abuse inside the workplace, they are frequently subjected to harassment once they leave their work premises, in the public spaces they must traverse before reaching home.

Women from impoverished backgrounds are the most at risk of this dual harassment, which derives legitimacy from culturally dominant associations between poverty, promiscuity, and public visibility.

'There's not a single woman in the world that hasn't suffered from this problem [of sexual harassment]. Of course, it's an entirely different story when it comes to the rich women.

'I'm the daughter of a poor man so I face danger with every step. God has reserved all danger for the poor (victim of rape inside factory)'.

'Just because I'm poor and I'm fair, I'm in danger (molested by Lineman threatened with dismissal if she reported it to the higher authority)'.

'The poor have endless problems on the roads. No one has the nerve to say anything to the rich and employers. Once a rickshaw puller whistled at a woman who was in her house [After the woman complained] the rickshaw puller had his vehicle taken away by its owner. He was subsequently dismissed'.

The predicament of garment workers is emblematic in this respect. The reputation of the industry and the conditions of work offer an implicit license for otherwise unacceptable behavior, making garment workers fair game for male attention inside the factory and beyond. For these women, the street—male public space—can be an extremely dangerous and intimidating space. Perceived 'low' status (which translates into a lack of social protection) combined with late working hours and inadequate transport facilities expose female workers to all sorts of insecurity and harassment.

At the individual level, subjects of harassment experience emotional stress, depression, fatigue, anxiety, an inability to concentrate, humiliation, and anger, among other things. It follows that work performance is significantly lowered. Tension, hostility and fear in the workplace hinder teamwork and collaboration, leading not only to decreased productivity but also to increased absenteeism, loss of interest in work and in severe cases to the resignation of valuable employees. The financial costs to enterprises can be huge.

Monowara,[39] a young garment operator was often sexually passed as the young male co workers made passes at her and tried to have affairs. But she sought the advice and guardianship of the production manager who ultimately turned out to be devious and amorous himself. Confessions later revealed that a friend of her was requisitioned to lure and trap Monowara but fortunately he became wise. Many have proposed marriage, some only illicit relationships. Monowara reported that usually the line chief, quality controller, supervisor etc. bothered her. But she was afraid to disclose their names. She further reported that most of her female colleagues were harassed in similar ways. But most of them never complained about harassment to the management because of fear of retrenchment from jobs. Monowara told that she knew many incidences of such retrenchment.[40]

Her male colleagues often teased Rokeya, another young garment worker. They often passed demeaning remarks at her. Some proposed an illicit relationship. But she did not disclose it to her colleagues since her colleagues may think badly about her. She also did not complain against them to the management to the factory since according to her; management never took any action against this type of harassment. Moreover, in some cases, the victims were retrenched since management thought that they disturb the production. To save herself she changed her job twice. However, she reported that recently she received a concrete marriage proposal from a cutting master.

Majeda,[41] another beautiful unmarried female garment worker, and aged only 18 narrated a more horrible story.

"One day I was kidnapped by four touts from the street when I was returning home a 10 p.m. after finishing my overtime work at a garment factory, about 2 kilometers away from my residence. They took me to a building which was under construction. Four touts raped me repetitively and left me in a senseless condition. Regaining my sense I came back home. Looking at my condition both my parents and neighbor could understand what happened to me. My father was very sympathetic to me. He went to the factory and requested the management to file a complaint against those touts to the police. But they refused. My father filed a complaint to the police on my behalf."

Representations of garments workers as always on the verge of sex work have serious material repercussions in the everyday lives of all female factory workers, most acutely in relation to sexual harassment. The presumption or justification for much of the sexual harassment of garment workers described in this report is that by virtue of their profession, these women are of 'easy virtue'; they can slide into prostitution at any moment and so do not deserve to have their rights respected either as workers or as women.

4.6 Night Shift: Is It Safe For Women Worker?

Workers who have to work night shifts face the risk of sexual assault or rape inside the factory which rises after work ends and before they are able to go home. If the shift ends very late—any time from midnight to 4 am and if the factory has no facilities for safe transport or for secure overnight stays—workers are forced to pass the night at the factory premises. Women bed down wherever space is available. After the lights are turned off, various people continue to have access to the shop floor. These include linemen, Promotion Manager, supervisors, security guards, owners, management or their close relatives.

The night is an especially vulnerable time for those women who catch the fancy of male superiors or colleagues but who succeed in staying off any personal encounter during the day. Called out with some excuse, such as apparent mistakes in their work that require urgent attention, women may be escorted into deserted or darkened areas (store rooms, office rooms, an unlit section of the sleeping area, or even just behind a column) and assaulted. According to the women interviewed, this is when the greatest numbers of attempted and actual rapes take place.

It has always been the matter of debate, "Should women be allowed to work in the night shift?". Women's security is the main concern behind the question. It's a bitter truth that our government has failed in providing security to women. Even though our constitution has given us the right to choose our profession irrespective of cast, religion or sex, we have a traditional society and people have different opinions on this issue. Large section of the society, still don't like to send their women to work in the night shift. Our society blames the woman herself if she gets assaulted outside in the night. They simply say that, 'What is the need to go outside in the night?' The nightscape is primarily an exclusive, male domain that often represents danger for women and in some cases, women who go out at night are associated with prostitution or questionable moral values. Apart from this there isn't any ample security for women traveling in the night though they are vulnerable to many dangers in this country.

4.6.1 Sexual Division

Bangladesh being an agrarian country with a low stage of economic development, the activities of men and women are explicitly divided and sex roles are strictly enforced. The labor market is, therefore, highly segregated. Possession of land and other means of production—the key to social and economic hierarchy in Bangladesh—are controlled by men and as such the work load is divided in their favor. Under such circumstance, female are pushed indoors onto seclusion and this restricts their mobility and enforces their dependency on men. Women are mostly involved in activities which bring "income in kind consisting of goods produced and services provided for family's need".

Restricted mobility of women to assume wage employment relegates them to an inferior position. In the organized sector, though a microscopic number of women are pursuing varied types of occupation from flying to judiciary, in general they tend to be concentrated in particular fields and jobs categories. In most cases women are at the bottom of the ladder holding jobs with no authority and little scope of promotion.

Occupational segregation of women may also be caused by labor laws which limit women's total hours of works and prohibit women's working at night or during pregnancy. Sometimes these are used as mechanisms through which firms could legally refuse to hire women for certain jobs. Sharp occupational segregation of women in Bangladesh has contributed to the persistence of male female wage gap. The incident below was narrated by one of the students of the same institution:

"Bangladesh University of Engineering and Technology has an enriched civil department comprising of almost 60 professors and lecturers in which about 30% are women. Besides teaching, the teachers get to do a lot of project work and consultancy which generates a substantial amount of their income. The people who come for consultancy always find out the male teachers for their purpose because according to them 'civil engineering projects' is a job for men and women engineers cannot be relied in these cases. As a matter of fact, when the male teachers get hoards of work and subsequently extra earning outside their own jobs, their women counterparts—even though having the same qualifications—has limited options to earn money more than their salaries."

A woman seeking employment is judged by the prevailing social norms and idea of typically "female jobs" rather than her individual ability. Discriminatory hiring and advancement of policies leave little options for women but to accept traditional jobs of lower ranks. Prejudicial attitude of employers and co-workers makes women shun challenging careers. So women are pushed to professions where they do not violate the rule of seclusion and which are not directly competitive with men's occupation.

4.6.2 Differential Wage Rate of Women

That women's earnings trend on average to be less than men's throughout all regions of the world is an oft-cited indicator of gender-based inequality in labor markets. Indeed, a recent report by the International Trade Union Confederation (ITUC) finds an average "global" gender pay gap of 16.5 per cent, with an average pay gap in Asian countries of 21.2 per cent based on countries with available sex-disaggregated earnings data. In Bangladesh, a country with low per-capita GDP and limited resources for conducting surveys on wages, relatively little is known about differences between women and men with regard to earnings and the extent to which any gender-based earnings differential can be explained by women's and men's relative endowments in productive factors such as human capital (education and experience) versus outright labor market discrimination. Bangladesh Occupational Wage Survey—2007 conducted by Bangladesh Bureau of Statistics (BBS) reveals very low average hourly wages of 16.8 taka, the equivalent of approximately 25 cents/hour in current 2007 US$, or about $1.21 per hour at purchasing power parity exchange rates. The survey results also highlight the existence of a significant and persistent gap in earnings between women and men: on average, men in the surveyed industries earn over 21 per cent more per hour of work than women. As wages provide a crucial link to living standards—particularly for the poor who rely on the earnings derived from their labor for survival—it is important to ascertain why wages vary among different groups, such as women and men. That is, the existence of a gender wage gap and failure to understand the root causes of the gap could result in a negative feedback loop: if it is seen that women earn less than men, this could discourage parents from investing in girls and lower girls' future employability. If, on the other hand, it is understood that women earn less than men because of differences in their endowments of productive factors (perhaps that they have less education due to poor access to schooling) or because they do not have access to the same types of jobs as men, policy measures could be enacted and awareness campaigns launched to address the specific underlying causes. A recent study by the ILO finds that women in Bangladesh are often considered to be lesser or inferior participants in the labor market, largely owing to traditional societal views that the primary role of women is to fulfill reproductive and domestic functions, rather than fully participate in education, training, and paid work. This, in turn, limits women's choice of income-earning activities and results in industry-level or occupational segregation, whereby women are relegated disproportionately to jobs viewed as less important, requiring lower skills, and with lower earnings. In terms of hourly wages, the largest gender gap is in construction, where the average hourly wage for women is approximately 60 per cent that of men; followed by hotels & restaurants (69 per cent); financial intermediation (71 per cent) and manufacturing (76 per cent). The smallest gaps are observed in the service industries in education, health & social work and other services—Industries in which women have a fairly high share of employment. Women earn less than men do even when they hold the same job.

Even in the operator and helper category jobs, which are dominated by female workers, they earn less than their male counterparts. The gender gap in earnings persists even after controlling for skill. The survey of 1997 by Bangladesh Bureau of Statistics shows that a female operator in the woven wears factories earns 74 percent of a male operator's earnings; in the knitwear factories, where operators use improved technology, a female operator earns only 69 percent of her male counterpart's earnings.[42]

With some exception the discrimination is more prominent in the employees of higher skill level and reduces as the skill level reduces. Helpers of both genders who are at the bottom of the skill ladder enjoy same level of wages whereas male supervisors enjoy a 21% salary advantage over their female counterparts. The equivalence of wages at the helpers' level is perhaps a result of the minimum wages for non-skilled labors fixed by the government and enforced by very strict monitoring mechanism of the buyers to ensure compliance with their code of conduct. On the other hand, better labor management skills of the male supervisors perhaps account for a part of their discriminatory salary level.

4.6.3 Training Bias

Women's participation in economic activities is generally conceptualized as offering them a program package containing functional literacy, health and family planning education and skill training, the last one being the major component. In fact, training is the most abused term in women's program though nearly all programs relating to income generation have major training component aiming towards skill development and infusing of family planning ideas to the target group. In program designing there is a tendency to over generalize the character, need and capabilities of women ignoring their class and regional diversity.

Although skill training is important, it is likely to create new problems rather than solve the old if it serves to retain in low growth and unprofitable sectors of the economy. There is a bias towards training women in discrete skills while "educating" men—a similar form of discrimination to the common division between income generating activities for women versus employment for men!

Analyses of the existing women's program reveals that most of the trainings are either not need based or poorly designed and therefore, fail to serve the purpose or impart any concrete skill to the clients. In most cases these short training courses can more appropriately be termed as fragmented information dissemination rather than the creation of skills among trainees with a commercial bias which could be used for creating income and alleviating poverty. As far as motivation to small family norm is concerned it is apparent from the current population growth that it has failed to achieve the desired objective. The trainees fail to make use of these training in the formal sector due to a lack of participation, and in informal sector due to the absence of linkage at the macro level for necessary input and technological support.

Thus most of the program for women shows a training bias irrespective of the need of the client. Out of 24 schemes undertaken by the Ministry of Women's Affairs, all except 4 had major components of training. Of the major training programs, Training-cum-production centers in 200 Upazillas, development centers in 38 unions, Socio—economic development Programs of BJMS etc. were important. However, findings of an evaluation team about one of these major training programs is quite significant, which says; "Rural women of these projects accept to receive something concrete . . . . but unfortunately these projects have not yet established any positive set of concrete and constructive examples . . . . As a result gradually they are losing their interest and developing some kind of negative attitudes to the project programs." Another evaluation carried out by the Planning commission, Bangladesh indicates that participation of women is relatively poor in those programs due to insufficient equipment, irregularity of funds and wrong choice of training items.

Due to poor planning training are offered without much consideration of their applicability in terms of individual or local needs. The quality of training fails to impart the requisite skill. Moreover there is no policy planning to provide the much needed support and follow-up services like credit, marketing, raw materials, etc.[43]

An evaluation of women's Skill Training and Day Care Services in 32 Centers conducted by the women's Affairs Directorate (1986) reveals that in all centers training in 3 trades were commonly offered—tailoring, weaving and sewing. In addition, some centers offered some other selected trainings, but nearly 40 % could not at all make any use of their training. Those who could use the training for earning income, earned about Tk. 150 per month or less and only 13 % could earn above Tk. 300 per month. These adequately depict the wrong policy of training.

4.6.4 Male Attitudes towards Female Workers

Ten men from the apparel sector were interviewed. Although this is a very small sample to draw conclusions about male attitudes—some interesting contrasts emerged from conversations with men.

It was clear from the interview that male workers feels considerable solidarity toward their female colleagues and that they are acutely aware of the power imbalances women have to negotiate in their work lives. Over half of the men interviewed said they have a high opinion of their female coworkers. In response to the question of whether any of their female coworkers had ever been sexually harassed, almost half replied in the affirmative. But it was striking that most of the men did not think sexual harassment had any particular impact on productivity. They did concede, however, that harassment would have psychological effects on women "because their honor was involved."

While most men had a high opinion of their female coworkers, a few of the respondents said they did not or would not allow their own wives to work outside the home. Perhaps too good a grasp of the realities of women's work environment generated this response.

The men interviewed gave practical solutions to the problem of harassment. Most felt that the best strategy for combating street harassment would be the provision of company buses for commuting. Notably, a significant number felt the solution lay in changing dominant social attitudes toward working women. At the same time, half of the respondents claimed that out of work, garments workers become sex workers. When they were asked how they knew, several replied that they had seen a program on Ekushey Television on the subject.

4.7 Parda as Resistance?

Women workers are clearly in a weak bargaining position when it comes to the point of negotiating incidents of harassment—be it inside the workplace or on the streets. Not surprisingly, the modes of resistance on which workers draw attention tend to rework existing ideological beliefs about the 'good' Bengali woman. With respect to verbal harassment on the streets, a third of the respondents felt it was best to ignore such incidents. This conscious passivity and conformity with patriarchal norms resonates with cultural ideals of submissive womanhood, thereby entitling women to some degree of social protection.

About a quarter (the interview was conducted with 40 garments workers) of the women interviewed said they wear a 'borkha' while almost one-third wear a large 'orna' to cover the hair and the body. That is, half the women interviewed use some visible form of 'parda'. This appeared to be the most common strategy to avoid unwanted male attention. Paradoxically, entry into modern wage labor encourages these women workers to take advantage of this so-called 'traditional' practice of female modesty. Very few of them covered themselves as a sign of personal piety. Their objectives were more practical than religious. The 'borkha' hides the shape of the body, thereby providing something akin to protective armor. Moreover, men are apparently more hesitant about approaching women in 'borkha's. Indeed, it appears that women who wear 'borkha's or cover their hair are much less likely to face harassment than those who do not, although they are not immune from it.

Wearing 'Borkha's has its own hassles because 'borkha' clad women are deemed less competent than other women who do not wear veils in case of most large companies.

Sonia, an employee of a mobile company, followed 'parda' strictly due to her family's perception that their daughter would face security problems at work if she did not do thus. But this had a completely disastrous effect at her workplace. Her job included dealing with foreign delegates on a regular basis from which she was exempted frequently as the company thought that both it would create an awkward situation for both the delegates and her, giving her other colleagues a chance to prove themselves and enhance their promotion opportunities and their public dealing skills.

There is an opposite side of this story. Sometimes women are forced to wear veils although they are unwilling to do so. Top of the company management do not allow women in their head office who do not wear veils while male employees are not restricted to do anything like this.

In one of the large company in Gulshan, Taslima worked as an office secretary for almost 15 years and she had to wear veils to work there although in her real life she never wear veils. She also complaint while all the five female employees had to wear veils as per company instructions, her male colleague has no such restrictions imposed upon them.

4.8 Child Care

The negative attitude of our society towards women's employment has mainly sprung from the cultural bias that a woman's prime duty is to rear her children, and that their interests are neglected when a mother assumes outside employment. Therefore, child care has been an important issue for all working mothers. Women in Bangladesh mostly take up employment due to economic necessity rather than for self—actualization or for filling up their leisure times.

One must also remember that a great advantage of increase in female employment in a poor economy is that children become the direct beneficiaries of mother's income. Several studies conducted by different NGO's and government organizations in Bangladesh indicate that working mothers raise healthier children as they can afford to supplement the poor family diet with their extra income. So in a poor country like ours the need for increasing the number of working mothers can hardly be overemphasized.

In the Section 94 of 'The Bangladesh Labor Code, 2006' provisions are provided regarding child care facilities for children of working mothers. Which are-

1. "In every establishment, wherein 40 (forty) or more female workers are ordinarily employed, there shall be provided and maintained one or more suitable room (s) for the use of their children under age of six.
2. Any such rooms shall provide sufficient accommodation, be adequately lighted and ventilated and maintained in a clean and sanitary condition, and shall be under the supervision of woman experienced and trained in the care of children.

3. Such rooms shall be easily accessible to the mothers of the children and so far as is reasonably practicable it shall not be situated in close proximity to any part of the establishment wherefrom vexation fumes, dust or odors come out in which excessively noisy workers are carried on.

4. Such rooms shall have to be soundly constructed and all its wall and roof shall be of suitable heat-resisting materials and shall be water-proof.

5. The height of such rooms shall not be less than 360 (three hundred and sixty) centimeter from the floor to the lowest part of the roof and the floor space for each child staying therein shall be at least 600 (six hundred) square centimeter.

6. Effective and suitable provisions shall have to be made in every part of such room for securing and maintaining adequate ventilation by the circulation of fresh air.

7. Such room shall have to be adequately furnished and equipped and specially there shall be one suitable cot or cradle with the necessary bedding for each child and at least one chair or equivalent seating accommodations for the use of each mother while she feeds or attends to her child and sufficient supply of suitable toys for the comparatively older children.

8. A suitable fenced and shady open air play ground shall be provided for comparatively older children;

Provided that chief inspector may, by order in writing, exempt any establishment from compliance with the provision of this sub section, if he is satisfied that the establishment does not have sufficient space for making such play-ground."

In spite of these provisions of law institutional child care facilities are absent in Bangladesh. As a result, working mothers are required to put considerable amount of their time, energy and effort to manage their children inside and outside working premise simultaneously. This not only restricts a woman's mobility outside home, but also takes away her productive energy. So establishment of baby homes, nurseries, day care center and children's health clinics for middle and lower income are pre requisites for women to take up wage employment. In Bangladesh as this is a new concept still to be accepted only those women who have some dependable female relatives (mother, mother-in-law etc.) at home to look after the children can take up employment outside.

At present the Ministry of Women's Affairs and Social welfare provides care for the children of working mothers through their programming to a limited extent. Besides these in Dhaka there are a few such centers run by voluntary and private organizations. Their number is however, too inadequate compared to the need.

4.9 Child Labor

The child labor issue is one of great concern throughout the world. It is quite common for children of all types of societies to be engaged in some forms of occupation depending on the economic structure and level of development. Child labor has been generally perceived more as a problem of poor developing countries, which are consistently facing challenges against poverty, high population growth, rising unemployment, natural disasters and so on.

In 2000, the ILO estimates, "246 million child workers aged 5 and 17 were involved in child labor, of which 171 million were involved in work that by its nature is hazardous to their safety, physical or mental health, and moral development. Moreover, some 8.4 million children were engaged in so-called 'unconditional' worst forms of child labor, which include forced and bonded labor, the use of children in armed conflict, trafficking in children and commercial sexual exploitation."

5.0 Child Labor in General

"Child labor" is the employment of children at regular and sustained labor. Generally speaking, work for children that harm them or exploits them in some way (physically, mentally, morally, or by blocking access to education).

But there is no universally accepted definition of "child labor". Varying definitions of the term are used by international organizations, non-governmental organizations, trade unions and other interest groups. For example: UNICEF defines child labor as work that exceeds a minimum number of hours, depending on the age of a child and on the type of work. Such work is considered harmful to the child and should therefore be eliminated.

- **Ages 5-11:** At least one hour of economic work or 28 hours of domestic work per week.
- **Ages 12-14:** At least 14 hours of economic work or 28 hours of domestic work per week.
- **Ages 15-17:** At least 43 hours of economic or domestic work per week.

ILO Convention No. 138 (1973) sets the minimum age for entry into work at 15 years (14 years for less developed countries) and at no less than the minimum age of completion of compulsory education; prohibits work for children less than 18 years.

On the other hand United Nations Convention on the Rights of the Child (1989) defines all those under the age of 18 as children.

Bangladesh Labor Act (2006) prohibits the employment or permission to work in any occupation or establishment for children under age of 15 years; prohibits adolescents (between the ages of 15-19) from being employed or permitted to work in establishments when the works are hazardous by definition. Bangladesh is a signatory to the United Nations convention on the rights of the child (1989) and has ratified ILO convention No. 182 on the worst forms of Child Labor (2001), but has yet to ratify the ILO Minimum Age Convention (No. 138).

5.1 Definition of "Child"

According to the Bangladesh Labor code, 2006—"Child" means any person who is yet to complete fourteen years of age.

Generally a child is defined as an individual under the age of 18 years based on the 1989 UN Convention on the Rights of the Child and the ILO Convention on the worst forms of Child Labor 1999 (No. 182). Since it is commonly accepted that a child under five years of age is too young to be engaged in work or to start schooling it considers only the child population aged 5-17 for the purpose of National child Labor statistics (NCLS) as well as for estimates.

Earlier in Bangladesh, under the Basic Remuneration Act 1961, the age of maturity is 18. The Employment of Children Act 1938 says that anyone under to that 15 is a child. The Child Labor Restriction Act 1933 agrees to that. However, the Child Act 1974 lays down 16 as the age of maturity. One cannot vote, though, until one is 18 according to the law.

In Bangladesh workers are engaged in both formal and informal sectors.

5.2 Estimates of Working Children and Child Labor

The number of children at work or engaged in economic activity is generally estimated by both (I) usual activity status and (ii) current activity status. For classification of children in the age groups, 5-9, 10-14 and 15-17 as working (employed), or not working but available or looking for work (unemployed) and outside of the work (inactive), the above two activity statuses have been used. The activity statuses are defined as follows:

1. Usual activity status with a reference period of 12 months preceding the day of survey enumeration.
2. Current activity status with a reference period of 7 days preceding the day of survey enumeration.

Working children under the usual activity status refers to those who have worked relatively longer time during the last 12 months preceding the day of inquiry. 'Children at work in economic activity' is a broad concept that encompasses most productive activities by children. "Economic Activity" includes paid and unpaid, causal, and illegal work as well as work in the informal sector. It is the only internationally agreed standard to measure work and employment.

5.3 Activity Status of Children

A simple activity status classification has been adopted for the purpose of estimation of working children. The activity status is defined in terms of three categories with a maximum of two levels:

At work in economic activity

  a. At work only.
  b. At work and at school

At school, and not at work in economic activity

Neither at work nor at school

  a. Household chores
  b. Others (e.g. sick, or disabled, beggar, or in informal education etc.)

The table below presents the number of child labors aged 5-17. The table breaks down the number by age as well as rural and urban area. It also gives the number of girls and boys separately. It is observed that the highest numbers of child labor in rural areas are aged 5-9, which is shocking. On the other hand in the urban area the number ranges between the ages of 10-14. This is probably because in the rural areas most of the children are engaged in urban areas, children are engaged in different industrial works which they start at an early age.

Gender and Age Group	Bangladesh			Urban			Rural		
	Total	Boys	Girls	Total	Boys	Girls	Total	Boys	Girls
Total	42387	22689	19698	9458	5062	4396	32929	17627	15302
5-9	18160	9340	8820	3826	1996	1830	14334	7344	6990
10	4295	2343	1952	896	486	410	3399	1857	1542
11	2376	1241	1135	560	291	268	1816	949	867
12	4364	2298	2066	924	501	423	3440	1797	1643
13	2646	1350	1296	624	320	304	2022	1030	992
14	3222	1692	1530	808	419	389	2414	1273	1141
10-14	16903	8923	7980	3812	2017	1795	13091	6907	6185
15	3025	1774	1251	689	391	298	2336	1383	953
16	2345	1421	925	598	340	258	1747	1081	667
17	1953	1231	722	533	318	215	1420	913	508
15-17	7324	4426	2899	1820	1049	771	5504	3376	2128

Table 13 : Child Population Aged 5-17 by Age and Number

5.4 Children Attending School and Engaged in any Activity

There is a direct link between child labor and education. Nearly 50% of primary school students drop out before they complete grade 5, and then gravitate towards work, swelling the number of child labors. The high drop-out rates are correlated with the low quality of public primary education, low adult literacy, low awareness of the importance of education, teacher-student ratio (sometimes this goes up to 1 per 100), non-availability of didactic and learning materials, and the cost of education. Basic primary education is free as far as direct costs and school books are concerned. But many indirect costs are involved as well, such as transport, pens, pencils and paper/reference books.

The number of children currently attending school or training and engaged in any activity (Economic or non-economic) before or after the school hours by gender has been presented below:

Gender and Age Group	Bangladesh			Urban			Rural		
	Total	Engaged	Not Engaged	Total	Engaged	Not Engaged	Total	Engaged	Not Engaged
Both Sex									
Total	33333	8321	25011	7524	1467	6057	25809	6854	18955
05-09	14986	1333	13653	3117	230	2886	11870	1103	10767
10-14	13986	5400	8586	3207	903	2304	4498	4498	6282
15-17	4360	1588	2772	1200	334	866	1254	1254	1906
Boys									
Total	16973	4270	3845	3845	715	3129	13129	3555	9574
05-09	7579	556	1595	1595	93	1501	5984	462	5522
10-14	7018	2899	1615	1615	458	1157	5404	2442	2962
15-17	2376	815	635	635	164	471	1741	651	1090
Girls									
Total	16359	4051	3679	3679	752	2927	12680	3300	9381
05-09	7408	777	1522	1522	137	1385	5885	641	5245
10-14	6968	2501	1592	1592	445	1147	5375	2056	3319
15-17	1984	773	564	564	170	395	1420	603	817

Table 14 : Children Attending School and Engaged in Any Activity

It is revealed from the table that of the total estimated 33.3 million currently attending school children of age group 5 to 17, only 8.3 million were engaged in economic and /or non-economic activities. The proportions of children engaged in economic or/and non-economic activities in the age group 5-9, 10-14 and 15-17 were 8.9 percent, 38.6 percent and 36.4 percent respectively.

The proportion of school attending children (78.4 percent) in rural areas was much higher than that of the urban areas (79.5 percent) and it is perhaps due to the fact that the rural school children generally engage themselves in farm activities after or before the school hours to support their family. Moreover, the currently school attending children in rural areas help their families in household chores as well as engage themselves in nonfarm economic activities due to poverty.

The next table shows the percentage distribution of child students (currently attending school) aged 5 to17 years engaged in economic and non-economic activities by gender.

Engaged in activity	Bangladesh			Urban			Rural		
	Total	Boys	Girls	Total	Boys	Girls	Total	Boys	Girls
Economic activity									
Total	100.0	100.0	100.0	100.0	100.0	100.0	100.0	100.0	100.0
Work for wages	18.0	20.6	9.9	21.4	21.6	20.5	17.3	20.4	7.7
Own household economic activity	77.6	74.6	86.5	73.7	73.5	74.4	78.3	74.9	89.0
Self/own economic activity	4.5	4.8	3.6	4.9	4.9	5.0	4.4	4.8	3.3
Non-economic activity									
Total	100.0	100.0	100.0	100.0	100.0	100.0	100.0	100.0	100.0
Take care of younger brother/sister	80.0	68.5	88.2	79.9	71.6	85.2	80.1	67.9	88.8
Take care of ill parents/ relatives	5.8	9.0	3.5	4.0	5.4	3.1	6.2	9.8	3.6
Other household work	14.2	22.4	8.3	16.1	23.0	11.7	13.7	22.3	7.5

Table 15 : Children Currently Attending School and Engaged in any Activity by Gender

The data reveal that the percentage of children who are currently attending school and at the same time also engaged in economic activity for wages is 21.4 in urban areas as against 17.3 percent in rural areas. Of those students engaged in economic activities, the proportion of boys is as high as 75.4 percent, as compared to 24.6 percent for girl students.

The next table presents the percentage distribution of school attending children aged 5 to 17 engaged in economic and non-economic activity by gender and age groups. It is seen from the table that about 83.1 percent students engaged in economic activities are age group 10 to 14; 12.2 percent in age group 15-17 and only 4.6 percent in age group 5-9. Analyzing the table shows that the number of girls engaged in economic activities are less than half of that of boys. But in case of non-economic activities the number is opposite that is more girl children are engaged in non-economic activities than boy children. Percentage distribution shows that as high as 92% of total girl child labors are aged 05-14. the case is same for boy child labor that is highest number of boy child engaged in economic activities are aged 05-14.

Age Group	Economic Activity			Non-Economic Activity		
	Total	Boys	Girls	Total	Boys	Girls
Number ("000")						
Total	2435	1836	598	5887	2434	3453
05-09	113	64	49	1220	491	729
10-14	2024	1522	502	3376	1377	1999
05-14	2137	1586	551	4596	1868	2728
15-17	298	250	48	1291	566	725
Percent						
Total	100.0	100.0	100.0	100.0	100.0	100.0
05-09	4.6	3.5	8.2	20.7	20.2	21.1
10-14	83.1	82.9	83.9	57.3	56.6	57.9
05-14	87.8	86.4	92.0	78.1	76.8	79.0
15-17	12.2	13.6	8.0	21.9	23.2	21.0

Table 16 : Children Aged 5 to 17 years currently studying and engaged by type of activity

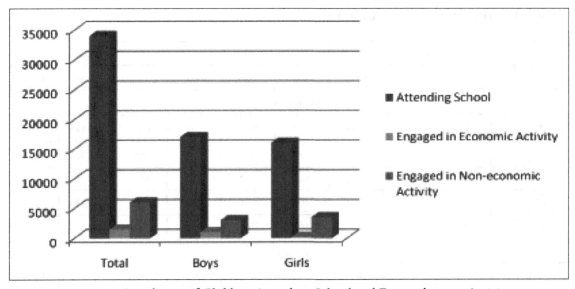

Figure 7 : Population of Children Attending School and Engaged in any Activity

Figure 7 is about the number of children attending in school. It is seen that the number of boys and girls engaged in non-economic activities is high in case of attending school. Those who are engaged in economic activities mostly do not attend schools or drops out in a very early stage. But in general the number of boys attending school is slightly higher than the number of girls.

The recent years have seen a lot of interest and discussion in the national media about the role of child labor. As a result of the awareness created and responding to both national and international pressure an innovative way of ameliorating the suffering of the child workers has been worked out by the relevant parties. A memorandum of understanding between Bangladesh Garment Manufacturers & Exporters Association (BGMEA), UNICEF and ILO, Bangladesh was reached regarding the placement of child workers in school programmes and elimination of child labor. The agreement was signed on July 4, 1995.

5.4.1 Breakdown of Child Laborer

Age Group	Bangladesh			Urban			Rural		
	Total	Boys	Girls	Total	Boys	Girls	Total	Boys	Girls
Number (000)									
Total	7904	5810	2094	1501	1096	404	6403	4714	1689
05-09	360	212	148	60	35	25	300	178	122
10-14	4631	3352	1280	845	617	229	3786	2735	1051
05-14	4991	3564	1428	905	651	254	4086	2913	1174
15-17	2912	2246	666	595	445	150	2317	1801	516
Percent									
Total	100.0	100.0	100.0	100.0	100.0	100.0	100.0	100.0	100.0
05-09	4.6	3.7	7.1	4.0	3.2	6.3	4.7	3.8	7.2
10-14	58.6	57.7	61.1	56.3	56.2	56.5	59.1	58.0	62.2
05-14	63.1	61.3	68.2	60.3	59.4	62.8	63.8	61.8	69.5
15-17	36.8	38.7	31.8	39.7	40.6	37.2	36.2	38.2	30.5

Table 17 : Economically Active Children Aged 5-17 by Gender (2002-2003)

The table shows that about 0.36 million children in 5-9 age category are reportedly working in economic activity. This means that roughly one in every fifty children aged 5 to 9 years was engaged in economic activity. It is also estimated that some 4.6 million children aged 10-14 years were at work in economic activity in 2002-2003. The figure in this category is significantly higher than that for the 5-9 years age group; about thirteenth times greater both in absolute and relative terms. About one in every fourth 10-14 years old children was working. A marked difference in the incidence of economic activity can be observed as one crosses the cutoff minimum age to work and employment of 15 years. The estimated number of working children in the 15-17 years age category was about 2.9 million or 39.8 percent of the population of that age group.

Gender and Age Group	Bangladesh			Urban			Rural		
	Economically active children (EAC)	Child Labor (CL)	Child Labor as Percentage of EAC in age group	Economically active children (EAC)	Child Labor (CL)	Child Labor as Percentage of EAC in age group	Child Labor (CL)	Child Labor (CL)	Child Labor as Percentage of EAC in age group
Both Sex									
Total	7904	3381	42.8	1501	747	49.8	6403	2635	41.1
05-09	360	360	100.0	60	60	100.0	300	300	100.0
10-14	4631	2285	49.3	845	477	56.4	3786	1808	47.7
05-14	4991	2645	53.0	905	537	59.3	4086	2107	51.6
15-17	2912	737	25.3	595	210	35.2	2317	527	22.8
Boys									
Total	5810	2581	44.4	1096	568	51.8	4714	2014	42.7
05-09	212	212	100.0	35	35	100.0	178	178	100.0
10-14	3352	1684	50.3	617	345	55.9	2735	1340	49.0
05-14	3564	1897	53.2	651	379	58.2	2913	1517	52.1
15-17	2246	685	30.5	445	188	42.3	1801	496	27.6
Girls									
Total	2094	800	38.2	404	179	44.3	1689	621	36.8
05-09	148	148	100.0	25	25	100.0	122	122	100.0
10-14	1280	600	46.9	229	132	57.9	1051	468	44.5
05-14	1428	748	52.4	254	158	62.1	1174	590	50.3
15-17	666	52	7.8	150	21	14.2	516	31	6.0

Table 18 : Child Labor by Age Group and Gender

There were about 5.0 million economically active children below the age of 15 and 7.9 million below the age of 18 years in 200-03 in Bangladesh. About 42 percent of the economically active children, that is, two-fifths were estimated to be in the child labor domain/group. It is particularly striking to see that the majority of these, about 2.6 million or 53.0 percent of the economically active were below the age of 15. Among children in the higher age group 15-17, there were about 0.7 million children in child labor.

5.4.2 Hazardous work

Hazardous work by children is any activity or occupation which by its nature or type has, or leads to, adverse effects on the child's safety, health (physical or mental), and moral development. Hazards could also derive from excessive workload, physical conditions of work and/or work intensity in terms of the duration or hours of work even where the activity or occupation is known to be non-hazardous or safe.

The following criteria are used for identification of hazardous child work:

1. Any child working in mining and construction was considered to be in a hazardous work;
2. Beyond mining and construction a number of occupations were considered to be of hazardous natures for example, work with heavy machinery or exposure to pesticides;
3. Any child below the age of 18 working 43 hours or more a week was considered to be in a hazardous work.

5.4.3 Worst forms of child labor (WFCL)

The unconditional worst forms of child labor include:

1. All forms of slavery or practices similar to slavery, such as sale and trafficking of children, debt bondage and serfdom and forced or compulsory labor, including forced or compulsory recruitment of children for use in armed conflict;
2. The use, procuring or offering of a child for prostitution, for the production of pornography or pornographic performance;
3. The use, procuring or offering of a child for illicit activities, particularly for the production and trafficking of drugs as defined in the relevant international treaties.

Gender and Age Group	No. of Children in hazardous work (000)	Percent
05-17		
Total	1291	100.0
Boys	1172	90.7
Girls	120	9.3
05-11		
Total	124	100.0
Boys	102	82.1
Girls	22	17.9
12-14		
Total	430	100.0
Boys	385	89.5
Girls	45	10.5
05-14		
Total	555	100.0
Boys	487	87.8
Girls	67	12.2
15-17		
Total	737	100.0
Boys	685	92.9
Girls	52	7.1

Table 19 : Children in Hazardous Work* by age group and gender

A total number of 1291 thousands children were estimated to be working in a hazardous situation in 2002-03. More boys than girls were engaged in hazardous work across all age groups. For instance, in the 5-14 and 15-17 years age groups, there were, respectively, 420 and 633 thousands more boys exposed to hazards at workplace than girls.

Gender and Age Group	Economically Active Children (EAC) million	Child Labor (CL) (in millions)	Children in Hazardous work (CHW) (in millions)	Child Labor As Percentage of EAC	CHW As Percentage of EAC	CHW As Percentage of CL
05-17						
Total	7423	3179	1291	42.8	17.4	40.6
Boys	5471	2461	1172	45.0	21.4	47.6
Girls	1952	718	120	36.8	6.1	16.7
05-11						
Total	841	841	124	100.0	14.8	14.8
Boys	609	609	102	100.0	16.7	16.7
Girls	232	232	22	100.0	9.6	9.6
12-14						
Total	3851	1601	430	41.6	11.2	26.9
Boys	2763	1167	385	42.2	13.9	33.0
Girls	1087	434	45	39.9	4.2	10.4
05-14						
Total	4692	2442	555	52.1	11.8	22.7
Boys	3372	1777	487	52.7	14.4	27.4
Girls	1319	666	67	50.5	5.1	10.1
15-17						
Total	2731	737	737	27.0	27.0	100.0
Boys	2099	685	685	32.6	32.6	100.0
Girls	632	52	52	8.3	8.3	100.0

Table 20 : Economically Active Children (Current Status), Child Labor and Hazardous Work by Gender and Age Group

The table indicates that out of the 7.4 million economically active children aged 5—17, a little less than 3.2 million were child labor and nearly 1.3 million of them were working in hazardous situations or conditions. In other words, children in hazardous work constituted about one-fifth the total number of economically active children (17.4%) and more than two-thirds of those in child labor (40.6%). Table 5.21 further, about 14.8 percent of child laborers (below12 years of age) are already working in hazardous occupations or situation, and the older the child worker, the more he/she is likely to be exposed to hazards at the work place.

5.5 Migrant Workers

Migration (human) is the movement of people from one place in the world to another for the purpose of taking up permanent or semi permanent residence, usually across a political boundary. An example of "semi permanent residence" would be the seasonal movements of migrant farm laborers. People can either choose to move ("voluntary migration") or be forced to move ("involuntary migration").[44]

ILO has given the following definition of Migrant workers:

'Migrant worker' means a person who migrates or who has migrated from one country to another with a view to being employed otherwise than on his own account and includes any person regularly admitted as a migrant worker. This part of the convention does not apply to—

  a. Frontier Worker
  b. Artists and members of the liberal professions who have entered the country on a short time basis
  c. Seamen
  d. Persons coming from specifically for purposes of training or education
  e. Employees of organizations or undertakings operating within the territory of a country who have been admitted temporarily to that country at the request of their employer to undertake specific duties or assignments, for a limited and defined period of time, and who are required to leave that country on completion of their duties or assignments."

International migration of labor has become an integral part of the global economy. Almost all countries are involved in the migration process in one way or other. Some are participating as labor sending countries, some as receiving, and others as transit countries.

5.6 Two Types of Migration Events Occur

5.6.1 External Migration

In case of external migration, residence changes occur between a residential unit and one outside it.

5.6.2 Internal Migration

Internal migration is a structural factor impacting on unemployment, involves people moving from rural to urban areas seeking employment. In this case residence changes occur from one residential unit to another in the same geographic location.

Despite having a labor intensive economy Bangladesh, has a significant imbalance in the human resources market in the country. Necessity forced Bangladeshi laborers to migrate to other countries for employment and better earning. From seventies; workers migrated in large numbers to the Middle East and other parts of the world, including Europe and Asia. Between 1996 and 2002 about 3.24 million Bangladeshis migrated for overseas employment that remitted 23.7 billion dollars during this period. These numbers excludes those who go abroad undocumented and made remittance through unofficial channels.

Bangladesh is a huge labor surplus country. On an average, it exports about 225,000 people annually (1990-99). According to UNDP (1995) over 125m people i.e., one out of every forty—five, live outside their country of origin for various reason. More than 25% of its foreign exchange earnings is derived from the remittances of the migrant workers. However, this sector is yet to be efficiently organized.

5.7 Destination

Bangladesh export migrant workers to 13 Middle Eastern and North African counties. Only 8 countries among them, account for more than 82% (24, 10,690) of the total migrants till now.[45] These countries are Saudi Arabia, UAE, Kuwait, Qatar, Iraq, Libya, Bahrain and Oman of which Kingdom of Saudi Arabia, alone accounts for nearly half of the total number of workers who migrated from Bangladesh during the period 1976-99.

Saudi Arabia is the largest employer of Bangladeshi migrant workers. From 1976 to February 1999 altogether 2,679,171 people have migrated from Bangladesh on overseas employment. Of this figure 1,126,539 have gone to Saudi Arabia during this period. From the late 1980s to 1997 Malaysia used to be the second largest employer of Bangladeshi migrant workers. Other major countries of destination for migrant workers are UAE, Kuwait, Oman, Qatar, and Bahrain.

Country Year	K.S.A	Kuwait	U.A.E.	Qatar	Iraq	Libya	Bahrain	Oman	Malaysia	Korea	S.Pore	Others	Total	Remittance Million (U.S)	Remittance Crore (tk.)
1976	217	643	1989	1221	587	173	335	113				809	6087	23.71	35.85
1977	1379	1315	5819	2262	1238	718	870	1492				632	15725	82.79	125.16
1978	3212	2243	7512	1303	1454	2394	762	2877	23			1029	22809	106.9	165.59
1979	6476	2298	5069	1383	2363	1569	827	3777			110	223	24495	172.06	266.95
1980	8695	3687	4847	1455	1927	2976	1351	4745	3		385	2	30073	301.33	492.95
1981	13384	5464	6418	2268	13153	4162	1392	7352			1083	1111	55787	304.88	620.74
1982	16294	7244	6863	6252	12898	2071	2037	8248			331	524	62762	490.77	1176.84
1983	12928	10283	6615	7556	4932	2209	2473	11110	23		178	913	59220	627.51	1568.76
1984	20399	5627	5185	2726	4701	3386	2300	10448			718	1224	56714	500	1265.49
1985	37133	7384	8336	4751	5051	1514	2965	9218			792	550	77694	500	1419.61
1986	27235	10286	8790	4347	4728	3111	2597	6255	53		25	254	68658	576.2	1752.85
1987	39292	9559	9953	5389	3847	2271	2055	440				711	74017	747.6	2313.94
1988	27622	6524	13437	7390	4191	2759	3268	2219	2			709	68121	763.9	2423.59
1989	39949	12404	15184	8462	2573	1609	4830	15429	401		229	654	101724	757.85	2446
1990	57486	5957	8307	7672	2700	471	4563	13980	1385		776	517	103814	781.54	2691.63
1991	75656	28574	8583	3772		1124	3480	23087	1628		62	585	147131	769.3	2818.65
1992	93132	34377	12975	3251		1617	5804	25825	10537		313	293	188124	901.97	3513.26
1993	106387	26407	15810	2441		1800	5396	15366	57938		1739	724	244508	1009.09	3986.97
1994	91385	14912	15051	624		1864	4233	6470	47826	1558	391	2012	186326	1153.54	4629.63
1995	84009	17492	14686	71		1106	3004	20949	35174	3315	3762	3975	187543	1201.52	4838.31
1996	72734	21042	23812	112		1966	3759	8691	56631	2759	5304	4904	211714	1355.34	5685.3
1997	105534	21126	54719	1373		1934	5010	5985	152844	889	27401	2762	381077	1525.03	6709.15
1998	158715	25444	38796	6806		1254	7014	4779	551	578	21728	2602	267667	1599.24	7513.18
1999	26286	3324	39120	854		239	666	713		136	1000	563	268182	1806.63	8882.74
2000 (Jan-March)	32701	278	7014	715		484	815	1220	30	264	2584	166	46271	478.50	2440.34
Total	1318693	302970	338114	90713		46686	75779	214620	385526	10854	78087	13139	2956243	18537.19	69783.48

Source: Prepared from BMET and Bangladesh Bank Data 2000

Table 21 : Migration by Country of Employment [1976-2000 March)]

5.7.1 Type of Employment

BMET has classified short-term migrants to Middle East and South East Asia into four categories: professional, skilled, semi-skilled, and unskilled. Doctors, engineers, teachers and nurses are considered as professional workers. Manufacturing or garment workers, drivers, computer operators and electricians are considered as skilled, while tailors and masons as semiskilled. Housemaids, agri-laborer, hotel boy and menial laborers, i.e., cleaners, cart loader, carton pickers are considered as unskilled workers. Only a small proportion of migrants are professionals (4.40%). 31% of them are skilled, 16% semi-skilled and 47% are unskilled workers.

Year	Professional	Skilled	Semi-skilled	Un-skilled	Total	Remittance (US Million)
1976	568	1775	543	3201	6087	23.71
1977	1765	6447	490	7022	15725	82.79
1978	3455	8190	1050	10114	22809	106.90
1979	3494	7005	1685	12311	24495	172.06
1980	1983	12209	2343	13538	30073	301.33
1981	3892	22432	2449	21014	55787	304.88
1982	3898	20611	3272	34981	62762	490.77
1983	1822	18939	5098	33361	59220	627.51
1984	2642	17183	5484	31405	56714	500.0
1985	2568	28225	7823	39078	77694	500.0
1986	22210	26294	9265	30889	68658	576.20
1987	2223	23839	9619	38336	74017	747.60
1988	2670	25286	10890	29356	68121	763.90
1989	5325	38820	17659	39920	101724	757.84
1990	6004	35613	20792	41405	103814	781.54
1991	9024	46887	32605	58615	147131	769.30
1992	11375	50689	30977	95083	188128	901.97
1993	11112	71662	66168	95566	244508	1009.09
1994	8390	61040	46519	70377	186326	1153.54
1995	6352	59907	32055	89229	187543	1201.57
1996	3188	64301	34689	109536	211714	1355.34
1997	3797	65211	193558	118511	381077	1525.03
1998	9574	74718	51590	131785	267667	1599.24
1999	8045	98449	44947	116741	268182	1705.74
2000 (Jan-March)	202	20853	5515	17791	46271	1949.32
Total	108569	798860	591506	1180146	2679171	19907.17

Source: Prepared from BMET and Bangladesh Bank Data 1999

Table 22 : Total No. of People Officially Migrated Yearly. Their skill Composition and Remittance Sent by them during 1976-2000[46]

5.8 Bangladeshi Migrants

Currently two types of voluntary international migration occur from Bangladesh. One takes place mostly to the industrialized west and the other to Middle Eastern and South East Asian countries. Voluntary migration to the industrialized west includes permanent residents, work permit holders and professionals. They are usually perceived as long term or permanent migrants. Migration to Middle East and South East Asia are usually for short term. The migrants return home after finishing their contract. Although long term migration is much older than short term yet; information on their types, extent and composition is not available with the government. Information on the short term labor migrants who officially go overseas for employment is available with the Bureau of Manpower Employment and Training (BMET).

The recruitment process of migrant workers in Bangladesh is complex. The whole process is characterized by a host of intermediaries, some official and legitimate, while others are clandestine and dubious. The recruitment of migrant workers is in the hands of the private recruiting agents and individuals.

In this context, though a migration friendly policy intervention by the Bangladesh government is desirable, in reality there is an absence of such policy perspective. The migrant workers send their remittances mainly through "hundi" system which is a method that by-passes the banking system. The remittances do have positive impact on Bangladesh economy. The remittances make substantial contribution to family welfare, social development and macroeconomic growth. There are mixed views about the costs and benefits of migration of workers from Bangladesh. However foreign laborers have remitted US$11.5 billion during 1977-99. The remittances are inexpensive source of foreign exchange available for economic development of Bangladesh. Migration of workers also helped in reducing the unemployment rate, which is one of the major problems of Bangladesh. Migrant households experienced enormous expansion of their income base during the post migration period. The benefit to cost ratio came out to be highly favorable to the individual as well as to the society.

Migrant workers, particularly in Asian countries, have to return to Bangladesh after stipulated contract period. There is absence of policy framework as well as program for facilitating reintegration of NRBs. Re-integration and rehabilitation of the returnees is the least explored area in labor migration scenario for Bangladeshis. Parameters of a policy framework for reintegration have been identified for action.

Globalization along with local factors has made the management of the labor migration a complex and difficult undertaking. The interest of migrant workers has been marginalized due to lack of rules, migration norms and expertise in migration management, both locally and globally. In Bangladesh, there is absence of institutional and policy framework to address the issues of institutional arrangements for skill development, protection of rights of the NRBs as well as evaluation of the measures to minimize the migration of undocumented workers.

Despite institutional limitations, Bangladesh, like other labor originating countries, has the goals of maximizing labor migration and ensuring protection and welfare of migrant workers abroad.

Extent

BMET data show that from 1976 to 2003, the total number of Bangladeshis working abroad as short-term migrants' stands at more than three million. It indicates a yearly average flow (1991-2002) of around 214,098. There is a slight decline in migration in 1991, perhaps because of Gulf War in that year. Again, dramatic increase is recorded in the following two years.

5.9 Age and Educational Level of Migrant Workers

Database of BMET is also not segregated according to age and educational level. Different micro studies conducted in migrant prone areas have shown that most of the migrants were young (15 to 30 years of age) when they first migrated (Siddiqui and Abrar, 2000; Afsar, 2000; Murshed, 2000) and a substantial majority were either illiterate or possessed educational background from class one to SSC.

6.0 Women in Trade Union

Global changes as a result of industrial restructuring had given momentum to women involvement in paid employment. Though statistics from the 1991 census estimates put women as constituting sixty percent of the population and about twenty-five percent of the actual workforce studies by Olajumoke (1985), Okoronkwo (1985), and Anugwon (1999) have shown that in spite of the above, their participation in active labor unionism is almost negligible.

The general attitude towards trade union in our country is that these matters are solely a male issue due to the personality clashes and the hooliganism associated with it. This lack luster approach of women to trade unionism is attributed to dynamic economic and social factors operating on both sides of the market. In the situation, where the competition for urban jobs is high, employers, influenced by the realities of differential labor costs or by discriminatory altitudes prefer to hire male labor who would not be encumbered by domestic and social demands. The few women, who have acquired some professional skill and are employed automatically falls into the elite class and unlike their counterparts in the informal sector, are unable to appreciate the importance of collective action to defend economic interests (Anugwon, 1999). Such elite conception has militated against women active participation in the workers struggle on the foray of trade unions. Thus the base provided by women action in the post war era could not project women into the realm of notice as labor leaders or activists.

In Bangladesh, it was found that almost all existing and active trade unions were engaged in one way or other with some of the garment workers' federations. No unionization process was found that could sustain itself for a considerable period without the help of existing federations. The reasons were: 1) high turnover of basic unit workers and/or sympathizers—who are mostly female—from one factory to another for economic betterment; 2) inactivity of the basic unit workers and/or supporters after a certain period of time because of the fear of harassment by the management or due to inducement on behalf of the management for refraining from becoming supporters and/or members of any such union; 3) expulsion or dismissal of the basic unit union leaders by the management on flimsy grounds such as "misconduct"; and, 4) the so-called "voluntary restraint" shown by the unit union leaders after being "bought off" by the management or being threatened with physical violence by the hired ruffians of the owners.

As far as the office records of the Directorate of Labor are concerned, there should now be four registered federations of garment workers unions operating in Bangladesh. However, despite the existence of four federations on paper, the investigation suggested the existence of only two federations in reality, whose name is not mentioned in order to protect the confidentiality of the respondents. One registered Federation is only partially active and is characterized by certain irregular labor-related activities, while the last Federation registered seems to be defunct. All of the three registered active federations claimed to have sufficient numbers of unions at the unit levels. Most of the unit unions, they claimed, were established with their direct support. Beside the above-mentioned registered federations, the study found—from different sources, including newspaper reports, the names of 10 more non-registered federations which were purportedly involved with garment workers. However, it is found that, among these 10 federations, only one non-registered Felderation is active on almost a full-time basis with various female labor related activities—for instance providing medical facilities to female garment workers, running night and weekend schools, conducting paralegal and socio-political awareness-building programs, extending legal support to individual workers and its affiliated unit unions, etc. For other federations, the investigation failed, despite all efforts, to trace either the office bearers or their offices or to find even one clue regarding their existence.

The study didn't intend to tap into the general problems affiliated with trade unions, so it excluded the office bearers of the federations from interview, who were mostly male. The interviewers sat independently on several occasions with only the unit union leaders, who were mostly female, as well as other female members and supporters of the federations in or outside their office premises. During group discussions with female members and supporters they were asked particularly to what extent their own issues and sentiments—such as, for example, ensuring separate toilets and changing room facilities at the work place, fighting against sexual harassment, ensuring personal security and safety both in and outside the workplace, overcoming various hazards of long working hours, ensuring health and childcare facilities and so on—were echoed in the activities and demand charters of the federations. The study also intended to verify whether any gender subordination existed in the hierarchy of the federations in terms of decision making. While most of the workers spoke positively about the inclusion of "all feasible women's issues" in the activities and demand charters of the unions, their responses on issues related to gender subordination within the unions were varied. Some were quite ambivalent in their expression of opinions. Some accepted the prevalence of male domination within union leaderships as inevitable given the existing socio-political conditions in Bangladesh which, to their mind, were not conducive to women's leadership, particularly when it came to industrial dispute resolution. For them, industrial disputes in Bangladesh are always confrontational, and therefore male leaders are better equipped to withstand the management in times of crisis. However, not all female unit union members are happy with the idea of delegating their right to negotiate to the federation leaders. In fact, this has remained the most controversial aspect of federation unit union relations. On the one hand, most female garment workers feel technically too weak to negotiate, both individually and through their unit unions, because owners are often quite autocratic and patrimonial in handling industrial disputes. Female garment workers thus welcome the intervention of federation leaders on their behalf in disputes with the management, both in bipartite negotiations and extended conciliation, as well as compulsory adjudication. On the other hand, many female garment workers and unit union leaders confessed to the interviewers that they are apprehensive about some male middle-class federation leaders, who might be pursuing their own interests. Some argued that given the opportunity and perhaps a little outside support, women workers would be equally able to lead their unions or federations. In support of their argument they pointed the fact that both the President and the General Secretary of the only active non-registered Federation—a federation established with support from an American-based NGO—were women. For the majority of them, however, the issue of leadership within unions or federations did not really matter because the women workers constituted more than 90 per cent of their total membership.

In order to have a clearer picture of the role played by interested male outsiders in the formation of these federations—whose membership comprised almost exclusively female garment workers—the study tried to know next about the socio-political background of the founding leaders. It was not surprising to find out that very few garment workers, particularly female workers, were able to establish federations themselves. Among the respondent federations, only in one case (non-registered Federation) did the leadership come originally from the garment workers themselves, and these leaders, incidentally, were female. However, it must be reiterated here that a foreign NGO played a significant role, both in terms of finance and organizational support, in promoting the above-mentioned female leadership. In six other cases, the leadership came either directly from former and active male political activists of various centrist or left leaning political parties, or from former student leaders or activists (again, mostly male) affiliated with student front organizations of different political parties. Although some of our respondent federations reported that they try to educate female garment workers and their unit union leaders regarding their legal rights and obligations through various workshops, group discussions and other means, during the survey it was observed that only the non-registered Federation is conducting weekly classes on various legal, social, and other issues related to female workers. The leaders of this federation, however, confessed that they often encountered difficulties in getting enough female garment workers to participate in the courses.

One's understanding of the status of women in Bangladesh society must be grounded on the conviction that women, like men, are human beings and are entitled to rights, benefits and status in equal measure to that of men in workplace. Unless accompanied by such conviction the quest to learn about women status in Bangladesh employment scenario is an exercise in futility. By merely knowing the present status, one only reaffirms the status quo, and does not question the validity of the status quo itself. Analysis and outcome of development inputs adopted with a view to improve women's status must be framed within a broad overview that the phenomena of women's subordination, exploitation and discrimination are not natural, but are products of history and social evolution.

In Bangladesh workers are engaged in both formal and informal sectors.

Informal sector

The informal sector is economic activity that is neither taxed nor monitored by a government; and is not included in that government's Gross National Product (GNP); as opposed to a formal economy. The concept of the informal sector was introduced into international usage in 1972 by the International Labor Organization (ILO) in its Kenya Mission Report, which defined informality as a "way of doing things characterized by (a) ease of entry; (b) reliance on indigenous resources; (c) family ownership; (d) small scale operations; (e) labor intensive and adaptive technology; (e) skills acquired outside of the formal sector; (g) unregulated and competitive markets". Since that time, many definitions were introduced by different authors and the ILO itself. The ILO/ICFTU international symposium on the informal sector in 1999 proposed that the informal sector workforce can be categorized into three broad groups: (a) owner-employers of micro enterprises, which employ a few paid workers, with or without apprentices; (b) own-account workers, who own and operate one-person business, who work alone or with the help of unpaid workers, generally family members and apprentices; and (c) dependent workers, paid or unpaid, including wage workers in micro enterprises, unpaid family workers, apprentices, contract labor, home workers and paid domestic workers.

In the light of the SNA 1993 as well as 15th International Child Labor Statistics (ICLS) and in the context of Bangladesh, the informal sector is defined as those economic activities which are run or operated by the households-

1. Either in household premises or outside household with a fixed location or without fixed location, including in uncovered spaces such as streets and parks.
2. Mostly operated by household members.
3. Outside the purview of the government regulation
4. Unregistered, no formal accounts keeping etc.

Formal sector

It includes mainly corporate and quasi-corporate types of establishments. Their operations are registered with a legal authority and are regulated by the concerned laws of the country.

CHAPTER II

Definitions of Industrial Relations

Definitions of Industrial Relations

The term 'Industrial Relations' comprises of two terms: 'Industry' and 'Relations'. "Industry" refers to "any productive activity in which an individual (or a group of individuals) is (are) engaged". By "relations" we mean "the relationships that exist within the industry between the employer and his workmen."

Industrial Relations have developed both a broad and a narrow meaning. Originally, 'Industrial Relations (IR)' was broadly defined to include the totality of relationships and interactions between employers and employees. From this perspective, "Industrial Relations' covers all aspects of the employment relationship, including human resource (or personnel) management, employee relations, and union-management (or labor) relations.

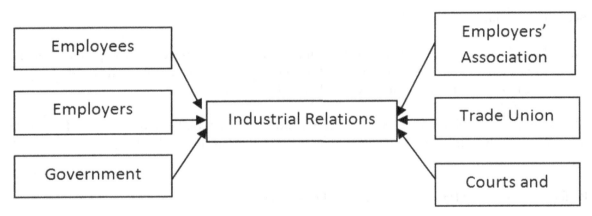

Figure 1 : Relationship between three major role players

But now a day its meaning has become more specific and restricted. Industrial relations now pertains to the study and practice of collective bargaining, trade unionism, and labor-management relations, while human resource management is a separate, largely distinct field that deals with nonunion employment relationships and the personnel practices and policies of employers.

The relationship which arise at and out of the workplace generally include the relationships between individual workers, the relationships between workers and their employer, the relationships between employers, the relationships employers and workers have with the organizations formed to promote their respective interests, and the relations between those organizations, at all levels. Industrial relations also includes the processes through which these relationships are expressed (such as, collective bargaining, workers' participation in decision-making, and grievance and dispute settlement), and the management of conflict between employers, workers and trade unions, when it arises.

Definitions of Industrial Relations given by different Scholars and Institutions

One of the very first definitions of industrial relations was given by J.H. Richardson (1954) in his book 'An Introduction to the Study of Industrial Relations'-

"Industrial Relations' is concerned with the relations between the parties in industry, particularly with the determination of working conditions."

But a more comprehensive definition was given by John Dunlop, founder of Systems theory of Industrial relations. This definition covers almost all aspects of Industrial Relations. This considers the interaction of the key actors that is labor and management with the government as well as the rules derived from this interaction that govern the employment relationship.

According to John Dunlop (1958)—

"An industrial relations system at any one time in its development is regarded as comprised of certain actors, certain contexts, an ideology which binds the industrial relations system together and a body of rules created to govern the actors at the work place and work community."

This definition by Professor John Dunlop does not cover industrial conflict and the origin of the work place rules. On the other hand in the definition of Professor Margerison's dominant is the concept of conflict.

Professor Margerison (1969) defined industrial relations as-

"The study of people in a situation, organization or system interacting in the doing of work in relation to some form of contract, written or unwritten . . . . The essential element in all industrial relations is conflict . . . the nature of and development of conflict itself."

Professor Margerison equates Industrial Relations (IR) to workplace conflict in his definition. Though the definition misses the most important aspect of IR which is the role of power, the definition of Hymen (1975) emphasizes the importance of power/control in industrial relations as well as the process rather than result or outcome.

Hyman (1975) says industrial relations is "The study of processes of control over work relations".

When Hyman talks about conflict he emphasizes on the relations between the employee and management, but the definition of Flanders emphasizes the institutions of regulation and "Industrial relations problems" seen to relate to the institutions.

Flanders (1975) defined Industrial Relations as

"The only aspect of business enterprise with which industrial relations is concerned is the employment aspect; the relations between the enterprise and its employees and among those employees themselves . . . . The study of industrial relations may therefore be described as a study of the institutions of job regulation."

This definition of Flanders does not consider behavioral variables of people at work. That is their attitudes, motivations, and perceptions. The definition of Arun Monappa citated the variables:

"Industrial relations are sets of functional interdependence involving historical, variables."

The definition given by Alistair McMillan includes all the three major parties involved in the system that is employer, employees and government. According to Alistair McMillan,

"Industrial Relations are interaction between employers, employees, and the government; and the institutions and associations through which such interactions are mediated."

In this definition all the four most important actors of an industrial relations system that is employer, employee, Government and trade unions as well, are identified. But the parties involved in industrial relations system are identified very well in the definition of Professor Barbash.

Professor Barbash (1980) defined industrial relations as

"the area of study and practice concerned with the administration of the employment function in modern public and private enterprise. This function involves workers, unions, mangers, governments and various publics."

The main problem with the definition is that it deals only with the administration of the workplace rules. Though this definition involves workers, unions, managers and government, but 'industrial relations' (IR) is actually a very broad term. It cannot be confined within these four elements. IR constitutes of some more aspects like collective bargaining, workplace disputes/ conflicts, negotiations etc.

Though the definition of J.H. Richardson focuses on the relationship between parties emphasizing on the working conditions of industry, he didn't identify the parties or actors unions, mangers, governments and various publics involved in industrial relations whereas the definition given by S. Nagaraju (1981) in the book "Industrial Relations System in India" attempts to identify the parties involved in the industrial relations system.

"The term 'Industrial Relations' can be described as a subject which includes in its purview all types of relationships that arises in the process of production between employers and employees, or employers and trade union workers, or among the unions themselves."

This definition though identifies some of the actors like: employers, employees and trade unions, it misses to mention 'government' as an actor in industrial relations.

On the other hand, though the definition of Arun Monappa as well as Flander doesn't define these variables, the definition of Deery and Plowman focuses particularly on the behavioral aspects of IR.

According to Deery and Plowman (1985)

"In its broadest sense, industrial relations is about the behavior and interaction of people at work. It is concerned with how individuals, groups, organizations and institutions make decisions which shape the employment relationship between management and labor."

A similar kind of definition was given by Momtaz Uddin Ahmed, Professor, Department of Economics, University of Dhaka:

"Industrial relations is defined as a study of the relationship between employer and employee in paid employment, the ways in which employees are paid, motivated, trained and disciplined and the manners in which these processes are influenced by the major factors such as management, trade unions and the government."

A definition similar to J.H. Richardson was given by Reeta Mathur (1986) in her book "Industrial Relations in Public Enterprise". According to her:

"The term 'Industrial Relations' refers to all type of relationships between all parties in an enterprise."

However may be the most comprehensive definition was given by Joris Van Ruysseveldt et Jelle Visser in the book "Industrial Relations in Europe".

Joris Van Ruysseveldt et Jelle Visser (1996) defined industrial relations as-

"The study of strategic choice and collective action of labor, business and governments, their mutual relationships of conflict, cooperation and power, affecting the content and regulation of employment relations and the use and distribution of physical and human resources."

In this definition "Industrial relations" is termed as a study of collective actions of labor and owners and government. Mutual relationship among them, conflict management, cooperation and power, regulation of employment, wages and other benefits are also included in this study.

The Dictionary of Business and Management defines 'Industrial relations' as the "relationship between the management of an organization and its workforce. If industrial relations are good, the whole workforce will be well motivated to work hard for the benefit of the organization and its customers. The job satisfaction in such an environment will itself provide some of the rewards for achieving good industrial relations. If the industrial relations are bad, both management and workers will find the workplace an uncongenial environment, causing discontent, poor motivation, and a marked tendency to take self-destructive industrial action."

So Industrial relations should be considered as the interactions among the relevant role players, which provides better environment in any organization through the implementation of government regulations like minimum wages, flexible/performance pay, cross-cultural management, dispute prevention, industrial relations/human resource management training, balancing efficiency with equity and labor market flexibility, freedom of association, labor rights and changing patterns of work, women, migration, human resource management, transition economies.

CHAPTER III

Perceptions of Industrial Relations

CONTENTS

1.0 Legal History of Bangladesh Industrial Relations and Management Approach

1.1 History of Industrial Relations in Bangladesh

In Bangladesh, the Industrial Relations practice is upheld by

a) The Constitution of the country
b) The ILO Conventions ratified by the government and
c) The Labor Policy and the set of legislations enacted by the Government on the basis of the ILO conventions by the Government of Bangladesh.[47]

The Labor Policy of the Government stresses the need for healthy Labor relations for achieving higher productivity, freedom of association, introduction of productivity linkage incentives, resolution of disputes through bi-partite negotiations, conciliation and adjudication etc.

The ILO Convention Nos. 87 and 91 concerning freedom of association and right to collective bargaining form the basis of Labor relations practice. Other ILO Conventions ratified by the Government are also of importance since they concern the conditions of employment of workers, wages, social security etc. which have direct bearing on the over-all Labor relations of the country.

The Constitution of the country provides for freedom of association which guarantees the right to form or join associations and trade unions. The relevant provisions in the Constitution of the People's Republic of Bangladesh are indicated as follows:

"Every citizen shall have the right to form associations or unions subject to any reasonable restrictions imposed by law in the interest of morality of public order."[48]

1.1.1 Evolution of Labor Policies and Laws

The growth of labor laws has its origin in British India. In the absence of any state control or organization of workers, the employers were free to do whatever they liked. Hours of work were very long, wages much below subsistence level and other conditions miserable. The Government of India felt the necessity of taking necessary for safeguarding the interests of workers and improving their working conditions.[49]

After liberation of Bangladesh as an independent country in 1971, a new phase of principles of labor policies was recognized. The Constitution of Bangladesh guarantees, among other things, that the fundamental responsibilities of the State would be to emancipate the toiling masses, peasants and workers and backward sections of the people from all forms of exploitation. In line with the

Constitutional responsibility, the first labor minister of Bangladesh announced the Labor Policy on October 27, 1972.[50]

On March 01, 1980, the then Minister for Labor announced a Labor Policy in pursuance to the government's 19-point program. The most distinguishing features of this labor policy are: tripartism, productivity and incentives and the limited scope of workers' participation in the management.[51]

1.2 History of Labor Laws in Bangladesh[52]

1.2.1 Act Regulating Working Conditions

Before the enactment of Labor Code 2006 the following laws (and rules made there under) regulate the working conditions of workers employed in factories, shops and establishments, road transport organizations and tea plantations of covering such aspects as working hours, health and hygiene, safely and welfare.

1. The Road and Transport workers Ordinance, 1961 (XXVIII of 1961)
2. The Tea Plantations Labor Ordinance, 1961 (XXXIX of 1962)
3. The Factories Act, 1965 (IV of 1965), and
4. The shop Establishments Act, 1965 (VII of 1965)

1.2.2 Acts Regulating Service Conditions

Matters such as conditions of employment, classification of workers leave holidays, disciplinary matters, grievances procedures, maintenance of service records, etc. are covered by the following laws (and rules and by-laws made there under):

1. The Working Journalists (Conditions of Service) Ordinance, 1960 (XVI of 1960)
2. The Apprenticeship Ordinance, 1962 (LVI 0f 1962)
3. The Employment of Labor (Standing Orders) Act, 1965 (VIII of 1965)
4. The Inland Water Transport Workers (Regulation of Employment) Act, 1992
5. The Newspaper Employees (Conditions of Services) Act, 1974 (XXX of 1974), Administered By The Minister of Ports, Shipping and Inland Water Transport.

1.2.3 ACT Regulating Wages

The following laws (and rules made there under) regulate the payment of wages, implementation of the wage commissions' recommendations and determination of minimum wages in specified industries:

1. The Minimum Wages Ordinance, 1961 (XXXIV of 1934)
2. The Coal Mines (Fixation of Rates of Wages) Ordinance, 1960 (XXXIX of 1960)
3. The Agricultural Workers (Minimum Wages) Ordinance, 1984 (XVII of 1984) administered by the Ministry of Agriculture.
4. The State-Owned Manufacturing Industries Workers (Terms and Conditions of Service) Act, 1974 (X of 1974)

1.2.4 Acts Regulating Industrial Relations

The Industrial Relations Ordinance, 1969 (XXIII of 1969)

This ordinance is intended to regulate trade union activities (including strikes, lockouts etc.) and relations between employers and workman and the avoidance and settlement of any differences or disputes arising between them. But The State-Owned Manufacturing Industries Workers (Terms and Conditions of Service) Ordinance, 1985 restricts collective bargaining in the nationalized sector on certain matters, viz., (a) wages, (b) leave, (c) house rent, (d) conveyance allowance, (e) medical allowance, (f) festival bonus and (g) provident fund.

1.3 History of Laws Regarding Labor Inspection

1.3.1 Historical Development[53]

In East Pakistan, after the subject 'Labor' was withdrawn from the Concurrent List of the Constitution of the country and made a provincial one, the most important Labor laws dealing with Labor administration and industrial relations were re-enacted in 1965 by amending the relevant previous laws.

These important laws are the Factories Act of 1965, the Shops and Establishments Act of 1965, the Employment of Labor (Standing Orders) Act of 1965, the Trade Unions Act of 1965, the Labor Disputes Act of 1965 and the Inland Water Transport (Regulation of Employment) Act of 1965. In 1969, the Trade Unions Act of 1965 and the Labor Disputes Act of 1965 were integrated into one law, namely, the Industrial Relations ordinance, 1969, and the Government enforcement machinery of Labor laws was separated from the Labor Directorate.

The Department for Inspection of Factories and Establishments thus came into existence in the year 1970 on functional lines under the administrative control of the Ministry of Labor and manpower as a distinct and unified inspection service for the enforcement of Labor laws.

1.4 History of Laws Regarding Labor Relations

1.4.1 Coordinating and Implementing Agencies[54]

The Ministry of Labor and Manpower is the central co-coordinating agency for Labor relations and the Department of Labor (DOL) provides the relevant Labor relations

The wages of workers engaged in manufacturing process in the public sector are determined by the Industrial Workers' Wages Commissions set up by the Government from time to time. The wages of other public sector employees are determined by the National Pay Commission. In small undertakings, where effective collective bargaining agents are not available, the minimum wages of workers' are determined by the Minimum Wages Board set up under the Minimum Wages Ordinance, 1961. Wages in the private sector establishments are determined through collective bargaining within the framework of the Industrial Relations Ordinance, 1969.

1.4.2 Historical Development[55]

Pre—Partition Context

Consequent upon the partition of British India in 1947, Pakistan inherited all the Labor laws from undivided British India. The setting up of a Works Committee at the plant level was designed to remove causes of friction between workers and the employer in the day-to-day operations of the enterprise. Certain minor amendments were made in this law from time to time. It was, however, repealed in 1959 by the Martial Law regime, and the Industrial Dispute Ordinance was promulgated in its place.

The Industrial Disputes Ordinance of 1959 was again amended in 1961. It made provision for the formation of Works Committees consisting of representatives of employers and workers engaged in industrial plants employing 50 or more persons empowered the Industrial Court to dismiss any application for reasons of it being frivolous or vexatious. Officers of trade unions were, however, protected by a provision that their service conditions could not be altered without the permission of the Industrial Court during the tendency of an industrial dispute. An amendment of the Ordinance in 1962 made a provision giving the right to appeal to the High Court against the awards of the Industrial Court. In 1965, the Industrial Disputes Ordinance of 1959 was repealed and substituted by the East Pakistan Labor Disputes Act, 1965. During this period many other Labor ordinance were promulgated by the Martial Law Authority and Rules and Regulations relating thereto were framed.

Registration and recognition, of trade unions were controlled by the Registrar of Trade Unions. The Labor Disputes Act, 1965, provided for collective bargaining, but for all practical purposes the use of strikes was made impossible. Under the East Pakistan Trade Unions Act, 1965, the Director of Labor was given vast powers in regard to trade union recognition.

The most unfavorable provision for workers in the Employment of Labor (Standing Orders) Act, 1965 was the termination of employment of workers, without showing any reasons, which was against the very spirit of collective bargaining. This led to mass discontent accompanied by agitation.

The Factories Act, 1965, incorporated some additional provisions. Under workers were entitled to not less than 10 days festival—1 holiday with pay, 10 days' equal leave pay, 14 days' sick leave on half the average pay and annual leave based on the working days. Similarly, the scope of the Shops and Establishments Act, 1965, was widened. The law extended its applicability to all establishments having five or more workers. Compared to the Trade Unions Act and Industrial Disputes Act and Industrial Disputes Act, the Factories and Shops and Establishments Acts were found to be wider in coverage.

Following mass agitation, combined with the rising tendency of industrial unrest, the Government announced an outline of the Labor Policy on 5 July 1969. Based on a broad policy statement, the Industrial Relations Ordinance, 1969, was promulgated on 13 November 1969, restoring the right to strike. In accordance with the policy guidelines, the Minimum Wages Ordinance was promulgated and minimum wages were fixed for certain categories of industrial establishments having 50 or more workers.

Post—Liberation Context

At the time of the independence of Bangladesh, it inherited all the Acts and Ordinance regulating the activities and governing the employment of the Labor force. It also inherited 29 ILO Conventions ratified during 1919-1971. Subsequently, Bangladesh ratified 2 more Conventions.

After liberation, the Government of Bangladesh nationalized the major industries and services, including banks and insurance companies. The working class of Bangladesh, with higher hopes and aspirations, demanded higher wages and fringe benefits. The Government, for the sake of uniformity and to meet the demands of the workers, constituted an Industrial Workers Wage Commission. The Commission within 6 months submitted its recommendations to the Government for fixing wages, bonus, medical allowance, house rent allowance, conveyance allowance and leave for workers engaged in nationalized industries. The recommendations of the Commission were also accepted by the Government. To implement these recommendations, the Government promulgated a law known as the State-Owned Manufacturing Industries Workers (Terms and Conditions of Service) Ordinance, 1974.

Trade Unions did not view this measure with favor as the workers' basic right to collective bargaining was taken away. The Pay Commission's Report was also published in 1973 for employees of Government, corporations, semi-autonomous units and other authorities created by the Government. However, large-scale agitation started among the jute and cotton industries, causing considerable loss of production. Employees engaged in autonomous and semi-autonomous organizations were also dissatisfied.

In 1975, the Government enacted the Industrial Relations (Regulations) Ordinance to regulate industrial relations. The Ordinance provided that unless the Government otherwise directed, there should be no registration of new trade unions. It was further provided that persons employed as members of the watch and ward, security staff and confidential assistants shall have no right to be members of trade unions. The law prohibited outsiders from holding office in trade unions. Elections for determination of collective bargaining agents were suspended. This situation created alarm in the minds of the workers of Bangladesh. The Government, by an executive order on 20 July 1977, withdrew the restriction on registration of trade unions and determination of collective beginning agents, but the restriction on trade union activities in the offices of corporations and semi-autonomous organizations continued.

The Industrial Relations Ordinance was further amended in 1977 to provide that a trade union should not be entitled to registration unless it has a minimum membership of 30 per cent of the total number of workers employed in the establishment or group of establishments from which it is formed. It was also laid that no trade union which was unregistered, or whose registration had been canceled, should function as a trade union.

The Government set up the Industrial Workers' Wages and Productivity Commission and Pay and Services Commission in 1976 for workers and employees engaged in nationalized industries and Government establishments respectively, and their recommendations, which were accepted by the Government, were declared in 1976 and made effective from July, 1977. It may be clarified that though legally, collective bargaining was not allowed in matters covering the Wages and Pay Commission recommendations, in practice, managements of corporations and semi-government organizations did negotiate with trade unions and federations on problems and anomalies that arose in the implementation of such recommendations. However, in the private sector the collective bargaining process remained the means for settlement of Labor disputes, including determination of wages.

To improve industrial relations, the Government set up a National Tripartite Consultative Committee on 23 September 1978, with representation from the Government, managements and workers. Subsequently, on 27 September 1979, the Government revoked the Emergency Power Rules, 1975, and as such, the restraints imposed on trade unions in the offices of autonomous or semi-autonomous organizations were withdrawn.

A comprehensive Labor policy was announced by Government on 1st March 1980, whereby full freedom of association and right of collective bargaining has been allowed to the workers. The policy recognizes the right to strike by the workers and that of lock-out by the employers as instruments of collective bargaining. It, however, suggests that in the interest of continuity of production of goods and services, strikes may be resorted to after exhausting all legal process. It further provides that right to strike may be exercised only after securing through secret ballot the support of majority workers of collective bargaining agents. It also stipulates that strikes and lock-outs will continue to be regulated in certain essential and public utility services, duly notified by the Government. The policy lays stress on the process of joint negotiation, conciliation and adjudication for settlement of industrial disputes.

The Industrial Relations Ordinance, 1969 which regulates the Labor relations and provides for settlement of industrial disputes, was amended in the light of the Labor policy declaration of 1980. The law contains detailed procedures to bringing about settlement of industrial disputes through the process of direct negotiation i.e. bipartite negotiation, conciliation, arbitration and adjudication by Labor Courts and Labor Appellate Tribunal as mentioned.

1.4.3 Collective Bargaining and Settlement of Industrial Disputes[56]

Direct Negotiation

Section 26 of the IRO, 1969 provides that "if at any time an employer or a collective bargaining agent finds that an industrial dispute is likely to arise between the employer or any of the workmen, the employer or as the case may be, the collective bargaining agent shall communicate his or its views in writing to the other party. Within ten days of receipt of such a communication, the party receiving it shall, in consultation with the representatives of the other party, arrange a meeting with the representatives of the other party for collective bargaining on the issue raised in the communication with a view to reaching an agreement through the procedure of dialogue. If the parties reach a settlement, a memorandum of settlement is recorded in writing and signed by both the parties and a copy thereof is forwarded to the conciliator and other specified authorities.

It is necessary to mention here that as per section 43 of the IRO 1969 "no industrial dispute shall be deemed to exist unless it has been raised in the prescribed manner by a collective bargaining agent or an employer." Section 22 and 22A of IRO 1969 deal with the manner of determining collective bargaining agent in an establishment or group of establishments. No union other than the collective bargaining agent can, therefore, legally raise any industrial dispute.

Conciliation

Section 27 A of the IRO 69 provides that where the parties to an industrial dispute fail to reach a settlement by negotiation under Section 26, any of them may report to the Conciliator that the negotiations have failed and request him in writing to conciliate in the dispute. The Conciliator shall, on, receipt of such request, proceed to conciliate in the dispute.

Section 27 of the above law empowers the Government to appoint as many persons as it considers necessary to be Conciliators specifying the area within which or the class of establishments or industries in relation to which each one of them shall perform his functions. The Director of Labor and the Additional Director of Labor have been notified to be Conciliator under this law for the whole of the country, while the Joint Directors of Labor, deputy Directors of Labor, Assistant Directors of Labor and Labor Officers posted in the divisions, regional offices and branch offices have been notified by Government to be Conciliators in their respective areas for the purpose of the Ordinance.

Section 28 of the IRO stipulates that if the Conciliator fails to settle the dispute within ten days of the receipt of a request under Section 27A, the collective bargaining agent or the employer may serve on the other party to the dispute twenty one days' notice of strike or lock-out, as the ease may be. But the collective bargaining agent is debarred from serving any strike notice unless three-fourths of its members have given their consent to it through a secret ballot specifically held for tins purpose. Where a party to an industrial dispute serves a notice of strike or lock-out under Section 28, it shall simultaneously deliver a copy thereof to the Conciliator who shall proceed to Conciliate or as the case may be, continue to conciliate in the dispute notwithstanding the notice of strike or lock-out.

Arbitration

It is stipulated in section 31 of the IRO 1969 that if the conciliation fails, the conciliator may try to persuade the parties to agree to refer the dispute to an arbitrator. In case the parties agree, they make a joint request in writing for reference of the dispute to an arbitrator agreed upon by the parties. The arbitrator forwards his award to the parties and to the govt. and the govt. publishes it in the official gazette.

Strikes/lock outs and Adjudication

If no settlement of the dispute is arrived at in course of conciliation proceedings and parties do not agree to refer the dispute to an arbitrator the workers may on strikes or as the case may be, the employer declares lock out, on the expiry of the period of notice or upon the issuance by the conciliator a certificate of failure on the dispute whichever is later. Section 32(a) provides that "the parties to the dispute may at any time either before or after the commencement of strike or lock-out make a joint application to the labor court for adjudication of the dispute." The govt., however has the authority to prohibit suck a strike or lockout if such strike or lockout lasts for more than 30 days and simultaneous refer the dispute to the labor court for adjudication.

Section 34 of the ordinance further provides that any collective bargaining agent or any employer or work man may apply to the labor court for the enforcement of any right guaranteed or secured to it or him under any law or an award or settlement.

A settlement arrived at in course of conciliation proceedings or an award of an arbitrator published under sec. 31 or an award or decision of labor court delivered under sec 37 or the decision of the tribunal under the sec.38 are binding on all the parties to the industrial disputes and any breach of any team or any settlement award or decision are punishable offense under the law.

The legal framework and machinery on labor administration and industrial relation system in the country have been briefly outlined above. These are designed for ensuring speedy and orderly resolution of industrial disputes and dealing with labor problems through the process of

1. Joint consultation between workers and management,
2. Collective bargaining
3. Mediation and conciliation

1.4.4 Bangladesh Employers' Association[57]

The Bangladesh Employer's Association (BEA) represents nearly 90% of the established employers in the private sector and all the sector corporations and autonomous bodies in the public sector. The BEA, in their Memorandum of Articles of Association, has included some laudable goals for promoting good relations and unanimity amongst employers, creating mutual interest and good feelings between such employers and their workmen, to encourage reasonable and admissible scheme for the general welfare and uplift of labor and other employers, to negotiate with trade unions and other labor organizations etc.

The BEA is represented on various national committee/bodies concerning Labor-management relations, like the:

a) Inter-Ministerial Cabinet Committee on Labor Matters:
b) Tripartite Consultative Council on Labor Matters, Ministry of Labor and Manpower:
c) ILO Tripartite Consultative Committee;
d) Bangladesh Minimum Wage Board;
e) Minimum Wages Boards for different industries where collective bargaining is not developed;
f) Bangladesh Family Planning Council;
g) Labor Courts in Dhaka, Chittagong, Khulna, Rajshahi;
h) Governing bodies of Bangladesh Management Development Centre and Institute of Business Administration; and
i) Managing Committee of different technical Training Institutions.

In the international field, the Association has representations in the ILO Governing Body, ILO Asian Advisory Committee, and the Executive Committee of the International Organization of employers (IOE). It also sends representative to attend various international conference and industrial relations seminars and symposiums organized from time to time by the ILO.

1.4.5 History of Trade Unions[58]

After Partition (1947-71)

In January 1948, Trade union Federation of Pakistan (TUFP) came into existence. East Pakistan Trade union Federation (EPTUF) was split in 1949. In April 1950, EPTUF and TUFP were amalgamated as trade Union Federation, Pakistan (TUFP). In 1951, another federation, named, Mashrequi Pakistan Federation of Labor (MPFL) was created by Kashen Chowdhry. The United Council of Association of Civil employees of Pakistan (UCACEP) were also formed in the same year with eleven government employees' unions. Inland Water Workers' Union (IWTWU) came into existence in 1952.

After liberation of the country in 1971, the Government of Bangladesh nationalized the major industries and services including banks and insurance companies. The working class of Bangladesh, with higher hopes and aspirations, demanded higher wages and fringe benefits.

It is interesting to note that after liberation, the government affiliated trade unions always dominated the trade union scene. In 1972, the number of registered trade unions in the country was 2523 with a membership of 682,923 workers. In 1975, the figures stood 3,161 and 921,152 respectively. This means, during 4 years following Liberation, 638 trade unions were registered with 238,229 members. The then government Labor front, namely, Jatiya Sramik Leagues JSL) dominated the field of Labor. During the period 1975-81, 372 new trade unions with a membership of 11,27,508 workers got registration. From 1982 to 1990, 1633 new trade unions with 672,060 members got registration. The government affiliated Jatiya Sramik Party played the dominated role. This federation had by then 279 basic trade unions with a total membership of 2,21,909 workers affiliated with it. On the contrary, BNP affiliated Jatiya Sramik Dal had only 35 basic union with 42,634 members with it. It is, therefore, clear from the statistical data that the government supported Labor from always dominated in the field of trade union in the country.

The statistical data regarding overall growth of trade unions in Bangladesh shows that in 1949 there were only 74 registered trade unions with a membership of 987,543 only. During the period 1949-71, it rose to 1,169 with a total membership of 4, 50,606 only. In 1992, a total of 4,065 registered trade unions with 16, 48,783 members existed in Bangladesh. This means, there is an increase of 1567.57% and 457.27% in the number of the trade unions and their members stands at 5493.24% and 1673.16% respectively. This clearly shows the rate of multiplicity of trade unions in Bangladesh.

1.4.6 Workers' Participation[59]

In Bangladesh, the Industrial Relations Ordinance, 1969 provides for constituting a Participation committee in each industrial establishment in which 50 or more workers are employed. The committee consists of representatives of employers and workers on equal basis workers representatives are nominated by the CBA of the establishment chosen from amongst the workers therein.

The company's Profits (Workers Participation) Act, 1968, however, provides for participation of workers in the profits of the company. This is administered through a Workers Participations Fund to which the company contributes certain percentage of its net profits every year.

1.5 Approaches towards Industrial Relations in Bangladesh

1.5.1 Managerial Approach

Perception of industrial relation is based primarily on a belief what is 'right' in respect of 'fairness' and the exercise of 'power' and 'authority'. Managerial approaches to industrial relations been characterized by in consistency, informality, lack of structure. Managers have also tended to be reactive in industrial relations situations rather than proactive.

As indicated, there is some evidence to suggest, however, that many more employers are beginning to think of themselves as adopting a more participative and consultative style of management than was once the case, with a proportion considering that they are more proactive than reactive. In analyzing the ways in which management approach to industrial relations we need to examine three key concepts: managerial styles, strategies and policies.[60]

Managerial Styles

Managerial style is related to a number of organizational and managerial variables and different classificatory systems have been used to analyze them, Fox, for example puts forward six patterns of industrial relations between management and employees varying according to the degree of legitimacy afforded by each side to the other which are 'traditional', 'classical conflict', 'sophisticated modern', 'standard modern', 'continuous challenge' and 'sophisticated paternal' patterns.

Strategies

Industrial relations strategies are defined as long term goals developed by management 'to preserve or change its products, practices or results of industrial activities over time'. That some organizations have such strategies is based on a number of assumptions, for example: that corporate management usually determine overall strategies to achieve their corporate goals; that strategic thinking is necessary for corporate success; that corporate leaders have some choice in the matter; and that choosing their industrial relations policies rationally implies that they should be linked to other objectives and policies.

Policies

One of the first formal definitions of industrial relations policy was provided by the Commissions on Industrial Relations (CIR). The CIR argued that a corporate industrial relations policy should form an integral part of the total strategy through which enterprises pursue their corporate objectives.

Factors contributing to the Management Approach

Concerning collective bargaining employers across the country studied have shown a clear preference for the active involvement of works councils rather than trade unions. Increasingly they have begun to distance themselves from centralized bargaining favoring decentralized enterprise bargaining.

However employers have by no means free reign. They have had to operate within the web of legislative regulations and different institutional contexts of Labor management relations. In many developing countries employers organization are not influential mainly because of the difficulty in coordinating the actions of the various sectors of the economy and writing diverging interests.

It is clear that employers generally want to introduce labor market flexibility by exercising their managerial rights without being subject to any restrictions resulting legislation or trade union action. However, their search for the full extent of possibility may have inherent limits arising from general conditions of competition and employer—employee relationships, ever without legislative and collective intrusion of management.

The Issues of employment Flexibility

Employers and their organizational are strong advocates of employment flexibility, as they regard rigid regulation of employment contracts as an obstacle to their efforts to adapt to changing market situations. Therefore they are increasingly calling for the removal of regulatory provisions over their power to hire and fire, such as relaxing the restrictions on resource to flexible forms of employment, including temporary agency work, part—time work and fixed term work.[61]

The Issues of Wage Flexibility

Employers has generally established a policy for various flexible compensation schemes over rigid wage structures such as seniority based systems which they believe lack elements to encourage higher productivity and performance by employees.[62]

They prefer flexible payments for two primary reasons-

First, they allow employees to adjust the total wage bill to the business cycle.

Second, they motivate employers to enhance their performance and productivity by creating a direct link with pay. In their view for example, gain sharing can help motivate workers and focus on their energy improve productivity and link pay to business results

The employers' dilemma in wage policy lies in the need to coordinate the bargaining process in order to secure wage moderation, while enhancing flexibility at the company level. However the increasing competition in both domestic and global markets has driven employers to pursue decentralized wage determination in order to gain wage flexibility. In particular multinationals tend to be more aggressive in pursuing decentralized wage bargaining while departing from centralized bargaining.

1.5.2 Management Approach

Bangladesh Employers' Association (BEA) is the only organization in the country representing employers in the field of industrial relations.

BEA's involvement in industrial relations both at national and unit levels are well established and very wide. All employers' representatives in the Labor Courts are nominated by the associations.

In the public sector management suffer from lack of authority and accountability. They have to wait for government guidelines and act on the basis of these. Private sector owner—managers continue to be reluctant to consider workers as equal partners. Industrial relations policies, practices and climate are usually considered far better in multinational companies, which are the harbingers of new practices

1.5.2.1 Styles of Management

In Bangladesh, theoretically employers' paternalistic approach is positive. There is a saying that guardian of the family knows the best. Like the owner have the responsibility to maintain the industry in a peaceful manner. So if industry is positive the paternalistic approach is positive. So here again comes the humanitarian approach. The demand of the workers is unlimited. This has to be fulfilled with limited resources. But if the owner wants to ensure their interest most then they maximize their interest by maximizing profit at the cost of the labor. The scenario of Bangladesh is similar to that.

Attitude	Behavior
Contempt	Dictatorial
Adversity	Paternal
Acceptance	Business-like
Cooperation	Participative

Table 1 : Employers' Style towards Union[63]

1.5.2.2 Policies of Management

Work Organization and skill Formation[64]

One notable trend is employers policies on work organization over the past decade has been growing recognition of the crucial link between work organization and competitiveness pressures of changes from number of sources. Intensified new technologies requiring multi skilling and enabling new work organization in practice new work concept as just-in-time total quality management, total productive management and changes in external labor market encouraging employers to take more systematic steps to develop and retain the skills of their key employees.

It is in the context that employers have shout organizational reform which enabled them to gain more benefit from employees' work relative knowledge and skills and to integrate quality control into production process. To bring about changes in work organization employers are increasingly eager to involve employees and/or union in the process of continuous quality and productivity improvement as well as promote teamwork.

However, in spite of the common pressures employers to pursue work organizational flexibility, employers' organization and individual employers have pursued a wide range of approaches to these matters.

In Bangladesh, the system between worker and owner sharing policy formulation, benefits talk with representatives are mandatory. Despite a short industrial history, labor-management relations have undergone several changes in Bangladesh. The major characteristics of labor-management relations in Bangladesh are as follows:

I. Lack of requisite leadership.
II. Lack of scientific management system.
III. Absences of necessary delegation of power to plant management of public sector enterprises.
IV. Lack of proper education and training to management and working groups.
V. Greater influence of politics in trade unionism.
VI. Violation of labor laws both by the management and workers.
VII. Violation of labor laws both by the management and workers
VIII. Absence of a sense of belongings.
IX. Irrational wages structure.
X. Absence of a matured industrial workforce on the one hand and industrial entrepreneurs on the other hand. In the former case the workforce is only one generation old and in the later case entrepreneurs.
XI. Absence of mutual trust and respect between management and trade union and
XII. Inadequate communication system.

1.5.2.3 Strategies of Management

The issue of Collective Bargaining

The Labor Code 2006 provides for regulation of trade union activities (including strikes and lockouts), the relations between employers and workers, and the avoidance and settlement of any differences and disputes arising between them. The confrontational character of relations makes it difficult to engage in effective collective bargaining.[65]

As such, further participation of all three partners is required to narrow differences and provide effective form of consultations and collective decision making. This requires high levels of political commitment, strengthening of tripartite institutions, encouragement of collective bargaining processes, and reform of the Labor law.

1.6 Public Policy and Industrial Relations

1.7 Introduction

Public Policy is the term used to describe the mixture of legislation, current government political priorities and the broad policy directives pursued by the civil service and public agencies at any given time. Public policy changes as govt. political priorities change and when Government change.

The existence of a clear public policy on industrial relations is important for all those concerned with developing and maintaining good relations between employers and trade unions and between managers and employees. Bangladesh is a developing country, and the government is striving relentlessly to attain rapid economic development in the country. Many programs taken so far have been carried out successfully. Despite a lack of resources faced by the government, development programs in the key sectors have continued. At the same time, considering the importance of the private sector, an all-out support is being provided to initiatives taken in this sector. As a result, a new kind of dynamism is under way in public policies in both the public and private sectors. In this backdrop, it is essential to examine various aspects of industrialization and its impacts on overall economic activities and influence of public policies on industries.

The graduation out of poverty is caused by the expansion of gainful employment, driven by expansion of productive capacity of an economy. The centrality of employment in reducing poverty is an obvious lesson from the history of development, especially demonstrated in the post second war years of golden age of capitalism. According to such analyses, the poor can be lifted out by a combination of strategies including an increase in wage employment; in real wages; in the opportunity of the poor to employ themselves; in the productivity of the poor in self employment; and increase in the terms of exchange of the output of poor's self employment.

The strategies pursued in the advanced industrial countries in post-war years in rebuilding their economies address the fundamental point of the inability of the poor to enter into more remunerative segments of labor market. This stems not only from low endowments and entitlements, but also is attributable to entry barriers and to both. The investment flows may not be creating enough labor demand; or may generate demand only for a certain type of work and workers; and labor demand that people who are poor in certain endowments and entitlements cannot meet. Because of existence of constraints on both sides, people who are poor in endowments and entitlements "create" their own employment—low productive, below-subsistence and subsistence type of activities—and join the army of 'working poor,' who do not earn enough to lift themselves out of poverty and the poverty continues to remain pervasive.

The continuance of high incidence of poverty[66] and increase in absolute number of poor in Bangladesh call for scrutiny into growth and its relationship to creation of employment.

Second, the efficacy of the current market-centric policy framework which assumes that economic growth, derived out of functioning of market induces an increase in productive and remunerative employment resulting into reduction of poverty has to be examined.

1.8 Public Policy in Bangladesh

The last decade of Bangladesh has been taken under consideration which is crucial both for economic and political reasons. An informed discussion on policies and subsequent choices for representation by, and for, the citizens warrant a deeper understanding of the political settlement that makes and breaks policies affecting their lives. On the economic policy-making, the country has witnessed an increasing mobility of pursuance of neo-liberal framework of deregulation, liberalization, privatization and withdrawal of state over the years. The period in transition has witnessed political transition as the BNP led four party alliances replaced the Awami League government in October 2001, but continuation of same framework, as their ancestors have followed.

Second, the anachronistic political paralysis has continued to persist, with less of engagement in policy based politics on real issues facing the country.

Third, the allocation rules remain adhoc, devoid of reflection of need, reality and rights while ideology-driven mantra of leaving everything to market has geared heightened speed, with deliberate attempt not to factor in institutional realities such as power, authority and social structure, implying unabated rise in primitive accumulation of natural and physical resource, state patronage, rent-seeking and resource-dependent syndicates. Fourth, the paradox is that less intervention in theory[67] has meant more intervention in practice, even when aid flow is lowest in the country. In this period of neo-liberal ascendancy, the so-called donors have been up in arms in every spheres and their prescriptions have been scaled up to encompass the reshaping, or transformation, of political and social (and, by implication, cultural) as well as economic institutions and practices. Therefore, both the political and economic factors have serious implications on macroeconomic state of the country. Taking both the economic and political factors under consideration the report provides a comparative analysis on major economic indicators dividing the period under consideration into two tenures of the two governments. In tune with its tradition, the current annual number also instead of treating the key macroeconomic indicators in isolation rather builds a chain relation between them so as to understand how one indicator is related with others and their aggregate implications to the economy as a whole.

1.9 Traditional Role of Government in Industrial Relations[68]

Bangladesh has achieved relatively good economic progress during the 1990s by adopting a series of structural and economic reforms. The GDP recorded an average of 5% annual growth during the period. As a result, improvements have been recorded in the area of poverty alleviation and other human development indicators like education, health, nutrition, life expectancy, infant mortality and dropout rates in primary schools. Despite the progress made, 45% of the population still lives below the poverty line. Unemployment and, more significantly underemployment, remain a huge problem as the economy is unable to absorb the new entrants to the Labor force not to mention the huge backlog of already unemployed persons. Between a third and a quarter of the Labor force remain unemployed or underemployed. In terms of employment, informal sector dominates the scene—about 90% of the Labor force work in the informal sector. Women workers are entering in ever increasing numbers in the Labor force, particularly in the service sector and export-oriented industries dominated by garments and textiles. But women continue to face discrimination and they dominate the low paid jobs. About 80% of women are unpaid family workers as compared to 20% for men. Child Labor is widespread—about 12% of the Labor force are working children.

Over the past two decades or so, the Government has instituted major reform programmes including reformation of the public enterprises. However, these reformations have not brought the desired results. Labor laws are quite comprehensive, but weak implementation capacity has resulted in frequent violations of laws, poor working conditions, discrimination in employment, and high incidence of child Labor. An act was passed by the Bangladesh Government announcing the withdrawal of restrictions imposed on trade union rights in the EPZs on 2004. On March 2008, for the first time in the country, 69 industrial units in Dhaka and Chittagong export processing zones (EPZ) have introduced workers' associations on the basis of referendums by workers. At the same time, workers of 22 industrial units have voted for not having any trade union body for themselves for yet another year.[69]

Although Parliamentary Democracy has been functioning in the country since 1991, the process needs to be further strengthened. Frequent hartals or general strikes continue to severely disrupt normal life of the people. Violent clashes leading to death or injury are quite common. These are serious implications for the growth of the economy and improvement of employment conditions.

Now, if we really think about the public policy that playing an important role in the industrial relations, it almost was absent in our country traditionally. Minimum wages and occupational safety are some of the concepts of the recent times. Mostly the industrial relations in Bangladesh were taking the form of landlord and servant where the government played a mere role traditionally. All the policies usually reflect the issues that are there between the owners and the government not the owners and the employees.

For example, the main legislation covering industrial dispute in Bangladesh are Bangladesh Labor Act 2006. The legislations lay down formal procedures for dispute resolution in Bangladesh. The procedures are quite comprehensive and takes into account most of the factors. However, these procedures are not properly implemented. Government should take a more stringent supervisory role in order to ensure effective implementation of the procedures. So, it will be more beneficial if the Government can take a more active role in the industrial relations. More active supervisory committees can be set up for each industry which will ensure the proper implementation of the industrial relations provided by the public policies incorporated in the regulatory framework of the country.

From some of the recent incidents one can see that the workers are trying to establish their rights for living a better life. The demand is to be fulfilled by the owners and the government and should be reflected in the public policies. The rights that are being demanded by the workers are very basic rights of the workers which are extremely essential for leading a normal happy life. One would easily see that the workers are struggling for the minimum wage which is a must for participating in any market of the world. The minimum salary of US $14 that was passed in 1992 can no longer support the workers in the 21st century. Afterward the workers are asking for the healthy and safe conditions. In US market one can see that there is a government association called Occupational Safety and Health Administration (OSHA) that is working for ensuring the safe working conditions for the workers. Institute like this can also solve the problem of Bangladeshi workers regarding safety.

Another very basic facility that the workers are asking is the proper environment where social facilities like schools and hospitals are there and the area is build for the workers. Demand like this is time consuming for its fulfillment so it is more a matter of the future than present. So, it is very clear that traditionally, hardly see any public policies that are really helping or guiding the industrial relations to reach an optimum level.

One other very important issue in the matter of industrial relations that was true traditionally but no longer can be ignored is the presence of the woman in the industrial relations. So, obviously there were no public policies that could support the issue of the female workers. In the garment industry it is the female workers who are working for considerably lower wages and thus allowing Bangladesh to enjoy a competitive advantage in the global market. Traditionally this role of female workers was not dominant in Bangladesh society.

The political parties or the government backed by the forces don't show their commitment toward the welfare of its citizens yet. The recent days scandals of the political leaders about their corruptions clearly show that the philosophy of the ruling governments of the county merely have any concern about the welfare of the society, let alone the issue of industrial relations. So, eventually very little of effective public policies are truly found in Bangladesh traditionally that can have an impact in the industrial relations.

2.0 The Changing Role of Govt. in Industrial Relation

2.0.1 Trade Unions in Bangladesh

Employment in growth sectors used to be a source of workers' empowerment through trade unionism. Unions are generally highly politicized, and unions are strongest in state-owned enterprises. Civil service and security force employees were forbidden to join unions because of their highly influential character. Teachers in both the public and private sector were not allowed to form trade unions. The history of the trade union movement in Bangladesh is linked with the development of a modern industrial society in the sub-continent beginning from 1850. In the Indo-Pak subcontinent the first labor organization was the All India Trade Union Congress (ITUC).[70] After the independence of Pakistan, East Pakistan Trade union federation was formed on 28th September 1947. In 1959, Pakistan federation of labor was formed; it was the only central labor organization in the whole of Pakistan.[71] After declaring the Industrial Relations Ordinance—1969, freedom was given to labor to form any trade union in any commercial or industrial establishments.[72] Industrial Relations Ordinance, 1969 provides that any worker or employer has the right to form a union without previous authorization. But such a union cannot function as a trade union without being registered under the law. After liberation of the country in 1971, the Government of Bangladesh nationalized the major industries and services including banks and insurance companies. The working class of Bangladesh, with higher hopes and aspirations, demanded higher wages and fringe benefits. It is interesting to note that after liberation, the government-affiliated trade unions always dominated the trade union scene. Industrial Relations Ordinance, 1969 deals with trade unions in Bangladesh. In any industrial and commercial establishment, a trade union may be formed with 30% of the total number of workers employed. If there is more than one union in any establishment, Collective Bargainly Agent (CBA) is determined by the Registrar of the Trade Union through secret ballot for a term of two years. Only the CBA is authorized to raise industrial disputes and negotiate with the management. The Director of labor of the government acts as the Registrar of Trade Union in Bangladesh. In 1972, the number of registered trade unions in the country was 2523, with membership of 682,923 workers. Till December 2004, 6492 trade unions (worker's union—5242 and employers' association—1250) exist in Bangladesh having 2,094,887 members. This clearly shows the rate of multiplicity of trade unions in Bangladesh.

2.0.2 The Role of the Unions

One of the major political weaknesses of the bourgeoisie in Bangladesh is the fragility of its democratic apparatus and as a result of democratic mystifications. There have been several military dictators in the short history of Bangladesh so far. The political process is characterized by gang wars, killings, and large scale bombings between main bourgeois factions—Bangladesh Nationalist Party (BNP) of Khaleda Zia and Awami League (AL) of Sheikh Hasina.

Due to this weakness of its state structures, bourgeoisie has not been able to set up a trade union apparatus, especially in the garment factories. This weakness of the bourgeoisie allowed workers to develop their revolt and give it such a sharp edge for several days. But once the bourgeoisie saw the danger of the situation they quickly set out to redress it. Union co-ordinations were quickly set up—mostly at formal level, with no presence in the factories. Agreement between them and bosses was widely propagated on radio, TV and newspapers. They were presented as standing up for workers. A demand for 'union rights' was pushed forward. Although workers have not been sucked in by these lies—as shown by persistence of workers revolt till 6th June 2006 and unions' inability to control it—in the absence of major development of workers self-organization, union lies have not been without influence.

The bourgeoisie itself has seen the danger of its present ways—especially of absence of unions. This has been expressed in numerous proclamations by bourgeoisie that if unions have been there, if 'democratic rights' of workers have been respected, the workers movement would not have exploded the way it did. "Trade union leader Mishu said 'if there had been trade unions in factories . . . the situation would not have turned violent'" (New Age 3rd June 2006). Another trade union boss declared, "The absence of trade unions is very much more dangerous than the presence of active unions" (Letter from International Textile, Garment and Leather Workers' Federation to Prime Minister Khaleda Zia). There has even been talk to take help of International Labor Organization in setting up the unions.

Experience of Bangladesh shows that physical absence of unions is not enough. Important thing is the ability of the working class to consciously reject the unions. Even more important is its ability to develop its own self-organization. Development at this level has been very rudimentary, if at all. Although this movement would not have developed if workers have not stood up to the repressive forces, in the absence of self-organization the revolt sometime took the character of rioting. While some of the weaknesses are expression of the lack of experience of the working class in Bangladesh, they also point toward the need for appropriating all the experience of the workers' movement worldwide. It is the responsibility of the revolutionary organizations of the communist left to contribute to the development of the workers' consciousness of their class identity and of their historic goal: the communist revolution which alone can put an end to the brutal exploitation of the working class not just in Bangladesh but throughout the world.

Existing labor rights and emerging trends of trade unions in Bangladesh call for re-thinking. Trade unions in Bangladesh contribute to a lack of solidarity and collaboration on certain issues. The union movements consider 'reaching out to the unorganized and vulnerable' groups as a way to ensure the future relevance of trade unions. By removing the political leadership from trade unions and other labor organizations; by reducing government intervention and at last by amending the existing labor-industrial laws, proper trade unions and labor rights can be ensured in Bangladesh.[73]

2.0.3 Privatization in Bangladesh

Privatization programs got its virtual start in Bangladesh in the mid-seventies. The first round of privatization was put to work following the post independence thrust on economic growth. The second phase of privatization (or denationalization) took place in the first half of the 1980s and covered jute and textile mills owned originally by Bangladeshi citizens prior to independence.

The Revised Investment Policy designed in 1975 put much emphasis in the development of private sector providing enormous incentives to spur private investment. A Disinvestment Board was set up and a total of 255 State Owned Enterprises (SOE) were privatized in between 1975 to 1981 and about 115 of these SOEs, were divested through the office of the then Director General of Industries (DGI). The New Industrial Policy (NIP) of 1982 marked a major shift towards privatization where total of 222 SOEs got privatized under the NIP' 1982.

The privatization programs gained gradual momentum and government made liberal Industrial Policy in 1991, where 42 enterprises were identified for privatization. On its further move, the number of enterprises was increased to 62 by adding 20 textile mills under the Asian Development Bank (ADB) sponsored Industrial Sector Program (ISP). In the meantime, the government created an Inter-Ministerial Committee on Privatization (ICOP) in the year 1991 to develop a privatization policy. In 1993 Privatization Board was setup and assigned with the responsibility of privatizing State Owned Enterprises identified by the Government. Subsequently, the Privatization Board was converted into a Commission delegating more administrative and financial authority to intensify the privatization program drive.

2.0.4 Achievement in the Privatization[74]

A World Bank study (1994) reveals that, around 305 state owned enterprises (SOEs) comprising industrial, commercial and financial institutions were put under public ownership by 1974-75. However, the size of the public sector enterprises have reduced considerably after the paradigm shift in the government's economic policy towards privatization.

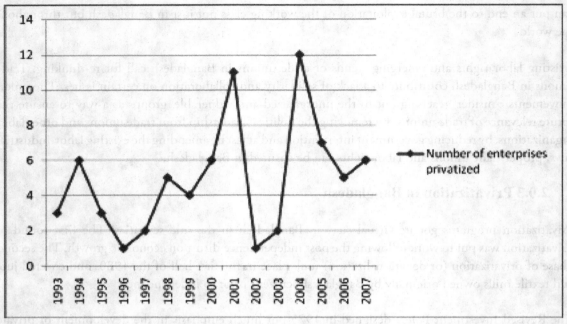

Figure 1 : Year-wise status of privatization

Since the establishment of the Privatization Board in 1993 and thereafter the Privatization Commission in 2000, 74 state owned enterprises were privatized of which 54 were privatized through outright sale and 20 through offloading of shares. Privatization activities are gaining a momentum. This reflects the increased participation of the private sector in privatization.

While considering the sector-wise distribution of privatized enterprises, the privatized 74 enterprises belong to textiles, jute, manufacturing, chemicals, food, leather and banking sector.

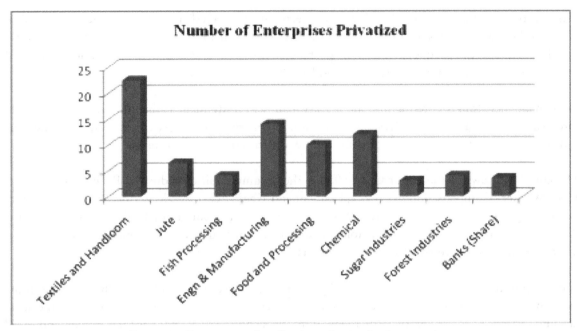

Figure 2 : Sector-wise distribution of privatized enterprises

According to a census, during the period 1993 to 2007, 54 Enterprises were privatized through tender and 20 were privatized by Sale of Govt. Shares.

2.1 Wages Councils and Pay Review Bodies

2.1.1 Background and Justification

Bangladesh is a developing country in South Asian region with 130 million of people. According to Labor Force Survey 2005-2006 of the Bangladesh Bureau of Statistics (BBS), the total estimated civilian labor forces of the country is 49.5 million and among them 24.44% are female.

The constitution of Bangladesh has recognized fundamental rights of the workers at work places including necessary social protection. Globalization and changing economic condition influencing traditional workplace values, nature of employment, working condition, welfare facilities, industrial relations and contemporary social protection system. The introduction of free market economic policies, unbalanced economic and industrial reforms posed serious challenges to job security and social protection of workers in different sectors.

The approximate ratio of formal and informal sector in Bangladesh is 20:80 and the ratio between public and private sector is 30:70. However 48.4% of employment is covered by agriculture—forestry and fishery sector, the production and transport sector cover 8.4% of employment, 2.1% of employed people in clerical occupation, 5.8% in sales and 14.2% in service sector.

Women are increasingly entering into job market mainly in ready-made garments and allied sector, tea gardens, NGOs, health care services, food processing industry, export processing zones, services sectors and commercial enterprises and informal sector i.e. construction, agriculture etc.

The core labor laws of the Labor Code 2006 is the accumulation of Industrial Relation Ordinance, 1969, Worker's Compensation Act, 1923, Payment and Wages Act, 1936, Maternity Act, 1939, Factory Act 1965, Shops & Establishment Act 1965, Employment of Labor (EoL) 1965 etc. Majority of the above laws are backdated with week enforcement by concerned authorities and most important face of it is that in does not covered all section of workers.

According to recognized international definition, the social safety nets can be broadly defined as those instruments aimed at providing extended social protection, guarantee of social security to the most needing sections of society particularly the working class and the social poor as their human and social rights not only for their human and social objectives in public policies and private participation, but as system of international convents, collective social contract and income redistribution. This means that social safety nets include both social security schemes such as guarantee of decent minimum wage; old age/ retirement benefits; unemployment insurance benefits; retrenchment compensations; medical care sickness and compensation for employment injury and death; maternity protection and issues specific to women as well as social and welfare programs, as determined in law, policy measures, contracts including collective bargaining agreements and international instruments.

In Bangladesh the root of social security system and laws are based upon rules and regulation introduced by the British Colonial regime. There is no specific national policy at present on safety-net issue and very little discussion took place in society on this regard.

Decent wage is one of an important factor to achieve the objective of decent work. Right to receive fair minimum wage is one of the human rights for all workingmen and women at workplaces and a key issue for the trade unions. It is also important to note that the UN Millennium Development Goal or poverty reduction strategy of Bangladesh would not success without having any minimum wage standard for the workers. But the reality is, there is no national minimum wage in Bangladesh yet.

But the wage structure determined by the Minimum Wages Board or Wage Commission or the Pay Commission is not based on minimum daily life requirement of a worker. For that reason, there is a huge gap between income and expenditure level of a worker and employees forced to live below the poverty line.

One of an important safety-net issue for all working women in maternity benefit right. But, in Bangladesh the majority of the women workers are deprived from this right for various reasons such as the weakness of relevant rules/acts and lack of enforcement, negative attitude of the employers to violate the rules/acts, lack of awareness among women workers about this special right, week role of trade unions to deal the issue, lack of seriousness from the part of the government on implementation and monitoring of relevant laws at workplace level. The scene is very much common in leading women worker intensive sectors such as the garments, private shops/establishments and services sectors.

The reasons behind this is that the concerned employers are not properly aware on impact of violating this basic right of women workers and the trade union organizations at different levels not giving priority the issue in their regular activities for discussion and action. Different women organizations working for the rights and empowerment of women are not vocal on maternity benefits rights of working women and media's are also not much active to address the issue.

2.1.2 Bangladesh Labeled as 'cheapest place' for Investment in Asia

A survey of investment-related cost comparison conducted by Japan External Trade Organization (JETRO) showed Bangladesh emerging as "the cheapest place" in Asia in terms of nine cost components, including legal minimum wages, social security burden ratio and charges of utility services as the cost of investment[75] is falling.

"The relative position of Bangladesh against the components like salary of mid-level manager, legal minimum wage, rate of increase in nominal wage, telephone installation fees and call charges, mobile phone subscription fee, monthly basic mobile phone charge, cost of general use of per cubic meter gas, and cost of diesel has improved," noted the survey.

JETRO conducted surveys in 30 Asian cities according to the 32 cost-components. Some hidden costs, which are abstract by nature but exist in matters related to legal, policy, procedural system and infrastructure, have been playing a vital role in case of elevation of cost of investment, the report noted. It said that in Bangladesh, poor law and order situation, delay in the settlement of letter of credit (L/C) payment, sudden changes in government policies, inadequate infrastructure facilities, and problem related to Chittagong port need attention of the government to reduce the hidden cost of investment.

"The cost related to the usage of mobile phone has gone down because of internal stiff competition among the mobile operators which belong to private sector," the survey noted. The survey also noted that due to the emergence of several new private cell phone operators, the new connection fee for mobile phones has become cheaper.

The wage for workers, salary of the mid-level managers, legal minimum wages, social security ratio, cost of land area of an industrial estate, telephone installation fee and call charges, electricity and water costs, and corporate taxes are among the other cost-components.

Bangladesh is, however, less competitive in the areas like cost of industrial estate land, monthly basic payment for broadband internet service, new connection fee for fixed telephone line, container transportation cost, and rate of corporate taxes. Particularly, the monthly basic payment for broadband internet service in the country remains one of the highest in Asia. Regarding telephone service, the charge per call in Bangladesh stands around the middle range among the Asian countries, but the new installation fee is quite high. Regarding the container transport, even after offsetting the proportional cost due to geographical longer distance, the cost of transportation from Chittagong Port is higher than that from Mumbai Port due to the fact that large container ships cannot come to Chittagong Port due to its shallow draft and, therefore, trans-shipment of containers becomes necessary either at Singapore or at Colombo. The survey mentioned corporate tax in Bangladesh, being 40 per cent for non-listed companies, is one of the highest in Asia.

In addition, the survey report said that the government would have to take care of the existing foreign investors to attract more investment. If the existing investors are not satisfied, then the probability of getting new FDI will gradually decrease in course of time and the prospective investors will go to other countries, the report warned. The JETRO suggested that the government should conduct occasional surveys among the foreign companies on the degree of their satisfaction and try to resolve any existing problem for further improvement.

2.1.3 Minimum Wage for RMG Sector

RMG sector is the one of the biggest export source of Bangladesh. Yet, to set minimum wage for these valuable workers, there were huge agitation throughout the economy. Unlike some countries, it is also difficult for Bangladesh to introduce a statutory minimum wage covering all employees as well as protecting the interest of the employers. Following serious Labor unrest in the country's premier export-earning garment sector, the government formed the wage board on May 31, 2006 and asked it to recommend a pay structure for the workers within three months. The minimum wage for workers in the RMG sector was then Tk. 930, which was fixed about 12 years ago.

While discussing about the minimum wage fixation, in answer to a question, Annisul Huq, BGMEA representative on the wage board, said a worker can survive somehow with an income ranging between Tk. 1,900 and Tk. 1,950 a month. But it is also true that owners are not in a position to pay as per the need of the workers. Around 50 per cent of the factories will be out of the business within six months if the proposed wage structure is implemented, Huq said

"Buyers come with a fixed CM (cutting and making) charge and ask whether we accept their offer. They tell us directly that they would shift their orders elsewhere if we are not ready to accept their price offer," said Khalilur Rahman, owner of KDS garments. "Who will pay the salary of the workers—the government or the Minimum Wage Board or the owners?" Rahman posed the question. It is true that the owners made money when there was quota system and the price was good, said garment owner Muzaffor U Siddiqui. But it is also true that they have invested their money in expansion of the industry, which has created more employment, he added. Buyers rush to Bangladesh not because they love this country but for cheaper prices of Bangladeshi apparels, he said.

As per the demand of the garments workers, on October 5th, 2006, the Minimum Wage Board announced the final pay structure for the workers in the readymade garment (RMG) sector fixing Tk. 1,662.50 as the minimum monthly wage including basic salary, house rent and other allowances for the entry-level workers.

Earlier a draft proposal with recommendation for three-tier pay package failed to get support from owners and workers. In the final proposal, the board announced two separate pay structures for the garment workers and the employees. There are seven grades for the workers and four grades for the employees. Minimum wage for grade one workers will be a total of Tk. 5,140 including basic salary, house rent and allowances, Tk. 3,840 for grade two, Tk. 2,449 for grade three and Tk. 2,250 for grade four, Tk. 2,046 for grade five and Tk. 1,851 for grade six. Total monthly wage for apprentice workers will be Tk. 1,200. Minimum wage for grade one employees will be Tk. 3,580 including basic salary, house rent and allowances, Tk. 2,800 for grade two, Tk. 2,449 for grade three and Tk. 1,851 for grade four.

After announcing the draft proposal, the board received more than 400 opinions and objections and prepared the final recommendation taking those into account. Annisul Huq, representative of Bangladesh Garment Manufacturers and Exporters Association (BGMEA) on the board, after finalizing the draft, said, "It will be very difficult for the owners to pay Tk. 1,662.50 (£13.27) for the seventh grade and minimum wages in other grades for the workers. We have agreed despite all limitations," He also said that around 95 per cent leaders of different workers' organizations in the RMG sector expressed their opinions favoring a minimum wage that would range between Tk. 1,650 and Tk. 1,800 although they were demanding Tk. 3,000 earlier.

2.2 Conciliation, Arbitration and Inquiry

2.2.1 Labor Arbitration

Labor arbitration usually resolves disputes involving Labor unions, employees, and employers. It is commonly divided into two distinct categories: interest arbitration and rights arbitration.

Interest arbitration resolves conflicts of interest over the establishment of the terms and conditions of employment, for example, the wage rate, working hours, and number of vacation days for each employee. In Labor relations, these terms and conditions are negotiated through collective bargaining, and agreements are formalized in collective bargaining agreements or union contracts. A breakdown in these negotiations typically results in a strike. Interest arbitration avoids or ends strikes.

2.2.2 Arbitration Law in Bangladesh

In Bangladesh, the present law of arbitration is contained mainly in the Arbitration Act, 1940, there being separate Acts dealing with the enforcement of foreign awards. There are also stray provisions as to arbitration, scattered in special Acts. Three types of arbitration are contemplated by the Arbitration Act of 1940, namely (i) Arbitration in the course of a suit, (ii) Arbitration with the intervention of the court, and (iii) Arbitration otherwise than in the course of a suit and without the intervention of the court in practice; the last category attracts the maximum number of cases.

Under the Act of 1940, an arbitration agreement must be in writing, though it need not be registered. The agreement might make a reference about present or future differences. The arbitrator may be named in the agreement or left to be designated later, either by consent of the parties or in some other manner specified in the agreement. Very often, the rules of prestigious commercial bodies lay down that a person who becomes a member of the association must accept the machinery of arbitration created or recognized by the rules of the association. This also amounts to an "arbitration agreement" for the purposes of the Arbitration Act, 1940.

Once an arbitration agreement is entered into for submitting future differences to arbitration, it is not, necessary to obtain the fresh consent of all the parties for a reference to arbitration at the time when the dispute actually arises.

2.2.3 Types of Institutional Arbitration

Arbitration has been used customarily for the settlement of disputes between members of trade associations and between different exchanges in the securities and commodities trade. Many contracts contain a standard arbitration clause, referring to the arbitration rules of the respective organization. Numerous arrangements between the parties in industry and commerce also provide for the arbitration of controversies arising out of contracts for the sale of manufactured goods, for terms of service of employment, for construction and engineering projects, for financial operations, for agency and distribution arrangements, and for many other undertakings.

2.2.4 Selection of Arbitrators

The matter of selecting arbitrators is an important aspect of the arbitration process, as the arbitrators' ability and fairness is the decisive element in any arbitration. The general practice is for both the parties to select an arbitrator at the time the arbitration agreement is concluded. Selection of arbitrators is also often made by agencies administering commercial arbitration, under pre-established rules of procedure. These organizations, including various trade associations, and Chambers of Commerce, maintain panels of expert arbitrators. The parties may either make their own selection or entrust the appointment of the arbitrators to the organization.

2.2.5 Law to be Applied in Trans-national Transactions

The statutory law of various countries and the rules of agencies administering commercial arbitration contain provisions on the form, certification, notification, and delivery of the award. The arbitrator must comply with these requirements.

2.2.6 Substantive Law

A much debated question in commercial arbitration concerns the substantive law to be applied by the arbitrators. Generally, the award must be based upon the law as determined by the parties in their agreements. This failing, the arbitrator must apply the law which he considers proper in accordance with the rules of conflict of laws. In both the cases, the arbitrator will have to take account of the terms of the contract and the usages of the specific trade.

2.2.7 The Arbitrator and the Court

Challenges to the process of arbitration are not uncommon. A party may claim, for example, that no valid arbitration agreement came into existence, because the person signing the agreement had no authority to do so or that a condition precedent to arbitration had not been fulfilled. More often, the validity of arbitration is contested on the ground that the specific controversy is not covered by the agreement. In such cases, the question whether the arbitrator has authority to deal with the conflict is usually determined by a court.

Challenges before the courts against the award cannot be excluded by agreement of the parties, since the fairness of the arbitration process as a quasi judicial proceeding has to be maintained by the legal system.

Challenges before the court are, however, confined to specific grounds and specific matters. A review of the award by a court will not generally deal with the arbitrators decisions as to facts or with his application of the law. The jurisdiction of the court is thus restricted. The arbitration process must be the end and not the beginning of litigation.

2.2.8 Filing the Award

An award of the arbitrator must be filed in the court and a decree obtained in terms thereof. The decree so obtained can be executed, like any other decree of the court. However, the court may, instead of confirming the award, remit it to the arbitrator, modify it or set it aside for the specified causes. Most of the orders passed by a court under the provisions of the Arbitration Act, 1940 in this regard are subject to appeal.

2.2.9 Competent Court

The court having jurisdiction under the Arbitration Act 1940 is the court in which a suit on the matter under dispute could be instituted.

Provisions have been enacted in the Act to deal with questions concerning the cost of arbitration and the procedure to be followed by the arbitrators regarding filing of the awards. In case of difference of opinion among an even number of arbitrators, the parties can provide for an umpire. Generally, most of the provisions applicable to arbitrators apply, with necessary modifications, to umpire also.[76]

2.3 Employing Organizations

2.4 Introduction

Organizations produce those goods and services demanded by individuals or corporate consumers who are prepared to pay for them either directly in the marketplace or indirectly through taxation and public funding. A wide variety of producers or service organizations exist in the world. They are found in the extractive, manufacturing, distributive, financial, educational and welfare sectors and incorporate a diverse range of enterprises and establishments including firms, factories, offices, universities, hospitals, banks, insurance companies and so on. Some are large organizations, others are small; some are privately owned, others are public bodies.

2.5 Classification of Organizations

A useful way of classifying organizations is by their orientation and ownership. An organization's orientation reflects the primary goals it seeks to achieve. And the structure of ownership determines the strategy by which it aims to achieve these goals. The orientation of an organization can either be profit motivation or social welfare motivation. As for ownership, organizations can be publicly or privately owned. In this type of classification, there can be 4 types of organizations:

(1) Private Business
(2) Voluntary Organizations
(3) Public Corporations
(4) Public Services

This classification is clearly illustrated i figure 3.

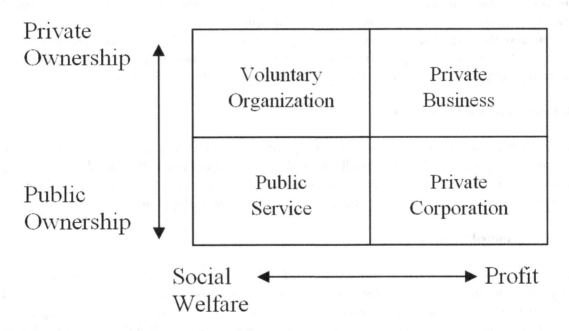

Figure 3 : Classification of Organizations

2.5.1 Private Business

Private businesses are organizations that are owned by the public and operate with a motive for earning profits. Private businesses can be classified into 4 major categories:

i. Sole Proprietorship

A sole proprietorship is a one man business owned and controlled by one person. These are usually small businesses and are owned and managed by one person. The employment in this type of business is quite small. Most professionals operate as sole proprietorships and so does very small businesses.

ii. Partnerships

Partnerships are similar to sole proprietorships except that they are owned by two or more persons. The partners share profits and losses in the ratio of their initial investment or in an earlier agreed ratio. Professionals are encouraged to work in partnerships rather than sole proprietorships so that they can pool their expertise to improve the quality of service provided by them. Example: Institute of Chartered Accountants of Bangladesh encourages the Chartered Accountant professionals to operate in partnership by giving the partnerships better rating that individually owned firms.

iii. Private Limited Companies

Private limited companies are a more formal type of partnership where the partner's liabilities are limited to the value of their shares. Small and medium sized enterprises in Bangladesh are becoming more and more private limited companies. In companies limited by shares, it is easier to introduce and practice corporate governance—where there is a separation of ownership from management.

iv. Public Limited Companies

Public limited companies are those whose shares are listed in one of the Stock Exchanges of Bangladesh. They are by the far the largest employers in the country. Usually, big organizations are public limited companies. In these organizations, there is usually a complete separation of ownership from management. The whole company is managed by employees with supervision from the Board of Directors who are the nominees of the shareholders.

2.5.1.1 Industries Comprised of Private Businesses

In terms of the types of industries, private sector[77] may includes organizations involved in agriculture and fisheries (including dairy/poultry farmers), manufacturing companies, transport companies, telephone companies, construction companies, housing societies, non-governmental publicity and news media, private educational institutes (private schools, colleges, universities, madrashas, medical and dental colleges etc.), private financial institutes, financial intermediaries, insurance companies and pension funds, financial auxiliaries and other non-financial corporations.

i. Manufacturing

Manufacturing companies include large and medium scale manufacturers and small-scale manufacturers. Jute mills, printing and dying industries, spinning mills, weaving mills, coconut oil mills, tobacco processing industries, cosmetics and toiletries industries, rubber and plastic industries, rice/flour/pulse mills, leather, textile mills, paper, wood manufacturing companies, pharmaceutical industries, garments factories, cement factories, fertilizer company, edible oil mills etc. are large and medium manufacturing companies in Bangladesh. Small-scale manufacturing companies include cottage industries, saw mills, hosiery, handicrafts factories etc.

ii. Banking

One of the most important service sectors in Bangladesh is the banking sector. There are approximately 47 private banks in Bangladesh out of which there are 30 commercial banks, 9 foreign banks and 8 specialized banks. The division is shown in the chart below:

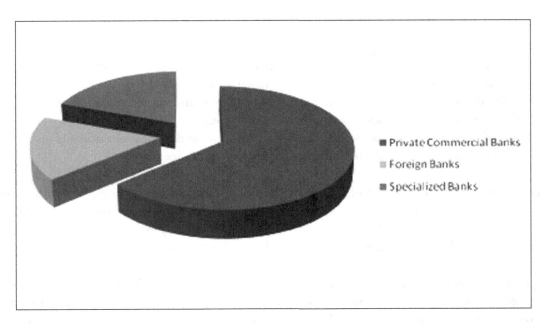

Figure 4 : Classification of various private banks in Bangladesh

Non banking financial institutions include insurance companies and there are around 60 insurance companies in Bangladesh. A detailed list of all the insurance companies is beyond the scope of this report. Other service industries in Bangladesh include entertainment services like cinema, amusement parks, hospitals and clinics, IT services (including cyber cafes), courier services, hotels and restaurants, beauty parlors, travel agencies etc.

iii. Education

Every year a large number of students aspiring for admission in the public universities were deprived of higher education due to limitations of available seats in the public universities of the country. With the view to solving the problem in the higher education available to the students the government has accorded permission for the establishment of private universities in the private sector by promulgating the Private University Act (PUA), 1992. Thus, the journey of establishing private university started from 1992. After some time the government in consultation with the University Grant Commission (UGC) has made some amendments of the Act in 1998.

According to the Private University Act, the pre-conditions for the establishment of a private university are as follows:

1. An academic plan to be approved by the UGC
2. At the initial stage a minimum of two faculties are needed to open & establish
3. Qualified teachers for each faculty to be approved by the UGC
4. Fixed deposit of Taka 5 (five) crore to be kept in any government recognized Bank
5. Curriculum and syllabuses to be approved by the UGC
6. 5% of the total seats are to be kept reserved for the poor and meritorious students
7. Salary of the teachers and tuition fees of the students to be described.

Apart from those conditions, one of the major conditions is that a house rented or owned having 10,000 sft. of floor space is required for Class rooms, Academic and Administrative activities, Library, Laboratories, Seminar room and other facilities. Complying with the above mentioned conditions 54 private universities have been established and operating in the country so far.

Excepting a few, most of the private universities are offering BBA, MBA, EMBA, B.Sc. in Computer Science & Engineering, B Sc. in computer science and information technology, B.Sc in information and communication technology. LL.B. LL.M, BA & MA in English and BA & MA in economics. Few universities have offered courses like BA & BFA, B-Music & M-Music, BA in Fashion and Product Design, Interior Architecture and Physiotherapy and Hospital Management etc.

iv. Others

Commerce and trade industries include importers and exporters, wholesale traders, retail traders etc.

2.5.1.2 Legislations

Although private businesses are profit oriented and the ownership is totally in the hands of private individuals, these are not completely beyond the purview of government. Government, through various legislations and policies, regulate the activities of these private businesses. Major laws related to private investment-both foreign and local-are:

- The Foreign Private Investment (Promotion and Protection) Act of 1980
- The Bangladesh Export Processing Zones Authority Act of 1980
- The Investment Board Act of 1989
- The Companies Act 1994
- The Bangladesh Private Export Processing Zones Authority Act of 1996
- The Industrial Policy 2005
- The Import Policy Order 2003-2006
- Bangladesh Export Policy 2003-2006
- Private Sector Infrastructure Guideline 2004

In addition, foreign investors are required to follow the regulations of the Bangladesh Bank—and the National Board of Revenue for taxation and customs matters.

According to the Board of Investment (BOI) the most important legislations are

- The Foreign Private Investment (Promotion and Protection) Act of 1980
- The Investment Board Act of 1989
- The Industrial Policy 2005

The literature published by the BOI focus on these three acts intensively. Though this paper has tried to focus all the activities relating to investment, the resource and purpose of this book constraint hampered the review of all 9 legislatures.

One of the most important tools of the government is the "Investment Policy" of the government. The synopsis of this policy is given below.

Investment Policy

Bangladesh economy is passing through a transitory stage from an agrarian economy to a structured industrial economy. Each year industry is gradually taking up major share of national income. In the last two decades this contribution has doubled to 29.01% of the GDP while agriculture's contribution has declined to 21.77%. The key aspect of this development is private sector investment rose significantly to 18.7% of GDP. FDI has picked up to $845 million in 2005. The recent legislature and policies have focused on these aspects. The government has envisioned raising private investment to 25% of GDP, driving industry's contribution to 40% of GDP, quadrupling FDI inflows, increasing GDP growth to 10%.

2.6 Public Corporations

Public Sector Enterprise often referred to as state sector, government owned undertakings/enterprises or state-owned enterprises. These are formed under the legal proceedings, wholly or partly owned and controlled by the government and produce marketable goods and services, have an explicit or extractable budget, and are supposed to finance their operating costs from their own resources. In a public sector enterprise, the majority of equity shares is owned by the government directly or indirectly through governmental institutions and the government has decision making control either directly or through its appointed bodies. Public sector enterprise normally has three forms of organizational structure, the departmental undertakings, statutory corporations and joint stock companies.

2.6.1 Features

Public corporations have five main features.

- Their capital is publicly owned and they are managed by government appointed executives.
- They are not subject to company law and have a different legal status.
- They obtain their current revenue, or part of it, from selling their goods or services; their capital expenditure is raised by borrowing from the Treasury or general public
- They are exempt from the normal parliamentary financial scrutiny exercised over government departments.
- Their boards are usually appointed by a secretary of state and their employees are not civil servants

2.6.2 Public Corporations of Bangladesh

In Bangladesh public sector enterprises, conceived basically as an instrument of economic development are active in almost all areas of the economy and engage a sizeable volume of resources. The total investment in the industrial sector in 1980-81 was estimated at Tk. 43.85 billion, three-fourths of which was in the public sector.

Departmental undertakings are not formed by or with the consent of the legislative authority. These are set up by the executive actions of government bodies without any capital structure and budget, and charged with the duty of carrying out specially defined functions within the purview of the government bodies that set them up. These undertakings are not independent entities, although they enjoy a fairly high degree of monopoly. They are subject to budgetary, audit and other controls of the government and are managed by civil servants. They are financed by annual appropriation from the Treasury, which also receives their revenues. A departmental undertaking is best suited where the main purpose of the enterprise is to collect revenue for the state and to provide public utilities and services at fair prices in larger public interest. Some examples of departmental undertakings in Bangladesh are the Bangladesh Railway, Postal Department, Telephone and Telegraph Board, Power Development Board, Water Development Board, Customs Department, National Board of Revenue, ordinance factories, overseas communication services, and multipurpose river projects.

Statutory corporations are enterprises normally engaged in economic or manufacturing activities and are set up by act of legislature. These corporations are legal entities separate from the government and also the persons who conduct their affairs. Bangladesh Bank, government owned life and general insurance companies and Biman Bangladesh Airlines are examples of statutory corporations. Shares of such corporations are in the name of the government and these are thus owned and controlled by the government. Statutory corporations enjoy extensive legal autonomy, and their rules, objectives, functions and duties are defined and specified in the act. Financing statutory corporations is not part of the Treasury and therefore, they can retain their revenues, and also spend as per the rules laid down by the statute. A statutory corporation set up by an Act cannot be regarded to fit in with the changed circumstances without legislative amendments.

Joint Stock Companies are set up under the provision of the companies act. Establishment of companies is easier and is best suited where the nature of the work is substantially commercial. Most joint stock companies are not public sector enterprises in the strict sense. They are free from day-to-day control by the ministry, and are not subject to government's budgetary discipline. They are managed by the board of directors, and are subject to audit and other provisions of the Companies Act. The distinctive feature of a government controlled joint stock company is that the government, except when it sets up a mixed enterprise, puts up the entire capital. Such a company is wholly autonomous and makes its own rules and decisions in respect of investment, finance, personnel and commercial audit. Bangladesh Shilpa Bank, Bangladesh Shilpa Rin Sangstha, Bangladesh Krishi Bank, and nationalized commercial banks (NCBs) are examples of joint stock forms of public sector enterprises in Bangladesh.[78]

2.6.3 Classification of Public Sector Enterprises

One of the classifications of public sector enterprises in Bangladesh is that as non-financial public enterprises and banking and other financial public enterprises. The number of non-financial public sector enterprise is 40, and according to Bangladesh Standard Industrial Classification (BSIC), these belong to 7 broad sectors.

i. Industrial Sector

Public sector enterprises in the industrial sector are under 6 public corporations-

- Bangladesh Textile Industries Corporation
- Bangladesh Steel and Engineering Corporation
- Bangladesh Sugar and Food Industries Corporation
- Bangladesh Chemical Industries Corporation
- Bangladesh Forest Industries Development Corporation
- Bangladesh Jute Mills Corporation

Those in the power, gas and utilities sector are Bangladesh Oil, Gas and Mineral Resources Corporation, Bangladesh Power Development Board, Dhaka Electric Supply Authority (DESA), Dhaka Water and Sewerage Authority and Chittagong Water and Sewerage Authority.

ii. The Transportation and Communication Sector

The transportation and communication sector comprises Bangladesh Shipping Corporation, Bangladesh Inland Water Transport Corporation, Bangladesh Biman Corporation, Bangladesh Road Transport Corporation, Chittagong Port Authority, Mongla Port Authority, Chittagong Dockyard Workers Management Board and Mongla Dockyard Workers Management Board. The commerce sector includes Bangladesh Petroleum Corporation, Bangladesh Jute Corporation, and Bangladesh Trading Corporation.

iii. Service Sector

Entities in the service sector are Bangladesh Freedom Fighter Welfare Trust, Bangladesh Film Development Corporation, Bangladesh Tourism Corporation, Bangladesh Civil Aviation Authority, Bangladesh Small and Cottage industries Corporation, Bangladesh Inland Water Transport Authority, Rural Electrification Board, Bangladesh Export Processing Zone Authority, Bangladesh Handloom Board, Bangladesh Silk Foundation, Bangladesh Water Development Board and Bangladesh Tea Board.

iv. Financial Sector

The financial sector includes the 4 nationalized commercial banks-

- Sonali Bank
- Janata Bank
- Agrani Bank
- Rupali Bank

And six development financial institution-

- Bangladesh Shilpa Bank
- Bangladesh Shilpa Rin Sangstha
- Bangladesh Krishi Bank
- Rajshahi Krishi Unnayan Bank
- Bank of Small Industries and Commerce Bangladesh
- Bangladesh House Building Finance Corporation.

v. Insurance Sector

The Insurance Sector includes the Life Insurance Corporation and the General Insurance Corporation.

vi. Others

The agricultural sector includes Bangladesh Fisheries Development Corporation, and Bangladesh Agricultural Development Corporation. The construction sector includes Chittagong Unnayan Kartippakka, Rajdhani Unnayan Kartippakka, Khulna Unnayan Kartippakka, and Rajshahi Unnayan Kartippakka.

2.6.4 Management of Public Sector Enterprises

The state-owned enterprises, as indicated in the guidelines of 1976, section 3(3) of the paragraph on 'Relationship between the Corporation/Autonomous bodies and Enterprises under them' are (i) to operate on commercial consideration having due regard to national interest, in the most efficient and economic manner within the policy framework and guidelines prescribed in the rules and regulations; (ii) to continuously strive to improve its performance and attain better result; and (iii) to earn additional revenue for the government. There is a provision in President's Order 27 for transfer of the government property, assets and liabilities to a corporation. The provision was later amended by the Ordinance No. VII of 1987, which enabled the government, among other things, to sell or transfer shares of the nationalized enterprises to corporations or to any other persons.

The general direction and administration of the officers and business of the corporations were vested in the respective board of directors, which could exercise all powers and do all acts and things that might be exercised or done by the corporation. The board could delegate its power to the chairman (the chief executive) for the purpose of efficient operation of the corporation. The corporation was authorized to appoint officers, employees and consultants for efficient performance of the corporation on such terms and conditions as it might determine. Under the system, the board operated under the supervision and control of the government and was guided in the discharge of its functions by such general or special instructions as might from time to time be given to it by the government. An annual budget statement for the corporation was to be prepared by the corporation and to be duly approved by the government. The system, however, emphasized more on an appropriate management system than on accountability. The government adopted some corrective measures in the form of directives to the ministries and corporations from improving efficiency in performance by the corporations. These included:

- Guidelines on the relationship between the government and the autonomous bodies/corporations and enterprises under them;
- Recommendations of the committee for reorganization of public statutory corporation;
- The Public Corporation (Management co-ordination) Ordinance No. 48 of 5 July 1986;
- Government Order regarding strict observance of the guidelines of 1976 and resolutions of 1983;
- The Bangladesh Industrial Enterprise (Nationalization) (Amendment) Ordinance relating to disinvestment and transfer of government shares of nationalized enterprises to the public corporations; and
- Notification (7 July 1988) of the Ministry of Industry relating to public issue of shares of the government enterprises and holding of 5% share of divested enterprises by the corporations under which they belong (e.g. BCIC, BSEC, or BSFIC).

There are many shortcomings and constraints in the structure of control and management of the state-owned enterprises in Bangladesh. Generally speaking, there are four hierarchical levels in the control supervision structure. At the bottom is the enterprise level control involving internal management matters. At the next tier is the corporation control involving supervision, coordination among units, and delegated policy matters. At the third tier is the ministerial control of bureaucratic nature, involving evaluation, coordination amongst ministries and non-delegated policy matters. Finally, at the top is the political control exercised by the minister and the government involving major policy issues. There exists an implied accountability to the Jatiya Sangsad of elected representatives.

At the bottom is the individual enterprise, which is the ultimate object of control and supervision. The enterprises have no policy-making options as they operate within approved budgets, plans, policies and norms. Even when there is an enterprise management board, they limit themselves to routine operational matters and refer everything to the corporation. This resulted from the absence of mutual trust, lack of professionalism and the uncertain and changing state of informal authority and accountability. Above the enterprises are the statutory corporations. The basic function of these juridical bodies as defined in presidential order/ordinances/acts of parliament is to supervise, coordinate and direct the enterprises.

These bodies control and supervise the enterprises directly and contribute towards coordination between enterprises in matters of foreign procurement, personnel, marketing, disposal of surplus, or arrangement of finance. But the statutory corporations are heavily dependent on ministerial decisions. In most matters of policy and in certain matters of operations, they do not enjoy any autonomy. However, the statutory corporation can move on matters of policy on their own behalf and on behalf of the enterprises under them. The third tier is the ministry, which retains all control over the policy matters, which they define in consultations with other ministries, after scrutiny of papers prepared by the corporations. The fourth tier, the minister, who is a people's representative or a guardian of the public interest, often gets involved in small details of day to day administration rather than the policy issues. The minister, however, conducts review meetings, pilot's policy proposals in the cabinet and responds to parliamentary scrutiny on behalf of the enterprises and corporations.

To increase the management skill efficiency, production capacity and marketing network of the state-owned enterprise, an attempt was made in October 1980 to form a forum under the name and style of 'Consultative Committee of Chairman and Managing Directors of Autonomous and Semi-Autonomous Bodies'. It was renamed in 1982 as Consultative Committee of Public Enterprises (CONCOPE). The objective was, among others, to continuously interact with the government for coordinated decision making on administrative and financial management across the public sector corporations and the enterprises under them. CONCOPE regularly holds sittings with the relevant government functionaries including the prime minister and the president for quick decisions on administrative, financial and related other matters.

2.7 Public Services

Public services is a term usually used to mean services provided by government to its citizens, either directly (through the public sector) or by financing private provision of services. The term is associated with a social consensus (usually expressed through democratic elections) that certain services should be available to all, regardless of income. Even where public services are neither publicly provided nor publicly financed, for social and political reasons they are usually subject to regulation going beyond that applying to most economic sectors. Public services are also a course that can be studied at college and/or university. These courses can lead entry in to the: police, ambulance and fire services.[79]

The following can be included in the public services sector in Bangladesh-

- Civil Services
- Education
- Police service

- Local authorities

2.7.1 Civil Services

The implementation of government policies and projects is the duty of the Bangladesh Civil Service, a corps of trained administrators who form the nation's most influential group of civilians.

2.7.2 Education

The educational system in Bangladesh is three-tiered and highly subsidized. The government of Bangladesh operates many schools in the primary, secondary, and higher secondary levels. It also subsidizes parts of the funding for many private schools. In the tertiary education sector, the government also funds around 21 state universities through the University Grants Commission.

The present education system of Bangladesh may be broadly divided into three major stages, viz. primary, secondary and tertiary education. Primary level institutions impart primary education basically. Junior secondary/secondary and higher secondary level institutions impart secondary education. Degree pass, degree honors, masters and other higher-level institutions or equivalent section of other related institutions impart tertiary education. The education system is operationally categorized into two streams: primary education (Grade I-V) managed by the Ministry of Primary and Mass Education (MOPME)) and the other system is the post-primary education which covers all other levels from junior secondary to higher education under the administration of the Ministry of Education (MOE). The post-primary stream of education is further classified into four types in terms of curriculum: general education, madrasah education, technical-vocational education and professional education

At the tertiary level, there are 73 universities in Bangladesh. Out of these, 21 universities are in the public sector, while the other 52 are in the private sector. Out of 21 public sector universities, 19 universities provide regular classroom instruction facilities and services. Bangladesh Open University (BOU) conducts non-campus distance education programmes especially in the field of teacher education and offers Bachelor of Education (B.Ed.) and Master of Education (M.Ed) degrees.

There is only one medical university namely, "Bangabandhu Sheikh Mujib Medical University", like other public universities, offers courses on a different system where FCPS Degree is offered in the disciplines of medical education; diploma courses are offered in 12 disciplines. MD degree in 15 subjects and MS courses on 8 subjects are also offered.

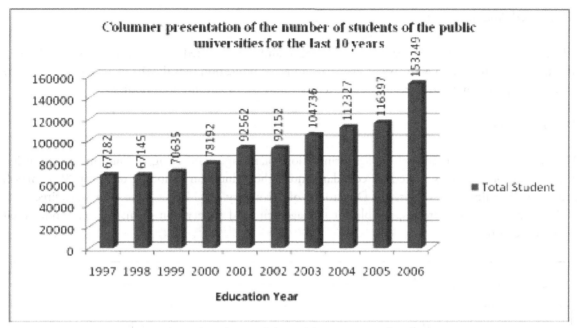

Figure 5 : Number of students of the public university for the last 10 years

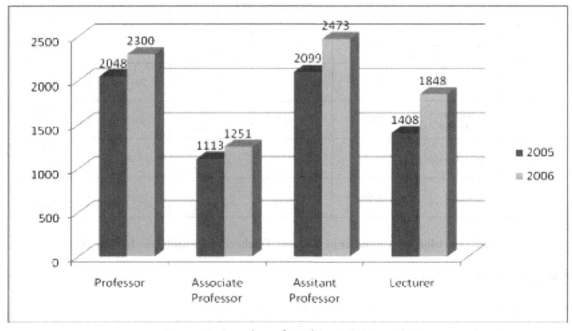

Figure 6 : Number of teachers in University

Educational Administration

Education Systems in Bangladesh is being managed and administered by two Ministries viz. Ministry of Education (MOE) and Ministry of Primary and Mass Education (MOPME) in association with the attached Departments and Directorates as well as a number of autonomous bodies.

Ministry of Education (MOE)

This Ministry is concerned with policy formulation, planning, monitoring, evaluation and execution of plans and programmes related to secondary and higher education including technical & madrasah education. The line directorates, viz. Directorate of Secondary and Higher Education and Directorate of Technical Education are responsible for management and supervision of institutions under their respective control.

Sl. No.	District	No. of Teachers			Enrolment	
		College	Total	Female	Total	Girls
01	Barishal Division		7051	1259 (17.9%)	86843	38257 (44.1%)
02	Chittagong Division	244	11345	2375 (20.9%)	233001	95535 (41.0%)
03	Dhaka Division	462	21116	5619 (26.6%)	435627	190951 (43.8%)
04	Khulna Division	758	15009	2327 (15.5%)	201409	97724 (48.5%)
05	Rajshahi Division	1081	33627	5468 (16.3%)	358005	134669 (37.1%)
06	Sylhet Division	127	2253	352 (15.6%)	52034	25293 (48.6%)
Total in Bangladesh		3150	90401	17400 (19.2%)	1367246	569337 (41.6%)

Table 2 : Division with number of College, Teachers and Enrolment by Sex, 2005

Other government bodies include:

a) Directorate of Secondary and Higher Education (DSHE)
b) The Directorate of Technical Education (DTE)
c) Bangladesh National Commission for UNESCO (BNCU)
d) Chief Accounts Office (CAO)

e) National Curriculum and Textbook Board (NCTB)
f) Bangladesh Bureau of Educational Information and Statistics (BANBEIS)
g) Directorate of Inspection and Audit (DIA)

Furthermore, a number of autonomous bodies have a share in the administration of education. These are:

i. University Grants Commission (UGC)
ii. National University
iii. Education Boards
iv. Madrasah Education Board
v. Technical Education Board

Ministry of Primary & Mass Education (MOPME)

Bangladesh is committed to the World Declaration on Education for All (Jomtein, March 1990) and the Convention on the Right of Children (New York, September 1990).

Recognizing the importance of primary and non-formal education in ensuring education for all and eradicating illiteracy, the Government created a new Division called Primary and Mass Education Division (PMED) in August 1992. This Division is now operating as a Ministry. The Ministry of Primary and Mass Education is responsible for policy formulation, planning, evaluation and execution of plans and initiating legislative measures relating to primary and non-formal education.

Other bodies include:

(a) Directorate of Primary Education (DPE)
(b) National Academy for Primary Education (NAPE)
(c) Bureau of Non-formal Education (BNFE)
(d) Compulsory Primary Education Implementation Monitoring Unit

2.7.3 Police Services

At present, the British Irish Constable System of police administration is in practice in the subcontinent including Bangladesh. The highest officer of police administration in Bangladesh is 'Inspector General of Police (IGP)', who controls all departments of police under indirect supervision of the Home Minister. Some senior police officers help him in his work at police headquarters. A Deputy Inspector General of Police is appointed for each range of civil administrative unit. He controls district level police administration under his range. There are six civil ranges and one railway range in Bangladesh. In each range there is a Deputy Inspector General of Police. Besides, police commissioners of three divisional cities (Rajshahi, Chittagong and Khulna), administrative head of Central Intelligence

Department (CID), head of Special Branch (SB) and Sarda Academy are of the rank of Additional Inspector General of Police.

At the district level, police super is the chief of police administration. An additional police super, few assistant police supers and official staff help him in his administrative work. An assistant police super controls the administration of a circle. In every police station under a circle, the administration is controlled by an inspector or by an officer in-charge (OC). In district headquarters some armed police are kept reserved under the district police super. This force is engaged on emergency basis when law and order falls rapidly. Activities of CID and SB police are extended at field levels parallel to district police in addition to their activities at central headquarters. Two police supers in two railway districts under Bangladesh railway range conduct the administrative activities of railway police. An additional police super and an adequate number of assistant police supers help police super in his job. A group of armed police named Railway Special Armed Force is appointed to work under him.[80]

2.7.4 Local Authorities

The local authorities provide both strategic services over wide geographic areas and essentially local services. They employ wide range of personal in manual and non-manual grades, including skilled and less skilled grades, as well as technical and professional staffs such as engineers, surveyors, accountants, lawyers, architects and teachers.

2.7.5 Voluntary Bodies

Voluntary bodies are usually small, privately owned organizations providing specialized services to their own members or special interest groups. An emerging element in the voluntary sector is worker or producer cooperatives where the enterprises are owned and managed by their members. Larger cooperatives are more likely to employ professional managers, though, responsible for implementing the policies determined by their memberships and management boards. Being small-scale organizations, and as they often have social rather than economic objectives, voluntary bodies do not usually have major industrial relations problems. Nevertheless, they employ people; their managers manage employees, where trade unions are recognized their managerial representatives negotiate with union representatives.

Voluntary organizations may be identified specially by their clientele i.e., the socio-economic classes and sub-classes of people for which they work. While some voluntary organizations may be concerned with development needs of all or most classes of people, others have orientation towards specific classes only. Non-profit institutions serving households consist mainly of associations such as trade unions; professional or learned societies; consumers' associations; political parties (except is included in general government); churches and religious societies (including those financed by government); social, cultural, recreational, and sports clubs; and organizations that provide goods and services for philanthropic purposes rather than for the units that control that. Non Governmental Organizations (NGOs) are one of the most important voluntary bodies.

2.7.6 NGOs in Bangladesh[81]

The growth of NGOs in Bangladesh began in the aftermath of the WAR OF LIBERATION in 1971 when such organizations stepped in to participate in the massive task of rehabilitating a war-ravaged country. As the need for relief and rehabilitation receded, some of these organizations moved on to support direct interventions to promote social and economic empowerment of the rural poor. Now they form an integral part of the institutional framework addressing issues such as poverty alleviation, rural development, gender equality, environment protection, disaster management and human rights. The phenomenal growth of NGOs in Bangladesh is also attributed to the limitation of the government to meet the enormous challenges of poverty. It is difficult to ascertain the exact number of NGOs in the country because they are not registered under one authority and many of them operate even without any registration at the central level. A major institution that gives registration to NGOs is the Department of Social Welfare, which registered more than 19,000 NGOs between 1961 and 2001. A great majority of them are small clubs or cultural groups.

Some major NGOs are:

1. BRAC
2. Caritas-BANGADESH
3. Care
4. Centre for Mass Education in Science (CMES)
5. Enfants Du Monde (EDM)
6. Grameen Bank
7. Heed Bangladesh
8. Helen Keller International
9. Proshika
10. Intermediate Technology Development Group (ITDG)
11. International Development Enterprises
12. International Voluntary Services (IVS)
13. Juba Jibon Unnayan Samity
14. Koinonia
15. Manabik Shahajya Sangssta (MSS)
16. International Urban Planning Organization (IUPO)
17. Marie Stopes Clinic Society (MSCS)
18. Nari Maitree (NM)
19. Nari Unnayan Samity (NMS)
20. Nayan Action Foundation (NAF)

21. NGO Forum for Drinking Water Supply & Sanitation
22. Organization for Mothers and Infants (OMI)
23. Oxfam

2.8 Employer-employee relationship

In our country the current employer—employee relationships is better than the past. Employers have started to understand that the more they invest in human resources the more output is likely which will lead them to emphasize on employee capability development. As such in many organizations, employee development is viewed as part of business plan. In these organizations, training budget is calculated as a percentage of total budgets of the organization.

Employers now recognize the importance of employees' participation in business planning, major decision making and organizational change process. Many organizations now conduct employee opinion surveys for collecting employee feedback and improve employer—employee relationships.[82]

In many organization employers are concerned about the job satisfaction of the employees. Some HR actions have legal implications. But in the country context legal explanation does not seem to be adequate. There is lack of uniformity of the interpretation of law that lead to practice by organizations in different way. There is also ambiguity of existing legal policy or detailed policy framework on HR actions seems to be incomplete.

In future the overall HR practice is expected to be brighter in Bangladesh because more are feeling the necessity of an established HR department in the organizational structure employer-employee relationship is expected to improve.

In Bangladesh now IT is becoming part of HR practices which will make HR actions, decision making process faster and accurate.

Effective HR practice can help employer-employee relationship to reach in a higher position.

But still there are some major problems. Such as:

- Many organizations still see their employees in traditional ways. They used to think that paying salaries and wages is there only duty to the employees. They think little about caring the employees, thinks little about the personal problem of the employees. They want to utilize employees as much as they can to earn profit. Such thing disrupt employee—employer relationship.
- Owners and in some cases employers too are the stronger part. Most of the Member of Parliament (MP)s are businessmen these days. They influence the Government to make rules

favoring them. Such things create negative impacts on the employees/labors mind. They think that owners are manipulating laws.

- Again labor laws are not implemented strictly in our country. In many cases employers take benefit of these.

2.9 Theories of Management

2.9.1 Maslow's Hierarchy of Needs

If motivation is driven by the existence of unsatisfied needs, then it is worthwhile for a manager to understand which needs are the most important for individual employees. In this regard, Abraham Maslow developed a model in which basic, low-level needs such as physiological requirements and safety must be satisfied before higher-level needs such as self-fulfillment are pursued. In this hierarchical model, when a need is mostly satisfied it no longer motivates and the next higher need takes its place.

2.9.2 Theory X and Theory Y[83]

Theory X

Theory X assumes that the average person:

- Dislikes work and attempts to avoid it.
- Has no ambition, wants no responsibility, and would rather follow than lead.
- Is self-centered and therefore does not care about organizational goals.
- Resists change.
- Is gullible and not particularly intelligent.

Essentially, Theory X assumes that people work only for money and security.

Theory Y

The higher-level needs of esteem and self-actualization are continuing needs in that they are never completely satisfied. As such, it is these higher-level needs through which employees can best be motivated.

Theory Y makes the following general assumptions:

- Work can be as natural as play and rest.
- People will be self-directed to meet their work objectives if they are committed to them.

- People will be committed to their objectives if rewards are in place that addresses higher needs such as self-fulfillment.
- Under these conditions, people will seek responsibility.
- Most people can handle responsibility because creativity and ingenuity are common in the population.

2.9.3 Expectancy theory

Expectancy theory predicts that employees in an organization will be motivated when they believe that:

- Putting in more effort will yield better job performance
- Better job performance will lead to organizational rewards, such as an increase in salary or benefits
- These predicted organizational rewards are valued by the employee in question.

2.9.4 Goal-setting theory

For goals to increase performance one must define them as difficult to achieve and as specific. Easily-attained goals tend to correlate with lower performance than more difficult goals. A vague goal does not seem likely to enhance performance. A goal can become more specific through quantification or enumeration (specifying a certain number or a list), such as by demanding "increasing productivity by 50%"; or by defining certain tasks that need completing.[84]

2.9.5 Behavioral Theory

Assumptions

Leaders can be made, rather than are born.

Successful leadership is based in definable, learnable behavior.[85]

Description

Behavioral theories of leadership do not seek inborn traits or capabilities. Rather, they look at what leaders actually do.

.

If success can be defined in terms of describable actions, then it should be relatively easy for other people to act in the same way. This is easier to teach and learn then to adopt the more ephemeral 'traits' or 'capabilities'.

2.9.6 Social Learning Theory

Social learning theory is a theory to explain how people learn behavior. People learn through observing others' behavior. If people observe positive, desired outcomes in the observed behavior, they are more likely to model, imitate, and adopt the behavior themselves.

2.9.7 Total Quality Management (TQM)

Total Quality Management (TQM)[86] is a management strategy aimed at embedding awareness of quality in all organizational processes. TQM has been widely used in manufacturing, education, government, and service industries, as well as NASA space and science programs.

TQM is composed of three paradigms:

- Total: Involving the entire organization, supply chain, and/or product life cycle
- Quality: With its usual Definitions, with all its complexities (External Definition)
- Management: The system of managing with steps like Plan, Organize, Control, Lead, Staff, provisioning and the likes

3.0 Relevance of Management Theories in Garments Sector-in Bangladesh

Garments sector is playing a vital role in our country. It's the biggest sector in terms of earning foreign exchange through export. Millions of labor and workers works here.

To have an idea about this sector a survey has been conducted on Sardar Apparels. Its factory and main office is in the same building at Uttara. Findings based on this garments are discussed below:[87]

- In the Sardar Apparels managers are held responsible for any failures by the top management. Specially production managers are always kept under pressure. They are seriously been held responsible in case of failing to meet the dateline of the shipment. Omni point view of management prevails among garments sector of Bangladesh. Under this view management are directly held responsible for the failure or success of the organization.
- Usually Sardar Apparels helps all the employees to adapt with system and culture of its own. When employees are hired then respective managers verbally instruct them about how they should work, how they should behave and what is right or wrong in the firm. Sardar helps its employees to fit with the culture of the firm.
- Sarder Apparels do believe in employee empowerment. But such practices are not done in case of making key decisions. Usually managers at lower level are allowed to make decisions when the matter is part of their daily work or not a bigger one. Sarder Apparels to some extent

practices employee empowerment, though such empowerment is not for the key decisions which have an overall effect on the organization.

- Usually unitary chain of command remains in Sardar Apparels. That means any employee is usually directly under only one boss.
- In Sardar Apparels span of control is larger in the lower level. A supervisor controls plenty of workers. But the span of control decreases as the management level goes up. Here top managers got less span of control, middle managers got relatively higher span of control then the respective top managers and lower level managers got the largest span of control.
- The firm mainly tries to follow relevant labor laws and BGMEA guidelines to guide its employees.
- The types of communication depend on the nature of the situation. Depending upon the situation downward, parallel and diagonal all types of communications go on here.
- Technology helps in different ways in case of communication. The main office and the factory office of the Sardar Apparels situated on the same building. There are some computers there having internet connection. So through internet the management can communicate with the employees as well as with the outside world. Another source of communication is through cell phone. Now cell phone service providers of Bangladesh have almost covered the whole Bangladesh under their network. So management can easily communicate with the employees through the cell phone. Plus telephone and fax facilities are also there.
- As labors of Sardar Apparels are not under any union so it can be said that this labor force are bit weak in terms of representing the different matters related with the labors. Especially labors here may not be very strong in demanding and getting those demand of the labors fulfilled.
- Sardar Apparel's management does not encourage collective bargaining. Rather the management prefers labors to apply if they get any problem or demand anything. And then management tries to solve the matter.
- Usually there are two different processes for hiring. One is for hiring labors and another is for hiring management employees. When there is a shortage of labors in the factory, the authority hangs a vacancy notice in the board. A committee of three members is assigned the selection process. All three members are selected from the supervisor level. Usually middle management selects those members from the supervisors. For employee selection usually top management makes the final decision. Sardar Apparels prefers employee referrals method and observation method for hiring employees. The firm does not go for advertising or others type of recruiting process.

Sardar Apparels collects information about different potential or existent employees from different sources such as from its employees or external people. If the company sees existence of any potential and/or qualified employees then the firm approaches to him as the need for having new employees' rises.

- Sardar Apparel's tries to sack employees according to the law. The firm usually gives three months prior notice to the respective employee before firing him. The firm also pays all the dues before the employee/labor leaves the company. Providing three months prior notice before firing gives the respective employee the fair chance of searching another new job so that he may not find any problem after losing his/her job at Sardar Apparels.

- Basically when a new employee is hired, his immediate senior officer gives him an oral orientation. Such orientation can be person to person, person to group or group to group. The senior officer welcomes the newcomer and tells him/her about the company, company rules and values etc. Also tells what the company expects from him/her. But no formal orientation period is held here when it helps the new comers to get familiar with the other employees and if possible also with the owners.
- Sardar Apparels does provide employee training.
- Usually Sardar Apparels provides two types of training. These are described below:
  - o On the job training: Here the senior officer shows his subordinates how to do a work while the subordinates are trying or before starting doing the job.
  - o Sometimes the company brings external experts to provide training to its employees. For example the company had hired external software experts to provide training its employees of accounting department so that the employees of department can use accounting software's. Providing training to the employees not only increases employees' skills but also increases employees' satisfaction.
- Mainly the company evaluates the performance of the employees on the basis of their work done. Every employee gets a target from the company. Such as each labor gets daily target of production and his performance is judged on the basis of the output he produced. Again the company also considers other factors such as physical condition of the labor, availability of electricity, political disturbance etc. Suppose for political disturbance a labor may come 20 minutes late and that may hinder to reach his given goal. Company then considers this fact. Performance evaluation is a very key issue. It helps the company to know how the employees are working. It also helps the employees to know how they are doing and how their performances are evaluating. Well the evaluation process should not be very strict. It should be fair otherwise it may degrade the relationship between the management and the employees
- The company provides various types of compensation and benefits to its employees such as:
  - o Monthly salary and wage
  - o Performance bonus
  - o Festival Bonus
  - o Transportation for the top management officials
  - o Commission
  - o Others

Compensation and benefits play a huge role in the relationship between the management and the employees. If the employees think that management is not paying them what they should get then conflict can arise between the management and the employees. This ultimately can degrade the relationship between the management and the employees. It also may discourage employees to give their best possible output. On the other side if the employees think that management is paying them what they should get then it will make the employees happy. It will help in increasing the relationship in a positive way.

- Sardar Aparals did not face any complain about sexual or racial harassment from its employees and labors.
- Sardar Aparals do provide different facilities to its employees and workers such as:
  o Drinking water: There is a water container (Gazi tank type) in every working floor and also arrangement of glasses so that workers can drink water whenever they feel thirsty.
  o There are water jars for the management employees.
  o Latrines:
    ■ There are eight latrines for the workers in every working floors of the factory.
    ■ In every working floor there are four latrines for the male workers and four for the female workers.
    ■ All latrines are placed in suitable places so that workers can easily go to.
    ■ The latrines and urinals are adequately lightened and ventilated.
    ■ Water is supplied through pipes to those latrines.
    ■ Each latrine has bathing facility and a pan.
    ■ Disinfectants are used to clean the latrine.
    ■ Shelters: There is a rest room for the labors.
    ■ Canteen: There is a canteen for the labors where labors can sit and have meal.
- Safety features of the company has been described below
  o There is an emergency exit for fire or any other calamity.
  o Good numbers of fire extinguishers are there.
  o There is a fire alarm in the factory building.
  o Plenty of lighting and air ventilators on each working floors.
  o Space is there for the free and safe movement of the workers.

Present of safety features also plays a good role in determining the relationship between the management and the employees

- Management of the Sardar Apparels believes that both X and Y types labor exists in there factory and office. According to the Management of the Sardar Apparels some labors are enthusiastic about their jobs while some are escapist.
- In case of key decisions top management makes the decision. Usually managers at lower level are allowed to make decisions when the matter is part of their daily work or not a bigger one.
- Basically Sardar Apparels corrects employees' performance by two ways
  o Providing training

- o   Guiding
- The following things make the employees believe that Sardar Apparels organization care about your employees:
  - o   Provides Training
  - o   Give sick leave
  - o   Allow maternity leave
  - o   Provides free medical treatment
  - o   Provides salaries and wages at due time.
- Sardar Apparels hires people randomly, when it requires.
- Sardar Apparels faced change in all the following cases:
  - o   Competitors changing organizational structure changing technology changing people

Usually Sardar Apparels gives leaves to reduce stress of the employees. For this the employees have to apply then the management considers the facts before granting the leaves. To get the leave to get rid of the stress employee has to submit application but the company itself does not automatically provide holidays to reduce employee stress.

3.1 Relevance of Management Theories in Pharmaceutical Sector—in Bangladesh

Another local company for our studying purpose, UniMed & UniHealth Manufacturers was taken as a sample in pharmaceutical sector.[88] The findings are described below.

- Consistency of the physiological need of motivation of Maslow's Need Hierarchy theory is found in providing rest room, drinking water, canteen and transportation facilities.
- The company sets specific goals to increase performance of employees which is too some extent similar with goal-setting theory. For Medical Promotion officers mainly the company targets sales on monthly basis and Medical Promotion officers have to meet the target.
- An implication of Theory X is accompanied by low-level employees like operation workers. What they are provided is just on hourly basis with no performance bonus except two festival bonuses.
- Expectancy theory of management states that employees in an organization will be motivated by providing them organizational rewards, such as an increase in salary or benefits. But the organization is not utilizing this perception.
- The organization does not have any standard rules and regulations for employee guidance (formalization).it is not so big a company and due to cost cutting tendencies it tries to keep paperwork and documentation as few as possible.
- 3 Pharmacists in UniHealth Pharma and 2 Pharmacists in UniMed Pharma groups are providing the product and brand management input for the different therapeutic group products. They are respectively supervised by a Marketing Services Manager and a Product Manager. Again overall

responsibility for the pharmaceutical and medical nutritional sales and marketing has been given to the Marketing Manager who provides leadership to all the three teams. So delegation and decision making authority is prominent here. But top management sets centralized goals and strategic plans. These are some features of the behavioral theory.

- The employees of the company do not have any labor union or trade union. As a result, collect bargaining is not encouraged.
- The structure of the company is not well defined and the type of span of control in the organization in different level does not show any specific characteristics, i.e., it is neither too high nor too low. The communication flow in the organization is always from up to bottom.
- Like many other private companies, the company provides different compensations and benefits for the employees. But these benefits are not for lower-level employees'. Only higher-level professional and managers are subject to it.
- The company has casual leave, sick leave, medical leave etc policies for its employees. Yearly each employee can enjoy 15 days of leave to free from their monotonous life and stress.
- The recruitment policy of the company is performed at a need basis.
- From the beginning of the company, many changes it confronted are changes in the in the technology and changes in the numbers of competitors. Ands to remain competitive it takes several plans which are fulfilled by employees of the organization.
- The company invests huge amount for the training and development of the employees especially for medical promotion officers. As they are key points to increase sales, these employees are always keep under observation.

3.2 Relevance of Management Theories in Real Estate Sector-in Bangladesh

To determine the implication of management theory and the specific qualification of managers in real estate sector, the construction firm "The Structural Engineers Ltd. (SEL)" was studied.[89] The findings are described below.

- The Company (SEL) provides drinking water, shelter or rest room for the employees. This is consistent with the physiological need of motivation of Maslow's Need Hierarchy theory. Moreover, the company also provides safety features like emergency exit, fire extinguisher, fire alarm etc. which is consistent with the safety need of motivation of this theory. In this regard, according to Maslow's model, low-level needs such as physiological requirements and safety are satisfied before higher-level needs such as self-fulfillment are pursued.
- In the company, most, but not all, of the employees, especially lower level workers do not inherently enjoy handling responsibility because creativity and ingenuity are not common. This is an example of employees described by Theory X. As a result, there is an opportunity to align personal goals with organizational goals by using the employee's own quest for fulfillment as the motivator. So, we can assume that some employees in the organization may not have reached

the level of maturity assumed by Theory Y and therefore needs tighter controls that can be relaxed as the employee develops. On the whole, the top level employees can be described by Theory X and middle and lower-middle level employees be described by Theory Y.

- The company does not set specific goals to increase performance of employees. Though, according to goal-setting theory, goals narrow attention and direct efforts to goal-relevant activities, and away from perceived undesirable and goal-irrelevant actions, the company is not following this concept. Again, according to expectancy theory, employees in an organization will be motivated when they believe that better job performance will lead to organizational rewards, such as an increase in salary or benefits. But the organization is not utilizing this perception, too. So, the company can use these two theories of management to increase the motivation of employees.

- When evaluating the employee, the company not only observes the attitude, behavior or special skills of employees but also the output of their work. We know, according to social learning theory, people learn through observing others' behavior. So, here the company is utilizing the concept of social learning theory as well as evaluating the output or productivity of individual employees.

- The empowerment of employees depends on the situation. For example, the organization has four persons in marketing department: one assistant general manager (marketing) and three deputy managers under him. The AGM is the head of marketing department and he can take any decision for the benefit of the company. But all the employees are not given the delegated authority in this way. Many times the company takes centralized decisions. These situations depict certain aspects of the behavioral theory.

- According to Organizational Change Management theory, it is a structured approach to transitioning individuals, teams, and organizations from a current state to a desired future state. From the beginning of the company, it has experienced many changes, for example, changes in the organizational structure, changes in the technology also changes in the competitors. But change must involve the people—change must not be imposed upon the people. As a result, the company gives training to its employees. It updates its technology. Change such as new structures, policies, targets, acquisitions, disposals, re-locations, etc., all create new systems and environments, which are explained to employees as early as possible, so that employee's involvement in validating and refining the changes themselves can be obtained.

- The company practices "Total Quality Management" (TQM) at its work places & has engaged a management consultant for imparting training to its work force on TQM. At SEL quality is considered as the key to success & survival.

- The employees of the company do not have any labor union or trade union. As a result, collect bargaining is not encouraged. This is a modern technology system in which workers' interests and loyalties are enterprise-based. In the company employment security and welfare is guaranteed by the employer. The recruitment system of the company is performed at a need basis. It is not done at annually or semi-annually basis.

- The company provides different compensations and benefits for the employees. For example, the company believes in profit sharing. It shares a certain percentage of profit with its employees. The percentage is based on the performance of individual employees. This is an excellent method to motivate them.

- In case of stress management for the employees, the company gives several benefits. The employees get casual leaves. Moreover, in each year, every employee gets two days' vacation leave with travel and staying cost. This helps the employees to reduce the stress of work life.

- The company spends a lot for the training and development of the employees. Massive trainings are given to the employees on a need basis. The company sends the employees to Japan for training. The company has a contract with Japan govt. Under this scheme, the Japan govt. pays 80% of the training cost and the rest is paid by SEL.

- The suppliers for raw material for construction are always fixed. The contractors of laborers are also fixed for the company. They only perform the construction work of SEL. The company trains the laborers at the top floor of their corporate office and also at the site. The company pays the workers on a daily basis. The workers work 6 full days with a half day on Friday. But they get full wages of 7 days.

- One of the most important functions of a manager is controlling. In this organization, the most important aspect of controlling employees is protecting the organization and the physical workforce. In this organization the managers are not directly responsible for the success or failure of any employee. The structure of the organization is not so structured. The line is not so well defined. As a result, at times it is not clear who is working under whom or who is an employee's superior. For the same reason, it is not possible to say whether the chain of command is unitary, dual or parallel.

- The employers of SEL help the new employees in adapting to organizations culture. The supervisor of an employee introduces the new employee to all the members of the department where he joins. Thus the orientation of the employee takes place, which is very important from the employers' as well as employee's point of view.

- The type of span of control in the organization in different level does not show any specific characteristics, i.e., it is neither too high nor too low. As pointed out earlier, the structure of the company is not well defined. The organization does not have any standard or formalized rules and regulations for employee guidance. But, the communication flow in the organization is always bottom to up.

- Technology helps a great deal in better communication within the organization as well as with different business parties, i.e., customers, suppliers etc. All the officers are provided with mobile phone from the company. The employees have adequate number of computers. They use different type of software to design buildings. The company has internet and intranet facility at their office. All of the officers are also provided with email account with the help of which they can communicate with different business parties. They also perform direct marketing through email.

3.3 Relevance of Management Theories in Banking Sector—in Bangladesh

Bangladesh is a third-world country where industrial relations are a complex issue. The employer does not go through most of the rules and regulations. They normally try to overlook the benefits and other support required for the employee. They do not also care for the organizational and management standards i.e. the theories of management in their operation. On the other hand employees also do not have sufficient support of the rules and regulations of the country as the governance system in Bangladesh is poorly implemented. This study tried to find out the relationships among the theories of management and their application in the context of Bangladesh. Here some observations about One Bank Limited is discussed below.

Though One Bank provides drinking water, shelter or rest room for the employees, it does not take any initiative for the inhabitation solution of its employees. This partially comply with the physiological need of motivation of Maslow's Need Hierarchy theory as the company only provide salary at the industry status which helps employees to solve their basic needs (physiological needs like food, shelter, sex etc). The company also provides safety features like fire extinguisher, fire alarm etc. which is consistent with the safety need of motivation of this theory. In this regard, according to Maslow's model, low-level needs such as physiological requirements and safety are more or less satisfied before higher-level needs such as self-fulfillment are pursued.

In the company, most of the employees, especially lower level workers are reactive in nature. They do not do any duty beforehand proactively before they are being assigned the duty. Commands from higher management level are necessary part for completion of any job. So it seems that employees do not enjoy their work but they feel it as a load every time. This is similar to the example of employees described by Theory X. So, we can assume that some employees in the organization may not have reached the level of maturity assumed by Theory Y in which the employees are proactive and enjoy their work and therefore needs tighter controls that can be relaxed as the employee develops. On the whole, the lower level employees can be described by Theory X and middle and top management can be described by Theory Y.

The company sets specific goals to increase performance of employees. At the beginning of each year managers are given a target to attain a certain goal. According to goal-setting theory, goals narrow attention and direct efforts to goal-relevant activities, and away from perceived undesirable and goal-irrelevant actions, the company is following this concept. Again, according to expectancy theory, employees in an organization will be motivated when they believe that better job performance will lead to organizational rewards, such as an increase in salary or benefits. This organization is utilizing this perception to some degree. For every manager there is an opportunity to have reward in the form of promotion. This helps the company to increase the motivation, productivity of employees.

When evaluating the employee, the company not only observes the attitude, behavior or special skills of employees but also the output of their work. We know, according to social learning theory, people learn through observing others' behavior. So, here the company is utilizing the concept of social learning theory as well as evaluating the output or productivity of individual employees.

The company does not believe in employee empowerment as almost every decision of the organization is taken centrally. Sometimes they proceed further. Sometimes they act as an autocratic body and interfere into the normal activity flow of the organization. These situations depict certain aspects of the behavioral theory.

In this company all the managers are directly responsible for the failure to do any job as per specification. It also discourages the empowerment of its employees. As a consequence, it prefers to take all the decision centrally.

In case of orientation of the new employees, new employees attend a meeting arranged by top management in which top management describe about the organization, its rules and regulations. It also provide a informal oral RJP that what the employees' duties and responsibilities to be performed in the specific job. Here the top management also demonstrate before the employees the objectives and goals and conveys its mission and vision. Employees also get a brief idea about their benefits and rewards they could be able to get on some basis normally performance.

As an integrated process One Bank has different training program for their employees. For the employees recruited from other banks got a probationary training for 3 to 6 months. For fresh entry level managers, the probationary training period is 1 year. Within this periods this employees get both off the job and on the job training. In on the job training, they learn through rotating into different desk of different work division. In off the job training there are two special course of training are carried out at Bangladesh Institute of Bank Management (BIBM). One of this training is a basic requirement regulated by Bangladesh Bank.

In case of the orientation of the culture to the employees it gives time to its fresh employees to be familiar with the organization's culture in different ways like attitude and behavior of peers, supervisors and top management, heritage and past history of the organization etc. Employees also learn the ethical issues from the organization. This company encourages people with high morale and ethics.

In case of evaluating employees company follows a specific method to evaluate what is called Behavioral Anchored Rating System (BARS). In this method, immediate supervisor (normally the operation in charge of the branch) gets tabulated lists of different aspects of behavioral and Operational to evaluate his/her subordinates. He puts points in every aspects of the form according to his judgment. This feedback is again received by HRD. They summarize the data and according to the accumulated points prepare a list of candidates for promotion. Besides this, organization also emphasizes on individuals who performed their job with excellence and helped significantly the org in increasing its number of clients, amount of revenues and the company image at last. Though the company has a specific appraisal method to evaluate its employee, all the efforts go in vein as top management interfere in the process.

This company also feels for their responsibility for the society. They included themselves in the rehabilitation and food support for the flood victims in the recent years. They also assist meritorious students by providing them financial benefit in the form of scholarships.

Technology plays a great role in the business of banking. It helps the company to provide better service for the customer and also makes the internal operations easier for the bank itself. For an example, it provides online banking which enable customers to bank from any of its branch offices. They also have Automatic Teller Machine (ATM) booth which helps customer to draw money any time from any convenient location.

Contacted Person: Mr. Uttam Kumar Roy, Officer, One Bank Ltd

3.4 Relevance of Management Theories in Textile Sector-in Bangladesh

3.4.1 The Present Structure of Textile Industry of Bangladesh:

The main sub-sectors of Textile Industry are: spinning, weaving/knitting, dyeing-finishing and export-oriented RMG. Sub sector-wise brief description of textile industry is given as under:

1. At present, there are more than 200 spinning mills[90] in the country of which 175 units are in the private sector and the remaining 25 units in the public sector. The annual requirement of raw cotton and artificial fibers for the spinning sub-sector is about 400 million kg. More than 95% of these raw materials are being met out of import and the rest are produced in the country.

2. In the weaving sub-sector at present there are 498,000 handlooms (of which 310,000 are in operation) and 43,000 power looms. The large weaving mills and small power looms units has a total production capacity of 1,000 million meters per annum. Moreover, there are 656 knitting units, which is capable to supply more than 80% of the knit fabrics required for the export-oriented knit RMG industry of the country. The growth of the weaving sub-sector is very slow while that of knitting sub-sector is comparatively faster.

3. There are 178 semi-mechanized and 115 mechanized dyeing and finishing units with annual fabric production capacity of 970 million meters. The semi-mechanized dyeing and finishing units have technological limitations for producing good quality fabric and as such these units are supplying fabrics mainly to meet the domestic demand of fabrics. A considerable number

of the mechanized dyeing and finishing units can produce and supply export quality fabrics required for the RMG industry.

4. At present there are more than 3,800 export-oriented RMG units in the country having production capacity of 180 million dozens of garments of various types with a workforce of 1.8 million, 90% of whom are women.

3.4.2 Square Textiles Limited

For our studying purpose, Square Textiles Limited was taken as a sample in Textile sector. The findings are described below.

3.4.2.1 Training and Development program of SQUARE textile

Training is a process of learning a sequence of programmed behavior. It is application of knowledge. It gives people an awareness of the rules procedures to guide their behavior. It attempts to improve their performance on the current job or prepare them for an intended job.

Development is a related process. It covers not only those activities which improve job performance but also those which bring growth of the personality; help individuals to the progress towards maturity and actualization of their potential capacities so that they become not only good employees but better men and women. In organizational terms, it is intended to equip person to earn promotion and hold greater responsibility.

There are many types of method practices in SQUARE. we discuss that method at bellow:

On the job training

On the job training is a training that shows the employee how to perform the job and allows him or her to do it under the trainer's supervision

On the job training is normally given by a senior employee or a manager like senior merchandiser or a manager. The employee is shown how to perform the job and allowed to do it under the trainer's supervision.

Job rotation

Job rotation is a training that requires an individual to teach several different some in a work unit or department and performer each job for a specified time period.

In job rotation, individuals learn several different job within a work unit or department. One main advantages of job rotation is that it makes flexibilities possible in the department. When one employee like junior merchandiser in absence of another merchandiser can easily perform the job.

Apprenticeship training

Apprenticeship training provides beginning worker with comprehensive training in the practical and theoretical expect of work required in a highly skilled occupation. Apprenticeship program combined of the job and classroom training to prepare worker for more than eight hundred occupation such as computer operator, sewing technician.

Length of selected apprenticeship courses of SQUARE[91]

Occupation	length (months)
1. Quality control manager	13
2. Quality control officer	15
3. Cutting Astt. Manager	07
4. Packing Astt. Manager	07
5. Ware house Astt. Manager	05
6. Production officer	03
7. Sewing technician	05
8. Sewing Supervisor	05

Classroom training

Classroom training is conducted off the job and probably the most familiar training method. It is an effective means of imparting information quickly to large groups with limited or no knowledge of subject being presented. It is useful for teaching factual material, concepts principle other theories. portion of orientation programs, some expects of apprenticeship training and safety programs are usually presented utilizing some form of classroom instruction. More frequently however, classroom instruction is used for technical, professional and managerial employee.

3.4.2.2 Development of the human resources

The long term development of human resources as distinct from training for a specific job is of growing concern to HR departments of SQUARE. Throw the development of current employees the department reduces the company's dependents on hiring new workers. If employees are developed properly the job openings found throw HR planning are more likely to be filled internally promotions and transfers also show employees that they have a career not just a job. The employee benefits from increased continuity in operations and from employees who fail a greater commitment.

HR department is also an effective way to meets several challenges including employee obsolescence, international and domestic diversity, technical challenges, affirmative action and employee turnover. By meeting these challenges the department can, maintain an effective workforce.

Steps in the Evaluation of training and development:
Evaluation criteria > pretest > trained or developed-
Workers > posttest > transfer to the job > follow-up studies.
Square Textiles Limited—Performance Management

3.4.2.3 Performance Management

Performance appraisal is the process of assessing employee's past performance, primarily for reward, promotion and staff development purposes.

'Performance appraisal (is) a process that identifies, evaluates and develops employee performance to meet employee and organizational goals.

Performance Appraisal doesn't necessarily use to blame or to provide a disciplinary action. Previous management theories used to view performance appraisal as a stick that management has introduced to beat people. Performance appraisals are now more clarified and they concentrate on developing organizational strengths and employee performance.

Purpose of Performance Appraisal in SQUARE

To review past performance
To assess training needs
To help develop individuals
To audit the skills within an organization
To set targets for future performance
To identify potential for promotion
To provide legal & formal justification for employment decision
To diagnose the hidden problems of an organization

Performance Appraisal Process

Who Appraises

- Supervisors
- Subordinates
- Peers
- Clients/customers
- Self appraisal
- 180/360 degree approach

Approaches to measuring performance in SQUARE textile

There are various kinds of method for measuring performance appraisal. But we get information that SQUARE uses only two type of performance method. These are at below:

1. 360-degree feedback
2. Experience based.

We describe those at below:

360-degree feedback

One currently popular methods of performance appraisal is called 360-degree feedback. With this method managers, peers, suppliers or colleagues are asked to complete questionnaire is generally lengthy.

Experience based

SQUARE measures the performance of employee by experience. For example MR. X has been working in SQUARE for three years and MR. Y has been working in SQUARE for two years. So SQUARE favors MR. X for his more experience.

3.4.2.4 Employee Relations

Employers and employees each have their own sets of needs and values, and successful relationship between these two sides requires that some sort of balance be struck. This balance often takes the form of a psychological contract, an understood agreement between employer and employees that defines the work relationship. This contract with or without support of a formal collective bargaining, agreement influence the outcome achieve by each side.

SQUARE group varies into three channel categories which are

1. Employee safety

2. Employee health
3. Employee working condition

1. Employee safety

SQUARE provides the employee with all kinds of job safety such as insurance of each employee: it provides insurance to the labors also.

2. Employee health

SQUARE provides free medical checkup, health card and also necessary medical facilities for each employee.

3. Employee working conditions

The working condition of employee is very hygienic and SQUARE is ISO 9001-2000 Certified company.

3.4.2.5 Benefits of SQUARE Textile Limited

Employee benefits & services, formerly known as fringe benefits, are primarily the in-kind payments that employees receive in addition to payments in the form of money.

In addition to paying employees fairly and adequately for their contributions in the performance of their jobs, organizations assume a social obligation for the welfare of employees and their dependents

Employees' benefits, usually inherent components of the non-compensation system, are made available to employees that provide:

—Protection in case of health and Accident

—Income upon retirement & termination

These benefits are components that contribute to the welfare of the employee by filling some kind of demand.

Legally required benefits of SQUARE

1. Social Security

—Social security benefits include the general benefits like unemployment insurance & benefits, old age insurance, and Medicare facilities.

2. Workers' Compensation

—Worker's compensation includes the compensation when an employee becomes injured or disable due to extreme working conditions or while working at the job site.

3. Family & Medical Leave

—Family leave includes the compensation continuation during the family leave such as maternity or paternity leave and other family leave.

4. Old age, Survivor, Disability Insurance requirements for getting compensation:

—Earn 40 quarters of credit, or

—Be employed for 10 years

—Be age 62 for partial benefits

—Be age 65 for full benefits

—Now the age has been extended to age 67 because more and more workers are retiring late.

—Widow aged 60 +

Medicare

Depends on the country's policy, Medicare facilities are generally government services to citizens. Organizations add some value to Medicare facilities. In some countries Medicare is financed together with employees' tax, employers and the government.

SQUARE provides insurance coverage for

—Hospitalization—Covers inpatient & outpatient hospital care & services.

—Major Doctors bills—Charges of visiting a doctor or specialist.

—Prescription drug costs.

—Provides unlimited in-home care in certain situations.

Workers' Compensation

1. Workers' compensation, a legally required benefit, is included in the compulsory disability laws of many countries. Mostly, employer is seen liable regardless of the fault.

2. Objectives of Workers' compensation

    —Provide income & medical benefits
    —Reduce litigation
    —Eliminate legal fees & time
    —Encourage employer safety
    —Promote accident study & avoidance

3. Workers' compensation claims

    —Injury
    —Occupational disease
    —Death

4. Workers' compensation benefits

    —Medical services
    —Disability income
    —Death benefits

Discretionary Benefits

1. Discretionary benefits are judgment based benefits that the organization provides to its employees. These benefits are not legally required benefits but enhance organizational culture and corporate image.

2. Benefits include:

    —Protection programs
    —Pay for time not worked
    —Other services

3.4.2.6 Pay for time not worked

- Holidays
- Vacations
- Funeral leave
- Marriage leave
- Sick leave
- Stress leave
- Blood donation or welfare work
- Personal leave
- Sabbatical leave/ For Muslims, leave after death
- Other religious leaves such as pilgrimage or preaching

3.4.2.7 Organizational considerations for job design

Effectiveness

In the context of job design, to remain effective, organizations may have to redefine jobs, monitoring, and using technology so that the firm can even compete against giant rivals.

Efficiency

Maximum outputs through minimum inputs of time, effort and other resources. In the context of job design, efficiency in time, effort, labor costs, and training should be done accordingly.

3.5 Relevance of Management Theories in Jute Sector-in Bangladesh

3.5.1 The Present Structure of Jute Industries of Bangladesh:

Jute Industries play an important role in the economic development of Bangladesh. At the beginning of the twentieth century, Bangladesh could boast of only one manufacturing industry—jute. It employed about a half of the total industrial workforce of Bangladesh.

Jute Industry Manifests it-self with a destined brightness for the significant role and contribution to the national economy of Bangladesh. Soon after independence of Bangladesh, Jute mills under private ownership including abandoned Jute Mills and the then EPIDC sponsored Jute Mills were nationalized through promulgation of the Bangladesh Industrial Nationalization Order-1972 (P.O. 27 of 1972) and the responsibility for managing, supervising, controlling and co-coordinating the activities of the mills were vested with Bangladesh Jute Mills Corporation (BJMC). Jute Goods is one the main sources of foreign exchange earnings and a large number of industrial workforce is engaged in the Jute Industry. A lion portion of raw jute produced in the country is consumed in the local jute mills. BJMC purchase raw jute through purchase centers spread over the country to ensure fair price to the growers. At present there are 35 mills under BJMC (Running 26 jute mills and 3 non-jute mills and 6 closed Mills.

3.5.2 Bangladeshi Jute Traders

Being the major playground of the long history of jute trade and having relatively finer fiber, Bangladesh always had advantage in raw jute trading. Still now Bangladesh is the largest exporter of raw jute in the world. After the liberation of Bangladesh from Pakistan in 1971, the jute trading was not limited to specific groups like India or Pakistan. Because, after the liberation of Bangladesh, most of the Pakistani owned Jute Mills were taken over by the government of Bangladesh.

Later, to control these Jute mils in Bangladesh, the government built up Bangladesh Jute Mills Corporation (BJMC). No other jute mills were allowed to grow in the private sector before 1975. This incident grew many raw jute traders from different corners of Bangladesh who used to supply raw jute to BJMC owned jute mills. This group of traders is called Beparis, who buy raw jute directly from the farmers.

Bangladesh Jute Mills Corporation (BJMC), a public corporation in Bangladesh, is the largest state owned manufacturing and exporting organization in the world in the jute sector.[1][2]

BJMC owns and operates a number of jute mills around Bangladesh:

- Dhaka Zone: Bangladesh Jute Mills, Karim Jute Mills, Latif Bawany Jute Mills, U.M.C Jute Mills, Qaumi Jute Mills, Rajshahi Jute Mills,
- Khulna Zone: Aleem Jute Mills, Carpeting Jute Mills, Crescent Jute Mills, Eastern Jute Mills, Jessore Jute Industries, Peoples Jute Mills, Platinum Jubilee Jute Mills, Star Jute Mills
- Chittagong Zone: Amin Jute Mills, Amin Old Field, Gul Ahmed Jute Mills, Hafiz Jute Mills, Karnafuli Jute Mills, Development of Decorative Fabric, M.M. Jute Mills, R.R. Jute Mills, Bagdad-Dhaka Carpet Factory, Furat Karnafuli Carpet Factory

3.5.3 Productivity improvement in Jute Industry

Whatever is produced with Jute, efficiency in the process of production must be ensured. Inefficient production is not likely to be cost-effective and quality-wise acceptable. Productivity is directly related to the men and machinery of an industry.

So far as the productivity of a plant is concerned, again 4 (four) factors are of paramount importance.

1. Duly trained workers capable of running/operating the machinery with optimum efficiency.
2. Good machinery which may ensure smooth running.
3. Congenial working atmosphere/environment so that workers may not suffer from fatigue / over-exhaustion/ monotony.
4. Reasonably good wages for the workers and compensation package for other grades of employees/supervisor/managerial staff.

Jute industries mainly feel importance for their improvement in production purpose in the following issues-

Workers of an industrial plant must be properly trained for running the machinery smoothly. Training of workers at the plant level should be a continuous process. Refresher courses for all grades of workers will definitely help improve the productivity of an industry.

Machinery must be good and smoothly operational. Good machines and workers' skill must go hand in hand to produce the desired result.

Working environment is a key factor in productivity improvement. Well ventilated factory, clean floors, good surroundings healthy living conditions in the workers' barracks, proper sanitation arrangements in those barracks, satisfactory water supply system etc. will definitely give impetus to the workers to put in their best efforts.

Needless to say, reasonably good wages for workers act as the silver tonic to inspire them to do their work with utmost efficiency.

There are other factors such as selection of right kind of Jute for appropriate batching for the goods to be produced. But these are routine matters for the factory/mill management.

3.6 Managerial qualifications in different sectors in Bangladesh

3.6.1 Qualifications of a Manager in Garment sector

- At least 5 years of experience in related field and in same types of job. Such if a person wants to be the manager of a garment, then he should have at least five years of experience of working in management level of another garments doing same/related types of production.
- At least graduate from any discipline
- Good interpersonal communicating skill. Means that he should be good and frank in communicating with others. Export oriented garments prefer to have managers having sound communicating ability in English.

- Good coordinating and controlling ability: As lots of employees and or labors work under a manager. The manager must have to have some coordinating and controlling ability. So that they can delegate, monitor, evaluate subordinate's works and can take necessary action.
- Skills in computer is preferred: As today's business world is more related with the computer and technology than ever, garments sector may prefer their managers to have some computer skill.

3.6.2 Qualifications of a Manager in Pharmaceutical sector

The leadership qualities concerned with this pharmaceutical company are being

1. **Dynamic and enthusiastic:** As this sector is highly growing and increasingly facing intense competition, the managers of this sector must be able to cope with this dynamic and changing situations. S/he also has to be enthusiastic to take the right decisions at right time
2. **Good interpersonal and communication skills:** As the manager has to communicate with people from different sectors like suppliers, operational workers, medical promotion office and key persons of various hospitals, s/he needs good interpersonal and communication skills.
3. **Control and coordination:** The manager of this sector must be capable of handing work force and have the ability to communicate with hospitals and other health care services throughout the country.
4. **In-depth knowledge:** The manager must have in—depth knowledge about the global and local market to remain updated.
5. **Sound educational background:** The qualification to become a manager as required by the company requires is minimum five years experience in concerned field with sound educational background. The manager as we consulted has B. Pharm/M. Pharm with MBA.

3.6.3 Qualifications of a Manager in Real Estate sector

1. **Communication capability:** In real estate sector, people of different type and background work together. Moreover, the sector is highly dependent on bottom level workers. As a result, it is very important for the manager to communicate with everybody. This requires excellent communication capability.
2. **Decision making power:** The manager in a real estate sector has to work in connection with different public organizations like Rajuk, WASA, DESA etc. At times it becomes very important to take strong decisions in difficult situations. So the manager must have the capacity to take realistic decisions.
3. **Engineering background:** As it is a mainly a sector of civil engineering works, it is highly preferable if the manager have a civil engineering background.
4. **Follower:** As stated earlier, people of different type and background work together in real estate business. Different people require different styles of leadership. For example, a new hire requires more supervision than an experienced employee. A person with a poor attitude requires a

different approach than one with a high degree of motivation. The manager must know his employees. The fundamental starting point is having a good understanding of human nature: needs, emotions, and motivation. He must know his employees' be, know, and do attributes.

3.6.4 Qualifications of a Manager in Banking Sector

- Good Interpersonal and Communication Skill: The objective of this bank is to enhance their business in terms of increased customer number, total revenue. For this purpose they focus on two basic requirements. Firstly, satisfying the existing customers and retaining them. Secondly, getting new customers. For attaining both goals, it is very much important to have excellent communication capabilities.
- Decision Making Ability: To satisfy both the goals stated above, every manager also requires having the ability to choose what the best way among the alternatives is. That is they are required to have good decision making power to make the job done perfectly.
- Banking related Education: As it is a mainly a sector of banking, it is highly preferable if the manager have a degree related to business administration, banking etc.

3.7 Trade Union in Bangladesh

According to Abraham Lincoln, "Labor is prior to, and independent of, capital. Capital is only the fruit of labor, and could never have existed if Labor had not first existed. Labor is superior to capital, and deserves much the higher consideration." Still, from the very beginning of civilization the rights of laborers have been ignored and laborers have had a lack of awareness of their own rights. Though "Labor is the source of all wealth" (Frederick Engles)—laborers are deprived of all kind of rights, all over the world. This deprivation puts the labor class in an extreme position, which requires them to reinstate their rights. So they have to organize themselves with the philosophy—'we must learn to live together as brothers or we are going to perish together as fools'. So comes into existence the idea of 'Trade Union'.

Everyone has the right to form and to join a trade union for the protection of their interests.[92] Sideny and Beatrice Webb defined a trade union as "continuous association of wage-earners for the purpose of maintaining or improving the conditions of their working lives". This classical definition of trade union remains true in substance, since it is the status of a person's work as an employee which determines his or her potential eligibility for trade union membership. Its fundamental objective according to Webb is "the deliberate regulations of employment in such a way as to ward off from the manual-working producers the evil effect of industrial competition." To Karl Marx the trade union was first and foremost an "organizing centre". The labor organization provided for Marx the focal point for the functional organization of the working class towards a change in the structure of the society.[93]

3.8 The origin and growth of trade union[94]

In the early stage of industrial development when there were personal contacts between employers (master) and workers (employee), there was no need of any organization to determine relations between the two. But under the modern factory system the personal touch is absent and the relations between the employer and the worker have come under strain. The conflict of interests between buyer and seller of labor power has become conspicuous and this has led to the rise of trade union movement throughout the world.

The history of the trade union movement in Bangladesh is linked with the development of a modern industrial society in the sub-continent beginning from 1850. In the Indo-Pak subcontinent the first labor organization was the All India Trade Union Congress.[95] After the independence of Pakistan, East Pakistan Trade union federation was formed on 28th September 1947. In 1959, Pakistan federation of labor was formed; it was the only central labor organization in the whole of Pakistan.[96] After declaring the Industrial Relations Ordinance—1969, freedom was given to labor to form any trade union in any commercial or industrial establishments.[97] The tradition of the parallel development of the nationalist and the trade union movement, which had originated in British India, continued through the Pakistan period down to the birth of Bangladesh.

During Pakistan period most trade union leaders held conflicting views and the trade unions were fragmented and weakened. As a result, the trade union movement met a setback and the trade union activities passed into the hands of petty bourgeoisie leadership. Moreover, the trade union movement in Pakistan was characterized by fragmentation of unions, prolonged strikes, retaliatory lockouts and picketing which sometimes led to violence. Although Pakistan was one of the first states which ratified the International Labor Organization (ILO) Conventions No. 87 and 98, its workers were virtually deprived of the right to collective bargaining and the right to strike. The Industrial Dispute Act 1947 of India was adopted in Pakistan with some amendments until 1959, when worker's right was further curtailed by the Industrial Dispute Ordinance, promulgated by the martial law authority. Between 1965 and 1969, the East Pakistan Labor Disputes Act was mainly responsible for regulating industrial relations.

In 1969 a new regime promptly promulgated The Industrial Relations Ordinance which classified disputes as either matter of "right", or matter of "interest". On matters of right, guaranteed by existing labor laws, disputes were banned, though in practice the ban was ineffective. On matter of interest, workers were for the first time given a limited right to strike. Although the government could prohibit strikes in the public service, strikes were allowed in non-public utility services for 30 days, after which the government could ban the strike and refer the dispute to the court for adjudication.

After 1971, most industries and services were nationalized. The Industrial Relations Ordinance 1969 continued to govern industrial relations, but labor management relations were often more turbulent. On 24 December 1974 the government declared a state of emergency, disbanding all political parties, banning strikes and lock outs and restricting trade union activities; the conciliation machinery of the Labor Ministry and the industrial courts was maintained. In 1972, the number of registered trade unions in the country was 2523, with membership of 682,923 workers. Until 1975 Trade Unions were mainly at root level, though there were loosely organized industrial federations. At the end of May, 1975 there were about 3230 registered trade unions, including 21 industrial federations and 173 employers' organizations There were constant struggles between rival unions and federations which often led to violence. As the trade union movement in Bangladesh originated in British India and Pakistan, it naturally retained its old character of working more as a nationalist force against colonial domination than as a class force vis-à-vis capitalist exploitation. As a result, the trade union movement of the region that had gained momentum in the hands of political leaders stood divided along the political and/ or ideological lines in independent Bangladesh. During this period, the trade union movement was marked by direct interference by the government and the ruling party in its internal affairs. In many industrial belts terrorism was let loose by the men of the labor front of the then ruling party and tried to drive out the honest trade unionists from the leadership of the unions. Moreover, the barring of outsiders from trade union leadership at the basic union level made the process of union hijacking very easy and turned the workers into a very weak and defenseless community. In the early 1980s, the military government of Bangladesh banned all trade union activities in the country. Then an alliance of the National Federation of Trade Unions (NFTUs) emerged in the name of Sramik Karmachari Oikka Parishad (SKOP) to establish the democratic rights of workers as well as to fulfill their economic demands. Most NFTUs were in SKOP and since 1983, most trade union movements in Bangladesh have been organized under the leadership of SKOP.[98] The opportunism and lenient attitude of the trade union leaders including SKOP gave the ruling regimes a chance to disregard the agreements signed between the government and the trade union leaders. At present, the leaders of nineteen of the twenty three NFTUs are included in the SKOP. After its formation, SKOP submitted a 5-point charter of demands for establishing their democratic rights and higher wages through rallies, torch processions, demonstrations, strikes, hartals, blockades etc. Till December 2004, 6492 trade unions (worker's union—5242 and employers' association—1250) exist in Bangladesh having 2,094,887 members. This clearly shows the rate of multiplicity of trade unions in Bangladesh.

3.9 Developments in trade unions

First of all, let us take a cursory glance at the labor scenario in Bangladesh:

Overall employment situation

Bangladesh offers an abundant supply of disciplined, easily trainable and low-cost work force suitable for any labor-intensive industry. Of late, there is an increasing supply of professionals, technologists and other middle and low-level skilled workers. They receive technical training from universities, colleges, technical training centers, polytechnic institutions etc. The expenditure incurred by an employer to train his employee is exempted from income tax. The minimum age for workers in Bangladesh is 16 years in factories and establishments. Contracts are made in the form of a letter of offer. Workers may also be engaged on verbal agreements. In Bangladesh 47 labor laws are now in operation. These relate to (a) wages and employment, (b) trade union & industrial disputes, (c) working environment and (d) labor administration and related matters. In the public sector, wages and fringe benefits of the workers are determined by the government on the recommendation of the National Wages Commission established from time to time. Such commissions were appointed in 1973, 1977, 1984, 1989 & 1992. Wages & fringe benefits declared by the government in 1977 have 20 grades of wages. Workers in the public or private sector remain at their job for eight and a half hours daily (including half an hour for meal or rest) with Friday a weekly holiday marking 48 working hours a week.

The current labor force statistics (2005-2006) shows that right now in Bangladesh, Economically Active Population (15+ Population in million) is 49.5 of which male is 37.4 and female is12.1 million. Whereas employed population is 47.4 million and unemployed population is 2.1 million.

Employment by major occupation (million)

Professional, technical	2.2
Administrative, managerial	0.2
Clerical workers	1.0
Sales workers	6.7
Service workers	2.8
Agriculture, forestry & fisheries	23.0
Production & transport laborers & others	11.5

Employment by major industry (million)

Agriculture, forestry & fisheries	22.8
Mining and quarrying	0.1
Manufacturing	5.2
Electricity, Gas and water	0.1
Construction	1.5
Trade, hotel and restaurant	7.8
Transport, storage & communication	4.0
Finance & business services and real estate	0.7
Health, education, public admin. & defense	2.6
Community and personal services	2.6

(Source: Bangladesh Bureau of Statistics, Key findings of Labor Force Survey 2005-2006)

In this backdrop, employment in growth sectors used to be a source of workers' empowerment through trade unionism. Unions are generally highly politicized, and are the strongest in state-owned enterprises. Civil service and security force employees are forbidden to join unions because of their highly political character. Teachers in both the public and private sector are not allowed to form trade unions. Industrial Relations Ordinance, 1969 provides that any worker or employer has the right to form a union without previous authorization. But such a union cannot function as a trade union without being registered under the law. After liberation of the country in 1971, the Government of Bangladesh nationalized the major industries and services including banks and insurance companies. The working class of Bangladesh, with higher hopes and aspirations, demanded higher wages and fringe benefits. It is interesting to note that after liberation, the government-affiliated trade unions always dominated the trade union scene. Industrial Relations Ordinance, 1969 deals with trade unions in Bangladesh. In any industrial and commercial establishment, a trade union may be formed with 30% of the total number of workers employed. If there is more than one union in any establishment, CBA is determined by the Registrar of the Trade Union through secret ballot for a term of two years. Only the CBA is authorized to raise industrial disputes and negotiate with the management. The Director of Labor of the government acts as the Registrar of Trade Union in Bangladesh.

3.9.1 Labor Rights under the Trade Unions

By the very Ordinance, freedom is also given to the laborers to form any federation of trade union.[99] Trade unions or federation of trade unions can be formed in any premises or any commercial or industrial establishments. The Registrar appointed under this ordinance may declare any of the trade unions formed in accordance with the provisions of this ordinance, as the CBA of that very establishment.[100] To declare a trade union as a CBA, the registrar is bound to abide by the provisions of the Ordinance. The function of the CBA is to bargain with the employers and with the government regarding labor interests and labor rights. So, it can be said that the labor organization is recognized by the state.

Forced or compulsory labor may be as a means of political coercion or education, or as a punishment for holding or expressing political views or views ideologically opposed to the established political, social or economic system, or by mobilizing and using labor for the purposes of economic development and as a means of racial, social, national or religious discrimination.[101] The laborers of Bangladesh enjoy full freedom to choose their own sector of work, and they have the choice to be a member of any trade union, federation of trade unions or to constitute a new trade union. Nobody can put pressure upon them to do a specific work in a specific factory or establishment, or to be a member in a specific trade union. In choosing the place of work and working sector, full freedom is the fundamental right of a worker in Bangladesh. All forms of forced labor are prohibited and any contravention of this provision shall be an offence punishable in accordance with law.[102]

The laid-off workers have their rights for compensation.[103] Retrenched workers have their rights of re-employment.[104] Every employer is responsible for the payment to the laborer concerned.[105] To keep the health of the worker up to a proper standard and to ensure the welfare of the workers the employers must comply with the provisions stated under the Factories Act, 1965. Every worker has the right to a proper medical examination by a qualified medical practitioner if he or she falls in an accident during working hours.[106] No worker is bound to work more than the working hours prescribed under the different Acts existing in Bangladesh. Overtime allowance must be at the rate of twice of the ordinary rate of wages.[107] Every worker is entitled to weekly holidays, festival holidays, annual leave, casual leave, and sick leave with full wages under the different Acts and Ordinances existing in Bangladesh regarding labor. Apparently it seems that laborers in Bangladesh enjoy full freedom in choosing their own work and own organization. They are provided with all kinds of rights by the employers and states. But the real phenomenon is quite different.

Every citizen shall have the right to form associations or union.[108] Obtaining these opportunities employers and other elite forces formed so called trade union and other labor organizations under the shadow of political authorities. They use the weaker worker class at their political interest. A poor and weaker worker who is hand to mouth is not capable of forming any trade union; and cannot express his/her own opinion regarding labor politics and different labor industrial issues. So freedom of association is meaningless to a worker in Bangladesh as there is a major lack of existing labor-industrial laws in Bangladesh. A worker may be dismissed without prior notice or pay in lieu thereof, if he or she is found guilty of misconduct.[109] Without giving prior notice, dismissal only on the grounds of misconduct is a violation of natural justice. A residual power is always vested upon the government in almost every section of the existing labor industry related Labor Code 2006 in Bangladesh, by which the government can do whatever it likes. At present most of the employers of factories and other establishments is somehow part and parcel of the government directly or indirectly. So, the existing labor-industrial laws are in favor of the employers and not in favor of the workers.

Changing pattern of labor market has changed the Trade Union situation also. Increase of women workers, home based workers, growing informal sectors, small commercial and service sectors have changed the organizational strategies.

TU organizations are divided under many National Centers and major National Centers are united in a common platform named Sramik Karmachari Oikko Parishad—SKOP. For long time all the national Labor issues have been raised and addressed by the SKOP as the common and united platform of the TU movement of the country. At present almost all the major National centers are working to establish a united organization, independent of political influence.

Besides its success the rate of unionized workers are still less than 5% and more than half of the basic and plant level unions are not affiliated with any National Centre. Out of a total 53.5 million of working people only 1.9 million are unionized. There is little unity among the Trade Union leaders. Most of the federations are financially weak and don't have in-house development programs for the activists. Education level of the workers is not in a satisfactory level. Offices are not equipped with modern communication system.

Trade Union Memberships (June 2005)[110]	
Total Members of Basic Unions	19,69,614
Total Basic Unions	5242 (organized worker: 4.44%)
National Trade Union Federations	31
Women's Committee	13
Total Union under NF	1274
Total Membership	12,54,500
Workers Organized with National Federation Membership	2.83%
Organized members but not within National Federations	7,15,114
Trade Union but not Affiliated with National Federation	3968

Table 3 : Trade Union Memberships (June 2005)

Basically the institutional form of trade union is termed as trade union structure. Trade union structure of a country indicates the co-ordination of the trade unions from the basic level unions to national level federations. For trade union movement, the structure of trade union is termed as an important Body-Politic.

A strong structure is indispensable for a trade-union movement of a country. But there is difference in the structures of trade union in different countries. In some countries there is only one national level federation to control and coordinate all the trade unions of a country, for example, TUC of UK and Australia. Again in some countries there are more than one national level federation. For example, the National Federation of Trade Unions (NFTU) of Bangladesh, India and Pakistan etc. In the trade union structure of Bangladesh there are three levels:

(1) NTUFs in the national level
(2) Industrial federations in the industrial levels
(3) Basic unions in the basic levels.

Change in Trade Union Figures[111]								
Financial Year	No. of Trade Union at the Beginning of the year	No. of Members	No. of Trade Unions Registered during the year	No. of Members	No. of cancelled Unions	No. of Members	No. of Trade Unions during the year	No. of Members
1991-92	3818	1292782	282	46294	104	16905	3996	1322171
1992-93	3996	1322171	298	44488	143	22328	4142	1344331
1993-94	4142	1344331	268	32547	48	10396	4362	1366482
1994-95	4362	1366482	322	43229	39	31526	4645	1378185
1995-96	4645	1378185	309	38423	46	18485	4869	1721061
1996-97	4869	1721061	145	16667	59	6917	4955	1730811
1997-98	4955	1730811	602	92750	50	9877	5507	1813684
1998-99	5507	183684	419	52459	175	29067	5751	1837076
1999-00	5751	1837076	266	31253	52	6947	5965	1861382
2000-01	6063	1869437	338	48182	52	8205	6349	1909414

Table 4 : Change in trade union figures

Besides these the presence of zonal or regional committee is observed. But IR Ordinance—1989 amends the trade union structure and rules out the zonal or regional committees. So if there is still the presence of zonal or regional committees, they have no legal basis.

The numbers of registered trade union under this department from 1991-92 to 2000-01 (up to January) is showing in the following table:

Figure 7 : Trade Union Membership Trend

The above figure is a graphical presentation of the trade union membership trend since the independence of Bangladesh till 2002. The figure clearly shows the rising trend of the membership. During this time period trade union activities declined only was once that is from 1980-1990. The reason behind this decline was mainly due to political situation as this period is marked by the autocratic regime of Hussain Mohammad Ersdhad.

Below is a list of some of the prominent trade union of Bangladesh.

Prominent Trade Unions of the country[112]			
Sl. No.	Name of National Federation	Number of Union	Number of Union Members
01.	Jatiya Sramik Federation	19	19,101
02.	Bangladesh Trade Union Kendra	60	50,180
03.	Bangladesh Sangiukta Sramik Federation	232	1,19,996
04.	Bangladesh Trade Union Sangha	12	19,303
05	Jatiya Sramik Jote	12	2260
06.	Bangladesh Jatiyatabadi Sramik Dal	279	2,47,454
07.	Bangladesh Mukta Sramik Federation	33	1,32,301
08.	Bangladesh Sramik Kalyan Federation	39	43,108
09.	Jatiya Sramik Federation Bangladesh	11	15,881
10.	Jatiya Sramik League	226	2,27,800
11.	Bangladesh Trade Union Federation	4	1648
12.	Bangladesh Free Trade Union Congress	35	97,540
13.	Bangladesh Sramik Federation	5	3639
14.	Bangladesh Labor Federation	122	1,00,844
15.	Bangladesh Jatiya Sramik Forum	10	31,077
16.	Bangladesh Jatiya Sramik Federation	18	23,055
17.	Samajtantrik Sramik Front	16	2285
18.	Jatiya Sramik Jote Bangladesh	20	7130
19.	Jatiya Sramik Karmachari Jote	26	5019
20.	National Trade Union Federation	5	1798
21.	National Workers Federation	10	10,467
22.	Bangladesh Workers Federation	24	24,756
23.	Bangladesh Sramik Sanghati Federation	12	3664
24.	Bangladesh Jatiya Sramik Karmachari Parishad	5	8465
25.	Jatiya Samajtantrik Sramik Jote	14	5545
26.	Bangladesh Jatiya Sramik Jote	5	2421
27.	Bangladesh National Council of Textile Garments Workers	4	34,246
28.	Jatiya Sramik Party	2	6400
29.	Bangladesh Garments and Industrial Sramik Federation	6	1425
30.	Bangladesh Garments and Shilpa Sramik Federation	5	1425
31	Bangladesh Sramajibi Kendra	3	5692
	Total Union	1274	12,54,500

Table 5 : Prominent Trade Unions of the country

Following is the list of Registered Trade Unions (Divisional Basis, 1996-1997)

Distribution of Trade Unions on the basis of division[113]					
Sl. No.	Divisional Office	1996		1997	
		No. of Union	Members	No. of Union	Members
1	Head Office	7	259	17	15071
2	Dhaka	147	10835	140	28859
3	Chittagong	95	6248	57	7607
4	Khulna	89	4512	86	8339
5	Rajshahi	128	7113	148	13222
Total	Five (5)	466	28967	448	73098

Table 6 : Distribution of trade unions on the basis of division

Here is another list showing the registered trade unions on sector basis, 1996-1997

Sl. No.	Industry/Sector	1996		1997	
		Union	Members	Union	Members
1	Miscellaneous	180	11265	201	22580
2	Transportation	144	7248	119	20544
3	Shop	83	4188	52	7546
4	Gas	4	263	3	475
5	Chemical	6	626	3	111
6	Jute	5	1554	5	925
7	C.T.	10	1359	20	4309
8	P.E.	2	369	1	114
9	E.N.G	11	683	13	724
10	T.O.	2	152	2	555
11	S.B.	8	459	8	12853
12	P.P.	1	29	4	476
13	Hotel	6	577	7	113
14	Dock	1	74	-	-
15	Food	1	98	3	237
16	C.F.	2	23	1	21
Sl. No.	Industry/Sector	1996		1997	
		Union	Members	Union	Members
17	B.K.			1	129
18	C.P.			1	29
19	T.R.			1	1049
20	J.P.B			3	308
Total		466	28967	448	73098

Table 7 : Registered Trade Unions on Sector Basis, 1996-1997

3.9.2 Factors influencing union membership

The factors influencing the level and density of trade union membership are many, varied and complex. They are also extremely difficult to measure quantify or rank in order of importance.

Factors influencing trade union membership[114]	
Positive Factors	**Negative Factors**
Low unemployment	Economic recession
Stable composition of employment and industrial structure	Rapidly changing composition of employment and industrial structure
Large employing organizations and workplace	Small employing organizations and workplace
Size of the public sector	
High inflation requiring defensive wage increases	Expansion in geographical areas with little trade union tradition
Willingness of management to recognize and negotiate with unions	Anti-union employers and mangers
Positive appeal of trade unions-image, leadership etc.	Unfavorable trade union image
High level of male full-time employment	High levels of female and part-time employment
Positive and favorable attitude by government to trade union membership and collective bargaining	Negative attitude of government to trade union membership and collective bargaining
Long established "brown-field" places of employment	Expansion of "green-field" sites
Low levels of product/services market competition	High levels of product/service market competition
Terms of employment determined by collective bargaining	Growth un private sector service employment and decline in manufacturing and public sector employment
A favorable political climate	Unfavorable political membership

Table 8 : Factors influencing trade union membership

Analytical purpose allows these to group into four categories: first, structural changes in pattern of national employment; second, growth and decline in the national economy; third' the political, legal and social climate of industrial relations; fourth, trade union image appeal and leadership.

3.9.3 Structural changes in the pattern of national employment

One common explanation of changes in the level and density of trade union membership focuses on the constantly changing pattern of national employment as old industries and occupations decline and new ones emerge. The membership pattern is also influenced by the growth in female, part-time and white collar employment. Structural change in industry and the patterns of employment also affects the size of workplace and establishments. Generally speaking, the larger the workplace and the more people employed the higher will be union membership and density.

The elasticity of demand for products produced in an industry and substitution availability are important industry characteristics which can influence collective bargaining. In industries where price can significantly influence demand, management will be extremely cost-conscious and tend to resist union wage demands. There consumers can use alternate products.

The nature of the production technology also influences labor relations. Some process industries, such as oil refineries, are easy for management personnel to operate during a strike. Others, such as steel mills, are impossible to operate without the regular work force. A strike in the former can mean no loss of production and is not very effective. A strike in the latter is the reverse.

More recently the issue of trade unions in the EPZ has re-surfaced. While the US is exerting considerable pressure on the Bangladesh government to fulfill an earlier commitment to allow trade unions to function in the EPZ, this is being strongly opposed by the foreign investors in the EPZ, who when they decided to invest were clearly attracted by the restrictions on trade union activities in the EPZs. What should the government of Bangladesh do? On the one hand to unionize could threaten the future of EPZs, which have flourished in the absence of any trade union activities. Not to unionize could threaten not only Bangladesh's GSP facilities to the US, but could threaten, in the long run, Bangladesh's RMG exports to the US, as well as the prospects of obtaining duty free access to the US market. Caught between the devil and the deep blue sea, something we have become quite habituated to, the government is anxiously, perhaps desperately, looking for a way out.

3.9.4 The political, legal and social climate

The attitude of government towards trade unions and the degree of public approval they enjoy is obviously important to their membership appeal. Favorable government attitudes in the nineteenth century towards responsible and constitutionally minded trade unions were essential for their early survival and growth.

The personalities of leaders of both the union and management and the type of leadership they provide are major determinates of a union management relationship.

Some union leaders have personalities strong enough to generate enthusiasm and trust among members so that they would follow him in whatever direction he leads while others fail to do so for their lack in charisma and credibility.

Economic conditions may well influence a union's willingness to settle and also the nature of its respective concerns in bargaining. When economic times are good, managements are often unwilling to take a strike and are thus more receptive to union demands. When times are bad, unions may be more concerned with security than money. Recently the economic conditions of high unemployment, high inflection and low profits have made bargaining difficult.

Socio economic condition of Bangladesh is characterized by exploitations on the part of the employers, lack of democratic environment, lack of educational qualification in Bangladesh workers, poor financial condition of the workers, equal presence of our workers, lack of nutrition and poor physical condition poor social status or our workers, poor base of the formation of working class, absence of industrial democracy absence of workers representative in the parliament, poor balance between the demand and supply of workers, big family size of the workers, lack of class consciousness in the working class etc.

All the factors above influence trade union movement heavily. As for example poor financial condition of the garment workers, according to many union leaders, is the main obstacle behind their lagging behind. Otherwise they could make the strongest movement in the country given the largest number of workers in the industry.

Legislation is probably the greatest outside force affecting labor relations. The law has created a whole framework within which unions and management operate. Many of the parties' actions, from the recognition of the union, to the negotiation and administration of a contract, to conciliation, mediation and sometimes arbitration are carried out because the law requires that they be done.

When the rules and regulations of a state do not intervene in the workers' right of association, workers can spontaneously participate in the trade union movement.

But in case of Bangladesh one can see different governments in different times have brought amendments in the IRO—1969 in most of the cases to; take away the freedom of association and democratic rights from the workers.

3.9.5 Relations between trade unions

In Bangladesh, many different unions represent identical grades or closely related grades of employees in the same industries and services and even in the sane firm. This is an inevitable consequence of the multi-union nature of the Bangladeshi trade unions.

When multi-union remains in play; it is not unusual that there are often conflicts of interest amongst the unions. There are many causes of inter-union conflict. The most frequent include: first, competition between unions for new members; second, the accusation that one union is poaching another union's members or potential members in its' sphere of influence'; third, the desire of a union not to lose promoted members to another union; fourth, problems of job demarcation at the workplace; fifth, disagreement over which union should have recognition and negotiating rights with particular employers; and sixth, differing policies on pay and conditions of employment towards the employers with which they negotiate.

Most, if not all, trade unions value membership growth as a vital element in their strength in relation to the employers with which they negotiate, and in terms of their influence within the labor movement generally. Large memberships also bring valuable financial economies of scale in providing services to members. The recruitment of members is therefore an important internal union objective. Potential and existing trade unions are strongly attracted by the protection offered by large, expanding and vigorous unions. Another major cause of inter-union conflict arises out of different policies to pay negotiations and other conditions of employment among trade unions in the same industries.

The nature of leadership is particularly important within unions, because unions are democratic institutions. Unlike management, union leadership serves at the pleasure of its constituency. All unions are democratic, but some unions are more democratic than others.

But our union politics is marked by internal conflicts and conflicts between unions. For internal conflict many leaders to toe form new unions breaking their old ones. Thus only the number of trade unions increases not the number of members. This only weakens the movement. Conflicts between unions are common phenomena in our trade union movement. One hundred workers killed in Barbakunda industrial area in Chittagong in 1973. It is a typical example of our conflicts between unions.

4.0 Main Challenges faced by the Trade Union movement

- Organizing the fast growing informal sector workers and the women and youth groups.
- Effective participation in the social dialogues on globalizations and reform agendas due to lack of information gathering and learning process and mechanism.
- Lack of own resources and establishments for continuous training and research activities to develop and update leadership skill specially the potential women and youth leadership.
- Winning public and media support in favor on TU agendas, campaigns and actions.
- Loosing membership due to the impact of globalization and closure of traditional big industries like jute, sugar, newsprint, textile silk etc.

4.1 Main Challenges faced by the Trade Union movement

- Organizing the fast growing informal sector workers and the women and youth groups.
- Effective participation in the social dialogues on globalizations and reform agendas due to lack of information gathering and learning process and mechanism.
- Lack of own resources and establishments for continuous training and research activities to develop and update leadership skill specially the potential women and youth leadership.
- Winning public and media support in favor on Trade Union agendas, campaigns and actions.
- Loosing membership due to the impact of globalization and closure of traditional big industries like jute, sugar, newsprint, silk etc.

4.1.1 Challenges to be faced by Trade Union in Future

There are some challenges to be faced by the trade unions which can be summarized as the following:

- Decrease of membership
- Negative effects of globalization
- Privatization of SOEs
- Contract labor system
- Image of trade unions
- Lack of technological skills
- Finding ways to organize workers in informal economy
- Limitations of labor laws.

4.1.2 Use of Information Technology (IT) within the trade unions

Bangladesh has a long glorious history of trade unionism, but when it is a question of modernization the movement is far behind of the rest of world especially in the sense of using information technology. 2/3 out of 33 national federations have computer in their offices. Those are not being properly used as the activists are not use to with the computer system.

In many cases the computers are used only for composing letters or notices. No national federation has its own web site. One or two have internet connections but trade unionists seldom browse the sites to get information and knowledge about the movement of the rest of the world.

The needs are to:

- Equip the trade union offices with IT supports.
- Train the office bearers on use of IT related equipments
- Equip the Education Committees and the Trainers Pools on modern training methodologies specially use of IT and distance education.
- Establish internet connection in all TU offices;
- Develop web page for all the federations so that they can share their information and views with all.

4.2 Motivation Theory and Bangladesh Perspective

4.3 Background

Motivation is a word used to refer to the reason or reasons for engaging in a particular behavior, especially human behavior as studied in psychology and neuro-psychology. These reasons may include basic needs such as food or a desired object, hobbies, goal, state of being, or ideal. The motivation for a behavior may also be attributed to less-apparent reasons such as altruism or morality. According to Geen,[115] motivations refers to the initiation, direction, intensity and persistence of human behavior

4.4 Motivational Concepts

Before going to details let discuss about some basic terms that come into play when one talks about motivation.

4.4.1 Rewards and Re-enforcements

A reward, tangible or intangible, is presented after the occurrence of an action (i.e. behavior) with the intent to cause the behavior to occur again. This is done by associating positive meaning to the behavior. Studies show that if the person receives the reward immediately, the effect would be greater, and decreases as duration lengthens. Repetitive action-reward combination can cause the action to become habit.

Rewards can also be organized as extrinsic or intrinsic. Extrinsic rewards are external to the person; for example, praise or money. Intrinsic rewards are internal to the person; for example, satisfaction or accomplishment.

Some authors distinguish between two forms of intrinsic motivation: one based on enjoyment, the other on obligation. In this context, obligation refers to motivation based on what an individual thinks ought to be done. For instance, a feeling of responsibility for a mission may lead to helping others beyond what is easily observable, rewarded, or fun.

A reinforce is different from reward, in that reinforcement is intended to create a measured increase in the rate of a desirable behavior following the addition of something to the environment.

4.4.2 Intrinsic and Extrinsic Motivation

Intrinsic motivation is when people engage in an activity, such as a hobby, without obvious external incentives.

Intrinsic motivation has been studied by educational psychologists since the 1970s, and numerous studies have found it to be associated with high educational achievement and enjoyment by students. There is currently no universal theory to explain the origin or elements of intrinsic motivation, and most explanations combine elements of Fritz Heider's attribution theory, Bandura's work on self-efficacy and other studies relating to locus of control and goal orientation. Though it is thought that students are more likely to be intrinsically motivated if they:

- Attribute their educational results to internal factors that they can control (e.g. the amount of effort they put in).
- Believe they can be effective agents in reaching desired goals (i.e. the results are not determined by luck).
- Are interested in mastering a topic, rather than just rote-learning to achieve good grades.

In knowledge-sharing communities and organizations, people often cite altruistic reasons for their participation, including contributing to a common good, a moral obligation to the group, mentorship or 'giving back'. In work environments, money may provide a more powerful extrinsic factor than the intrinsic motivation provided by an enjoyable workplace.

The most obvious form of motivation is coercion, where the avoidance of pain or other negative consequences has an immediate effect. Extreme use of coercion is considered slavery. While coercion is considered morally reprehensible in many philosophies, it is widely practiced on prisoners, students in mandatory schooling, within the nuclear family unit (on children), and in the form of conscription. Critics of modern capitalism charge that without social safety networks, wage slavery is inevitable. However, many capitalists such as Ayn Rand have been very vocal against coercion. Successful coercion sometimes can take priority over other types of motivation. Self-coercion is rarely substantially negative (typically only negative in the sense that it avoids a positive, such as forgoing an expensive dinner or a period of relaxation), however it is interesting in that it illustrates how lower levels of motivation may be sometimes tweaked to satisfy higher ones.

Intrinsic motivation is the motivation that comes from inside the performer. They compete for the love of the work, competition and position in the organization. Extrinsic motivation comes from outside of the performer. The colleagues honor and praise the performer; this motivates them to do well, or to beat a PB (Personal Best). Another example is trophies or a reward. It makes the performer want to win and beat the other competitors, thereby motivating the performer.

4.4.3 Self Control

The self-control of motivation is increasingly understood as a subset of emotional intelligence; a person may be highly intelligent according to a more conservative definition (as measured by many intelligence tests), yet unmotivated to dedicate this intelligence to certain tasks. Yale School of Management Professor Victor Vroom's "expectancy theory" provides an account of when people will decide whether to exert self control to pursue a particular goal.

Drives and desires can be described as a deficiency or need that activates behavior that is aimed at a goal or an incentive. These are thought to originate within the individual and may not require external stimuli to encourage the behavior. Basic drives could be sparked by deficiencies such as hunger, which motivates a person to seek food; whereas more subtle drives might be the desire for praise and approval, which motivates a person to behave in a manner pleasing to others.

By contrast, the role of extrinsic rewards and stimuli can be seen in the example of training animals by giving them treats when they perform a trick correctly. The treat motivates the animals to perform the trick consistently, even later when the treat is removed from the process.

4.5 Employee Motivation: Theory and Practice

The job of a manager in the workplace is to get things done through employees. To do this the manager should be able to motivate employees. But that's easier said than done! Motivation practice and theory are difficult subjects, touching on several disciplines.

In spite of enormous research, basic as well as applied, the subject of motivation is not clearly understood and more often than not poorly practiced. To understand motivation one must understand human nature itself. And there lies the problem!

Human nature can be very simple, yet very complex too. An understanding and appreciation of this is a prerequisite to effective employee motivation in the workplace and therefore effective management and leadership.

4.5.1 Need Hierarchy Theory

Abraham Maslow's hierarchy of human needs theory is the most widely discussed theory of motivation. The theory can be summarized as thus:

- Human beings have wants and desires which influence their behavior; only unsatisfied needs can influence behavior, satisfied needs cannot.
- Since needs are many, they are arranged in order of importance, from the basic to the complex.
- The person advances to the next level of needs only after the lower level need is at least minimally satisfied.
- The further the progress up the hierarchy, the more individuality, humanness and psychological health a person will show.

The needs, listed from basic (lowest, earliest) to most complex (highest, latest) are as follows:

- Physiological
- Safety and security
- Social

- Self esteem
- Self actualization

4.5.2 Herzberg's Two-Factors Theory

Frederick Herzberg's two-factors theory, intrinsic/extrinsic motivation, concludes that certain factors in the workplace result in job satisfaction, but if absent, lead to dissatisfaction.

He distinguished between:

- Motivators; (e.g. challenging work, recognition, responsibility) which give positive satisfaction and
- Hygiene factors; (e.g. status, job security, salary and fringe benefits) that do not motivate if present, but, if absent, result in de-motivation.

The name Hygiene factors is used because, like hygiene, the presence will not make you healthier, but absence can cause health deterioration.

The theory is sometimes called the "Motivator-Hygiene Theory."

4.5.3 Alderfer's ERG theory

Clayton Alderfer, expanding on Maslow's hierarchy of needs, created the ERG theory (existence, relatedness and growth). Physiological and safety, the lower order needs, are placed in the existence category, while love and self esteem needs are placed in the relatedness category. The growth category contains our self-actualization and self-esteem needs.

4.5.4 Self-Determination Theory

Self-determination theory, developed by Edward Deci and Richard Ryan, focuses on the importance of intrinsic motivation in driving human behavior. Like Maslow's hierarchical theory and others that built on it, SDT posits a natural tendency toward growth and development. Unlike these other theories, however, SDT does not include any sort of "autopilot" for achievement, but instead requires active encouragement from the environment. The primary factors that encourage motivation and development are autonomy, competence feedback, and relatedness.[116]

4.5.5 Goal-setting theory

Goal-setting theory is based on the notion that individuals sometimes have a drive to reach a clearly defined end state. Often, this end state is a reward in itself. A goal's efficiency is affected by three features; proximity, difficulty and specificity. An ideal goal should present a situation where the time between the initiation of behavior and the end state is close. This explains why some children are more motivated to learn how to ride a bike than mastering algebra. A goal should be moderate, not too hard or too easy to complete. In both cases, most people are not optimally motivated, as many want a challenge (which assumes some kind of insecurity of success). At the same time people want to feel that there is a substantial probability that they will succeed. Specificity concerns the description of the goal in their class. The goal should be objectively defined and intelligible for the individual. A classic example of a poorly specified goal is to get the highest possible grade. Most children have no idea how much effort they need to reach that goal. For further reading, see Locke and Latham (2002).

4.5.6 Unconscious motivation

Some psychologists believe that a significant portion of human behavior is energized and directed by unconscious motives. According to Maslow: "Psychoanalysis has often demonstrated that the relationship between a conscious desire and the ultimate unconscious aim that underlies it need not be at all direct."[117] In other words, stated motives do not always match those inferred by skilled observers. For example, it is possible that a person can be accident-prone because he has an unconscious desire to hurt himself and not because he is careless or ignorant of the safety rules. Similarly, some overweight people are not really hungry for food but for attention and love. Eating is merely a defensive reaction to lack of attention. Some workers damage more equipment than others because they harbor unconscious feelings of aggression toward authority figures.

Psychotherapists point out that some behavior is so automatic that the reasons for it are not available in the individual's conscious mind. Compulsive cigarette smoking is an example. Sometimes maintaining self-esteem is so important and the motive for an activity is so threatening that it is simply not recognized and, in fact, may be disguised or repressed. Rationalization, or "explaining away", is one such disguise, or defense mechanism, as it is called. Another is projecting or attributing one's own faults to others. "I feel I am to blame", becomes "It is her fault; she is selfish". Repression of powerful but socially unacceptable motives may result in outward behavior that is the opposite of the repressed tendencies. An example of this would be the employee who hates his boss but overworks himself on the job to show that he holds him in high regard.

Unconscious motives add to the hazards of interpreting human behavior and, to the extent that they are present, complicate the life of the administrator. On the other hand, knowledge that unconscious motives exist can lead to a more careful assessment of behavioral problems. Although few contemporary psychologists deny the existence of unconscious factors, many do believe that these are activated only in times of anxiety and stress, and that in the ordinary course of events, human behavior from the subject's point of view—is rationally purposeful.

4.5.7 Mcgregor's Theory X and Theory Y

Douglas McGregor in his book, "The Human Side of Enterprise" published in 1960 has examined theories on behavior of individuals at work, and he has formulated two models which he calls Theory X and Theory Y.

Theory X Assumptions

The average human being has an inherent dislike of work and will avoid it if he can.

- Because of their dislike for work, most people must be controlled and threatened before they will work hard enough.
- The average human prefers to be directed, dislikes responsibility, is unambiguous, and desires security above everything.
- These assumptions lie behind most organizational principles today, and give rise both to "tough" management with punishments and tight controls, and "soft" management which aims at harmony at work.
- Both these are "wrong" because man needs more than financial rewards at work; he also needs some deeper higher order motivation—the opportunity to fulfill himself.
- Theory X managers do not give their staff this opportunity so that the employees behave in the expected fashion.

Theory Y Assumptions

- The expenditure of physical and mental effort in work is as natural as play or rest.
- Control and punishment are not the only ways to make people work, man will direct himself if he is committed to the aims of the organization.
- If a job is satisfying, then the result will be commitment to the organization.
- The average man learns, under proper conditions, not only to accept but to seek responsibility.
- Imagination, creativity, and ingenuity can be used to solve work problems by a large number of employees.
- Under the conditions of modern industrial life, the intellectual potentialities of the average man are only partially utilized.

4.6 Why study and apply employee motivation principles

- Quite apart from the benefit and moral value of an altruistic approach to treating colleagues as human beings and respecting human dignity in all its forms, research and observations show that well motivated employees are more productive and creative. The inverse also holds true. The schematic below indicates the potential contribution the practical application of the principles this paper has on reducing work content in the organization.

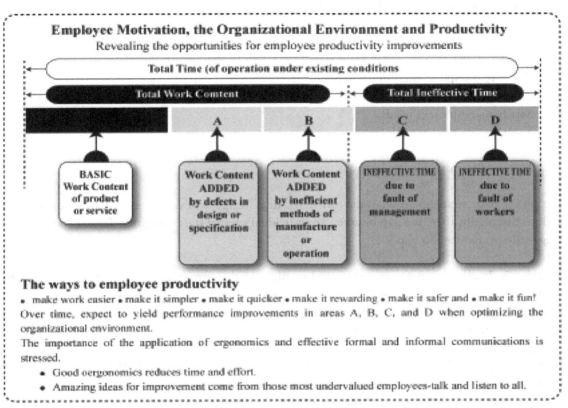

Figure 8 : Motivation and Productivity

4.6.1 Motivation is the key to performance improvement

There is an old saying—you can take a horse to the water but you cannot force it to drink; it will drink only if it's thirsty—the same goes with people. They will do what they want to do or otherwise motivated to do. Whether it is to excel on the workshop floor or in the 'ivory tower' they must be motivated or driven to it, either by themselves or through external stimulus.

Are they born with the self-motivation or drive? Yes and no. If no, they can be motivated, for motivation is a skill which can and must be learnt. This is essential for any business to survive and succeed.

Performance is considered to be a function of ability and motivation, thus:

• Job performance = f(ability)(motivation)

Ability in turn depends on education, experience and training and its improvement is a slow and long process. On the other hand motivation can be improved quickly. There are many options and an uninitiated manager may not even know where to start. As a guideline, there are broadly seven strategies for motivation.

- Positive reinforcement / high expectations
- Effective discipline and punishment
- Treating people fairly
- Satisfying employees needs
- Setting work related goals
- Restructuring jobs
- Base rewards on job performance

These are the basic strategies, though the mix in the final 'recipe' will vary from workplace situation to situation. Essentially, there is a gap between an individual's actual state and some desired state and the manager tries to reduce this gap.

Motivation is, in effect, a means to reduce and manipulate this gap. It is inducing others in a specific way towards goals specifically stated by the motivator. Naturally, these goals as also the motivation system must conform to the corporate policy of the organization. The motivational system must be tailored to the situation and to the organization.

In one of the most elaborate studies on employee motivation, involving 31,000 men and 13,000 women, the Minneapolis Gas Company sought to determine what their potential employees' desire most from a job. This study was carried out during a 20 year period from 1945 to 1965 and was quite revealing. The ratings for the various factors differed only slightly between men and women, but both groups considered security as the highest rated factor. The next three factors were;

- Advancement
- Type of work
- Company—proud to work for

Surprisingly, factors such as pay, benefits and working conditions were given a low rating by both groups. So after all, and contrary to common belief, money is not the prime motivator. (Though this should not be regarded as a signal to reward employees poorly or unfairly.)

4.7 Employee Motivation in Bangladesh

This section will cover the various aspects of the employee motivational activities practiced by the different local and multinational companies in Bangladesh. One problem in Bangladesh in the workplace is the lack of performance appraisal in the part of the managers, making it very hard for an employee to go up the ladder in the organizational hierarchy or be rewarded in any other way.

4.7.1 Different Methods of Worker Motivation

All the employees of an organization including the temporary as well as the part-time ones donate their times for the betterment of the company and add value to it. So it is natural that they expect to be rewarded by some means for their contribution. The methods of this "reward" can be defined in many ways. It can be

- Motivation through monitory compensation
- Motivation through employee participation
- Motivation through quality of work life program

4.7.1.1 Motivation through monitory compensation

In this category, management mainly concentrates on monetary rewards as money is the universal extrinsic reward. In Bangladesh, it plays a very important role in motivating the employees as the other types of motivational methods are still very new to the people. A hefty starting salary can make an employee work much harder than a congenial work atmosphere, at least in the short term. But at the same it is not always money that an employee wants. He/she may be more comfortable with power in the workplace that a high salary, if he/she is financially secured. Although most of the employees seek security through monetary means, that may not go the same for all the employees. That is why it is very important to customize each package for the taste of the employees. This ploy known as cafeteria compensation plan can be used to satisfy the need of the employees.

So it can be said that the results of company strategy must meet the need of the individuals.

It is imperative to put the belief in employees mind that if they work hard and show continuing performance and decision making skills in the job, they will be rewarded and their performance will not go unnoticed. That is why different methods like profit sharing, stock options, merit pay etc can be introduced. In this way the employee can feel a more personal touch with the company and work that much harder to add value to it.

The third point brings about the point of equity, both social and personal. Once an employee believes that he is getting more or less salary than he/she deserves, then eith because of frustration or guilt his/her performance will go downhill. In Bangladesh in the garments industry, where the workers are grossly overpaid. Still their productivity is very high, but comparing to the few organizations where their salary is fairer, the workers are more motivated and the productivity also is much higher. In Social equity, one cannot receive more or less than a person, his/her peer, who has the same level of experience and shows the same level of productivity.

Finally, one must be fair while judging the right rewards for the employees. Steps have to taken for stand out performance among the employees and they can not be done by traditional means like hourly wage. That is another big set back for Bangladesh, where the good performance is rewarded with mostly a shrug or even a scorn from the peers. By making sure that those who give an extra little get an extra little, the managers can increase productivity many folds.

4.7.1.2 Motivation through employee participation

This kind of motivation is still unique in the traditional sectors of Bangladesh. In this method, the workers are encouraged to give their inputs and be a part of the team. They are taken into making the decision for the future of the organization and their opinions are given much importance while making the future plans of the company. As a result the employees have a sense of pride and responsibility which encourages them to give their best efforts. In Bangladesh, this practice is continuing only in the board meetings, where the members participate and make future plans. But further down the line the employees only take orders from their supervisors and almost follow them blindly. If this system can be changed and the employees can be involved more in the decision making process, they will be more motivated and their performance will improve.

The multinational companies, at least some of them are already taking the initiative. It helps them in more than one way. Firstly, they can encourage the employees and get a higher performance out of them. Secondly, they can find out from the decision making skills and team meetings who would be best picked for future leadership of the company. And finally, it lowers the burden from the shoulders of the managers and they can make better decisions, as they are getting inputs from a wide range of people. All these reasons make it imperative for the organizations to adopt this motivational tool.

4.7.1.3 Motivation through quality of work life program

In this method, the flexibility and accommodation of the employees get the main focus as monetary needs alone will not suffice when it comes to having a motivated employee. In this category, tools like flexible work schedule, family support system and wellness can be mentioned. Unfortunately, in Bangladesh all this are relatively new terms. Apart from maternity leave which is not always paid, there is rarely any kind of family support given to a mother or a family. Organizations can easily adopt programs like baby care in the office of the working mothers. Above all they will have to acknowledge that the employees have a life outside the office too and if they can give them the feeling that their family is well taken care of, they will be happy and perform more for the organization.

4.7.2 Training Methods

In respect of on-the-job training, both local companies and multinational companies have shown similar trends. Two of each of the types practices this by placing each employee in different departments while three of each does it by understudy assignment (having employees work under a specific senior).

With regard to Off-the-job training, five Bangladeshi and six Multinational Company (MNC's) use "indoor lectures". Two MNC conducts "Vestibule training" (learning tasks on the job equipment) singly while two from each type combines "indoor lectures" and "Vestibule training" and two from each does them all. So, Bangladeshi companies clearly shows a preference to "indoor lectures" while MNC's preferences are varied.

	Category		Total
	Local Companies	Multi-national Companies	
Indoor lecture	5	5	10
Vestibule training (learning tasks on the job equipment)		2	2
All	2	2	4
Lecture & Vestibule	2	2	4

Table 9 : Training Methods

Sources: Primary

An interesting fact reveals in the findings that Bangladeshi companies do not provide for cross-cultural training to the expatriates as there are fewer expatriates working in such companies compared to Bangladeshis working in MNC's. On the other hand, two MNC's arrange for cross-cultural training to the expatriates.

4.7.3 Employee Development

Job rotation is the preferred employee development method used by both types of companies. Six Local companies and seven multinational companies use it two Local companies and one MNC use outdoor training. One MNC uses Lecture courses & Outdoor training while one from each type practices Assistance and Committee and Lecture & Outdoor training.

	Category		Total
	Bangladeshi	MNC	
Job rotation	7	7	14
Outdoor training	2	1	3
Lecture courses & Outdoor training	0	1	1
Assistance & Committee & Lecture & Outdoor training	1	1	2

Table 10 : Employee Development Methods

Source: Primary

4.7.4 Employee Rewards/Compensations

Both Bangladeshi and MNC's like to reward their employees with Promotion and Performance bonus, three local companies and two MNC provides only promotion, one provides promotion and profit sharing and one provides with all but commission.

	Category		Total
	Bangladeshi	MNC	
Promotion	3	2	5
Promotion & Profit sharing	0	1	1
Promotion & Performance bonus	5	6	11
All except Commission	1	1	2
More responsibilities & Performance bonus	0	0	1

Table 11 : Employee Rewards/Compensations

Source: Primary

None from each group found to provide responsibilities and performance bonus. Two Bangladeshi and two MNC reward with cash incentive.

As compensation, three Bangladeshi companies provide life insurance premium, one provides retirement accounts, three provides base payment (Scale increment) and three provides Life insurance and Base payment. Most of the MNC's prefer to provide a combination of all as compensation programs.

	Category		Total
	Bangladeshi	MNC	
Life insurance premium	3	1	4
Retirement accounts	1	0	1
Base payment (Scale increment)	3	2	5
Life insurance & base payment	3	1	4
All	0	6	6

Table 12 : Compensation Programs

Source: Primary

4.7.5 Other Benefits

Compared to local companies, multinational companies give importance to providing health insurance and social securities like source of income for retirees, disabled workers and surviving dependents of late workers. Besides social security and health insurance benefit, Bangladeshi companies also provide other different benefits.

	Category		Total
	Bangladeshi	MNC	
Social security (Source of Income for retires, disabled workers and surviving dependents of workers who have died)	2	5	7
Health Insurance	3	5	7
Others	3	4	7
Social security and Health Insurance	2	5	7

Table 13 : Employee Benefits

Source: Primary

Both local and multinational companies are found to provide provident fund and gratuity facilities. Few provide either one of them and Most of them provide both of them.

	Category		Total
	Bangladeshi	MNC	
Provident Fund	3	2	5
Provident Fund & Gratuity	7	8	15

Table 14 : Retirement Benefits

4.7.6 Types of Working Leaves

In case of casual leaves, multinational companies are found to provide less leaves than the local companies. Many of them do not allow any casual leave. Some of the companies from both groups are found to allow 10 days casual leaves. More local companies are found to provide casual leaves for 14 days or more.

Days	Bangladeshi	MNC	Total
0	2	5	7
10	3	3	6
14	6	3	9
18	0	2	2
21	0	1	1

Table 15 : Casual Leaves

Both local and multinational companies prefer 14 days as sick leave (Table 1.8). Some Local companies also provide 10 days of sick leaves. Few of them of both types are found to provide more sick leaves—21 days in a year.

Days	Category		Total
	Bangladeshi	MNC	
10	4	1	5
14	6	6	12
18	1	2	3
21	0	1	1

Table 16 : Sick Leaves

Only one local company is found to provide single day earned leave for every 18 days of work. Both local and multinational companies are found to prefer single day earned leave for every 21 days of work. Few local companies are found to provide at a very low ratio—a single day for every one month.

No. of working days for every 1 day leave	Category		Total
	Bangladeshi	MNC	
18 days	1	2	3
21 days	6	6	12
1 month	3	2	5

Table 17 : Earned Leaves

Source: Primary

All local companies are found to provide the facility to encash the leaves if not taken. But most of the multinational companies do not provide that facility.

CHAPTER IV
Theories of Industrial Relations

CONTENTS

1.0 Unitary Theory: The Unitary Perspective of Workplace Relations

1.1 Introduction

In unitarism, the organization is perceived as an integrated and harmonious system, viewed as one happy family. A core assumption of unitary approach is that management and staff, and all members of the organization share the same objectives, interests and purposes; thus working together, hand-in-hand, towards the shared mutual goals. Furthermore, unitarism has a paternalistic approach where it demands loyalty of all employees. Trade unions are deemed as unnecessary and conflict is perceived as disruptive.

Consequently, trade unions are deemed as unnecessary since the loyalty between trade unions and organizations are considered mutually exclusive, where there can't be two sides of industry. Conflict is perceived as disruptive and the pathological result of agitators, interpersonal friction and communication breakdown.

From employee point of view, unitary approach means that:

- Working practices should be flexible. Individuals should be business process improvement oriented, multi-skilled and ready to tackle with efficiency whatever tasks are required.
- If a union is recognized, its role is that of a further means of communication between groups of staff and the company.
- The emphasis is on good relationships and sound terms and conditions of employment.
- Employee participation in workplace decisions is enabled. This helps in empowering individuals in their roles and emphasizes team work, innovation, creativity, discretion in problem-solving, quality and improvement groups etc.
- Employees should feel that the skills and expertise of managers supports their endeavors.

From employer point of view, unitary approach means that:

- Staffing policies should try to unify effort, inspire and motivate employees.
- The organization's wider objectives should be properly communicated and discussed with staff.
- Reward systems should be so designed as to foster to secure loyalty and commitment.
- Line managers should take ownership of their team/staffing responsibilities.
- Staff-management conflicts—from the perspective of the unitary framework—are seen as arising from lack of information, inadequate presentation of management's policies.
- The personal objectives of every individual employed in the business should be discussed with them and integrated with the organization's needs.

1.2 The Essence of Unitary Theory

The essence of the unitary theory as held by Halford Reddish[118] and others are that every work organization is an integrated and harmonious whole existing for a common purpose. It is assumed that each employee identifies unreservedly with the aims of the enterprise and with its methods of operating. By this view, there is no conflict of interest between those supplying financial capital the enterprise and their managerial representatives, and those contributing their and job skills. By definition, the owners of capital and are joint partners to the common aims of efficient production, high profits and good pay in which everyone in the organization has a stake. It follows that there cannot be 'two sides' in industry. Indeed managers and managed alike are merely parts of the same 'team'. This team, however, is expected to be provided with strong leader from the top to keep it working and to ensure commitment to the tasks to be done and to its managerial office holders.

Briefly stated, the unitary perspective derives from the view that work organizations essentially resemble smoothly operating functional machines. While they may occasionally break down, due to lack of maintenance or poor management, they are fundamentally harmonious entities which exist for a common purpose. All organization members share common interests and identify with its aims and objectives. There is therefore no inherent conflict of interests between the owners of capital and of, the two being complementary partners in the production from which flows the income of the organization and on which both relies for their financial rewards. Thus, maximizing these revenues is in their mutual interests and is best served by total and unstinting cooperation between them. The organization is seen as a team, of which all employees are members, even though their roles and responsibilities may differ. Like all successful teams, the organization requires leadership to ensure effective coordination and commitment to the organization's objectives and its methods of operation. Sustaining this 'team spirit' requires certain styles of behavior, particularly by managers. They must inspire loyalty by recognizing the human dignity of each individual, be firm but fair in the administration of discipline, and maintain suitable communication system to keep employees informed. Authority in the organization has one source (rather like a commanding officer in a military unit), is undivided, and is exercised for the benefit of all. It follows that there cannot be 'two sides' of industry; all are on the same side. Consequently, all employees owe loyalty to the organization and to its management as the latter grapple with the problems of the firm's operation and environment.

The unitary approach requires management to display a paternalistic approach towards subordinate employees or, at the other extreme, a more authoritarian one, together with a suitable communication structure to keep employees informed of managerial and enterprise decisions. Conversely, employees are expected to remain loyal to the organization and to its management in deference to the common problems facing managers and subordinates alike. Thus the unitary theory of industrial relations emerges from a belief that work enterprises, whether privately or publicly owned, are very much like a professional football team; 'Team spirit and undivided management authority co-exist to the benefit of all.' Work organizations in short, are viewed as unitary in their structure and unitary in their purposes, and as having a single source of authority and a cohesive set of participants motivated by common goals. Consequently industrial relations is assumed to be based on mutual cooperation and harmony of interest between management and managed within the enterprise.

1.3 Conflicts and the Unitary Approach and Criticism Thereof

Factionalism within the enterprise, or in a part of it, is seen as a pathological social condition in the unitary approach. Subordinate employees are not expected to challenge managerial decisions or the right to manage, while trade unionism is viewed as an illegitimate intrusion into the unified and cooperative structure of the workplace.

Unitarian approach sees little or no role for independent trade unions, certainly not inside the workplace. Unions are regarded essentially as intruders, which foster differences, create discontents and interpose themselves between workers and management as an alternative focus for loyalty. The existence of unions is explained largely by the faults or excesses of earlier generations of managers, but the need for them has disappeared as enlightened policies have superseded earlier conditions. If union recognition has been conceded and cannot easily be removed, managements must limit the union's influence and wean employees away from it by demonstrating that management is in better position to know and act in the 'best interests' of employees.

Conflict is regarded as pathological rather than potentially constructive. Conflicts which occur in industry are either (a) merely frictional, e.g., due to incompatible personalities or 'things going wrong', or (b) caused by faulty 'communications', e.g., 'misunderstanding' about aims or methods, or (c) the result of stupidity in the form of failure to grasp the communality of interest, or (d) the work of agitators inciting the supine majority who would otherwise be content (Fox 1966, p. 12).

Thus in this harmonious model, occasional frictions and conflicts are not seen as fundamental, but as the result of human frailties and error.

Some firms base their operations on this concept in which they seek to induce a height degree of loyalty in their employees. This is particularly true of some American firms such as IBM and Kodak, but it is seen in some British firms as well. The approach may be viewed as paternalistic whereby the firm itself is best able to look after the interests of their employees. This unitary perspective may be prevalent amongst managers who merely tolerate the existence of trade unions but who firmly believe that they are better able to maintain and improve the conditions of employment of the work force.[119]

Frequently this view of the organization is criticized as being impracticable, particularly with the adamant refusal to acknowledge conflict as a healthy part of organizational life. To eliminate conflict is to force the organization into an unnatural state and this in itself generates friction which has to be eliminated for the organization to remain true to its basic belief in the unitary perspective.

However, this approach of the Unitary perspective is what formed a basis of an entirely new school of management, which is described in the next section.

1.4 Results of Unitary Perspective: Human Relations

We saw in the previous section that the Unitary approach considers conflict to be taboo and tries to avoid and ban it like a plague. This perspective thereof is may be expected to appeal to many managers, for it offers reassurance about their greater authority and about its broader purpose. It is, however, not only a perspective held by managers, but may be supported by workers at various levels. It is not asserted that, in its purer forms, it is a view widely held as describing the way things are. Rather it is more like to describe what people think 'ought' to be, and thus a goal towards which managerial policies should be directed. Much of the work of the 'Human Relations School' rests on this scenario, arguing that conflict can largely be attributed to poor human relations in industry.

A unitary perspective underlies two rather different lines of development, one of which can be traced back to some of the earliest writers about organizations who directly addressed managerial problems, devising and advocating various methods and techniques of management. The main thrust of their work was the search for the optimum or the 'best' methods of work organization in industrial undertakings, and it was based on, among other things, very simple theories of motivation.

F. W. Taylor, working in the USA at the turn of the century, sought to replace the approximate, rule-of-thumb methods used by managers by the concept of 'scientific management'. Taylor advocated careful study of working methods, using time-and-motion study to identify the optimum way of performing tasks. Management's job then was simply to explain the best method to the operative, and to ensure that it was adopted. Taylor felt that individual workers could be related to their work rather like machines (to be made as efficient as possible), and that the single motivating factor was money. This last assumption was perhaps not so surprising given that much of Taylor's work involved immigrants to the United States. Indeed, it also accorded with the simplified assumptions often attributed to economists about the behavior of individuals, whether as workers or as entrepreneurs—namely, that they exist as unorganized or isolated individuals, each acting in a manner calculated to maximize their own self-interest. An essential feature of Taylor's approach was the individual piece-rate system of payment. He considered that this provided maximum satisfaction for the worker interested in high wages and for the employer interested in low costs, and would thus secure the harmonious cooperation of both groups.

Taylor's ideas aroused much controversy and opposition even at that time. 'Taylorism' was frequently associated with 'speed-ups', for employers often cut piecework rates when earning rose; and then, as now, earnings were affected by machine breakdowns and production bottlenecks beyond the control of employees. However, many strands of the scientific management approach remain today, not least in the form of work study.

1.5 Elton Mayo and the Human Relations School[120]

A major change in emphasis in the study of human behavior in work organizations followed the investigations by Elton Mayo and his colleagues at the Hawthorne Works of the Western Electric Company in Chicago between 1927 and 1932. (Rothlisberger and Dickson, 1939). Mayo's early work was on physiological factors and the effect on output levels and turnover of rest periods, changes in lighting, etc. the Hawthorne studies have been very influential, becoming the basis for the Human Relations 'movement' with its emphasis on 'rational-economic man'. Briefly, these studies led to the 'discovery of the importance of workgroups. Experiments with a small group of women workers in the relay assembly test room led to the initially perplexing result that output levels were independent of carefully monitored changes in lighting, hours worked, length of rest periods and methods of payment. When conditions, which had been subject to many improvements, were returned to those applying before the experiments started, output was the highest ever recorded. The increases in output were attributable to the fact that the workers as a group were aware that they were the subject of a study, and this together with the interest the researchers showed in them gave them a sense of identity and importance both individually and as a group.

A further study of 14 men in the bank-wiring room, using less obvious, indirect observation techniques, revealed that they had evolved complex 'informal' social organization and group control over levels of output and other forms of behavior. That group had developed norms of behavior which, if transgressed, would lead to social sanctions against offenders. Thus, although there was a financial incentive to produce more, the group had fixed upper and lower limits to individual output. If too much was produced, the worker was branded as a 'rate-buster', while too little led to labeling as a 'chiseler'. Failure to fall into line with group norms meant becoming the butt of jokes, exclusion from conversation at break times etc.

Significantly, from a management perspective, the group put their own interpretation on company rules, and its 'leaders' were not those officially designated as such by management, and had more influence over the group than did the official leaders. The norms developed by the group were not those that management would have preferred, or indeed assumed, and some (as with the limitation of output) were antithetical to them.

These findings have been interpreted in various ways. Certainly the research suggests that workers could no longer be regarded as socially isolated individuals acting independently of their workmates to maximize income. The Hawthorne research produced a reaction against the individualistic and over-rational emphases of scientific management, and research in human relations was pursued in a variety of directions, such as styles of supervisions and group participation in decision making. These tended to show high levels of group satisfaction with democratic rather than authoritarian or laissez-faire leadership in small groups, and reductions in resistance to change when groups were allowed to participate in planning the changes. Mayo saw conflict in organization as pathological, and advocated the development of social skills, especially by managers, and exhorted managers to establish and maintain a sense of shared purpose and 'spontaneous cooperation' in industry (Mayo 1949).

Their ideas emanating from the Human Relations movement have influenced managemental practice and ideologies. The main emphasis has been advocacy of 'supportive' rather than 'controlling' styles of behavior by managers or supervisors, on participation in decision making by primary workgroups, training in man-management or social skills and improved communications from senior management. These policies offer the attractive suggestion that productivity can be raised, conflict reduced and cooperation increased by 'being nice to people'. However, as with Taylor's work, there have been qualifications and criticisms.

One of the most important criticisms of the human relations approach is of its strong but narrow emphasis on inter-personal relations, especially supervisor-worker relations, in isolation from the wider organizational and social setting. As a consequence, little account is taken of wider factors either inside the factory, such as technology, or beyond the factory gates. Second, the emphasis on group membership and the functions of groups has been criticized as too generalized and simplistic. Third, the human relations approach largely ignores trade unions, and questions concerning the distribution of the income of the enterprise as wages or profits. In addition some techniques of man-management developed in the human relations tradition have, on occasion, been seen by workers as somewhat empty gestures; and managers have not always found them successful.

1.6 Unitary Perspective Held by Employees

Some employees also hold unitary theories of work and of industrial relations; it seems likely for example that the churches and the armed services have traditionally tended toward unitary structures and consensus values which have generally been accepted by their managerial cadres and their subordinates alike. Whether these circumstances will continue, however has to be seen in the light of European developments. The growth of unionization has already substantially proceeded within some of the armed forces in Western Europe, for example, whilst both the Anglican and Catholic churches have become internally factionalized and pluralized in recent years.

1.7 Neo-Unitarianism

A variant of unitary theory, 'neo-unitary' theory, appears to have emerged in some organization since the 1980s. It builds on existing unitary concepts but is more sophisticated in the ways it is articulated and applied within enterprises. Its main aim seems to be to integrate employees, as individuals, into the companies in which they work. Its orientation is distinctly market centered, managerialist and individualist. By gaining employee commitment to quality production, customer needs and job flexibility, employers embracing this frame of reference have expectations of employee loyalty customer satisfaction, and product security in increasingly competitive market conditions. Companies adopting a neo-unitary approach to managing people share a number of ways in which they do this: they try to create sense of common purpose and shared corporate culture, they emphasize to all employees the primary of customer service; they set explicit work targets for employees; they invest heavily in training and management development; and they sometimes provide employment security for their workers.

The personnel management techniques used to facilitate employee commitment, quality output and worker flexibility include, performance related conditions, employee involvement, and a human resources management functions, rather than a personnel management function. The emphasis of neo-unitary approaches to industrial relations' or what some of its protagonists describe as 'employee relations'-is that committed, motivated and well-trained people are there to corporate success.

1.8 Analysis of Industrial Relations Unitary Theory

Industrial relation is not just about trade unions. Its institutions are trade unions, third parties, employer organizations, educational and research bodies. Major role players are shop stewards, full-time trade union officials, HR managers and officers, third-party actors. Role of the state, role of collective and individual law, and political decision-making are the major issues in industrial relation.

There are two types of approach in the literature of industrial relation. These are unitarism and pluralism. Unitary theory stems from the unitarism concept. Unitarism is an unconscious approach to people management. It assumes no contradictions in the employment relationship. On the other hand pluralism deals with the conscious approach to manage the tensions in the employment relationship. These lead to differing IR practices and policies.

Analysis of Unitary Theory proposes the following assumptions:

- All employment units are cohesive, with each member striving for a common goal.
- There is one source of authority, accepted and recognized without question.
- Conflict is not normal—and is caused by agitators or a breakdown in communication etc.
- Managerial vision is the key to change
- There is no need for unions.
- Unions are divisive in that they constitute a second focus for loyalty.
- Unitarism implicitly underlies HRM approaches.

Unitary Theory does not accept the following assumptions:

- Ownership and management are separate entities.
- Workplace is comprised of differing interest groups, each in pursuit of their own sectional interests.
- Conflict is accepted and recognized as endemic in the employment relationship.

- IR system is regulated through representative organizations, institutions and processes.
- Temporary compromises on both sides are achieved through collective bargaining.

One comment that goes with unitary theory is that it is influential enough but subsequently modified in practice. One last thing is that there is no universally accepted global theory in industrial relation.

1.9 Unitary Theory Related to Industrial Relations System

The view of industrial relations of Unitary Theory is based on the concept that organizations have a single, common objective that everyone works towards that objective with loyalty by accepting the authority structure of the organization. Such organizations work from this presumption and proceed to generate harmony and single-mindedness of purpose by creating the right kind of environment. On the other hand, The Enterprise—Corporatist System[121] is a modern technology system in which workers' interests and loyalties are enterprise-based. In this system, enterprise unions behave as though they share with the employer an interest in the well-being of the enterprise. From this point of view, the unitary theory is related to enterprise—corporatist system.

One implication of unitarism is that factionalism within the enterprise, or in a part of it, is seen as a pathological social condition. Subordinate employees are not expected to challenge managerial decisions or the right to manage, while trade unionism is viewed as an illegitimate intrusion into the unified and cooperative structure of the workplace. More than this, it is suggested, trade unionism competes almost malevolently with management for the loyalty and commitment of the employees to their employer. In other words, unitary theory in its traditional or classical form denies the validity of conflict at work whether between management and employees, between management and unions, or even between the organization and its customers.

The enterprise-corporatist system produces relationships of a paternalistic quality where—at least in the expectations of people if not always in reality—there is reciprocity on dependency and loyalty on the part of the worker with an obligation of support and protection on the part of the employer. The paternalistic relationship is total and diffuse, involving the whole personality and many aspects of life and work. Paternalistic relations may be very durable in a society which does not change very much, but if the economics of the system render observance of mutual obligations difficult—for example, when it produces rapid turnover—tensions will arise within the system between expectations and reality and the issues of legitimacy and of system change may be posed. According to unitary theory, on the part of management, at the minimum a paternalistic approach towards subordinate employees or, at the other extreme, a more authoritarian one, together with a suitable communication structure is required to keep employees informed of managerial and enterprise decisions. Conversely, employees are expected to remain loyal to the organization and to its management in deference to the common problems facing managers and subordinates alike. Thus the unitary theory of industrial relations emerges from a belief that work enterprises, whether privately or publicly owned, are very much like a professional football team; 'Team spirit and undivided management authority co-exist to the benefit of all.'

In the Enterprise—Corporatist system worker is reduced in exchange for employment security and welfare guaranteed by the employer. This is a modern technology system in which workers' interests and loyalties are enterprise-based. Trade unions, when they exist, are primarily enterprise unions, behaving as though they share with the employer an interest in the well-being of the enterprise. In some cases the security and welfare provided by the corporation may act as a deterrent to the formation of unions. Paternalism is impersonal and bureaucratized through internal rules. Industrial relations are dealt with in large measure autonomously within the corporation without significant control by the political system.

The spread of Enterprise—Corporatist system was assisted by its inclusion in political ideologies which sought to formalize the links between the economic and political systems, deny the inevitability of class conflict and grant legitimized power and prestige to corporations. According to unitary theory, conflict is either merely frictional, e.g., due to incompatible personalities or 'things going wrong', or caused by faulty 'communications', e.g., 'misunderstanding' about aims or methods, or the result of stupidity in the form of failure to grasp the communality of interest, or the work of agitators inciting the supine majority who would otherwise be content.

2.0 Practical Implications of the Unitary Theory

Unitary Theory of industrial relations is practiced in Bangladesh in most service level organizations. One reason for such widespread use of this theory is probably the development of corporate management system in Bangladesh. In such a system, the management is separated from ownership and whole organization is treated as a cluster of employees working at different levels to achieve a common goal, which is the basic essence of the unitary theory.

Another reason for the widespread use of unitary theory in Bangladesh, especially in the service level organizations is because of the narrow definition of worker in the Act 2006. Act 2006 defines worker as 'any person including an apprentice employed in any establishment or industry, either directly or through a contractor, to do any skilled, unskilled, manual, technical, trade promotional or clerical work for hire or reward, whether the terms of employment be expressed or implied, but does not include a person employed mainly in a managerial or administrative capacity'. As a result of exclusion of personnel employed in management or supervisory capacity, most officers in an organization will be excluded from the definition of worker. Unless it is manufacturing organization, it is very difficult to include people in the definition of worker.

Even in manufacturing organizations where trade unions exist, the neo—unitary theory is used. In those organizations, trade union is only seen as a mere facilitator of the harmonious relationship between all the employees in the organization.

The unitary theory was practiced in Bangladesh for a long period of time. However, it became more widespread with the development of the service industry and the entry of large foreign companies in Bangladesh. For the purpose of practical analysis of the unitary theory, two organizations have been considered in this paper. One is GrameenPhone Limited, a large joint venture multinational organization employing more than 5,000 people at different levels in the organization. The other one is a small local company, Keari Limited, where the number of employees is less than 200.

2.0.1 GrameenPhone Ltd

GrameenPhone was established in 1996 as a telecommunication service provider. The company has a very well integrated Human Resource Team. Since it is a service organization there are no factory level workers in the company. The lowest level in the organizational hierarchy is the position of "officer" who sometimes has considerable management functions. As a result, all permanent employees of GrameenPhone are excluded from the definition of worker as provided in the Labor Act 2006.

There are no existing trade unions in GrameenPhone. Although there are personnel in Grameen Phone who might fall under the definition of workers, e.g. cleaners and security guards, they are usually hired through third party sources and hence GrameenPhone cannot be treated as employer of these employees.

The participation of owners in the management of the organization is very negligible. The organizational head is the Chief Executive Officer (CEO). The major decisions regarding the direction and action plan of the company are taken by him. These are then circulated to the individual divisions, which formulate their own plans and strategies which are complimentary to the master plan forwarded by the CEO.

The whole organization works as a team in reaching the objectives of the organization under the direct and indirect guidance of the CEO. Although the CEO is the central source of authority he is also treated as an employee of the company. Thus there is only one body in the organization, which they term as human resources, who work together with no conflict or power struggle in order to achieve the organizational goals.

2.0.2 Keari Limited

Keari Limited started its operation as a real estate business in 1997. Initially it started with very few employees. Over the years, it has grown to a bigger organization employing approximately 200 employees.

Keari was initially managed and run by the 5 shareholders and founding directors. There was a separation between management and ownership and there were mainly two groups: owners and employees. However, the employees were mainly employed in capacities that excluded them from the definition of worker. As a result, there was no trade union. The day Laborers and the other workers working on construction sites are usually hired to third party contractors.

Over the years, Keari has gone for a more corporate management system, delegating more power and authority from the owners to the management units. Although, even now the main sources of authority are the five founding directors, they work more in the capacity of management committee rather than owners.

By talking to the employees, we found that almost all the employees feel that there is no power struggle between them and the owners. They treat the organization as a whole and work towards reaching its objectives. The board of directors is looked up as the only source of authority and till today there was no conflict between the employers and the employees.

Thus, although Keari limited is a very small local organization which is still managed by the owners, they practice the unitary theory of industrial relations in that all the employees and the employers treat the organization as whole and work together as a team towards fulfilling its objectives.

2.1 Conflict Theory

2.2 Introduction

One of the theories in industrial relations is conflict theory. This theory is based on two interrelated views of society and of industrial relations between employers and employees. The first is that although Britain and western societies are still class based, they are essentially 'post-capitalist' as political and industrial conflict are increasingly separated within them and industrial conflict has become less violent due to its existence has been accepted and its manifestation has been socially regulated through agreed constitutional agreements. Second one is that that as society comprises of a variety of individuals and social groups each with own self-interests and objectives, it is argued those controlling and managing work enterprises thus have to accommodate the differing values and competing interests within them. Actually in this view industrial relations between employers and unions and between managers and trade unionists, are an expression s of the conflict and the power relations between organized groups in society. However industrial conflict between managers and their subordinates has to be recognized as an endemic feature of work relationships and managed thereby.[122]

2.3 Conflict Theory

Conflict theory emphasizes the role of coercion and power, a person's or group's ability to exercise influence and control over others, in producing social order. It states that a society or organization functions so that each individual participant and its groups struggle to maximize their benefits, which inevitably contributes to social change such as changes in politics and revolutions. The theory is mostly applied to explain conflict between social classes, proletarian versus bourgeoisie; and in ideologies such as capitalism versus socialism. It is the theory that a continual struggle exists between all different aspects of a particular society. The struggle that occurs does not always have to involve physical violence. It can pertain to an underlying struggle for each group or individual within a society to maximize its own benefits. The theory was founded by Karl Marx, and later developed by theorists including Max Weber. Variants of conflict theory may depend on radical basic assumptions (society is eternally in conflict, which might explain social change), or moderate ones (custom and conflict are always mixed). The moderate version allows Functionalism as an equally acceptable theory since it would accept that even negative social institutions play a part in society's self-perpetuation.

2.3.1 Essence[123]

The essence of conflict theory is best epitomized by the classic 'pyramid structure' in which an elite dictates terms to the larger masses. All major institutions, laws, and traditions in the society are created to support those who have traditionally been in power, or the groups that are perceived to be superior in the society according to this theory. This can also be expanded to include any society's 'morality' and by extension their definition of deviance. Anything that challenges the control of the elite will likely be considered 'deviant' or 'morally reprehensible.' The theory can be applied on both the macro level (like the US government or Soviet Russia, historically) or the micro level (a church organization or school club). In summary, conflict theory seeks to catalogue the ways in which those in power seek to stay in power. The conflict theory basically states that all problems are caused by different groups and their status and how they compete for the necessities in life.

2.3.2 Basic Conflicts

In conflict theory there are a few basic conflicts. One of the basic conflicts in conflict theory is that of class. There are low and high ranks in class, and that gives a certain group more power over another group which causes conflicts. For the most part, when an individual is part of a high ranked class they usually own a lot of property. That means that if you are of a lower class, then you don't own as much property. This usually causes conflict on who owns the most property and what property one does own. In Marx's original conception, ownership of property was the most essential determinant of the class structure. On the other hand Weber thought that property ownership was only one factor determining class structure. Another basic conflict in conflict theory is that of race and ethnicity. Much like in the class system, groups in this system are ranked by their prestige and power. This means that if a certain race or ethnicity has more education, prestige, and power then it is considered the better race or ethnicity which creates conflict. Other basic conflicts in conflict theory are that of religion, region, gender, etc. All of these groups seek to gain power and use it to reshape society the way they see it best. It seems that this is the determining factor in the ruling class.

2.3.3 Modes of Conflict

In conflict theory there are different modes of conflict. One mode of conflict theory is that of warfare and revolution. Warfare and revolutions take place in phases due to the rocky "collations among a variety of social classes." An example of warfare is that going on currently in Burma, where there is military versus population fighting for control over the country's government. Another mode of conflict in conflict theory is that of strikes. Modern society has created a main social divider between workers and managers. When workers feel they have been treated unfairly, they go on strike to regain their right to power. Another mode of conflict in conflict theory is that of domination. Most social classes don't form their ideologies the same. Different groups will struggle in conflict over what they think is right, what the norms are, and their ideologies. Higher classes have more abstract ideologies, while subordinated classes that are much less to their advantage but still reflect the want in their own lives. The ideas of the ruling class are the ruling ideas, where the ruling material force is the ruling intellectual force.

2.3.4 Assumptions[124]

The following are four primary assumptions of modern conflict theory:

1. **Competition:** Competition over scarce resources (money, leisure, sexual partners, and so on) is at the heart of all social relationships. Competition rather than consensus is characteristic of human relationships.
2. **Structural inequality:** Inequalities in power and reward are built into all social structures. Individuals and groups that benefit from any particular structure strive to see it maintained.
3. **Revolution:** Change occurs as a result of conflict between competing social classes rather than through adaptation. Change is often abrupt and revolutionary rather than evolutionary.
4. **War:** Even war is a unifier of the societies involved, as well as war may set an end to whole societies.

2.4 Post-Capitalism

A major element in post-capitalist theories of contemporary society and industrial relations is the proposition that the nature of class conflict has substantially changed from that suggested by Marx in his nineteenth-century analysis. Firstly, it is argued that, we now live in a more open sand socially mobile society compared with the class-based social divisions associated with nineteenth-century and early twentieth-century capitalism. he widening of educational opportunity, the democratization of politics and the growth of public sector industry, for instance, have opened up recruitment to a whole range of sought-after roles in society, including those within industry, politics, education, the professionals, the arts and so on, which would have been inconceivable a hundred years ago. Moreover, the creation of the welfare state, it is suggested, mitigated the worst effects of social deprivation, economic inequality and abject poverty.

Secondly, the post-capitalists argue, the distribution of authority, property and social status in society is more widely diffused than in the past. The positions which individuals occupy in the authority structure of industry, for example, do not necessary correlate with their positions in the political structure or with their social standing in the community. The village postal worker can become the local councilor, the schoolteacher a Member of Parliament and the trade unionist a Justice of the Peace. Similarly the union convener within the workplace might have potentially more industrial power than the senior management with which he or she negotiates. Such individuals may also have had more political power if they were on the selection panel of the local constituency Party responsible for selecting the prospective parliamentary candidate in a safe seat. In other words, post-capitalists take the view that the dominant and subordinate classes within industry need no longer necessary correspond with the political or social divisions of society generally.

Above all, these theorists believe, these theorists believe, the institutionalization of conflict in industry not only has decreased in intensity but also has changed its form. Several changes seem to be particular importance in this respect:[125]

- The organization of conflicting interest groups itself:
- The establishment of 'parliamentary' negotiation bodies in which these groups meet:
- The institutions of mediation and arbitration;
- Formal representations of within the individual enterprise; and
- Tendencies toward and in institutionalization of workers' participation in industrial management.

Thus, it is argued, the emergences of trade unionism, employers' organizations and collective bargaining, together with union representation at enterprise and workplace level, now effectively regulate the inevitable social conflicts arising between management and subordinates at work. Even where these conflicts seem irresolvable, third-party invitation, usually through state agencies providing conciliation and arbitration services, is now available to provide workable remedies. By this analysis, extending worker participation in managerial decision making, as happens in broad levels worker representation in countries like Denmark, the Netherlands and Germany, is seen as a logical progression in institutionalizing the power relations between managers and subordinates at work. Post-capitalist society, in short, is viewed as an open society in which political, economic and social power is increasingly dispersed and in which the regulation of industrial and political conflict are of necessary's dissociated.

2.4.1 Post Capitalism in the Context of Bangladesh: Capitalism to Post-Capitalism

In Bangladesh the number of the organized working class people is not very big. There are some reasons for that. The history tells that Bangladesh was a British colony for almost 200 years. Basically in that period almost all the force was engaged in the agricultural activities for producing raw materials. In that period 'Zamindar Protha' was going on. Under this system there was a particular Zamindar or Land-lord for a particular area that used to take tax from the farmers of that area. The Zamindars or the Land-lords were the capitalists of that time. Many times farmers were bound to grow the crops that the respective Zamindar wanted. Farmers in those period followed very old way of cultivation. This system got resembles with the Peasant—lord system.

With the introduction of British rule in the urban areas important changes took place at the level of urban social stratification. A pristine 'Bhadralok' or gentlemen class consisted of educated professionals (lawyers, teachers, doctors, engineers, service holders and others) emerged in urban Bengal reaping the benefits from the new educational and occupational opportunities. The size of the newly emerged business class was small and characteristically not comparable with the bourgeois counterpart of the West. Earlier, the social status enjoyed by the traders or 'Banians' was lesser than the higher caste like the Brahmans and it changed during the colonial time. Business class also became educated and the vice versa. Thus the society of our country gradually was turning from capitalism to post-capitalism.

One of the significant developments immediately after the partition of the subcontinent was the abolition of zamindari land system in Bangladesh. Since historically most Zamindars came from the Hindu community, their migration to India after partition created a sort of vacuum in social structure. The Muslim traditional wealthy class linked to agriculture came to occupy that vacuum.

The following agrarian classes and groups are found to constitute rural society with hierarchical status and prestige: capitalist farmers, rich peasants, middle peasants, marginal peasants and the landless. The capitalist farmers are wealthy, own land and technology, hire outside and carry out cultivation for the market. Rich peasants are also wealthy and hire outside but they are still engaged in cultivation. Middle peasants are primarily subsistence cultivators with occasional market participation and primarily depending on household. Marginal peasants combine cultivation and labor sale to ensure subsistence. The landless people were the wage workers primarily engaged in agriculture. About three-fourths of rural households belong to the categories of marginal peasants and landless.

Economic status of a rural household is found to be subject to mobility when examined over a long span of time. There are different forces what result in the changes of the economic condition of rural households. Many surplus producing rural households gradually turned into subsistence and later deficit households. On the other hand, many deficit households gradually became surplus ones. Market forces, demographic forces, inheritance laws, household splitting are some of the important factors causing such mobility.

The above mentioned period matches with the Primitive labor force market system, mentioned in the Interim report on 'Future Industrial Relations' prepared by Robert W. Cox, Jeffrey Harrod & others, in many cases. The following table will show the number of labors of different years of that period.

Year	Population (In Millions)	Labor Force (In Millions)	Participation Rate %	Total Dependents Per 100 Labor Force
1901	28.97	9.64	33.3	201
1911	31.61	9.98	31.6	217
1921	33.24	10.53	31.7	216
1931	35.57	8.96	25.2	297
1941	-	-	-	-
1951	41.93	12.87	30.7	225
1961	50.84	17.44	34.3	192

Table 1 : Total Labor Force of Our Country in Late Colonial Stage and in Pakistan Period[126]

The flow of people from the village towards the town increased more after 1947. After 1947, the custom of Zamindars was abolished and it started the introduction of post capitalism.[127]

At present, in Bangladesh, the position which individuals occupy in the authority structure of industry does not always necessarily correlate with their position in the political structure or with their social standing in the community. Now, the village postal worker can become the local councilor, the school teacher a Member of Parliament, a trade unionist a Justice of the peace which shows the characteristics of post capitalism.

But still in our country rural people are rushing towards town for jobs. Basically scarcity of cultivable land, poverty, lack of employment in agro-sector, regular erosion of river, drought, flood and other natural calamity etc. are forcing people to come from rural areas to the city areas. In that way every year countless agro-based workers are becoming industrial workers in our country.

The labor market of Bangladesh is very competitive. Because still there are hundreds of thousands of workers are remained jobless. It gives the owners/employers the opportunity to employ these helpless workers in a comparative lower wage rate.

In Bangladesh, at present, the distribution of authority power and social status in society is more widely being diffused than the past. According to post capitalism, the emergence of trade unionism, employers' associations and collective bargaining together with union representation at enterprise and workplace level, now plays an important role to regulate the social conflict arising between management and subordinates at work. These facts are described below:

2.4.2 Trade Union in Bangladesh[128]

Trade Union a history of long struggle: The trade union movement, which started its journey in the area called Bangladesh now in around 1921, has a long history of struggle, playing a significant role to protect workers' rights and their fight against colonial oppression both during British and Pakistani regime. It has outstanding participation in all the democratic movements including the war of liberation of the country.

The attitude of the workers towards the employers is historically adverse. The country was ruled by the British for about 200 years. After the independence in 1947 then again the workers visualized the employers as not being their own men. The profit made in the industry was believed to be taken away, not to be used for the welfare of the workers and the people of the region-present Bangladesh. This situation created an altitude of indifference and opposition to the decision of the employers and affairs of the industry. Then after the glorious liberation war and Independence in 1971, due to wrong planning this attitude of the workers prevails. Thus a sense of participation, belong in guess and responsibility could not has been established till today.

Many organizations don't allow trade union: Beside the lawful restriction, due to administrative manipulation many workers especially in private industries and informal sectors could not enjoy the right to be organized in trade union. Even a huge number of workers of nationalized sectors those who enjoy the TU rights could not bargain for salary and wage. There is no law regarding the TU rights of agriculture workers.

Trade Union pattern changed: Changing pattern of labor market has changed the Trade Union situation also. Increasing of women workers, home based workers, growing informal sectors, small commercial and service sectors have changed the organizational strategies.

Trade Union Movement: Trade union organizations are divided under many National Centers and major National Centers are united in a common platform named Sramik Karmachari Oikko Parishad—SKOP. For long time all the national labor issues have been raised and addressed by the SKOP as the common and united platform of the TU movement of the country. At present almost all the major National centers are working to establish a united organization, independent of political influence.[129]

No. of Registered Union—	6492 (As on 2006-07)
No. of members—	2 Million
No. National Centers—	26
Women's' Committees—	13

Only 5% workers are organized: Besides its success the rate of unionized workers are still less than 5% and more than half of the basic and plant level unions are not affiliated with any National Centre. Out of a total 53.5 million of working people only 1.9 million are unionized. There is little unity among the Trade Union leaders. Most of the federations are financially weak and don't have in-house development programs for the activists. Education level of the workers is not in a satisfactory level. Offices are not equipped with modern communication system.

In Bangladesh trade unions are organized at three levels: basic unions at the establishment level, industrial unions at the sectoral level, and national unions.

Sl. No.	Type of Union	Union		Industrial Federation		
		Number	Membership	Number	Affiliated Union	Membership
1.	Basic Union					
(a)	Workers' Union	4440	1,699,991	-	-	-
(b)	Employees' Association	879	93,083	-	-	-
	Total	5319	1,793,074	-	-	-
2.	Industrial Federation					
(a)	Workers' Federation	-	-	105	816	5,95,318
(b)	Employees' Federation	-	-	4	25	45,081
	Total	-	-	109	841	6,40,399
3.	National-level Federation					
	Grand Total	5319	1,793,074	109	841	6,40,399

Table 2 : Statement of Registered Trade Unions[130]

Year	No. of Unions	No. of Members
1971	1160	450606
1972	2523	682923
1973	3096	859735
1974	3320	946977
1975	3161	921152
1976	3037	895904
1977	3005	873120
1978	3178	1006516
1979	3357	1041080
1980	3613	1097757
1981	3533	1127508
1982	2156	946048
1983	2126	947281
1984	2488	1075496
1985	2593	1090338
1986	3132	1164279
1987	3387	1195704
1988	3625	1421834
1989	3908	1517567
1990	3789	1619008
1991	3956	1642915
1992	4065	1648783
1993	4238	1674945
1994	4484	1681694
1995	4678	1720679
1996	5178	1730927
1997	5319	1793074
2007	6492	2094887

Table 3 : Growths of Registered Trade Unions[131]

As of 2006-2007, Bangladesh had 6492 trade unions at the establishment level with a membership of 2094887 members,[132] representing one-third of the workforce of the organized sector (Table 2). Nearly one-third of this membership was organized into 109 industry federations. Trade unions have flourished in the post-independence and post-liberalization period. As seen from Table 3, between 1971 and 1997 the number of unions rose 4.5 times and the membership nearly four times. The country had 23 national federations of which the following three are large, namely, the Jatio Sramik League (JSL), Bangladesh Jatiyatabadi Sramik Dal (BJSD) and Jatiyo Sramik Party (JSP), which claim to represent nearly two-thirds of the union members in the country (Table 4).

Trade unions have low membership density (about 5 per cent), and are financially starved and politically weak. Weaknesses/Imperfections in the functioning of trade union movements and persistent poverty and unemployment and the challenges of economic liberalization have together rendered workers and trade unions more vulnerable than ever before.

Sl. No.	Name of Federation	No. of Affiliated Unions	No. of Members Affiliated Unions
1.	National Sramik Federation	18	18000
2.	Bangladesh Trade Union Centre	63	36881
3.	Bangladesh Sanjukta Sramik Federation	41	26136
4.	Bangladesh Trade Union Sangha	15	21562
5.	Jatio Sramik Jote	18	4345
6.	Jatiyatabadi Sramik Dal	69	168065
7.	Bangladesh Jatio Sramik Dal	87	47007
8.	Bangladesh Sramik Kalyan Federation	11	5764
9.	Bangladesh Ganatantrik Sramik Federation	3	5937
10.	Bangla Sramik Federation	3	294
11.	Jatio Sramik League	111	150832
12.	Bangladesh Trade Union Federation	4	1648
13.	Bangladesh Free Trade Union Congress	22	50206
14.	Bangladesh Sramik Federation	8	3482
15.	Jatio Sramki Party	174	127553
16.	Bangladesh Jatio Sramik Forum	2	1540
17.	Bangladesh Jatio Sramik Federation	2	1540
18.	Samajtantrik Sramik Front	16	1323
19.	Jatio Sramik Jote Bangladesh	6	1669
20.	Jatio Sramik Karmachari Jote	10	1606
21.	National Trade Union Federation	5	1798
22.	National Workers' Federation	10	10497
23.	Bangladesh Workers' Federation	4	10500

Table 4 : Registered National-level Trade Union Federation[133]

2.4.3 Problems Regarding Trade Union in Bangladesh[134]

- **Fragmentation of unions:** One of the major problems of trade union movement in Bangladesh is the fragmentation of unions. All unions associated with different political parties and groups have entrusted the national scene. This multi-unionism has posed a serious threat to industrial harmony in Bangladesh has evolved a Labor Code which provides that a union can claim recognition of its members can constitute 30 percent of the total workers in that industry.

- **Workers Participation:** Workers participation is yet another issue, which has been taken up under the broad category of Industrial Relations because the concept of workers participation emerged within the framework of the tripartite system of labor-management relations in Bangladesh. The major actors of labor-management relations in Bangladesh are the Government, the employers and the employers. The issue of workers participation has great relevance in the industrial relations scene in Bangladesh because it emerged as a measure for promoting harmony between labor and management. In Bangladesh, worker participation schemes had their beginning after independence.

- **Labor Legislation:** This is another important area, which has a great impact on the industrial relations system. Labor legislation has been instrumental in shaping the course of industrial relations in Bangladesh. Establishment of social justice is the principle, which has guided the origin and development of labor legislation in Bangladesh. The international labor organization (ILO) gave an impetus to the consideration of welfare and working conditions of the workers all over the world and also to the growth of labor laws in all parts of the world, including Bangladesh.

- **Wage and industrial relations:** The government of Bangladesh always plays significant role in the determination of wages in the organized sector. There are number of laws in Bangladesh to ensure payment on time of a certain minimum wage. In addition, there are wage boards appointed by the Govt. to determine the wages in particular industries. The Government has also established Labor-courts and industrial tribunals to settle wage disputes by adjudication. In unionized situation, bilateral process of collective bargaining is evident and in case of deadlock or dispute between the employer and the union, recourse is taken to the government Labor machinery, labor tribunals and even law courts.

- **Technological Changes and Industrial Relations:** Technological changes do have an impact on industrial activity. Its impact on employment is an important short-term economic aspect of automation. Installation of a large number of automatic machines at the same time may create serious problems of unemployment, because by introducing automatic the number of workers for the same output is likely to be less. One of the growing problems in Bangladesh is large-scale unemployment and under-employment. Cottage and small-scale industries, which are Labor-intensive, provide large-scale employment. In this connection the government of Bangladesh is fully aware of the situation and has taken steps to the effect that in the application of advanced techniques of production, adequate care is taken to see that the traditional Labor intensive sector which provides employment to a large Labor force continues to exist.

2.4.4 Overall Issues addressed regarding Trade Union in Bangladesh[135]

1. In this region an adversarial relation exists between trade union and management so rate of participation becomes less.
2. Frequent violations of collective bargaining agreement negotiation by the management create volatile environment of non-co-operation by the trade unions.
3. The management's paternalistic attitude towards the trade unions discourages participation of trade unions to the industrial relations system.
4. Passive and ineffective government role as well as tax law enforcement discourages the unions to participate in the industrial relation system.

5. In the collecting bargaining process the trade unions tend to go co-opted either by the government or the management so it discourages trade union to participate in the industrial relations system

6. Most of the unions are tied up with the political parties very often instead of Labor benefit and this factor affects the morale of other unions. The above mentioned clauses are the major problems in relations to the participation of trade unions in the industrial relations.

2.4.5 Arbitration

According to the post-capitalism view of conflict theory, if conflict seems irresolvable, third party intervention, usually through state agencies provide conciliation and arbitration services. In Bangladesh the mode of settlement of Industrial Dispute using third party intervention has been described in Sections 31 of the Industrial Dispute Ordinance 1969 as follows:

Section: Arbitration

If the conciliation fails, the Conciliator shall try to persuade the parties to agree to refer the dispute to an Arbitrator. In case the parties agree, they shall make a joint request in writing for reference of the dispute to an Arbitrator agreed upon by them.

The Arbitrator to whom a dispute is referred under sub-section (1) may be a person borne on a panel to be maintained by the Government or any other person agreed upon by the parties.

The Arbitrator shall give his award within a period of thirty days from the date on which the dispute is referred to him under sub-section (1) or such further period as may be agreed upon by the parties to the dispute.

After he has made an award, the Arbitrator shall forward a copy thereof to the parties and to the Government who shall cause it to be published in the official Gazette.

The award of the Arbitrator shall be final and no appeal shall lie against it. It shall be valid for a period not exceeding two years or as may be fixed by the Arbitrator.

2.4.6 Settlement of Labor Disputes[136]

Contract or agreement is usually made between the management and the Collective Bargaining Agent (CBA) on settlement of industrial disputes as per provisions of Industrial Relations Ordinance, 1969. In case a bipartite negotiation fails, conciliation machinery of the government is requested by the aggrieved party to intervene and the conciliation process is undertaken. If succeeds, agreement is signed between the parties and the Conciliation Officer becomes a witness. If it fails, the party raising the dispute may go for strike or lockout as the case may be. The government may, however, prohibit the same after one month in the interest of the public. In the essential services like, (a) electricity, gas, oil & water supply etc. (b) hospital & ambulance service, (c) fire brigade, (d) railway & Bangladesh Biman and (e) ports etc., strike is prohibited.

2.4.7 Wages and Fringe Benefits[137]

In the private sector, the wages & fringes benefits of the workers and employees are determined through collective bargaining process. Sometimes private industries follow the public sector wages & salary structure for their workers and employees respectively. In the public sector, wages and fringe benefits of the workers are determined by the government on the recommendation of the National Wages Commission established from time to time.

2.4.8 Labor Union[138]

Industrial Relations Ordinance, 1969 deals with trade union in Bangladesh. In

1. Official website of Board of Investment, Bangladesh—Investor's Guide—Human Resources & Employment.

In any industrial and commercial establishment, a trade union may be formed with 30% of the total number of workers employed. If there is more than one union in any establishment, Collective Bargaining Agent is determined by the Registrar of Trade Union through sector ballot for a term of two years. Only the Collective Bargaining Agent is authorized to raise industrial disputes and negotiate with the management. The Director of Labor of the government acts as the Registrar of Trade Union in Bangladesh. Till December 1996; 4955 trade unions (worker's union—4104 & employers association—851) exits in Bangladesh having 17, 30, 927 members.

2.4.9 Post capitalism theory and Cox's Classification:

The relation between the Post Capitalism theory and the classifications of Industrial Relations mentioned in the Interim report on 'Future Industrial Relations' prepared by Robert W. Cox, Jeffrey Harrod & others has been discussed below:

1. Peasant-lord System:

The class conflict mentioned in the Marx theory was found in the era of peasant lord system. At that period the Lords were controlling the workers and their family. Lords and their family members were treated as blue blood. They always got a better and different treatment than others. The workers were always treated as lower class people. Their fate was almost controlled by the land-lords. The workers had to do what their respective lords wanted. Workers almost had no freedom. Moreover this trend went on generation after generation. The son of the Lord became the next lord and worker's generation became workers. The child of the workers got little benefit in terms of education, health etc. So they had little chance to get proper knowledge to shift to other recognized occupations. At this period the indicators of the Post-capitalism theory were not existed.

2. Primitive Labor Market system:

According to the Cox's report at the time of primitive labor market the labor class began to gain some power, though the workers were not organized. This indicates that a change was to come. And at the last the change came indeed. This change gave more power to the workers to gain more facilities.

3. An enterprise Labor Market system:

Under this system the worker had got some power through the existence of the trade unions, though these trade unions may be not that strong in case of determining wages and working condition. Their activities were basically towards welfare and education. It resembles with two of the characteristics of post capitalism era that are emergence of trade union and widening of educational opportunity.

4. Enterprise-corporatist system:

Though trade unions exist under this system but less conflict exists here. Because of some characteristics of this system:

- Workers' interests and loyalties are enterprise based.
- Trade unions act as they were interest share-partner of the enterprises.
- Enterprise provides sound deal of security and welfare facilities.

Under this system the children of the labors get educational facility and can participate in the future management after getting required qualification. These resemble with the post-capitalism theory.

5. Bipartite system:

Under Bipartite system the trade unions are very strong and have huge collective bargaining power. So they may pose strong conflict with the management in different issues and labors get good democracy to be involved in politics. Such thing resembles with the characteristics of the post capitalism theory.

6. Tripartite System:

Under tripartite system Govt. does intervene and plays a crucial role in industrial relations as a third party player. Usually Govt. does this thing through the following ways:

- Making related laws and implementing those.
- Parliamentary negotiating bodies
- Setting Govt. institution of mediation and arbitration.
- Through different policies such as privatization.

Some of these steps show the existence of the post-capitalism supposition. Such as: existence of parliamentary negotiating bodies and institution of mediation and arbitration.

2.4.10 State Corporatism

State Corporatism is a type of political system which includes a 'subordinate industrial relation system.' According to Robert H. Cox, this system is found in those countries where competitive party politics are suppressed or only formal, but semi-autonomous organizations of employers and workers exist. The ideologies of this system place a high value on consensus and peaceful labor relations.

Though the scope of conflict in this system is very little but conflict arises here also from labor groups of different organization. To resolve the conflicts between employee and employer, the bureaucrats or the officials of the ruling political party leads the vital role. It can be said that this system is a modified or advanced form of post capitalism as the conflict is in reduced to a minimal and resolved through some institutional processes which are similar to that of the post capitalism.

2.5 Pluralism[139]

Pluralism is, in the general sense, the acknowledgment of diversity. The concept is used, often in different ways, in a wide range of issues. In politics, pluralism is often considered by proponents of modern democracy to be in the interests of its citizens, and so political pluralism is one of its most important features.

The term pluralism is also used to denote a theoretical standpoint on state and power—which to varying degrees suggest that pluralism is an adequate model of how power is distributed in societies. This pluralism holds that political power in society does not lie with the electorate, or with small concentrated elite, but is distributed between a wide numbers of groups. These groups may be trade unions, interest groups, business organizations, and any of a multitude of formal and informal coalitions.

Pluralists emphasize that power is not a physical entity that individuals either have or do not have, but flows from a variety of different sources. Rather, people are powerful because they control various resources. Resources are assets that can be used to force others to do what one wants. Politicians become powerful because they command resources that people want or fear or respect. The list of possibilities is virtually endless: legal authority, money, prestige, skill, knowledge, charisma, legitimacy, free time, experience, celebrity, and public support.

Pluralists also stress the differences between potential and actual power. Actual power means the ability to compel someone to do something; potential power refers to the possibility of turning resources into actual power. Cash, one of many resources, is only a stack of bills until it is put to work. Martin Luther King Jr., for example, was certainly not a rich person. But by using resources such as his forceful personality, organizational skills, and especially the legitimacy of his cause, he had a greater impact on American politics than most wealthy people. A particular resource like money cannot automatically be equated with power because the resource can be used skillfully or clumsily, fully or partially, or not at all.

The pluralist approach to the study of power, states that nothing categorical about power can be assumed in any community. The question then is not who runs a community, but if any group in fact does. To determine this, pluralists study specific outcomes. The reason for this is that they believe human behavior is governed in large part by inertia. That said, actual involvement in overt activity is a more valid marker of leadership than simply a reputation. Pluralists also believe that there is no one particular issue or point in time at which any group must assert itself to stay true to its own expressed values, but rather that there are a variety of issues and points at which this is possible. There are also costs involved in taking action at all-not only losing, but expenditure of time and effort. While a structuralist may argue that power distributions have a rather permanent nature, this rationale says that power may in fact be tied to issues, which vary widely in duration. Also, instead of focusing on actors within a system, the emphasis is on the leadership roles itself. By studying these, it can be determined to what extent there is a power structure present in a society.

Three of the major tenets of the pluralist school are (1)resources and hence potential power are widely scattered throughout society; (2) at least some resources are available to nearly everyone; and (3) at any time the amount of potential power exceeds the amount of actual power.

Finally, and perhaps most important, no one is all-powerful. An individual or group that is influential in one realm may be weak in another. Large military contractors certainly throw their weight around on defense matters, but how much sway do they have on agricultural or health policies? A measure of power, therefore, is its scope, or the range of areas where it is successfully applied. Pluralists believe that with few exceptions power holders usually have a relatively limited scope of influence.

For all these reasons power cannot be taken for granted. One has to observe it empirically in order to know who really governs. The best way to do this, pluralists believe, is to examine a wide range of specific decisions, noting who took which side and who ultimately won and lost. Only by keeping score on a variety of controversies can one begin to identify actual power holders. Pluralism was associated with behaviorally.

2.5.1 Pluralism in the Context of Bangladesh

In Bangladesh, according to the concept of pluralism, the govt. ought to depend on the consent and cooperation of different cooperatives before taking any decision regarding their interest. For example, the govt. cannot take any decision unilaterally regarding the interest of BGMEA. As the garment sector is a major contributor in the economy of our country, the govt. has to listen to them. Again, the govt. has to discuss with different labor unions and cooperatives to take any interest concerning them. Since then the Department of Labor has been functioning and endeavoring continuously for facilitation effective Labor management relations, collective bargaining and negotiation and ensure prompt and efficient settlement of Labor disputes in the industrial sectors of Bangladesh.[140]

But, attempts to form workers' associations in the textile industry were routinely suppressed and the organizers fired. Major worker unrest and riots sparked by a litany of abuses and poor working conditions led to violent repression, including the killing of one striker and the arrest and beating of union leaders. Systematic government and employer opposition to the exercise of union rights in EPZs continued. Reform of the Labor law resulted in increased restrictions on the right to organise unions and to strike and excessive force was again used by police and military forces against protesting workers throughout the country.[141]

However, in this view, trade unions are viewed as legal representatives of employee interests at work with the right to challenge and the right to manage. Collective bargaining is recognized as being the institutional means by which conflict between employers and employees over the wage work bargaining and its adaptation is regularized and resolved. These aspects are described in the context of Bangladesh:

2.5.2 Trade Union Activities in Bangladesh[142]

Laws Relating To Trade Unions and Settlement of Industrial Disputes:

1. The Industrial Relations Ordinance, 1969
2. The Industrial Relations Rules, 1977

Under the provision of law it is clearly shown that a "Trade Union" is not only the combination of workers but the combination of employers also. And to function as an organization it has to be registered. There are organizations of the employers like the "Employers Federations".

The trade union have so far been bargaining only increase in money and financial facilities. The other important aspects of wellbeing and welfare activities and proper participation in the production process are not addressed for the workers. As a less advantageous and less privileged section of our society the initiative to bring about change in this pertinent aspect should come from the Government and the employers if we really mean good Labor relations.

On careful examination of the trade union movement, a peculiar trend is discovered. Instead of healthy and organized trade union movement the workers often found resorting to pressure tactics under the cover of political or any other social turmoil. Hence it is manifested that when there is strong political movement against the Government the workers realized most of the demands at that time.

In Bangladesh at present trade union is not functioning as they required doing. For example in garments industry in real sense there is no trade union. So image building is not there. In Bangladesh the trade unions are not getting support from the government. Although the workers are unjustly fired the trade unions are not there to support them. The question is whether trade union is there in enterprise Labor market. In case of garments industry there is a shortage of skilled Labor. The workers have not they say, owner is the autocrat. Trade union is not there. So workers are not happy. Owner is not giving wage, overtime and no guarantees of service because of the availability of workers.

Besides garments industry, in the private spinning mills this situation exists. In government industry owners cannot do unjust behavior.

In Bangladesh Enterprise Corporatist System reveals the relation between selection of workers and trade union. For example—there are many multinational companies. They are doing business by contractual agreements. For example in BATB few is permanent. There is a trade union but they do not work for the workers. They want to ensure their membership in the permanent membership of the organization. The trade unions real support is to give facilities. But in reality they are supporting the owners to give less profit to contractual employees. In this context trade union is worker's discretion. They are not eligible to permanent benefits. In other ways constituents are set by the interest of the unions.

Trade union activities under Bipartite System in Bangladesh is low because

- Political influence
- Literacy of industry
- Workers are not literate so there choice of leader is not literate

The problem in Bangladesh can be solved through bipartite system because of its joint mechanism, openness and flexibility. Only then by integrating with the humanitarian approach industrial relation can solve the crucial issues.

Although labor rights are now an established fact these rights are yet to be realized. While Bangladesh is on its way to becoming a middle-income country with hundreds of thousands of workers engaged in productive activities in the various sectors of the economy and in the international labor markets, in many cased they continue to be deprived of fair wages and subjected to other degradations at their workplace. Despite the presence of several national and regional trade organizations and unions in the country, our overseas workers who's back breaking work and hard earned foreign currency significantly to our foreign exchange reserves, continue to toil under challenging conditions.

In this more needs to be done to ensure that rights of both underage and adult workers in the small and medium enterprises that dot the economic landscape of Bangladesh are looked after. Furthermore, the hardship caused by redundancy of workers without proper compensation should be avoided.

Against the backdrop of the economic slump worldwide, what proves most outstanding is the improvement in industrial relations and working conditions for the labor force. Training for the workers for raising the level of skills as well as turning them more productive is in the interest of everyone:—workers themselves, owners of factories and industries as also the nation as a whole. This has to be complemented by developing entrepreneurship at the grassroots level so that the villagers are not left behind. If this done, the country can hope for and all-round development.

Better Opportunities can be created:

1. By raising the international standards—National minimum unskilled Labor salary is 1500 taka. Government gives bonus in two Eids. This is mandatory. But for multinationals this is not mandatory. They can give more bonuses. This is why they decrease their salary. Because 1 bonus = basic salary. For this they increase other benefits like children's education. In case of rent 55% is off in government sector but 100% off in private organizations. In this sector union can bargain with charter of demand.

2. By maintaining international standard and bargaining with workers owners can deal with positive paternalistic approach. So workers can realize the limitations of the owners.

The concept of pluralism is seen in different sectors of Bangladesh. Between May 20 and 24, the South Asian country of Bangladesh underwent the most severe and widespread industrial rioting in its history, as workers in its booming textile export industry torched 16 factories, ransacked 300 more and went on a general rampage, destroying cars, blocking roads, intimidating perceived adversaries and looting.[143]

The significance of the riot is that they mark one of the first instances of successful mass direct labor action against the export manufacturing sector in a developing country. Development will be achieved in an environment of free trade and investment in which poor countries utilize their comparative advantage in labor costs to generate and attract capital, leading to expanded employment. The riots reveal resistance to the working conditions and compensation levels that are partly behind comparative advantage, raising questions about the political viability of the neoliberal model.

The other significance of the riots lies in the fact that they reveal the weakness of the Bangladeshi. The failure of the government to contain the violence quickly and opting instead for half measures that satisfied neither side and did nothing to bring them to an agreement points to an implosion of governability. This has implications for the stability of the South Asian region. Thus the pluralism concept can be implemented in Bangladesh.

The pluralism theory emphasizes on parliamentary democracy and collective bargaining. Disputes disrupt productions processes and causes massive loss in production. In such disputes continue, it will be harder for Bangladesh to compete with the other industrial nations of the world. It is up to the Government and all other actors in the dispute to take a positive stance towards minimizing industrial dispute.

For creating a more pluralistic situation in Bangladesh, the government has to depend more on the consent and cooperation of the concerned parties. Barriers such as 30 per cent of workers in an enterprise have to be members before a union can be registered should be eased for freedom of the associations.

Workers who try to create a trade union has to be protected before registration and should not be persecuted by their employers for this reason. The minimum wages of the workers have to be ensured. RMG sector has women workers of about 60%. So their rights must be protected by the employer. The women should be protected from any kind of harassment, excess Labor, and should be given maternity leave.

Humanitarian approach from the employers is also needed. The factory owners should be more interactive and open to the workers, listen to their problems and complains and try to come to a solution before the workers start to get frustrated and agitated. The salary and wage as well as the overtime pay should be cleared without much delay. Government Regulatory Board has lots of work in this regard. They must ensure that all the factories comply with the requirements of Labor Code 2006. Health and safety issues must be ensured in factories.

2.5.3 Pluralism and Cox's classification:

The relation between the Pluralism theory and the classifications of Industrial Relations mentioned in the Interim report on 'Future Industrial Relations' prepared by Robert W. Cox, Jeffrey Harrod and others has been discussed below:

1. Peasant-lord System:

Under peasant-lord system period the Lords were controlling the workers and their family. They were the source of all power. Lords used to make the ultimate decision and controlled the workers. Workers got no such power to conflict with the lords. So pluralism theory does not have any effect on this system.

2. Primitive Labor Market System:

According to the Cox's report under the primitive labor market the labor class begins to gain some power, though the workers were not organized. Neither have they had collecting collective bargaining power. So this labor market does not have different groups to create conflict. So pluralism theory does not have any effect on this system.

3. An Enterprise Labor Market System:

Under this system the worker had got some power through the existence of the trade unions, though these trade unions may be not that strong in case of determining wages and working conditions. Their activities were basically towards welfare and education.

Since labor unions exist under this system some group interest may grow up. So under this system industrial conflict can be taken place due to different group interest.

4. Enterprise-Corporatist System:

Though trade unions exist under this system but less conflict exists here. Because of some characteristics of this system:

- Workers' interests and loyalties are enterprise based.
- Trade unions act as they were interest share-partner of the enterprises.
- Enterprise provides sound deal of security and welfare facilities.

Under this system the worker groups or the trade unions think less about own group interest and think more about the interest of the respective enterprises interest. Again as employers are also bit kind to the work force, employers also consider workers' need and take their views. Here workers' organizations work more as cooperative nature rather than as pressure groups.

5. Bipartite System:

Under Bipartite system the trade unions are very strong and have huge collective bargaining power. So they may pose strong conflict with the management in different issues. Here interest of the different groups may arise conflict. Such as:

- Interest of the different workers' group. Such as one group may prefer to have hourly basis wage rate while another group may want piece rate. In addition one group may like to start daily-work from 8 am, another group may like to work from 9 am due to transportation and locality problem.
- Political conflict between the workers. Such as supporters (among workforce and management) of conservative and right sided political parties may have different views in many issues related with the industrial system with the supporters of the progressive and left sided political parties.

6. Tripartite System:

Under tripartite system Government does intervene and plays a crucial role in industrial relations as a third party player. Usually Government does this thing through the following ways:

- Making related laws and implementing those.
- Parliamentary negotiating bodies
- Setting Government institution of mediation and arbitration.
- Through different policies such as privatization.

Now in case of conflict between labor and management, the Government may take side of any one party due to political, economical influence. In that case but the other party may strongly oppose Government's decision and force the government to make decisions by taking all parties consents. Such things resemble with the characteristics of the pluralism theory.

7. State Corporatism:

It is obvious that conflict, if any, arises from some groups of employees from different organizations and the State go for negotiation to some extent. So it can be said that here collective bargaining and joint consultation takes place here to a limit which is an indicator of pluralism. So pluralism to some extent is a feature of State Corporatism which is called 'Soft Pluralism.'

8. The Mobilizing System:

The Mobilizing System is also a political system in which the aim of the political elite is revolutionary that is to mobilize the non-participants segment of society through mass movements especially among peasants and the urban marginal populations, those not assimilated into modern modes of production.

The conflict can be raised if any group opposes such revolution commenced by the politicians. Especially such conflict can be very strong if the revolution intends to bring huge organizational or industrial change. Because the new system may have an effect on the lifestyle, working ways, economic condition of the workforce so here the opposing group may come up and show conflict to protect such revolution. This scenario conforms to pluralism aspects of conflict theory.

9. Socialist System:

In Marxism-Leninism, Socialism is the intermediate system between capitalism and communism, when the government is in the process of changing the means of ownership from privatism, to collective ownership.

Socialism refers to the goal of a socio-economic system in which property and the distribution of wealth are subject to control by the community. This control may be direct-exercised through popular collectives such as workers' councils-or indirect-exercised on behalf of the people by the state. As an economic system, socialism is often characterized by collective ownership of the means of production, goals which have been attributed to pluralism as all the employees are represented as groups or class i.e. the proletariat.

Later the conflict among different proletariat groups dominated through out the century. It is obviously the indication of the presence of pluralism. For an example, various adherents of socialist movements are split into differing and sometimes opposing branches, particularly between reformists and revolutionaries. Some socialists have championed the complete nationalization of the means of production, while social democrats have proposed selective nationalization of key industries within the framework of mixed economies. Some Marxists, including those inspired by the Soviet model of economic development, have advocated the creation of centrally planned economies directed by a state that owns all the means of production. Others, including Communists in Yugoslavia and Hungary in the 1970s and 1980s, Chinese Communists since the reform era, and some Western economists, have proposed various forms of market socialism, attempting to reconcile the presumed advantages of cooperative or state ownership of the means of production with letting market forces, rather than central planners, guide production and exchange. Social Anarchists, Luxemburgists (such as those in the Socialist Party USA) and some elements of the United States New Left favor decentralized collective ownership in the form of cooperatives or workers' councils over government ownership of the means of production.

10. Capitalist System:

Global capitalism is not working for the working class. That is neither the headline nor the pluralism. It is, indeed the conclusion of a rigorous 'analysis of Michael Spence, recipient of the Nobel Prize in economic sciences. He found that value added per worker increased sharply which is geek speak for these businesses integrated integrated into global economy. But even as productivity soared, wages and job opportunities stagnated. The take—way is this; Globalization is making many companies more productive but the benefits are mostly being enjoyed by the owner—class. The middle class worker, meanwhile, is struggling to find work, and many of the jobs available are poorly paid.

11. Employment Promotion:

Bangladesh is in the low skill, poor job quality and low—price bracket. So Bangladesh may need to move-up to high skill, better job quality and high value bracket through improving the strategies among the different trade. For the health and peaceful workplace job is also related with better work as better work is also a part of decent work. Better work ensures the fair wages, implementation of rights, at work which is also a strategies element in social protection which promote social dialogue and employment production. Job needs better work in all formal and informal sectors.

2.6 Social Action Theory

The theory of social action is that part of Sociology that examines collective human action independent of its content. It attempts to discover how individuals of our Species are able to coordinate their physical actions in order to achieve some common end, any end, without reference to any specific time or place.

Social Action Theory in industrial relation emphasizes on the individual response to social factors such as managers, employees and union representatives to given situation. It contrasts with systems theory which suggests that behavior in an industrial relations system is explicable in terms of structural features. Social action theory is preeminently associated with the studies of Max Weber. According to Weber, action is social by virtue of subjective meaning attached to it by the acting individual . . . . it takes account by the behavior of others and is thereby oriented in its course.[144] He insisted that in order for social actions to be explained they must be interpreted in terms of their subjectively intend meaning, not there objectively valid ones. If only observable behavior is examined, it is argued that the significance and value with individual actors place upon their behavior is likely to be misinterpreted.

Social action then is behavior having subjective meaning for individual actors, with social action theory focusing on understanding particular actions in industrial relation situations rather than on just observing explicit industrial relations behavior. This contrasts with system theory which regards behavior in industrial as reflecting the impersonal process external to systems social factors over which they have little or no control. In emphasizing that social action derives from personal meaning which individual attach to their own another peoples action, social action theorist are suggesting that social actions are constrained by the ways they are construct their own social reality. 'On the other hand it seems society makes man, on the other, man makes society'.[145] Individual actors however do not share same value system, which means individual attach to their different meaning to their interaction'.[146] Manager and union representatives, for example do not come together because they have same goals and values but because for, a while at least, their differing ends may be served by the same meas'.[147]

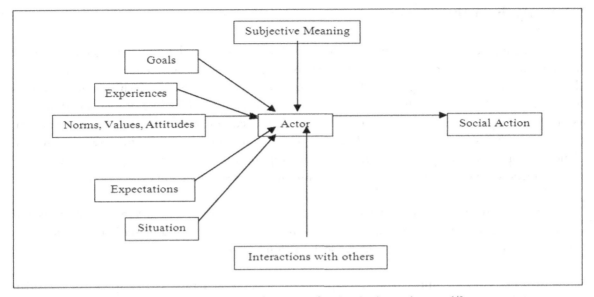

Figure 1 : The main influences of individual social action[148]

Figure 1 indicates the main influences affecting individual choice and social actions. The fundamental point is that, social action emerges out of meaning and circumstances attributed by individual to particular social situations, thereby defining their social reality. Through interaction between actors and union officers, line manager and personal specialist and union representatives, and their members, individuals as well as having an element of interpreting their own roles, and in acting out their intentions, also modify, change and transform social meaning for themselves and for others. The major difference between a social action approach in examining behavior in industrial relation and a system approach is this: action theory assumes an existing system where action occurs, but cannot explain nature of the system, 'while the systems approach is unable to explain satisfactorily why particular actors act as they do'.[149] The first view of industrial relation system as a product of the action of its parts, the other aims to explain of its parts in terms of the nature of the system as a whole.

Social action theory also has its critics. Marxist argues, for example that those supporting the action frame of reference neglect the 'structural influences' of which the actors themselves may be unconscious. While the consciousness of individual actor in industrial relations system to its politico—economic structures can be some extent autonomous, it is limited in practice. This is because 'Definitions of reality are themselves socially generated and sustained, and ability of men to achieve their goals is constrained by the objective characteristic of their situation'.[150] Perhaps the most useful feature of social action theory in industrial relation is the 'way in which it stresses that the individuals retain at least some freedom on action and ability to influence events'.[151] Although the structure of industrial relation system may influence the action of the actors, these in turn also influence the system as a whole, including its outputs.

2.7 Analysis of the Theory

Social action approach emphasizes the way the 'actors' see things, how they define the situation rather than how it looks to an outsider. The social action approach makes no attempt at explanation in advance—everything is contingent on the views, perspectives and meanings which situations have for those concerned. Such an emphasis is a useful reminder of the specific nature of each situation, that action is taken by people, and that the institutions and procedures are created and operated by them. The theory emphasizes on individuals' freedom of action and ability to influence events. Industrial relation actions best understood in terms of their subjectively intended meanings. The actions not solely influenced by specific work situations but also by attitudes, values and expectations.

There has been, Ackroyd argues, an increase in the interest shown towards Weberian concepts and perspectives by sociologists of this industrial behavior' in recent years.[152] Manifestations of this interest can be seen in the growing popularity of the social action approach.

Actors own decisions are initial basis for explanation: The social action has its origins in Weberian sociology although some of its recent manifestations move away from a strict adherence to the Weberian tradition. The social action approach is one in which 'actors' own definitions of the situations in which they are engaged are taken as an initial basis for the explanation of their social behavior and relationships'.[153] In contrast to approaches which being with some general and normative psychology of individual needs in work, or with some conception of the 'needs' of an efficiently operating industrial enterprise an action frame of reference directs 'attention systematically to the variety of meanings which work may come to have for industrial employees'.[154]

Contrast with the System Approach: The social action approach has been contrasted with the systems approach; while the system approach 'tends to regard behavior as a reflection of the characteristics of a social system containing a series of impersonal processes which are external to actors and constrain them',[155] the action approach stresses the way in which man influences the social structure and 'makes society'.[156] As described the social action approach can be viewed as the opposite side of the coin to the system approach (that is, that it does not pay sufficient attention to behavioral influences).

A number of studies have claimed that they have used a social action approach in their analysis; one of the best known of such studies carried out in recent years is that of Goldthorp and Lockwood et al.[157] They argued that they found an instrumental orientation to employment amongst their sample of 'affluent workers' and that although their 'affluent workers' need not be typical of works in general there were trends in modern industrial life which suggested that an instrumental orientation to work was likely to be adopted by many other workers.

An Action Frame of Reference: The trends in modern industrial life which they pointed to centered on changes in family life and structure; for example, the growing importance of the conjugal family might strengthen the tendency for the workers to seek expressive and affective satisfactions through family relationships, rather than from the workplace, with the result that work increasingly may be seen as a way of providing the means to obtain satisfaction elsewhere. However, the details of their arguments are relatively unimportant, for as they state, their discussion of, for example, the changes in family relationships, is intended as an outline of' some probable consequences working class economic life of already observable trends of change within society at large' rather than as an 'unconditional prediction about the future course of events'.[158] What is more important is their approach and method; what they have tried to do is to discover the sources of orientation to work by looking at the non-work experiences of the people concerned. Thus, they argue that what they have done (and what others in industrial sociology increasingly should do) is to adopt an action frame of reference.

The Goldthorpand and Lockwood thesis had a major impact on sociology and, therefore, has been the subject of careful scrutiny. A number of writers have challenged their conclusion on the 'orientation to work' them; such challenges have been important because they have raised questions not only about the detail of the case made but also about the approach and method. Bowey, in a review of this debate[159] cites the works of Brown[160] who argues that although the Goldthorpand and Lockwood was an improvement on the view that behavior at work is determined by such factors as the quality of human relations management, or the nature of technology and other structural factors, it is nevertheless still deficient in that it seems to view, in this case, orientations to work 'as independent of the work place' and fails to stress that socialization at work can affect orientations.[161] The crucial point implied by the last criticism is that work experience can determine as well as be determined by worker attitudes.

Social Action as an influencer: It is clear that while the social action frame of reference has many adherents it is also open to a variety of interpretations and emphases. For example, at one extreme the emphasis placed on individual meaning can be such that the approach moves very close to ethno methodology and phenomenology; at times it becomes impossible to distinguish it from them. Silverman, in some of his earlier work,[162] was clearly moving in this direction, and his later work indicates an almost total acceptance of such a point of view. For example, he now stresses the importance of examining the 'taken-for-granted' assumptions. To discuss reality without doing this, he suggests, is erroneous for what is 'reality' to one person may be different from what is 'reality' to another. Such an approach clearly raises many questions, most of which are outside the scope of this discussion. However, it is important to stress that this approach can lead one to disregard social structure as an influence on behavior almost completely.

Assumptions about Social Action Approach: Others would reject this stance and argue that a social action frame of reference cannot merely be based on an analysis of the meaning of reality for individuals but needs to make some kind of assumption about the nature of social structure as a starting point. Thus, Eldridge argues that social action cannot be understood in a totally free floating way[163] but needs to be grounded on some appreciation of the likely influence of social structure on behavior.

Eldridge's approach would find sympathy with that of writers like Bendix,[164] Banks[165] and Hyman. Hyman, for example, argues that much of the social action approach is an over-reaction against positivism. Such an over-reaction creates the danger that structural influences of which the actors themselves may be unconscious, will be ignored, which means, in effect, that the views and definitions of the actors may be treated as a sufficient explanation of the social situation being investigated. Hyman argues that such an approach is misguided, for while men's consciousness does have a certain independence from such structural factors as the level of technology, the system of economic relations and the institutions of political and industrial control; and it can influence the development of these components of the social structure, such consciousness is not wholly autonomous. Definitions of reality are themselves socially generated and sustained, and the ability of men to achieve their goal is constrained by the objective character of their situation.[166]

Relationship between Social Structure and Behavior: The challenge, if one accepts Hyman's point of view, is to find some way of showing the reciprocal nature of the relationship between social structure and behavior. This might be done by adopting a step-by-step[167] an 'incremental' approach. From this point of view the social structure, at any one point in time limits social action. Thus, a worker's ability to take strike action or an entrepreneur's ability to invest in machinery may be limited by his personal and by more general economic conditions may themselves be strongly influenced by their previous experience which in turn may, at least in part, be a function in their own position in the social structure.

Choice of Actors determines the Social Structure: The choice made by the actor, in part, will determine a social structure. To continue with the example, when the worker takes his decision on strike action and the entrepreneur takes his decision on investment, they will be helping to determine the environment for future similar decisions. If the worker decides to take strike action, he may gain extra income as well as experience in industrial conflict. This will affect his ability to take strike action and his perception of possibilities in the future. He will also change, however marginally; the established pattern of strike action is general. Similarly, if the entrepreneur decides to invest, he may increase his product base and gain experience in a different market. This may affect his long term financial stability and increase his knowledge of investment possibilities. In turn, this will also affect the position of his competitors, and to some extent, the market and the willingness of financiers to invest in certain products. In this way the actor can be seen as creating the social structure and step-by step may help to change it. Thus, the relationship between social structure and the actor is not one way: there is a complex interrelationship.

It should be stressed, though, that the use of the terms 'step by step' and 'incremental' should not be taken to imply that change in society must necessarily be gradual. These terms should be applied to the individual's ability to influence and change the social structure, not to the possibility of change in the social structure per se. Many have argued, for example, that inconsistencies in the social structure mean that change, fundamental and even revolutionary change, is inevitable, it certainly would not argue that it is impossible.

Probably one of the most important features of the social action approach is not contained in detail of its variants, but in the way in which it stresses that the individual retains at least some freedom of action and ability to influence events. In this it has links with the approach to industrial relations developed by a number of economists and labeled 'action theory' by Schienstock.

2.8 Relation of Social Action Theory with Cox's Classification of Industrial Systems

2.8.1 Peasant Lord System:

Norms, Values and Attitudes

- Workers and their family units are subject to an economic hierarchy and through it they are bound to their traditional occupations.

Interaction with Others

- The lord is the most powerful one in relation to the worker and his family, but his power may be tampered by custom and by an ethic of paternal obligation.
- State does not enter the relationship between lord and peasant except to extract some of the product.

2.8.2 Primitive Labor Market System

Subjective Meaning

- Technology of production remains primitive.

Experience

- No collective power as labor organizations do not exist.

Interaction with Others

- State does not usually enter the work relationship.

2.8.3 Enterprise Labor Market System

Interaction with others

- The state and trade unions intervenes only in a very limited or ineffective way in labor relations.

Subjective meaning

- The enterprise is the only meaningful domain in decision making

2.8.4 Enterprise—Corporatist System

Goal

- Worker is reduced in exchange for employment security and welfare guaranteed by the employer.

Situation

- Workers' interests and loyalties are enterprise-based.

Interaction with Others

- Trade unions behave as though they share with the employer an interest in the well-being of the enterprise

2.8.5 Bipartite System

State plays a minimum role, administering labor protective legislation and applying minimum standards. One of the most important stabilizing factors is that the system is well established and regarded as basically functional by the actors in it and the society at large. The other factor is the law, which is at present as much a factor for stability as it was an instrument of change in one historical period.

2.8.6 Tripartite System

Interaction with Others

- Government plays a more active role as a third party, bargaining with nongovernmental employers and trade unions.

- Government is concerned with the regulation of conflict and with the outcomes of collective bargaining.

2.8.7 State Corporatism System

Interaction with others

- Worker and employer organizations both seek satisfaction through direct relations with state bureaucracy or officials of ruling political party.

2.8.8 Mobilizing System:

In some enclaves, social relations in production may be of mobilization type, even though the political system of the country is not. For example, the Kibbutzim of Israel

2.9 Social Theory in Bangladesh Perspective

The Industrial Relations System in Bangladesh represents multi-pronged relationship between government, management, trade unions and workers.

2.9.1 Government Action

Apart from the legal framework of control of the trade unions in Bangladesh, extra constitutional action on the part of the various governments in the field of trade unions are used from time to time to control the trade unions of Bangladesh. The various governments when using extra—constitutional or oppressive powers to curb the activities of the militant unions have tried to justify the use of extra-constitutional power by claiming those are necessary for the security and progress of the country. But a deeper analysis of the intentions of the governments shows that the main motive behind such measures undertaken by the Governments are totally politically directed, i.e. the various governments simply try to control trade unions for their own political ends.

The government of Bangladesh always plays significant role in the determination of wages in the organized sector. There are number of laws in Bangladesh to ensure payment on time of a certain minimum wage. In addition, there are wage boards appointed by the Govt. to determine the wages in particular industries. The Government has also established labor-courts and industrial tribunals to settle wage disputes by adjudication. In unionized situation, bilateral process of collective bargaining is evident and in case of deadlock or dispute between the employer and the union, recourse is taken to the government labor machinery, labor tribunals and even law courts.

The provisions of the basic laws in the field of labor relations are in conformity with the principle upheld by these ILO Conventions already ratified by the Government of Bangladesh. There are also provisions in the laws for settlement of industrial disputes through negotiations, conciliation or adjudication.

2.9.2 Government-Management Action

Bangladesh is a country which is characterized for its patron-client relationship between state and business groups' i.e. employers and also politicization of trade union. All the major political parties maintain relationship with the business class. For example, after independence jute and specially textile mills grew very fast and were highly dependent upon government patronage in the form of contracts, loans, and credits. All are well connected politically and some are very active in politics. For instance, Beximco group is very active in politics. If we look at the MPs of the last few parliaments, we will see business groups have manned the parliament. Even if we have a glance at the various chambers of commerce of last decades the presidents were supporters of the ruling parties. There is provision in the Industrial Relations Ordinance, 1969 that the employers also have been given right to declare lock-out under certain circumstances.

2.9.3 Government—Trade Union Action

According to the Industrial Relations Ordinance, 1969 (IRQ) a Collective Bargaining Agent (CBA) is entitled to raise labor disputes on behalf of workers and to bargain collectively with the employers on the issues of the labor disputes. There is, however, some exception in the public sector industries where no dispute can be raised by CBA on wages, bonus, leave, medical allowance, house rent allowance, conveyance allowance, gratuity and night shift allowance which are determined by the Government on the basis of the recommendation of either of the National Pay Commission or of the Industrial Workers Wages and Productivity Commission.

2.9.4 Government—Worker Action

The provisions of the basic laws in the field of labor relations are in conformity with the principle upheld by these ILO Conventions already ratified by the Government of Bangladesh. The law provides that workers may raise industrial disputes on issues relating to wages, fringe benefits, service conditions, leave benefits, welfare measures, etc. The right of strike has also been enshrined in the law.

3.0 Management Action

Management approach towards itself presupposes management as a social task. Since life is based on conflict, the management task in the long run is directed towards in harmonizing the conflicts inside and outside the enterprise. The art and science is sophisticated with theories concepts and models of management.

Critical internal and external environmental change factors which are likely to affect the management principles and practices, organization and its mode of operating in future maybe given as:

a. Changes in public opinion
b. Changes in government-business relations
c. Changes in organization and management
d. Changes in workforce composition

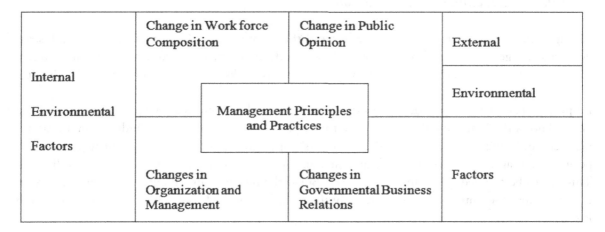

Figure 2 : Management Principles and Practices[168]

In the public sector management suffer from lack of authority and accountability in Bangladesh. They have to wait for government guidelines and act on the basis of these. In the private sector owner-managers continue to be reluctant to consider workers as equal partners. Industrial relations policies, practices and climate are usually considered far better in multinational companies.

3.0.1 Management-Trade Union Action

Management and trade unions action is based on increasing realization that trade unionism has come to stay as a necessary concomitant of the contemporary capitalist system and the trade union movement is the expression of the workers' collective determination to recover emotional security lost through industrial revolution.

Although multiplicity of trade unions and weaknesses of trade union structures are considered constraints to free play of collective bargaining, there are other problems in Bangladesh. The most serious ones are very narrow conceptions about collective bargaining and the process settlement of disputes as set in the law. Collective bargaining is generally perceived as power relationship and only practiced with the attitude for settlement of disputes concerning wage questions only. The basic factors which normally determine such settlement are elements of confrontation, interventions by outside conciliators and threats to adjudication by courts.

In private sector, especially in MNCs, the practice of resolution of disputes through the process of collective bargaining is still there; but the same practice is almost absent in the public sector and other enterprises.

3.0.2 Management-Worker Action

Management and workers action revolves around the themes like attitude towards work; industrial democracy; urge for greater degree of control over work situation; search for an environment, where worker can take roots and where he sees the purpose of his works and feels important in achieving it.

Employers' paternalistic approach is positive only theoretically. There is a saying that guardian of the family knows the best. Like the owner have the responsibility to maintain the industry in a peaceful manner. So, in the Labor market, if the employers' approach is positive, the paternalistic approach is positive. Here again comes the issue of humanitarian approach. The demand of the workers is unlimited. This has to be fulfilled with limited resources. But if the owner wants to ensure their interest most, they maximize their interest by maximizing profit at the cost of the Labor. The scenario of Bangladesh is similar to that.

In Bangladesh, the system between worker and owner sharing policy formulation, benefits talk with representatives are mandatory. Trade union is a voluntary wish of workers. But in Bangladesh the scenario is different. There is a lack of trust between employers and workers. Especially in RMG the situation is highly volatile. Workers activities have proved detrimental in many aspects. It has been considered as a serious bottleneck to the success of business and industry. Considering violence, death, terrorism and corruption committed by the workers in the industrial enterprises of Bangladesh, different sections of the community have made frequent demands for imposing ban on workers' activities.

Despite a short industrial history since 1971, labor-management relations have undergone several changes in Bangladesh. The major characteristics of Labor-management relations in Bangladesh are as follows:

(i) Lack of requisite leadership.
(ii) Lack of scientific management system.
(iii) Absences of necessary delegation of power to plant management of public sector enterprises.
(iv) Lack of proper education and training to management and working groups.
(v) Greater influence of politics in trade unionism.
(vi) Violation of Labor laws both by the management and workers.
(vii) Violation of Labor laws both by the management and workers.

(viii) Absence of a sense of belongings.

(ix) Irrational wages structure.

(x) Absence of a matured industrial workforce on the one hand and industrial entrepreneurs on the other hand. In the former case the workforce is only one generation old and in the later case entrepreneurs.

(xi) Absence of mutual trust and respect between management and trade union and

(xii) Inadequate communication system.

3.1 Trade Union Action

In Bangladesh at present trade union is not functioning as they required doing. For example in garments industry in real sense there is no trade union. So image building situation does not exist there. In Bangladesh the trade unions are not getting support from the government. The workers are unjustly fired the trade unions are not there to support them. In case of garments industry there is a shortage of skilled Labor. The workers do not have the authority to talk about their rights; owners behave like an autocrat. Since there is no trade union, workers are not happy. Owners are reluctant to give wages and overtimes; and guarantees of service due to the availability of workers. Trade union activities in Bangladesh is low because

- Political influence
- Literacy of industry
- Workers are not literate so there choice of leader is not literate

In Bangladesh there are many multinational companies. They are doing business by contractual agreements. For example in BATB few employees are permanent. There is a trade union but they do not work for the workers. They want to ensure their membership as permanent membership of the organization. The trade unions real support is to give facilities to the workers. But in reality they are supporting the owners to give less profit to contractual employees. In this context trade union is workers discretion. The permanent employees are served as the confidential assistants and fire assistants. They are not eligible to permanent benefits. In other ways constituents are set by the interest of the unions.[169] Besides garments industry, in private spinning mills this situation exists.

3.1.1 Trade Union-Management Action

Trade union and management action is conditioned by accepting the fact that management presents an indissoluble partnership amongst interests, power, and responsibility in the social context, whereby it is expected to serve:

Shareholders—	Success and results
Customers—	Price, quality and service
Employees—	Fair—dealing and continuing growth opportunities
Industry—	Development, productivity ethical action
Nation—	Economic and social advancement

3.1.2 Trade Union—Worker Action

Trade union and workers action implies that it should appreciate workers aspirations and expectations that trade union is essentially a protective, friendly society, meant primarily to manage and handle their economic, social and cultural problem. Often aspirations of workers are at variance with those of leaders in the trade union movement. Trade union approach towards itself is based on the premise that trade unionism is a management system. Trade unions as organizations generally viewed themselves as an end rather than as a means, centering on cause and not on man, which, in turn, creates an attitude of convalescence and the cause of unconsciousness. There is often a tendency in trade unionism to promote mass movement instead of organization, and membership often based on calamity features rather than on positive factors.

In a changing situation ideological postures are of limited relevance in the realm of trade unionism, which has to undertake responsibilities in a dynamic situation, influenced by external and internal environment and focusing on:

—The primary purpose
—Organization
—Adjustment and adaptation
—Attitudes
—Representation
—Economic responsibilities
—Discipline

3.2 Labor Market Situation

A Labor market is defined as a pool of all potential workers who compete for jobs. It also includes the employers who compete for workers. Labor markets are based on the supply and demand of Labor in a country or a specific location that are able and willing to work. These markets occur because different conditions characterize different geographical areas, industries, occupations, and professions at any given time. The attitude of the Government towards development of Labor relations is not significant. The present situation in the Labor relations system can be characterized by the following factors

i. The attitude of the government, employers and workers
ii. The existing Labor laws
iii. The application and enforcement of the Labor laws
iv. The trade union structure

The present state of Labor relations in Bangladesh can be said to be poor. Although we have a liberal Labor policy and a set of good Labor laws, our industrial relations are chaotic and productivity below standard. The result is foreign investors are scared of investment and skeptical in accepting our factor advantage as cheap production base. Although there is a comprehensive legal enactment to cover the various aspects of Labor relations questions, these are neither applied nor complied with properly.

Healthy growth of trade unionism and Labor relations practice has been greatly hampered due to intervention by external forces. Disputes on political causes are gradually increasing. Of the total number of disputes received by the government conciliation machinery involving stoppages of work 66.77% of them constituted disputes on political causes.

Constraints of Labor Market Condition in Bangladesh

1. Labor indiscipline: Harmonious labor management relations are essential pre-requisite for higher productivity. In Bangladesh, the labor indiscipline is acute that both foreign and local investors are hesitant to explore investment opportunities. Many foreign investors, despite their keen interest, changed decision to invest in Bangladesh mainly because of labor indiscipline, low productivity and chaotic industrial relations.

2. Politicization of trade unions: Politicization of trade unions is a major problem. Most of the political parties in Bangladesh have their own labor front. The result is that due to outside influence, the labor management relations at the plant level remains tense all the time and it is very difficult to carry out the production programme on schedule.

3. Government's intervention in wage determination: In 1985, the wages of unskilled workers at entry level were increased by 48% on the recommendation of the wages commission. Thereafter ad hoc concessions were given to the workers at frequent intervals through announcement in public meetings. Many of the mills and factories in the private sector were compelled to raise wages in proportion to the increase in the public sector because of strong union and political pressure.

4. Low labor productivity: Since 1986-87 labor productivity in the industrial sector declined between 10% and 17%. Such decline in labor productivity accompanied by an increase of 72% in wages has ruined the financial viability of many of the public sector enterprises. Similar is the situation in most of the cases in private sector. Bangladesh is, perhaps, the only country where workers are paid more than generation of value added. Estimate of over employment is also very high and in some cases it is more than 40%.

5. Lack of proper enforcement of labor laws: Bangladesh has a good set of labor laws. Unfortunately, the laws were not properly enforced. Timely and proper enforcement of labor laws in industrial sector have ignored for long. The government inspection machinery is so weak that proper enforcement of the various provisions of labor laws cannot be ensured.

6. Ineffectiveness of the present dispute settlement system: The present system of dispute settlement has neither succeeded in stopping the rising trend of disputes involving loss of man days, nor contributed to promotion of an atmosphere of good-will and understanding amongst employers and workers. According to the labor journal published by the Department of Labor for 1976-1989 the conciliation machinery could settle only 10.87%, 5.57% and 6.25% of the disputes involving stoppages of work during 1986, 1987 and 1989 respectively. The adjudication machinery also proved inadequate to dispose of cases in time and during the same years only 42.66%, 54.47%, 37% and 30% of the pending cases could be disposed of by the Labor Courts. Delay in speedy disposal of cases by the Court creates frustration amongst the workers, which ultimately causes labor unrests.

7. Lack of training in labor relations: Ignorance about the basic provisions of labor laws is one of the causes of labor unrests and misunderstanding amongst employers and workers. The scope of training in labor relations is grossly inadequate. Although there are a few industrial relations institutes run by the Department of Labor, they suffer from non-performance.

3.3 The Action of Technology as a Situation

Workplace change has become a prominent issue for business, labor and government globally as well as in Bangladesh. Management, organized labor and technology can be seen as the three most important or primary initiators of social—and workplace change.

Action towards employment relationship: Improvements in technology, and particularly information technology, have fundamentally impacted on the employment relationship. Firstly, and most obviously, technology is often used as a substitute for labor. Production lines have increasingly become automated and expert and other information systems are being used in organizations to replace the middle and lower tiers of management.

Complement the labor: Improvements in technology have also served to complement labor. The work process itself has become increasingly efficient. Secretaries and other administrative have access to vastly improved computer technologies that assist them in processing and storing data. Managers at all levels use various decision-making systems that help them to scan the environment and make informed decisions about laborers.

Action towards Manual Workers: Manual workers such as mechanics, plumbers, and electricians are able to complete jobs more quickly with the use of technologically advanced power tools, computer-assisted diagnostic equipment, and the like. Technology also impacts on the design, location and nature of work itself. A prime example of this is the concept of the virtual office place, and telecommuting, where workers are able to interface with the central office by means of information and telecommunications technology and thus work from home instead of commuting to work. It is thus as a complement to the employment relationship, rather than a substitute, that technology has had the greatest impact on the society actions.

In case of technology, it is clearly evident that it is playing a significant role in changing the employment structure of the county and is thereby leading a rapidly changing path of industrial relations system from social actions perspective.

3.4 Defense of Social Action Theory

Social action is an action that regards the reactions of other people. When the potential reaction is not desirable, the action is modified accordingly. Sociology is the study of society and behavior, the heart of interaction, and thus the study of social action. Social action states that human vary their actions according to social contexts and how it will affect other people. Sociology studies that alteration.

One of the fundamental tasks of industrial relations research is to describe and explain the behavior of in industry-level social relations. There are few regulations structuring exchange relations, thus giving social actors a great deal of leeway in the formation of such relations. Scholars of industrial relations therefore have to conduct theory-based research to determine the typical exchange relations that emerge in different industry. The response to this is the social action theory.

3.5 Effectiveness of Social Action Theory

Sociologists have put forth two competing models to explain why the effectiveness of works councils varies across firms. Macro theoretical models, such as those of system theorists and neo-Marxist labor process theorists (e.g., Burawoy, 1985; Hyman, 1989),[170] attempt to explain the behavior of collective actors by reference to the social structures and systems in which these actors are embedded. Micro theoretical explanations, such as those proposed by strategic choice theorists (e.g., Crouch, 1982; Kochan, Katz,and McKersie, 1986; Walton and McKersie, 1965)[171] and symbolic interactionists, identify the intentions, interests, and attitudes of individuals as the deciding factors structuring exchange relations in the firm.

3.5.1 A Non-reductionistic Model

In order to provide a non-reductionistic explanation of the collective behavior of management and the workforce, a theory of industrial relations has to link the macro level of the structural conditions impinging on action to the micro level of specific individual actions (Alexander et al., 1987; Archer, 1995).[172] Such an explanatory model would be based on at least two basic assumptions:

1. Social phenomena can be explained solely through the actions of individuals.
2. Individuals select these actions from a variety of possibilities that emerge from the nature of the social situation (cf. Coleman, 1990).[173]

Social action provides the ground in this regard. According to this theory if we are to explain collective phenomena in the workplace, then, we must first recognize that such phenomena result from the actions of individuals. Because the behavior of individual members of works councils, workers, and managers varies across firms, we are able to observe different levels of effectiveness of codetermination. The behavior of individual actors results from their decisions regarding the action to be taken. Both the decisions made and the spectrums of possible courses of action are influenced by firm-endogenous and firm-exogenous social phenomena. To explain the effectiveness of codetermination, we must, therefore, take into account:

(1) The system or macro-level phenomena that determine the situation of individual actors.
(2) The action we expect to result from these conditions, and
(3) The effectiveness of the codetermination resulting from these individual actions.

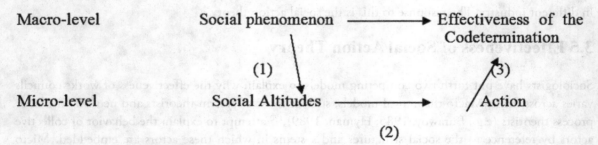

Figure 3 : A formal explanatory model of firm-level codetermination[174]

Figure 3 depicts the elements of this model and the relationships (1-3) it attempts to explain.

3.5.2 Linking the Micro and Macro Levels of Analysis of Society

An important step in explaining the effectiveness of social action theory is the identification of the social phenomena on the micro level that are influenced by the macro level, and that, at the same time, are relevant for individual actors.

- Social attitudes are especially relevant here: They reflect, to a certain degree, the social situation in which actors are embedded (Relation 1), and they serve to orient actors toward specific courses of action (Relation 2). Social attitudes reflect how individuals perceive their social world and which social conditions they consider desirable (Eagley and Chaiken, 1993).[175]
- Empirically, individuals sharing general structural characteristics such as gender, age, education, occupation, or membership of a social group or cultural community also display similarities in their social attitudes (House, 1981; Kluegel, Mason, and Wegener, 1995).[176]

Individual perceptions and preferences are thus significantly influenced by the structural and cultural context (Schooler, 1996).[177] This is why the dominant social attitudes in a society often reflect the social structural or institutional uniqueness of that society.

In the terminology of the social action model, the macro-level social structure influences individual attitudes at the micro level. This effect is not restricted to the societal macro level, however. Melvin Kohn and colleagues have shown that the social structure and organizational culture of a firm can also influence social attitudes. In research including an international comparative study, Kohn and his colleagues have demonstrated that organizational factors such as the position in the company's hierarchy, the extent of bureaucratization, the level of supervision, the structure of ownership, and the composition of work groups all affect workers' attitudes. It follows that not only the societal but also the organizational macro-level impacts on the perceptions of social reality and preferences of individual workers. In other words, social action also reflects the structural and cultural conditions of the workplace.

Although the structures of the industrial relations system may influence the action of its actors, it also influences the whole system.

3.6 The Issues to be addressed

As a part of industrial relations the problems regarding the system can co-ordinate through the implementation of actions of social actors. The issues are:

1. In Bangladesh an adversarial relation exists between trade union and management so rate of participation becomes less. The experiences can affect the relationship among the actors.

2. Frequent violations of collective bargaining agreement negotiation by the management create volatile environment of non-co-operation by the trade unions. Workers expectation can be achieved through successful negotiation

3. Frequent violations of collective bargaining agreement negotiation by the management create volatile environment of non-co-operation by the trade unions. Workers expectation can be achieved through successful negotiation.

4. The managements' paternalistic attitude towards the trade unions discourages participation of trade unions to the industrial relations system. There can be a interaction among them.

5. Passive and ineffective government role as well as lack of law enforcement discourages the unions to participate in the industrial relation system. Government role can be enhanced by understanding mutual needs.

6. In the collecting bargaining process the trade unions tend to go co-opted either by the government or the management so it discourages trade union to participate in the industrial relations system. By taking social action approach there can be specific goals to achieve.

7. The technological action can create a positive situation where all the actors can interact with each other.

3.7 System Theory

3.8 Background

Industrial relations are as old as industry and being inherent in industry, will always remain as a feature of industrial life. As a field of study as distinct from an area of activity, it has a much shorter history both in Britain and most other countries. Much of the early writing on industrial relations tended to place considerable emphasis on an institutional and factual approach. Authors concentrated their efforts on describing the situation as they saw it. They mainly described the situations and issues about the industrial activities and structures of unions and the impact of changes of their frame.

Different authors scrutinized the industrial relations from different point of views consequently, each of them behaved as if he or she were in different social situations. May be one of them perceived the issues in managerial, corporate or middle class terms where as the other viewed from the union and working class terms. Among the approaches, today industrial relations tended to place considerable emphasis on institutional and factual approach.

Though the institutional and the factual approaches best exemplified in Britain by the work of Oxford Group in recent years the dominance of the institutional approach to industrial relations has been challenged. The first and probably the most influential, major challenge have been linked to the work of Dunlop.

Dunlop, an economist, modified the work of sociologists, in particular that of Parsons and Smelser, to enable him to discuss the industrial relation system. Dunlop's aim was to develop a combined theory which by stressing the interrelationship of institutions and behaviors would enable one to understand and explain industrial relation rules. If conflict theory has dominated much British thinking in the field then Dunlop's system approach or theory has been the major American contribution to industrial relation theorizing. System theory has also influenced British and European students of industrial relations, including those supporting conflict theory.

System theory was first articulated by John Dunlop in his seminal book Industrial Relation System, published in the United States in 1958. Its purpose is to present a general theory of industrial relations and to provide tools of analysis to interpret and to gain understanding of the widest possible range of industrial relations facts and practice.

3.9 Definition of System Theory

According to John Dunlop—

"An industrial relation system at any one time in its development is regarded as comprised of certain actors, certain contexts, an ideology which binds the industrial relation system together and a body of rules created to govern the actors at the work place and work community."

To Dunlop, an industrial relation system is not part of a society's economic system but a separate and distinctive subsystem of its own, partially overlapping the economic and political decision making system with which it interacts. In his view, system theory provides the analytical tools and the theoretical basis to make industrial relations an academic discipline in its own right rather than merely a field of study or a subject which might be looked at by a number of other disciplines.

4.0 Theoretical Views and Aims of Dunlop

Dunlop's aim was to develop an "all embracing theory "which by stressing the interrelationship of institutions and behaviors, would enable one to understand and explain industrial relation rules.

Dunlop emphasized this point when he reviewed the development of the study of industrial relations. He said that for many years it had merely been a crossroads where a number of disciplines met—history, economics, government, sociology, psychology and law. What it needed in order to be considered a discipline, he argued, was a theoretical core, that was provided. Through such a study industrial relations would be accepted as a genuine discipline.

Essentially Dunlop's theoretical framework views the industrial relation system as a subsystem of the wider society or the total social system. Thus the wider society is seen as providing certain external influences and constraints but not as a completely dominating industrial relation. Therefore the industrial relations system has a similar status to, for example, the economic and political systems, with which it can overlap.

On the other side, the creation of rules is seen to be the central aim of the industrial relations system and the procedures for deciding their applications to particular situations which are the products of the system. The establishment and the administration of these rules is the major concern or output of the industrial relations subsystem of industrial society. These rules are of various kinds and may be written, oral or custom or practice. They include managerial decisions, trade union regulations, laws of the state, and awards by governmental agencies, collective agreements and work place traditions. Furthermore, they cover not only pay and conditions but also disciplinary matters, methods of working, the rights and duties of employees as well as employers and so on. Thus it is the rules of industrial relation which have to be explained by the independent variables of an industrial system. Actors, context and ideology of the systems are these variables.

Dunlop isolates three main groups of actors who take part in the rule making processes. They are-

A hierarchy of managers and their representatives in supervision,

A hierarchy of workers (non managerial) and their spokesmen,

Specialized government agencies (and specialized private agencies created by the first two actors) concerned with workers, enterprises and their relationships

However, the actors are not completely free agents. They are confronted by the environment and are influenced and limited by it. Dunlop argues that managerial hierarchies need not own the capital assets and may be located in either private or public

Enterprise. He also suggests that employees may be organized into a number of competing or complementary employee organizations. However, totalitarian societies normally have governmental agencies which are also powerful that they over-ride managers and employees on almost all matters.

4.1 Important Features and Aspects of Environment

The important features of the environment though, are determined by the larger society and its other sub systems and are not explained within an industrial relation system. The significant aspects of the environment are:

The technological characteristics

- The market or budgetary constraints which impinge on the actors
- The distribution of power in the larger society.

These aspects of the environment can influence the industrial relations system in a variety of ways. For example, the technology can influence the form of management and the employee organization and the problem posed for supervision. On the other hand, market and budgetary constraints can influence the ease with which products can be sold and the availability of labor and the distribution power within the industrial relations system will be greatly affected by and responsive to the locus and distribution of power in the wider society.

The industrial relation system is held together by an ideology or a common set of ideas and beliefs. The ideology defines the role and place of each actor in the system and that defines the ideas which each actor holds towards the place and function of others in the system. It is recognized that each of the actors in the industrial relation system may have their own ideology. However, an industrial relation system requires that these ideologies may be sufficiently compatible and consistent so as to permit a common set of ideas which recognize an acceptable role of each actor.

The rules that govern behavior in the workplace and work community can be expressed in a variety of forms. For example they can be the regulations produced by the management hierarchy, the rules laid down by any worker hierarchy etc.

4.2 Impact and Success of Dunlop's System Theory

Dunlop's work has had a tremendous impact. It has dominated industrial relation research for the past decade. It has been used as a starting point by most influential commentators.

It is not difficult to appreciate its attraction. It provided a way of broadening the subject area previously considered by industrial relation writers; in particular, enabling them to move away from a narrow concentration on collective bargaining and directly related questions. It gave commentators the opportunity to claim that industrial relation was a discipline in its own right rather than merely a field of study or a subject which might be looked at by a number of other disciplines. Dunlop emphasized this point when he reviewed the development of the study of industrial relations.

The industrial relations systems approach, as developed by Dunlop, has found many supporters. In Britain, it has greatly influenced the work of Flanders. He has used the notion of an industrial relation system to argue that the core of the subject involves the study of certain regulated or institutional relationships in industry. According to him it is clear that not all the relationships associated with the organizations of industry are relevant. Only those associated with the employment function need to be considered and not for example trade relationship between two enterprises or an enterprise and its customers. This leads Flanders to define industrial relations as a study of the institutions of job regulations.

Dunlop's work has also been used by Gill to show how industrial relations teaching might be developed around the notion of industrial relations systems. Gill argues that the systems approach enables the students to reach a deeper understanding of the nature of the system under consideration and provides him at a minimum with a useful classifying device and at a maximum with a level of analysis which may claim to be predictive of resistance to change.

Qualified support has been given by others; Eldridge, despite his many reservations, argues that it can be useful in analyzing industrial conflict because it reminds the practitioner of the whole range of factors that have to be considered in attempting to explain strikes.

4.3 Weakness and Deficiencies in Dunlop's Theory

A number of people have argued that although there is considerable merit in Dunlop's work but it is deficient in certain respects and modifications are essential. The kind of comments and suggestions they made can be illustrated by references to work of four well known writers. They are Bain & Clegg, Banks, and Hyman. Although each has his own emphasis but they all note similar defects.

Bain and Clegg argue that there are two central defects in the system approach. First, there are certain ambiguities in the way the concept of a system is used. Dunlop's work is closely linked to the Parsonian analysis of social system and his argument that it is an ideology or a set of ideas and beliefs commonly held by the actors that helps to bind or integrate the system together as an entity might be taken to imply that an industrial relation system is naturally stable and integrative and necessarily strives to perpetuate itself. Such a notion has conservative implications and is unacceptable. They sympathetically quote Eldridge who argues that in sociology the source of conflict, co-operation, order and instability must have an equally valid claim to problem status.

Secondly, the systems concept does not point to all of the important explanatory variables. Dunlop's formulation of an industrial relation system largely omits such behavioral variables as human motivation, perception, and attitude while Flanders has argued that personal or in the language of sociology unstructured relationships have their importance for management and workers but they lie outside the scope of a system of industrial relation. Bain and Clegg argue that if Dunlop and Flanders are attempting a full explanation of industrial relations behavior and its determinants then behavior variables co not be completely dismissed. The extent to which behavior variables will be important will differ but clearly they will be important in certain circumstances. To ignore the aims and interpretations of the actors would seem to hinder significantly an understanding of the process of job regulation.

Banks also puts forward two main criticism of Dunlop's work. First that when Dunlop identifies three main sets of actors in the industrial relations system he fails to make reference to the owners of industrial property. Dunlop fails to do so because he believed that decisions in the industrial relation are made by managers not owners. Banks argues that by adopting such an approach Dunlop fails to recognize the importance of profit for negotiations in particular and industrial relations in general and that what happens to profits is related to who owns the enterprise.

Bank's second criticism has many similarities to one of the comments made by Bain and Clegg. He argues that Dunlop's idea of a system is of essentially deterministic mechanism. Although Dunlop is persuasive in explaining the forces that shape the more substantive aspects of industrial relations, he leaves out of his explanations the way in which key leaders in enterprise, trade unions, employees associations and governmental agencies are able to influence events. Dunlop's actors are not persons. Even when he admits that each of them may be said to have its own ideology, he appears to have in mind a set of ideas and beliefs commonly held by the actors as a class of role players rather than the individual attitudes of people. Thus when Banks call for greater recognition to be given to the importance of behavioral factors he is clearly echoing the words of Bain and Clegg.

4.4 Dunlop Model and Cox Classification

Before we move on to relate Dunlop's Model with the classification of Cox, let us briefly summarize the Dunlop Model

4.4.1 Dunlop Model in a Gist

Dunlop Model consists of Rules which include

- Managerial decision
- Trade union regulation
- Laws of the State
- Awards by Governmental agencies
- Collective agreements
- Workplace traditions

These rules cover:—Pay and condition, the rights and duties of employers and employees. Rules are explained by three sets of independent variables: The actors, the contexts, and the ideology.

The actors are:

A hierarchy of managers and their representatives, A hierarchy of non managerial employees and their representatives, Specialized third party agencies whether governmental of private

Dunlop assumed:

Managerial hierarchies need not own the capital assets of production, Employees may be organized into numbers of employee organizations, Dunlop describes three environmental contexts:, The market conditions and budget constraints, State of development of technology and, Distribution of power in the larger society

Technology influences:

The size of workforce, Concentration or dispersion, Location, proportion of skills, Ratio of male to female workers, Health and safety etc.

Distribution is conditioned by:

Social relationships, Historical events like ethnical or colonial superimposition, Different Legal and Political norms.

In this environment these actors interact with each other, negotiate, and use economic and political power or influence in the process of determining the rules that constitute the output of the industrial relations system.

In a reasonably stable system, an ideology or shared understandings commonly held by the actors help to define their roles and to integrate the system as a whole.

As changes take place in the several contexts, or within the actors and their hierarchies themselves, or in their relationships and interactions, or in their shared understandings, the rules of the work place may be expected to change. The task of industrial relations is to understand and to explain such changes in the rules of work places, recognizing the interdependencies of the system as a whole.

If workers were devoid of any voice or organization, an industrial relations system would still set the rules of the work place with the involvement of the managerial and government actors.

Considering all these points, we can co-relate different key-points of Dunlop model to different class of Cox classification—

4.4.1.1 SUBSISTENCE System

In Subsistence system, family units have hierarchical economical authority. There is also political and social hierarchy. This is somehow related to Dunlop's model as it also describes about hierarchy. Family economical hierarchy can be compared to managers and their representative, with family head being the manager and other family members being the representatives.

Political and social hierarchy can be compared to as Special Third party agencies who can be Governmental or Private.

Also, in Dunlop model, it has been assumed that, managerial hierarchy need not own any capital asset; which is true for Subsistence system's Family units.

4.4.1.2 Primitive Labor Market

A part of this can be explained by the technology effect of Dunlop Model. Primitive Labor Market system states that, due to technological improvement, the less skilled workers are being relatively mobile and have some choices of employment.

In Dunlop Model, the effect of technology included dispersion of workers and proportion of skills. Surely since some places will require more skills, the less skilled workers are dispersing somewhere else, where the proportion of skills is still relatively low.

4.4.1.3 Enterprise Labor Market

Employment and conditions are regulated through the operation of an open Labor market in this system. This generally falls in one of the three environmental context of Dunlop Model.

Also, it talks about trade unions and governmental agencies. Though their intervene is very limited.

This classification is highly considered in terms of technology. More skilled Labor force, concentration of skilled workers in modern sectors relates this with Dunlop Model.

4.4.1.4 Enterprise Corporatist System

This system is similar to enterprise Labor market system, with an addition—co-relation to Dunlop's Model rules which cover 'Pay and Condition'. In this system, employment security and welfare is guaranteed by the employer.

4.4.1.5 Bipartite System

This system follows the Dunlop Model in terms of the assumption of Dunlop model that employees are organized into number of employee organizations. Also, this implicates Dunlop Model's rules like trade union regulation, laws and collective agreements.

4.4.1.6 Tripartite System

In addition to the relation of Dunlop model to Bipartite system, tripartite system adds to the relation of Government's Role to Dunlop model. So, now Tripartite system has the three actors of Dunlop model, rules like laws, collective agreement, workplace conditions. Thus, tripartite system has more co-relation with Dunlop than previously discussed classes.

4.4.1.7 Socialist System

Socialists system is related to Dunlop model in the following ways:

- Technology playing a great role in selecting skilled workforce
- Greater decentralization of decision making—a hierarchical system for the 3 actors.
- Employee organizations play a great role and works collectively with other players.

4.4.1.8 Self-Employed System

This system is related to Dunlop model in the following ways:

- Technology playing a much greater role.
- A stronger employee organization
- Collective bargaining power through employee organizations
- Have all the players—employee and organization, industry and Government.

So, by considering all the classification of Cox, it can be said that, apart from 1 or 2 classes, all other classes include at least 1 or 2 features of Dunlop model. If one out of these is asked to be chosen to be most closely related to Dunlop model, it would be Tripartite system, as it has the most number of features included in it that relates to Dunlop model in some way.

4.5 Relevance of Dunlop's Industrial relation model in Bangladesh

Following Dunlop we may explain the industrial relation system of Bangladesh in terms of certain groups, certain context and a body of rules which govern the interaction of groups at work place. The principal groups identifiable in the system and which constitutes the structure of industrial relation system are as follows-

Bangladesh Employers Federation (BEF). This is an employers' organization in Bangladesh established and registered in 1951 under the companies act 1913. It represents all formal sectoral employer's association, accounting for about 90% of employers in the private sector and all the public sector corporations and autonomous bodies. Its major functions are providing employers with guidance and assistance in the field industrial relation; bringing their concerted views on Labor matters to the attention of the government, representing them in national forums. It has a stake in government socioeconomic policy, Labor legislation and relations with kindred national and international bodies.

Workers Representative Organizations, i.e trade union. Bangladesh, being a signatory of ILO convention, allows its workers to form their own associations, commonly known as trade union in order to protect, promote, and improve their economic, social and political interest. Trade unions in Bangladesh have grown from 1160 with 450606 members in 1971 to 6349 with 1909414 members in 2000. Despite the absolute increase in their numbers over time, unionized workers and other employees account for only 3% of the total Labor force and 1/3 of the total regular formal employees, reflecting a very low rate of unionization in the country.

According to Dunlop, the interaction between the three actors—Labor, management and government-produce the network of rules governing industrial relation. Beside these three actors there are three environmental contexts that play up decisive part in shaping the rules of an industrial relation system with which three actors interact.

4.6 Trade Union and Bangladesh

Trade Unions in Bangladesh are highly politicized. Most unions are affiliated with industrial as well as national federations with affiliation to measure political parties. Most trade union officials try to perpetuate their leadership through strong political affiliations, particularly with the ruling party, without any approval or consent of the common worker, which works to the employees' detriment. Politicization of trade unions has made way for Labor in discipline, and is working as a blanket for inefficient and corrupt trade unions. By and large, trade unions no longer have the credibility to protect and promote workers interest. Trade union is weak in the private export oriented sector. It is absent in shrimp exporting firms finished leather good sector, pharmaceuticals because of relatively high wage levels and regular monitoring of workers problems and dissolving them through mutual discussion. In the RMG sector, unions have been low—key due to very poor employment relationships, reflecting very limited social protection of the workers. In the EPZ trade union is legally prohibited. The informal sector, which accounts for more than 90% of the total employment in the country, has no provision for social protection of workers.

4.6.1 Role of state in industrial relation

In Bangladesh, the state or government intervene in the industrial policy through different machineries, such as Labor Court, Industrial Tribunals, Wage-boards, Investigating and Enquiry committee.

State had emerged as the third important force determining industrial relations system in Bangladesh since the very beginning of its industrialization. Although, recently the role of state has declined due to deregulation and privatization, still the state itself has become an employer of millions of industrial workers and it is its moral and ethical responsibility to ensure that the rights of the workers are suitably safeguarded. Government is thus responsible for the maintenance of a balance between the interests of the two parties in industrial relations Dunlop (1978), and Memoria (1998) also place emphasis on the role of state in regulating employer and employee relationships. They contend that industrial relation is the complex of inter-relationship among workers, employers and Government. The government tries to regulate the relationship of employer and employee and keeps an eye on both parties to keep each in line.

4.6.2 State and Trade Union

The state has always tried to control trade union in Bangladesh through the judicial, legislative, executive and extra legislative power of the state. In Bangladesh, the register of trade union hold immense power to refuse and cancel the registration of a union and it was found that various governments used these powers to their own advantage. Apart from the legal framework of control of the trade unions in Bangladesh, extra constitutional action on the part of the various Governments in the field of trade unions are used from time to time to control the trade unions of Bangladesh. The various Governments when using extra—constitutional or oppressive powers to curb the activities of the militant unions have tried to justify the use of extra-constitutional power by claiming they are necessary of the intentions of the governments shows that the main motive behind such measures undertaken by the Governments are totally politically directed, i.e. the various Governments simply try to control trade unions for their own political ends.[178]

After independence, the Awami League Government in 1972 nationalized more than 90% of large-scale industries. The concept of workers' participation was also given serious consideration. The Government appointed various committees and also invited an ILO mission to explore the possibilities of introducing a Yugoslavian-type of workers' participation in management (known as self-management) in Bangladesh (ILO, 1973). In October 1972, the Government introduced its Labor Policy whereby workers' participation in management was finally agreed and a Workers' Management Council in every nationalized industry was also agreed. But this policy also severely curtailed the scope for collective bargaining by placing wages and fringe benefits outside the scope of collective bargaining. Moreover, they said labor policy took away the right to strike. The Government's argument at this stage was that the collective bargaining model applicable to a capitalist economy was not applicable in a socialist economy where large-scale nationalization and workers' participation had taken place. The trade unions fiercely opposed this plan. They were especially most reluctant to give up their rights to wage bargaining and strike. The Government labor policy also faced opposition from the management side. The traditional authoritative managerial structure could not accept the concept of workers participation in management. Moreover, the internal contradiction within the Government, mainly between rightist and leftist forces. also worked against the implementation of the aforesaid labor policy (Islam, 1977; Sobhan and Ahmad, 1980). In 1974, the Awami League Government went for a one party socialist-corporatist state system where a single trade union organization, as part of the state-party machinery, wds proposed. In the above system trade unions were to become a part of the Government in a socialist—corporatist framework. But before the scheme could be fully implemented an army coup overthrew the Awami League Government in 1975. So, we find that even a political party like the Awami League, whose coming to power was largely facilitated by the trade unions, was reluctant to lose control over the trade unions (Ahmad, 1979). It rather wanted to use trade unions as an arm of its party machinery to attain the party's political objectives. To accomplish this aim, the Awami League Government did not even hesitate to control trade unions by extra-constitutional measures and imposing a ban on strikes. This phenomenon simply represents the inclusions corporatist tendency of a typical Third World populist government. The Military Government that took power in 1975 adopted a policy on the industrial labor front similar to that of General Ayub in Pakistan, who ruled Pakistan from 1958 to 1968. In the industrial sector, the army Government encouraged private investment from both home and abroad, and took an 'exclusionist' policy in respect to trade union activities. The Government, by promulgating the Industrial Relations (Regulation) Ordinance of 1975, banned strikes and the formation of new unions. With the gradual pressure from the politicians and trade unions, the army Government in 1977 and in 1980 relaxed the rules regarding trade unions. At this stage the Government plan was to encourage the depoliticalisation process of the trade unions as well as to 'buy off' trade union leaders by offering them various opportunities (Islam, 1983). But after an army coup in 1982, the right to strike and lockout was again suspended by applying extra—constitutional measures in Bangladesh. This ban continued till 1991. The elected government in 1992 gave the right to strike and lockout. From the above discussion it is clear that the various Governments of Bangladesh, starting from the Pakistani rule up to the present time, have tried to control the trade unions through the Government's legislative, executive and judicial machinery. And whenever necessary, the various Governments resorted to extra constitutional means to control trade unions. The various measures of the Governments may be broadly divided into two categories. The various army Governments in the initial stage mostly adopted a policy of discouraging trade union organization mainly because of political affiliations and at a later stage when pressure was mounting on the army Governments to civilianize the administration, they mostly were for economic unionism and tried to de-politicalise the trade union movement. The various nationalists-populist Governments, on the other hand, in their initial stage of rule tolerated the trade unions mainly because trade unions mostly played a part in bringing them into power. But soon they wanted to use trade unions as extensions of their party. Thus, the various nationalist-populist Governments adopted an inclusions-corporatist framework regarding trade unions and thereby making trade unions part of the state decision-making process, whereas the various army Governments followed an exclusionist-corporatist policy in respect of trade unions and tried to ban them from the political arena, although they adopted two different methods of dealing with trade unions, yet both the populist and army Governments had one thing in common, they both tried to control and contain the working class militancy and to foster a kind of leadership that would accept the Government prescribed procedure for the industrial relations system.

4.6.3 Role of State in Wage Determination

In Bangladesh, government participation and intervention through the various Labor Policies and subsequent laws led to a situation whereby collective bargaining based on a concept of bilateral contractual obligation between the employer and employee has been virtually eliminated from the industrial relations scene. A discussion of this aspect of collective bargaining in Bangladesh, especially in the context of wage determination and the legal framework of collective bargaining, will be carried out now.

Having abandoned the market mechanism to determine the wages of the industrial workers, there are three widely used instruments for wage determination in the world. These are: wage determination through collective bargaining, statutory regulation and quasi-judicial settlements. The predominance of collective bargaining in wage settlement is very much in evidence in the developed industrialized countries of the West, whereas wages in Third World countries are mainly determined by statutory legislation and quasi-judicial settlements. The imperfection of the labor market, inequality of power between bargaining parties, i.e. labor and employer, and most importantly the intervention of the state in the wage determination process are the reasons for the limited use of collective bargaining as an instrument in wage determination in the Third World. Bangladesh is no exception to this rule'. Such intervention by Government on issues, which are subject matter of collective bargaining, should be stopped for all time to come.

After the independence of Bangladesh in 1971, due to the extensive nationalization program, the Government became almost the sole owner of the modern industrial sector of the country. In 1972, the Government declared its Labor Policy where among others it outlined the following policy:

The setting-up of a Management Board in each nationalized industries, which would run the nationalized industries. The Board would include two representatives each from employers and workers and one from financial institutions to ensure the smooth functioning of such industry.

A National Wage Board would be formed consisting of the representatives of employers, workers and other experts to determine and review the periodical wage structure and other fringe benefits of the workers employed in nationalized/state owned and taken over industries. The Government also felt that in the interest of the country such matters should always be decided on the basis of the recommendation of the regarding wage determination.

As regards the wages of workers of industries in the private sector, on reference by the Government, the existing Minimum Wages Board would review such wage structure from time to time. This would be suitably reconstituted for this purpose. Moreover, in relation to private industries and establishments, to achieve improved terms and conditions of employment for the workers, improve the physical environment at the workplace and other welfare measures through the process of collective bargaining.

The functions of the trade unions in relation to industries and establishments owned and managed directly by the Government, nationalized and taken over industries would be to promote measures for the well-being of the working class. Take care of the safety and protection of labor at the workplace, provide training, education and other welfare facilities for the workers and thereby create conditions for higher productivity in the overall interest of the country.

Thus, after independence, wages were fixed in the private sector through Government appointed Minimum Wage Board established under the Minimum Wage Ordinance of 1961, as well as through collective bargaining under the provisions of the Labor Code 2006. In the public sector, however, the Government appointed Wage Board from time to time to fix wages. The Industrial Workers' Wages Commission (IWWC) was constituted on 1st June 1973 in order to review the wage structure including fringe benefits and to make suitable recommendations for the same. On 1st September 1973, the Commission submitted its recommendations for fixing wages, bonuses, medical allowances, house rent allowances, conveyance allowances and leave for workers of public sector manufacturing industries.

The recommendations of the Industrial Wages Commission so far accepted by the Government had been enforced by a new Law, the State-Owned Manufacturing Industrial Workers (Terms and Conditions of Service) Act of 1974. A new Government, which came to power after 1975 also constituted another Wage Commission in 1977, named the industrial Workers' Wages and Productivity Commission (IWWPC) in order to recommend to the Government about wages and fringe benefits of the workers of the public sector industries. All the subsequent Governments of Bangladesh up to the present have followed this policy of determining wages in the public sector through Government appointed Wage Commissions and in the private sector through the Minimum Wage Boards as well as through a limited amount of collective bargaining. Apart from the comprehensive state machinery in the field of wage determination, the scope of collective bargaining in other aspects of the employer-employee relation is also very limited in Bangladesh because of the comprehensive legal framework enacted by the Government at various times. In all bargaining processes, the Government machinery plays the most important part and thus the limited scope for bargaining that exists in Bangladesh is tripartite in nature where workers, employers and representatives of the Government take part.

4.6.4 Role of State in Collective Bargaining

As per the Industrial Ordinance of 1969, the conciliation process starts when the parties to an industrial dispute fail to reach a settlement by direct negotiation. Any of the parties of the direct negotiation may report to the Conciliator that the negotiations have failed and request him in writing to conciliate in the dispute and the Conciliator, on receipt of such request, proceeds to conciliate in the dispute. If the Conciliator fails to settle the dispute within ten days of the receipt of a request for conciliation, the collective bargaining agent or the employer may serve on the other party to the dispute 21 days' notice of strike or lockout, as the case may be. The collective bargaining agent is debarred from serving any strike notice unless three-fourths of its members have given their consent to it through a secret ballot specifically held for this purpose. Where a part to an industrial dispute serves a notice of strike or lockout it must simultaneously deliver a copy thereof to the Conciliator who proceeds to conciliate or, as the case may be, continue to conciliate in the dispute notwithstanding the notice of strike or lockout.

The right to strike or lockout has been granted as a last resort. Even during the period of the notice of strike or lockout, the conciliation process must continue. The Conciliator on receipt of the notice of strike or lockout continues conciliation in the dispute and calls a meeting of the parties for the purpose of bringing about a settlement. The representatives of the parties are under legal obligation to attend the meetings called by the Conciliator. The Conciliator has the authority to call for and inspect or to seize any register, document or certificate which he has reason to believe to be relevant to the dispute. The Conciliator also has the authority to enter the premises occupied by any establishment to which the dispute relates and require any person whom he finds in the establishment to give such information relating to the dispute as are within his knowledge.

The workers may go on strike or, as the case may be, the employer may declare a lockout, on the expiry of the period of notice or upon the issuance by the Conciliator a certificate of failure on the dispute, whichever is later. The Government has, however, the authority to prohibit such a strike or lockout, if such a strike or lockout lasts for more than 30 days (in the case of non-public utility services) and simultaneously refer the dispute to the Labor Court for adjudication. In the case of public utility services the Government has the authority to prohibit a strike or lockout at any time before the commencement of the strike or lockout and also forthwith refers the dispute to the Labor Court for adjudication. The awards of the Labor Court are binding on all the parties to the dispute, unless appealed against to the Labor Appellate Tribunal and in such a case the decision of the Tribunal is final.

It is worth mentioning that the list of public utility services since the enactment of the Industrial Relations Ordinance of 1969 has been increasing. The Government, on various occasions, has declared many industries as public utilities and thus prohibited a strike or lockout in those industries. It has been found that the various Governments have used the concept of public utility service for their own convenience, i.e. to stop a strike or lockout in a particular industry without seriously considering its public utility value.

So we find that under the legislative framework of collective bargaining both the employers and workers hold little power in the negotiation process and, moreover, there is little scope for collective bargaining. It is the various state mechanisms, like conciliation, the Registrar of Trade Unions, Labor Court and Labor Tribunal that hold the real power in the bargaining process. Moreover, even the little powers that workers and employers hold in calling strikes and lockouts has most of the time been suspended by the various Governments by applying the extra-constitutional measures. For example, from 3rd January 1975 to March 1980 the right to strike and lockout was prohibited under such extra—constitutional measures. The right to strike and lockout was only restored after March 1980 for a brief period of two years. After an army coup in April 1982 the right to strike and lockout was suspended again by applying extra-constitutional measures in Bangladesh. This ban continued till 1991. The army government was overthrown and elected government came to power in 1992 Workers and employers were again given right to strike and lockout.

The above discussion clearly reveals the dominant role of the state in the industrial relations system of Bangladesh. In the past, the various Governments of Bangladesh, either through an exclusionist-corporatist or exclusionist-corporatist framework (depending on the character of the Government, i.e. populist or authoritarian) have tried to establish a predominant position for the state in the industrial relations system. Both the capitalist and the working classes of Bangladesh, due to their weakness had to live with this. The working class, as we saw in the previous discussion, had not yet completely yielded to the pressures of the various Governments in the past. On various occasions in the past, they rebelled and tried to resist the Government attempt to subordinate them completely under the State machinery. But the working class was not very successful in freeing itself from the Government control up to the present time.

4.7 Role of Bangladesh Employer Federation (BEF) in Industrial Relation

BEF has conducted a number of seminars and workshops on major issues of industrial relation at the plant level, wage productivity linkage, collective bargaining, Labor-management, cooperation. In the same way several training programs have been carried out by the BEF in order to raise awareness on relevant issues among mid and top level management personnel in different enterprises and to apprise them of the Labor management cooperation.

Historically, the attitude of employers associations towards the workers trade union movement has not been encouraging. Employers association does not recognize SKOP simply because it is not registered. In a sizable number of enterprises, however management has been undergoing an attitudinal change towards workers and trade unions. It has come to realize that the reduction of excess workforce alone will not make enterprises competitive. Enhanced productivity, quality, and better delivery systems are not achievable without the cooperation of the workers.

In Bangladesh there is very little interaction between the three actors. There is lack of trust between employers and workers. They have clash of interest, consider each other as opponent. They have a tendency to put blame on each other for failure or dispute. They are not guided by mutuality of interest. Beside Bangladesh is a country which is popular for its patron-client relationship between government and business group i.e the employers. In the lights of above discussion it can be concluded that interaction and coordination regarding formulation of industrial rules and regulations between these three groups are at minimal level. Dunlop emphasized on State to act as a regulatory body and as check of balance between employers and employees to maintain industrial relation. Rather every government of Bangladesh has a tendency to dominate the relationship and use it for their own advantage.

4.8 Conclusion

The Dunlop model gives great significance to external or environmental forces, with the key actors being held to respond in a relatively uniform and mechanical manner to a given environmental change. In other words, management, labor, and the government possess a shared ideology, or consensus that defines their roles within the relationship and provides stability to the system.

Dunlop's model worked well to organize the labor-management relationship into a framework in the 1960s and 1970s, but it worked only as long as there existed stability in the environmental forces and a shared consensus of the key actors in the employment.

The application of the Dunlop system to developing countries necessitates a rather wide interpretation of the model as Dunlop himself concedes expressis verbis. It is valid already for the term "rules" with respect to the communications between actors in developing areas. The term actor, too, can be applied in a narrower sense only to employers and workers, while the position of the state as actor is somewhat doubtful in developing countries. In this context we can refer to a supplementary remark of Dunlop[179] himself when he alludes to the possible passivity of an actor. "Actor" therefore means generally: "Subjects responsible for interpersonal relations in connection with human work".

The criticism of neglecting internal divergence and differences within the actor groups which has been expressed in relation to industrialized countries is even more valid for developing countries. It cannot be assumed that all employers and workers show the same behavior. The same is true for the governmental agencies. This aspect of the internal divergence of the groups is of special importance in developing countries.

Finally, the term "industrial relations" itself has to be interpreted in a wide sense, e.g. "All conditions, which exist in or result from the employment (of human beings)."[180] Fürstenberg tends also to such a wide interpretation; from his point of view, the term industrial relations "characterizes the factual area of all relations between employers and workers to each other, their consequences and their influencing factors."[181]

Even after all these criticism, Dunlop theory still is used to explain industrial relations, as it is a theory which altogether integrates all the key features of the Cox-Classifications. This theory undertakes all the features of an Industry's key factors like employee, employers and environment. In some cases, this theory may not be totally applicable for all the countries, but it creates a platform for other theories to evolve, to expand from Dunlop's Model to explain and gather all the possibilities of third world as well as developed countries.

4.9 Marxist theory

The philosophy of Marxism is materialism. But Marx did not stop eighteenth century materialism. He developed philosophy to a higher level. He enriched it with the achievements of German classical philosophy, especially of Hegel's system, which in its turn had led to the materialism of Feuerbach.

5.0 Emergence and Development of Marxist Philosophy[182]

The main achievement of Marxism was dialectics, i.e., the doctrine of development in its fullest, deeper and most comprehensive form, the doctrine of the relativity of the human knowledge that provides us with a reflection of eternally developing matter. Marx deepened and developed philosophical materialism to the full, and extended the cognition of nature to include the cognition of human society. His historical materialism was a great achievement in scientific thnking.

Creation of dialectical materialism is focused as a revolution in philosophy can be shown as the following diagrams:

Economic and socio-political conditions Development of the contradictions of capitalism and organization of the proletariat's class struggle	Theoretical sources Classical German philosophy: Hegel's idealist dialectics Feuerbach's philosophical materialism	Prerequisites in natural science Three great discoveries of the 19th century: Discovery of the cell, The law of conservation and transformation of energy. The theory of evolution

Source: Marxist-Leninist Philosophy, by T. Vlasova, 1987, page-22

5.1 Laws and categories of materialist dialectics[183]

It is from the history of nature and human society that the laws of dialectics are abstracted. They are nothing but the most general laws of these two aspects of historical development, as well as of thought itself.

5.1.1 Structure of materialist dialectics

Principles	Laws	Categories
Principles of universal interconnection of objects and phenomena	Law of the unity and struggle of opposites	Individual, particular and general
		Cause and effect
Principles of motion and development	Law of the transformation of quantity into quality and vice versa	Necessity and chance
		Content and form
	Law of the negation of the negation	Essence and appearance
		Possibility and reality and others.

Source: Marxist-Leninist Philosophy, by T. Vlasova, 1987, page-22

5.1.2 Dialectical concept of development

Dialectical Concept of development furnishes the key to the self movement of everything existing; it alone furnished the key to "leaps", to the "break in continuity", to the "transformation into the opposite", to the "destruction of the old" and the emergence of the new. The main points are:

1. The world is an integral whole, where phenomena are mutually conditioned in accordance with the law of matter in motion
2. The source of the motion of matter lies in matter itself, development is a struggle of opposites
3. At a definite stage quantitative changes lead to the emergence of a new quality(law of the transformation of the quantity into quality and vice versa)
4. Development which seemingly repeats past stage, but which in effect repeats them on a new and higher basis (law of the negation of the negation)

5.1.3 Fundamental contradiction of capitalism

Production with profit and loss has become a social act. Exchange and appropriation continue to be individual acts, the acts of individuals. The social product is appropriated by the individual capitalist. Fundamental contradiction, whence arise all the contradictions in which our present day society moves.

1. Severance of the producer from the means of production. Antagonism between the proletariat and the bourgeoisie.
2. Contradiction between socialized organization in the individual factory and social anarchy as a whole.
3. Producers are divorced from ownerships and the owners are divorced from production.

4. On the one hand, perfecting of machinery made by competition compulsory for each individual manufacturer and complemented by a constantly growing displacement of laborers. Industrial reserve army. On the other hand unlimited extension of production, also compulsory under competition for every manufacturer. On both sides, unheard of development of productive forces, excess of supply, over demand, over production, glutting of the markets, crisis. The vicious circle: excess here, of means of production and products—excess there, of laborers, without employment and without means of existence.

5.1.4 Pace of development of socio—economic formations

The primitive communal system lasted over 1,000,000 years. W here as, the slave holding system—over 10,000 years and the feudal system-over 1000 years. The capitalist system exists 200-300 years. Socialism has been developing faster than capitalism.

5.2 Materials production as the basis of the society's existence and development[184]

Marx discover the law of development of human history: the simple fact, hitherto concealed by an overgrowth of ideology, that mankind must first of all eat, drink, have shelter and clothing, before it can pursue politics, sciences, art, religion, etc. therefore the production of the immediate material means of subsistence and consequently the degree of economic development attained by a given people or during a given epoch form the foundation upon which the state institutions, the legal conceptions, art and even the ideas on religion, of the people concerned have been evolved, and in the light of which they must, therefore, be explained, instead of vice versa, a shad hitherto been the case.

5.2.1 Labor process

The major elements of the labor process are the followings:

1. **Purposeful activity:** Labor is a process in which both man and nature participate and in which man of his own accord starts, regulates, and controls the material reactions between him and nature

2. **Object of labor:** An object of labor is anything at which human labor is directed: the land and the mineral and other resources, plants and animals, diverse materials, etc.

3. **Instruments of labor:** An instrument of labor is a thing, or a complex of things which the laborer interposes between him and the subject of his labor and which serves as the conductor of his activity.

5.2.2 Structure of material production

In production, men enter into relation not only with nature. They produce only by cooperating in a certain way and mutually exchanging their activities.

Mode of production

In mode of production, the relationship between two aspects is in consideration; the productive forces and relation of production

Productive process

Initially it deals Men with production experience, labor skills and knowledge. And finally means of production created by the society.

Relations of production

Production process to consumption has a particular cycle and needs to complete some definite steps.

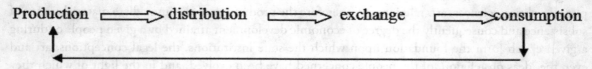

Figure 4 : Steps in Production Process

5.3.3 Types and forms of production relations

Whatever the social form of production, laborers and means of production always remain factors of it. For production to go on at all they must unite. The specific manner in which this union is accomplished distinguishes the different economic epochs of the structure of the society from one another.

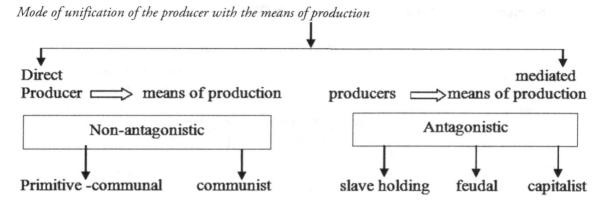

Mode of unification of the producer with the means of production
Direct
Producer means of production
mediated
producers means of production
Non-antagonistic
Antagonistic
Primitive -communal
communist
slave holding
feudal
capitalist

Figure 5 : Types and forms of production relations

5.3.4 Dialectics of development of the productive forces and the relations of production

The productive forces determine the development of the relations of production. A contribution arises and intensifies between the constantly growing productive forces and the relatively stable relations of production. The contradiction is resolved through a replacement of old relations of production with new ones, which corresponds to the growing productive forces. The relations of

Production has an active influence on the development of the productive forces: new ones accelerate and obsolete one obstructs their development.

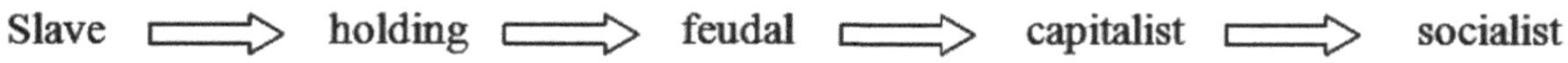

Slave
holding
feudal
capitalist
socialist

Figure 6 : Progressive development of the productive forces

5.3.5 Scientific and Technical Revolution (STR)

Main lines of the STR under socialism

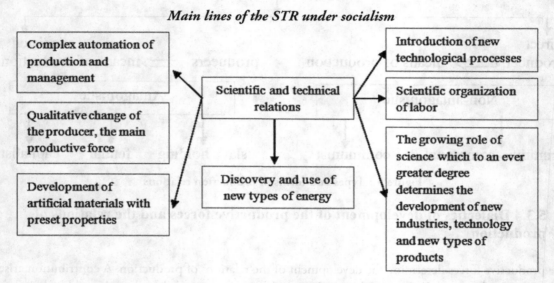

Figure 7 : Main line of the STR under socialism[185]

5.4 Social Structure of the Society[186]

The social structure of a class society based on classes, which exert a decisive influence on the behavior of the other social groups. With a change of the mode of production, the society's social structure changes as well.

5.4.1 Elements of the society's social structure

The totality of classes, social strata and groups and the system of their interrelations constitute the society's social structure. Social groups are large (on the scale of the society as a whole), medium (local), and small. Classes (antagonistic and non—antagonistic) involves:

1.   Ethnic communities, tribe, nationality, nation.
2.   Territorial communities: the inhabitant of a village, town or region.
3.   Family
4.   Special purpose groups: educational, sports.
5.   Primary production unit
6.   Production associations of persons working at one and the same enterprise
7.   Social strata

5.4.2 Emergence of classes

The first great social division of labor, by increasing the productivity of labor that is wealth and enlarging the field of production, necessarily carried slavery in its wake. Out of the first division of labor arose the first great division of society, into two classes: masters and slaves, Exploiters and exploited.

Pre requisites for the emergence of classes

- Emergence of primitive property in the means of production
- Existence of groups of people without any means of production
- Production of a surplus product.

5.4.3 Social class structure of antagonistic societies

According to Marx philosophy social class can be structured as:

Socio economic formation	Main Classes	Other Classes	Social Groups	Declassed Elements
Slave Holding	Slave Owners Slaves	Traders, handicraftsmen		
Feudal	Feudal Lords serfs	Bourgeoisie, handicraftsmen, manufactory workers	Clergy Intelligentsia	Lumpen-proletariat, beggars
Capitalist	Bourgeoisie Proletariat	Land owners, peasant		

Table 5 : Social Class Structure[187]

5.4.4 Main process of proletariat's class struggl

The main process consists of the interrelationship between economic, political and ideological aspects.

Economic	Ideological	Political
Struggle for better terms of selling Labor power: higher wages, shorter working hour, better working conditions	Struggle against the bourgeoisie's spiritual oppressions, to equip the working class with the Marxist Leninist ideology. Which is the theoretical expression of its vital interest.	Struggle against the power of the bourgeoisie and its anti popular policy. For democratic rights and freedoms. For dictatorship of the proletariat, to abolish exploitation

Figure 8 : The interrelationship between economic, political and ideological aspects

5.5 Political organization of the society[18]

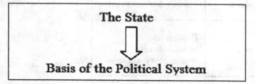

Political Parties   The State   **Social organization**

⇩

Basis of the Political System

Figure 9 : Structure of Society's Political Organization

The society's political organization is formed with the emergence of private property in the means of production and society's division into classes. In the course of historical development, it is complexified and perfected. In the building of socialism and communism, the political organization goes through several stages of development and is gradually converted into communist social self-government.

5.6 Antithesis between Socialist and Bourgeois Ideology

In the modern world, there is a bitter struggle between the two ideologies: communist and bourgeois. That struggle reflects the historical process of transition from capitalism to socialism.

Bourgeois Ideology Socialist Ideology

Totality of political, legal, ethical, aesthetic, philosophical, religious and other views, expressing the fundamental interests of the bourgeoisie an integral and harmonious system of scientific, socio-political, legal, ethical, aesthetic and philosophical views, expressing the vital interests of the working Class and all the other working people.

Bourgeois Ideology	Socialist Ideology
Totality of political, legal, ethical, aesthetic, philosophical, religious and other views, expressing the fundamental interests of the bourgeoisie	An integral and harmonious system of scientific, socio-political, legal, ethical, aesthetic and philosophical views, expressing the vital interest of the working class and all the other working people.

5.7 Marxist Theory in the Context of Bangladesh[189]

5.7.1 Political factors in development planning

1. Evolution of thinking on economic systems and policies of Marxist theory:

The attitude of the ruling party to the choice of economic system and policies in particular, whether to adopt socialism or a mixed economy, can be gauged partly from the election manifesto in 1970, the last election before independence, even the main issue of the election campaign was not the choice of the economic system but the demand for autonomy of East Pakistan.

Economic development policies and problems occupied an important place in the election manifesto and policy announcement of the ruling party before and after the independence. Therefore Awami League's popularity and appeal to the people of Bangladesh, rested on its promise of a higher rate of development expansion of economic opportunities. The Awami League election manifesto in1970 made specific pledge in the sphere of socialistic economic policy as follows:

2. Establishment of a socialistic economy and, and as a first step towards the achievement of this objective, nationalism of banking and insurance companies, jute industries, cotton textile as well as other basic and heavy industries.

The next important step in the enunciation of the fundamental state policies in the economic sphere was the framing of the constitution for an independent Bangladesh in 1972. The constitution reflected the economic objective of Bangladesh, as they were conceived by ruling Awami Party which framed the constitution then. The fundamental principles of the constitution were Democracy, Nationalism,

Secularism, and Socialism. Nationalism and Socialism was the very basis of the creation of the independent state of Bangladesh.

More than any other principle of the state policy it was the principle of the Socialism which had important ramifications in the economic field. The constitution described the essential features of a socialistic society as follows:

- An exploitation free society and emancipation of the toiling masses from all forms of exploitation;
- Equal opportunity for all citizens. 'The state shall adopt effective measures to remove social and economic inequality between man and man need to ensure the equitable distribution of wealth amongst citizens and of opportunities in order to attain a uniform level of economic development throughout the Republic;
- Limitation of private ownership by the means of production of law;
- Parliamentary democracy to the transition to socialism.

The lack of consensus as to the nature of the socialistic economy which Bangladesh should establish in the transition phase as well as in the long run was thus not a matter of differences between the ruling party and the opposition parties, there existed differences of opinion between the factions of the ruling party and among the members of the parliament as well as of the cabinet. The leftist opposition parties did not have the faith in the evolutionary path to the socialism, through prolonged co-existence of the private and public sector, was that so long as the ideological foundations were not changed, and the profit motive remained the prime mover in a large part of the economy, nationalization would be used to promote the interest of the of the private sector because the state apparatus itself was not in the hands of the poor and property less. This was the belief of almost all leftist parties except Pro-Moscow national Awami party.

Question was raised as to whether democracy was consistent with socialism in Bangladesh. So long as socialism was to be achieved through an evolutionary process, by popular will and consensus, democratic institutions were a necessity for the emergence of socialism in Bangladesh.

3. The five year plan and socio-political perspective based on socialism:

It was not only the constitution of Bangladesh and the manifesto of ruling party that attempted to set out the guidelines relating to the future economic system of Bangladesh; the five year plan prepared and published in 1973 also attempted to elaborate the socio-political perspective at length. In fact plan attempted to set forth the socio-political aspect of Bangladesh's future course of economic development on the basis of its understanding of the public announcements political parties in the power. It elaborated the implications of a policy of transition towards socialism which the political leadership accepted as the constitutional goal.

5.8 Industrial policies based on socialism: public versus private sector[190]

1. Nationalization Measures:

In march 1972 the took over public ownership all industrial units abandoned with assests above tk. 1.5 millions; furthermore, while promising to pay compensation, it nationalized all units owned by Bangladeshi citizens in three large scale industries, i.e. cotton textile, jute manufacturing and sugar manufacturing. Before independence, cotton textile, jute and sugar mills were partly owned by Bangladeshi citizens, either singly or jointly with the public sector and partly by Pakistanis; the proportion of total assets owned by Bangladesh nationals is jute and cotton textile industries as 34% and 53% respectively. In other industries Bangladesh private enterprise-which was anyway insignificant compared with that of Pakistan-was unaffected. Before independence, total industrial assets under Pakistani ownership constituted 43% of all industrial assets under private ownership. As a result of nationalization, the share of the public ownership in total industrial assets went up 36% before independence to 86%.

It is a moot question whether Bangladesh so early after independence would have embarked upon such a significant nationalization policy if she had not automatically gained public ownership of a large part of the industrial sector by simply talking over the units left behind by Pakistanis; in any case it acted as a catalytic element.

The extension of public ownership to the abandoned industrial units provided an occasion for series of consideration of the electoral pledge given by the ruling party that heavy or basic industries including jute, cotton and sugar industries would be nationalized. Heavy industries such as iron and steel, fertilizer, heavy chemical, etc. were already placed under public ownership before the emergence of Bangladesh. The electoral pledge before liberation was carried over into the post liberations period. In the objective circum stances of Bangladesh obtaining in the early days of 1972, the opposition to the policy of nationalization was weak; the private vested interest and the nascent industrialists were small, ill organized and mostly on the defensive, given their passive role in the liberation struggle. Moreover, the nationalization of a few Bengali owned enterprises was not considered a heavy burden on a greatly extended public sector caused by the phenomenon of abandoned properties.

2. Limits of private investment and role of socialism

New private investment was to be allowed in units with assets of no more than tk. 2.5 million, which could grow up to tk. 3.5 million through reinvestment of profits. The public sector was however debarred from investing in enterprises with assets below tk. 2.5 million. There was a moratorium for the next ten years on further nationalization of private enterprises, either existing or to be established within the Five-Year Plan period. The basic rationale behind the ceiling was that the private industrialists were not to be allowed to grow into big capitalists through the expansion of the existing enterprises wither by reinvestment of profits or by means of external financing. The expansion of assets of the private industrial units from tk. 2.5 million to tk.3.5 million and no more was considered adequate for meeting their growth objectives. It was presumed that such an expansion financed mainly by the reinvestment of profits would take place mainly in response to technological change and in order to realize economies of scale. Putting the investment in terms of assets rather than employment was also expected to stimulate labor-intensive techniques of production. While there was a limit on the size of an individual enterprise, there was no limit on the number of units a particular individual or groups of individuals could own.

While demarcating the respective roles of public and private investment in 1972, the government recognized that there were alternative ways of achieving such a demarcation. It was possible, for example, to reserve a few selected sectors for public investment, especially those requiring large capital, sophisticated technology and managerial expertise, and the rest could be kept open for private investment. But it was rejected by the government even though there were divergences of opinion in the cabinet on this issue.

In 1972 there was a strong section of opinion in government which visualized the relative roles of public and private enterprise very differently. They conceived the private enterprise as a transitional phenomenon, in the progress towards the socialist transformation phenomenon, in the progress towards the socialist transformation of the economy. In this view, to prevent the growth of large scale industrial bourgeoisie was an essential component of the policy of pre-empting the growth of anti-socialist forces in the future. A few, if not all, within the policy making circles, felt that any opportunity for private and public enterprises to co-exist in the field of large scale industry, either independently or as joint enterprises, would keep the door open for the pressure of anti-socialist forces, i.e. pressure by private industrialist themselves for the expansion of the scope of private investment. Moreover, private interest groups in the field of industry could in turn become a lobbying force for the expanded role of private enterprise in the other sectors of economy. Within this vision of the future economic system, the ceiling on the size of private investment was set so as to allow it only limited opportunities in the sector of small-scale and cottage industries.

3. Private foreign investment and socialism

The attitude towards domestic private enterprise, as enunciated in the industrial policy statement in 1972, determined in turn the policy towards foreign investment. Foreign direct investment was only allowed in collaboration with the public sector corporations and only with minority equity participation of 49% or below. However, no specific field of activity was excluded from participation by foreign investors; public enterprise could invite foreign collaboration in any field. All acts of foreign collaboration however were to be approved by the government. The exclusion of foreign private enterprise from partnership with domestic private interest was designed to forestall the possibility of a powerful pressure group being created for the expansion of the private sector. In particular this might have created pressure for the upward revision of the ceiling on private investment, since small scale investment industries were unlikely, in view of their requirements of capital and technology, to attract private foreign investment. Since Bangladesh is too heavily dependent on liberal economic assistance from rich capitalist countries, pressure for a change in domestic policy could gain added strength. Restricting the association of foreign private investors with the public corporations was expected to contain the influence and reduce the pressure, which might be potentially exercised by foreign interests on the domestic economy and policy, while at the same time allowing Bangladesh to secure access to technology and capital. A large public corporation would also have bargaining power in its negotiation with the foreign investors, which would far exceed that of small, private domestic enterprises competing for or seeking foreign collaboration.

Subsequent discussion with potential foreign investors revealed that they were less worried about compulsory participation with the public corporations than about the requirement of their majority participation. Exclusion of private domestic investors from joint participation was seen by them, more than anything else, as reflection of an unfriendly and unfavorable attitude of the Bangladesh government towards private enterprise in general and, therefore, by implication and at least potentially, towards foreign private investment.

The domestic private investors, on their side, felt that the willingness of the public sector to accept foreign, but not domestic, private investors as partners, was an inconsistent policy and was an act of discrimination against them.

4. Management of nationalized industries

The appropriate institutional framework of and the policy guidelines for the nationalized industries was a matter of continuing debate and discussion in Bangladesh. The basic question underlying the debate related to the optimum degree of autonomy to be enjoyed by the nationalized industries in their investment and production decisions. The most important aspect of the management of the nationalized enterprises was the relationship between the Ministry of Industry and sector corporations.

There is the need to deal with competing labor unions, linked up with conflicting political parties, as well as the need to contain the demands for increased wages and improved conditions of work.

The Five-Year plan advocated decentralized administrative structure for the nationalized industries; it conceived of the ministry of industry as performing the task of coordination and evaluation.

- Present constitution of Bangladesh and the role of socialism[191]

The constitution of Bangladesh which was first declared in 1972 was changed in 1978. And this changed constitution still exists. In the present constitution full dependence on Allah, social and economic development takes place instead of secularism and socialism. So the present constitution is as follows:

1. Full dependence on Allah
2. Nationalism
3. Democracy
4. Social and economic development

So by constitution we can say that Bangladesh is no more following socialism.

- Land reform and role of bourgeois class

Compared to the land area, the population of Bangladesh is huge, and the vast majority live in poverty, super-exploited by the bourgeois class, itself under the direct control of imperialism. The low level of industrializations has kept nearly 90% of the people in the countryside, where lack of infrastructure of all kinds means everyday existence is a struggle.

Land reform is a well-discussed issue in Bangladesh, yet a solution to the problem has proved elusive. Over the last few hundred years the toiling masses have repeatedly tried to build movements to overthrow the landowners, which for lack of political ideology and organization have ended mostly in defeat. The rare instances of success have led merely to a reconstitution of the rural tyranny.

Political parties of all shades in Bangladesh raise the slogan of land reform. Real progress on this question would have a great impact on the lives of the toiling masses in this country. But the bourgeois parties try to fool people with promises of land reform when elections draw near. Time and again it is shown to be nothing more than cynical manipulation of a rural population desperate for change.

Since 1971 all the governments of Bangladesh have introduced some sort of land reform programme, at least on paper. But in most cases land turned over for this purpose has ended up in the hands of rich landowners, a result of corruption, unwieldy bureaucracy and the poverty of the landless. The failure of bourgeois land reform proves our prognosis that land reform cannot be carried out without nationalization of the land under the direct control of urban and agrarian workers. The eviction of the bourgeois forces from power is the necessary first step to carry out land nationalization.

The Bangladesh Landless Association (BLA) has been involved in the movement for land reform over the last two decades. We stand for revolutionary change in land ownership, administration and use. Land must be managed with the aim of ensuring the welfare of the majority of the population, in an ecologically sustainable way. The present exploitative and discriminatory system of land ownership must be replaced with equitable ownership, as well as equitable distribution of agricultural products. For more effective utilization of arable land, improvements have to be made in agricultural infrastructure, including mechanization, irrigation, pest control and natural disaster mitigation schemes. Local communities, organized in a transparent, democratic manner, must have control over agricultural investment for maximum efficiency.

The agrarian question is bound up with the democratic and national issues, all historically bourgeois questions. However in the imperialist epoch it is no longer possible to fully resolve these questions under capitalism. The military, political and economic dependence of the semi-colonies, their backwardness and economic unevenness, are fundamental to the imperialist world order. There can be no separate stage of agrarian revolution in which the capitalist class could carry out the progressive reform of land.

Recent history shows that, in many parts of the world, the bourgeois nationalists have proved unwilling to take any radical measures, which could threaten their alliance with semi-feudal landlords or big capitalist farmers, when faced with demands for a comprehensive solution to land hunger. Any major land reforms that have been introduced—in Bolivia, Peru, and Punjab in India—have always been in order to side-track a revolutionary solution to the question. The reformist solution to land hunger can only temporarily quieting the calls for land reform. In effect, the measures carried out have simply created a new layer of small peasants—in need of credit and machinery—that has fallen into the hands of usurers, banks and rich farmers.

The most desperate group in the countryside are the landless peasants, or agri-laborers, robbed of their inheritance by the oligarchy, colonial planter and "green revolution" alike. Today there are over 600 million landless peasants in the semi-colonies. In Bangladesh, Pakistan and India, between a quarter and a half of the rural population are landless and in Central America over half is landless. Most face severe privations, a situation relieved occasionally by day or seasonal labor. Many migrate to the towns in the hopeless search for work. These people constitute a necessary ally of the proletariat.

5.9 Collectivism and Individualism in Industrial Relations

'Industrial relations consist of a web of institutionalized relationships between employees and their representatives (trade unions), employers and their representatives (employers' association), and the state . . . The relations exist on different levels and between different actors.' This definition includes further aspects of industrial relations: the relationships are considered as institutionalized and ongoing on several levels, and the state is mentioned as a third actor.

From various definitions of industrial relations we can identify the areas cover by the subject:[192]

- Processes of control over work relations and regulations of interests;
- Web of institutionalized relationships between actors, organizations and institutions;

- Collective relations;
- Different actors (employees and representatives/employers and representatives) and arenas;
- Different levels of industrial relations and interplay between them;
- Legal and institutional framework and public policies;
- Cooperative and conflictual relationships;
- Industrial relations as social, economic, political and cultural relations;
- Diversity between existing national models; and
- New supranational industrial relations.

This relationship can be identified from the diagram below:[193]

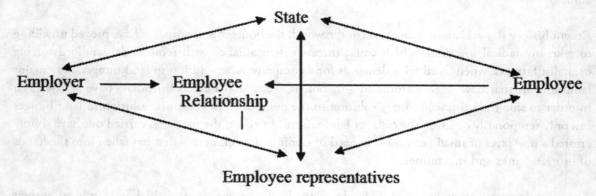

Figure 10 : The employment relationship

Industrial Relations have been studied using different angles. Explaining it is crucial to identify the dynamics that will dominate the behavior between workers, employers and regulators. It has been influenced by different things e.g. industry type, development stage of the country, structure of the relationship, political system, education etc.

We have seen at least five perspectives that have tried to make a sense out of the field:[194]

a) Unitary and its neo-unitary variant
b) The conflict-pluralist
c) The social action
d) The system
e) The Marxist

Each of these has its own set of underlying assumptions about human behavior. There is little relationship between one another. Important thing is to find out "The One" theory that will answer to all our need or at least explain the dynamics that is governing the interaction found in industry.

6.0 Unitary Theory

In unitarism, the organization is perceived as an integrated and harmonious whole with the ideal of "one happy family", where management and other members of the staff all share a common purpose, emphasizing mutual cooperation. Furthermore, unitarism has a paternalistic approach where it demands loyalty of all employees, being predominantly managerial in its emphasis and application.

Consequently, trade unions are deemed as unnecessary since the loyalty between trade unions and organizations are considered mutually exclusive, where there can't be two sides of industry. Conflict is perceived as disruptive and the pathological result of agitators, interpersonal friction and communication breakdown.

If we consider traditional Unitary Theory, we can see that it provides an ideal world scenario where everything is all right. In more specific terms industrial relation stability exists and conflict is absent. It views society's organization as orderly and stable mechanism that are instilled with senses of common purpose and a value consensus which are shared and supported by all the members of organization. It does not accept that there is competition and conflict between those seeking the control and allocation of limited and scarce resources in work enterprises and in society. Industrial relations exist to advance what are perceived to be the common goals of management and subordinate employees through mutual cooperation at work. At the same time management has the exclusivity to make the decision relating to everything. The theory justifies the considerable differentials and inequalities in income, status and power which exist between managers and non managerial employees. It provides a major source of support for managers and a sense of security for the subordinates with its underlying assumption of enlightened managerialism and conflict free industrial relations.

This view underlay much taken-for-granted managerial thinking about everyone in an enterprise having shared goals, and also underpinned several academic approaches, notably the 'human relations' tradition.[195] Unitarism was often used as a straw man representing old-fashioned and unrealistic ideas, but surveys found that many managers continued to believe in a harmony of interest, and, as should already be clear, a resurgence of managerial self-confidence and a reassertion of market individualism underpinned a revival of unitarism from the 1980s. During the 1990s, HRM often implied that management was the sole or at least key authority.

	Personnel and IR HRM	*Personnel and IR HRM*
Nature of relations	Pluralist	Unitarist
Conflict	Institutionalized	De-emphasized
Labor Management	Collective bargaining contracts	Towards individual contracts
Thrust of relations with stewards	Regularized through facilities and training	Marginalized

Table 6 : HRM and the management of labor[196]

HRM	High skills and commitment, direct communication with workforce, managerially led agenda
Unitarist social partnership	Similar to HRM, plus systems for employee consultation, agenda still managerially led
Pluralist social partnership	As above, but more independent voice for workers organized as a collectivity (in practice in a trade union)

Table 7 : Different Viewpoints[197]

Bangladesh Context:

As with the world trend unitarialism emerge in Bangladesh around 1990s. The wave of privatization that we have seen in the country during the 70s and 80s has finally reached its peak at that period. With the opening up of different sectors of the country we see a radical change in the way amongst the relationship that dominates industry. More flexibility in parts of the labor was apparent as more private sector venture starts to dominate the scene. Rather than following the previous years destructive path we started to see change in the viewpoint. The theory became dominant throughout the 90s and took dominant position during with the turn of millennium. But in recent years we can see that a tendency to return back to older years conflict viewpoint with the hassle relating to minimum wage and worker's right issues.

6.1 Conflicts-Pluralistic Theory

In pluralism the organization is perceived as being made up of powerful and divergent sub-groups, each with its own legitimate loyalties and with their own set of objectives and leaders. In particular, the two predominant sub-groups of in the pluralistic perspective are the management and trade unions.

Consequently, the role of management would lean less towards enforcing and controlling and more toward persuasion and co-ordination. Trade unions are deemed as legitimate representatives of employees, conflict is dealt by collective bargaining and is viewed not necessarily as a bad thing and if managed could in fact be channeled towards evolution and positive change.

An alternative view can be found in Conflict-Pluralistic Theory. The basic argument here is diverse pressure groups, pursuing their own self-interest through intergroup negotiation and compromise, are a basic feature of our society. The key goal of society's industrial relations institutions is to resolve conflict within and between different organizational and employment interest groups. Industrial relations focus on collective ad representative relations between employers and employee organization. It is a pragmatic interpretation of society and of its power relations but it does not necessarily justify them. The weakest and at the same time the strongest element in the industrial conflict and pluralist position is, somewhat paradoxically, its attempt to avoid absolute moral value judgments.

Pluralists see conflict as inevitable because, to cite Clegg (1979:1),[198] various organizations participate in determining the rules of employment. These have their own bases of authority, and 'whenever there are separate sources of authority there is the risk of conflict'.

Pluralism was particularly salient in the approach of management: instead of a unitary denial that there was any rational basis for conflict, managers should recognize the inevitability of disputes and seek means to regulate them. In Flanders's (1970: 1972)[199] oft-quoted dictum, 'the paradox, whose truth managements have found it so difficult to accept, is that they can only regain control by sharing it'.

Bangladesh Context

This theory became dominant after the Second World War. Everywhere around the world we see its effect, Bangladesh was no exception. After the independence this viewpoint regains its popularity and played a dominant role in governing the relationship of the industry. The industrial policies of those times prove the fact. The paternalistic view of the state with the wave of nationalization is two incidents that enabled the view to flourish.

6.2 Social Action Theory

Key contribution of Social Action Theory in industrial relations is the importance attached to individual managers and actions in work relationship. The relations covered here are inter-managerial relationships, relationships between managers and union representatives, amongst union representatives and between union representatives and their members. The industrial worker's own definitions of their work situations are taken as the basis for explaining their behavior and relationships. It emphasizes the relevance of individual actors in perceiving the nature of their work, in making personal choices, in interacting with others, and in taking industrial relations decisions. The action of industrial relations participants are not viewed as being determined solely by their structural constraints within which they operate, but by the expectations ad values of the individual actors and the meaning they assign to particular industrial relations situations.

6.3 System Theory

System Theory emphasizes on the diverse form of industrial relations rules in existence, the different rule-making methods, and the ways in which rules are applied. Its key contribution comes in the form of identification of the variety of industrial relations variables and the complex ways in which they interact. By focusing in the 'outputs' or rules of industrial relations systems, on their 'processes' such as the collective bargaining and other types of rule making and on their 'inputs' actors involved in rule making, systems theory provides a useful framework for classifying and describing the elements within any industrial relations structure. The major drawback here is it is a static theory from which it is difficult to explain industrial relations changes. Key criticism of the theory is by concentrating on the structure rather than upon change, it does not necessarily justify the existing social order when it is used as a tool to analyze and describe an industrial relations structure.

6.4 Marxist Theory

This view of industrial relations looks the nature of the capitalist society, where there is a fundamental division of interest between capital and Labor, and sees workplace relations against this background. This perspective sees inequalities of power and economic wealth as having their roots in the nature of the capitalist economic system. Conflict is therefore seen as inevitable and trade unions are a natural response of workers to their exploitation by capital. Whilst there may be periods of acquiescence, the Marxist view would be that institutions of joint regulation would enhance rather than limit management's position as they presume the continuation of capitalism rather than challenge it.[200]

One of the strongest features of Marxist Theory is its dynamic approach to industrial relations and its explanations of its inner logic and of social change. With its strong moral condemnation of capitalist values and its rejection of the ethics of liberal political economy, Marxist theory is overtly subjective and critical about industrial relations in what it describes as capitalist societies. In practical terms the strength of Marxism as a means of interpreting industrial relations is that it provides a theoretical perspective which not only analyses what is perceived as social reality, but also rejects it on moral grounds and suggests means from changing it. Marxist theory focuses the inherent class nature of liberal democracies-which is particularly reflected in their industrial relations institutions—it provides a useful analytical tool for understanding those conflicts in industrial relations deriving from competing class and power interests at work and in society.

From Collectivism to Individualism

The above discussion hopefully gives a grasp of the main theoretical approaches to analyzing industrial relations. By analyzing the past trends it can be concluded that the dominant doctrine during the 1960s and 1970s was conflict theory and pluralism. It was in fact the consensus model of industrial relations broadly accepted by management, especially in the large corporate and public sectors, by the trade unions and by successive governments as a matter of public policy. Classical unitarism was prevalent in small-scale private businesses; it took the form of a niche. Neo-unitary approaches to industrial relations were virtually limited to some USA and Japanese firms. But with the 1980s, pluralist and collectivist perceptions of industrial relations begin to lose its dominance. It began to be sidetracked as the preferred frame of reference in the determination of government policy on industrial relations. In short, in the 1980s and 1990s the theory got challenged first by, softer form of pluralism (no-strike agreements, and single union recognition) second by, renascent unitary and individualist ideas. The following diagram explains the different stance that the management can take while governing over the relationship that is going to decide upon industry dynamics.

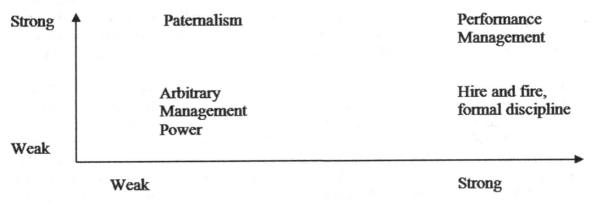

Figure 11 : Status and contract[201]

Unitary perception of industrial relations, by contrast, is distinctly managerial in orientation and emphasis. They reinforce managerial values and organizational norms in the work situation. They are therefore aimed at legitimizing the right to manage and the freedom to manage within organizations, without the intervention and intrusion of unions and their representatives in the processes of industrial relations. The values insist the handling of subordinates by management through the use of authoritarian or paternalist styles of management. Alternatively, neo-unitary or human resource management results in the application of manipulative or reward centered styles of managing employees. These seek to incorporate employees as individuals within the enterprises in which they work, by getting their commitment to organizational goals and objectives, whilst aiming at a homogeneous corporate culture with which all employees can identify.

It's quite apparent that the major contrasts in industrial relations theory at present are between pluralist and unitary theory. Whilst pluralist theory was the dominant intellectual and policy emphasis in industrial relations in the period up to the mid-1980s, unitary theory has seemed to enjoy some degree of renaissance during the late 1980s and early 1990s. In addition the pluralist theory comes closely in allied with systems and conflict theory and is traditionally associated with a number of specific features of political economy. The features include: consensus politics, demand-management economic policies, bipartisan public policy on industrial relations, tripartite relations amongst government, employers and unions and collectivism in industrial relations. Unitarism in contrast is more closely allied with social action theory and human relations management theory. The main features in work here: conviction politics, supply-side economic policies, partisan public policy on industrial relations, collective bargaining, market led wage determination and market economy and employee relations individualism.

One of the most widely cited perspectives on individualism and collectivism comes from the consideration of cross-national cultural differences by Hofstede (1984).[202] Hofstede saw individualist cultures as placing priority on personal goals and self-actualization, whereas collectivist cultures place priorities on the family and group, and seek satisfaction from a job well done as defined by the group rather than by oneself. People in collectivist cultures are especially concerned with relationships; those in individualistic societies give priority to their own goals over those of groups (Triandis 2001:909).[203]

A closely related concept to that of collectivism is 'social capital', defined by Robert Putnam (1995:67)[204] as referring to 'features of social organization such as networks, norms and social trust that facilitate coordination and cooperation for mutual benefit'. The link to collectivism is seen in Earley and Gibson's comment that 'individualism-collectivism refers to the social connectedness among individuals' (1998:266).[205] Putnam uses a wide range of indicators for social capital, including participation in conventional voluntary associations (including 'such diverse organizations as the PTA, the Elks club, the League of Women Voters, the Red Cross, labor unions, and even bowling leagues' (Putnam 1996);[206] measures of 'collective political participation', including attending a rally or speech, attending a meeting on town or school affairs, or working for a political party; and opinion poll data on 'social trust'.

While there is a substantial body of research examining collectivism and individualism in cultural and psychological studies (see Earley & Gibson 1998; Triandis 2001),[207] there is relatively little research integrating these broader notions of collectivism with industrial relations. Kelly and Kelly (1994, cited in Earley & Gibson 1998) indicated that collectivist orientations predicted participation in a wide range of union activities. Ilmonen and Jukiviori (2000:140, citing Zoll 1993 and Lash & Urry 1994)[208] indicate that it has been argued that 'cultural individualization has a great influence on the relationship between unions and their members'. They argue that 'One of the central consequences of individualization is the weakening of people's bonds to, for example, their families, birthplaces, traditions and social groups such as Labor unions.' (2000:138). As mentioned, Putnam (1995&1996) included (the decline of) union membership in the US as an indicator of (the decline of) social capital in that country. Jarley and Johnson (2003)[209] urge unions to adopt a 'social capital' approach to unionism as a means of redressing union decline, while Bailey and Brown (2004)[210] also critically examine the concept of unions as social capital. If, however, any decline of collectivism in industrial relations is due to wider shifts in society away from collectivism, then we should, as a minimum be able to identify declines in collectivism in society more generally—though this in itself would not indicate a causal link.

6.5 Dimensions of Collectivism and Individualism in Industrial Relations

While the broader social notions of collectivism discussed above provide important context, our focus in this report is on collectivism in industrial relations. Here, the central concept in the collectivist model is that of collective bargaining. Collective bargaining 'is the method of fixing the terms of employment and settling grievances arising from those terms by negotiation between union(s) and employer(s)' (Isaac 1958: 348).[211] Definitions of collective bargaining commonly refer back to Flanders (1970:41),[212] who described collective bargaining as also being 'a rule-making process'. Through collective bargaining, unions are 'interested in regulating wages as well as raising them; and, of course, in regulating a wide range of other issues pertaining to their members' jobs and working lives.' In turn, a trade union is 'a continuous association of wage-earners for the purpose of maintaining or improving the conditions of their working lives' (Webb & Webb 1920).[213]

Collective bargaining arises because of an imbalance in the power of employers (typically, collectively organized shareholders) and individual employees (e.g. Fox 1974:28).[214] The making of individual employment contracts is the antithesis of collective bargaining.

However, individual contracts do not equate to 'individual employment arrangements'. Unfortunately there is a degree of imprecision in the use of the term 'individualism' when referring to employment arrangements, arising from the different definitions adopted by various people, the different concepts to which the term may be used to refer and the conflation of meanings in some rhetoric.

There are four areas in which individualism and collectivism in employment relations arrangements can be assessed.

Collective bargaining arises because of an imbalance in the power of employers (typically, collectively organized shareholders) and individual employees (e.g. Fox 1974:28). The making of individual employment contracts is the antithesis of collective bargaining.

6.5.1 'Procedural individualization' or 'individualism in industrial relations'

Brown et al (1998:i)[215] defined 'procedural individualization' as referring to 'the removal of collective mechanisms for determining terms and conditions of employment'. This corresponds to what Storey and Bacon describe as individualism in the area of 'industrial relations'. They cite three major indicators of collectivism in industrial relations: central management orientations towards unions, employee orientations towards unions, and collective bargaining, i.e. 'the extent to which managers recognize the collective basis for industrial relations'. Where these are low then procedural individualism exists: the making of 'individual contracts' is an exemplar of procedural individualism. The central element of procedural individualism is the use of 'individual contracts'. These need to be distinguished from contracts of employment.

6.5.2 'Substantive individualization' or 'individualism in personnel/HR'

Brown et al (1998:i) define 'substantive individualization' as referring to 'the differentiation of individual employees' employment contracts'. That is, substantive individualization occurs where there is differentiation in employees' pay and non-pay terms and conditions of employment. Similarly, Storey and Bacon refer to individualism in the personnel or 'human resource' aspects of management strategy. Like Brown et al, they focus on the nature of the pay system, terms and conditions but they also add 'culture' to the list (arguably, inappropriately). An individualistic HR system would involve performance-related pay, a high number of temporary workers, divergent terms and conditions and low identification with common symbols, myths and values. A collective HR system would have a pay system which valued tenure and rates for the job, high job security, permanence of contract, converging terms and conditions and (in Storey and Bacon's model) high identification with the myths, symbols and values of the workplace (Storey & Bacon 1993:675)[216]

6.5.3 'Functional individualization' or 'Individualism in work organization'

Storey and Bacon also refer to collectivism and individualism in work organization, and focus on the technical and social organization of work, control over features of job operation and relationship to authority. Hence a workplace that has collective organization of work would be characterized by teamwork, a low division of Labor, low job segmentation, group-based joint regulation, and high involvement in management decisions providing a collective distribution of authority. Individualistic organization of work would feature isolated working, high division of Labor, infrequent job rotation, and low involvement in managerial decisions among lower grade staff (Storey & Bacon 1993:675). It is convenient to refer to this dimension as 'functional individualism'.

6.5.4 'Culturist collectivism': corporate culture and collective ties to the organization

As mentioned, Storey and Bacon include 'culture' in their list of elements of collectivism/individualism in HR, while Brown et al exclude it from their otherwise analogous list of elements of 'substantive' individualism or collectivism. Analytically, the approach of Brown et al seems preferable, as the other elements of this category (pay and conditions) and conceptually similar to each other but distinct from organizational culture—'the set of shared, taken-for-granted implicit assumptions that a group holds and that determines how it perceives, thinks about and reacts to its various environments' (Schein 1996:236).[217] It also enables a link to Hofstede's analysis of collectivism to be drawn, as Hofstede's dimension of individualism/ collectivism refers in part to the whether and how much people see themselves as dependent on a group such as the organization.

6.6 Bangladesh Perspective

Despite a short industrial history, Labor-management relations have undergone several changes in Bangladesh. The major characteristics of Labor-management relations in Bangladesh are as follows:[218]

(i) Lack of requisite leadership.

(ii) Lack of scientific management system.

(iii) Absences of necessary delegation of power to plant management of public sector enterprises.

(iv) Lack of proper education and training to management and working groups.

(v) Greater influence of politics in trade unionism.

(vi) Violation of Labor laws both by the management and workers.

(vii) Lack of pro-labor approach by the management.

(viii) Absence of a sense of belongings.

(ix) Irrational wages structure.

(x) Absence of a matured industrial workforce on the one hand and industrial entrepreneurs on the other hand. In the former case the workforce is only one generation old and in the later case entrepreneurs.

(xi) Absence of mutual trust and respect between management and trade union and

(xii) Inadequate communication system.

Bangladesh Labor Code 2006 provides for regulation of trade union activities (including strikes and lockouts), the relations between employers and workers, and the avoidance and settlement of any differences and disputes arising between them. Despite the existence of such a legal framework, industrial relations in Bangladesh are frequently confrontational and at times politically motivated. This is most notable in the case of particular state-owned enterprises. The confrontational character of relations makes it difficult to engage in effective collective bargaining. It is estimated that over 60 per cent of loss of working hours is due to political factors, while the remaining 40 per cent can be attributed to economic reasons. There is also reluctance on the part of employers, trade unions and the government to accept responsibility for what has gone wrong, to identify solutions and to co-operate for the effective functioning of the industrial relations system. As such, further participation of all three partners is required to narrow differences and provide effective fora for consultations and collective decision making. This requires high levels of political commitment, strengthening of tripartite institutions, encouragement of collective bargaining processes, and reform of the Labor law.

In general though the employers in Bangladesh recognize the necessity of Labor-management cooperation for productivity improvement, yet they think that non-cooperation of workers is the main cause of low Labor productivity. They strongly feel that wage fixation should be done at the plant level and it should be linked to productivity. Accordingly to them, political determination and commitment is necessary to relate wages to productivity. They demand that government should take necessary steps to maintain proper law and order situation for undisturbed production process. Further they demand that trade unions should not be affiliated to the political parties, so that trade unions can pay more attention to the matters related to the total economic welfare of the industry which can benefit both workers and the employers.

The Trade Unions in Bangladesh judge the role of management as a negative one. They consider the management unfair, greedy and reluctant to accept trade unions as a positive social force but only as an inevitable evil. All these factors have resulted in mistrust, antagonism and even estrangement. Low level of wages is considered one of the major causes of abnormal Labor-management relations and low productivity. The trade unions consider the existing Labor laws inadequate, faulty and ineffective; the state apparatus interferes in every dispute. Adjudication takes time, and conciliation and arbitration are arbitrary.

In important aspect of government's labor relations policy is to take steps to increase industrial production and productivity. It is necessary to create congenial environment in which labor and management works in the basis of identify of interest and unity of purpose. In the regard the Government of Bangladesh has taken a series of steps through legislation and institutional arrangement.

The Government of Bangladesh has announcement its latest labor policy in March 1980. The basic objective of the said policy is to ensure, in consonance with the fundamental principles of the constitution of the country, healthy labor relations needed for increased production and overall national economic development for improving the conditions as well as the standard of living of the people. The salient features of the above Labor policy are:

(i) Tripertism.
(ii) Productivity and Incentives.
(iii) Distribution of fair wages and development of manpower resources through education and training.
(iv) Industrial relations.
(v) Labor relations.
(vi) Amendment and adaptation of labor laws.

Technological changes also have an impact on industrial activity. Its impact on employment is an important short-term economic aspect of automation. Installation of a large number of automatic machines at the same time may create serious problems of unemployment, because by introducing auto system the number of workers for the same output is likely to be less. One of the growing problems in Bangladesh is large-scale unemployment and under-employment. Cottage and small-scale industries, which are labor-intensive, provide large-scale employment. In this connection the government of Bangladesh is fully aware of the situation and has taken steps to the effect that in the application of advanced techniques of production, adequate care is taken to see that the traditional labor intensive sector which provides employment to a large labor force continues to exist.

CHAPTER V

Cox's Model

CONTENTS

1.0 Introduction

'Industrial Relations' is defined by Robert W. Cox as 'social relations in production' in his research project on future industrial relations. According to him the traditional definitions of industrial relations were too narrow or specific to be useful to an enquiry of universal scope which needed a definition capable of including all forms of labor everywhere in the world. Thus the concept 'social relations in production' covers all form of economic activity or production and all forms of labor relationship regardless of the presence, absence or variety, of formal organizations.

1.1 Dimensions of Industrial Relations Systems

As Industrial relations are defined as "Social relations in production", at the outset of an inquiry of world-wide scope of industrial relations, it was obvious that there are many different kinds of social relations in production. So the techniques adopted by Cox, to reduce the variety of systems to manageable proportions has been to identify criteria of classification which will permit development of a set of broad types of social relations in production of models. Thus a useful classification was expected to cover all existing forms of social relations in production.

Four basic criteria have been used in making a classification and each of these classifications have also been revised and a relevancy analysis is done from the perspective of the labor, social, political and historical perspective of Bangladesh. The criteria's are: a) **The technological context of production:** Very broadly, there is a distinction between patterns of relations based upon a primitive technology, and those characteristics of modern technology. Technology as used here includes organization.

As in Bangladesh, when our farmers still use cows to plough their land in food production, we don't include them under our labor force. At the same time, when people are making food items (such as beverages, chips, canned food, tea) in our modern factories, we call them labor and they are part of our big labor force. b) **The power relations of the parties:** The degree of worker organization is a crucial factor in enhancing worker control over decisions: thus systems in which workers enter the labor market as individuals are to be distinguished from those in which they organize collectively in trade unions.

In Bangladesh, the power relations can be viewed in three different phases. When a daily labor works on hourly basis (say he/she removes soil on the site of building construction), he/she has no power for negotiation. Hence there is no party here.

Again in the case of rickshaw puller or CNG driver, they have to give a certain amount of money to their 'Mohajon' but they have the right to work independently and keep the rest of the earned money as their income. They can freely negotiate with their clients. Their 'Mohajon' is only concerned about the certain amount of money they pay him. Hence two parties are here.

Next comes the labors works in the factories and participate in production. Here comes the interaction of three parties—workers, management and the Government. None of them entirely enjoys power. Rather they share power. c) **The domain of decisions:** Some systems function primarily at the enterprise level, others organize decision-making at broader levels for groups of enterprises, e.g. for a whole industry or geographical area. A third group, the most complex systems, functions simultaneously at several levels, from the enterprise to the national level, taking different kinds of decisions at different levels while attempting to coordinate all levels of decision-making. The latter can be called integrated systems of decision-making. d) **Relationship to the political system:** This concerns the degree to which the industrial relations system is subordinated to the political system or is autonomous in relation to it. At one extreme, the industrial relations system is but one aspect of the political system (and can be designated appropriately by the same name as the political system); at the other, the industrial relations system has little connection with the political system. In intermediate situations, there is a good deal of interrelationship between the two systems.

1.2 Classification of Industrial Relations

Eleven broad types of social relations in production have been defined covering the gamut of existing systems:

1. Subsistence system
2. Peasant—Lord System
3. Primitive Labor Market System
4. Enterprise labor Market
5. Enterprise-corporatist System
6. Bipartite system
7. Tripartite system
8. State corporatism
9. Mobilizing system
10. Socialist system
11. Self—employed

1.3 Subsistence System

1.4 Characteristics

- Peasant economies where family units produce mainly for their own consumption limited specialization in artisan products products exchanged on a local basis primitive technology of production family units are largely independent of hierarchical economic authority

1.5 Approaches

The anthropological study of subsistence, often termed cultural ecology, covers the basic tools, techniques, and organizational arrangements (technology) that people have developed to obtain food and other material resources from their natural surroundings (environment).

The 3 most important terms related to the system are:

1. Cultural Evolution—emphasis on general subsistence types depending on technologies of food production.
2. Cultural Ecology—emphasis on adaptation to local environments through use of technology and patterns of social organization.
3. Indigenous Knowledge Systems—emphasis on local systems of classifying, utilizing, and managing environmental resources.

The subsistence system of social relations in production is widely spread, appearing in 106 countries or territories out of 153, the main areas of its incidence are in Africa, low economic growth Asian countries and to a lesser extent in Latin America and the Caribbean. Most densely populated peasant societies form part of large markets and cannot be considered as subsistence systems.

Subsistence system has some major disadvantages. If social relations are seen as determining work rules and return to producers, then the subsistence system is almost out of definition. The level of return depends on three basic factors which are:

1. Quality and size of land
2. Technology of production and
3. Climatic conditions.

The subsistence system is different from others in that it is politically inert. The main reason behind this is the isolation and independence of labor within the system. Changes occurring in the subsistence system are therefore a function of changes occurring in elsewhere. Thus land reform or commercialization of agriculture invariably results in a network of social relations transforming former subsistence farmers into peasants tied to a market. The number of workers in the system is, therefore, decreasing.

Social conflict is virtually impossible within the system, but the individual bitterness, frustration and disappointment which arises from subsistence experience may be an important factor in conflict situations arising in other systems.

In overall view, this is a naturally declining system in both relative and absolute terms. Population increase cannot be absorbed by subsistence farming except by extending to new land which is not likely to be available. Almost any change, economic or technological, will propel those involved into the peasant—lord and primitive labor market relationships. Political changes could incorporate subsistence farmers into mobilizing systems.

1.6 Reviews in the Context of Bangladesh

In Bangladesh, the subsistence system is not much seen in practice. It primarily is because in subsistence system, family units produce for their own consumption. But in Bangladesh, production is done for market rather than for personal consumption. Though peasant economy is the base of subsistence system, it also has limited specialization. In subsistence system, products are exchanged on a local basis, which is not common incident in Bangladesh. Here it is exchanged both in local as well as international basis. Of the two, the international basis should be considered prime because of its significant contribution to the country's economy. The technology used for production in subsistence system is primitive. Technology for production in Bangladesh is not latest, but at the same time, it is not entirely primitive. Day by day, more and more latest technological equipments are getting introduced for production. Again in the subsistence system, families are largely independent of hierarchical economic authority. But in Bangladesh, now-a-days, it is not quite the case. Now-a-days, there is a thin line of difference in families on the basis of economical authority. This can more be referred to a change in the social infrastructure.

Agricultural sector dominates Bangladesh economy in terms of contribution to national income as well as employment. In subsistence system primitive technology is used in production. But in the recent times the primitive technology is no more in use in agricultural production.

More than two-thirds of the labor force depends on agriculture for employment. Bangladesh's export mainly consists of jute, jute goods, and tea. Crop production dominates Bangladesh agriculture accounting for more than 60% of agricultural value added in 1993/94. Alauddin and Tisdell (1991) noted that if supporting activities like transport and marketing of agricultural products are taken into account, the share of agricultural sector GDP is likely to be over 60% of total. Within the crop sub-sector, food grain production is central to the economy dominated by rice monoculture. About 80% of the gross cropped area is planted with rice which accounts for about 93% of total cereal production.[219] In recent times, wheat is also gaining importance though its coverage remained extremely low.

Over the past thirty years, the major development influence in Bangladesh agriculture has been the introduction of "green revolution" technologies. This bio-chemical "land-saving" technology which transformed much of the Asian region were introduced at a relatively later stage (during the late 1960s) and at a much slower pace.[220]

Though the basic aim of agricultural development policies over the last four decades remained at increased food production, the program components underwent vast changes shifting from one category to the other. In the early 1960s, flooding during the monsoon and lack of irrigation facilities during the dry periods was identified as the major constraints hindering use of modern agricultural inputs. As such, the government aimed at building large scale irrigation and drainage facilities.[221] In the late 1960s, when major thrust was given in promoting "green revolution", the program strategies shifted from building large scale irrigation installations to more divisible and modern techniques of irrigation (e.g., shallow tube well (STWs), deep tube wells (DTWs) and low-lift pumps (LLPs)) coupled with increased distribution of highly subsidized chemical fertilizer and HYVs of rice. In the early 1970s, HYVs of wheat were introduced. As noted by Alauddin and Tisdell (1991), during the initial years until the early 1970s, HYVs of rice (e.g., IR-8, IR-5, and IR-20) used to be imported directly. However, subsequently the Bangladesh agricultural research system adapted and indigenously developed different varieties of rice and wheat which were then multiplied and released for farm production.

Finally, the subsistence system is seen fading in a number of places day by day. Sometime in near future, it will be completely gone from Bangladesh as well.

1.7 Peasant-lord system

1.8 Characteristics

- production is by primitive technology
- workers and their family units are subject to an economic hierarchy and through it are bound to their traditional occupations
- The lord is all-powerful in relation to the worker and his family, but his power may be tampered by custom and by an ethic of paternal obligation.
- State does not enter the relationship between Lord and peasant except to extract some of the product.

1.9 Approaches

The peasant-lord system is one of the most primitive forms of labor relations in its existence. Despite of new discoveries and technological innovations, peasant-lord system still prevails in many Asian and Latin American countries. But since its inception it has gone through many modifications, its main changing forces being population growth and variation in its composition, technological innovations especially in agriculture, urbanization and industrial development, increasing investment pattern and various social developments. Few of the characteristics of the system are enumerated as follows:

1. Prevails in densely populated rural areas

This is mainly because the feudal system is practiced by the people in the rural areas mainly in the form of tenant farming. The zamindar or the lord is the influential person in the village who manipulates his power to deceive the poor farmers off their legal right to their part of the harvest. These kinds of practices are not present in the urban areas where the state law is strictly followed and also mainly because the peasant lord system works where traditional occupations like farming are followed.

2. Production is by primitive technology

As the peasant lord system mainly follows a traditional method of production therefore the technology used is also primitive. The workers are often not educated enough to carry out their tasks with the help of the modern technology.

3. Workers and their family units are subject to an economic hierarchy and through it are bound to their traditional occupations.

4. The lord is all-powerful in relation to the worker and his family, but his power may be tampered by custom and by an ethic of paternal obligation.

As mentioned, the peasant lord system works mainly in the form tenant based farming. Therefore the influence of the lord is very significant in the life of the workers. But sometimes their authority may be somewhat dampened due to different cultural and religious customs. In Bangladesh, however, the influence of the zamindar or the lord is highly felt and affects each and every aspect of the workers' activities.

5. State does not enter the relationship between lord and peasant except to extract some of the product.

The peasant lord system practiced in the rural areas is completely out of reach of the state laws and regulations. The government does impose any direct regulation on the lords or the workers thus further facilitating exploitation of the poor workers.

2.0 Reviews in the Context of Bangladesh

Zanindars or the revenue collectors were the most powerful class in the agrarian structure since the pre-colonial time in Bengal and the new colonial land policy of 1793 did not disturb the basic equilibrium. There was change of hands in land ownership but the class did not disappear. Below the class of zamindar there was a vast peasant cultivator class. Subsequent land policy in the colonial period, particularly the sub-infeudation (MADHYASVATVAS or pattanidari) created intermediate rent collecting interests resulting in the emergence of numerous agrarian layers, known as Jotedar, Gantidar, Howladar, or Talukdar, or Bhuiyan, etc. The aggregate effect of introducing different land tenure measures was the emergence of a highly stratified society based on land interests.

One of the significant developments immediately after the partition of the subcontinent was the abolition of zamindari land system in Bangladesh. Since historically most zamindars came from the Hindu community, their migration to India after partition created a sort of vacuum in social structure. The Muslim traditional wealthy class linked to agriculture came to occupy that vacuum, although it was a fact that their size was minuscule. The same period also witnessed the strengthening of the process of emergence of a rich peasant/agraricultural capitalist class owing to the introduction of agricultural modernisation in the early 1950s and they became strong contenders for the upper echelon of social stratification. Another important class that emerged was the educated Muslim middle class who also mastered sufficient status in society and came to be known as Muslim 'Bhadralok' gentleman just before and following the partition.

2.0.1 Trend of Urbanization in Bangladesh

Bangladesh is still an agrarian society though nearly one quarter of the population lives in the urban areas. Table 1, which gives the trend of urban growth in Bangladesh for last one century, shows a very slow and retarded urban growth for Bangladesh. The overall trend is curvilinear, unstable and periodically fluctuating. It reflects both global and internal dynamism as well as statistical manipulation by the politicized administration of a peripheral state.

Census Year	Urban Population	Total Population	% Urban	Variation	Exponential Growth
1901	28,928,000	702,035	2.43	-	-
1911	31,555,000	807,024	2.56	14.95	1.39
1921	33,254,000	878,480	2.64	8.85	0.85
1931	35,604,000	1,073489	3.02	22.20	2.00
1941	41,997,000	1,537,244	3.66	43.20	3.59
1951	42,063,000	1,819,773	4.33	18.38	1.69
1961	50,840,000	2,640,726	5.19	45.11	3.72
1971	71,479,000	6,273,602	8.78	137.57	6.66
1981	87,120,000	13,228,163	15.18	110.85	10.66
1991	106,314,000	20,872,204	19.63	57.79	4.56
2001	123,851,120	28,605,200	23.10	37.05	3.15

Table 1 : Urbanization in Bangladesh, 1901-2001

2.0.2 Evolution of the Working Class

Bangladesh was a British colony for almost 200 years. In that period the British authority used this country as a source for the raw materials of different industry. The British authority showed disinclination to set up industrial establishment in eastern part of Bengal. Rather they preferred the labor force of Bengal to produce the raw materials which the British authority shipped to the abroad. So basically in that period almost all the labor force was engaged in the agricultural activities for producing raw materials. The number of the organized working class people is also almost absent.

Under the 'Zamindar Protha' there was a particular Zamindar or Land-lord for a particular area, who used to take tax from the farmers of that area. Many times farmers were bound to grow the crops that the respective Zamindars wanted. Farmers in those period followed very old way of cultivation. This system got resemblances with the Peasant—lord system mentioned in the Interim report on 'Future Industrial Relations' prepared by Robert W. Cox, Jeffrey Harrod & others. Farmers in those period followed very old way of cultivation.

Agrarian society during the colonial time also witnessed the emergence of a rich peasant class who happened to occupy an important position in social stratification. At least one specific development created the pre-condition for the emergence of rich-proto-capitalist peasants: the market integration of Bengal agriculture with the global economy particularly with the onset of indigo and jute cultivation. The rich peasant class enjoyed economic wealth and power in rural society. On the other hand, agrarian society during colonial time also went through the process of proletarianization/pauperization with the consequent emergence of landless class. While different land tenure measures influenced the class composition of the agrarian structure and in turn social stratification, the growing capitalization facilitated the emergence of agricultural wage workers. The social stratification pattern that emerged during the colonial time comprised the superior landed class, landed intermediaries with several layers, rich peasants/proto-capitalists, poor peasants/sharecroppers, and agricultural working class coming from the landless and marginal peasants.

Important changes took place at the level of urban social stratification with the introduction of British rule in the urban areas. A pristine 'Bhadralok' or gentlemen class consisted of educated professionals (lawyers, teachers, doctors, engineers, service holders and others) emerged in urban Bengal reaping the benefits from the new educational and occupational opportunities. On the other hand, the size of the newly emerged business class was small and characteristically not comparable with the bourgeois counterpart of the West. Earlier, the social status enjoyed by the traders or 'Banians' was lesser than the higher caste like the Brahmans and it changed during the colonial time. Business class also became educated and the vice versa.

2.1 Agrarian Classes and Groups

The following agrarian classes and groups are found to constitute rural society with hierarchical status and prestige:

1. **Capitalist Farmers**: wealthy, own land and technology, hire outside labor and carry out cultivation for the market.
2. **Rich Peasants:** they are also wealthy and hire outside labor but they are still engaged in cultivation.
3. **Middle Peasants:** primarily subsistence cultivators with occasional market participation and primarily depending on household labor.
4. **Marginal Peasants:** they combine cultivation and labor sale to ensure subsistence.
5. **The Landless:** the wage workers primarily engaged in agriculture.

In rural stratification there are other traditional groups such as kamars (blacksmiths), swarnakars (goldsmiths), sweepers, tantis (weavers), kalus (oil pressers), and others who enjoy minimum status. The roles of some of these groups are now taken over by the professional producers. For example, edible oil comes from the mill.

2.2 Peasant Revolutions in Bangladesh

Bengal is famous for peasant revolution dating back to Mughal time. In Jessore, a local Hindu Raja by the name Pratapaditya gave leadership to a rebellion against the mighty Mughal, which nearly cost him his life during 1610-1612.

In the middle of twentieth century right before Bengal was partitioned based on M.A. Jinnah's dubious two-nation theory, an uprising by the name Tebhaga Andolon (sharecroppers' movement) had exemplified the supreme sacrifice and tenacity of rural folks. The Nachole uprising near Kansat, Chapai Nawabganj in 1950 by Santal tribe was patterned after Tebhaga Andolon. In the next fifty-six year there is no such organized peasant movement.

In the beginning of 2006, the peasants from villages near Kansat, Chapai Nawabganj organized a movement to demand their fair share of electricity which is required to do their farm chores. In one sense their livelihood is linked with the availability of electricity. However, due to political involvements the issue took a turn towards a bloody conflict between the peasants and the state police. 20 people were killed in the clash and caused the villagers to flee their home for safety. The uprising had surprised many people inside and outside the country. The Amnesty International also made an appeal along with Mukto-Mona forum in the Internet for government's restraint and to assist the peasants to gain their fair rights.

2.3 Primitive labor market system

2.4 Characteristics

- Lack of skills required in modern organization
- A surplus of unskilled labor
- Technology of production remains primitive
- Wage contract appears
- Workers are relatively mobile
- Have some choice of employment and thus some individual bargaining power
- No collective power as labor organizations exist
- State does not usually enter the work relationship.

2.5 Approaches

A primitive labor market comes into existence when some workers have lost status or broken the ties of the peasant-lord relationship or abandoned the subsistence economy so as to become landless laborers. Although, currently, the conditions of employment and wages are determined by the availability of labor, this system is untouched by the minimum wage legislation, social security, and other protective activities of the State. Their conditions are lower and largely unaffected by those prevailing for established workers in the enterprise labor market or other highly organized systems.

The system falls under the systems associated with marginality and transition. However, this direct transition does not take place. Instead, a large marginal sector of workforce grows with the exodus from the primitive rural systems. The marginal workers are not fully integrated in the industry and are often recent migrants from rural villages who retain possibilities of earning from agriculture. They may be engaged in petty trading and menial personal services or they may be totally without income derived from any legitimate activity.

But it is found that movement out of the primitive labor market is blocked or insignificant. The number of workers in this system of social relations in production is determined by the flow from rural areas and the natural increase in the marginal production. Industrialization can absorb only a few into enterprise labor market or other modern systems.

2.6 Reviews in the Context of Bangladesh

2.6.1 Primitive Labor Market in Bangladesh

In 1951, few years after independence of Pakistan, the first labor market was reviewed with the number of 12.886 million of workers employed in different sectors. In 1956 one of the earliest studies on the extent of unemployment was carried out in four sub-divisions of four different regions of Bangladesh: Narayanganj, Rangpur, Rajbari and Feni. The percentages of unemployed adult male were found to be in Narayanganj 41.3%, in Rangpur 11.5%, in Rajbari 26.1%, and in Feni 45.2%. The farm families showed a much smaller proportion of unemployed males in the whole year. The percentages of unemployed among the farm families were recorded as 0.27% at Narayanganj, 0.09% at Rangpur, 0.6% at Rajbari, and 45.2% at Feni sub division.

During the period of 1901-1961 there has been increase in the size of the labor force in Bangladesh from 9.6 to 17.44 million while total population rose from 28.97 to 50.84 million. The higher population growth rate, therefore, was responsible for elevating the dependency of 201 persons per 100 labor force to 192 in 1961. An examination of the trend participation rates shows that there has been a continuous decline during the period, resulting in the number of dependents per labor force rising from 201 in 1901 to 297 in 1931.with the improved labor force conditions during the 1950s, it declined to 192 in 1961.

It should be noted here that the increase in the labor force participation had not been consistent with that of population growth rate throughout the successive decennial periods.

2.6.2 Current Situation of the Primitive Labor Market System in Bangladesh

The Primitive labor market systems still, to some extent, prevails in Bangladesh. This market comprises of none other than household help (servants) which often bring from villages via social or family connections and are engaged in occasional or frequent tasks of a menial nature. The other type of labor market is comprised of cart pullers (thela gariwala, in Bengali or van pullers) who come from the villages and become part of the urban population and engage in frequent tasks that require tremendous hard work. There is also a surplus of these unskilled labors (servants) However, these helping hands use their primitive knowledge to help in our daily chores. They are completely unaware of the use of modern equipments (e.g. microwave oven, blender, etc.). Again the surplus of unskilled labors, which are often seen sitting idle in front of furniture shops, big organizations and different busy areas however are people who use their primitive knowledge to help in daily lives. Both types of labor are often hired on a wage contract basis but also have the opportunity of some individual bargaining power. Moreover, these groups of people are quite mobile as well. The State plays no role in the work relationship between the helping hands or the cart pullers, acquired from the villages and us.

Bangladesh continues to have a labor-surplus economy where the problem is less one of open unemployment than of disguised unemployment, underemployment and low returns to labor. Returns to female labor continue to be even lower than those to male labor because women have lower levels of education and are 'crowded' into a far more limited range of productive opportunities. Estimates by Rahman (2000) suggest male underemployment rates of 12 per cent in 1995-96 compared to 71 per cent for female, and male unemployment-equivalent rates of 8 per cent compared to 31 per cent for female. In other words there was, and continues to be, a large reserve pool of female labor, much of it located in the countryside. While cultural norms, discrimination by employers and trade union practices all help to explain women's exclusion from the wider labor market, it was also reinforced in the past by a policy environment which protected employers from the consequences of such discrimination. Sheltered from global market forces by policies which promoted and protected domestic industry, competition within national labor markets was also suppressed, giving male workers privileged access to better paid formal employment. The participation of women in paid work was extremely low and confined to marginal informal activities which did not appear in the national statistics.

2.7 Enterprise Labor Market System

2.8 Characteristics

- Production is by modern technology.
- Employment and conditions are regulated through the operation of an open labor market.
- The state and trade unions intervenes only in a very limited or ineffective way in labor relations.
- The enterprise is the only meaningful domain in decision making.
- The power of the individual employer is not necessarily absolute as labor market conditions will considerably influence his behavior.

2.9 Approaches

An Enterprise Labor Market exists where production is by modern technology, employment and conditions are regulated through the operation of an open labor market, and both the state and trade unions or employers' organizations intervene only in a very limited or ineffective way in labor relations.

Two or three trends within the system can be identified:

1. The changing personnel of management.
2. Foreign investment demand for increased skills in both industrial and agricultural enterprises, and
3. Growth of workers organizations.

The principal feature of the enterprise labor market is that management is the prime source of decision-making in the system.

Typically this system exists in small manufacturing enterprises which form part of the modern sector in developing countries. The concept of modern enterprise, however also, covers plantations and commercial establishments. Workers tend to have acquired more modern skills than those in the primitive market.

3.0 Reviews in the Context of Bangladesh

In the Enterprise Labor Market, if there are very few skilled labor coupled with no unskilled labor, there cannot be unrest of workers. As legal benefit is ensured, no question of dispute as to allocation of legal benefits arises. The trade union is not a factor. The system between worker and owner sharing policy formulation, benefits talk with representatives are mandatory. Trade union is a voluntary wish of workers. However, they must be registered by government. Trade unions can only be established at the discretion of the workers.

In Bangladesh at present trade union is not functioning in the desirable way. For example, in garments industry, in real sense, there is no trade union. So image building is not there. In Bangladesh the trade unions are not getting support from the government. Although the workers are unjustly fired the trade unions are not there to support them. The question is whether trade union is there in enterprise labor market? In case of garments industry there is a shortage of skilled labor. Autocratic behavior on the part of the employers ensures an oppressive attitude towards the workers and unions, thereby highlighting the inefficiency of the unions. Thus, workers are not happy. Owner is not giving wage, overtime and no guarantees of service because of the availability of workers. Besides garments industry, in the private spinning mills also, this situation exists.

In Bangladesh, employers' paternalistic approach is positive only theoretically. There is a saying that guardian of the family knows the best. Like the owner have the responsibility to maintain the industry in a peaceful manner. So, in the enterprise labor market, if the employers' approach is positive, the paternalistic approach is positive. Here again comes the issue of humanitarian approach. The demand of the workers is unlimited. This has to be fulfilled with limited resources. But if the owner wants to ensure their interest most, they maximize their interest by maximizing profit at the cost of the labor. The scenario of Bangladesh is similar to that.[222] With high unemployment of labor; the social cost of labor is less than the market wage.[223] Thus, the private sector will employ too few workers and the output will be lower because social marginal cost of output is less than marginal private cost of output. In this circumstance, privatization is welfare-reducing if it leads to labor redundancy.

The institutional framework for resolving industrial relation disputes are not yet developed. Interests of workers in terms of health, or safety, are generally ignored. In the public sector there is little scope for peaceful negotiation of labor conflicts due to the lack of an effective mechanism for arbitration of disputes. Work stoppages, strikes, lockouts, sabotage of production, violence, and terrorism characterize industrial relation in Bangladesh. Trade unions' practices are autocratic and arbitrary.[224]

In a 'labor-surplus' economy such as Bangladesh, the developments in the labor market are crucial to bringing about desirable changes in growth possibilities and meeting poverty reduction and other social goals. For ensuring such a process of growth, public policies and investments need to ensure more equitable income and asset distribution and economic growth needs to be inclusive such that it generates more income and employment for the poor. In particular, a key challenge is to expand decent employment opportunities through both wage and self-employment to absorb the growing labor force. For this, an important agenda is to address some key issues in the country's labor market and adopt a consolidated and gender-sensitive strategy toward developing the labor market with capacity of sustaining rapid growth of productivity-enhancing employment in the economy.[225]

Sector	2005-06	FY 07 (estimated)	FY 08 (estimated)	FY 09 (estimated)
Agriculture	22.83	22.89	23.41	24.07
Crop and horticulture	2.93	20.95	21.37	21.96
Forestry	0.74	0.75	0.79	0.82
Fisheries	1.16	1.19	1.24	1.29
Industry	6.90	7.08	7.20	7.43
Mining and quarrying	0.10	0.11	0.12	0.13
Manufacturing	5.20	5.26	5.27	5.33
Electricity, gas and water supply	0.10	0.11	0.11	0.12
Construction	1.50	1.61	1.70	1.85
Services	17.70	18.52	19.13	19.55
Trade, hotel & restaurants	7.80	8.29	8.46	8.50
Transport storage & communication	4.00	4.02	4.21	4.32
Finance, business services and real estate	0.70	0.71	0.75	0.80
Health, education, public admin and defense	2.60	2.77	2.86	2.91
Community, social and personal services	2.60	2.72	2.85	3.02

Table 2 : Projected Employment in Major Sectors (in millions)

Bangladesh's labor market is burdened by inflexible employment regulations that hinder job creation and productivity growth. The non-salary cost of employing a worker is low, but dismissing a redundant employee can be difficult.

3.1 The Enterprise—Corporatist System

3.2 Characteristics

- Worker is reduced in exchange for employment security and welfare guaranteed by the employer.
- Modern technology system.
- Workers' interests and loyalties are enterprise-based.
- Trade unions behave as though they share with the employer an interest in the well-being of the enterprise.
- Security and welfare provided by the corporation may act as a deterrent to the formation of unions.
- Industrial relations are dealt with in large measure autonomously within the corporation without significant control by the political system.

3.3 Reviews in the Context of Bangladesh

In Bangladesh Enterprise Corporatist System in the private sector refers to having a pet union and controlling the labors by that union. Union works more for the employer than for the employees. So the actual benefit of Enterprise Corporatist System is not observed by the Employees.

On the other hand the public sector management suffers from lack of authority and accountability. They have to wait for government guidelines and act on the basis of these. Private sector owner-managers continue to be reluctant to consider workers as equal partners. Public sector employees are highly organized, and arguably the most politicized faction of the working class. Public sector wage increases, as result of apex trade union bargaining with the state and the employers' organizations, acts as a trendsetter for the private sector. The institutional framework for resolving industrial relations disputes are not yet developed. The trade unions are allied with bourgeois national political parties and are subservient to the paramount party leaders rather than rank and file membership of the unions.[226]

Industrial relations policies, practices and climate are usually considered far better in multinational companies, which fall under enterprise corporatist system. Also under enterprise corporatist system there are observations regarding Multi-national Companies (MNC) in Bangladesh. In Bangladesh there are many multinational companies. They are doing business by contractual agreements. There are trade unions in these organizations but they do not work for the workers. They want to ensure their membership in the permanent membership of the organization. The trade unions real support is to give facilities. But in reality they are supporting the owners to give less benefit to contractual employees. In this context, the unions are failing to bring prosperity to the workers and rather working against them.

They can serve as the confidential assistants and fire assistants. They are not eligible to permanent benefits. In other ways constituents are set by the interest of the unions.

By reviewing the existing company policy and strategy pertaining to employees or workers a study showed that 68.9 percent of the companies have an established public corporate framework for human resources which ensures respect for core labor standards, management of employee relations and communications, training for skill development, health and safety and equal opportunities. In 66.7 percent of the cases this policy is not applicable for part-time or temporary staff members. Most of the companies claim that they maintain a fair recruitment procedure where only merit and efficiency prevail rather than kinship or prejudice. Although the study found that only 32.3 percent of the companies have formal policies on recruitment and promotion which is gender, race or religion blind, the ratio could be higher in case the question did not include some of the sensitive issues like sexual orientation.

3.4 Recommendations

Recommendations to change the overhead scenario are as follows:

1. Non discrimination with regard to

Wage: Often is the case, that workers are not getting the expected wages, which in turn is creating problems and issue inside the organizations and in effect the slump in the working of the enterprise corporatist system. This is a serious contentious issue and needs to be resolved by setting wages in such a fashion so that wages are given fairly among all employees. Big local companies like Square are practicing this trend very well. The companies should also not make any discrimination in wage between male and female workers.[227]

Religion: Creed discrepancies and individual moral values have to be kept aside in order for an effective system of enterprise corporatist system to function. Friction might arise if discrimination practices are used. Many corporations follow the policy of not being biased towards any such religion. Again, multinationals can be used as a good example of bias free attitude towards religious belief.

Job status (permanent or non permanent): This is another area which needs to be looked into to make the system effective. Job status must be made mutually exclusive of any discrimination. Bonus, benefits and other amenities must be consistently provided.

2. Ensuring fair practice of labor law:
Application of fair labor law practices will ensure a healthy environment to work in. The current system lacks these mechanisms. So care must be taken to deal with the law strictly. Only then can the system be more effective.

3. Non permanent workers must have representatives in the union: Yet another contentious issue is the involvement of non permanent workers in the union. Currently, the non-permanent workers are deprived from having any CBA. That way, they can also have a motivation and certain level of commitment to work for the organizations if they see that their needs are felt by the top-level management. Often is the case that the corporatist system fails to deliver because of the union's apathy towards the temporary workers. The temporary workers also do not have any united voice to inform the management about their problems or requirements. But in reality, these workers might represent a high proportion of some organizations and in that case, it becomes very essential to get these people under the unions' vicinity.

4. Continuous Improvement: Over the years many irregularities, ignorance's have been prevailing in the enterprise—corporatist labor system in Bangladesh. Therefore, it is not possible to drastically improve in all these sectors at one go or in a very short time. The corporate companies can take measurable and specific time bound goals to improve this situation. This goal setting and implementation has to continue till these anomalies are fixed. After this goal is achieved, the company's should continuously strive to further improve and enhance the labor situation in Bangladesh and become an example for company's operating in other countries.

5. Government Supervision, Monitoring and Support: The government has a very crucial role in this field. The government's responsibility does not cease only by imposing a law or regulation. Rather, the government should play a very friendly part in helping the organization's to implement these new laws / regulations and at the same time the government should ensure very strict monitoring on the implementation of these law's, so that the law becomes a practice for these companies. The government before making and imposing any law should consult with both the parties to understand their side of the story and try to create a perfect balance between the requirements of the workers and the resources available to the employers.

3.5 Bipartite System

3.6 Characteristics

- Labor specialized, skilled and mobile and are associated with modern-technology production.
- Trade unions are strongly organized on a basis broader than the enterprise.
- Employers tend to be effectively organized.
- Relationship is contractual and workers identify with the skills and profession, not the enterprise.
- State's role is limited to administering labor protective legislation and applying minimum standards.
- More appropriate for groups of enterprises rather than for individual enterprises.

- The outcomes of bargaining do not systemically take account of interests beyond those of the parties directly concerned.

3.7 Approaches

Bipartite cooperation involves a system of bilateral relations with the participation of the employers and the employees, that is, their representative interest organizations. Industrial relations have different levels both in bipartite cooperation. Economic and social characteristics and the traditions of a country determine which level of industrial relations will become decisive in a given period. In general, at different levels different actors get involved in cooperation. Thus, for instance, participants in bipartite relations are usually the following:

- **At macro level:** confederations of trade unions and employers' associations;
- **At medium level:** Sectoral or regional federations of trade unions and employers' associations
- **At micro level:** workplace unions or works councils and individual employers.

Bipartite system is well established and regarded as basically functional by the actors in it and the society at large. Another important stabilizing factor is the law, which is at present as much a factor for stability as it was an instrument of change in one historical period. The basic features of the law will remain constant but government intervention through non-legislative means will continue to increase, just as the government's role in other type of economic activity seems destined to become more important. The nature and form of government intervention, possible value changes among section of the labor force and membership change in union represent the major sources of changes expected in the system.

3.8 Reviews in the Context of Bangladesh

In Bangladesh, the Industrial Relations Ordinance, 1969 (presently labor code 2006) is the main Instrument provided for the above mechanisms. There is clear provision to form "Participation committee", a bipartite mechanism comprising of equal number of representation of workers and the employer to meet every 2 month. This mandatory provision is not complied in 98% of the establishments due to very poor inspection and weak enforcement of law by the government.

3.8.1 Trade Unions Activities under Bipartite System in Bangladesh

Trade union activities under Bipartite System in Bangladesh are low. There are quite a few reasons behind it.

- Political influence: Government, particularly caretaker government had called a ban on trade union movement and thus the scope of trade union activities was very limited inside the organizations.

- Illiteracy of industry: Industry's lack of knowledge on the trade union's power and impact has led to a lowering influence of trade unions in various sectors. The trend is akin among almost all the major industries with some rare exceptions.
- Workers are not literate so their choice of leader is not literate: It is only expected that illiterate workers cannot choose an ideal leader to run their labor union. This case is valid for multiple sectors such as in jute, railway, garment, tea, leather etc.

3.9 Recommendations

The problem in Bangladesh can be solved through bipartite system because of its joint mechanism, openness and flexibility. Only then by integrating with the humanitarian approach industrial relations can solve the crucial issues.

In Bangladesh, better opportunities under bipartite system can be created:

By raising the international standards—National minimum unskilled labor salary is 3000 taka. Government gives bonus in two Eids. This is mandatory. But for multinationals this is not mandatory. They can give more bonuses. This is why they decrease their salary. Because 1 bonus is equal to basic salary. For this they increase other benefits like children's education. In case of rent 55% is off in government sector but 100% off in private organizations. In this sector trade unions can bargain with charter of demand.

By maintaining international standard and bargaining with workers owners can deal with positive paternalistic approach. So workers can realize the limitations of the owners.

4.0 Tripartite System

4.1 Characteristics

- Government plays a more active role as a third party, bargaining with nongovernmental employers and trade unions.
- Government is concerned with the regulation of conflict and with the outcomes of collective bargaining.
- The governmental initiative is to pursue public policy goals and its judicial action is as arbitrator.
- Political system and industrial system are interrelated.
- Outcomes affect the attainment of the economic and social goals of public policy.

An attempt to reach integrated decisions which merge all relevant group interests in a consideration of the general interest.

4.2 Approaches

Tripartite system exists in the modern sectors of some developing countries, where governments seek sometimes to compensate for weakness in the trade unions' bargaining power, sometimes to prevent industrial conflict from obstructing economic development, and sometimes to advance social equity by limiting the part of the national product going to the more organized groups. It comes to being when the government plays a more active role as a third party, bargaining with non-governmental employers and trade unions. The government is concerned with the regulation of conflict and with the outcomes of collective bargaining, both because, it is a large employer and, more particularly, because these outcomes affect the attainment of the economic and social goals of public policy.

4.3 Reviews in the context of Bangladesh

Bangladesh has ratified the ILO Convention on Tripartite Consultation (C144) in June 1979. The principles of tripartism found expression for the first time when the government, in order to improve industrial relations, set up the National Tripartite Consultative Committee (NTCC) on 27 September 1978 with equal representation of the government, employers and workers. The NTCC, now renamed into Tripartite Consultative Committee (TCC), is composed of 60 members. As of 18 February 2007, 20 of them are Trade Union (TU) representatives. Furthermore, the TCC engages in discussions on various ILO Conventions and Recommendations.

Bangladesh has established a policy of involving workers and employers as social partners of the government in formulation and implementation of policies with respect to labour administration as well as social, economic and political issues. Within the framework of this policy, sectoral representation has been installed, in both the legislative and executive branches of government, particularly in government boards and commissions. Currently, there are the following tripartite institutions at national level, even though in some cases, they are not consulted on a regular basis:

- Tripartism and the Labor Policy
- Tripartism in Wage Determination
- Tripartism in Minimum Wage Fixing
- Tripartism in Dispute Settlement
- Tripartism in Labor Judiciary
- Tripartism in Plantation Employee's Provident Fund
- Tripartism in Apprenticeship Training
- Tripartism in Labor Law Reforms, etc.

Additional tripartite institutions are:

- The National Council for Skill Development and Training
- Tripartite Productivity Committee

On top of these regular institutions, two adhoc tripartite institutions are convened at irregular intervals; the National Pay Commission (NPC), and the National Wage Commission (NWC).

The labor court is tripartite with equal number of representation from workers and the employer. This is not very affective and useful to the workers due to merger number of labor courts and long time required for disposal of cases. Available evidence suggests that these tripartite institutions are not working effectively in improving industrial relations at the national, sectoral, or plant levels. A variety of actors explain this. First, there is the multiplicity of tripartite institutions, which are assigned different functions, but few of which address the most fundamental issues of globalization, including industrial relations. An upgraded and strengthened TCC might perform most, though not all, of the tripartite functions. The NWC is virtually a sterile body and works only half-heartedly. There is no reason why the salaries of employees other than workers should be fixed by the NPC and not by the NWC. Moreover, the competence of the NPCs, NWCs, and the MWB is limited only to wage extermination, which constitutes only one part of the entire gamut of labor processes. The competence of the TCC is also limited only to reviewing domestic labor standards and ratifying ILO Conventions. Most importantly, all the tripartite bodies, including the MWB, suffer from inadequate staff and other support facilities. Secondly, while efforts are being made to create a climate for free market forces, the Government plays the predominant role in all the tripartite bodies. Government intervention seriously limits closer labor-management co-operation. Moreover, the authority for approval and implementation of tripartite body recommendations lies with the Government, which often creates conflicts and disrupts industrial relations at the national level with country-wide strikes and "hartal" (general strikes), In this context, mention may be made of important recent developments relating to policy on wages. While the workers are arguing for a basic needs (nutritional requirements) approach to determining minimum/floor wages, and making general wage adjustments in accordance with skill and experience, employers insist on linking wages to productivity. The position of the Government is dependent more on the availability of funds and keeping the minimum wage close to the 1995 NPC award of Tk. 1500/month. Despite a number of limitations of the existing tripartite bodies, there is huge potential hr their becoming involved in successful social dialogue in bringing about harmonious industrial relations. In many countries, social dialogue now involves not only the three traditional parties, but also new actors in civil society and the informal sector. In Bangladesh, however, no associations outside the traditional industrial actors play any significant role in the tripartite/bipartite social dialogue. NGOs among other civil society groups, do work behind voluntary initiatives that address corporate citizenship and workers' welfare such as codes of conduct and social labeling. There are several ways in which the traditional three parties can work more effectively in partnership with the NGOs to pursue shared goals and objectives.

Forging links with civil society is essentially a matter of recognizing the power of civil society as a base for alliance in meeting shared goals, and thereby strengthening the traditional social partners.

Under Tripartite System, there are three role players:

- State/Govt.
- Employers/Management
- Union/Labor

4.3.1 State/Government

As the trade union movement in Bangladesh originated in British India and Pakistan, it naturally retained its old character of working more as a nationalist force against colonial domination than as a class force vis-à-vis capitalist exploitation. As a result, the trade union movement of the region that has gained momentum in the hands of political leaders stood divided along the political and/or theological lines in Bangladesh.

State had emerged as the third important force determining industrial relations system in Bangladesh since the very beginning of its industrialization. Although, recently the role of state has declined due to deregulation and privatization, still the state itself has become an employer of millions of industrial workers and it is its moral and ethical responsibility to ensure that the rights of the workers are suitably safeguarded.

After 1971, most industries and services were nationalized. The Industrial Relation Ordinance 1969 continued to govern industrial relations, but labor management relations were often more turbulent. On 24 December 1974 the government declared a state of emergency, disbanding all political parties, banning strikes and lock outs and restricting trade union activities; the conciliation machinery of the Labor Ministry and the industrial courts were maintained. However, President Ziaur Rahman (1976-1981 in power) adopted a policy in the late 1970s for a return of substantial part of the nationalized sector to private ownership.

After a decade of disturbed political conditions, power was assumed in April 1982 by Gen. Hussain Mohammad Ershad, the Army Chief of Staff. General Ershad, in June 1982, announced a major program of decentralization. In December 1990 Ershad government was thrown out by a mass movement, especially guided and dominated by the student forces. Eventually, a fairly elected democratic government took over the power through the national pole in February 1991. A parliamentary government headed by the leader and chairperson of Bangladesh Nationalist Party (BNP), Begum Khaleda Zia assumed the power and continued to exercise it for the consecutive three and a half year. Then alike the past scenario, a political unrest upsurges the whole country led by the opposition leader Sheikh Hasina. Another national pole took place in 1996 which put Bangladesh Awami League in power.

During this period, the trade unions movement was marked by direct interference by the government and the ruling party in its internal affairs. In many industrial belts, terrorism was set loose by the men of the labor front of the then ruling party. They tried to drive out the honest trade unionists from the leadership of the unions. Outsiders were barred from trade union leadership at the basic union level thus making the process of union high jacking very easy. It also succeeded in turning the workforce into a very defenseless and weak community.

Government is thus responsible for the maintenance of a balance between the interests of the two parties in industrial relations. Dunlop (1978) and Memoria (1998) also place emphasis on the role of state in regulating employer and employee relationships. They contend that industrial relations is the complex of inter-relationship among workers, employers and Government. The government tries to regulate the relationship of employer and employee and keeps an eye on both parties to keep each in line.'

The process, as mentioned before, started during the colonial period and still continues in present Bangladesh. The aim of such control by the various governments in the past was to create a brand of unionism within the image and likeness of those who were in state power.

4.3.2 Employers

In Bangladesh, there is Bangladesh Employers Federation (BEF), which was registered in 1998 as employers association. After its founding in 1998, the BEF took over the activities of the Bangladesh Employers' Association (BEA) which, registered earlier in 1951, had so far been representing the employers as an all-country organization of the employers. The BEF with a wider membership representation, cover all major industrial associations in the country as well as established individual enterprises. The objectives of the Federation are to promote, encourage and protect the interest of the employers in industrial relations, and through such efforts, to establish good relations amongst employers and workers so as to provide the vital supporting role in the country's economic development.

Having a wider representative character, the Federation has been endeavoring to promote and protect the interest of the employers giving them guidance and assistance in the field of industrial relations, bringing their concerted views on labor matters to the attention of the Government, labor and others concerned. It also represents them both at national and international levels. Being the apex body of the employers, it has been involved in the task of promoting and protecting the interests of employers. Today, the Federation is the only organization of its kind dealing with industrial relations in Bangladesh.

The membership of the Federation is the source of the policy making process. The policies and activities are formally given shape by the Managing Committee with the active involvement of the Secretariat.

The Managing Committee for the management of the affairs of the Federation consists of one President, one Vice-President and eighteen members. The Managing Committee is elected of two annual terms.

The Committee in its activities is assisted by Sub-Committees each of which is headed by a Committee member and consists of representatives of the sectors where the activities of the Sub-Committees are focused.

The Secretariat has the responsibility of implementing the decisions under the supervision of the Managing Committee. The Secretariat is headed by the Secretary-General.

The Federation's services to member-firms cover a wide range of areas:

1. Direct advisory services on labor problems and help with guidance to employers in their collective bargaining with the unions

2. Fortnightly meetings in Dhaka and Chittagong in order to facilitate exchange of views on current topics and come to an agreed solution to the same. A large number of representatives from the Public and Private Sector units participate at the meetings.

3. Keeping members informed of the up-to-date labor situation through weekly reports and monthly bulletins.

4. Collection, collation and, if necessary, circulation to member-firms of various comparative information on pay scales and the terms of service to maintain uniformity of action.

5. Preparation of index of various facts and figures so as to make them available to member-firms and Government agencies, as and when required.

6. Apart from organizing training for management officials abroad, the BEF also participates in the promotion of management and vocational training by associating itself with the Governing Bodies of the Bangladesh Institute of Management, National Council for Skill Development and Training, Industrial Relations Institute and such other bodies.

7. Organizing regular seminars/workshops/symposiums on industrial health and safety and working conditions for managers of member firms with assistance from ILO and other International Agencies.

8. The Federation is also represented on all national tripartite committees and institutions such as the Labor Courts, Minimum Wages Board, National Tripartite Consultative Committee on Labor Matters.

The Federation's membership structure has undergone a lot of change since the employer-group organized itself under the BEA umbrella in 1951. From a few direct members, the membership now includes all Public Sector Corporations, and all major national level Associations.

The Federation now represents almost 80 % of the established employers in the organized sector. The Federation is a member of the IOE and participates in ILO activities, representing the employers of Bangladesh.

4.3.3.1 State of the Trade Unions in Bangladesh

Trade Union Membership

The following figures provide a quantitative overview of the trade union membership in Bangladesh:

—**Total Basic Unions : 5242**
—**Total Members of Basic Unions** : 1.969.614

(Organized workers: 4.44%)

—**National Trade Union Federations** : 32
—Total Union under National Trade Union Federations : 1269
—**Total Membership** : 1.262.765
—Workers organized with national federation membership : 2.83%
—Organized members but not within national federations : 715.114
—Trade Union but not affiliated with National Federations : 3.968

Year	No. of registered trade unions	Total no. of their members
1971	1160	4,505,06
1975	3161	9,21,152
1980	3613	10,97,707
1982	2156	9,46,048
1985	2593	10,90,338
1990	3789	16,19,008
1994	4434	16,81,898
1996	5178	17,30,927
2000	6304	19,05,451
2001	6528	19,38,269
2002	6809	19,95,307

Table 3 : Number of Registered Trade Unions and their Members from 1971 to 2002

(Source: Bangladesh Labor Journal 2002)

4.3.4 Relation between Trade Union and the State/Govt. in Bangladesh

Apart from the legal framework of control of the trade unions in Bangladesh, extra constitutional action on the part of the various Governments in the field of trade unions are used from time to time to control the trade unions of Bangladesh. The various Governments when using extra—constitutional or oppressive powers to curb the activities of the militant unions have tried to justify the use of extra-constitutional power by claiming they are necessary for the security and progress of the country.[228]

But a deeper analysis of the intentions of the governments shows that the main motive behind such measures undertaken by the Governments are totally politically directed, i.e. the various Governments simply try to control trade unions for their own political ends.

After independence, the Awami League Government in 1972 nationalized more than 90% of large-scale industries. The concept of workers' participation was also given serious consideration. The Government appointed various committees and also invited an ILO mission to explore the possibilities of introducing a Yugoslavian-type of workers' participation in management (known as self-management) in Bangladesh (ILO, 1973). In October 1972, the Government introduced its Labor Policy whereby workers' participation in management was finally agreed and a Workers' Management Council in every nationalized industry was also agreed. But this policy also severely curtailed the scope for collective bargaining by placing wages and fringe benefits outside the scope of collective bargaining. Moreover, the said labor policy took away the right to strike.

The Government's argument at this stage was that the collective bargaining model applicable to a capitalist economy was not applicable in a socialist economy where large—scale nationalization and workers' participation had taken place. The trade unions fiercely opposed this plan. They were especially most reluctant to give up their rights to wage bargaining and strike. The Government labor policy also faced opposition from the management side. The traditional authoritative managerial structure could not accept the concept of workers participation in management. Moreover, the internal contradiction within the Government, mainly between rightist and leftist forces also worked against the implementation of the aforesaid labor policy.[229]

In 1974, the Awami League Government went for a one party socialist—corporatist state system where a single trade union organization, as part of the state—party machinery, was proposed. In the above system trade unions were to become a part of the Government in a socialist—corporatist framework. But before the scheme could be fully implemented an army coup overthrew the Awami League Government in 1975. So, one by find that even a political party like the Awami League, whose coming to power was largely facilitated by the trade unions, was reluctant to lose control over the trade unions.[230] It rather wanted to use trade unions as an arm of its party machinery to attain the party's political objectives. To accomplish this aim, the Awami League Government did not even hesitate to control trade unions by extra—constitutional measures and imposing a ban on strikes. This phenomenon simply represents the inclusions corporatist tendency of a typical Third World populist government. The Military Government that took power in 1975 adopted a policy on the industrial labor front similar to that of General Ayub Khan in Pakistan, who ruled Pakistan from 1958 to 1968. In the industrial sector, the army Government encouraged private investment from both home and abroad, and took an 'exclusionist' policy in respect to trade unions activities.

The Bangladesh Government, by promulgating the Industrial Relations (Regulation) Ordinance of 1975, banned strikes and the formation of new unions. With the gradual pressure from the politicians and trade unions, the army Government in 1977 and in 1980 relaxed the rules regarding trade unions. At this stage the Government plan was to encourage the depoliticalisation process of the trade unions as well as to 'buy off' trade union leaders by offering them various opportunities (Islam, 1983). But after an army coup in 1982, the right to strike and lockout was again suspended by applying extra—constitutional measures in Bangladesh.

This ban continued till 1991. The elected government in 1992 gave the right to strike and lockout. From the above discussion it is clear that the various Governments of Bangladesh, starting from the Pakistani rule up to the present time, have tried to control the trade unions through the Government's legislative, executive and judicial machinery. And whenever necessary, the various Governments resorted to extra constitutional means to control trade unions. The various measures of the Governments may be broadly divided into two categories. The various army Governments in the initial stage mostly adopted a policy of discouraging trade union organization mainly because of political affiliations and at a later stage when pressure was mounting on the army Governments to civilianize the administration, they mostly were for economic unionism and tried to depoliticalise the trade union movement. The various nationalists-populist Governments, on the other hand, in their initial stage of rule tolerated the trade unions mainly because trade unions mostly played a part in bringing them into power. But soon they wanted to use trade unions as extensions of their party. Thus, the various nationalist-populist Governments adopted an inclusions-corporatist framework regarding trade unions and thereby making trade unions part of the state decision-making process, whereas the various army Governments followed an exclusionist-corporatist policy in respect of trade unions and tried to ban them from the political arena, Although they adopted two different methods of dealing with trade unions, yet both the populist and army Governments had one thing in common, they both tried to control and contain the working class militancy and to foster a kind of leadership that would accept the Government prescribed procedure for the industrial relations system.

4.3.5 Relation between Trade Unions and Management in Bangladesh

In general though the employers in Bangladesh recognize the necessity of Labor-management cooperation for productivity improvement, yet they think that non-cooperation of workers is the main cause of low labor productivity. They strongly feel that wage fixation should be done at the plant level and it should be linked to productivity. Accordingly to them, political determination and commitment is necessary to relate wages to productivity. They demand that to government should take necessary steps to maintain proper law and order situation for undisturbed production process. Further they demand that trade unions should not be affiliated to the political parties, so that trade unions can pay more attention to the matters related to the total economic welfare of the industry which can benefit both workers and the employers.

The Trade Unions in Bangladesh judge the role of management as a negative one. They consider the management unfair, greedy and reluctant to accept trade unions as a positive social force but only as an inevitable evil. All these factors have resulted in mistrust, antagonism and even estrangement. Low level of wages is considered one of the major causes of abnormal labor-management relations and low productivity. The trade unions consider the existing labor laws inadequate, faulty and ineffective; the state apparatus interferes in every dispute. Adjudication takes time, and conciliation and arbitration are arbitrary.

In important aspect of government's labor relations policy is to take steps to increase industrial production and productivity. It is necessary to create congenial environment in which labor and management works in the basis of identify of interest and unity of purpose. In the regard the Government of Bangladesh has taken a series of steps through legislation and institutional arrangement.

The Government of Bangladesh has announcement of its latest labor policy in March 1980. The basic objectives of the said policy is to ensure, in consonance with the fundamental principles of the constitution of the country, healthy labor relations needed for increased production and overall national economic development for improving the conditions as well as the standard of living of the people. The salient features of the above labor policy are:

(i) Tripertism.
(ii) Productivity and Incentives.
(iii) Distribution of fair wages and development of manpower resources through education and training.
(iv) Industrial Relations.
(v) Labor relations.
(vi) Amendment and adaptation of labor laws.

4.4 Major Challenges

The challenges facing the three partners in the context of globalization are many. Most of these issues, however, emanate from structural rigidities and narrow focus of the existing tripartite and bipartite institutions and inadequacies in their efforts to meet the challenges.

4.4.1 Challenges to the Government/State

By and large, business confidence in Bangladesh appears to be fragile. One compelling reason for this is the political situation, which continues to remain confrontational among major political parties. Pervasive corruption and rampant 'toll collection' by hired goons or political parties add to the cost of doing business and discourage the business community. There is frustration that the political leadership, both those in power and those in opposition, have been unable to work together to end the impasse created by the public sector's extreme inertia and weak capacity. Uncertainty also prevails about the direction of economic and labor policies and the slowdown in the pace of economic and labor reforms in recent years. The privatization program is virtually at standstill. Following an initial spurt, the pace of financial sector reform has slowed no detriment of labor market reforms conducive to globalization. Any attempt to promote tripartism at the national level and bipartism at the plant level or to strengthen workers' and employers' institutions is most likely to be abortive, unless the major political parties reach a national consensus on these virtual issues.

4.4.2 Challenges to the Employers/Management

It is important that the employers understand the emerging business environment and respond to growing expectations on the part of workers and the government to work together for a common good. The employers cannot dispense with sound practices regarding HRD and industrial relations. They have to share insights in restructuring and in shaping economic and social policies. Although there is an institutional base for promoting industrial relations at the sectoral and national levels, plant level industrial relations suffer from inadequate institutional support.

4.4.3 Challenges to the Workers/Trade unions

Specific issues of trade unions governance can be seen in the light of four distinct categories of good governance.

- Legitimacy of trade unions, which hinges upon whether the trade union leaders have the consent of the common workers and can be removed by peaceful labor processes
- Accountability of the trade union leaders, which requires a network of checks and balances between labor institutions and defined performance standards for both common workers and trade union leaders
- Competence of the trade union leaders, which involves the capacity to formulate appropriate charters of demand, make timely decisions, and implement them effectively; and
- Respect for workers' rights and privileges, and a rule of law where the government has a duty to guarantee individual and group rights and provide a framework for economic and social activity.

4.5 Recommendations

Government action in support of globalization has to rely on policy planning and delivery services provided by the public sector. This sector has to be restructured to meet the demands of, or overcome problems arising from, globalization (e.g., demands from MNC's and domestic firms for less "red tape"; and the problem of enterprises having to rely on inefficient public enterprises for provision of basic services). In this regard, Ministries of Labor often have a narrow and reactive role. Given the importance of industrial relations to economic development, they should be working more actively with planning and finance Ministries to generate development options, create more coherent and coordinated strategies and, generally, improve public sector efficiency. There is also a need for governments to include trade unions in any public sector reform process and take account of their major concerns.

Finally, governments should continue to promote bipartite and tripartite institutions and processes to establish appropriate labor policy and standards. Inputs from all relevant parties should be considered. Not only will this limit potential conflict in the future, but (particularly where major business and investment interests—including those of MNC's—are involved) it should establish a sound basis for investment and economic and employment growth.

4.6 State Corporatism

4.7 Characteristics

- Leadership is conditional upon loyalty to the ruling political party or government leaders.
- Covers enterprises with modern technology, but not include marginal or rural components of labor force.
- Worker and employer organizations both seek satisfaction through direct relations with state bureaucracy or officials of ruling political party.
- Industrial conflicts are usually limited or repressed by political leadership.

4.8 Approaches

State corporatism is a type of political system which includes a subordinate industrial relations system to which the same name applies. Such systems are to be found in some countries where competitive party politics have been suppressed or are only formal, but semi autonomous organizations of employers and workers exist under state tutelage. It may be define as "a process by which the state uses officially-recognized organizations as a tool for restricting public participation in the political process and limiting the power of civil society."[231]

By establishing itself as the arbitrator of legitimacy and assigning responsibility for a particular constituency with one sole organization, the state limits the number of players with which it must negotiate its policies and co-opts their leadership into policing their own members. This arrangement is not limited to economic organizations such as business groups or trade unions; examples can also include social or religious groups. One such example would be the People's Republic of China's "Islamic Association of China", in which the state actively intervenes in the appointment of imams and controls the educational contents of their seminaries, which must be approved by the government to operate and which feature courses on "patriotic reeducation". Another example is the phenomenon known as "Japan, Inc.", in which major industrial conglomerates and their dependent workforces were consciously manipulated by the Japanese MITI to maximize post-war economic growth.

4.9 Reviews in the Context of Bangladesh

4.9.1 History

The drive for nationalizing different sectors in Bangladesh formerly under the Pakistani control started immediately after the end of liberation war. The statist economic model adopted by its early (Pakistani and Bangladeshi) leadership, including the nationalization of the key jute industry, had resulted in inefficiency and economic stagnation[232] Bangladesh nationalized most industries in 1972 and set up nine corporations to oversee them. The switch from a state-sponsored capitalist mode of industrial development to private sector-led industrial growth in Bangladesh began in the mid 1970s. With the famine of 1974, rising prices and a dwindling economy led to gradual shifts in the government's policies toward encouraging private sector participation in manufacturing and reducing the role of the public sector through disinvestment.[233]

One of the earliest decisions of the new Awami League Government was to create a national Planning Commission for Bangladesh under the chairmanship of the then President Sheikh Mujibur Rahman. The planning committee. Immediately came under fire, as its problems began with the publication of the country's First Five Year Plan. While the Commission insisted that the Plan presented a coherent set of social and economic objectives for the new nation, critics charged that the Plan was little more than a declaration of pious exaltations. The real problem was the lack of political support for the Plan. In addition the political leadership had a limited understanding of socialism and its policy implications and many Awami Leaguers had a weak commitment to socialist principles; the planners, on the other hand, made overly optimistic assumptions in drawing up the Plan and the members of the Planning Commission had an inadequate understanding of the importance of governance in the implementation of the Plan. As a result the Plan failed to achieve its objectives.[234]

4.9.2 Nationalization of Industries

Among the most controversial decisions taken by the Awami League Government, was the decision to nationalize both Pakistani and Bangladeshi owned industries. The decision was a product of a long series of Awami League political commitments over the years including the party's 1970 election manifesto. Although the cabinet was divided on the issue, Sheikh Mujib supported the policy of nationalization due to the party's past commitments, intense pressure from radical students, workers and leftist parties and the low political costs of alienating a weak and divided business community . . . . the long-term impact Awami League nationalization policies were to have on private sector investment behavior.[235]

4.9.3 Shift from Nationalization in Bangladesh

The privatization process in Bangladesh evolved gradually before taking concrete shape in 1993. The switch from a state-sponsored capitalist mode of industrial development to private sector-led industrial growth in Bangladesh began in the mid 1970s. With the famine of 1974, rising prices and a dwindling economy led to gradual shifts in the government's policies toward encouraging private sector participation in manufacturing and reducing the role of the public sector through disinvestment. After the political change in August 1975, the new government declared a revised industrial policy, through which the public sector-led industrialization strategy was abandoned. Between 1975 and 1981, a number of important changes in the policies and institutions were introduced (i.e. declaration of Industrial Investment Schedule 1976, withdrawal of the private investment ceiling in 1978, etc.) to broaden the scope for private sector participation in the industrialization process.

The major elements in the policy to bring about a decisive shift toward a private sector-driven industrialization during this period included:

- Elimination of ceiling on private investment,
- Reduction in the reserve list of industries under the public sector and creation of "free sectors",
- Relaxation of investment sanctioning procedures,
- Amendment of the Constitution to allow disinvestment and denationalization of both abandoned and taken-over industries,
- Establishment of a Disinvestment Board in 1975,
- Reopening of the stock market,
- Shift to a floating exchange rate and
- Introduction of various export promotion measures.

As the author has found out, this shift from state corporatism has been hugely benefited for the country, as shown from the booming the textile industry, a primarily government owned sector in the country.

Year	No. of Mill	Spindle Capacity	Growth in spindle capacity compared with previous year (0%)
1983	21	511 084	-
1992	49	922 938	-
1994	76	1 423 366	43.34
1995	84	1 701 823	19.56
2000	116	2 289 280	34.51
2001	145	2 352 310	02.75
2002	163	3 390 026	44.11
2003	174	3 419 504	0.87
2004	198	3 931 624	4.90
2006	230	7 937 353	25.85
2006	260	5 500 000	11.39

Source: Bangladesh Textile Manufacturers Association

Table 4 : Growth Pattern of Primary Textile Mills in Bangladesh

Beginning in 1975, the government gradually increased private sector participation in the economy, including privatization of more than 30 state enterprises. In the mid-1980s encouraging, if halting, signs of progress appeared. Economic policies to encourage private enterprise and investment, denationalize public industries (including jute, textiles, and banking), reinstate budgetary discipline, and liberalize the import regime were accelerated. In 1985, the government also began an economic structural adjustment program with the International Monetary Fund.

4.9.4 Present State Corporatism in Bangladesh

Bangladesh is a country which is characterized for its patron-client relationship between state and business groups' i.e., employers and also politicization of trade unions. All the major political parties maintain relationship with the business class. For example, after independence jute and specially textile mills grew very fast and were highly dependent upon government patronage in the form of contracts, loans, and credits. All are well connected politically and some are very active in politics. For instance, Beximco group is very active in politics. If we look at the MPs of the last few parliaments, one will see business groups have manned the parliament. Even one like to have a glance at the various chambers of commerce of last decades the presidents were supporters of the ruling parties. Now, let's look at the workers' side. Bangladesh being a signatory of ILO convention, allows their worker to form their own associations commonly known as trade unions in order to protect, promote and improve their economic, social and political interests. In a study, it was revealed that union leaders and general workers are undone; they cannot realize even a reasonable demand without the support of the political parties. They require political support and political parties are also ready to provide the support. Union leaders argued that unlike the western countries, trade unions in Bangladesh are weak and unable to pursue their objectives through the normal machinery of trade union's methods. Union leaders opined that the employers or managers are so strong that workers along could not cope with them. They firmly believed that it was easier to realize demand if they had political backing. For instance, in Bangladesh CBA are not allowed to fix wage and other benefits of the industrial workers rather these are fixed by the NPC (National Pay Commission) and Wage Board. The Government direct involvement in wage setting for workers has caused them to have affinity and loyalty towards the state bureaucracy and ruling party. Also in order to secure jobs and to resolve intra union and inter union conflict workers have loyalty towards the ruling party. In state corporatism theory it is seemed that both parties place a high value on consensus and peaceful labor relations which means there is little industrial conflict. But in Bangladesh the scenario is different. There is a lack of trust between employers and workers. Especially in RMG the situation is highly volatile. Workers activities have proved detrimental in many aspects. It has been considered as a serious bottleneck to the success of business and industry. Considering violence, death, terrorism and corruption committed by the workers in the industrial enterprises of Bangladesh, different sections of the community have made frequent demands for imposing ban on workers' activities.

So, there is little consensus between employers and workers. State corporatism works in Bangladesh up to the loyalty part only.

5.0 Mobilizing System

5.1 Characteristics

- Penetrates and encompasses different economic sectors and social groups.
- Tends to become transformed into other types. For example, the Mexican revolution
- In some enclaves, social relations in production may be of mobilization type, even though the political system of the country is not. For example, the Kibbutzim of Israel.

5.2 Approaches

"Collective interests also require workers to believe in the efficacy of collective action."—Sandra Cockfield in 'Mobilizing at the Workplace: State Regulation and Collective Action in Three Workplaces, 1900 to the 1920s'

The concept of mobilization first got popular during World War II. Literally, mobilization is the process of assembling and organizing troops, materiel, and equipment for active military service in time of war or national emergency. As such, it brings together the military and civilian sectors of society to harness the total power of the nation. It is the mechanism that facilitates the successful prosecution of any conflict.

From the perspective of industrial relations, mobilizing system is a political system which organizes social relations in production in a particular way. In this case, the role of the state in the radical reconstruction of industrial relations systems is very significant. In this case, the aim of the political elite is revolutionary to mobilize the hitherto non-participant segments of society through mass movements, especially among peasants and the urban marginal population, i.e., those not assimilated into modern modes of production. Workers are exhorted inspirationally to dedicate themselves to constructing a new society. The system counteracts market forces and acts to restrain the tendency of trade unions of established workers in modern production processes to advances the interests of their particular members (economism). The political elite put the force of the state behind its mobilizing effort and there by weakens or eliminate the power of non-state employers. Success in mobilization depends upon the health of the national industrial base, the availability of manpower, the state of international trade, and the condition of the nation's foreign relations. Mobilization levels depend upon the existence of forward bases, the level of industrial infrastructure, propositioned equipment, industrial preparedness, preparedness planning, and public and congressional support. Ideally, high levels of any or all of those factors ease the entire process. Naturally, all are influenced by perceived threat or some massive inspiration. Generally, the higher the level of perceived threat, the higher the corresponding levels of support.

In Rethinking Industrial Relations,[236] John Kelly argued that social movement literature allowed industrial relations to move beyond analyses based on bargaining structures and institutions and examine the social processes at play in the employment relationship. Drawing on the works of Tilly, McAdam and Gamson, Kelly presented mobilization theory as a framework for understanding how individuals transform into collective actors and conversely why this transformation may fail to occur. Following Tilly, Kelly's framework is based on five components beginning with the identification of worker interests and the extent to which these are in opposition to management and defined collectively. Additionally, the framework explores how workers are organized (such as union density, structure, and the like) and mobilized, that is, those processes that turn individual workers with collective orientations into collective actors. The last two components are the opportunities available to groups to pursue their claims collectively, as shaped by the policies and actions of the state and the employer and the prevailing balance of power, as well as the recognition that collective action can take many different forms. From the standpoint of industrial relations systems the major importance of the mobilizing system is that it attempts to solve, through complete control of economic life, the dichotomies which are inherent, if unchecked, in the industrializing process. That if this is attempted does not mean that it succeeds, or more importantly that it is the only possible way of achieving balanced growth and social and economic harmony. Full mobilization is the state that exists when all units in the current industrial structure are called to active duty, fully equipped, fully manned, and sustained.

5.3 Current Global Scenario

The mobilizing system is numerically the most important system but it is in 10th position out of eleven with reference to its presence in countries and territories of the world. In the nineteenth century the working class was strongly collectivist in outlook because of the deprivations of working life, particularly poverty, job insecurity, unemployment and employer power. This common set of conditions created a widespread sense of mutual interdependence and solidarity, features of the working class that were reinforced by employment concentration in large factories and by housing. The decline of trade union membership and collective action in Britain and other advanced capitalist countries during the 1980s was initially addressed in the literature through familiar ideas such as the business cycle and changing class composition. But a growing number of commentators began to argue that what underlay the sharp and dramatic decline of the labor movement was a pervasive and secular transformation in popular attitudes, a decline in the collectivist values intimately associated with post-1945 patterns of industrial relations. The People's Republic of China has implemented mobilizing industrial[237] relations system in a successful way to some extent; other cases exist or have existed in some smaller poorer countries. Though it was predicted by Cox[238] that China will move with greater vigor in the world 15 years ago, it was not the scenario After the 1980s, the governments of China and Taiwan, across the Taiwan Strait, promoted reform, a more transparent policy, and democratization, in order to compete in a globalizing world. In the 1980s, China had begun to emphasize economic reform and Taiwan had begun to emphasize political reform. Both ignored reform on the social dimension. Employment relations were subordinated to the priorities of economic and political reform. In the 1990s, Taiwan's democratic transformation created a pluralistic society and gave the trade unions room to take root. However, free collective bargaining has not been realized due to the marginalizing of both employer organizations and trade unions. In China, the state decentralized the business sector, allowing unilateral employer activities in employment relations. Statutory rules were enacted after the 1994 labor law. Again, the distinctive pattern of low union density, high bargaining coverage, politically divided union confederations, and recourse to political mobilization found in Southern Europe suggests there is a distinctive system of Mediterranean industrial relations. In UK, the government indirectly is using mobilization for solving the industrial relations or labor problems. Though there is a tripartite system existing in UK, there has been a dismantling of institutions that dealt with industrial relations issues and which provided industrial relations actors with an influence over the system.

The idea of long waves in industrial relations focuses our attention on recurring periods of worker mobilization and state and employer counter-mobilization. With its underpinning in a Marxist analysis of labor's exploitation and domination it suggests that the class struggle between labor and capital is a perennial feature of capitalist society.

5.4 Reviews in the Context of Bangladesh

Mobilizing system is more of a political type. Socialism is one of the prerequisites. Bangladesh after its inception incorporated socialism as one of its state philosophies which aims to ensure that individuals enjoy equal freedom in every spheres of life and state will control production, distribution, and exchange, which was impossible then.

In the time of socialism everything was nationalized in Bangladesh. The then government formed BAKSAL. Processes for mobilization of peasants were taken but because of the coup everything was stopped. Later on with change of state philosophy and new regime that came into power, it was not in favor of this type of mobilizing system.

Mobilizing system can work even if the country's political system is not stable. It has been observed that various governments in the Gram Sarkar, Upazilla has worked for mobilization of resources and people of the country in Bangladesh. But the system was used to achieve political end.

Urban marginal population in Bangladesh has always actively participated in all types of political movements like those of '69s, '71s, or '90s (which was again dominated by the students only). Now a days, NGO's in rural areas, through micro credit and others socio economic programs are trying to reduce poverty. But each NGO is doing it in isolation. There is no co-ordination and they are not working for mass mobilization.

5.5 Reasons behind the failure of mobilizing system in Bangladesh

A focus on interests and power, conflict and cooperation in the employment relationship allows us to identify four central and enduring problems in the field. First, how do workers come to define their interests in collective or individual terms? This is a central problem for several reasons. There is such a wide and diverse range of employee interests that can be pursued through the employment relationship, e.g. job security, higher wages, training, equal opportunities and career progression, that we need to find some way of categorizing and conceptualizing these interests if we are to explain their variation. Whereas employers are necessarily and primarily concerned with profitability, because of market competition, there is no corresponding mechanism amongst workers that can assign equivalent priority to any one of their many interests (Offe and Wiesenthal 1985:179). Since workers occupy a subordinate position in the employment relationship, their collective definitions of interest are subject to repeated challenges by employers as they try to redefine and realign worker interests with corporate goals.

So, firstly, the system counteracts market forces and acts to restrain the tendency of trade unions of established workers in modern production processes to advances the interests of their particular members. In our country labor union is in a good position. It can be difficult to mobilize the workers without unionizing them

Secondly, Bangladesh is a small country and is more susceptible to external influences. Mobilizing system cannot work under external influence.

The political elite put the force of the state behind its mobilizing effort and there by weakens or eliminate the power of non-state employers. This attitude will decrease the activity of NGO's and other private organization. But, our foreign investment policy encourages foreign investment and NGO's co-operation. That's why mobilizing system is not going to work properly.

5.6 Socialist System

5.7 Characteristics

- Weakness and contradiction inherent in the capitalist system would result in revolution and the ascendancy of socialism over capitalism.
- Capitalism would foster monopolies.
- Wages (costs to the capitalist) would be minimized to a subsistence level.
- Capitalists and workers would compete/be in contention to win ground and establish their constant win-lose struggles would be evident.

5.8 Approaches

The view of socialism in industrial relations is a product of a theory of capitalist society and social change.

This perspective focuses on the fundamental division of interest between capital and labor, and sees workplace relations against this background. It is concerned with the structure and nature of society and assumes that the conflict in employment relationship is reflective of the structure of the society. Conflict is therefore seen as inevitable and trade unions are a natural response of workers to their exploitation by capital.

Socialist system is logically a development of mobilizing system. Whereas the mobilizing system functions to transform a primitive technology society into a modern technology society, the socialist system is a modern—technology system. Its characteristic institutional feature is central planning of all economic, activities. Trade unions and management are conceived each as functionally related agencies for the implementation of an economic policy integrally planned through the State with the participation of these agencies.

The socialist system tends to encompass the whole labor force; but some socialist modes of social relations in production may exist alongside smallholder farming. The smallholder sector is taken into account in planning, though not directly controlled through planning.

5.9 Socialist System in subcontinent

Socialist industrial system exists in country like India. In post-colonial India labor came to be closely associated with industrial work. The agrarian-rural mode of production would come to an end soon to be replaced by large—scale enterprises making use of modern technology and situated in urban localities. The drift of labor from the countryside towards middle—and large-sized cities seemed to herald the approaching transformation towards the type of society that had emerged in the developed part of the world. Employment in the organized sector of the urban economy, although absorbing only a minor portion of the total workforce outside agriculture, became the main focus of studies on work and labor. India is socialist democratic republic state. Every elected government of the country has as its bounden duty to secure upliftment of all citizens and to that extent the constitution provides for rules and regulations through a system of laws that would facilitate progress, redress of grievances and thereby would maintain peace and harmony in the society. As regards "labor" while the State is committed to promote industrial growth through bilateral relations between employers and employees for mutually healthy existence, cooperation and progress, the state is not oblivious to the fact that despite best intentions and efforts, sometimes the issues between the parties may not get resolved at bilateral level and unless a way to resolve is sanctified through the constitution of the country and the system of law, there would be impediments to progress and the expected peace and harmony may get vitiated. Against this backdrop, it is simple to accept and appreciate that the State of India has reserved a role of an "Umpire or a Referee" in the game of industrial relations in the country. It provides all kinds of mechanisms to parties through law to resolve their own problems bilaterally and has further taken care to provide a quasi judicial/judicial system for determination of disputes. Personally and professionally, one feels that this is an ideal system. Unfortunately, the experience shows that corrupt administration, adventurous unionism, sluggish judiciary and tight fisted managements have made a virtual mockery of the concept. But the idea essentially is excellent in the State becoming an Umpire and to help parties become mature in resolving problems amongst themselves. The role of the State in Indian Industrial Relations is that of an Umpire, Elder brother and well-wisher.

6.0 Reviews in the context of Bangladesh

Bangladesh is not a socialist country with a centralized planning of all economic activities. And as socialist system indicates to a nation-scaled planning, Bangladesh automatically excludes from this system of industrial relations. And this finding is of no surprise, because it is not necessary for all systems to be existed in the same economy.

The imperatives of organization, technology, and planning operate similarly in both capitalist and Marxist systems. Differences in behavioral outputs (such as organizational productivity, industrial relations behavior, or the outcomes of different health services systems) can be explained by adopting a framework of an interactional value theory. The interactional approach links together ethical theory and various issues in social philosophy, especially in the context of the resolution of conflict among values. The dynamics of economic and social change stem from differing values held by key actors in society—government, business and the public. Values are not categorical but integrative, and values held by various parties converge.

6.1 Self-employed System

6.2 Characteristics

- The kinds of activity covered are quite heterogeneous which includes independent farmers, shopkeepers, independent service providers and independent professionals.
- Some of these groups have created associations through which they determine terms of work and return labor by fixing their own rules and rates, by bargaining with client groups or by putting pressure on the state.
- In the less advanced "early modern" economies, most of those included in this category are small cultivators, whose independence has been guaranteed by land reform and complementary institutions such as cooperatives and agricultural credit.
- In the more advanced modern economies farmers tend to be less numerous and other service providing self-employed numerically more important.
- The proportion of self-employed workers in the developed or industrialized countries is much less than that of the developing countries, particularly reflecting the self-employed agriculturist producers.

6.3 Approaches

From the standpoint of spread among the countries and territories of the world and as a percentage of the world labor force, the workers covered by the self-employed category are important. Almost every country or territory has a proportion of its labor force within this category. The concept of social relations in production for self-employed sector excludes primitive production in which individual or family unit producers are covered by the subsistence and primitive labor market systems.

This category tends to relate to the type of worker such as independent agriculturalist, shopkeepers, professionals and personal service suppliers.

In the farming sector the number of self-employed is decreasing in the developed countries. In developing countries the situation is more complex. Some trends in agriculture (development of cooperatives, collectivization) are reducing the number of self-employed, while other trends (land reform, technological innovation) are increasing it.

Shopkeepers in developed countries are facing considerable change in last two decades. The retailing revolution, begun in United States and Europe in 1960s, is eliminating the independent shopkeeper in the developed countries. This retailing revolution has entered our country also some years ago and gave rise to some big retailing shop such as Meena Bazar, Agora. In near future these shops will eventually take the place of the small retail shops and will eliminate the independent shopkeeper gradually in our country.

For professionals, there are also indications of decline in independent status. In developed countries the trend towards salaried rather than fee employment for professionals is growing. Independent professionals are also increasingly form groups to share the cost. Professionals are organizing more overt forms than in the past, which is considered in both developed and developing country.

The large service sector of developed countries has been subjected to more enterprise organization. Thus services which are often supplied by the individual, is now supplied by the corporations, with the individual taking a wage or salary rather than collecting their own charge. But, a counter-tendency of the growth of the artisans or the re-emergence of the individual craftsman is more frequent in the developing countries as well as in our country. The emergence of this group is often associated with the change in social values, as people are more ready to take risks and sacrifice income opportunities for greater personal freedom and more opportunity to personal creativity.

6.4 Reviews in the context of Bangladesh

In Bangladesh, salaried wage employment in the formal sector is not large enough to employ the huge workforce. Majority of the women are engaged in household work without remuneration. Youths belonging to the age group of 15-30 constitute more than one-third of the total population. A large number of them in spite of being educated remain unemployed. A possible answer to this vast problem is to inculcate the motto of self-employment among the unemployed and the underemployed.

According to the Labor Force Survey 2005-06, More than forty two percent labor force is self employed, employer or entrepreneur. In 1990-91, this amount was only 26.8%. Table-1 shows the summary of the labor force statistics:

Characteristics	LFS 1990-91	LFS 1995-96	LFS 1999-2000	LFS 2002-03	LFS 2005-06
Labor Force Composition (in millions)	50.0	54.6	39	44.3	47.4
Self-employed (in millions)	13.45	16.16	18.33	20.02	20.00
Percentage	26.8	29.6	47	45.2	42.2

Table 5 : Percentage of self-employed in the total labor force[239]

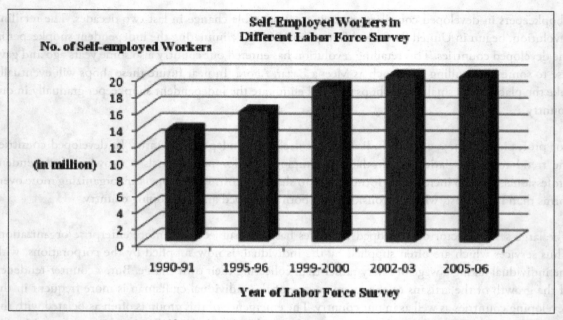

Figure 1 : Self-Employed Workers in Different Labor Force Survey

The graphical presentation of the self employed workers in Bangladesh shows that the number of self employed workers was increasing gradually (almost 3% a year) up to 2002-03. But from 2002-03 to 2005-06 the number of self employed worker remained same (almost 20 million). Probably one of the main reasons of this is huge expansion of private sector especially RMG sector that creates a lot of salaried wage employment.

6.4.1 Woman in Self-Employed System

The table below shows the Frequency, Percent Distribution, and Mean Weekly Earnings of Self-employed Workers in Bangladesh, by Gender:

Characteristics	Number of Workers				Mean Weekly Earnings (in taka)	
	Male		Female			
	Frequency	Percent	Frequency	Percent	Male	Female
Self-employed	16,909,706	54.1	1,767,930	17.2	1,631.6	1,390.1
Total	31,243,469	100.0	10,294,540	100.0	1,226.5	939.7

Table 6 : Frequency, Percent Distribution and Mean Weekly Earnings of Self-employed Workers in Bangladesh[240]

The table shows that 54.1% of total male labor force is self-employed, whereas only 17.2% of total female labor force is self-employed. Besides, it was found that the mean weekly earnings of female self-employed worker is almost 30% low than that of male self-employed worker.

6.5 Government Role in Self-Employment System

With some training, credit facilities, advisory assistance and, above all, initiative arid organizational efforts a self-employment program can be initiated. The relevant agencies of the Government, namely the Ministry of Social Welfare and Women's Affairs, Ministry of Youth and Sports, Bangladesh Small and Cottage Industries Corporation, Bangladesh Rural Development Board and Bureau of Manpower, Employment and Training (BMET), under the Ministry of Labor and Manpower, have already contributed in this respect. The self-employment programs of all these agencies are not necessarily the same. Each of them has a different approach and emphasis.

CHAPTER VI

Trade Union

Contents

1.0 Introduction

After World War II socio-economic activities in Zanzibar—an island of Tanzania, were limited in scope and employment opportunities were minimal. The few employed felt the pain of poor working conditions and poor pay. The few workers in different work places knew their problems, but they had no institution that united them and gave voice to their grievances. In 1948 the dock workers of Zanzibar staged a strike to demonstrate to the colonial authorities how great was their dissatisfaction with the poor working environment and wages that in no way tallied with their output. This held the very first legend of the Trade Union tale.

Later on, the trade union movements in the southwest continent of the world were led mainly by the progressive and leftist politicians, but the movement has ground to a halt due to the 'derailment' of many of the leftist leaders and their cooperation with the major political parties.

The current condition of Trade Union is in between somewhat due to some positive and negative activities occurred by some of them. Among the positive activities—competitive wage, job security for workers, benefit are the prime issues. On the other hand, strikes, political influences, violation of organizations rule are the main negative activities done by labor leaders. Recently, due to these unconstructive activities labor union faces some image problems that is more people having the negative idea about this institution. The labor unions of Bangladesh, associated mostly with political parties, usually demonstrate some violent activities. Violence and the threat of violence by some trade unions have produced wage increases, raising unit labor costs, and decrease the productivity and efficiency of the organization. Moreover, worker layoffs, or the mere threat of reductions-in-force, can be expected to cause some of the most serious and confrontational labor disputes. Labor disputes do not necessarily need to be heard before a legal court. Many companies have found it effective to resolve issues before a Labor Tribunal. Labor in private sector enterprises is mostly not unionized and comparatively more productive.

Productivity in Bangladesh has been affected by hartals (general strikes) called by political parties and movements. These hartals, enforced by political activists, essentially close down business throughout the country and raise the cost of doing business in Bangladesh due to the downtime they impose on commercial activity.

Theoretically, Trade Union; recognizes that for improvement to occur in the lives of working people it is necessary for effective collective organization through the trade union movement, without trade unions Bangladeshi's societies will be less democratic and more unequal.

Also that for unions to remain relevant to the needs of working people they must be democratic, representative, non-discriminatory, active on the workplace and also concerned and involved with other organizations in areas such as the environment and social justice.

1.1 Definition of Trade Union

Trade Unions are the organizations which are engaged in protecting the rights of the labor force of the country. They are the registered unions which are devoted for the betterment of the workforce.

The Bangladesh Labor Code 2006 of Bangladesh defines TRADE UNION as:

"Trade Unions means any combination of the workmen of an employer's formed primarily for the purpose of regulating the relations between the workmen and employers or workmen and workmen or employers to employers or for imposing any restrictive conditions on the conduct of any trade or business and includes a federation of two or more trade unions"

Section 2 (Clause—XXVI)

Provided that this Act shall not affect—

Any agreement between partners as to their own business;

Any agreement between an employer and those employed by him as to such employment; or any agreement in consideration of the sale of the goodwill of a business or of instruction in any profession trade or handicraft.

So the primary concern of trade Unions are-

    a. Regulating the relations of:
    b. Employers to workmen
    c. Workmen to Workmen
    d. Employers to employers

And Impose restrictive conditions on the conduct of business and trade.

Trade Unions are also of some other important Labor relation betterment, as such are:

    a. Quality of Work Life (QWL)
    b. Legal Proceedings
    c. Resolving Industrial Disputes
    d. Working Conditions
    e. Welfare of the Work force etc.

Trade Union movements are essential for a country, especially for the betterment for the existing and potential workforce. Trade unions are the Collective Bargaining Agents (CBA) which speaks for their rights.

1.2 Types of Trade Union

Theoretically, Trade unions are classified into the following types:

1.3 Craft union

This is an organization of wage-workers engaged in a single occupation, as, for example, in glass-bottle blowing, horseshoeing, locomotive engineering. The occupation may be limited strictly to one simple task or may include a number of closely allied tasks or crafts. The strict test of a craft union seems to be that each member of the organization performs or may perform all the tasks included in the occupation. Usually a craft union covers but a fraction of the work of a given industry. Example: Dhaka Mahanagar Nirman Sromik Union

1.4 General trade union

This type of unionism proposes the organization of all workers regardless of craft or industrial divisions into homogeneous groups. Example: For the novice and the unskilled.

1.5 Industrial unions

This type, as the name implies, is organized on the basis of the industry rather than the craft. That is to say, it attempts to unite into one homogeneous organic group all the workers, skilled and unskilled, engaged in turning out and putting on the market a given finished product or series of closely related products. For example, it would organize into one union all the workmen in and about a coal mine including actual miners, miners' helpers, shot firers, drivers, spraggers, trappers, trackmen, timbermen, hoisting engineers, check-weighmen, dumpers, etc. "Patkal Sramic Union" in Bangladesh is a good example of this type.

1.6 Blue Collar Unions

This type of union is formed with the laborers directly concerned with the production process. This type of unions plays important roles in trade union movement. Example: General Labor Unions

1.7 White Collar Union

This type of union is formed with the staffs of industries. They are not directly connected with the production process. "Sonali Bank Karmachary Union" is an example.

1.8 Mixed Union

Labors and pen-workers together make this type of union. This type of union can have more members than others. "Popular Jute Mill Sramik Union" is an example.

Besides the above types there are some other types of trade unions. They are described below:

1.9 Reformist Trade Union

There are two types of reformist trade unions:

1. Business Unionism

It is essentially trade-conscious rather than class-conscious. That is to say, it expresses the viewpoint and interests of the workers in a craft or industry rather than those of the working class as a whole. It aims chiefly at more here and now for the organized workers of the craft or industry, in terms mainly of higher wages, shorter hours, and better working conditions, regardless for the most part of the welfare of the workers outside the particular organic group, and regardless in general of political and social considerations except in so far as these bear directly upon its own economic ends. It regards unionism mainly as a bargaining institution and seeks its ends chiefly through collective bargaining supported by such methods as experience from time to time indicates to be effective in sustaining and increasing its bargaining power. It favors voluntary arbitration, deprecates strikes, and avoids political action, but it will refuse arbitration and resort to strikes and politics when such action seems best calculated to support its bargaining efforts and increase its bargaining power. This characteristic is found in North American unions. vii

2. Uplift Unionism

It may be trade-conscious, or broadly class-conscious, and at times even claims to think and act in the interest of society as a whole.

It aspires chiefly to elevate the moral, intellectual, and social life of the worker, to improve the conditions under which he works, to raise his material standards of living, give him a sense of personal worth and dignity, secure for him the leisure for culture, and insure him and his family against the loss of a decent livelihood by reason of unemployment, accident, disease, or old age.

2.0 Revolutionary Unionism

It is distinctly class-conscious rather than trade-conscious. That is to say, it asserts the complete harmony of interests of all wage-workers as against the representatives of the employing class and seeks to unite the former, skilled and unskilled together, into one homogeneous fighting organization. It repudiates, or tends to repudiate, the existing institutional order and especially individual ownership of productive means, and the wage system. It looks upon the general fabrications of the employing class designed to secure the subjection and to further the exploitation of the workers.

2.1 Socialistic

This finds its ultimate ideal in the socialistic state and its ultimate means in invoking class political action. For the present it does not entirely repudiate collective bargaining or the binding force of contract, but it regards these as temporary expedients. It looks upon unionism and socialism as the two wings of the working-class movement.

2.2 Quasi-anarchistic Unionism

This type of revolutionary unionism repudiates altogether socialism, political action, collective bargaining, and contract. Socialism is to it but another form of oppression, political action a practical delusion, collective bargaining and contract schemes of the oppressor for preventing the united and immediate action of the workers. It looks forward to a society based upon free industrial association and finds its legitimate means in agitation rather than in methods which look to immediate betterment. Direct action and sabotage are its accredited weapons, and violence its habitual resort.

2.3 International Unions

This type of unions is extended across the world. National unions and federations of different counties usually become the members of these unions. International Confederation of Free Trade Union and World Federation of Trade Union are examples.

2.4 Structure of Trade Unions in Bangladesh

Basically the institutional form of trade union is termed as trade union structure. Trade union structure of a country indicates the co-ordination of the trade unions from the basic level unions to national level federations. For trade union movement, the structure of trade union is termed as an important Body-Politic.

A strong structure is indispensable for a trade-union movement of a country. But there is difference in the structures of trade union in different countries. In some countries there is only one national level federation to control and coordinate all the trade unions of a country. As for example, TUC of UK and Australia. Again in some countries there are more than one national level federations. As for example, the NFTUs of Bangladesh, India and Pakistan etc. In the trade union structure of Bangladesh there are three levels:

1. NTUFs in the national level
2. Industrial federations in the industrial levels
3. Basic unions in the basic levels

Besides these the presence of zonal or regional committee is observed. But Labor Code 2006 amends the trade union structure and rules out the zonal or regional committees. So if there is still the presence of zonal or regional committees, they have no legal basis.

2.5 Strength of Trade Union Structure in Bangladesh

The merits of Bangladesh trade union structure are the following:

The federation level leaders do not change their political affiliation as frequently as the basic union leaders. So there is less chance of opportunism in federation level leaders. So federations are necessary to strengthen the trade union movement.

Many trade unions leaders who lead trade union movement are in the more than one level. Thus the coordination becomes easier. As for example, the name of Mr. Md. Mukaddem Hussain can be mentioned who is at the same time General Secretary of Bangladesh Sanijukta Sramic federation (BSSF), a national level federation of Bangladesh, President of Bangladesh Sanjukta Building & Wood Workers Federation (BSBWWF), an industrial level federation, President of Bangladesh Sanjukta Truck Bandabastakari Paribahan Sramik Federation and the Secretary General of Asian Trade Federation of Transport Workers (ATF-TW). This type of one person's association indifferent levels of the trade union structures is a meant of Bangladesh trade union structure.

The formation of SKOP and bringing of national level federations in the same platform under the umbrella-SKOP is another merit of trade union structure of Bangladesh. SKOP can be called the CBA of national level federations.

Leaders of industrial and federation levels are external who have no fear of job-less and so they can play effective roles in the movement.

When any dispute is raised among union and management in the basic level, the federations guide the basic unions. As the federation level leaders are literate and experienced and have affiliations, management cannot easily ignore them.

2.6 Weakness of Trade Union Structure in Bangladesh

To achieve the goals and objectives of trade union, a strong trade union structure is necessary. But the following weaknesses in the structure of the trade unions are noticed.

Conflicts of trade unions and internal conflicts of unions are common phenomena of trade union. This impedes a strong trade union movement.

Economically the trade unions are very weak. Fund crisis constitutes problems in structuring the movement.

In the highest level (national level) there is not a sole national level federation. Though SKOP is formed is some nation level federation's are get to join in the SKOP-umbrella. According to many federations level leaders, they differ in their political views and this difference has been working for the division of SKOP several times (followed by reunions) SKOP leader Mr. Md. Mukaddem Hossain says there is hope that SKOP will remain united and that the rest of the national level federations will join SKOP. Leaders think if any time SKOP breaks, it can only happen because of political reasons.

For the continual divisions of trade unions, though the number of unions has increased, the number of members has not increased proportionately.

The long channel of the structure of trade union sometimes creates confusion among basic union leaders.

2.7 Brief History of development of Trade Unions in Bangladesh (1947 to till)

The tradition of the parallel development of the nationalist and the trade union movement, which had originated in British India, continued through the Pakistan period down to the birth of Bangladesh.

For the first time in India the Bombay Mill Hands Association was formed on 24 April 1890. This gave impetus to the trade union movement in British India. The establishment of ILO in 1919 provided a source of inspiration for the workers to organize themselves and shape their destiny. India's membership of the same exerted great influence in the formation of a central organization of workers called 'All India Trade Union Congress' (AITUC) in 1920 for the purpose of conducting and coordinating the activities of the labor organizations.

The period from 1924 to 1935 may be considered as the era of revolutionary trade union movement. MN Roy, Muzaffer Ahmed, SA Dange and Shawkat Osmani led the trade unions movements and as a result the political consciousness among industrial workers increased. To control the movement, the British government adopted ruthless measures (e.g. Kanpore Conspiracy Case and Meerat Conspiracy Case) against the militant workers and trade union leaders, but no strategy could suppress the trade unions movement; rather the colonial resistance invigorated the movement against the colonial power. Later, the trade unions movement was closely linked with nationalist movements and the working class started vigorous struggle for emancipation from extreme repression and economic exploitation by the colonial regime.

At the time of Partition of India (1947), most trade union leaders were Hindus and when they migrated to India, a void was created in leadership in the trade union movement of Pakistan, especially in its eastern wing. Moreover, the institutions to advance workers' interest were mostly situated in areas outside Pakistan. There were barely 75 registered trade unions in the whole of Pakistan, compared to 1987 in undivided India in 1946. Of this small number of trade unions, the larger share fell to West Pakistan, leaving only a very few for the eastern wing, where there were only 141 factories with 28,000 workers and 30 unions in all with a total of 20,000 members.

During Pakistan period most trade unions leaders held conflicting views and the trade unions were fragmented and weakened. As a result, the trade unions movement met a setback and the trade unions activities passed into the hands of petty bourgeoisie leadership. Moreover, the trade union movement in Pakistan was characterized by fragmentation of unions, prolonged strikes, retaliatory lockouts and picketing which sometimes led to violence.

As the trade unions movement in Bangladesh originated in British India and Pakistan, it naturally retained its old character of working more as a nationalist force against colonial domination than as a class force vis-à-vis capitalist exploitation. As a result, the trade union movement of the region that had gained momentum in the hands of political leaders stood divided along the political and/or ideological lines in independent Bangladesh.

During this period, the trade union movement was marked by direct interference by the government and the ruling party in its internal affairs. In many industrial belts terrorism was let loose by the men of the labor front of the then ruling party and tried to drive out the honest trade unionists from the leadership of the unions. Moreover, the barring of outsiders from trade union leadership at the basic union level made the process of union hijacking very easy and turned the workers into a very weak and defenseless community.

In the early 1980s, the military government of Bangladesh banned all trade union activities in the country. Then an alliance of the National Federation of Trade Unions (NFTUs) emerged in the name of Sramik Karmachari Oikka Parishad (SKOP) to establish the democratic rights of workers as well as to fulfill their economic demands. Most NFTUs were in SKOP and since 1983, most trade union movements in Bangladesh have been organized under the leadership of SKOP.

The opportunism and lenient attitude of the trade union leaders including SKOP gave the ruling regimes a chance to disregard the agreements signed between the government and the trade union leaders. At present, the leaders of nineteen of the twenty three NFTUs are included in the SKOP. After its formation, SKOP submitted a 5-point charter of demands for establishing their democratic rights and higher wages through rallies, torch processions, demonstrations, strikes, hartals, blockades etc.

Ironically, SKOP failed to yield any tangible results for the working class people of the country. The effectiveness of the trade union movement under the leadership of SKOP gradually weakened because most SKOP leaders have political affiliations and therefore, cannot escape the influence of their respective political parties. Moreover, lack of active support by the major political parties to SKOP's programs, excessive pressures on government by the private employers and donor agencies to disregard SKOP's demands using repressive measures to disrupt the trade union movement, forcible occupation of unions, bribing of trade union leaders, opportunistic and compromising attitude of the union leadership rendered the SKOP demands ineffective. In fact, SKOP has become a moribund forum of the working class with little to offer to the country's future trade union movements.vi

The Jatiobadi Sramik Dal (formed) joined the federation and this unity named them "Sramik Karmachari Oikka Parishad" (SKOP) (workers unity organization). SKOP called 24 hour nationwide strike on the basis of 5 point strike. This was the first successful nation side strike called by trade unions alone. Patient work of leaders' innumerable struggle of workers at enterprise and trade levels, martyrdom and imprisonment, contribution of WFTU leaders and political leaders lead to the advancement of trade union movement. Efforts of the government to divide and confuse the workers failed.

The SKOP again called country wide strike for 48 hours on 22 and 23rd May. The military government ultimately had to bow down and sign an agreement with SKOP. This was a historic event bringing forward the immense potential of working class and its radical impact on politics.

The employers association, the bourgeois politicians were alarmed. The cunning bourgeois leadership helped by a left, lacking vision and determination subordinated the trade union movement to their power game.

Realization of workers demands and requirements of policy changes were ignored and only change of govt. that is one point demand, as it was called, was stressed. Several govt. changes could not bring about any change in the life of the working people. Workers became disillusioned about SKOP. Yet they did not give up. Action committees were formed at trade levels. Several strike actions of Jute, Textile, Chemical and other workers shook the country. On one single day 17 workers were shot dead. One can say the working class of Bangladesh which during 1984 and around showed its tremendous potential was betrayed by the political as well as the trade union leadership. Nevertheless the workers made a fighting retreat as was evident in such movements which led to killing of many workers and people in one day.

2.8 Industrial Relations

Development of trade union of a country depends on the industrial relations of that country. Industrial relations refer to the relationship between the employer and the employee. It is also called the relationship between labor and capital. W.V. Owen & H.V. Finston gives the following definition:

"Industrial relations deals with people at work or that Industrial relations is concerned with many problems related to employer employee relations"

J.E.T. Dunlop says "an industrial relations system, at any one time in its development is regarded as comprised of certain actors, certain contexts, an ideology which binds the industrial relations system together and a body of rules created to govern the actors at the place of work and work community."

So industrial relation can be expressed by the following equation:

(IR)=f (a, c, r and i) a = Trade unions leaders, employers/management and the government. c = Market, technology and power. r = Procedural and substantive rules. i = Ideology f = Unspecified function.

2.9 Varity of relations

Union and management interactions or relationships display almost infinite variety. The relationship between unions and management has been characterized as a challenge-response process: union challenge and management response. The challenge is dual: a negotiation challenge and a grievance challenge. The challenge and the response can be militant, moderate, or weak to the point of virtual nonexistence. The nature of the challenge and the response—whether it is militant or nonmilitant—is a reflection of how the parties use the power they have and how they tend to relate to each other as human beings.

David A. Peach and David Kuechle (The Practice of Industrial Relations) arranged union—management relationships on a spectrum, ranging from conflict to collusion. Any particular union-management relationship can be placed on this spectrum in relationship to certain key or bench-mark relationships.

3.0 Conflict

In a relationship characterized as "conflict," the parties may be said to be actively attempting to "do each other in." Both the challenge and the response are likely to be extremely militant. Management does not want its employees represented by a union and will do everything in its power to see that the union is destroyed. In turn, the union is fighting for survival—on its own terms—and will do everything it can to survive, returning the company's actions tit-for-tat even if it means destroying the company. Many of the activities which used to characterize conflict are now illegal: employer blacklists, yellow-dog contracts, the use of spies, or massive, violent picketing.

3.1 Containment-Aggression

In a relationship characterized as containment—aggression the parties tolerate the existence of one another—but just barely. The union challenge and management response can be characterized as militant. Management acts to restrict the degree of authority which it shares with the union. The union actively works to increase the scope of its influence. In this type of relationship the parties tend to be very legalistic, insistent on following the contract to the letter. The scope of arbitration is frequently restricted.

Jealous of their rights, the parties may engage in petty bickering. The General Electric—International Union of Electrical Workers relationship was for many years a typical containment—aggression relationship. Virgil Day, a company vice president, characterized the union as "attempting to perform a hysterectomy on the goose that lays the golden egg." When several company officers were sent to prison in the United States for violating the antitrust laws, the union President, James Carey, sent them games of Monopoly to help them pass the time.

3.2 Accommodation

Further along the spectrum is a relationship described as accommodation. Here, while still watchful of their rights, the parties are actively attempting to adjust to each other. They are learning to live with each other, even though the relationship is not always happy. They are tolerant of one another, and the union challenge is somewhat moderate.

3.3 Cooperation

The collective bargaining agenda is much broader in scope under a cooperative relationship. It includes almost any matter of normal concern to management: production scheduling, prices, waste elimination, technological change, work measurement and methods analysis. The union and the workers it represents are seen as full partners in the enterprise. The two parties jointly deal with problems to the mutual benefit to both. Companies and unions that have adopted "Scanlon plans" provide examples of cooperative relationships. Few union-management relationships can be called cooperative.

3.4 Collusion

This final type of relationship is found where union and management are colluding to the detriment of another party. Sometimes those being harmed are the workers which the union supposedly represents. This type of unionism, known as "gangster" unionism or "predatory" unionism, is rare. The union (for a fee) signs a collective-bargaining agreement with the employer, and this effectively prevents another union from organizing employees (an existing contract is generally a bar to an organizing attempt). That agreement, called a "sweetheart contract," does not provide very significant benefits to the workers.

There is probably no union-management relationship which fits neatly into one of the categories described above. Most collective bargaining relationships probably fall somewhere in between containment aggression and accommodation. However, this brief enumeration shows that a variety of relationships are possible. The exact nature of the relationship depends on both union and management, and the parties are responsible for their relationship, whatever it is like. Generally parties get exactly the kind of relationship they deserve.

3.5 Factors Affecting Development of Trade Union

A number of factors influence the parties as they evolve a relationship. These factors can be differentiated into two types: those internal to the relationship and under the control of the parties, and those external to the relationship and somewhat beyond the control of the parties.

3.6 Internal factors influencing labor relations

History and tradition:

The impact of history and tradition in a relationship can be seen in a number of ways. Historically, certain work groups may have received a wage differential. Management may have responded only to the use of pressure tactics—wildcat strikes or slowdowns—by the union. Works may have traditionally received a certain benefit, such as a coffee break or a Festival bonus.

In so far as history and tradition influence the parties' expectations about each other, rapid change cannot usually be accomplished without some upheaval. A company that has followed a set of policies designed to implement containment—aggression relationship with the union could not logically expect to change that relationship to one of accommodation overnight, Mutual trust is earned over time.

History of Industrial Relations of Bangladesh shows that industrial relations is one of oppression from the owners/employers' part. The workers had to undergo colonial suppression and the employers' only attention was on their capital not on labors. Laborers were treated as animals. Any objection from the part of the labor used to mean death on the hands of the owners, and the trend is still visible.

3.7 Nature of Leadership

The personalities of leaders of both the union and management and the type of leadership they provide are major determinates of a union management relationship.

Some union leaders have personalities strong enough to generate enthusiasm and trust among members so that they would follow him in whatever direction he leads while others fail to do so for their lack in charisma and credibility

There are dedicated leaders in Bangladesh who have led the trade union movement to the present state. But at the same time there is alleged opportunism in trade union leadership in Bangladesh. Trade union leadership is in part still under the control of bourgeois who have no real respect for the class-struggle of the working class and who maintain secret relation with the employer class and seek their own ends in the name of working for the working class. In many cases basic unions are the pocket unions of the management. For this disease trade union movement in Bangladesh has not yet developed as per expectation.

3.7.1 Union Politics

The nature of leadership is particularly important within unions, because unions are democratic institutions. Unlike management, union leadership serves at the pleasure of its constituency. All unions are democratic, but some unions are more democratic than others.

But in Bangladesh union politics is marked by internal conflicts and conflicts between unions. For internal conflict many leaders to toe form new unions breaking their old ones. Thus only the number of trade unions increases not the number of members. This only weakens the movement. Conflicts between unions are common phenomena in Bangladesh trade unions movement. One hundred workers killed in Barbakunda industrial area in Chittagong in 1973. It is a typical example of conflicts between unions of Bangladesh.

3.7.2 Policies

Perhaps the most important determinants of the relationship between the parties are the policies adopted by the unions and management, or lack thereof.

A policy is a statement as to how an organization will act in a given situation. While leaders of most organizations believe that their actions are policy-guided, those actions frequently are not in fact so guided. Actions frequently are impromptu and often made with short-run considerations rather than long-run considerations in mind. Those companies with successful labor relations are successful because they companies with successful labor relations are successful because they manage by policy. The same is true for unions.

Management and the union face some fundamental policy decisions in their response to each other and to collective bargaining in general. What kind of a relationship do they want? How hard are they willing to work to achieve that relationship? In general, the tone of the relationship is the result of management initiative and not union initiative.

Both parties must make policy decisions concerning the content and administration of collective agreements. These decisions must encompass a host of specific subject areas, including wage payment systems, benefit level and structure, seniority systems and discipline. The parties must determine whether and to what extent they will use or resist pressure in the pursuit of their goals. Both sides must have implementing and procedural policies for translating their goals into action.

For example, a management may decide to accept the union and to be "firm but fair" in dealing with it. In terms of discipline this basic policy may give rise to a substantive policy of administering discipline for just cause. The discipline policy may, in turn, be implemented by a policy of following a progressive disciplinary system. Detailed procedural policies would then follow to outline the specifics of the systems, such as the penalties associated with absenteeism. A union could make a set of policies in the same way.

The policies adopted by the parties may be identical, may be different, or may be amenable to compromise. In any event, these policies and the extent to which they exist will influence the general relationship of the union and management and their specific actions within that relationship.

3.8 External Influences on Labor Relations

External factors influencing labor relations can be divided into the following categories:

3.8.1 Industry Characteristics

The elasticity of demand for products produced in an industry and substitution availability are important industry characteristics which can influence collective bargaining. In industries where price can significantly influence demand, management will be extremely cost-conscious and tend to resist union wage demands. There consumers can use alternate products, for instance aluminum instead of steel, or can obtain products from other markets, substituting Japanese steel for Canadian steel for example, management may be cost-conscious but also reluctant to take a strike lest customers turn permanently to the substitute product or source of supply. In some industries, such as education, medical care, or construction, there may be no available substitute for the product[241].

The labor cost as a percentage of the total cost of a product may well influence the parties in their relationship. In industries where labor costs are a significant cost item, such costs as construction, education, transportation will be monitored closely. In other industries, such as utilities, which are capital intensive and where labor costs are not as important as other costs, management may be less inclined to strongly resist wage demands.

So in case of garments workers, our employers are extremely cost—conscious and tend to resist union wage demands that is why we see the movements of our garment workers center round wage though they have other substantial issues.

Another factor about industry characteristics is that it matters what percentage of workers of a particular industry is involved in the movement. Though there is a huge number of garments workers only a very low percentage of them are involved in trade union movement. That is way the movement is very weak here garments industry.

3.8.2 Technology

The nature of the production technology also influences labor relations. Some process industries, such as oil refineries, are easy for management personnel to operate during a strike. Others, such as steel mills, are impossible to operate without the regular work force. A strike in the former can mean no loss of production and is not very effective. A strike in the latter is the reverse.

Socio economic condition:

Economic conditions may well influence a union's willingness to settle and also the nature of its respective concerns in bargaining. When economic times are good, managements are often unwilling to take a strike and are thus more receptive to union demands. When times are bad, unions may be more concerned with security than money. Recently the economic conditions of high unemployment, high inflection and low profits have made bargaining difficult.

Our socio economic condition is characterized by exploitations on the part of the employers, lack of democratic environment, lack of educational qualification in our workers, poor financial condition of the workers, equal presence of our workers, lack of nutrition and poor physical condition poor social status or our workers, poor base of the formation of working class, absence of industrial democracy absence of workers representative in the parliament, poor balance between the demand and supply of workers, big family size of the workers, lack of class consciousness in the working class etc.

All the factors above influence our trade union movement heavily. As for example poor financial condition of the garment workers, according to many union leaders, is the main obstacle behind their lagging behind. Otherwise they could make the strongest movement in the country given the largest number of workers in the industry.

3.8.3 Legislation

Legislation is probably the greatest outside force affecting labor relations. The law has created a whole framework within which unions and management operate. Many of the parties' actions, from the recognition of the union, to the negotiation and administration of a contract, to conciliation, mediation and sometimes arbitration are carried out because the law requires that they be done.

When the rules and regulations of a state do not intervene in the workers' right of association, workers can spontaneously participate in the trade union movement.

But in case of Bangladesh we see different governments in different times have brought amendments in the IRO—1969 in most of the cases to; take away the freedom of association and democratic rights from the workers. The following is the amendments of the ordinance[242].

Industrial Relations (amendment) Ordinance 1970

Industrial Relations (Regulations) Ordinance 1973

Industrial Relations (regulations) Ordinance 1975

Industrial Relations (Regulations) Ordinance 1977

Industrial Relations (Amendment) Ordinance 1980

Industrial Relations (Regulations) Ordinance 1982

Industrial Relations (Amendment) Ordinance 1985

Industrial Relations (Regulations) Ordinance 1989

Industrial Relations (Regulations) Law 1990

Industrial Relations (Amendment) Ordinance 1990

And the last amendment occurred in 2006. The new ordinance is "Bangladesh Labor Code, 2006" which rules not the following previous ones—

The Workmen's Compensation Act, 1923 (viii of 1923)

The Children (Pledging of Labor) Act, 1933 (ii of 1933)

The Workmen's Protection Act, 1934 (iv of 1935)

The Dock Laborers Act, 1934 (xix of 1934)

The Payment of Wages Act, 1936 (iv of 1936)

The employer's Liability Act, 1938 (xxiv of 1938)

The Employment of Children Act, 1938 (xxvi of 1938)

The Maternity Benefit Act, 1939 (iv of 1939)

The Mines Maternity Benefit Act, 1941 (xix of 1941)

The Motor Vehicles (Drivers) Ordinance, 1942 (v of 1942)

The Maternity Benefit (Tea Estate) Act, 1950 (xx of 1950)

The Employment (Records of Service) Act, 1951 (xix of 1952)

The Bangladesh Plantation Employees Provident Fund Ordinance, 1959 (xxxi of 1959)

The Coal Mines (Fixation of Rates of Wages) Ordinance, 1960 (xxxix of 1960)

The Road Transport Workers Ordinance, 1961 (xxvii of 1961);

The Minimum Wages Ordinance, 1961 (xxxiv of 1961);

The Plantation Labor Ordinance, 1962 (xxix of 1962);

The Apprenticeship Ordinance, 1962 (lvi of 1962);

The Factories Act, 1965 (iv of 1965);

The Shops and Establishment Act, 1965 (vii of 1965);

The Employment of Labor (Standing Orders) Act, 1965 (viii of 1965)

The Companies Profits (Worker's Participation) Act, 1968 (xii of 1968);

The Industrial Relations Ordinance, 1969 (xxiii of 1969);

The Newspaper Employees (Conditions of Service) Act, 1974 (xxx of 1974);

The Dock Workers (Regulation of Employment) Act, 1980 (xvii of 1980)

Whatever the laws and regulations are, the matter of regret is that they are not reflected in real life situations. In garments sector the real pictures is that the workers do not even enjoy the right of joining a trade union. An attempt to join a trade union is still in many cases translates into the loss of job of a worker.

3.9 Trade Unions in Different Industries in Bangladesh

In Bangladesh there are many industries off which a few are very prominent and active such as garments, textile, agriculture, ship breaking and pharmaceuticals.

4.0 Trade Union in Garments Industry

The registered garment federations in Bangladesh

As far as the office records of the Directorate of Labor are concerned, there should now be four registered federations of garment workers unions operating in Bangladesh. However, despite the existence of four federations on paper, it has found the existence of only two federations in reality, which we designate here as registered Federation A and registered Federation B in order to protect the confidentiality of our respondents. Registered Federation C is only partially active and is characterized by certain irregular labor-related activities, while registered Federation D seems to be defunct. It should be mentioned in this connection that after repeated attempts people failed to locate even the office of registered Federation D from the address that was submitted to the office of the Registrar of Trade Unions while applying for registration, and also failed to find out the whereabouts of its office bearers. All of the three active registered federations claimed to have sufficient numbers of unions at the unit levels. Most of the unit unions, they claimed, were established with their direct support. They extend, they stressed, all kinds of legal support to the workers of their unit unions in case of dismissal or any other wage or work-related disputes. They also claimed to have negotiated with the owners of some factories on behalf of their unit unions. Registered Federation A and registered Federation B further emphasized that they also provide paralegal and other job related training to members and supporters at the unit union level[243].

The non-registered garment federations in Bangladesh

Beside the above-mentioned registered federations, it is found from different sources, including newspaper reports, the names of 10 more non-registered federations which were purportedly involved with garment workers. However, among these 10 federations, only the one the surveyors designate non-registered Federation G was active on almost a full-time basis with various female labor related activities—for instance providing medical facilities to female garment workers, running night and weekend schools, conducting paralegal and socio-political awareness-building programs, extending legal support to individual workers and its affiliated unit Trade unions, gender issues and the ready-made garment industry of Bangladesh 187 unions, etc. For four other federations, we failed, despite all our efforts, to trace either the office bearers or their offices or to find even one clue regarding their existence.

Of the remaining five non-registered federations, one is a comparatively new organization established by a former left-leaning female student leader, which had yet to start any significant activity at the time of the study. A federation designated non-registered Federation F is the second best organization among the non-registered federations in terms of organizational activity. Besides providing legal and institutional help to its unit unions, it also conducts, from time to time, it claims, various socio-political and paralegal awareness building programs for garment workers. The remaining three federations are mostly engaged in mousumi (seasonal) activities such as organizing rallies and demonstrations in front of factories or the National Press Club, arranging processions to the National Press Club, sending workers' delegations to the management on behalf of the garment workers in respective factories and so on in times of labor management disputes. viii

4.1 Trade Union in Ship Breaking Industry

The industry is in a very introductory stage in the country. The trade union here is yet to be developed but this needs to be taken care of very seriously. The workers risky job responsibilities make them vulnerable to fatal accidents. The welfare of the workers is of most important.

4.2 Trade Union in Textile Industry

Trade union in textile industry especially in the government sector is very disappointing. As the number of government cotton mills is diminishing and are closing the labors have almost nothing to do. As the trade unions lack collective bargaining the workers interest are not taken care of. The workers lead their life in a dilapidating condition.

4.3 Growth of Trade Union in Bangladesh

Bangladesh, since after inception of the country, has trade union activities. At the very beginning the number of trade unions was slightly more than one thousand. As the industrial activities of the country increases, the number and member of trade union increases too many folds. Now the country has around seven thousand trade unions which are six times more than the initial number.

The following table represents the registered trade union numbers and total number of their members:

Year	No. of registered trade unions	Total no. of their members
1971	1160	4,505,06
1975	3161	9,21,152
1980	3613	10,97,707
1982	2156	9,46,048
1985	2593	10,90,338
1990	3789	16,19,008
1994	4434	16,81,898
1996	5178	17,30,927
2000	6304	19,05,451
2001	6528	19,38,269
2002	6809	19,95,307
2003	6492	20,94,887
2004	6740	21,29,698
2005	6777	21,31,800

(Source: Bangladesh Labor Journal 2006)[244]
Table 1 : Number of registered trade unions and their members from 1971-2005

The following graph shows the growth of trade union members in the country. It is clearly assumed from it that during the military regime trade union movements were slashed down and after the democratic regime it started to accelerate very rapidly.

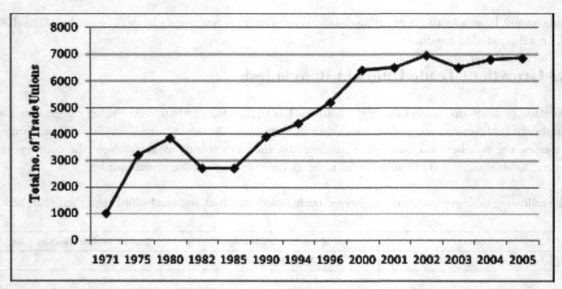

Figure 1 : Growth of Trade Unions in Bangladesh

The same thing happened in case of the number of trade union members in the country. The number even decreased during the army ruled regime. The following graph shows the growth of total number of members in the trade unions:

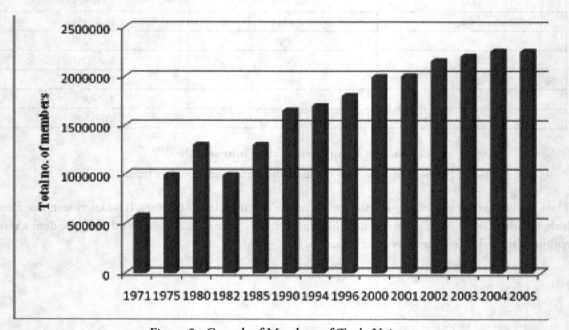

Figure 2 : Growth of Members of Trade Unions

The department of Labor accords registration of trade unions, regulates their activities and also tries to resolve the inter-union and intra-union rivalries through informal discussion, etc., under the provision of Industrial Relations Ordinance, 1969. The Director of Labor is the registrar of Trade Union for the whole of Bangladesh. While the join Directors of Labor are the registering authorities for respective divisions. Statement showing the numbers of registered trade union under this department from 1991-92 to 2000-01 (up to January) is showing in the following table:

Year	No. of Trade Unions Registered during the year	Total no. of Trade Unions	No. of Members during the year	Total no. of Members
1970	21	21	2489	2489
1971-83	Do not available			
1984	127	726	72568	75587
1985	45	771	94254	169841
1986	273	1044	125486	295327
1987	109	1153	168548	463875
1988	86	1239	185478	649353
1989	99	1438	208954	858308
1990	105	1543	244254	1102561

(Source: Bangladesh Labor Journal, 2002)

Table 2 : Trade Union Registered in Bangladesh

Trade unions, though, homogeneously distributed across the country, are concentrated in the capital city when the number of members is counted. Dhaka division singly comprises more than fifty percent members of the whole country. The following table shows the division-wise segmentation of the trade unions across the country.

HQ/Division	National Federation	Ind. Federation	Garments Federation	Basic Unions	Emp. Association/ GU	Total
Head32 quarters	108	15	208	57	420	
Dhaka Division	X	X	11	2119	Gar. Un 123	2253
Chittagong Division	X	X	2	1419	Gar. Un 21	1442
Khulna Division	X	X	X	960	X	960
Rajshahi Division	X	X	X	1562	X	1562
Total 32	108	28	6268	144	6647	

Table 3 : Number of Registered Trade Union in Different Division (As on 1st January, 2008)

Reg. National Federation: 32 Aff. Unions: 1269   Membership: 12,62,765

Total Reg. Federation: 168 Aff. Unions: 1269   Membership: 12,62,765

Reg. Basic Union: 6402   Membership: 21,90,473

(Source: Register of Trade Unions, Govt. of Bangladesh)

While trade unions are counted according to the type of industry, it is found that transportation sector has the highest number of trade unions in Bangladesh. Transportation sector is followed by shop which is almost half of the preceding sector. Other than these two sectors all have very small number of trade unions. The following table and graph distribute the trade union among different sectors or industries of Bangladesh.

Sl. No.	Industry/Sector	1996		1997	
		Union	Members	Union	Members
1.	Miscellaneous	180	11265	201	22580
2.	Transportation	144	7248	119	20544
3.	Shop	83	4188	52	7546
4.	Gas	4	263	3	475
5.	Chemical	6	626	3	111
6.	Jute	5	1554	5	925
7.	Hotel	6	577	7	113
8.	Dock	1	74	-	-
9.	Food	1	98	3	237

(Source: Bangladesh Labor Journal, 2002)

Table 4 : List of Registered Trade Unions (Sector Basis, 1996-1997)

The above table can be graphically represented as follows:

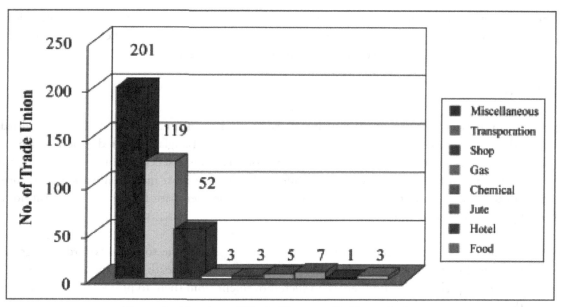

Figure 3 : Number of Trade Union in Different Industry

4.4 Workers Opinion from Different Industries

The workers opinion can be categorized in two different categories. First the government sector and second is the non-government sector. The non-government sector can further be classified into two: the multinationals and the local companies.

After conducting interviews with some of the different organization's trade union members, the following assumptions can be taken:

The trade union in the government sector is very bureaucratic and the workers are bound to register to join the trade union in most of the cases though they are suppose to be the member when they are employed by the government. The political affiliation is very important to get promoted in a higher position and to get few others benefit. The workers always try to have a good relation with the leaders to get support from them.

The multinationals trade union is very organized. The workers after getting their employment letter become a member of the trade union. There is no political activity within the organization. The workers get their benefit according to their performance and experience. The payment of them is higher than the floor selected by the government. Once a problem occurs within the organization regarding the workers, the dispute is solved by the higher authorities. The leaders of the trade union only abide by the decision made by the decision makers.

In the local private companies the trade union is in between the government and the multinational organizations. The trade unions in most of the cases are organized and the workers get their benefits from the trade union leaders. The collective bargaining process is very strong.

4.5 Conclusion

Opportunism, corruption, undue political interference, workers' disunity and the ideological divide between the leaders have stalled the trade union movement in Bangladesh for decades, which has allowed the workers' rights to be crushed across the country. The absence of constructive unionism has imperiled the workers in both formal and informal sectors as most industrial workers have been deprived of the right to form trade unions. General workers, on their part, have gradually learnt not to expect anything from trade unions.

Workers in the construction sector, which involves many people due to its backward linkage, are also in the same disarray. Their workplaces are still considered to be death traps and the frequency of accidents is unacceptably high and there is no such movement from them to protect the workers from the Death Valley.

In the garments sector, which earns the lion's share of the country's foreign exchange, workers have hardly any right to form unions. More than two million workers, mostly women, get the lowest ages in the world and cannot even buy enough food. Moreover they have to work in dangerous conditions since most factories do not take even the most basic safety measures. Their ruthless exploitation has sometimes led to violent unrest, which the unrepentant factory owners term 'a conspiracy' against the sector.

The wholesale divestment of industries has shattered the workers' unity and weakened the trade union movement throughout. An 'upstart' section sheltered by the mainstream political forces has emerged in the trade unions, which has slowed down the movement.

The country's political leaders do not seem to realize that an active and constructive role played by trade unions is good for industrial growth. Industrial unrest would have been lessened if there were constructive bargaining agents free of political influence. In other countries, trade unions promote better management of industries, and such sound trade union activism would also help Bangladesh to grow.

Some blame political division among the trade unionists and union leaders' opportunism for the state of inertia in the trade union movement. Moreover the labor fronts of the mainstream political parties prioritize the party's interest instead of the workers' rights.

A holistic approach is needed to organize the trade union movements of Bangladesh. The union leaders need to be more educated and devoted to the need of the owners as well as the workers from the existing way of devoting towards their own benefit and the owners benefit. The workers need to know what their rights are and what the appropriate way of demonstrating a demand is. The owners as well as the government has to be more concerned about the well-being of the workers and need to concentrate on the development of collective bargaining.

CHAPTER VII

Functions of Min

CONTENTS

1.0 Role of Ministry of Labor

1.1 Coordinating Ministry: Ministry of Labor and Manpower

In 1971, Bangladesh came into being as a sovereign independent country. The Constitution of Bangladesh provides for a unitary form of government and so, Ministry of Labor and Manpower is vested with the responsibility for labor ministration. In 1974, the Office of Registrar of Trade Unions was merged with Department of Labor. In 1976, the employment service and vocational functions of the Department of Labor were transferred to a newly-tied agency, the Bureau of Manpower, Employment and Training (BMET). It also took over the responsibility of overseas employment administration which enjoins the responsibility of emancipating the toiling masses, peasants and workers, i.e. ensuring the right to social security. Everyone will be paid for work and persons will not be able to enjoy unearned income. It also enjoins upon the obligation of creating conditions in which human labor of every form—intellectual and physical—will become a fuller expression of creative endeavor and of the human personality. Under the provisions of the Constitution, equality of opportunity in public employment has also been protected as fundamental right and thus a form of forced labor has been abolished. The epitome of fundamental rights is built under the provisions of Article 38, which confers on citizens the right to form associations and unions subject to any responsible restrictions imposed by law in the interests of morality and/or public order.

In Bangladesh, the Ministry of Labor and Manpower is responsible for policy formulation and overall supervision of the departments and offices under it. As per schedule-1 of the Rules of Business, the Ministry performs in relation to the following functions[245]:

1. Welfare of labor including labor under non-agricultural employment
2. Industrial unemployment and insurance
3. Trade unions, industrial and labor disputes, labor courts, wages boards and industrial workers' wages commission;
4. Labor statistics
5. Administration of labor laws
6. Labor research including compilation of labor statistics;
7. Dealings and agreements with international organizations in the field of labor and manpower
8. International Labor Organization (ILO)
9. Labor Conferences
10. National Institute of Labor Administration and Training
11. Employees' Social Security and Social Insurance Laws
12. Welfare of merchant navy seafarers, employment of seamen (except the administration of seamen's pool for national shipping and training of seamen
13. Administration of Essential Services (Maintenance) Ordinance

14. Administration of laws connected with safety and welfare in mines and quarries
15. Administration of Minimum wages Act
16. Workers' education
17. Discipline in industry
18. Constitution of wages boards for individual industries
19. Regulation of working conditions of industrial workers
20. Evaluation of implementation of labor and industrial welfare laws and policies
21. Social security measures
22. Co-ordination of activities of other ministries and organizations in connection with labor and industrial welfare
23. Manpower research including compilation of manpower statistics

1.2 Implementing Agencies

The Ministry of Labor and Manpower has under it the following implementing agencies:

1. Department of Labor
2. Department of Inspection for Factories and Establishments
3. Bureau of Manpower, Employment and Training (BMET)
4. Minimum Wages Board
5. Labor Appellate Tribunal and seven labor courts
6. Labor attaché offices attached to the Bangladesh embassies in Saudi Arabia, Kuwait, UAE, Qatar, Bahrain, Oman, Libya and Malaysia
7. Plantation Employees' Provident Fund.

1.3 Labor Laws and Role of Ministry of Labor as Administrative Applications of Labor Laws

The following laws (and rules made there under) regulate the working conditions of workers employed in factories, shops-and establishments, road transport organizations and tea plantations covering such aspects as working hours, health and hygiene, safety, and welfare. Matters such as conditions of employment, classification of workers leave holidays, disciplinary matters, grievances procedures, maintenance of service records, etc. are covered by the following laws (and rules and by-laws made there under);

1. The Railways Act, 1980 {Chapter VI-A) and the Railway Servants (Hours of Employment) Rules, 1931
2. The Inland Water Transport Workers {Regulation of Employment) Act, 1992
3. The Newspaper Employees (Conditions of Services) Act, 1974 (XXX of 1974), administered by the Ministry of Information and Broadcasting.

4. The Dock Workers (Regulation of Employment) Act, 1980 (XVIII of 1980), administered by the Ministry of Ports. Shipping and Inland Water Transport.
5. The Agricultural Workers (Minimum Wages) Ordinance. 1981 (XVII of 1984)—administered by the Ministry of Agriculture.
6. The State-owned Manufacturing Industries Workers (Terms and Conditions of Service) Act, 1974 (X of 1974)
7. The National Service Ordinance, 1970 (XXII of 1970)
8. The Emigration Ordinance, 1982 (XXIX of 1982)
9. The Bangladesh Merchant Shipping Ordinance. 1983 (XXVI of 1983)

This Ordinance is intended to regulate trade union activities (including strikes, lockouts etc.) and relations between employers and workmen and the avoidance and settlement of any differences or disputes arising between them. But the State-owned Manufacturing Industries Workers Ordinance-1985 restricts collective bargaining in the nationalized sector on certain topics, viz. (a) wages, (h) leave, (c) house rent, (d) conveyance allowance, (e) medical allowance, (f) festival bonus and (g) provident fund.

The following Acts and Ordinance provide that the Industrial Relations Ordinance:

a. Bangladesh Agriculture Research Institute (BARI) Ordinance, 1976
b. Bangladesh Rice Research Institute (BRRI) Act, 1974
c. Fire Services (Amendment) Act 1974 for Fire Service Department
d. Jute Research Institute Act, 1974
e. Civil Aviation Authority Ordinance, 1985
f. The Rural Electrification Board/Samity (Amendment) Ordinance, 1987

1.4 Role of Director of Labor

The Department of Labor was established during the British Indian Rule. Initially it was established to look into the welfare of Indian Immigrant Labor, and was called the Department of Indian Immigrant Labor. With the gradual expansion of the indigenous segment of the labor force, the colonial rulers were compelled to look beyond their limited scope of looking into the welfare of Indian Immigration Labor and had to take measures for the welfare and well-being of all the workers alike. Accordingly, in 1931 the Department of Indian Immigrant Labor was transformed into the General Department of Labor—the state agency responsible for ensuring welfare of both Indian Migrant Labor as well as indigenous labor. Initially the head of the department was designated as Commissioner of Labor, but in 1958 the head was re-designated as Director of Labor and later according to a Govt. order, memo no—230/s—111/1A—8(2)/69 dated 5—3—70, the name of labor Commission office was changed to the Department of labor. Since then the Department of labor has been functioning and endeavoring continuously for facilitation effective labor management relations, collective bargaining and negotiation and ensure prompt and efficient settlement of labor disputes in the industrial sectors of Bangladesh.

Department of labor is responsible to maintain industrial peace and healthy labor management relations throughout Bangladesh. Every Office of this Department administers and implements the provisions of Industrial Relations Ordinance 1969 (before Labor Act 2006) to keep harmonious industrial peace, uninterrupted production process and solves the raised industrial disputes using its conciliation machinery. Moreover through its four IRIS (Industrial Relations Institutes) situated in 4 divisional cities training courses of various duration are being conducted with a view to achieve higher productivity and to make healthy labor management relations.

The Director of Labor (according to Bangladesh Labor Code 2006—Chapter XX) acts has following powers and functions to control Trade Union Movement in Bangladesh:

1. Registration and maintaining registers of trade unions under Chapter Thirteen i.e. anything related to trade union and industrial relations.
2. Filing complaint to the Labor Court for any offence or unfair labor practices or for contravention of any provisions of trade union and industrial relations issues.
3. Determining as to whether an establishment or group of establishments shall be certified to work as a CBA.
4. Election of executive committee of trade unions and supervision of any secret election;
5. Performing as a conciliator in any industrial dispute.
6. Supervise the work of any participation committee; and
7. Perform any other functions imposed by the Labor Code 2006.

The main functions of Director of Labor are-

a. Trade Union Registration
b. Dispute Mitigation
c. Training, and
d. Health Care

So, during any type of dispute mitigation Director of Labor takes the following steps to mitigate the issue:

• If the parties filed to resolve problems by themselves then within next fifteen days they ask for a conciliator to conciliate the dispute.
• With request from the Govt. the conciliator within 10 days calls a meeting between the parties.
• If the settlement is reached then a memorandum of settlement is sent to the Government signed by the parties in dispute.

- If within 30 days of recipient of request by the conciliator no settlement is reached then the conciliation is either considered to be failed or it may continue on the basis of agreement between the parties.
- If the conciliation fails, the conciliator tries to persuade the parties to agree for an Arbitrator for settlement.
- If the parties don't agree to go for an Arbitrator then the conciliator within three days of failure of conciliation gives a certificate to the parties.
- With this certificate the disputed parties go to the labor court for settlement. If they find the award of the court unsatisfactory then they may prefer an appeal to the Labor Appellate Tribunal within 60 days of award delivery but the decision of the Tribunal in such appeal shall be final.
- If the parties agree to go an Arbitrator then he will give his award within thirty days of receiving the request for settlement and the award of the arbitrator shall be final and no appeal shall lie against it.

1.5 Training Institute for Skill Development

Vocational and skill development programmes in Bangladesh are carried out by both public and private sectors. The public sector training system is mainly implemented by two ministries: the Ministry of Labor and Manpower (MOLM). The programmes of the Labor—Ministry are—implemented by BMET, which also acts as the Secretariat of NCSDT. BMET operates 11 Technical Training Centers (TTCs), located in large urban areas, and the Bangladesh Institute of Marine Technology (BIMT). The estimated enrolment capacity of the TTCs and BIMT are 5715. TTCs offer two one-year (9 months' institutional and 3 months' industrial attachment) self-contained trade courses, one leading to national skill standard (NSS) III and the other, leading to NSS II. The BIMT, in addition to offering courses of various duration similar to TTCs, offers three-year diploma courses in marine technology. Besides their regular courses, both TTCs and BIMT offer self-supporting courses and upgrading training programmes for the workers of various enterprises on request from employers.

Besides above institutional trainings, BMET implements (a) the apprentice training programme under the Apprenticeship Ordinance, 1962 and (b) In-plant training programme, a scheme for "Development of in-plant and Apprenticeship Training within Industry" is in operation from July 1992 and will continue for 5 years. Its main objective is to strengthen craftsman skill training within the framework of national policy for development as outlined in the Fourth Five Year Plan (FFYP). The output of the project is estimated to be 21200, trained manpower in different levels of skills. The other important factor in vocational training is the Ministry of Education. Fifty-one Vocational Training Institutes (VTJs), run by MOE through the Directorate of Technical Education (DTE), has an enrolment capacity of about 5000. The private institutes affiliated with the Bangladesh Technical Education Board (BTEB) have an enrolment capacity of about 2500. Thus; the combined enrolment capacity of TTCs, VTls and private institutes is a little over 13000 trainees per year.

1.6 Role of Chief Inspector

The Department of Inspection for Factories and Establishments has zonal and regional offices for inspection of factories, shops, commercial establishments, plantations, ports, docks, railways, inland water transport and road transport for enforcement of labor laws relating to safety, health, hygiene, factory lay-out design, hours of work and rest, payment of wages and compensation etc.

The specific functions allocated to the Chief of this Department are:

1. Inspection of factories, shops, commercial establishments, tea plantations, ports/docks, railways, inland water transport and road transports under labor laws for enforcement of the provisions relating to safety, health, hygiene, labor welfare, payment of wages, regulation, hours of work, conditions and terms of employment, social security etc. of workers
2. Prosecution against the violations of labor laws in different courts; Approval of construction and extension of factories;
3. Approval of lay-out plans of factories;
4. Issue of registration and licenses of factories and realization of fees for the purpose;
5. Maintenance of liaison with different government departments, employers' organizations and trade unions on enforcement of labor laws;
6. Grant of exemption to the managements from operation of different provisions of labor laws;
7. Collection and compilation of data for preparation of animal and oilier periodical reports under various labor laws;
8. Assistance to the Government in formulation of policies about enforcement of labor laws and framing labor laws including amendment of various acts and rules;
9. Preparation of replies [of the ILO questionnaires relating lo adoption of ILO Conventions and Recommendations;
10. Assistance to other international agencies in preparing survey reports relating to labor inspection, wages administration, working conditions, and Occupational health and safety;
11. Representing the Government in national and international seminars, meetings, forums on labor inspection, labor administration, productivity etc.
12. Approval of Service Rules of the workers as and when applied for by the management of different establishments;
13. Examination and checking of the certificates issued by the competent authority relating to safe operations of gears, derrick, winches and other accessories of ports and ships ensuring safety. Also inspects ships touching at Chittagong and Mongla ports for enforcement of safety and welfare provisions of law.

The Department of Inspection for Factories and Establishments is expected to ensure safe operation of factories and establishments in the country. It is assigned the responsibility of approving the factory lay-out plan and overview the scheduling of work and enforcement of legal provisions relating to hours of work, safety, health, welfare facilities, hygiene-, payment of wages, conditions and terms of employment and social security of workers. It is also responsible for the registration and licensing of factories. Before issuing any license, an Inspector should satisfy himself with the provisions for control of dust, fumes, humidity, accidents, environment etc.

Inspectors are expected to go on physical inspections of factories and establishments on a regular basis and give on-the-spot advice to managements in compliance with the legal standards. They may, as well, give written actions, including prosecution for non-compliance of legal provisions and instructions. The Department also initiates programs for training of employers and workers in relevant subjects like health, hygiene, safety, and hazards, etc.

CHAPTER VIII

Objectives of Trade Union Movement in Bangladesh

CONTENTS

1.0 Trade Union

A trade union or labor union is an organization run by and for workers who have banded together to achieve common goals in key areas and working conditions. The trade union, through its leadership, bargains with the employer on behalf of union members (rank and file members) and negotiates labor contracts (Collective bargaining) with employers. This may include the negotiation of wages, work rules, complaint procedures, rules governing hiring, firing and promotion of workers, benefits, workplace safety and policies. The agreements negotiated by the union leaders are binding on the rank and file members and the employer and in some cases on other non-member workers.

1.1 Overall Objectives of Trade Union

Representation

Trade unions represent individual workers when they have a problem at work. If an employee feels he is being unfairly treated, he can ask the union representative to help sort out the difficulty with the manager or employer. Unions also offer their members legal representation. Normally this is to help people get financial compensation for work-related injuries or to assist people who have to take their employer to court.

According to the Bangladesh Labor Code 2006

1. A workman who is a party to an industrial dispute shall be entitled to be represented in any proceedings under the ordinance by an officer of a collective bargaining agent and subject to the provisions of sub section (2) and sub section (3) any employer who is a party to industrial dispute shall be entitled to be represented in any such proceeding by a person duly authorized by him.
2. No party to an industrial dispute shall be entitled to be represented by a legal practitioner in any conciliation proceedings under this ordinance.
3. A party to an industrial dispute may be represented by legal practitioner in any proceedings before the Labor Court, or before an arbitrator, with the permission of the court or the arbitrator as the case may be.

Negotiation

Negotiation is where union representatives, discuss with management, the issues which affect people working in an organization. There may be a difference of opinion between management and union members. Trade unions negotiate with the employers to find out a solution to these differences. Pay, working hours, holidays and changes to working practices are the sorts of issues that are negotiated. In many workplaces there is a formal agreement between the union and the company which states that the union has the right to negotiate with the employer. In these organizations, unions are said to be recognized for collective bargaining purposes.

The term "negotiation" originates from the Latin word negotiari, which means "to carry on business". Negotiation may be defined as a process whereby two or more parties seek an agreement to establish what each shall give or take, or perform and receive in a transaction between them (Saner, 2000). Alternatively, it is an act of discussing an issue between two or more parties with competing interests, with an aim to identify acceptable trade-offs for coming to an agreement (Raihan, 2004). Negotiations are of different types and forms, and various nomenclatures have been developed to classify them (for example, see Monning and Feketekuty, 2004). In this paper, the focus is on multilateral trade negotiations, which may be defined as inter-governmental negotiations on trade-related issues involving all members of the World Trade Organization[246].

Negotiation is one of the fundamental and crucial tasks of every trade union and through effective and successive bargaining on wages, working condition, workers rights and other facilities from the employers.

Voice in decisions affecting workers

The economic security of employees is determined not only by the level of wages and duration of their employment, but also by the management's personal policies which include selection of employees for layoffs, retrenchment, promotion and transfer. These policies directly affect workers. The evaluation criteria for such decisions may not be fair. So, the intervention of unions in such decision making is a way through which workers can have their say in the decision making to safeguard their interests.

Member services

During the last few years, trade unions have increased the range of services they offer their members. These include:

a) Education and training—Most unions run training courses for their members on employment rights, health and safety and other issues. Some unions also help members who have left school with little education by offering courses on basic skills and courses leading to professional qualifications.

The education and training program include the following things:

1) "awareness-raising as to the dramatic number of work-related accidents and the generally rapid deterioration of the health of workers as a consequence of the poorly controlled silent assassins that seriously compromise their health";

2) "Information about laws, the official goal of which is to protect health";

3) "The various dimensions of the means unions have of taking action . . . to protect members health and ensure our physical integrity". These three stages correspond to the three "blocks" of the training program and are identified as such in the trainer's manual:

- work-related accidents and threats to health;
- workers' rights, as far as health and safety are concerned;
- Trade union action[247].

b) Legal assistance—As well as offering legal advice on employment issues, some unions give help with personal matters, like housing, wills and debt.

What are trade union legal services?

Trade union legal services are legal services which one become entitled to after join a trade union. In many cases one will not need to pay for legal services or they will be discounted because they are a benefit of your membership. It is needed to remember that each trade union offers different specific legal services. Trade unions help thousands of people at work with a wide range of different problems. Examples of the some common issues in the workplace today include accidents at work, unfair discrimination in the workplace, pension schemes closing and manufacturing/service sector jobs being transferred to overseas locations[248].

c) Welfare benefits—One of the earliest functions of trade unions was to look after members who hit hard times. Some of the older unions offer financial help to their members when they are sick or unemployed[249].

1.2 Objectives of Some Bangladeshi Trade Unions

1.2.1 National Garments Workers Federation (NGWF)

National Garments Workers Federation is a countrywide registered Independent, Democratic and Progressive Trade Union Federation of garment workers in Bangladesh. The federation was established on 1984. There are 28 registered trade unions (plant unions) affiliated with the NGWF. Beside these, the federation has 1016 factory committees. From 1984, the federation is involved in all the important movements including several countrywide strikes in the garment sector. Total membership of the federation is: 20.000 paying member: 5.100 and non-paying: 14.900.

The federation is run by its written constitution and participations of its members in a democratic way.

Aims and Objectives

- Ensure fair wages.
- Establish the Workers Rights and Human Rights.
- Ensure the equal wages and equal rights for the women workers.
- Improve the working condition and environment in working places.
- Struggle for a democratic, developed and progressive society.

Source: Constitution of National Garments Workers Federation NGWF

1.2.2 Daily Ittefaq (New Nation Printing Press) Workers' Union

The Daily Ittefaq (New Nation Printing Press) workers' union, Dhaka has a trade union according to Labor Code 2006. Its registered office is located at 1, R.K. Mission Road, Dhaka.

Objectives:

1. To ensure economic and better working environment related rights of its members.
2. To motivate workers towards unity and self—dependency.
3. To settle any dispute between the members and employers through negotiation.
4. To ensure financial, legislative and other aids during union approved strike and lockouts.
5. To create responsibility towards newspaper industry and the country.
6. Quality improvement of skill and discipline of the workers.

Source: Constitution of Daily Ittefaq (New Nation Printing Press) workers' union

1.2.3 Bangladesh Parishangkhan Bureau Shangsthpan Karmachari Kallyan Shamiti

Bangladesh Parishangkhan Bureau Shangsthpan Karmachari Kallyan Shamiti was established in July, 2001 with a view to support the workers in many respects and to bargain with the higher authority for the members' rights.

Some of the objectives of this union are:

- To build better relation among the employees.
- To help poor members financially.
- To organize recreational activities.
- To train the dependents of the members in social welfare related works.
- To support members n distress.

- To bargain with the higher authority to achieve legal rights of the members[250].

1.2.4 Bangladesh Choturtha Sreni Sharkari Karmachari Shamiti (Bangladesh fourth class government employee association)

Workers' union for the 4th class government worker of Bangladesh was established in 1950. This union is not specific to a particular organization rather a common union for all the 4th class government workers working in Bangladesh. The head office is situated in Dhaka. There are branch offices in most of the districts, than, locality and unit. The union has a flag and also a monogram but not registered.

The union was mainly established for the welfare of its members and also to bargain with government in various issues related to workers' demands. Some of the objectives of the union are:

- To work for the benefit of the 4th class government workers and to inspire them to work with honesty and sincerity.
- To present different problems and demand of the workers before the government and confirm the rights of them in a regulated manner.
- To increase the quality of work, discipline in the workers.
- To help poor workers financially[251].

1.3 Common Purposes of Bangladeshi Trade Unions

1. To bargain with higher authority:

Owing to a combination of worker inexperience, employer reluctance and barriers to strikes, there is little collective bargaining in practice. The large number of unions further reduces workers' weak bargaining power. Collective bargaining agreements only cover around 10% of workers in the formal economy.

2. To ensure fair wages:

"Fair" compensation of worker wages is a complex one, especially in light of the many different national economies in which workers reside. For fair wages workers should receive the full wages and other compensation they are due without deductions for fines, deposits, or recruitment fees. But in our country fair wages is a major reason of workers' demonstration. For example we can consider the situation of garments workers.

Bangladeshi garments workers are in bad conditions. In 2006, sewing helpers are receiving tk.930/ ($16) per month. Operators are receiving tk. 1500/ to Tk. 2200/ ($25 to $ 37) per month. Their other facilities are low. Working conditions are also poor. Why this bad condition? Bangladeshi garment owners are exploiting the garment workers. On the other hand, the MNCs are main responsible for these bad conditions. MNCs sell a Bangladeshi T-Shirt in $20 to $25 in USA or other developed countries. But they buy this T-shirt from Bangladesh against of $2.Sameway MNC,s sell a Bangladeshi Denim Shirt in $30 to $40 in USA or other developed countries. But they buy this shirt from Bangladesh against of only $4 to $5.This is not the Fair trade or fair price. They also mentioned that this unfair and unjustified trade of the MNCs are also responsible for the bad conditions of the Bangladeshi garment workers. USA and their other institutions always prescribing about the Open Market and Free Economy. But they are not giving Duty Free and Quota Free access of Bangladeshi garments products in the USA market. As a result, garment workers are in more threat[252].

3. To improve better working conditions:

Accidents due to poor working conditions are very common in the workplaces of Bangladeshi work places. Following is a survey of such accidents conducted by Bangladesh Institute of Labor Studies—BILS

Workplace Safety Report-2006
Accident and Violence at Work in Bangladesh
Prepared By-
Bangladesh Institute of Labor Studies-BILS
At a glance:

	Killed	Injured	Raped
			436597408
Sector Basic			
	Killed	Injured	Raped
Garments	141	1578	31
Construction	07	195	
Domestic Workers	35	31	13
Ship Breaking	14	05	-
Transport	30	01	-
Fishermen	509	15	41
Migrant Workers	13	-	-
Shop Workers	19	12	-
Port Workers	09	05	-
Stone Collectors	11	30	-
Tea Workers	04	12	-
Electric Workers	09	01	-
Rice Mill Workers	07	31	-
Cleaners	12	-	-

Other	54	208	4

1.4 Legal Framework of Registrations of a Trade Union

1.5 Special Definition of Worker

According to The Bangladesh Labor Code, 2006 "Worker" means any person including an apprentice employed directly or by a contractor in any establishment or industry to do any skilled, unskilled, manual, technical, trade promotional or clerical work for hire or reward, whether the terms of employment expressed or implied, but does not include any such person who is employed mainly in a managerial or administrative capacity. For the purpose of any proceedings in relation to an industrial dispute includes a person who has been dismissed, discharged, retrenched, laid off or otherwise removed from employment in connection with or as a consequence of that dispute or whose dismissal, discharge, retrenchment, lay off or removal has led to that dispute, but does not include a person employed as a member or the watch and ward or security staff or fire service staff or confidential assistant of an establishment.

1.6 Workers' and Employers' Trade Unions

Subject to provisions the trade unions and industrial relations—

a. Workers, without distinction whatsoever, shall have the right to establish and subject only to the rules of the organization concerned, to join associations of their own choosing primarily for the purpose of regulating the relations between workers and employers or workers and workers.

b. Employers, without distinction whatsoever, shall have the right to establish and subject only to rules of the organization concerned, to join associations of their own choosing primarily for the purpose regulating the relations between employers and workers or employers and employers.

c. Workers' and employers' trade unions shall have the right to establish and join federations and any such union or federation shall have the right to affiliate with international organizations and confederations of workers' and employers' organizations.

d. Trade unions and employers' associations shall have the right to draw up their constitutions and rules, to elect their representatives in full freedom, to organize their administration and activities and to formulate their programs.

1.7 Application for Registration

Any trade union may, under signatures of its President and the Secretary, apply for the registration of trade union to the Registrar of Trade Unions of the concerned area.

1.8 Requirements for Application

1) Every application for registration of trade union shall be made to the Director of Labor or to an officer authorized in this respect.
2) The application shall be accompanied by the following particulars, namely-
    a) A statement showing the following information, namely-
        i) the name of the trade union and the address of its Head Office;
        ii) date of formation of the union;
        iii) The titles, names, age, addresses and occupations of the officers of the trade union.
        iv) Statement of the total membership
        v) Name and number of total workers of the establishment with which the trade union is associated; and
        vi) In case of federation of trade unions the names addresses and registration number of member unions.
    b) Three copies of the constitution of the trade union together with a copy of the resolution by the members of the trade union adopting such constitution bearing the signature of the Chairman of the meeting;
    c) A copy of resolution by the members of the trade union authorizing its President and the Secretary to apply for its registration; and
    d) In case of federation of trade unions, a copy of the resolution from each of the constituent unions agreeing to become a member of the federation.
3) Upon receipt of an application the Director of Labor or the officer authorized in this respect shall immediately forward a copy thereof (together with a list of the officers of the union) to the employer concerned for his information.

Provided that I case of a group of establishments, the Registrar of Trade Unions shall cause public advertisement together with a list of the officers of the union at the cost of the applicant.

1.9 Requirements for Registration of a Trade Union

1) A trade union shall not be entitled to registration under this ordinance unless the constitution thereof provides for the following matter, namely-
    a) The name and address of the trade union;
    b) The objectives for which the trade union has been formed;
    c) The manner in which a worker may become a member of the trade union specifying therein that no worker shall be enrolled as its member unless he applies in the form set out in the constitution declaring that 'he is not a member of any other trade union';
    d) The sources of the fund of the trade union and the purposes for which such fund shall be applicable;

e) The conditions under which a member shall be entitled to any benefit assured by the constitution of the trade union and under which any fine or forfeiture may be imposed on him;

f) The maintenance of a list of members of the trade union and of adequate facilities for the inspection thereof by the officers and members of the trade union.

g) The manner in which the constitution shall be amended, varied or rescinded.

h) The safe custody of the funds of trade union, its annual audit; the manner of audit and adequate facilities for inspection of the account books by the officers and members' of trade union.

i) The manner in which the trade union may be dissolved.

j) The manners of election of officers by the general body of the trade union and the term, not exceeding two years, for which an officer may hold office upon his election or re-election.

k) The numbers of officers, as prescribed by rules, must not be less than five and more than thirty five;

l) The procedures for expressing want of confidence against any officer of the trade union; and

m) The meetings of the executive and of the general body of the trade union, so that the executive shall meet at least once in every three months and the general body at least once every year.

2) A trade union of workers shall not be entitled to registration under this ordinance unless it has a minimum membership of thirty percent of the total number of workers employed in the establishment in which it is formed.

Provided that more than one establishment under the same employer, which are allied to and connected with one another for the purpose of carrying on the same industry—irrespective of their place of situation, shall be deemed to be one establishment for the purpose of this subsection.

3) Where any doubt or dispute arises as to whether; any two or more establishments are under the same employer or whether they are allied to or connected with one another for the purpose of carrying on the same industry, the matter may be referred to the Director of Labor for disposal.

4) Any person aggrieved by the decision of the Director of Labor within thirty days from the date of the decision, appeal to the Labor Court and the decision of the Labor Court on this shall be final.

5) There shall be no more than three registered trade unions in an establishment or group of establishments at a time.

2.0 Disqualification for Being an Officer or Member of a Trade Union

There are several criteria under which the applicant can be disqualified for being an officer or member of a trade union:

1) Not withstanding anything contained in the constitution or the rules of a trade union, a person shall be entitled
   a) To be or to be elected as, an officer of a trade union if he has been convicted of an offence involving moral turpitude or an offence under clause (d) of sub-section (1) of section 16 or section 61; and
   b) To be a member or officer of a trade union formed in any establishment or group of establishments if he is not, or was never, employed or engaged to that establishment or group of establishments.
2) Nothing in clause (ii) clause (a) and clause (b) sub-section shall apply to any federation of trade unions.

2.1 Registered Trade Union to Maintain Register

According to Sec 7B, Bangladesh Labor Code 2006 every registered trade union shall maintain in such form as may be prescribed:

A register of members showing particulars of subscriptions paid by each member;

a) An account book showing, receipts and expenditure; and
b) A minute book for recording the proceeding of meetings.

2.2 Process of Registration

After application and fulfillment of the requirement by the trade union the registrar completes the registration and a certificate of registration is given to the trade union as conclusive evidence. According to Sec 8, Bangladesh Labor Code 2006 the process is as follows:

1) The registrar, on being satisfied that the trade union has complied with all the requirements of this ordinance, shall register the trade union in a prescribed register and issue a registration certificate in the prescribed form 'within a period of sixty—days from the date of receipt of the application. In case the application is found by the registrar to be deficient in a material respect or respects he shall communicate in writing his objections to the trade union within a period of 15 days from the receipt of the application and the trade union shall reply thereto within a period of 15 days from the receipt of the objections.

2) When objections raised by the registrar have been satisfactorily met, the Registrar shall register the trade union as provided in sub section (1). In case the objections are to satisfactorily met, the registrar may reject the application.

3) In case application has been rejected or the registrar has after settlement of the objections delayed disposal of the application beyond the period of sixty days provided in sub section (1) the trade union may appeal to the labor court who for reasons to be stated in their judgment may pass an order directing the registrar to register the trade union and to issue a certificate of registration or may dismiss the appeal.

2.3 Certificate of Registration

The registrar, on registering a trade union under section under section 8, shall issue a certificate of registration in the prescribed form, which shall be conclusive evidence that the trade union has been duly registered wider this ordinance.

2.4 Cancellation of Registration

According to Sec 10, Bangladesh Labor Code 2006 the registration of the trade union can be cancelled as follows:

1) Subject to the other provisions of this section the registration of a trade union may be cancelled by the registrar if the trade union has

    a. Applied for cancellation or ceased to exist;
    b. Obtained registration by fraud or by misrepresentation of facts;
    c. Contravened any of the provisions of its constitution;
    d. Committed any unfair labor practice;
    e. Made in its constitution any provision, which is inconsistent with this ordnance or Ns rule;
    f. A membership which has fallen short of 30% of the workers o f the establishment or group of establishments for which it was formed;
    g. Failed to submit its annual report to the registrar as required under this ordnance
    h. Elected an officer, a person who is disqualified under section 7A from being elected as or from being, such officer; or
    i. Contravened any of the provisions of this Ordnance or the rules.

2) Where the Registrar is of opinions that the registering of the trade union should be cancelled, he shall submit an application to the labor court praying for permission to cancel such registration.

3) The Registrar shall cancel the registration of a trade union within seven days from the date of receipt of permission from the labor court.

4) The registration of a trade union shall not be cancelled on the ground mentioned in clause (d) of sub-section (1) if the unfair labor practice is not committed within three months prior to the date of submission of the application to the labor court.

2.5 Appeals against Cancellation

According to Sec 11, Bangladesh Labor Code 2006 a trade union aggrieved by the order of cancellation of its registration under section 10 may, within sixty days from the date of the order, appeal to the labor appellate Tribunal which may uphold or reject the order. But once cancelled according to Secl lA and 11B no union can function without registration and no worker can possess dual membership. In detail it is as follows:

1) No union to function without registration: a) No trade union which is unregistered or whose registration has been cancelled shall function as a trade union. b) No person shall collect any subscription for any fund of a trade union mentioned in sub-section (1).

2) Restriction on dual membership: a) No member shall be entitled himself as; or to continue to be, a member of more than one trade union at the same time.

2.6 Registrar of Trade Unions

According to Sec 12, Bangladesh Labor Code 2006 the government shall, by notification in the official gazette, appoint as many person as it considers necessary to be Registrar of trade unions and, where it appoints more than one registrars, shall specify in the notification the area within which each one of them shall exercise and perform the powers and functions under this ordnance.

According to the Labor Code 2006, the following are considered as the powers and functions of the registrar

1. The registration of trade unions under the ordnance and the maintenance of a register for this purpose;
2. To lodge complaints with the labor courts for action against the trade unions for any alleged offence or any unfair labor practice or violation of any provision of this ordnance;
3. The determination of the question as to which one of the trade unions in or an industry is entitled to be certified as the collective bargaining agent in relation to that establishment or industry", and
4. Such other powers and functions as may be prescribed.

2.7 Unfair Labor Practices on the Part of Employers

1) No employer or trade union of employers and no person acting on behalf of either shall

   a) Impose any condition in a contract of employment seeking to restoration in the right of a person who is a party to such contract to join a trade union or Continue his membership of a trade union; or

   b) Refuse to employ or refuse to continue. To employ any person on the ground that such person is, or is not, a member or officer of a trade union; or

   c) Discriminate against any person in regard to any employment, promotion, condition of employment or working condition on the ground that such person is, or is not, a member or officer of a trade union; or

   d) Dismiss, discharge, remove from employment or threaten to dismiss, discharge or remove from employment a workman or injure or threaten to injure him in respect of his employment by reason that the workman

       i. Is or proposes to become, or seeks to persuade any other person to become, a member or officer of a trade union

       ii. Participates in the promotion formation or activities of a trade union; or

   e) Induce any person to refrain from becoming, or to cease to be a member or officer of a trade union, by conferring or offering to confer any advantage, on or by procuring or offering to procure any advantage for such person or any other person;

   f) Compel any officer of the collective bargaining agent to sign a memorandum of settlement by using intimidation, coercion, pressure, threat, confinement to a place, physical injury, disconnection of water and telephone facilities and such other methods;

   g) Interfere with, or in any way influence the balloting provided for in section 22

   h) Recruit any new workman during the period of a notice of strike under section 28 or during the currency of a strike which is not illegal except where the conciliator has, being satisfied that complete cessation of work is likely to cause serious damage to the machinery or installation, permitted temporary employment of a limited number of workmen in the section where the damage is likely to occur.

2) Nothing in sub-section (1) shall be deemed to preclude an employer from requiring that a person upon his appointment or promotion to managerial position all cease to be, and shall be disqualified from being, a member or officer of a trade union or workmen.

2.8 Unfair Labor Practices on the Part of Workmen

No workman or trade union of workmen and no person action on behalf of such trade union shall-

   a. Persuade a workman to join or refrain from joining a trade union during working hours; or

b. Intimidate any person to become, or refrain from becoming, or to continue to be, or to cease to be a member or officer of a trade union; or

c. Induce any person to refrain from becoming, or cease to be a member or officer of a trade union, by conferring or offering to confer any advantage on" or by procuring or offering to procure any advantage for such person or any other person; or

d. Compel or attempt to compel the employer to sign a memorandum of settlement by using intimidation, coercion, pressure, threat, confinement to a place, physical injury, disconnection of telephone, water and power facilities and such other methods; or

e. Compel or attempt to compel any workman to pay, or refrain from paying, any subscription towards the fund of any trade union by using intimidation, coercion, pressure, threat, confinement to a place, physical injury, disconnection of telephone, water and power facilities and such other methods.

It shall be an unfair practice for a trade union to interfere with a ballot held under section 22 by the exercise of due influence, intimidation or bribery through its executive or through any person acting on its behalf.

2.9 Rights, Privileges and Functions of Registered Trade Unions

A trade union registered under this ordinance is called a Registered Trade Union. As per IRO a registered trade union has the fallowing rights & privileges:

- Law of Conspiracy Limited in Application
- Immunity from 0'61 Suit in Certain Cases
- Enforceability of Agreement
- Federation of Trade Union

3.0 Law of Conspiracy Limited in Application

- As per section 17, no officer or member of a registered trade union or a collective bargaining agent as determined by the Registrar shall be liable to punishment under sub-section (2) of section 120B of the Bangladesh Penal Code (Act XL V of 1860) in respect of any agreement made between the members thereof for the purpose of furthering any such object of the trade union as is specified in its constitution referred to in section 7, unless the agreement is an agreement to commit an offence, or otherwise violate any laws than this Ordinance.

- Per section 18 (1) No suit or other legal proceedings shall be maintainable in any 0-61 Court against any registered trade union or a collective bargaining agent or any officer or member thereof in respect of any action done in contemplation or furtherance of app, dispute of which the trade union is a party on the ground only that such act induces some other person to break a contact of employment, or that is an interference with the right of some other person to dispose of his capital or of his labor as he wills.

- A trade union shall not be liable in any suit or other legal proceedings in any Civil Court the respect of any tortuous act done in contemplation or furtherance of an industrial dispute by an agent of the trade union if it is proved that such person acted without the knowledge of, or contrary to express instructions given by, the executive of the trade union.

3.1 Enforceability of Agreement

As per section 19, notwithstanding anything contained in any other law for the time being in force, an agreement between the members of a trade union shall not be void or voidable by reason only that any of the objects of the agreement are in restraint of trade:

Provided that nothing in this section shall enable any Civil Court to entertain any, legal proceedings instituted for the express purpose of enforcing, or recovering damages for the breach of any agreement concerning the conditions on which any member of a trade union shall or shall not sell their goods, transact business or word, employ or be employed.

3.2 Registration of Federation of Trade Unions

(1) Any two or more registered trade unions may, if their respective general bodies so resolve, constitute a federation by executing an instrument of federation and apply for the registration of the federation.

Provided that a trade union of workmen shall not join a federation which comprises a trade union of employers; not shall a trade union of employer join a federation which comprises a trade union of workmen.

(2) An instrument of federation referred to in sub-section (1) shall among other things, provide for the procedures to be followed by the federated trade unions and the rights and responsibilities of the federation and the federated trade unions.

(3) An application for the registration of a federation of trade unions shall be signed by the Presidents of all the trade unions constituting the federation or by the officers of these trade unions respectively authorized by the trade unions in this behalf and shall be accompanied by three copies of the instrument of federation referred to in sub-section (1).

(4) Subject to sub-sections (1), (2) and (3) the provisions of this Ordinance shall, so far as may be and with the necessary modifications apply to a federation of trade unions as they apply to a trade union.

As per IRO, a registered trade union has to perform the following functions:

- Submit Returns
- Act as CBA and Perform all the duties and responsibilities of CBA, if elected
- Perform all the functions under Industrial. Relations Rules ORR), 1977

3.3 Returns

As per section 21 (I) There shall be sent annually to the Registrar, on or before such date as may be prescribed, a general statement, audited in the prescribed manner, of all receipts and expenditure of every registered trade union during the year ending on the 31st day of December, next preceding such prescribed date, and of the assets and liabilities of the trade union existing on such 31st day of December, as may be prescribed.

Together with the general statement there shall be sent to the Registrar a statement showing all changes of officers made by the trade union during the year to which the general statement refers, together also with a copy of the constitution of the trade union corrected up to-the date of the dispatch thereof to the Registrar.

A copy of every alteration made in the constitution of a registered trade union and of a resolution of the general body having the effect of a provision of the constitution shall be sent to the Registrar within fifteen days of the making of the alteration or adoption of the resolution.

In case the registered trade union is member of a federation, the name of the federation shall be given in the annual statement.

3.4 Submission of General Statement

The general statement which a registered trade union or federation of trade unions is required to mid annually to the Registrar under sub-sections (1) of section 21, shall be sent the 'Form K.' on or before the 30th April of the next year following the year in respect of which the statement relates.

3.5 Participation Committee

1) The employer of every establishment in which fifty or more workers are employed shall, in the manner prescribed by rules, constitute a Participation Committee in his establishment.
2) The participation committee shall consist of representatives of the employer and the workers.
3) The representatives of the workers in the committee shall not be less than the number of the representatives of the employer.
4) The representatives of the workers shall be appointed on the basis of the nomination made by the trade unions of the establishment.

5) Apart from the collective bargaining agent of the establishment concerned all other trade unions shall nominate equal number of representatives and the collective bargaining agent shall nominate such number of representatives which shall be one more than the total number of representatives nominated by the other trade unions.

6) In establishment where there are no trade union representatives of the workers in the participation committee of such establishment shall be nominated in the manner prescribed by rules from amongst the workers engaged in the establishment.

7) In an establishment where there is a unit employing at least fifty workers, a Unit Participation Committee may be formed for such unit in the manner prescribed by rules on the recommendation of the Participation Committee.

8) Such Participation Committee shall consist of the employer and the representatives of worker engaged in and under that unit.

9) The provision of this section applicable to Participation Committee shall also apply, as per as practicable, to the Unit Participation Committee.

3.6 Functions of the Participation Committee

1. The functions of the Participation Committee shall be to inculcate and develop a sense of belonging and workers' commitment and, in particular: a) To endeavor to promote mutual trust, understanding and cooperation between the employer and the workers. b) To ensure application of labor laws. c) To foster a sense of discipline and to improve and maintain safety, occupational health and working condition. d) To encourage vocational training, workers' education and family welfare training. e) To adopt measures for improvement of welfare services for the workers and their families and f) To fulfill production target, reduce production cost and wastes and raise quality of products.

2. Any participating unit of a committee shall, under the supervision of the main participation committee, execute its functions mentioned in subsection (1)

3.7 Meetings of the Participation Committee

1. The Participation Committee shall meet at least once in every two months to discuss and exchange views and recommend measures for performance of the functions under section, 206

2. The proceedings of every meeting of the Participation Committee shall be submitted to the Director of Labor and the Conciliator within seven days of the date of the meeting.

3.8 Implementation of the Participation Committee's Recommendations

1. The employer and the trade union of an establishment shall take necessary measures to implement the specific recommendations made by the Participation Committee within the time prescribed by it.
2. If, for any reason, the employer or the trade union faces problems in implementing the recommendations of the Participation Committee within the prescribed time, the Committee shall be informed of it and all possible endeavors shall have to be taken to implement the recommendations as early as possible.

3.9 Trade Union Situations in Bangladesh: A Criticism

Trade Unions Rights in Law

The constitution provides for the right to form or joins unions. There are many restrictions, however. Before a union can be registered, 30 percent of workers in an enterprise have to be members and the union can be dissolved if its membership falls below this level. Unions must have government approval to be registered, and no trade union action can be taken prior to registration.

Candidates for union office have to be current or former employees of an establishment or group of establishments. The Registrar of Trade Unions has wide powers to interfere in internal union affairs. He can enter union premises and inspect documents. The Registrar may also cancel the registration of a union, with Labor Court approval.

4.0 Exclusions from union membership

Under the Bangladesh Labor Code 2006, workers in the public sector and state enterprises may not belong to a trade union, with the exception of railway, postal and telecommunications workers. No teachers may form trade unions, in either the public or private sector. Managerial and administrative employees are also denied the right to join a union.

4.1 Right to strike not recognized

The right to strike is not specifically recognized in law. Three quarters of a union's members must agree to a strike before it can go ahead. The government can ban any strike if it continues beyond 30 days (in which case it is referred to the Labor Court for adjudication), if it involves a public service covered by the Essential Services Ordinance or if it is considered a threat to national interest. In this last case, the 1974 Special Powers Act can be used to detain trade unionists without charge. The government may ban strikes for renewable periods of three months.

Sentences of up to 14 years' forced labor can be passed for offences such as "obstruction of transport".

4.2 Collective Bargaining Agent

Only registered unions can engage in collective bargaining, and each union must nominate representatives to a Collective Bargaining Agent (CBA), which is subject to approval by the Registrar of Trade Unions. The National Pay and Wages Commission, whose recommendations are binding, set public sector workers' pay levels and other benefits.

4.3 EPZs—Recognition of Union Rights Delayed

Bangladesh's six export processing zones (EPZs) are currently exempt from the major laws establishing freedom of association and the fight to bargain collectively, so no professional or industry-based unions is allowed. However, faced with the threat of losing trade preferences for its exports to the US and Canadian markets, the government was to allow trade unions into the zones as from January 1, 2004.

Pressure from a group of 22 South Korean companies based in Chittagong EPZ has caused the government to reverse that decision. They filed a petition with the High Court in December 2003 challenging the proposed changes in status. Key ministers and the Bangladesh EPZ Authority (BEPZA) Chairperson met on December 28 to discuss the issue. At the meeting, they agreed that the World Bank Country Director would mediate the process and that a decision would be reached by Jan 1, 2004.

The same day, the US announced that it would not suspend the Generalized System of Preferences (GSP) benefits immediately, but rather work with Bangladesh towards an agreement. A further two month was granted. The GSP facility was worth $35m to Bangladesh during the 2002-2003 fiscal years alone.

CHAPTER IX
Employers Associations in Bangladesh

CONTENTS

1.0 Introduction

Bangladesh has achieved relatively good economic progress during the 1990s by adopting a series of structural and economic reforms. The GDP recorded an average of five percent annual growth during the period. All employers are expected to comply with the government's labor laws, which specify employment conditions, working hours, wage levels, leave policies, health and sanitary conditions, and compensation for injured workers. At the same time the employers' rights must be looked after also. This is the main reason for the formation of the employers association.

1.1 The Federation of Bangladesh Chambers of Commerce and Industry (FBCCI)

1.1.1 Background

The Federation of Bangladesh Chambers of Commerce and Industry (FBCCI) is the apex representative organization safeguarding the interest of the private sector in trade and industry in Bangladesh.

1.1.2 Role

FBCCI's Broad Objectives and Functions[253]

- To coordinate and promote the interest of its federating units-Chambers of Commerce, Trade and Industrial Association;
- To aid and stimulate investment, development of trade, commerce, industry, agriculture, tourism, human resources and communication sectors in Bangladesh;
- To project, encourage and safeguard the cause of the private sector through effective participation in the process of consultation and inter-action with the Government, Ministerial Consultative Committees and other inter-ministerial bodies and agencies;
- To assist the Chambers of Commerce and Industry and Associations in organizing of Trade and Industry Fairs in different parts of Bangladesh;
- To collect and disseminate statistical and other information for advancement of trade and industry;
- To make efforts for the spread of commercial, technical and economic knowledge for promotion of commercial, technical, industrial and scientific education in the country;
- To study and undertake research for promotion and growth of trade and industry;
- FBCCI is involved in forging strong bilateral ties between and among different countries of the world through counterpart organizations for commercial and economic cooperation. It helps promote Foreign Direct Investment (FDI) including Joint Ventures in Bangladesh and identify appropriate partners;

- It maintains close relation with Overseas National Chambers of Commerce and other Trade and Industrial Associations including related economic organization;
- The FBCCI as the Apex Trade Organization plays the pivotal role in consultative and advisory capacity in formulation of Commercial, Industrial and Fiscal policies at the national level. It has been playing a very vital role in all Forum of the Government and Economic Development organizations for mutual sharing of views on all vital issues concerning and affecting the national economy;
- FBCCI represents the Private Sector in different permanent committees of the Government and autonomous bodies;
- FBCCI also represents the Private Sector in various Committees and Task Forces on specific issues, constituted by the Government from time to time.

In general it can be said that the purpose of employers' associations is to bargain collectively for their members with trade unions and to protect the interests of those members in their dealings with unions.

Objectives of Employers' Association are-

Political: to effectively represent employers' views to Government and other appropriate bodies.

Economic: to create an economic environment that supports the free enterprise system

Social: to ensure any social or legal changes best represent the interests of affiliated employers.

Employee relations: to ensure a legislative and procedural environment which supports free collective bargaining and to co-ordinate employers' views and approaches to employee relations matters?

1.1.3 International Links

FBCCI is the member of different international bodies, such as International Chambers of Commerce (ICC), Islamic Chamber of Commerce and Industry (ICCI), Confederation of Asia-Pacific Chambers of Commerce and Industry (CACCI) and the SAARC Chamber of Commerce and Industry (SCCI). To safeguard and protect the interest of business community in the international arena, FBCCI maintains close communication with these International Organizations.

The Federation of Bangladesh Chambers of Commerce and Industry has collaboration agreements with the General Union of Chambers of Commerce and Industry and Agriculture of the Arab Countries, Karnataka Chamber of Commerce & Industry and Mizoram Chamber of Commerce of India, Kunming Chamber of Commerce & Industry of China and Singapore Chinese Chamber of Commerce & Industry of Singapore. The FBCCI has also established a Joint Chamber viz., Bangladesh

India Chamber of Commerce and Industry (BICCI) in cooperation with the Federation of Indian Chambers of Commerce and Industry and signed an agreement of understanding with the United States Bangladesh Business Council (USBBC).

1.2 Bangladesh Employers Federation (BEF)

1.2.1 Overview

Bangladesh Employers Federation (BEF) was registered as the national organization of the employers in 1998. It embodies all associations representing major industries in the country as well as established individual enterprise.

The mission of (BEF) is to promote and defend the interests of employers in Bangladesh, particularly in the International Labor Organization (ILO), and to this end works to ensure that international labor and social policy promotes the viability of enterprises and creates an environment favorable to enterprise development and job creation. At the same time it acts as the Secretariat to the Employers' Group at the ILO International Labor Conference, the ILO Governing Body and all other ILO-related meetings.

The BEF is well-known as a progressive body, having a pro-active approach on social issues. It is the only body of the employers recognized by the Ministry of Labor and Employment and accordingly. It enjoys the sole representative capacity in the Tripartite Consultative Council, Labor Courts, Minimum Wages Board, National Wages and Productivity Commission, etc. closely inter-acts with the Ministry of Labor and employment on all policy issues. Similarly, it maintains close touch with other relevant Ministries of the Government on issues concerning industrial relations, enterprise efficiency, competitiveness, etc.

In order to ensure that the voice of business is heard at the international and national level, the BEF is actively engaged in the creation and capacity building of representative organizations of employers, particularly in both the developing world and those countries in transition to the market economy.

1.2.2 History

After its founding in 1998, the BEF took over the activities of the Bangladesh Employers' Association (BEA) which, registered earlier in 1951, had so far been representing the employers as an all-country organization of the employers. The BEF with a wider membership representation, cover all major industrial associations in the country as well as established individual enterprises. The objectives of the Federation are to promote, encourage and protect the interest of the employers in industrial relations, and through such efforts, to establish good relations amongst employers and workers so as to provide the vital supporting role in the country's economic development.

1.2.3 Scope of Activities

The federation handles all the issues in Bangladesh regarding Social, labour and economic affairs. The BEF activities cover a wide range of issues other than industrial relations. Training and skill development is a major activity along with enterprise-level programmers for productivity improvement, safety and health, good management practices, etc.

1.2.4 Present Structure

The membership of the Federation is the source of the policy making process. The policies and activities are formally given shape by the Managing Committee with the active involvement of the Secretariat.

The Managing Committee for the management of the affairs of the Federation consists of one President, one Vice-President and eighteen members. The Managing Committee is elected of two annual terms. The Committee in its activities is assisted by Sub-Committees each of which is headed by a Committee member and consists of representatives of the sectors where the activities of the Sub-Committees are focused.

The Secretariat has the responsibility of implementing the decisions under the supervision of the Managing Committee. The Secretariat is headed by the Secretary-General.

1.2.5 Roles of Bangladesh Employers Federation (BEF)

Having a wider representative character, the federation has been endeavoring to promote and protect the interest of the employees giving them guidance and assistance in the field of industrial relation, bringing their converted views on labor matters to the attention of the government, labor and other concerned. It also represents them both at national and international levels. Being the apex body of the employers, it has been involved in the task of promoting and protecting the interests of employers. Today, the federation is the only organization of its kind dealing with industrial relations in Bangladesh. It has lots of contribution and success in the field of industrial relations of Bangladesh.

The main roles of Bangladesh Employers federation are as follows-

1.2.5.1 Advisory Roles

BEF gives a wide range of services to its members, which cover almost every aspect of industrial relation. It's secretarial and labor advisers posted in Dhaka and Chittagong are available to members for consultation, advice and information. Advisory services include issues such as wage negotiations, labor-management relations, disciplinary actions, interpretation of labor laws etc.

1.2.5.2 Information Roles

The Federation brings out a monthly bulletin, the labor News, which contains news about labor relation situation, articles on management and human resources development, import IR and labor-related court cases, economic and labor-related data. It also issues weekly reports on industrial relation situation. Another important feature of the federations' activities is monthly meeting of officers, of member organizations dealing with labor and administrative matters which serves as a training ground for them. These meetings focus of examining labor problems in different aspects so as to arrive at a consensus for information and guidance of the members.

1.2.5.3 Productivity Improvement Roles

The federation helps its member identifying the scope of improving productivity through the application of modern management technique. It assists members mainly in the fields like work study, production planning and control, fixation of wage structures, job evaluation, setting recruitment standards, method improvement, value analysis, maintenance management etc.

1.2.5.4 Training

Management training is a regular feature of the federations' activities. Senior officials engaged in respective management functions participate in various seminars and workshop. The seminars and workshop are organized by the federation and the facilitated by national and international experts.

1.2.5.5 Labor Court Assistance

The federation represents employees in the seven labor courts of the country. It monitors the cases that come up before the courts through its representative on the panels and carefully ensures that legitimate interests of employers are duly highlighted.

1.2.5.6 National Policy Issues

The federation renders expert assistance, advice and services to the government, particularly to Ministry of labor and employment in the formulation of various plans and policies. Its involvement in the formulation of plans and policies especially in the field of industrial relation is well known. It represents employers' viewport at the Tripartite Consultative committee.

1.2.6 Success Story

1.2.6.1 Labor Court

It has a lot of success history in labor court assistance to its members. it took pioneer role in initiation, discussion with various parties, draw the attention of the legislative body, formation, and pass of the Bangladesh labor law,2006 in the parliament. It also helped the employees can be member of trade union. The trade unions advocated for a provision in labor law, 2006 that the terminated employees would be allowed to become member of a trade union. But the BEF appealed to the government against this provision and they effectively convinced the government that this is not logical and they were successful in excluding this provision in the law.

1.2.6.2 Minimum Wage Board

The federation represents and safeguards the interests of the employers in the minimum wage board. On October 5, 2006 the Bangladesh Minimum wage board announced the first raise to the minimum wage for the garment workers since 1994 and BEF have played pioneer role in setting this minimum wage. This gross minimum monthly wage has been announced as Tk 1,662.50 including basic salary plus house rent and other allowances for entry level worker.

The board decisions are crucial for smaller firms because these firms survive mainly on the basis of competitive labor costs.

1.2.7 Functions

The Federation's services to member-firms cover a wide range of areas:

- Direct advisory services on labor problems and help with guidance to employers in their collective bargaining with the unions
- Fortnightly meetings in Dhaka and Chittagong in order to facilitate exchange of views on current topics and come to an agreed solution to the same. A large number of representatives from the Public and Private Sector units participate at the meetings.
- Keeping members informed of the up-to-date labor situation through weekly reports and monthly bulletins.
- Collection, collation and, if necessary, circulation to member-firms of various comparative information on pay scales and the terms of service to maintain uniformity of action.
- Preparation of index of various facts and figures so as to make them available to member-firms and Government agencies, as and when required.

- BEF officials, in direct interview, said that they organizing regular seminars and workshops on industrial health and safety and working conditions for managers of member firms with assistance from ILO and other international Agencies
- Apart from organizing training for management officials abroad, the BEF also participates in the promotion of management and vocational training by associating itself with the Governing Bodies of the Bangladesh Institute of Management, National Council for Skill Development and Training, Industrial Relations Institute and such other bodies.
- Organizing regular seminars/workshops/symposiums on industrial health and safety and working conditions for managers of member firms with assistance from ILO and other International Agencies.
- The Federation is also represented on all national tripartite committees and institutions such as the Labor Courts, Minimum Wages Board, and National Tripartite Consultative Committee on Labor Matters.

1.2.8 Membership[254]

The Federation's membership structure has undergone a lot of change since the employer-group organized itself under the BEA umbrella in 1951. From a few direct members, the membership now includes all Public Sector Corporations, and all major national level Associations.

The Federation now represents almost 80 % of the established employers in the organized sector. The Federation is a member of the IOE and participates in ILO activities, representing the employers of Bangladesh.

1.3 The Dhaka Chamber Of Commerce & Industry (DCCI)

1.3.1 Background

The Dhaka Chamber of Commerce & Industry (DCCI) is the first point of contact for business in this country. It facilitates commerce for the local as well as foreign entrepreneurs to catering their demands in penetrating into a new market. The DCCI is a limited company incorporated under the companies Act. It was established in 1956. It is largest chamber of the country.

The DCCI is a high profile non-profit service organization whose function is very relevant to the innovators business community. Both local and foreign entrepreneurs come to the DCCI with request of services they need-they are unaware of the other services that the DCCI offers.

1.3.2 Structure

It has four classes of membership: General, Associate, Town Association and Trade Group. The Chamber is run by a Board of twenty-four Directors representing all classes of membership. One third of the Directors retire every year. A President, a Senior Vice-President and a Vice-President are elected by the Board for a term of one year. The President is the Chief Executive of the Chamber. The Board of Directors is assisted by a number of Standing Committees on various important business-related subjects and by a fully fledged Secretariat.

1.3.3 Functions of the DCCI[255]

- The basic functions of the DCCI relate to promotion and development of trade, commerce and industry. Some of these are: to give market oriented inputs for formulation and implementation of government policies in respect of import, export, industry, investment, banking, insurance, fiscal measures, annual budget etc. and brief materials for conferences relating to WTO, UNCTAD, SAPTA, SAFTA, BIMST-EC etc;
- to represent trade, commerce and industry on various advisory or consultative committees at different Ministries and Departments of the Governments;
- to give views and comments on legislative measures affecting trade, commerce and industry;
- to function as a forum for exchanging views on trade and economy among different Chamber members, Government agencies, DCCI members and local/foreign delegations;
- to issue Certificate of Origin (CO) and authenticate documents for promotion of exports;
- to disseminate business information to members by Electronic Communication, Fortnightly Trade Bulletin, DCCI Monthly Review, Circulars, Notifications, Statistical data etc;
- to organize training courses, seminars/ workshops/symposia, trade delegations, trade fairs to participle in them at home and abroad and to receive delegations from abroad;
- to undertake activities like survey, research etc. to suggest for favorable business related policies; to prepare Economic Policy Papers (EPPs) for conducting policy advocacy for the benefit of the business sector;
- to prepare position papers, fact sheet on different business issues to lobby with the Government;
- to sign Memorandum of Understandings (MOUs) with overseas Chambers of Commerce and Industries and other business organizations for promotion of bilateral trade and investment;
- to prepare, implement and evaluate projects for entrepreneurship development and other trade related matters and
- to develop business through internet/web page of its own.

1.3.4 Ongoing Services[256]

DCCI helps its members to face the challenges of stiff competition in a globalised economy by providing various services:

- To create awareness amongst the members about the various policies, regulations, norms and practices concerning all sectors of economic activities of the country.
- To critically evaluate the fiscal and other measures and policies of government and recommend necessary changes to create an enabling and business-friendly environment.
- To ventilate the needs, problems and grievances of the business community and suggest suitable remedial and supportive measures while commenting on major economic issues and policies.
- To represent, uphold and focus on the interests of private sector in various Advisory & Consultative Committees.
- To disseminate information relating to problems & prospects of the trade & investment through the publication of research papers, circulars, manuals, survey reports, annual reports, news bulletins, tax guides, trade bulletins etc
- To provide a forum for interaction and exchange of views among the members of the business community by way of holding Seminars, Symposia, Discussion Meetings and Representations.

1.3.5 Role of DCCI

It plays a pivotal role in

- Business matching services.
- Subcontracting and Franchising.
- Documentation Processing etc.
- To conduct need-based training & orientation courses.
- To extend logistic services like Fax, Phone, Telex, E-mail, Photocopy, Internet fax, Conference facility etc.
- To issue Certificate of Origin of export consignments.
- To undertake settlement of trade disputes by arbitration.

The Dhaka Chamber of Commerce & Industry (DCCI) the voice of SMEs serves as the first point of business contact for penetration into new market and a vibrant platform putting forward facts-based opinions, suggestions and recommendations for a brighter tomorrow in the sphere of trade, commerce and the overall economy. DCCI, the largest and most active Chamber of the country, established in 1958, was incorporated under the companies Act, V11 of 1913 as a limited company on March 10, 1959. It serves as a model of non-profit, service-oriented organization. It has rendered more than four decades of very useful services for the development of business and industry in Bangladesh.

1.3.6 Achievement (Success Story) of DCCI[257]

- The Dhaka Chamber of Commerce and Industry (DCCI) is the premier Chamber of Bangladesh having more than 4500 members. They consist of different business sectors of the country represented by mostly SMEs. From the very inception DCCI has been rendering useful services for the development of private sector business and industry in Bangladesh.

- The Dhaka Chamber of Commerce & Industry (DCCI) has reached an exalted position by achieving high-status "2007 World Chambers Competition" Award in the category of Best Skills Development Programme organized by World Chambers Federation-ICC's Specialized Division for Chamber Affairs co-organized with the Union of Chamber & Commodity Exchanges of Turkey (TOBB).

- DCCI puts forward its suggestions and recommendations to the Government of Bangladesh on all policy matters, such as industrial policy import policy, export policy, fiscal policy, annual budget and many other business-related policies. DCCI represents in about 70 government, semi-government and autonomous bodies for promotion and development of private sector of Bangladesh.

- DCCI in its endeavor to accelerate the pace of development of Bangladesh organizes on regular basis seminar, symposium, round table discussion, training and workshops; takes part in trade fairs and exhibitions; receives & sends delegation; implements various useful projects, arranges one to one business meetings with the delegates of different countries for trade and investment promotion.

- DCCI introduced "DCCI Business Award" for encouraging women, young, new and innovative entrepreneurs which were highly appreciated by all.

- The DCCI Business Institute (DBI) imparts Training for development of entrepreneurs and business executives. It offers Certificate, Advanced Certificate and Diploma courses on International Purchasing and Supply Chain Management (IPSCM), as an Authorized Examination Body of ITC—UNCTAD WTO, Geneva and holds examinations. Recently introduced EMBA programme in its premises of Motijheel Commercial Area in cooperation with IIUC.

- DCCI knowledge Centre, established in cooperation with South Asia Enterprise Development Facility (SEDF), provides internet based Internet training and service" to SMEs, students, NGOs and other services providers.

- Since 1999 under its DCCI-CIPE project, DCCI has prepared research-based 38 policy papers on different trade related issues and submitted them to the government for appropriate policy formation for creating a private sector friendly investment climate in the country. Many of the recommendations of these policy papers have been accepted and implemented. The growth of GDP by 6.71% in 2005-06 is a testimony to this development. l Policy advocacy is the primary activity of the chamber. The representatives of DCCI in committee of many national and government organizations raise the voices of private sector in order to create business friendly environment for economic development of the country.

- SME-Help Line Centre (Online—Based)
- The Dhaka Chamber of Commerce and Industry (DCCI) in cooperation with Ministry of Industries (MOI), GoB has established the SME Helpline Centre (SME-HC) in the DCCI to provide better services to the Small and Medium Enterprises (SMEs).
- Key objective of the SME-HC is to provide necessary assistance and advisory support services and facilitate SMEs' access to get government services, laws, rules & regulations, registration and licensing requirements etc.

1.3.7 Services

- To maintain close contact with SME Foundation (SMEF), other SME supporting organizations and 26 SME HCs to share information stocks;
- To provide necessary linkages with sources of technology;
- To aware about SME Web Portal and utilize its resources;
- To organize training workshops, seminars, dialogues etc.
- To provide electronic information on different SME related issues, facility for advertisement of SMEs products, buyer-seller meet, trade fairs etc.;
- To provide assistances with advisory, documentary and support services;
- To prepare required research-based publications and disseminate the same.

1.4 The Bangladesh Garment Manufacturers and Exporters Association (BGMEA)

1.4.1 Background

Apparel makers are eyeing to fulfill a target to export garments worth $30 billion within the next three years, against a backdrop of current trends. It has been reported in different newspapers too that the total export of garments would cross the $30 billion mark in the next three years.

The country achieved more than 40 percent growth in apparel exports in the July-March period this fiscal year, against the same time last year.

Manufacturers hope to achieve the target in the next three years, as a significant number of orders are shifting to Bangladesh from China, the largest apparel supplying country world-wide.

The flow of orders from international buyers is also increasing rapidly as production costs in China have climbed steeply.

In addition, work orders from international buyers are also rising as the country now enjoys a zero-duty benefit from the EU.

The Eurozone relazed the rules of origin (RoO) from January this year for the least developed countries (LDCs). Being a member of the LDCs, Bangladesh enjoys duty-free access to some major export destinations, like Canada and Japan. Bangladesh also enjoys a duty-free quota in garment exports to some countries like China, South Korea and India. While the prospect of achieving a target of $30 billion is bright, it is also time for a question of capacity to arise. Will the country be able to meet the work orders with the present workforce, utility and infrastructure? With present capacities, the country exported knitwear products worth $6.70 billion and woven garments worth $6.00 billion in July-March this fiscal year.

Among other elements, manufacturers often complain about a shortage of skilled workers. At present, the sector suffers from a 25 percent shortage of skilled workers.

Moreover, the internal migration of workers from factory to factory is another problem for the sector, manufacturers complained.

Manufacturers say productivity in the garment factories is not improving because of the low skills of the workers.

In fiscal 2009-10, manufacturers exported 465.50 million dozen garments-172.80 million dozen woven goods and 292.70 million dozen knitwear items, according to Export Promotion Bureau data.

The Bangladesh Garment Manufacturers and Exporters Association (BGMEA) is the only recognized trade body that represents all the export oriented garment manufacturers and exporters of the country. It is the officially recognized apex apparel export trade body of 4,490 apparel manufacturing units.

The primary mission objective of the BGMEA is to

"Establish a healthy a business environment for a close and mutually beneficial relationship between the manufacturers, exporters and importers in the process ensuring a steady growth in the foreign exchange earnings of the country"

The BGMEA secondary mission objective is to

"Implement all legitimate rights and privileges of garment workers regarding Health, Welfare and Safety"

1.4.2 History

The readymade garment (RMG) sector is a success story for Bangladesh. The industry started in the late 1970s, expanded heavily in the 1980s and boomed in the 1990s. The quick expansion of the industry was possible because of the use of less complicated technology, cheap and easy to operate sewing machines, and relatively cheap and abundant female workforce.

But, apparel firms in the country have moved into a challenging position in the new millennium. The challenge is now to offer high-quality, low-cost products within a short lead time; and to meet health, social and environmental compliances in the face of increasingly stiff competition. To face these challengers, the apparel makers should focus on effective supply chain management as it will ensure delivering the right product to the right place at the right time at the right price.

However, the concept of a 'complete under-standing of supply chain management' is absent in most organizations in Bangladesh because of a lack of a basic understanding of the subject.

But, the country needs plenty of supply chain resources to benchmark itself against the best in the world like Toyota and Wal-Mart.

Therefore, the government, the RMG units, the textiles units and all other supporting partners of the apparel supply chain need to come together to become a part of one chain, define a common competitive strategy and align its supply chain capability accordingly.

The BGMEA commenced activities in the late 1970s when the Bangladeshi readymade garments (RMG) industry was a negligible non-traditional sector with a narrow export base. Since its inception, the BGMEA has been working to promote and protect the interests of the RMG sector—it has helped boost RMG exports by 500%, allowing Bangladesh to become one of the chief RMG exporters worldwide.

The BGMEA set up its regional office in Chittagong in 1985. Chittagong is a strategically important commercial port and the gateway for all RMG exports.

The BGMEA is run by a 27-member elected Board of Directors. Four Vice Presidents and an administrative office assist the President in formulating and implementing the policies and programmes of the organization. The President is the highest executive authority of the BGMEA.

The BGMEA is committed to protecting the interests of its members, mainly readymade garments (RMG) manufacturers who rely on it to advocate private sector-led economic growth.

The BGMEA also acts as a pressure group to protect the interests of the RMG sector and acts as a facilitator of trade negotiations with global trade bodies such as the WTO, ILO, and UNCTAD.

BGMEA, The pioneer Trade Association of 4700 garment factory owners in Bangladesh gets the credit of contributing to the national exchequer for the last 24 years. The RMG sector has earned US$ 9.2 billion in the export basket in the fiscal year 2006-07. Besides this financial aspect, BGMEA has greatly been contributing to the development of Social Sector of the country that acclaimed national and international reputation including the appraisement of the United States Department of Labor (USDOL) for the last decade. BGMEA is committed to ensure that the labor laws of the country is being followed. Sensitive issues such as maternity leave, payment of minimum wages, overtime, appointment card, ID card are being addressed by the BGMEA. BGMEA is also operating a number of projects and programs to ensure improved healthcare, workplace safety and labor rights of the garment workers in consonance with the Labor Standards set by the Govt. and ILO.

1.4.3 Functions of BGMEA[258]

BGMEA performs the following functions as the governing body of the garments industry:

1. Support globalization of the economy and liberalization of trade
2. Influences government to formulate pro-growth policies for the sector
3. Constantly persuade government to deregulate control over private sector.
4. Provide trade information to its members.
5. Keeps its members updated on contemporary business trend.
6. BGMEA bridges interaction between the local exporters and international buyers by arranging Fairs in Bangladesh and participates with its member in international fair
7. Maintain liaison with local and global trade bodies and UN Agencies
8. Encourage its members constantly to attain development of skill and efficiency for the development of competency in the global marketplace
9. Research on global trend in garment business, major global trade arrangements and WTO guidelines
10. BGMEA has recently opened the countries first B2B web portal directly linking both the RMG exporters and buyers around the world.
11. Promote automation and use of modern technology in RMG sector.

1.4.4 Services to Factory Members

1.4.4.1 Legal Advice

BGMEA Labor Cell provides legal advice to its member-units in various labor and compliance related issues.

1.4.4.2 Bi-Lateral Committee

BGMEA has formed a Bi-lateral committee on 30th June 1997 with Registered Trade Union Federation to solve labor issues such as maternity leave, overtime, payment of wages, minimum wages.

1.4.4.3 Conciliation-Cum-Arbitration Committee (CAC):

Since 26th April 1998 CAC in accordance to Industrial Relations Ordinance (IRO)-1969 performs the following activities:

- The committee solves the grievances of the owners and the workers rapidly to keep production uninterrupted.
- The committee tries to solve the disputes without any charge that arise between the owner and the employees of the factory before referring the matter to court.
- Provides trade information to its members.
- Keeps its members updated on contemporary global business trends.
- Endorses ICT solutions for better management of RMG units.
- Manages a 'B2B web portal' directly linking RMG exporters and buyers.
- Organizes seminars and dialogues for recommending on key policies for trade and industry.
- Provides advisory services to its member on how to improve environmental standards.
- Publishes a newsletter about RMG business news, events and activities in Bangladesh.
- Fosters relationships between the local exporters and international buyers by arranging Fairs in Bangladesh and participates with its members in international Fairs.
- Helps members to honor national and international compliance.

1.4.5 Roles of BGMEA

1.4.5.1 Implementation of Rules in Workplace

BGMEA do not have the right to make any legislation. But it pressurizes Government to make legislation in the parliament if required for the betterment of the industry. BGMEA play a very big role regarding the enforcement of national and international Laws in the RMG sector. BGMEA has a monitoring team that monitors and report at least 10 member organizations whether they are in compliance with the national and international role.

BGMEA look over their member garment factories for compliance with minimum standards related to structural/Building regulations, health and safety through their watchdog committee and suggests corrective actions for those factories that do not sufficiently implement these standards, said BGMEA officials in direct interview.

BGMEA is trying to implement the tri-partied agreement, which has been recently worked out among the BGMEA, trade unions and the government of Bangladesh.

1.4.5.2 Bargaining

BGMEA represent employers who are one the three parties that are involved in industrial Relations. The main two parties in Industrial Relations is employer and employee. At the time of bargaining BGMEA try to protect the interest of the employers.

1.4.5.3 Policy Matters

BGMEA also play a pivotal role in various policy matters. BGMEA arrange workshops, seminars and consult with government, civil society and other stake holders regarding what should be export, import trade policy etc. they suggest government their view.

1.4.5.4 Legislation

BGMEA suggests government regarding the ratification of various rules that affects industrial relations, for example, rules regarding union, collective bargaining process, labor relations, job-contract and implement the provision of weekly holiday and working hours per week, pay settlement and also so on, and the implementation and enforcement of these rules.

1.4.5.5 Making Economic Policy of the Country

It also plays roles in areas that affect in industrial relation indirectly as well (for example, economic policy of the country). We know industrial relations are not an independent subject rather it has an interdisciplinary focus. It affects lot of other area (for example, employment structure of the labor market, production, development of trade and overall socio-economic condition of the country)

1.4.5.6 Resolving Conflict in Workforce

Some times BGMEA directly handles the conflict between workers and workmen. For example, if a member organization takes any undue action against the workers, or fails to meet the rights of interest of the workers, willingly or unwillingly, then the workers may complain BGMEA through the federation of their trade unions and a common complaint is that the employees are not receiving their salary for the past few months. In this case BGMEA has no legislative right to handle to dispute (at least there is nothing in the legislation that they will handle the conflict by themselves but there is no bar for handling the matter informally). So they call the parties, investigate the matter and induce the employer to pay the salary as per law.

1.4.6 Success Stories

1.4.6.1 Elimination of Child Labor

BGMEA along with ILO and UNICEF has been working for the elimination of child labor from this sector. This is one of the main conditions of the foreign purchasers/ buyers while they place any order to any manufacture

1.4.6.2 Corporate Social Responsibility

While direct interview, BGMEA officers claimed that they encouraging their member garment owners to contribute in social programs like

1. Setting up safe and human residential, health and transport facilities for the workers
2. Improving safety measures in production units
3. Training and development of workers skills.
4. Ensuring the workers benefit and compensation package under the national laws and ILO Convention

1.5 Bangladesh Plastic Goods Manufacturers and Exporters Association (BPGMEA)

Bangladesh Plastic Goods Manufacturers & Exporters Association (BPGMEA) is a private sector association which represent all kinds of plastic goods manufacturers of Bangladesh and it has got about 1,000 members. The principal object of this Association is to safeguard the interest of the plastic sector in Bangladesh and development of trade between national and international fields. It is a private sector association and also representing our country's total plastic goods industries with more than 700 members. [3]

The industrial growth in plastic sector in Bangladesh began at around the year 1980. Prior to that plastic sector industry was on such a small that it was not worth mentioning. A gradual growth in the plastic industry was noticeable from the year 1980 to the year 1990. A large number of injection grade and film grade plastic industries were set up during this period and this sector started to play a significant role in the national economy. Since then the plastic industries started to move faster than the other sectors. [3]

The processing technology and the equipment initially came from India, followed by Thailand, Korea, Japan, China, Singapore and some European countries.

Today, there are around 3000 small, medium and large size plastic goods manufacturing units with around 1 million workforces directly or indirectly employed in this sector.

The main activities of the association are to assist the industries related to plastic goods manufacturing. It represents the plastic industry as a whole to deal with matters relating to Government regulations, patent rights, import and export regulations etc. The association serves as a contact point for overseas companies who desire to buy or sell or create a contact in Bangladesh for Plastic products.

1.6 The Leather Goods and Footwear Manufacturers and Exporters Association of Bangladesh (LFMEAB)

LFMEAB is an Association established and registered in August 2003.

The fundamental objective of LFMEAB is to establish a healthy business environment for a close and mutually beneficial relationship between the local manufacturers & exporters of leather footwear & leather goods and foreign buyers.

1.6.1 Aims and Objectives

The Leather goods and Footwear Manufacturers and Exporters Association of Bangladesh. (LFMEAB) is the recognized trade body that represents most of the major export oriented manufacturers & exporters of leather goods & footwear in Bangladesh.

It has been established with the aim and object of uniting all the leather goods & footwear manufacturing companies by encouraging co-operation amongst the members and provide them with a platform to have local and international exposure, creating awareness amongst international buyers and making representations to the government and concerned public bodies on behalf of the members for resolving their regulatory problems.

LFMEAB carries out its activities through an Executive Committee consisting of:

President	1
Vice President	1
Sr. Vice President	1
Vice President (Finance)	1
Executive Members	3
Secretary	1

1.6.2 Functions[259]:

- Collecting, collating and disseminating world market intelligence
- Updating the information on global trends in fashion & design, product development and adaptation
- Dissemination of information of commercial and technological nature through seminars, news bulletins and magazines
- Organizing participation of exporters in international fairs and buyer seller meets
- Sponsoring sales-cum-study teams and trade delegations
- Inviting foreign experts for providing technological inputs to leather exporters
- To affiliate or be affiliated to other institutions having kindred objects and to further or participate directly or indirectly, in the work or purpose of an Association or anybody corporate or Association having its objects for the furthering of the interests of the Leather Science and its profession.
- To amalgamate with any other Association having objects altogether or in part similar to those of this Association.
- To extend and improve Scientific and technical education and the professional training of those seeking to become fully qualified Scientific or technical workers by organizing training facilities, conducting proper examination, and in other ways.

1.7 Bangladesh Knitwear Manufacturers & Exporters Association (BKMEA)

1.7.1 History

Bangladesh Knitwear Manufacturers & Exporters Association (BKMEA) was formed in 1996 by the all out efforts of few knitwear manufacturers. Soon after the formation it undertook activities to look after the interest of the knitwear sector of the country. Today it an association of about 1500 knitwear manufacturers and exporters that represent the largest export earning sector of the country.

BKMEA has grown enormous network in home and abroad. The members are the strength and primary network support of BKMEA. Besides BKMEA works closely with International agencies and maintains close relationships with Diplomatic Offices in Dhaka. It also works with similar organizations in Europe and USA on common interest like Global Alliance for Fair Textile Trade (GAFTT) and American Manufacturing Trade Action Coalition (AMTAC). To boost up trade and to enhance cooperation between Bangladesh and China, BKMEA and Yunnan Light & Textile Industry Association signed a MoU on 10th June, 2005.

BKMEA is putting tireless efforts to enhance productivity of its members, enhance social compliance status and workers welfare, diversify export market, and better market access of the country's knitwear products to EU, USA, China, and other countries. BKMEA is working with German Technical Cooperation (GTZ), and other international organizations in this regard. BKMEA has signed MoU with GTZ on March 16, 2005.

BKMEA is run by a 27-member Board of Directors led by the President. The Board of Directors is elected for a 2-year period. To run the association efficiently there is 21 different committees.

1.7.2 Functions

BKMEA performs the following functions:

- Protect the Interest of the Sector
- Promotion & Development of the Market
- Promotion & Development of the Sector
- Capacity Building of the Sector
- Social Compliance Status Enhancement
- Basic Rights Education and Awareness Raising

1.7.3 Services

BKMEA's Services to the Member Units are as follows

- Product & Market Promotion
- Social Compliance
- Research & Development
- Productivity Improvement
- Arbitration
- One stop service point regarding UD/UP
- Other necessary services at the shortest possible time

1.7.4 Governance

BKMEA is run by a 27 member Board of directors led by the presidents. The board of directors is elected by the members for a 2 years period. To run the associations efficiently there are 27 different committees.

1.8 Role of Government in Declaring Minimum Wage

It was difficult for Bangladesh to introduce a statutory minimum wage covering all employees. Bangladesh has very recently set minimum wage for RMG workers. RMG sector is the one of the biggest export source of Bangladesh. Yet, to set minimum wage for these valuable workers, there were huge agitation throughout the economy.

Rejecting outright the proposed pay structure for the garment workers, owners urged the government to return the matter to the Minimum Wage Board immediately and fix a revised lowest wage instead of a full-fledged scale.

Hurried declaration of a pay scale was made to gain cheap popularity and accepting the pay scale would be suicidal for the garment owners, he said. Annisul Huq, BGMEA representative on the wage board, said a worker can survive somehow with an income ranging between Tk. 1,900 and Tk. 1,950 a month. As the owners are not in a position to pay as per the need of the workers, they offered to pay a package of Tk. 2,000 including two-hour overtime, he said. Around 50 per cent of the factories will be out of the business within six months if the proposed wage structure is implemented, Huq said, adding that as the workers have their own rights, the owners also have the right to close their factories. BGMEA Vice-president Lutfor Rahman Matin (2006) said those who have declared an unrealistic wage structure will be responsible for the factory closure and making the workers unemployed.

"Buyers come with a fixed CM (cutting and making) charge and ask whether we accept their offer. They tell us directly that they would shift their orders elsewhere if we are not ready to accept their price offer," said Khalilur Rahman, owner of KDS garments. "Who will pay the salary of the workers—the government or the Minimum Wage Board or the owners?" Rahman posed the question. It is true that the owners made money when there was quota system and the price was good, said garment owner Muzaffor U Siddiqui. But it is also true that they have invested their money in expansion of the industry, which has created more employment, he added. Buyers rush to Bangladesh not because they love this country but for cheaper prices of Bangladeshi apparels, he said. Urging the government to fix only the minimum wage, he said the owners will negotiate with the workers for fixing salaries of other grades on the basis of their efficiency. The owners are not bound to implement a three-tier pay scale for the workers; rather they would shut their factories if it is imposed unilaterally, said garment factory owner Shah Alam.

Ariful Huq, another factory owner, said he will need to pay Tk. 72 lakh more if the proposed pay scale is implemented in the first year. "I made a profit of Tk. 70 lakh last year. Now who will pay the rest two lakh?" he said, adding, "It seems that joining a garment unit as an employee will become more profitable than running a factory." Foreign buyers tend to come with a reduced CM, Sardar Liakat Hossain said, adding that it would be better for the owners to shut their factories as they do not know how to adjust with a situation that would force them to implement over 100 per cent wage hike.

Factory owner Bahauddin Md Yossuf said banks and insurance companies will also be forced to close their operations if the proposed pay scale is implemented.

Finally, on 5th October, 2006, The Minimum Wage Board announced a final and single pay package for the workers in the readymade garment (RMG) sector recommending around Tk. 1,700 as the minimum wage for the entry-level workers.

Earlier a draft proposal of neutral member of the MWB with recommendation for three-tier pay package failed to get support from owners and workers. The final proposal also have seven grades like the draft proposal but there would be significant reduction of pay in the grades other than the seventh, sources said, adding that the final proposal is likely to be accepted by all the six members of the board. Besides, there may be a marginal change in the pay offer of Tk. 1,200 for the apprentice workers.

Around 30 organizations representing garment workers sent their opinions about the draft proposal urging the board to increase the minimum wage for the workers that would range between Tk. 1,650 and Tk. 1,800, sources said. "In the face of severe opposition from the garment owners, there has been an understanding that instead of a three-tier proposal a single pay structure will be sent to the government for consideration," Zafrul Hasan, permanent representative of the workers on the board, said.

"After a hectic discussion among all parties, it has been agreed that a single pay structure will be finalised. Bangladesh Garment Sramik Karmachari Federation General Secretary Kamrul Ahsan said, "A chaotic situation has been going on for few months. As we would not like to see things deteriorate, we are trying to reach a stage where workers will get some benefits."

The wage board at its 25th meeting on September 12 announced a three-tier proposal to be implemented in three years with Tk. 1,604 as gross minimum salary for the entry level workers in the first year. Following a labor unrest in the country's premier export-earning garment sector, the government formed the wage board on May 31 and asked it to recommend a pay structure for the workers within three months. The minimum wage for workers in the RMG sector is now Tk. 930, which was fixed about 12 years ago.

The government, garment factory owners and workers' leaders at a meeting on June 12 inked a 10-point memorandum of understanding (MoU) after a series of discussions and decided to implement the MoU in phases to address the unrest.6

1.9 Government Interventions in Running of FBCCI

FBCCI has threatened to consult lawyers and take legal steps on a government order to incorporate a controversial clause in its Memorandum of Articles of Association (MAA) in 2004.

The clause the governments seek to insert in the MAA of Federation of Bangladesh Chambers of Commerce and Industry (FBCCI) would enable its board members to remove its president or vice-president if their conducts are deemed detrimental to the federation's interests. [11]

In the board meeting it was decided to convene an extraordinary general meeting (EGM) on June 12 where around 1,200 general members of the country's apex trade body would decide whether the clause will be incorporated in the MOU or not, meeting sources said.

On May 17, 2004, the commerce ministry sent a letter to the FBCCI president asking him to take measures to incorporate the clause in Articles 14 of its MOU within four weeks.

The FBCCI thought government move was aimed at paving the way to remove the then FBCCI president, "As some political aides to the Prime Minister and a section of business leaders did not like the political views he expressed at a press conference on April 26."

In the April-26 press conference, ex President FBCCI Awwal Mintoo presented a set of proposals to reform key areas of governance and politics, which he described as extremely confrontational.

The FBCCI chief's proposals were for increasing the president's power, reducing the number of ministries to 20, strengthening the Supreme Judicial Council, introducing two posts of deputy speaker in parliament—one each from the treasury and the opposition benches—and formation of citizens' committees to curb police corruption.

Another member of the FBCCI board of directors, who was also present in the emergency meeting, compared the government's order to amend the federation's MOU with what he said was its controversial role in 2003 election of Bangladesh Garment Manufacturers and Exporters Association (BGMEA).

"The government interfered in the BGMEA election last year, as a state minister and some other influential ruling BNP lawmakers favored a certain panel and were against holding the election in time. At one stage, the Prime Minister's Office asked the commerce ministry to defer the election," the ex FBCCI director recalled. He deplored such government interference in trade associations terming it utterly undemocratic.

Appendix

Definition

Government [1]

The Government of Bangladesh is currently the deputy member of the ILO Governing Body. ILO assistance to the Ministry includes programrs in the area of international labor standards, child labor, skills training, women's empowerment and health, industrial relations, and occupational safety and health.

Employers [1]

ILO's main focal point is the Bangladesh Employers Federation (BEF) which presents more than 90 percent of the employers in the country. It is affiliated with the International Organization of Employers (IOE). Mr. Alamgir T. Rahman is the current President. ILO provides assistance to employers in the areas of human resources management, occupational safety and health, industrial relations, and non-discrimination in employment. Bangladesh Garments Manufacturers and Exporters Association (BGMEA), which is receiving assistance from ILO in the area of child labor, is a member of BEF.

Workers [1]

There are over 22 national trade union federations in the country of which four are ICFTU affiliates. The trade union movement is severely fragmented and politicized. Unionization in the private sector industries is generally low and participation of women in the trade unions is even lower. The ILO has encouraged the formation of the Bangladesh National Committee for Women Workers' Development and continued to provide support for its capacity building. Currently, sixteen federations have formed a loose group known as the National Coordination Committee on Workers' Education (NCCWE). ILO has been collaborating with the NCCWE in various activities which include training courses, workshops and seminars on collective bargaining, industrial relations, leadership development, and awareness about labor law and trade union rights.

[1] http://www.ilo.org/public/english/region/asro/bangkok/arm/bgd.htm

CHAPTER X
Jatiya Sramik League

Contents

1.0 Emergence Final

Jatiya Sramik League (JSL) was emerged at a very critical point of the nation. It was founded in 12th October, 1969. 1969—the year which has immense significance in our national history, has no less importance to JSL. Not because that was the year JSL was formed, but because it was founded for a great cause. The then President of Awami League, prominent political party in the East, Sheikh Mujibur Rahman was farsighted enough to foresee the future as uncertain. He could feel the forth coming domestic war which later on took place in 1971. He felt the necessity to organize the prevailing labor force into a unit. It is not that there was not labor support, but there was. They had to be unified, because they were presumed to make a major contribution in the upcoming war, which came out very true after wards.

So, according to Sheikh Mujibur Raman's instructions, and under his full supervision, the organization was formed. The process took place in the Engineers' Institute in Dhaka. It was a conference attended by the representatives of labourers from all over the country. JSL is actually a supportive organization of Awami League, which has no written base. On the very day of its inception Jatiya Sramik League got registered.

Central Offices

There has been always political instability in the country and JSL had to change itself a number of times. This change was observed in the locations of its central office too.

Periods	Addresses
Before War	15/Ka, Purana Paltan, Dhaka
After War	21, Purana Paltan, Dhaka
1975-81	91, Nawabpur Road, Dhaka
1982-Till today	23, Bangabandhu Avenue, Dhaka

1.1 History of Jatiya Sramik League

1969-75

As stated earlier, the Jatiya Sramik League officially started its journey in 1969. The JSL played an active role in the war of independence giving training 40000 Sramik league fighters. Bangladesh emerged as an independent nation after a prolonged struggle and tremendous sacrifice in terms of human sufferings and bloodshed. After independence Awami League became the ruling party of the new republic but a number of political parties of different orientation were in existence and most of them supported their own trade union organizations. Jatiya Sramik League also continued with their activities with the registration number B-11 which they still hold today. The government was faced with a war torn economy, disrupted communication system, social dislocation due the return of industrial workers from the refugee camps in India after nine months. They were driven out from the country by the settlers (Non Bengali workers) with the assistance of Pakistan army in 1971. When they returned home they found their home either destroyed or burnt and government had to arrange their rehabilitation which by itself was a tremendous task because the number of refugees who started returning every day in hundred and thousand could not be rehabilitated immediately as the government had no fund of its own. Most of the ready currency notes were either looted by the Pak army or burn to ashes from the state bank vault. Industrial undertakings most of which were owned and managed by Pakistan employers were suddenly abandoned by those owners and managers who left the plants uncared for. However in 1972, the government took a decision to pay nine months salary to all workers who were absent during the war. Also May Day was observed as a public holiday in Bangladesh—Jatiya Sramik League look upon these events as one of their principal achievements in the post liberation period. During the liberation war a number of workers organized their 'red shirts' (private army) and effectively used sophisticated arms distributed to them to fight against the Pakistani army. However after the liberation war the same arms continued to be used against the rival trade unions to secure the dominating position among the workers in the name of socialism or one party government. In fact intense rivalry ensued and there was a polarization between the JSL on one side and all other leftists' trade unions like BSF (Bangladesh Sramik Federation) on the other side. As result rowdyism in different mill and factories ensuing from inter union rivalry became almost daily occurrence. And on hind sight it can be said that JSL failed during those days to act responsibly and showed a tendency dictatorial rather than democratic attitude to build up the nation, depending more on muscle men rather than reasonable men. While the finance Minister was running with the beggar's bowl JSL and BSF continued to show their strength in various industrial areas and continued making irresponsible demands to government only to gain popularity for their groups in the field of rivalry at the cost of the country. Even some leftists party began to burn the jute go down so that the government may not earn the foreign exchange by exporting them and by the beginning of 1974 Bangladesh was really an international basket. At the same time Bangladesh was hard hit by the rise of the price of foodstuff and other necessities as a result of the oil embargo of 1974. The situation deteriorated fast and the result was turned from industrial area to rural areas. It must be said that JSL failed to serve as responsible labor union during that time instead surrounding the Prime Minister Sheikh Mujibur Rahman with flatterers, permit hunters and intriguers who went to Ganabhaban (Prime Minister Office) everyday for their own interest and misguided him. On 3rd January 1975 emergency was declared and all kinds of strikes and lock out was banned by the government. On June 1975, the constitution of BAKSAL was announced declaring it as the only political party. According to this constitution Jatiya Sramik League became the only recognized labor party. But on the 15th August 1975, Khandakar Mushtaque Ahmed took over power as the president of the country after the assassination of Sheikh Mujibur Rahman and from the 15th of August three federations became more active. They are-

1. Bangladesh Sramik Federation
2. Jatiya Sramik Federation
3. Bangla Sramik Federation

However in August the new government dissolved all national trade union centres. Although grass root trade unions continued, JSL activities faded and eventually the most active and powerful federation during three year after the independence—Jatiya Sramik League became more or less inactive.

1978-90

After 1978 a breakaway group from the BJSL formed an organization affiliated to the WFTU. But understandably the activities of JSL were very limited with its parent party. The Awami League being ousted out of power and being portrayed in a more or less villainous role by the new regime of General Ziaur Rahman who came to power after a bloody coup attempt. Then another general grabbed national power. General Ershad came to power and he declared martial law in the country. During the martial law period, trade unionism was banned for the period of 1982-84. After 1984 trade union activities were reinstated and Sramik League officially resumed its activities with Rahmatullah Chowdhury as president and Mahboob ul—Alam as General Sectretary. As general Ershad continued with his martial fisted rule of the country, annoyance and discomfort grew among the democracy—loving citizens. The two biggest political party of the country Bangladesh Nationalist Party (BNP) and Awami League along with the help of students and workers launched series of hartals and others anti government rallies to oust the military ruler, the Jatiya Sramik League also played its rule in this struggle for democracy by stirring up the labor forces. Finally in the 1990 Ershad's regime was toppled in a mass up rise in which JSL played its role with its influence over the working group and by rallying them in the mass protests against the military ruler. Obviously, the JSL looks at its participation in this mass uprising as its chief achievement during this period.

1991-96

In 1991 in a free and fair election the rival party of the Bangladesh Awami League-The Bangladesh Nationalist Party and the BNP came into power. Apart from smaller industrial disputes the major activity of the JSL during this period included the minimum wage offensive. In fact the major labor event of 1992-1993 was the winning by the labor federation (of which the JSL was a major member) known by the acronym SKOP (Sramik Karmachari Oikya Parishad) of a higher industry wise minimum wage for public sector industrial workers. The SKOP had demanded a TK 1000 per month minimum wage since 1992 and in support of these demands mounted a series of nationwide transport blockades in the first half of 1993. Eventually the government agreed to give SKOP most of what it wanted. The SKOP also demanded (and won) government agreement and consult the labor organization over future government privatization efforts and workers retrenchments. The government had refused to bargain with SKOP in its first 3 blockades earlier in 1993. Police were deployed to keep roads and railways open and the SKOP action were largely unsuccessful. In July however, in the face of a simultaneous 72-hours blockade by SKOP and a nationwide hartal by the major opposition Awami League and Jatiya Party, the government was agreed to sign an agreement with SKOP. The agreement provided a minimum wage of TK 950 per month and productivity increases of about TK 45 and various allowances for housing, medical and food which could double the compensation, depending on the skill and wage scale of the employee. In early June 1994, the National Labor Law Commission submitted a report codifying a new labor law to consolidate and supersede a series of previous laws. Obviously the Jatiya Sramik League looks backs at these events as a major victory for them during this period.

Another important labor issue during this period was the burning issue of child labor. Child labor and potential fallout of Bangladesh's garment industry of the so-called Harkin Bill occupied center stage in labor issues in 1993. The Harkin Bill was directed specifically against the import of goods into the U.S made by child labor. The Bangladesh garment industry exported over $1.2 billion in FY 1993, more than half the value of the country's total exports. By some estimates, in early 1993, some 50000 children of 14 years old were working in the garment industry (out of an estimated total of 800000 workers). The bill was introduced for the first time in 1993. As word spread of its provision to ban imports, if it is proven they are manufactured using child labor, many mill owners reportedly began terminating child employees. However, labor unions like the JSL and other labor parties failed to come up with any plan to provide better opportunities for these children.

In 1996 the term of BNP came to an end in February 1996 the national parliamentary election was held which the main opposition Awami league and other opposition parties had boycotted. The new government of BNP was sworn in but the opposition staged nationwide series of strikes that were supported by workers of Jatiya Sramik League too. Finally the government and other semi-government employee joined the so-called "Janatar Mancha" or the stage of the people and JSL played an important role here too. As a result of movement like this the government was forced to resign and fresh elections were held at which Awami League came out as winners after being out of power of 21 years.

1996-2008

In 1996 the parent party of Jatiya Srmik League—the Awami League formed the government after being out of power of 21 years. Naturally there was a surge in the membership of the JSL the number of affiliated unions jumped from near 750 to about one and a half thousand. As customary various commemorations and salutary activities became order of the day. In the 90s along with its parent party, the JSL had undergone Philosophical shifts with a changed belief in a "free and democratic trade union movement" in contrast to the one party rule and nationalization of industries that it once believed in. During this period there was relative calm in the industries as Bangladesh recorded her first self sufficiency in food grains. Also the government announced a minimum wage policy, which JSL and most other labor unions accepted. Nine textile mills were handed over to the workers. In fact during this period the parent party Awami League came to the fore and the activities of the JSL became somewhat limited to observance of different days and basking in the glory of shared power which is a common happening in Bangladesh for the labor wing of the ruling party. In the election of October 2001 the rival party registered an unprecedented victory and sure enough following in the culture of Bangladeshi labor union the JSL had to go back stage and rival Jatiyatabadi Sramik Dal had captured center stage. But after the national election of 2008 the scenario reversed as Awami league got two third majorities. The officials of JSL said that with the change in government many workers are to change their affiliation to the trade union because of fear of losing their jobs. Also there are harassments from law—enforcing agencies. Such is the legacy of trade unionism in Bangladesh, being in power by hook or by crook is more important than true labor welfare if a labor union wants to maintain its support among workers.

1.2 Role of Some Leaders

Abdur Rahman

The president of Bangladesh Jatiya Sramik League Late Abdur Rahman was born at Senbag thana under the district of Noakhali. He was an employee of Bangladesh Jute Mill at Palash in the district Norshingdi. Late Abdur Rahman was a very influential trade union leader in the Jute sector. He contributed a lot in establishing labor movement before and after liberation. He was the member of the central committee of East Pakistan Federation of Labor. He formed the Pakistan Jute Mills labor Union in 1966 and was elected the General Secretary of the union. He was one of the significant organizers of the liberation war. He was popular not only in the labor movement but also in national politics. After liberation he was elected parliament member from his own constitution. A group of assassinator killed him while he was on the way home after attending a seminar on Labor act.

Ruhul Amin Buiah

Ruhul Amin Buiah was born in a village named Kesharpara under Senbag than in the district of Noakahli on 23rd March, 1943. He started his service life in CNB Workshop in 1953. From the very beginning of his service life he started he involved himself with labor movement. He was elected the General Secretary of Tejgaon regional committee of Mojumder Federation in 1960.In that year he was arrested for being involved in trade union. He formed Tejgaon Trade Union Association in 1961. He played a leading role in the political movements. He was accused and arrested because of giving lead in the 6-point demand movement of Awami League in 1966 and Mass movement in 1969. He was in jail for three years for participating in the 69's movement. Immediately after being released from jail he took part in formation of Sramik League and was elected the Joint Secretary. After liberation he was elected the Secretary of Labor affairs of Bangladesh Awami League. In that very year he was elected the General Secretary of Jatiya Sramik League. Again he was arrested on 6th December, 1972. He was released from jail after six years in 1978. In that year he gave lead to form Jatiya Sramik Jote and he was elected General Secretary of that party. He participated in the liberation war in 1971 and played a very courageous role being the General Commander of B-Zone of Noakhali district. His contribution in the formation of SKOP is mention worthy.

Roy Ramesh Chandra

Roy Ramesh Chandra, is present (2011) General Secretary of Jatiya Sramik League,

He was born in Magura on January o1, 1953 and passed his SSC from Sripur High School in 1969 and passed his HSC from Sripur College in 1971. After HSC he took admission into Rajshahi University. He did his B.Sc Honours and M.Sc in Chemistry. He was politically conscious from his student life and actively related with the activities of Chatra League when he was the student of Rajshahi University. Roy Ramesh did his post graduation from Bulgeria. He also did diploma on Globalization and Mass Communication from ILO Touring Centre Italy. He also studied on Trade Union in Japan. He took part many seminar, symposium and world conference. He was arrested in 1977 for being involved with the movement demanding trial of the killers of Sheikh Mujibur Rahman. He passed 33 months in jail and there he came into contact with some communist leaders. From them he got the inspiration to work for the workers. Three leaders played a vital role in bringing him in the Sramik League. They are Phoni Bhushan Mojumder, Abdus Samad Azad and Abdur Razzak. From July 03, 2003 he occupying the post of General Secretary of Jatiya Sramik League and playing active role in establishing the rights of the workers, improve the overall condition of the workers and to expedite the movement of trade union for the workers of formal and informal sector. His continuous endeavor is to solve the problems of workers and establish a strong industrial relations in the industrial sector of Bangladesh. Presently he is occupying many positions in different national and international committee and federation. Roy Ramesh Chandra is the Executive Board Member of International Trade Union Confederation Asia Pacific; Vice chairman of Trade Union and Human Rights Committee; General Secretary of Bangladesh Truck Chalok Sramik Federation and also President of United Federation of Garments Workers.

1.3 Objectives of Jatiya Sramik League

(As stated in Section 3, Constitution of JSL)

1. To create awareness, motivate and organize labor force and working-class for establishing nationalism, democracy, socialism and an unsuppressed society.
2. To combat against all sorts of repression imposed on the labor force and the working class people by both internal and external force.
3. To establish the five fundamental rights for the labor force and working—class: food, clothing, housing, education and medical facilities.
4. To take necessary steps for conserving the rights of the working—class in economical, social and cultural field.
5. To strengthen the independence and sovereignty of the country.

6. To protect the labor force against all sorts of internal and external repression and conspiracy and help the patriotic and the progressive labor force to achieve the goal.

7. To create unity, solidarity, and friendship among the trade unions.

8. To become an active participant of the world labor federation and Internal Trade Unions and maintain a close and amiable relation with them. To become affiliated member and associate of the International Trade Unions and participate in the movement to establish the lawful rights of the labor force and working class throughout the world.

9. To become a legal representative body of the labor force in various industrial establishment and factories to create a healthy and amicable relation between the labor force and the occupier/authority for the sake of better production.

10. To bargain with the occupies for the sake of the labor force and expedite movements in the question of trade union and other democratic rights as claimed by working—class.

11. To ensure proper salary, wage, allowance, gratuity, bonus as well as period of the job, security, salient working environment, insurance, pension, damage for r accidents, job for the relatives of any deceased person in accordance with the present market value and living standard and thus preserve the rights of the labor force.

12. To create provision of laws for the sake of the labor force.

13. To represent in the various labor court, different committees and communities and related industry and labor, salary commission, wage commission on behalf of the labor to bargain with the occupier for the sake of the labor force and expedite movements in the question of trade union and other democratic rights as claimed by working—class and present their lawful demand and arguments.

14. To take necessary initiatives for labor welfare and ti eztend elaborate programs to eliminate the course of illiteracy of the labor force and run training program for the enhancement of their professional skills.

15. To establish cooperative societies for the economic betterment of the working class as to improve their living standard by establishing cooperative shops.

16. To express solidarity with all the combatant labor forces of the world and expedite movement to establish peace and friendship among the nation and for the social progression of their own society.

17. To ensure the equal right for the female labors and to uproot corruption from every sphere of life. To protect working—class from any sort of narrowness of fundamentalism and nationalism

18. To take democratic steps to attain the aforesaid goal and objectives through talk, discussions and creating public opinion. The organization shall always abide by the existing ruled and regulations and the other provisions of laws concerning to this matter.

1.4 Achievements of Jatiya Sramik League

Since the formation, Jatiya Sramik League is actively participating in many activities regarding establishing the rights of workers and also participating in the political activities when necessary. During its long journey from 1969 it has a long list of achievements. It played important role in the liberation war 1971 and also participated in the movement against the autocratic government of General Ershad. Time and often JSL pressed the government to uphold the right of workers and to formulate policy and declare minimum wage for the workers. Here is some list of the achievements of the Jatiya Sramik League.

1. Influencing the government to pay nine months wage during the liberation war.
2. Inducing the government to form industrial workers' wage commission and declare minimum wages.
3. Concerning effort to establish overall rights of trade unions.
4. Making May Day to observe nationally.
5. Playing a role in the nationalization of the industries.
6. Working together with the transport workers to achieve their demands.
7. With the approval of central council, this federation has already established relationship and a network of communication with the trade unions of different countries and with international labor organization.
8. Time and often the federation publish journals and magazines, and other trade union related books and articles. They also facilitate the training for members, employees and other workers of the federation.
9. This federation has already determined whether there is any barrier to the labor interest and has prepared a comprehensible suggestion to protect the labor interest regarding the legal issues. If the trade union or any workers of the trade union needs assistance regarding the legal issues, the secretary of the 'legal issues and Bargaining' performs the responsibilities of resolving the problems. Again, in this regard, the secretary also resolves the bargaining of the rights of the labor, provided that such any situation arises. The secretary also informs all this legal issues to the general secretary or to the central council.
10. The federation has already arranged the provision for improving the living standard of the labor and ensured the welfare of the labor. They have already compensated the distressed and suffered labors of the federation.
11. They have already established communication network and coordination with the incorporated trade unions.
12. They have helped to form the craft federation among other organizations as much as possible.
13. If the leaders suffer and become victimized due to natural disaster, the federations help and rehabilitate them.
14. Dock Sramik League, an affiliated organization of Bangladesh Jatiya Sramik League, was elected as Collective Bargaining Agent (CBA) on behalf of entire trade unions of Chittagong Sea Port and successfully completed its period with good reputation.

1.5 Relationship between Objective and Achievement

The objectives that are mentioned in the constitution of Jatiya Sramik League are very much worker welfare oriented and in most cases it sounds good. Actually determining objectives is much easier job in comparison to establishing those objectives. Here is a analysis of how many of the achievements of JSL actually fulfill their objectives.

If analyze the objectives and the achievements of the Jatiya Sramik League so far some relations and gaps between the objectives and achievements become obvious. Just consider the first objective of the organization and give a look on the achievements of the organization, it becomes clear that the organization has not yet been able to achieve a society that is a combination of democracy, socialism, nationalism and free from suppression. Still garments manufacturing sector is the highest export earners in Bangladesh and there is no trade union in most of the garments factories. That is the indication that still the organization has lots of responsibilities to establish workers rights of union and collective bargaining agent. Since many organizations do not allow trade union in their organizations because of the fear of interruption in production and daily operations there is no body to raise voice to act as safeguard of the workers.

One of the core objectives of JSL is to ensure five fundamental needs of the workers but so far there is no concentrated effort by JSL to fulfil those needs. It is obvious that it is not possible for any particular organization to ensure five basic needs of the workers. But what most they can do is that they can collaborate with other federations to place the pressure on the concerned authority that can help ensuring the fundamental needs for the workers. In our country two major Sramik federations are JSL and JSD. But because of their affiliation with two major political parties of the country they often do not agree upon on any issue regarding labor welfare because of their rivalry attitude towards one another. That is why they lag behind to achieve the aforementioned objective of establishing five fundamental rights of work force.

Another core objective of JSL is to create unity, solidarity and friendship among trade unions. But it is still a far dream in Bangladesh to establish good relationships among the trade unions. Only the trade unions which belong to the same trade unions maintain good relation among them. There is no exception for JSL. Though the organization is articulate of having good relations with trade unions it was obvious from the interview of the leaders of JSL that they actually maintain relations with the trade unions whose political ideology match with that of JSL to greater extent.

It is the objective of the organization to establish relation with international trade union federations and to work in collaboration with ILO to establish workers rights. In this area JSL has gained their objective. With the approval of central council, this federation has already established relationship and a network of communication with the trade unions of different countries and with international labor organization.

In the objectives section of the constitution there is an objective to ensure equal right for the female laborers and uproot corruptions from every sphere of life. But in reality the organization has not yet been taken any such steps to achieve the objective. There is no any mentionable achievement in this area.

1.6 The Popular Sectors of JSL and Reasons behind the Popularity

JSL has a total member of eleven lac members including formal and informal sector and 1765 trade unions are affiliated with Jatiya Sramik Leagues of 2011. It is a very old wing of Bangladesh Awami League and from emergence of JSL in 1969 the leaders of JSL is working relentlessly to establish the rights of the workers. JSL has huge popularity in some sectors such as Jute, Transport, Rickshaw puller, Vendor (Especially at Sadar Ghat), Service sector especially in banking and insurance sector.

The reasons behind the popularity are given below-

1. Uncompromising attitude:

JSL is uncompromising in establishing the rights of workers. According to the General Secretary of JSL, they always try to pursue to achieve the demands they think are relevant in improving the condition of mass workers.

2. Continuously organizing activities:

JSL organize activities on a continuous basis. They never halt organizing activities whether their parent party is in power or not. They organize meetings, seminar, rally, procession time and often and observe the May Day with great enthusiasm. JSL organized a grand rally on May Day.

3. Solve day to day problem:

JSL tries to solve the problem of workers day to day basis. As long as the problem is under the control of JSL they try to solve the problem immediately after being known of the nature of the problem.

4. Patient hearing of workers:

All the workers have access to the JSL and they are very much concern about the problem of the workers. They hear the problem with great patience of the grass root level workers and try to address all the problems.

5. Good relation with the political parties:

JSL maintains good relation with Bangladesh Awami League, with the leftist parties and with parties who pro-liberation and who are in favor of sovereignty of the country. Some of the workers belong to the Awami League and its wings. That is why the workers are interested to get into JSL. Another reason for the popularity of JSL is that JSL was formed by Sheikh Mujibur Rahman who is the father of Bangladesh and there are a lot of followers across the country.

6. Implementation of rules and regulations:

Every organization should implement the rules and regulations regarding labor issue properly. Jatiya Sramik League always tries to implement the rules and regulations for the betterment of the working class. Jatiya Sramik League arranges time to time development programs for its affiliated trade unions.

1.7 Privilege of being the Member of Trade Union

Jatiya Sramik League follows some basic criteria to enlist a new member. There are some requirements one has to meet to be the member of Jatiya Sramik League. The conditions of being the member of Jatiya Sramik League are given below.

1. To be the member of Jatiya Sramik League one must has to be worker.
2. One has to be above 18 years to be the member of Jatiya Sramik League as JSL does not allow child labor.
3. He has to give the commitment to abide by the principles, ideals, purpose, constitution and rules and regulations.
4. Have to pay admission fee along with other fees determined by the central council.
5. Any Sramik Karmochari Union has to show obedience towards the ideals, vision, goals and programmes of the Sramik League and has to give written resolution with signature to abide by the rules and regulations mentioned in the constitution.
6. Every member has to pay his affiliation fee along with other fees set by the central committee to retain his membership. Any violation of this rule will result in cancellation of the membership.

1.8 Relationship with Political Parties

Organized labor is organized for more than bargaining with employers, it also organized for political actions. Politicians who are running for office are seeking votes. Union has the power to supply votes. Union on the other hand is seeking the adoption of government policies in Bangladesh favorable to them. More importantly connected with big political parties gives the union leaders power and position they otherwise would not enjoy. Especially in Bangladesh the trade union movement has been marred by the relationship with the political parties. The workers here are much familiar with trade unionism but they still do not realize the paramount need of independent trade unionism for promoting their collective group interest. This is because there has been too much politics with Bangladeshi trade union movement, which discourages independent trade unionism in the country. Because of the heavy politicalization of the trade unions, workers are often used by their respective 'parent parties' to provide crowd and muscles. In some cases the use of labor by leaders in search of political and financial aggrandizement has crossed the line of legality and reduced the unions to practicing extortion and intimidation.

The political process in Bangladesh today operates through a two party system. Many smaller parties do make their appearances in elections, but their influence in the political scenario and labor union is meager to say the least. Jatiya Party tried to establish its own labor union branch but the effort has not been very successful. But one trend that is visible as a result of this party oriented system is that in Bangladesh has not developed a truly labor oriented trade unionism. In the romantic periods of post liberation the leaders thought of building Bangladesh in the socialist model and hence there were thought of a labor dominated political process. But the scenario has changed considerably since 1972. Today as regard the political alignment more than the parties class orientations, the labor union has developed party orientation. This generally true in today's political climate aristocracy where someone's to be son, daughter or widow to get political support. In fact today the general line for trade unions is formulated primarily by the political parties for maintaining or changing the existing status quo. Too often strikes instigated by the trade unions are politically motivated—intended at embarrassing the government and not for true labor—welfare.

Although all the labor unions deny such relationships but a deeper analysis reveals the degree of dependence of such labor unions on their parent parties—as is the case for JSL. When asked by the writer to describe their relationship with political parties the officials and leaders iterated that their constitution is different from that of Awami League (AL) and they are not bound to follow the agenda of AL. But in reality braking way from the political party is extremely difficult for the Jatiya Sramik League because they are at present inter-twined like the Siamese-twins. Such perpetuation of political unionism in Bangladeshi industry has led to trade union rivalry, which has a harmful effect on industrial relations. Rivalry between the Jatiya Sramik League and the Jatiyatabadi Sramik Dal is on account of their political affiliation, which has resulted in the fragmentation of work force in the same industry or their political affiliation, which has resulted in the fragmentation of workforce in the same industry of establishment. Demonstrations have been staged and bloodshed on labor unrelated issues like not calling someone the father of the nation or not recognising someone as the announcer of independence. This is why, although the labor federations like JSL and JSD claim not to be influenced by the mother party, a close inspection reveals the hollowness of their claims. Both Awami League and BNP favoured unduly their own trade union wings and gave step-motherly treatment to trade unions affiliated to opposing political parties during their term in power and this trend is continuing today leaving its complicated legacy in the industrial scenario of Bangladesh.

1.9 Role and Contribution of JSL in Labor Movement

Actually the contribution of JSL is not limited to only one sector. The inception of JSL was held before the liberation war. And from the inception in 1969, JSL is a distinct name in the field of labor movement. In the war of independence the role of JSL is quite mentionable. About 40000 Sramik League fighters were trained up and took participation in the war. And after the war they influenced the government to pay the wages of labor for the nine months of liberation war. After the war when the country's economy was at broken situation and unrest was prevailing in the industrial sector their role was not positive. They did nothing but to flattering then Prime Minister Sheikh Mujibur Rahman. When they need to play a significant role in the trade union movement they failed to do so.

After the independence of Bangladesh all the industry were nationalized. Naturally nationalization was a welcome decision for the trade unionist working class and the people at large. However the purpose of nationalization was not materialized later on. The already small manufacturing sector which accounted for only 10 of the Gross Domestic Product faced severe crisis. It was not only the failure of the political leadership or Government, administration or management or failure due to various restraints but the trade union generally also could not perform their due role.

The ruling party men mostly busied themselves in making quick money. Its trade union front Sramik League also ran after wealth. Machines, fund and industrial products were looted. Many trade union leaders got involved in corrupt deals of the sales and purchases in the enterprises. Sramik League took full advantage of its party rules, organized volunteer corps called "Lal bahini" (red brigade). Large number of trade union leaders and "Lal bahini" people used to get wages and salaries without working. This vitiated working atmosphere in the enterprise level. To suppress their misdeeds they even raised unreasonable financial demands which the enterprises were unable to fulfill.

Other trade unions not belonging to the government backed Sramik League was mostly engaged in the struggle for higher wages and benefits. Unions or workers influenced by opposition used every means to bring out workers on the street and unrest.

At the regime of General Zia and General Ershad the party has little scope of doing something for the labors. Because most of the time of that two regimes trade union movement was banned for a long time. Emergency was installed and all kinds of movement were banned. But JSL actively participated in the movement of restoring democracy in 1991 against the autocratic government of General Ershad. When democracy was installed JSL activities took momentum and they form SKOP (Sramik Karmochari Oikka Parishad) and through which all the labor federations jointly participated in placing demand for the workers to concerned authority.

At present JSL is in a good position since the party with which they are affiliated are in power. They have scope to place their charter of demand that will truly reflect the welfare of the working class.

2.0 Relationship with ILO and International Perspective

Jatiya Sramik League maintains good relations with the organizations which work for the betterment of the working class. ILO is an international organization which is working to ameliorate the condition of workers across the globe. Bangladesh ratified some of the conventions of the ILO. When any government ratify any convention of ILO, it becomes mandatory for that government to implement the content of that convention within a given time frame. The government includes different Sramik federation in implementing the conventions of ILO. When ILO organize any meeting, rally, seminar regarding labor issues they usually invite the president and general secretary of different Sramik federation. Actually ILO cannot get the true picture of the condition of the labor only relying on the information provided by the different organization of the government. That is why they do not rely fully on the government organization rather they also keep relations with different Sramik federation. There is no such formal affiliation with ILO by the Jatiya Sramik League but they work in collaboration to establish the rights of the workers and establish the rights of trade union of formal and informal workers. They also work for collective bargaining with the government to have better industrial relations.

In the earlier stages, Sramik league worked as a group with the International Confederation of Trade Union (ICFTU). The so-called Jatiya Sramik League is still working as a part of that.

In accordance with the four state policies of secularism, socialism, democracy and nationalism, JSL started working with the World Federation of Trade Union (WFTU), which is the international organization of the labourers from the socialistic world. This started after 1975. JSL supporting 'Bakshal' also included itself with WFTU. Presently, JSL is still working with it. It is to be mentioned here that JSL is also a member of the General Council of the WFTU. JSL had also participated in the international labor conferences organized by ILO and a few foreign countries. It is still very much in touch with those organizations and their plans. The seminars and conferences have been very useful for the Bangladeshi labourers, as the experienced gathered there were reflected in practice here. The members could also uphold our ideals, boosting the image of our labourers.

2.1 Leadership Development

The 11th and 14th no. section of the constitution of JSL describes how leaders, officers and members of JSL would be selected. Even to select the officers and members there are provisions in the constitution. It is a good sign to build up leaders in the federation. But the first condition of build up present and future leaders is to hold election on a regular basis. As mentioned in the constitution that after every two years national council will held and executive committee will be selected but in practical holding of national council on a regular basis is not a common phenomena in JSL. Many factors affect the holding of election. If the country's national political situation remain stable and the party with which it is affiliated permit or give green signal only then the election held. The holding election also depends on the willingness of existing executive committee. Sometimes they differ the holding election to longer their tenure. And it is seen that the previous leaders elected year after year. That is why the scope of being new leaders is limited.

2.2 Practice of Democracy in JSL

JSL claims that there is democracy in the organization but in reality there is no such practice of democracy in the organization. The first and foremost condition of democracy is to hold election on a regular basis so that there is change in the leaders to make the organization more active. In the eleventh section of the constitution of JSL there are some provisions describing how the executive committee would be selected. There is a provision of holding the national council after every two years. The central executive committee elected by the national councilors will be considered as the chief committee. The election will be held by the confidential ballot box.

The officers and members of Central Executives Council will be elected by the National Council. The Election Commission will be constructed of five members making one chairman who will not attend the Central Council Election. This council will collect confidential poll. Those candidates who will get most of the votes will be considered as the officers and members of the new Central Council. If there is not more than one candidate for a post there would be no election for that post. The only candidate is declared elected without any contest.

The aforementioned provision of the constitution makes it clear that leaders of JSL are elected through election. It indicates that there exist practice of democracy in federation but question is to what extent the provisions of the constitution are followed by the leaders. One of the key leaders mentioned that whatever decision is made it is made according to guide lines of the constitution. But the constitution has no provision of how many times a leader would be able to contest for the same post.

2.3 Conclusion

From the discussion of the history and achievements of the Jatiya Sramik League it is clear that this labor union had an important role to play in our struggle for independence. However it must be stated that the post-liberation era till to date the contribution of JSL toward labor and national welfare has not always been a boon. Like most other labor unions in Bangladesh the JSL has not gained inherent strength because of a lack of common cause, common goal and common philosophy of bread and butter unionism. Politically motivated leaders who secured their position only to strengthen their power base have been responsible for much harmful intra union and inter union rivalry sometimes sacrificing the workers interest to those of the party to which they belong. Even more damage has been done by the leaders who used the labor union movement for their own personal ends. But at the same time it is also true that there were some leaders who sacrificed their whole life to ensure the welfare of the labor. Healthy industrial relations are desired to move the country forward. If the there is unrest and dissatisfaction among the workers it is the country who has to count the loss. There must be a good relation among the trade unions and trade union federations. Otherwise the workers would not be able to uphold their rights. If the workers are fragmented into different segments and if the workers cannot be unified and cannot come under one umbrella they would be exploited by the "aristocracy of leadership" backed by capitalists. The workers must be aware of their interest and also be aware that they are no longer used as the political tool to achieve the goals of the bourgeoisie.

CHAPTER XI
Bangladesh Jatiyatabadi Sramik Dal

CONTENTS

1.0 Bangladesh Jatiyatabadi Sramik Dal (BJSD)

1.0.1 Overview

Bangladesh Jatiyatabadi Sromik Dal (BJSD) is the labor wing of Bangladesh Nationalist Party (BNP). It is one of the largest National Trade Union Federations of Bangladesh. It has 279 registered trade unions affiliated with it and 2,47,454 registered members. It is enlisted in the International Trade Union Confederation (ITUC) and its registration number is BNF-7. Its head quarter is in 28/1, Naya Paltan, (4th floor), VIP Road, Daka-1000. [7]

1.0.2 History

Bangladesh Jatiyatabadi Sromik Dal was founded on April 26, 1979 under the supervision of the president of Bangladesh of that time, Ziaur Rahman, for the welfare of the labor force and workers of the different industries of Bangladesh. At that time Nazrul Islam Khan, Iskandar Ali, Abdul Baten, Mijanur Rahman Chowdhury, Abul Kashem Chowdhury, Abdullah Al Noman, Jafrul Hasan and many other leaders were in the front line to build Jatiyatabadi Sramik Dal. [3]

After the independence of Bangladesh in 1971, when the trade unions in different industries all across the country were more or less inactive, this organization was established to ensure the interests of the workers. During this time, the industrial relations between the owners of the industries and the workers were not very satisfactory. According to the personnel of 'Bangladesh Jatiyatabadi Sramik Dal' these are some reasons that led to the inception of the organization and no political or any other issues other than the welfare of worker led to the establishment of this organization. [3]

1.0.3 Objectives

According to the constitution (Section 1, Clause 3) of Bangladesh Jatiyatabadi Sramik Dal the main objective of BJSD is to unite all labor force and influence them for motivating trade union movement to—

- Establish social justice on the basis of democracy and, production oriented political view for national development and economic improvement of mass people.
- Make the labor force productive and creative to ensure the welfare of their lives and thus establish social value in national life.
- Ensure all basic needs such as food, health, education, shelter, and clothing of the citizens of Bangladesh together with the labor forces by effective and realistic development activities.
- Provide profitable employment to all the active men and women and young person's by effective training opportunities and thus ensure proper utilization of human resources.

The other objectives of the federation are—

- Without stopping the production, it tries to achieve solutions of all the complaints of labor forces by discussions, arbitrations, and law.
- To ensure social justice through the economic development of the labor forces and increased production.
- To support all the legal movements against any kind of oppression and torture in any national or international level and to establish unity of all national and international labor unions.
- To preserve the interest of the labor force and improve their status in national and international level.
- To acquire universal support and implement the right of collective bargaining and form trade unions according to the convention of international labor organizations.
- To represent the labor forces of Bangladesh in international organization related to the social, economic, and professional activities of labor forces.
- To supply the information to the affiliated trade unions regarding economical, wages, and working conditions of the labor forces of different classes within and outside the country.
- To coordinate, direct, assist, and order to the national union / craft federation / unions about the activities of economical, social, and political interest of labor forces of entire Bangladesh.
- To try to strengthen the national unity on the basis of Bangladeshi nationalism.
- To give effective support for the preservation fundamental and democratic rights of labor forces of other countries.
- To preserve freedom of speech, freedom of newspaper, and freedom of organization
- To make an effort to the improvement of labor management relations by increasing production for achieving better economic condition and a better life.
- To represent the labor force to the government and make an effort to formulating laws for improving the interest of the labor force.
- To help, order, and train the workers about the fundamental trade union principles.
- To increase the family income for improving financial conditions of the workers and encourage and develop cooperative movement through establishing cottage industries in industrial areas for solving unemployment problems.
- To eliminate illiteracy of the workers and their family members through education of older people and free primary education for all.
- To make an effort to introduce social security activities such as pension allowance for illness, accidents, unemployment, and death.
- To ensure the representation of workers in the planning process of—national economy and industrialization.
- To encourage cooperative firm and ensure just wages of agricultural workforce and save the workers from environmental danger.
- To make an effort to improve the working and natural environment within and outside the workplace.

- To encourage the development of national culture, literature and sports.
- To improve the family system through the betterment of family members and to encourage for a planned family. [1]

1.1 Critical Analysis of the Objectives of BJSD

Now with a close look on these objectives, it can be said that none of these objectives have been fulfilled completely for the workers of all across the country. The first objective is to establish social justice for the workers. At first we should define social justice. According to socialists and social democrats social justice is based on the concepts of human rights and equality. Social justice, sometimes called civil justice, refers to the concept of a society in which "justice" is achieved in every aspect of society, rather than merely the administration of law. It is generally thought of as a world which affords individuals and groups fair treatment and an impartial share of the benefits of society. It can also refer to the distribution of advantages and disadvantages within a society.[10] From the perspective of Bangladesh, in most of the cases the poor workers do not get fair treatment and benefits from the society. And according to political left the term "social justice" is a society with a greater degree of economic egalitarianism, which may be achieved through progressive taxation, income redistribution, or even property redistribution, policies aimed toward achieving that which developmental economists refer to as equality of opportunity and equality of outcome. But in Bangladesh most of the workers are very poor and live under the poverty line and the economic equality is not present in Bangladesh society. Many of them do not have the opportunity to get employed. And most of the employed workers get a very low wage which is not enough to ensure the basic needs of the worker and his/her family. So it is obvious that the third objective of BJSD which is to ensure all basic needs such as food, health, education, shelter, and clothing for the workers is not fulfilled yet.

The last of the four main objectives of BJSD is to provide profitable employment to all the active men and women by effective training opportunities. But as the unemployment problem remains one of the biggest problem of Bangladesh, so it is needless to say that BJSD could not fulfill this objective yet. Though they have taken some initiatives to provide training for workers, those were not enough to reduce the unemployment rate of our country.

Another objective of BJSD is to achieve solutions of all the complaints of labor forces by discussions, arbitrations, and law without stopping the production. But most of the cases it was seen that where there was a labor dispute, the first step that the labor takes is stopping the production and workers goes for strike, hartal, road blockade, and even destroying the machines and equipments of factories. Recent incident (2009-2010) of labor disputes in Savar, Dhaka is an example of that. And most of these cases, the national trade union federations were unable to stop this destructive activities, rather sometimes they gave inspiration to workers to go for such massacre.

1.2 Achievements

Within 30 years, this trade union walks a long path and establishes many bench marks in their way. Starting from 6 unions and 11000 members, it has now more than 750 basic unions and more than 7.5 lacks members. From the very beginning it strives for the improvement of the quality of the life of the exploited workers and achieved a lot. Though it yet not fully successful with their demand, but it has achieved some of the following issues partially:

- Active role in reformation of labor act 2006
- Provide training for workers through international agency
- Positive support in fixing minimum wages for the workers
- Provide help to establish trade unions in different organizations (such as in banking sector)
- 50% dearness allowance.
- Stop generalize privatization
- Bargaining with the government about the future of losing mills, factories and restrict the government in laying-off the workers.
- Delaying the privatization of railway, electricity and T.N.T. sector.
- Stopping transfer for the purpose of harassment.
- Regularize the payment of wage, provident fund and gratuity of the workers.

However, according to Mr. Shafiul Islam, the former office secretary of BJSD and current education secretary of BJSD, the organization is not fully successful in achieving its goals yet. There are still some issues that haven't yet been ensured such as: a minimum wage scale for all the workers across the country, the abolition of child labor from dangerous work. In addition to its activities relating to the labor welfare, BJSD also undertakes several social activities for the welfare of the families of the poorly paid workers. For instance, they teach the women of these poor families sewing and give them sewing machine. [3]

1.3 Critical Analysis of the Achievements of BJSD

Now, with a close look on the achievements of BJSD, one can find that most of them were achieved through the Sramik Karmochari Oikka Porishod (SKOP), the common platform of all national trade union federations. So these achievements such as reformation of labor law 2006, fixation of minimum wages for the workers, stopping generalize privatization, bargaining with the government about the future of losing mills, factories and restrict the government in laying-off the workers etc are the combined achievements of the different national trade union federations. Some of them were achieved during the period of last democratic government ruled by BNP. As it is mentioned earlier that BJSD is the labor wing of BNP, one of the largest political party of Bangladesh that ruled the country several times, it has the power or ability to put pressure on the government to achieve the demands of workers. But unfortunately, where the labor agitation for demands went against the interest of the then government ruled by BNP, BJSD remained silent or even played a negative role.

Many of the successes of BJSD were achieved within one or some organizations and is not true for the whole industry (such as fixing minimum wages in different organization, reestablishment of fired workers, stopping transfer for the purpose of harassment, regularize the payment of wage, provident fund and gratuity of the workers). And in reality, many of their achievements did not help the economic growth of the country, rather they slowed it down. For example, delaying the privatization of railway and electricity sector hampered the quality of services of these organizations and thus made the customers of these sectors suffer for a long time.

1.4 Role of 'BJSD' in the Trade Union Movement

After the establishment of Bangladesh Jatiyatabadi Sramik Dal (BJSD), their first movement was to hold a conference for women workers. This was the first ever women workers conference that was held on 7th October, 1979. On the conference a 10 point demand was published. [4]

After the assassination of President Ziaur Rahman and re-imposition of military rule by General Ershad in 1982, the trade unions were the first to resist the military dictatorship of Ershad. BJSD was one of the trade unions that stand against the autocracy of General Ershad. [4]

BJSD was one of the 11 national trade union federations those united on the basis of 5 points demand against the then autocratic government of Ershad. The unity of 11 national federations on the basis of 5 point demands was a historic land mark in trade union movement. The demands included trade union and democratic rights, stoppage of denationalization, building independent national economy better wage and benefits. The 11 federation unity called for general strike on 1st March 1984 which was a grand success. After the joining of the Bangladesh Jatiyatabadi Sramik Dal (BJSD), this unity of 11 federations took a name of "Sramik Karmachari Oikka Parishad" (SKOP). So BJSD played a prominent role in the formation of SKOP which is till the common platform of all the national trade union federations of Bangladesh. And now SKOP is the spoke-person of the national trade union federations and generally all the federations publish their charter of demand through SKOP. [4]

After the formation of SKOP, it called a 24 hour nation-wide strike on the basis of 5 points demand. The strike was a huge success. After this strike SKOP again called country wide strike for 48 hours on 22 and 23rd May. 2000. And ultimately the military government down and sign an agreement with SKOP. This was a historic event bringing forward the immense potential of working class and its radical impact on politics and thus BJSD along with SKOP put a landmark on the trade union movement in Bangladesh. After the fall of Ershad, the labor movement was not strengthened as the labor parties got in connection with the political parties in power. [4]

1.5 Organizational Structure of 'BJSD'

Organizational Structure of
Bangladesh Jatiyatabadi Sramik Dal—BJSD [9]

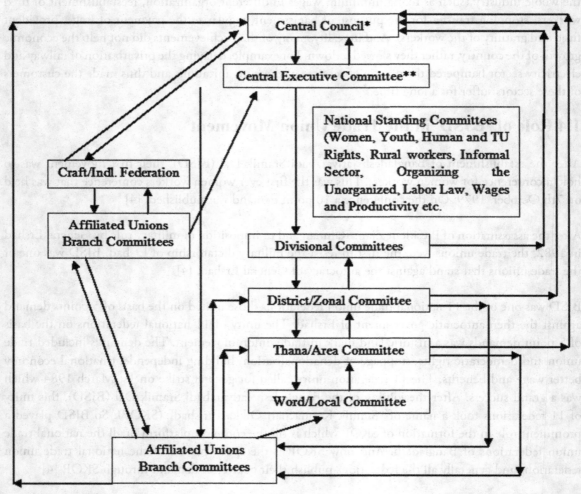

* Comprised of the Councilors nominated by Basic Unions, Craf/Industrial. Federations, Divisional, District, Zonal, Thana/Area Committees.

- All elected Office Bearers and Members of the outgoing Central Executive Committee are also entitled to participate the Central Council as Councilors.

** Elected by the Central Council.

Shows the route of command and representation

From the organizational structure of Bangladesh Jatiyatabadi Sramik Dal, it is found that the Central Council is the subject committee that controls the whole federations. The councilors of this committee are nominated by the Basic unions, Craft/Industrial federations and Divisional, District, Zonal, Thana/Area Committees. This Central Council elects and announces the officers and members of the Central Executive Committee (also known as Central Committee). The Central Committee was elected in 2003. The next election was due in 2008. But during the Caretaker Government the activities of all Trade Unions was prohibited. As a result, the central committee election was not held in the due time.

The name of the office bearers excluding the members are enlisted below: [2]

Sl. No.	Position	Name
1	President	Nazrul Islam Khan
2	Senior Asst. President	Abul Kashem Chowdhury
3	Assistant President	Professor Jahan Ara Begum
4	Assistant President	Md. Muzibur Rahman Sarowar MP
5	Assistant President	Kazi Mosharraf Hossain
6	Assistant President	Md. Mohiuddin
7	Assistant President	Abdul Malek (Khulna)
8	Assistant President	Rafiqul Islam Dulal (Rajshahi)
9	Assistant President	A.M. Nazim Uddin (Chittagong)
10	General Secretary	Md. Jafrul Hasan
11	Joint General Secretary	Anwar Hossaqin (Chittagong)
12	Joint General Secretary	B.M. Bakir Hossain (Banks)
13	Asst. General Secretary	Syed Shamsul Alam (Khulna)
14	Asst. General Secretary	Abul Khaer Khaja (Dhaka)
15	Asst. General Secretary	Matiar Rahman Faraji (Jessore)
16	Asst. General Secretary	Md. Kabir Hossain (Rail)
17	Asst. General Secretary	Firoz Mia (T&T)
18	Finance Secretary	Abdus Sobhan (Rail)
19	Organizing Secretary	Salahuddin Sarker (Dhaka)
20	Organizing Secretary	M. A Gafur (Chittagong)
21	Organizing Secretary	Nurul Islam Khan Nasim (Dhaka Metropolitan)
22	Organizing Secretary	Shohidur Rahman (Rajshahi)
23	Organizing Secretary	M. G. Faruk (Barishal)
24	Organizing Secretary	Rezwan Ahmed (Sylhet)
25	Secretary (International)	Nimai Pada Shingho Roy (WDB)
26	Education Secretary	Md. Shafiul Islam (BCIC)
27	Press Secretary	Md. Abul Hossain (DESA)
28	Social Welfare Secretary	Rafiqul Islam (Rail)
29	Youth Secretary	Sheikh Nurullah Bahar (Chittagong Port)
30	Secretary of Women's Committee	Ramiza Begum (Women's Committee)

According to the constitution, the central committee should have 101 members including one president, one senior assistant president, five assistant presidents, one general secretary, two joint general secretaries, five assistant general secretaries, five organizing secretaries and seven other secretaries of different departments and seventy members. But the central committee that has been created in 2003 has seven assistant presidents, six organizing secretary and 109 members. So it is clear that there is some violation of the constitution in the creation of the central committee.

1.6 Craft/Industrial Federations

There are eight craft federations under Bangladesh Jatiyatabadi Sramik Dal. The names of these craft federations are—[3]

- Bangladesh Jatiyatabadi Pat Sramik Dal
- Bangladesh Jatiyatabadi Sutakol Sramik Dal
- Bangladesh Metal Workers' Federation
- Bangladesh Ispat O Prokoushol Songstha Sraomik Kormochari Federation
- Bangladesh Chemical Workers' Federation
- Bangladesh Bank Employees Federation
- Bangladesh Jatiyatabadi Garments Federation
- Bangladesh Jatiyatabadi Biddyut Federation

1.7 Sector-wise Distribution of Unions and Members of 'BJSD'

As mentioned earlier, Bangladesh Jatiyatabadi Sramik Dal has more than 750 trade unions along with more than 7.5 lakhs members. But unfortunately, the personnel of BJSD failed to provide the information about the distribution of these 750 trade unions and 7.5 lakhs members in different sectors (such as jute, textile, chemical, tobacco, tea, press, mining and quarrying, construction, utility, transportation, bank and insurance etc). According to Mr. Shafiul Islam, in the bank sectors they have the highest number of trade unions and members. Besides, in utility, transportation, and tea sectors they have many trade unions and members. The largest basic trade union they have is the trade union of Public Works Department which has more than 10,000 members. [3]

1.8 Reasons behind the Popularity of 'BJSD' in Certain Sectors

Clearly, Bangladesh Jatiyatabadi Sramik Dal has some popularity among the workers in different sectors. The number of trade unions and members of BJSD certainly proves this popularity. When asked why BJSD has the popularity, Mr. Shafiul Islam informed that 95% of the leaders and collective bargaining agents of BJSD came from the grass-root level. As example he referred the former and current president of BJSD. According to his opinion, as the leaders came from the grass-root level, they know the original demands and needs of the workers. As a result, when they play the role of collective bargaining agent with the management, they are very much able to put the demands of the workers in front of the management. Besides, their achievements through uncompromising role in bargaining with the management made them and the BJSD popular among the different sectors. As an example, he informed us that in very recently BJSD has won the election in 'Uttara Bank' competing against the 'Jatiya Sramik League', the labor wing of the ruling party Awami League. [3]

1.9 Leaders of Bangladesh Jatiyatabadi Sramik Dal

The first committee, formed for Jatiyatabadi Sromik Dal, was presided over by Iskandar Ali and the General Secretary was Nazrul Islam Khan. After the death of Iskandar Ali in 1996 Abdullah Al Noman took charge as the President. The current president is Nazrul Islam Khan and General Secretary is Md. Jafrul Hasan. [3]

President	General Secretary	Duration
Iskandar Ali	Nazrul Islam Khan	1979-1996
Abdullah Al Noman	Nazrul Islam Khan	1996-2003
Nazrul Islam Khan	Md. Zafrul Hasan	2003-Ongoing

Iskandar Ali: Iskandar Ali, the founder and president of Bangladesh Jatiyatabadi Sramik Dal and one of the advisors of Bangladesh Institute of Labor Studies (BILS), was born in 30 December, 1938 at the village of Pakhazipur of Nabinagar thana of Brahmanbaria. In 1960, his job life started at the Fenchuganj Fertilizer Factory. And his trade union activities also started from there. He was elected the joint-secretary of the labor union of the fertilizer factory in 1961. Later, he became the general secretary and then the president of that labor union. He was a member of the central committee of 'East Pakistan Federation of Labor' from 1962 to 1970. According to Md. Shafiul Islam, the education secretary of BJSD, Iskandar Ali fought as a freedom fighter and played a vital role as the commander of the freedom fighters of Fenchuganj Thana in the independence war. After the independence, in 1973 he became the vice president of 'Jatiya Sramik Federation' and till 1978 he fulfilled his duty there. In 1979, the BJSD was established and from then Iskandar Ali was the president of the federation till death. He was the general secretary and acting president of the 'Bangladesh Chemical Workers' Federation' from its establishment in 1992 till death. Besides, he was an honorable member of Bangladesh Government Labor Court, Tripartite Advisor Council, and National Wage Commission. In 1991 he was elected the organizing secretary of the then East Pakistan Industrial Development Corporation (EPIDC) Trade Union Federation. Iskandar Ali was a member of the Advisor Council of BILS from the very beginning. He was the member of the executive committee of International Confederation of Free Trade Union (ICFTU) and represented the labors of Bangladesh for three consecutive years in International Labor Conference. To enrich the labor movement in Bangladesh he visited many countries including USA,

UK, Australia, Switzerland, Japan, Turkey, Germany. He was also one of the assistant presidents of Bangladesh Nationalist Party (BNP). In 24 November, 1996 he died at the BIRDEM Hospital. [5]

Abdullah Al Noman: After the death of Iskandar Ali, Abdullah Al Noman took charge as the president of BJSD. He was the president of BJSD from 1996 to 2003. Like Iskandar Ali, he was also in the front line to establish the BJSD. Abdullah Al Noman was also a renowned politician of BNP and was elected MP for more than once. [3]

Nazrul Islam Khan: Nazrul Islam Khan was born in Islampur Upazilla of Jamalpur in 3rd January, 1948. He completed his graduation from the department of Political Science of Dhaka University in 1974. He earned a degree in Trade Union, Journalism and Publication from the ASEAN University of New Delhi. He started his trade union activities in Jayadebpur Machine Tools Factory. He was the one of the collective bargaining agent of the labor union of the stated factory. Alike Iskandar Ali, Nazrul Islam Khan was also a member of the 'East Pakistan Federation of Labor'. One of his great achievements was that he was elected the member of the Governing Body of International Labor Organization (ILO) for two consecutive terms. He was one of the 14 labor representatives of ILO Governing Body who were elected from all over the world. Nazrul Islam Khan was with the BJSD from its establishment and was the first general secretary of BJSD. In 2003, Abdullah Al Noman resigned from the post of president and Nazrul Islam Khan took the charge. Till today he is the current president of BJSD. He is also the joint secretary of BNP. Besides, from 1985 to2000 he worked as the general secretary of BILS. He is the first labor leader who became the ambassador of the country. He earned Deshbondhu Chittoranjan Desh gold medal and Sorojini Naidu gold medal for his contribution to the labor welfare. [5]

2.0 Practice of Democracy and Leadership Development in 'BJSD'

As a labor wing of a political party, it is expected that there will be a practice of democracy in Bangladesh Jatiyatabadi Sramik Dal. Central Committee is the source of all power in the federation and this committee decides what will be the activity or role of the federation in different issues. Since this committee is comprised of the Councilors nominated by Basic Unions, Craft/Industrial, Federations, Divisional, District, Zonal, Thana/Area Committees, so according to the personnel of BJSD, there is a practice of democracy in the federation.

But if one takes a look at the list of the presidents and general secretaries of BJSD, then he will see that the first president, Iskandar Ali, was in the charge for 17 years. The second president was in charge for 7 years. Obviously this scenario does not represent the presence of democracy in BJSD.

In the question of leadership development, Mr. Shafiul Islam replied that many leaders have been created since its inception in 1979. But he failed to name some of these leaders. With a close look to the list of the leaders of BJSD, one can easily find that the previous and current leaders (presidents, general secretaries) of BJSD are the known faces, and they are with the federation since its establishment in

1979. The names of the former and current presidents of BJSD are Iskandar Ali, Abdullah Al Noman and Nazrul Islam Khan. Jafrul Hasan is the current General Secretary and Abul Kashem Chowdhury is the Senior Assistant President. All of them were in the front line to build Jatiyatabadi Sramik Dal in 1979. So it can be said that there is no appearance of new leaders in BJSD during the last 30 years which means that there is merely any development of leadership in BJSD.

2.1 Rules and Conditions of Becoming a Member of 'BJSD'

Anyone can be a member of the basic trade union affiliated with BJSD by obeying the following rules and conditions:

- He/She must be a permanent worker.
- He/She must believe in the idealism, moral principles, and activities of the BJSD.
- He/She must obey the decisions made by the appropriate committee.
- He/She must support the objectives and goals of the organization as stated in the constitution.
- He/She must ensure his/her democratic characteristics by their activities.
- He/She must give promise to fulfill their duties as a member of BJSD. [3], [1]

2.2 Relationship with 'ILO' and International Confederations

As mentioned earlier, Bangladesh Jatiyatabadi Sramik Dal is enlisted in the International Confederations of Free Trade Unions (ICFTU) and its registration number is BNF-7. The ICFTU and the World Confederation of Labor (WCL), another international labor organization based in Europe, merged together to form the world's largest labor trade union federation, 'International Trade Union Confederation' (ITUC), on November 1, 2006. So automatically BJSD has become affiliated with ITUC. According to the 4th General Council of ITUC, held in Brussels, BJSD has 180,000 members. But earlier it is mentioned that the organization has more than 750,000 members. When asked about this huge difference in number of members, Mr. Shafiul Islam informed that every organization which is affiliated with ITUC, has to give an amount of money per member yearly to ITUC. Since there is a huge fund crisis in BJSD as well as in the national federations, the organization is unable to give this huge amount of money. The reason of the crisis is due to not collecting the monthly fee from its member which amount in terms of money is BDT 1/= only. [3]

2.3 Relationship with the Political Parties

Bangladesh Jatiyatabadi Sramik Dal (BJSD) is a labor front of Bangladesh Nationalist party (BNP). BNP is one of the main political parties of Bangladesh. According to the personnel of BJSD, it always tries for the betterment of the mass people through the improvement of economical condition of labor forces. It always tries to earn facilities from the government for the workers. They protest any activities against workers from the government or employees. But it also supports any positive activities from the government for the betterment of workers. [3]

The federation has its own constitution, own governing body and own objectives and targets. It does not follow all activities of Bangladesh Nationalist Party. It only follows and supports the activities for developing the nation. It supports the 19 points declarations of Late President Ziaur Rahman as a nation-building manifesto. Bangladesh Jatiyatabadi Sramik Dal supports and tries to fulfill the historical 19 points declarations and activities of President Ziaur Rahman, which was declared in the 30th May, 1978 for building a successful and independent Bangladesh. The 19-point activities are: [8]

1. To protect independence and sovereignty of the country at any cost
2. To reflect four main objectives of constitution i.e. faith and confidence on Almighty Allah, Democracy, Jatiyatabad and socialism based on social and economic justice in all fields of national life.
3. To make the nation self—dependent at any cost.
4. To ensure participation of mass people in the development activities of all fields of administration and law and order situations.
5. To strengthen the national economy through improving economy of villages with greater emphasis.
6. To make the nation self sufficient in foods so that nobody remains without foods.
7. To ensure supply of cloths to all by increasing production of cloths in country.
8. To take necessary steps for shelters so that no citizens remain without shelter.
9. To free the nation from the curse of illiteracy.
10. To supply minimum medical facilities for all the citizens of the country.
11. To establish proper respectful situation to women and influence the young person's to build the nation.
12. To encourage the private sector for economic development of the country.
13. To improve the condition of workers and develop sound employer-employee relations together with increasing production.
14. To encourage helping people and nation-building mentality among government employees.
15. To resist population problem.
16. To develop friendship with all foreign countries on the basis of equity and tie the special relationship with Muslim countries.
17. To decentralize administration and development programs and make the local government administration stronger.
18. To achieve a corruption free and justice-centered society.
19. To preserve the rights of all citizens irrespective of religion, color, caste etc and thus strengthen national unity and co-operation.

2.4 Conclusion

The labor forces are the main driving force of national economy. The trade unions are formed for protecting the rights of labor forces. The main functions of Trade Unions are to ensure adequate wages, secure better conditions of work employment, reduce hours of work, get better treatment from employers and to secure some share in the profit and also control of industry. Its motive is to help increasing production by maintaining good employer-employee relationship. So, for any democratic country the trade union becomes an essential part of development.

Bangladesh Jatiyatabadi Sramik Dal is one of the popular labor-wing of Bangladesh Nationalist Party (BNP). Starting from 6 unions and 11000 members, it has now more than 750 basic unions and more than 7.5 lakhs members. According to the personnel of Bangladesh Jatiyatabadi Sramik Dal, from the very beginning it works for the interest of workers. It does not hesitate to protest any oppression against the labor forces within or outside the national domain. Though it is a wing of BNP it has a strong central administrative committee consists of 109 members and 30 officials.

But there is a widespread allegation against them that they are only engaged to such activities that align with the activities of BNP's, rather for the common interest of the workers. In response to this allegation the leaders of BJSD informed that they only support and actively participated all social, cultural and developmental activities of BNP. Being one of the leading labor organizations of the country it is essential for them to work for the utmost economical development of the huge work force irrespective of the political parties. The leaders informed that the reasons behind not building up trade union movement countrywide are ethnocentricity attitude of the labors, weak leadership, insufficient fund for trade unions and not looking after the actual interests of the labors.

The labor forces are a unit class of society. But in Bangladesh, they are not unique forces. They are divided under many political parties. There are lots of collaborators and the opportunistic leaders in trade unions of Bangladesh. These forces along with the elite forces try to divide the workers as well as make them enemies of one another. These forces have to be removed from the trade unions. So, the labor forces have to remove these opportunistic leaders from trade unions and they have to remember that their fight should be focused on their employers' illegal decision and harmful government laws and not against another group of workers.

In past, in the labor movement against any misrule many times the labor forces are influenced. The leaders of labor forces are managed by the employers. So the general workers do not get any benefit from the leaders. As a result, now the general labor forces do not have any confidence and faith on their leaders. So, they hesitate to go into any movement. This confidence and faith will have to be achieved again through good leadership.

Some labor leaders believe that there is no scope to belong a trade union under any political party. But, in perspective of Bangladesh it is not possible now. So the labor politics should be removed from direct contact of political party. The labor party will have to be engaged mainly into the interest of labor forces. So, it is the basic duty of labor forces to unite themselves for their own interest, make people conscious about the labor interest and above all to make a co-operative state for workers.

At the end it can be concluded that though BJSD yet not fully successful with their demand, it has touched some landmarks in different issues. Being the labor front of BNP, it had the opportunity to make a significant contribution for the welfare of the workers of Bangladesh. But unfortunately the federation did not make the proper use of the opportunity due to absence of constructive unionism, opportunism, corruption, undue political interference, workers' disunity and the ideological divide between the leaders.

CHAPTER XII

Strike and Lockout

Contents

1.0 Definition of Strike[260]

A strike is a very powerful weapon used by trade unions and other labor associations to get their demands accepted. It generally involves quitting of work by a group of workers for the purpose of bringing the pressure on their employer so that their demands get accepted. When workers collectively cease to work in a particular industry, they are said to be on strike.

According to Industrial Disputes Act 1947, a strike is "a cessation of work by a body of persons employed in an industry acting in combination; or a concerted refusal of any number of persons who are or have been so employed to continue to work or to accept employment; or a refusal under a common understanding of any number of such persons to continue to work or to accept employment". This definition throws light on a few aspects of a strike. Firstly, a strike is a referred to as stoppage of work by a group of workers employed in a particular industry. Secondly, it also includes the refusal of a number of employees to continue work under their employer.

In a strike, a group of workers agree to stop working to protest against something they think is unfair where they work. Labors withhold their services in order to pressurize their employer or government to meet their demands. Demands made by strikers can range from asking for higher wages or better benefits to seeking changes in the workplace environment. Strikes sometimes occur so that employers listen more carefully to the workers and address their problems.

1.1 Causes of Strikes

Workers may engage in a strike for several reasons. Those are-

- To obtain some improvement in the conditions of employment, such as higher wages or shorter working hours; to forestall an adverse change in the conditions of employment, such as a lowering of wages.
- To prevent the employer from carrying out actions viewed by the workers as detrimental to their interests, such as the employment of nonunion labor or the discharge of a worker without adequate justification.
- Strikes may also be conducted with the aim of compelling an employer to recognize a labor union as the legal collective-bargaining representative of the employees, and to conclude a labor contract with the union.
- The political strike may be used as a means of compelling a government to accede to certain demands of the workers, or as a revolutionary weapon designed to help secure the overthrow of a government.

A strike is usually undertaken as a measure of last resort, adopted, for example, when the employer has rejected settlement of an existing dispute by methods provided for in a labor contract, such as negotiation or mediation.

1.2 Types of Strike

Economic Strike: Under this type of strike, labors stop their work to enforce their economic demands such as wages and bonus. In these kinds of strikes, workers ask for increase in wages, allowances like traveling allowance, house rent allowance, dearness allowance, bonus and other facilities such as increase in privilege leave and casual leave.

Sympathetic Strike: When workers of one unit or industry go on strike in sympathy with workers of another unit or industry who are already on strike, it is called a sympathetic strike. The members of other unions involve themselves in a strike to support or express their sympathy with the members of unions who are on strike in other undertakings. The workers of sugar industry may go on strike in sympathy with their fellow workers of the textile industry who may already be on strike.

General Strike: It means a strike by members of all or most of the unions in a region or an industry. It may be a strike of all the workers in a particular region of industry to force demands common to all the workers. These strikes are usually intended to create political pressure on the ruling government, rather than on any one employer. It may also be an extension of the sympathetic strike to express generalized protest by the workers.

Sit down Strike: In this case, workers do not absent themselves from their place of work when they are on strike. They keep control over production facilities. But do not work. Such a strike is also known as 'pen down' or 'tool down' strike. Workers show up to their place of employment, but they refuse to work. They also refuse to leave, which makes it very difficult for employer to defy the union and take the workers' places. In June 1998, all the Municipal Corporation employees in Punjab observed a pen down strike to protest against the non-acceptance of their demands by the state government.

Slow Down Strike: Employees remain on their jobs under this type of strike. They do not stop work, but restrict the rate of output in an organized manner. They adopt go-slow tactics to put pressure on the employers.

Sick-out (or sick-in): In this strike, all or a significant number of union members call in sick on the same day. They don't break any rules, because they just use their sick leave that was allotted to them on the same day. However, the sudden loss of so many employees all on one day can show the employer just what it would be like if they really went on strike.

Wild cat strikes: These strikes are conducted by workers or employees without the authority and consent of unions. In 2004, a significant number of advocated went on wildcat strike at the City Civil Court premises in Bangalore. They were protesting against some remarks allegedly made against them by an Assistant Commissioner.

1.2.1 Picketing & Scabs

Many people associate strikes with picket lines. Workers bearing placards with slogans supporting their position file around the gate of their workplace, often chanting or even singing songs. The purpose of picketing is to draw public attention (and sympathy) to their cause, inform the public of the goals and the reasons behind the strike and discourage anyone from violating the strike order and going to work. Anyone who does this literally has to cross the picket lines, and they usually are called scabs.

Scabs can be union members who decide to work instead of striking, or they can be non-union workers specially hired by the employer to fill the positions of the striking workers. The term goes back to the 18th century, and probably refers to diseases common in that era that left victims with infectious scabs. Workers crossing picket lines would be "scabb'd" by the other union members (shunned and forced out of their jobs).

In 1806, the Cordwainers Union of Philadelphia went on strike, and several union members became scabs. This was recounted in the ensuing trial by cordwainer Job Harrison.

Sometimes union members will picket without striking. This is known as informational picketing. Prior to the air traffic controllers' strike in 1981, the controllers picketed outside airports during their off hours, holding signs and handing out pamphlets that explained their position.

1.3 Strike Action[261]

Strike action, often simply called a strike, is a work stoppage caused by the mass refusal of employees to perform work. A strike usually takes place in response to employee grievances. Strikes became important during the industrial revolution, when mass Labor became important in factories and mines. In most countries, they were quickly made illegal, as factory owners had far more political power than workers. Most western countries partially legalized striking in the late 19th or early 20th centuries.

Strikes are sometimes used to put pressure on governments to change policies. Occasionally, strikes destabilize the rule of a particular political party. A notable example is the Gdaosk Shipyard strike led by Lech WASA. This strike was significant in the struggle for political change in Poland, and was an important mobilized effort that contributed to the fall of governments in Stalinist East Europe.

1.3.1 History

The strike tactic has a very long history. Towards the end of the 20th dynasty, under Pharaoh Ramses III in ancient Egypt on 14 November 1152 BC, the artisans of the Royal Necropolis at Deir el-Medina organized the first known strike or workers' uprising in recorded history. The event was reported in detail on a papyrus at the time, which has been preserved, and is currently located in Turin. The strike is narrated by John Romer in Ancient Lives: The story of the Pharaohs' Tomb makers.

The use of the English word "strike" first appeared in 1768, when sailors, in support of demonstrations in London, "struck" or removed the topgallant sails of merchant ships at port, thus crippling the ships. [3][4] Official publications have typically used the more neutral words "work stoppage" or "industrial dispute".

The Mexican Constitution was the first, all over the world, that constitutionally guaranteed the right to strike, in 1917.

1.3.2 Characteristics of Different Types of Strikes

Most strikes are undertaken by labor unions during collective bargaining. The object of collective bargaining is to obtain a contract (an agreement between the union and the company) which may include a no-strike clause which prevents strikes, or penalizes the union and/or the workers if they walk out while the contract is in force. The strike is typically reserved as a threat of last resort during negotiations between the company and the union, which may occur just before, or immediately after, the contract expires.

Sometimes a union will strike rather than sign an agreement with a no-strike clause. Such an action was documented in Harlan County, USA, a video about a United Mine Workers strike.

In some industrial unions, the no-strike clause is considered controversial.

Generally, strikes are rare: according to the News Media Guild, 98% of union contracts in the United States are settled each year without a strike.[citation needed] Occasionally, workers decide to strike without the sanction of a labor union, either because the union refuses to endorse such a tactic, or because the workers concerned are not unionized. Such strikes are often described as unofficial. Strikes without formal union authorization are also known as wildcat strikes.

In many countries, wildcat strikes do not enjoy the same legal protections as recognized union strikes, and may result in penalties for the union members who participate or their union. The same often applies in the case of strikes conducted without an official ballot of the union membership, as is required in some countries such as the United Kingdom.

A strike may consist of workers refusing to attend work or picketing outside the workplace to prevent or dissuade people from working in their place or conducting business with their employer. Less frequently workers may occupy the workplace, but refuse either to do their jobs or to leave. This is known as a sit-down strike.

Another unconventional tactic is work-to-rule (also known as an Italian strike, in Italian Sciopero bianco), in which workers perform their tasks exactly as they are required to but no better. For example, workers might follow all safety regulations in such a way that it impedes their productivity or they might refuse to work overtime. Such strikes may in some cases be a form of "partial strike" or "slowdown".

During the development boom of the 1970s in Australia, the Green ban was developed by certain more socially conscious unions. This is a form of strike action taken by a trade union or other organized Labor group for environmentalist or conservationist purposes. This developed from the black ban, strike action taken against a particular job or employer in order to protect the economic interests of the strikers.

United States labor law also draws a distinction, in the case of private sector employers covered by the National Labor Relations Act, between "economic" and "unfair labor practice" strikes. An employer may not fire, but may permanently replace, workers who engage in a strike over economic issues. On the other hand, employers who commit unfair labor practices (ULPs) may not replace employees who strike over ULPs, and must fire any strikebreakers they have hired as replacements in order to reinstate the striking workers.

Strikes may be specific to a particular workplace, employer, or unit within a workplace, or they may encompass an entire industry, or every worker within a city or country. Strikes that involve all workers or a number of large and important groups of workers, in a particular community or region are known as general strikes. Under some circumstances, strikes may take place in order to put pressure on the State or other authorities or may be a response to unsafe conditions in the workplace.

A sympathy strike is, in a way, a small scale version of a general strike in which one group of workers refuses to cross a picket line established by another as a means of supporting the striking workers. Sympathy strikes, once the norm in the construction industry in the United States, have been made much more difficult to conduct due to decisions of the National Labor Relations Board permitting employers to establish separate or "reserved" gates for particular trades, making it an unlawful secondary boycott for a union to establish a picket line at any gate other than the one reserved for the employer it is picketing. Sympathy strikes may be undertaken by a union as an organization or by individual union members choosing not to cross a picket line.

A jurisdictional strike in United States labor law refers to a concerted refusal to work undertaken by a union to assert its members' right to particular job assignments and to protest the assignment of disputed work to members of another union or to unorganized workers.

A student strike has the students (sometimes supported by faculty) not attending schools. Unlike other strikes, the target of the protest (the educational institution or the government) does not suffer a direct economical loss but one of public image.

A hunger strike is a deliberate refusal to eat. Hunger strikes are often used in prisons as a form of political protest. Like student strikes, a hunger strike aims to worsen the public image of the target.

A "sickout", or (especially by uniformed police officers) "blue flu", is a type of strike action in which the strikers call in sick. This is used in cases where laws prohibit certain employees from declaring a strike. Police, firefighters, and air traffic controllers are among the groups commonly barred from striking: usually by state and federal laws meant to ensure the safety and/or security of the general public. So are teachers in some U.S. states (see below). Workers have sometimes circumvented these restrictions by falsely claiming inability to work due to illness.

Newspaper writers may withhold their names from their stories as a way to protest actions of their employer.

1.4 Legal Prohibitions on Strikes

1.4.1 In the People's Republic of China and the Former Soviet Union

In "Marxist-Leninist" regimes, such as the former USSR or the People's Republic of China, striking is illegal and viewed as counter-revolutionary. Since the government in such systems claims to represent the working class, it has been argued that unions and strikes were not necessary. In 1976, China signed the International Covenant on Economic, Social and Cultural Rights, which guaranteed the right to unions and striking, but Chinese officials declared that they had no interest in allowing these liberties.[6] (In June 2008, however, the municipal government in Shenzhen in southern China introduced draft Labor regulations, which Labor rights advocacy groups say would, if implemented, virtually restore Chinese workers' right to strike.[7]) At one point Stalin remarked that strikes were completely unnecessary, as workers would be striking against themselves[citation needed]. Trade unions in the Soviet Union served only as propaganda machines to indoctrinate common workers-"Schools of Communism."

1.4.2 In France

A "minimum service" during strikes in public transport was a promise of Nicolas Sarkozy during his campaign for the French presidential election. A law "on social dialogue and continuity of public service in regular terrestrial transports of passengers" was adopted on August 12, 2007, and it took effect on 1 January, 2008

This law, amongst other measures, forces certain categories of public transport workers (such as train and bus drivers) to declare to their employer 48 hours in advance if they intend to go on strike. Should they go on strike without having declared their intention to do so beforehand, they leave themselves open to sanctions.

The unions did and still do oppose this law and argue these 48 hours are used not only to pressure the workers but also to keep files on the more militant workers, who will more easily be undermined in their careers by the employers. Most importantly, they argue this law prevents the more hesitant workers from making the decision to join the strike the day before, once they've been convinced to do so by their colleagues and more particularly the union militants, who maximize their efforts in building the strike (by handing out leaflets, organizing meetings, discussing the demands with their colleagues) in the last few days preceding the strike. This law makes it also more difficult for the strike to spread rapidly to other workers, as they are required to wait at least 48 hours before joining the strike.

This law also makes it easier for the employers to organize the production as it may use its human resources more effectively, knowing beforehand who is going to be at work and not, thus undermining, albeit not that much, the effects of the strike.

However, this law has not had much effect as strikes in public transports still occur in France and at times, the workers refuse to comply by the rules of this law. The public transport industry—public or privately owned—remains very militant in France and keen on taking to strike action when their interests are threatened by the employers or the government.

The public transport workers in France, in particular the "Cheminots" (employees of the national French railway company) are often seen as the most radical "vanguard" of the French working class. This law has not, in the eyes of many, changed this fact.

1.4.3 In the United Kingdom

The Industrial Relations Act 1971 was repealed through the Trade Union and Labor Relations Act 1974, sections of which were repealed by the Employment Act 1982.

The Code of Practice on Industrial Action Ballots and Notices, and sections 22 and 25 of the Employment Relations Act 2004, which concern industrial action notices, commenced on 1 October 2005.

Legislation was enacted in the aftermath of the 1919 police strikes, forbidding British police from both taking industrial action, and discussing the possibility with colleagues. The Police Federation which was created at the time to deal with employment grievances, and provide representation to police officers, has increasingly put pressure on the government, and repeatedly threatened strike action [8].

The current government is considering reintroducing the ban on strikes by prison staff, a law which itself was repealed in the last decade. This is in the face of a proposed strike by 20,000 staff members.

1.4.4 In the United States

The Railway Labor Act bans strikes by United States airline and railroad employees except in narrowly defined circumstances. The National Labor Relations Act generally permits strikes, but provides a mechanism to enjoin strikes in industries in which a strike would create a national emergency. The federal government most recently invoked these statutory provisions to obtain an injunction requiring the International Long shore and Warehouse Union return to work in 2002 after having been locked out by the employer group, the Pacific Maritime Association.

Some jurisdictions prohibit all strikes by public employees, under laws such as the "Taylor Law" in New York. Other jurisdictions impose strike bans only on certain categories of workers, particularly those regarded as critical to society: police and firefighters are among the groups commonly barred from striking in these jurisdictions. Some states, such as Michigan, Iowa or Florida, do not allow teachers in public schools to strike. Workers have sometimes circumvented these restrictions by falsely claiming inability to work due to illness—this is sometimes called a "sickout" or "blue flu", the latter receiving its name from the uniforms worn by police officers, who are traditionally prohibited from striking. The term "red flu" has sometimes been used to describe this action when undertaken by firefighters.

Postal workers involved in 1978 wildcat strikes in Jersey City, Kearny, New Jersey, San Francisco, and Washington, D.C. were fired under the presidency of Jimmy Carter, and President Ronald Reagan terminated air traffic controllers and the PATCO union after the air traffic controllers' strike of 1981.

1.5 Strikebreakers

A strikebreaker is someone who continues to work during strike action by trade unionists or temporary and permanent replacement workers hired to take the place of those on strike. Strikebreakers are commonly given derogatory terms like scab and blackleg. The act of working during a strike—whether by strikebreakers, management personnel, non-unionized employees or members of other unions not on strike—is known as crossing the picket line, regardless of whether it involves actually physically crossing a line of picketing strikers. Crossing a picket line can result in passive and/or active retaliation against that working person.

The classic example from United Kingdom industrial history is that of the miners from Nottinghamshire, who during the 1984-85 miners' strike did not support strike action by fellow mineworkers in other parts of the country. Those who supported the strike claimed that this was because they enjoyed more favorable mining conditions and thus better wages. However, the Nottinghamshire miners argued that they did not participate because the law required a ballot for a national strike and their area vote had seen around 75% vote against a strike.

Irwin, Jones, McGovern (2008) believe that the term 'scab' is part of a larger metaphor involving strikes. They argue that the picket line is symbolic of a wound and those who break its borders to return to work are the scabs who bond that wound. Others have argued that the word is not a part of a larger metaphor but, rather, originates from the old-fashioned English insult, "scab." The OED gives the etymology of 'scab' in this sense as a term of abuse or depreciation derived from the MDu. schabbe, applied to women with the senses 'slut' and 'scold' and 'scurvy'.

"Blackleg" is an older word and is found in the late-nineteenth/early-twentieth century folk song from Northumberland, Blackleg Miner. The term does not necessarily owe its origins to this tune of unknown origin. The song is, however, notable for its lyrics that encourage violent acts against strikebreakers.

1.5.1 Union Strikebreaking

The concept of union strikebreaking or union scabbing refers to any circumstance in which union workers, who normally might be expected to honor picket lines established by fellow working folk during a strike, are inclined or compelled to cross those picket lines or, in some manner, otherwise engage in workplace activity which may prove injurious to the strike.

Unionized workers are sometimes required to cross the picket lines established by other unions due to their organizations having signed contracts which include no-strike clauses. The no-strike clause typically requires that members of the union not conduct any strike action for the duration of the contract; such actions are called sympathy or secondary strikes. Members who honor the picket line in spite of the contract frequently face discipline, for their action may be viewed as a violation of provisions of the contract. Therefore, any union conducting a strike action typically seeks to include a provision of amnesty for all who honored the picket line in the agreement that settles the strike.

No-strike clauses may also prevent unionized workers from engaging in solidarity actions for other workers even when no picket line is crossed. For example, striking workers in manufacturing or mining, produce a product which must be transported. In a situation where the factory or mine owners have replaced the strikers, unionized transport workers may feel inclined to refuse to haul any product that is produced by strikebreakers, yet their own contract obligates them to do so.

Historically the practice of union strikebreaking has been a contentious issue in the union movement, and a point of contention between adherents of different union philosophies. For example, supporters of industrial unions, which have sought to organize entire workplaces without regard to individual skills, have criticized craft unions for organizing workplaces into separate unions according to skill, a circumstance that makes union strikebreaking more common. Union strikebreaking is not, however, unique to craft unions.

1.6 Methods Used by Employers to Deal with Strikes

Most strikes called by unions are somewhat predictable; they typically occur after the contract has expired. However, not all strikes are called by union organizations—some strikes have been called in an effort to pressure employers to recognize unions. Other strikes may be spontaneous actions by working people. Spontaneous strikes are sometimes called "wildcat strikes"; they were the key fighting point in May '68; most commonly, they are responses to serious (often life-threatening) safety hazards in the workplace rather than wage or hour disputes, etc.

Whatever the cause of the strike, employers are generally motivated to take measures to prevent them, mitigate the impact, or to undermine strikes when they do occur.

1.6.1 Strike Preparation

Companies which produce products for sale will frequently increase inventories prior to a strike. Salaried employees may be called upon to take the place of strikers, which may entail advance training. If the company has multiple locations, personnel may be redeployed to meet the needs of reduced staff. Companies may also take out strike insurance prior to an anticipated strike, to help offset the losses which the strike would cause.

1.6.2 Strike Breaking

Some companies negotiate with the union during a strike; other companies may see a strike as an opportunity to eliminate the union. This is sometimes accomplished by the importation of replacement workers, strikebreakers or "scabs". Historically, strike breaking has often coincided with union busting. It was also called 'Black legging' in the early 20th century, during the Russian socialist movement.

1.6.3 Union Busting

One method of inhibiting a strike is elimination of the union that may launch it, which is sometimes accomplished through union busting. Union busting campaigns may be orchestrated by labor relations consultants, and may utilize the services of labor spies, or asset protection services. Similar services may be engaged during attempts to defeat organizing drives. A modern example of a union buster is The Burke Group.

1.6.4 Lockout

Another counter to a strike is a lockout, the form of work stoppage in which an employer refuses to allow employees to work. Two of the three employers involved in the Caravan park grocery workers strike of 2003-2004 locked out their employees in response to a strike against the third member of the employer bargaining group. Lockouts are, with certain exceptions, lawful under United States labor law.

1.6.5 Violence

Historically, some employers have attempted to break union strikes by force. One of the most famous examples of this occurred during the Homestead Strike of 1892. Industrialist Henry Clay Frick sent private security agents from the Pinkerton National Detective Agency to break the Amalgamated Association of Iron and Steel Workers strike at a Homestead, Pennsylvania steel mill. Two strikers were killed, twelve wounded, along with two Pinkertons killed and eleven wounded. In the aftermath, Frick was shot twice in the neck and then stabbed twice by Alexander Berkman, surviving the attack. Generally, though, Carnegie and J.P. Morgan, as well as other capitalists, have used the U.S. military to gun down and kill strikers, such as in the Seattle General Strike, the Haymarket Massacre, the Minneapolis Teamsters Strike of 1934, during the 2006 Oaxaca protests, the Toledo Autolite Strike, the 1934 West Coast waterfront strike, among dozens and dozens of other strikes.

1.7 ILO Principles Concerning the Right to Strike[262]

It may be surprising to find that the right to strike is not set out explicitly in ILO Conventions and Recommendations. It has been discussed on several occasions in the International Labor Conference during the course of preparatory work on instruments dealing with related topics, but for various reasons this has never given rise to international standards (Conventions or Recommendations) directly governing the right to strike.1 However, the absence of explicit ILO standards should not lead to the conclusion that the Organization disregards the right to strike or abstains from providing a protective framework within which it may be exercised. Two resolutions of the International Labor Conference itself—which provide guidelines for ILO policy—in one way or another emphasized recognition of the right to strike in member States. The "Resolution concerning the Abolition of Anti-Trade Union

Legislation in the States Members of the International Labor Organization", adopted in 1957, called for the adoption of "laws . . . ensuring the effective and unrestricted exercise of trade union rights, including the right to strike, by the workers" (ILO, 1957,p. 783). Similarly, the "Resolution concerning Trade Union Rights and Their Relation to Civil Liberties", adopted in 1970, invited the Governing Body to instruct the Director-General to take action in a number of ways "with a view to considering further action to ensure full and universal respect for trade union rights in their broadest sense", with particular attention to be paid, inter alia, to the "right to strike" (ILO, 1970, pp. 735-736). The right to strike has also been affirmed in various resolutions of the ILO's regional conferences and industrial committees, as well as by other international bodies.

1.8 How Does A Strike Happen[263]?

Contrary to the myth that union leaders simply call strikes at will, there is a specified process that must be followed before a strike can occur.

1.8.1 Direct Negotiation

Section 26 of the IRO, 1969 provides that "if at any time an employer or a collective bargaining agent finds that an industrial dispute is likely to arise between the employer or any of the workmen, the employer or as the case may be, the collective bargaining agent shall communicate his or its views in writing to the other party. Within ten days of receipt of such a communication, the party receiving it shall, in consultation with the representatives of the other party, arrange a meeting with the representatives of the other party for collective bargaining on the issue raised in the communication with a view to reaching an agreement through the procedure of dialogue. If the parties reach a settlement, a memorandum of settlement is recorded in writing and signed by both the parties and a copy thereof is forwarded to the conciliator and other specified authorities.

It is necessary to mention here that as per section 43 of the IRO 1969 "no industrial dispute shall be deemed to exist unless it has been raised in the prescribed manner by a collective bargaining agent or an employer." Section 22 and 22A of IRO 1969 deal with the manner of determining collective bargaining agent in an establishment or group of establishments. No union other than the collective bargaining agent can, therefore, legally raise any industrial dispute.

1.8.2 Conciliation

Section 27 A of the IRO 69 provides that where the parties to an industrial dispute fail to reach a settlement by negotiation under Section 26, any of them may report to the Conciliator that the negotiations have failed and request him in writing to conciliate in the dispute. The Conciliator shall, on, receipt of such request, proceed to conciliate in the dispute.

Section 27 of the above law empowers the Government to appoint as many persons as it considers necessary to be Conciliators specifying the area within which or the class of establishments or industries in relation to which each one of them shall perform his functions. The Director of Labor and the Additional Director of Labor have been notified to be Conciliator under this law for the whole of the country, while the Joint Directors of Labor, deputy Directors of Labor, Assistant Directors of Labor and Labor Officers posted in the divisions, regional offices and branch offices have been notified by Government to be Conciliators in their respective areas for the purpose of the Ordinance.

Section 28 of the IRO stipulates that if the Conciliator fails to settle the dispute within ten days of the receipt of a request under Section 27A, the collective bargaining agent or the employer may serve on the other party to the dispute notice of strike or lock-out. But the collective bargaining agent is debarred from serving any strike notice unless three-fourths of its members have given their consent to it through a secret ballot specifically held for this purpose. Where a party to an industrial dispute serves a notice of strike or lock-out under Section 28, it shall simultaneously deliver a copy thereof to the Conciliator who shall proceed to Conciliate or as the case may be, continue to conciliate in the dispute notwithstanding the notice of strike or lockout.

1.8.3 Arbitration

It is stipulated in section 31 of the IRO 1969 that if the conciliation fails, the conciliator may try to persuade the parties to agree to refer the dispute to an arbitrator. In case the parties agree, they make a joint request in writing for reference of the dispute to an arbitrator agreed upon by the parties.

1.8.4 Strikes/lock outs and Adjudication

If no settlement of the dispute is arrived at in course of conciliation proceedings and parties do not agree to refer the dispute to an arbitrator the workers may on strikes or as the case may be, the employer declares lock out, on the expiry of the period of notice or upon the issuance by the conciliator a certificate of failure on the dispute whichever is later. Section 32(a) provides that "the parties to the dispute may at any time either before or after the commencement of strike or lock-out make a joint application to the labor court for adjudication of the dispute." The govt., however has the authority to prohibit such a strike or lockout if such strike or lockout lasts for more than 30 days and simultaneous refer the dispute to the labor court for adjudication.

1.9 General Prohibition of Strike

The provisions of section 23 are general in nature. It imposes general restrictions on declaring strike in breach of contract in the both public as well as non—public utility services in the following circumstances mainly:—(a) During the pendency of conciliation proceedings before a board and till the expiry of 7 days after the conclusion of such proceedings; (b) During the pendency and 2 months after the conclusion of proceedings before a Labor court, Tribunal or National Tribunal; (c) During the pendency and 2 months after the conclusion of arbitrator, when a notification has been issued under sub—section 3 (a) of section 10 A; (d) During any period in which a settlement or award is in operation in respect of any of the matter covered by the settlement or award.

The principal object of this section seems to ensure a peaceful atmosphere to enable a conciliation or adjudication or arbitration proceeding to go on smoothly. This section because of its general nature of prohibition covers all strikes irrespective of the subject matter of the dispute pending before the authorities. It is noteworthy that a conciliation proceedings before a conciliation officer is no bar to strike under section 23.

2.0 Legal and Illegal strike

When a strike takes place following all the procedures it is called legal strike. Now a days in Bangladesh most of strikes that takes place in different industries, doesn't follow the hard and fast rules and these are all termed as illegal strike.

Section 24 provides that a strike in contravention of section 22 and 23is illegal. This section is reproduced below: (1) A strike or a lockout shall be illegal if, (i) It is commenced or declared in contravention of section 22 or section 23; or (ii) It is continued on contravention of an order made under sub section (3) of section 10 or sub section (4-A) of section 10-A. (2) Where a strike or lockout in pursuance of an industrial dispute has already commenced and is in existence all the time of the reference of the dispute to a board, an arbitrator, a Labor court, Tribunal or National Tribunal, the continuance of such strike or lockout shall not be deemed to be illegal;, provided that such strike or lockout was not at its commencement in contravention of the provision of this Act or the continuance thereof was not prohibited under sub section (3) of section 10 or sub section (4-A) of 10-A. (3) A strike declared in the consequence of an illegal lockout shall not be deemed to be illegal.

2.1 Consequence of Illegal Strike

2.1.1 Dismissal of Workmen

In M/S Burn & Co. Ltd. V, Their Workmen, it was laid down that mere participation in the strike would not justify suspension or dismissal of workmen. Where the strike was illegal the Supreme Court held that in case of illegal strike the only question of practical importance would be the quantum or kind of punishment. To decide the quantum of punishment a clear distinction has to be made between violent strikers and peaceful strikers. In Punjab National Bank v. Their Employees, it was held that in the case of strike, the employer might bar the entry of the strikers within the premises by adopting effective and legitimate method in that behalf. He may call upon employees to vacate, and, on their refusal to do so, take due steps to suspend them from employment, proceed to hold proper inquires according to the standing order and pass proper orders against them subject to the relevant provisions of the Act.

2.1.2 Wages

In Cropton Greaves Ltd. v. Workmen, it was held that in order to entitle the workmen to wages for the period of strike, the strike should be legal and justified. A strike is legal if it does not violate any provision of the statute. It cannot be said to be unjustified unless the reasons for it are entirely perverse or unreasonable. Whether particular strike is justified or not is a question of fact, which has to be judged in the light of the fact and circumstances of each case. The use of force, coercion, violence or acts of sabotage resorted to by the workmen during the strike period which was legal and justified would disentitle them to wages for strike period. The constitutional bench in Syndicate Bank v. K. Umesh Nayak decided the matter; the Supreme Court held that a strike may be illegal if it contravenes the provision of section 22, 23 or 24 of the Act or of any other law or the terms of employment depending upon the facts of each case. Similarly, a strike may be justified or unjustified depending upon several factors such as the service conditions of the workmen, the nature of demands of the workmen, the cause led to strike, the urgency of the cause or demands of the workmen, the reasons for not resorting to the dispute resolving machinery provided by the Act or the contract of employment or the service rules provided for a machinery to resolve the dispute, resort to strike or lock-out as a direct is prima facie unjustified. This is, particularly so when the provisions of the law or the contract or the service rules in that behalf are breached. For then, the action is also illegal.

2.1.3 Right of Employer to Compensation for Loss Caused by Illegal Strike

In Rothas Industries vs. Its Union, the Supreme Court held that the remedy for illegal strike has to be sought exclusively in section 26 of the Act. The award granting compensation to employer, for loss of business though illegal strike is illegal because such compensation is not a dispute within the meaning of section 2(k) of the Act.

2.2 Conclusion

The right to strike is not fundamental and absolute right in India in any special and common law, whether any undertaking is industry or not. This is a conditional right only available after certain pre-condition are fulfilled. If the constitution maker had intended to confer on the citizen as a fundamental right the right to go on strike, they should have expressly said so on the basis of the assumption that the right to go on strike has not expressly been conferred under the Article 19(1) (c) of the Constitution. Further his Lordship also referred to the observation in Corpus Juris Secundum that the right to strike is a relative right which can be exercised with due regard to the rights of others. Neither the common law nor the fourteenth Amendment to the federal constitution confers an absolute right to strike. It was held in the case that the strike as a weapon has to be used sparingly for redressal of urgent and pressing grievances when no means are available or when available means have failed to resolve it. It has to be resorted to, to compel the other party to the dispute to see the justness of the demand. It is not to be utilized to work hardship to the society at large so as to strengthen the bargaining power. Every dispute between an employer and employee has to take into consideration the third dimension, viz. the interest of the society as whole.

CHAPTER XIII

How Government Keeps Liaison with Trade Union

CONTENTS

1.0 How Government keeps liaison with Trade Unions

Labor Rights Now strongly protested the jailing of top leaders of the largest union in Bangladesh. Police arrested Rajendra Prashad Boonerjee, president of the Bangladesh Cha Sramik Union (BCSU) on March 24, 2006. In a letter to Shamsher M. Chowdhury, the Bangladesh ambassador to the U.S., Labor Rights Now President Don Stillman urged his immediate release along with that of Narendra Boonerjee and Bupesh Sind, also officials of the BCSU. The BCSU represents more than 80,000 tea workers in Bangladesh. Unfortunately, when BCSU workers demonstrated against the arrests in front of the union office, the police employed brutal force to halt the protest.

"American trade unionists are particularly concerned about these arrests and want to see justice done here," Stillman told the ambassador.

Bangladesh is a member of the International Labor Organization (ILO) and has an obligation to uphold its conventions, such as the right to freedom of association and the right to collective bargaining.

"If trade union leaders cannot carry out their duties without being arrested and jailed, then Bangladesh is failing to honor its ILO commitments," Stillman said.

1.1 Exclusions from Union Membership

Under the Industrial Relations Ordinance, workers in the public sector and state enterprises may not belong to a trade union, with the exception of railway, postal and telecommunications workers. No teachers may form trade unions, either in the public or private sector. Managerial and administrative employees can form welfare associations, but they are denied the right to join a union.

1.2 Collective Bargaining Agent

Only registered unions can engage in collective bargaining, and each union must nominate representatives to a Collective Bargaining Authority (CBA) committee, which is subject to approval by the Registrar of Trade Unions. The National Pay and Wages Commission, whose recommendations are binding, set public sector workers' pay levels and other benefits.

1.3 EPZ's—New Law on Union Recognition

It provides for the formation of trade unions in EPZs from 1 November 2006. In the meantime, workers are allowed to set up "Welfare Committees", provided over 30 per cent of the workforce take part, with elected representatives who have the power to negotiate and sign collective agreements. However, they are not allowed to strike or organize demonstrations. The trade unions will be subject to the same 30 per cent threshold, as for all unions in the country, and will also have to hold a referendum, in which over 50 per cent of the total workforce must participate. Trade unions have effectively been outlawed in Bangladesh's six export processing zones (EPZs) since their launch in 1980, as the zones have so far been exempt from the major laws establishing freedom of association and the right to bargain collectively. Faced with the threat of losing trade preferences for its exports to the US and Canadian markets, however, the government was to allow trade unions in the zones as from 1 January 2004. It then caved in to pressure from Korean and Japanese companies based in the EPZ's, delaying its decision until it found this compromise solution. There are still some limitations on the freedom of association in the new law, in addition to the 30 per cent rule. While trade unions in a particular EPZ will be allowed to form a federation, there can only be one federation in the area. Federations will not be allowed to form a single body or join any national trade union.

1.4 Strike Bans

The government makes use of the Essential Services Ordinance, hereby it can ban strikes. It continues to apply it to the Power Development Board, the Dhaka Electric Supply Authority and the Chittagong Port Authority. In May 2003, it also imposed the Ordinance on the Bangladesh Petroleum Corporation.

1.5 Restrictions on Bargaining and Union Meetings

The government does not allow any collective bargaining authority in jute mills during production time. Only pro-government supporters are allowed to hold meetings during work time and unions not affiliated with the government's labour grouping are not allowed to hold protests even on their day off.

1.6 Garment Industry Anti-Union

Textile workers outside the zones fare no better. Estimated two million women workers, working for 3,300 employers, make clothes for export from Bangladesh. Unions are registered in only 127 factories and fewer than a dozen employers actually negotiate with them. Workers are regularly sacked, beaten up or subjected to false charges by the police for being active in unions. The General Secretary of the United Federation of Garment Workers (UGFW) has been arrested 12 times. Meanwhile, the country's garment workers are among the lowest paid in the world. They work long hours with very little leave, and face physical, verbal and sexual abuse.

1.7 Ship Recycling Industry outlaws Unions

The Bangladeshi ship recycling industry is based at Chittagong Port. Workers are contracted on an as-needs basis, have no contract and do not sign any document which could link them to a specific yard. Thus workers have no legal recourse in the event of a dispute. Largely owing to the fear instilled in them—through violence and the precariousness of their employment situation—workers have no way of standing up for their rights or even claiming their dues. Any claim would provoke instant dismissal. Unions are de facto forbidden on the sites and union organizers find it very difficult to gain access.

1.8 Mass Arrest of Women Trade Unionists

The police arrested 350 women trade unionists on 20 April, 2004 when they were taking part in activities to mark Women's Day organized by the ICFTU-affiliated Jatio Sramik League (JSL). Among those arrested was the General Secretary of the JSL's Women's Committee, Shamsur Nahar Bhuiyan. They were released on bail on 25 April, and were due to face possible charges in court on 5 May, although the nature of those charges was unclear.

1.9 Government's Initiatives to grow awareness of negative aspects of Trade Union movement

Opposition to trade unions comes from a variety of groups in society and there are many different types of argument on which this opposition is based. Attempts to reduce the effects of trade unions may include union busting activities by private companies or state action. A distinction maybe drawn between absolute opposition to trade unions and opposition to specific practices associated with trade unions.

2.0 Unemployment

By raising the price of labor, the wage rate, about the equilibrium price, unemployment rises. This is because it is no longer worthwhile for businesses to employ those laborers whose work is worth less than the minimum wage rate set by the unions. As such, Governments may seek to reduce union powers in order to reduce unemployment. Trade unions are often accused of benefiting the insider workers, those having a secure job and high productivity, at the cost of the outsider workers, consumers of the goods or services produced, and the shareholders of the unionized business. The ones that are likely to lose the most from a trade union are those who are unemployed or at the risk of unemployment or who are not able to get the job that they want in a particular field. While the disadvantage to exceptional workers, who are forced to take lowest common denominator pay, is obvious, as they could have commanded higher wages by themselves, union contracts also harm inexperienced or below-average workers, as they cannot negotiate lower pay in order to be worth hiring while they seek to improve their skills and experience. Some union-negotiated contracts may impose limits on companies' power to dismiss their employees. In cases where a company needs to dramatically restructure, this can result in more layoffs than would otherwise be necessary, or in extreme cases, a company filing for bankruptcy.

2.1 Negative Salary Effects

Unions prevents workers from negotiating their own pay, making them settle for "lowest common denominator" wages which may represent the minimal value of a worker of their tenure. Some believe, furthermore, that promotions (and even full-time positions} in a union workplace are typically given by seniority only, with little or no regard to qualifications. Unions can force workers to take specific benefits instead of higher pay, again because of the collective

2.2 Harm to Un-Unionized Labor

Advocates of unions claim that the higher wages that unions bring come at the expense of profits. However, profits aren't high enough. Profits are invested leading to an increase in capital: which raises the value of labor, increasing wages. If profits were totally removed, this source of wage increase would be removed. Instead of harming profits, unions increase the wages of about 10 to 15% of workers by about 10 to 15% by reducing the wages of the other 35 to 90% of workers by about 4%. However, Austrian economists dispute this, arguing that the increase in the cost of labor simply means that less of other goods can be bought.

2.3 Efficiency

The effect of TU Movement activities to influence pricing is potentially very harmful, making the system ineffective.'8' By raising the price of labor, above the market rate deadweight is created. Additional non-monetary benefits exacerbate the problem.

2.4 Undemocratic

One "benefit" of Trade Union Movement sometimes cited by corporate advocates is that unions impose uniformity and predictability on workers. Corporate management often negotiates in secret with union management rather than directly with employees. Many unions have pro-democracy factions which seek greater rank and file involvement in the process of running the union, but such efforts often face a significant challenge.

Many people feel that unions tend to act in their own interests rather than in the interests of their members. For example, a union may be doing actions for purposes of increasing its membership that existing union members may not approve of.

CHAPTER XIV

The Role of Federation in Trade Union Movement

CONTENTS

1.0 The Role of Federation in Trade Union Movement

A trade union or labor union is an organization of workers who have banded together to achieve common goals in key areas and working conditions. The trade union, through its leadership, bargains with the employer on behalf of union members (rank and file members) and negotiates labor contracts (Collective bargaining) with employers. This may include the negotiation of wages, work rules, complaint procedures, rules governing hiring, firing and promotion of workers, benefits, workplace safety and policies. The agreements negotiated by the union leaders are binding on the rank and file members and the employer and in some cases on other non-member workers. The immediate objectives and activities of trade unions vary, but may include:

- Provision of benefits to members: Early trade unions, like Friendly Societies, often provided a range of benefits to insure members against unemployment, ill health, old age and funeral expenses.
- Collective bargaining: Where trade unions are able to operate openly and are recognized by employers, they may negotiate with employers over wages and working conditions.
- Industrial action: Trade unions may enforce strikes or resistance to lockouts in furtherance of particular goals.
- Political activity: Trade unions may promote legislation favorable to the interests of their members or workers as a whole. To this end they may pursue campaigns, undertake lobbying, or financially support individual candidates or parties (such as the Labor Party in Britain) for public office.

Workers realized what unionism was all about through the configuration of mechanics association and many people followed in their footsteps. The strike gave others hope that they could get their concerns out by word of mouth. Before this time many people did not speak about their concerns because of the lack of bodies. However, with more people comes more confidence. Strikes were a new way of speaking out minds and getting things done. Unions may organize a particular section of skilled workers (craft unionism), a cross-section of workers from various trades (general unionism), or attempt to organize all workers within a particular industry (industrial unionism). These unions are often divided into "locals", and united in national federations. These federations themselves will affiliate with Internationals, such as the International Trade Union Confederation.

In many countries, a union may acquire the status of a "juristic person" (an artificial legal entity), with a mandate to negotiate with employers for the workers it represents. In such cases, unions have certain legal rights, most importantly the right to engage in collective bargaining with the employer (or employers) over wages, working hours, and other terms and conditions of employment. The inability of the parties to reach an agreement may lead to industrial action, culminating in either strike action or management lockout, or binding arbitration.

In other circumstances, unions may not have the legal right to represent workers, or the right may be in question. This lack of status can range from non-recognition of a union to political or criminal prosecution of union activists and members, with many cases of violence and deaths having been recorded both historically and contemporarily. Unions may also engage in broader political or social struggle. Social Unionism encompasses many unions that use their organizational strength to advocate for social policies and legislation favorable to their members or to workers in general. As well, unions in some countries are closely aligned with political parties.

Unions are also delineated by the service model and the organizing model. The service model union focuses more on maintaining worker rights, providing services, and resolving disputes. Alternately, the organizing model typically involves full-time union organizers, who work by building up confidence, strong networks, and leaders within the workforce; and confrontational campaigns involving large numbers of union members. Many unions are a blend of these two philosophies, and the definitions of the models themselves are still debated. Although their political structure and autonomy varies widely, union leaderships are usually formed through democratic elections.

Trade unions have been accused of benefiting the insider workers, those having secure jobs, at the cost of the outside workers, consumers of the goods or services produced, and the shareholders of the unionized business. Those who are likely to be disadvantaged most from unionization are the unemployed, those at risk of unemployment, or workers who are unable to get the job they want in a particular line of work. Trade unions have been said to have ineffective policies on racism and sexism, such that a union is justified in not supporting a member taking action against another member. The finding was that in the event of the union offering assistance to the complainant it would be in violation of the union's duty to protect the tenure of the accused member and the judgment still sets the precedent for cases of this kind that union members who make complaints to the employer of racist or sexist harassment against member(s) of the same union cannot obtain union advice or assistance.

The largest organization of trade union members in the world is the Brussels-based International Trade Union Confederation, which today has approximately 309 affiliated organizations in 156 countries and territories, with a combined membership of 166 million. Other global trade union organizations include the World Federation of Trade Unions. National and regional trade unions organizing in specific industry sectors or occupational groups also form global union federations, such as Union network International, the International Federation of Journalists or the International Arts and Entertainment Alliance.

Trade Union Movement organized activities of workers to improve their working conditions. In the early stage of industrial development when there were personal contacts between employers (master) and workers (employee), there was no need of any organization to determine relations between the two. But under the modern factory system the personal touch is absent and the relations between the employer and the worker have come under strain. The conflict of interests between buyer and seller of labor power has become conspicuous and this has led to the rise of trade union movement throughout the world. The tradition of the parallel development of the nationalist and the trade union movement, which had originated in British India continued through the Pakistan period down to the birth of Bangladesh.

1.1 The World Federation of Trade Unions

The World Federation of Trade Unions (WFTU) was established in the wake of the Second World War to bring together trade unions across the world in a single international organization, much like the United Nations. After a number of Western trade unions left it in 1949, as a result of disputes over support for the Marshall Plan, to form the International Confederation of Free Trade Unions, the WFTU was made up primarily of state-run unions from communist countries and unions affiliated with or sympathetic to communist parties elsewhere. A number of those unions, including those from Yugoslavia and China, left later when their governments had ideological differences with the Soviet Union.

The WFTU has declined precipitously in the past twenty years since the fall of the communist regimes in the Soviet Union and Eastern Europe, with many of its former constituent unions joining the ICFTU. It maintains its headquarters in Prague, Czech Republic but focuses now on organizing regional federations of unions in the Third World, campaigning against imperialism, racism, poverty, environmental degradation and exploitation of workers under capitalism and in defense of full employment, social security, health protection, and trade union rights. The WFTU continues to devote much of its energy to organizing conferences, issuing statements and producing educational materials. As part of its efforts to advance its international agenda, the WFTU develops working partnerships with national and industrial trade unions worldwide as well as with a number of international and regional trade union organizations.

The recent International Labor Organization (ILO) survey reports that in Pakistan, 35% of transport workers did not believe they should join a trade union, against 24<1<) who wanted to. In Gujarat, only 20% of respondents knew about trade unions, while in Bangladesh it was 38%. 33% of respondents show a completely negative attitude to unions, as against the 21% that had a positive attitude. In Gujarat, 33% of the respondents believed the best means of representing work-related interests was by direct representation to employers, as against 7.4% who preferred the union and 14.8% that preferred direct collective action.

Trade unions must recognize that they are the products of the industrial revolution, while the current labor market structure is the result of the structural changes of the 80's and the 90's. They had enjoyed oligopolistic rights over the factory and public sector workers and have created a type of 'industrial citizenship' that is in contrast to the speedily growing employment in other sectors. If they become more inclusive and expand their base, they will be hard-pressed to resolve the contradictions among member-segments. Hence, they remained elitist rather than mass-based. In the process, they continued with archaic rhetoric that now appears jarring even to their own members. The ILO pointed out a lot of flaws in the different segments of the trade union movements of Bangladesh. A few examples are highlighted:

- In 2006, number of employed inspectors responsible for health or safety in factories or docks was 20, even lower than 1984
- In the office there are four 'safety' inspectors and three "health" inspectors responsible for 11,665 premises
- No dock labor inspector for the port in Mongla

The following Trade Unions Internationals are constituted within the WFTU:

- Trade Unions International of Agriculture, Food, Commerce, Textile, and Allied Industries
- Trade Unions International of Public and Allied Employees
- Trade Unions International of Energy, Metal, Chemical, Oil and Allied Industries
- Trade Unions International of Transport Workers
- Trade Unions International of Building, Wood and Building Materials Industries
- World Federation of Teachers Unions

The trade unions listed in Bangladesh are:

- Bangladesh Free Trade Union Congress
- Bangladesh Ganotantrik Sramik Federation
- Bangladesh Jatio Sramik League
- Bangladesh Jatiyo Sramik Jote
- Bangladesh Jatyatabadi Sramik Dal
- Bangladesh Labour Federation
- Bangladesh Mukto Sramik Federation
- Bangladesh Sanjukta Sramik Federation
- Bangladesh Trade Union Kendra
- Jatio Sramik Federation
- Jatyo Sramik League
- Samajtantrik Sramik Front

1.2 Trade Union Rights Law in Bangladesh

Restrictions: The Constitution provides for the right to form or join unions. There are many restrictions, however. Before a union can be registered, 30 per cent of workers in an enterprise have to be members and the union can be dissolved if its membership falls below this level. The ILO has informed the government that this is a clear barrier to freedom of association and recommended the law be amended, but that advice has been continuously ignored.

Unions must have government approval to be registered, and no trade union action can be taken prior to registration. Unions can only be formed at the factory/establishment level, with some exceptions (such as private road transport, private inland river transport) where union formation can take place based on geographic area. There can be no more than three registered trade unions in any establishment. Membership in a union is restricted only to the permanent workers currently working at an establishment, meaning that severance from employment also results in the end of a worker's membership in the union.

Candidates for union office have to be current or former employees of an establishment or group of establishments. The Registrar of Trade Unions has wide powers to interfere in internal union affairs. He can enter union premises and inspect documents. The registrar may also cancel the registration of a union, with Labor Court approval.

Exclusions from union membership: Under the Labor Code 2006, workers in the public sector and state enterprises may not belong to a trade union, with the exception of railway, postal and telecommunications workers. Members of the security forces are also denied the right to form unions. Teachers are also forbidden to form trade unions, in either the public or private sector. Managerial and administrative employees can form welfare associations, but they are denied the right to join a union.

Right to strike not recognized: The right to strike is not specifically recognized in law. Three quarters of a union's members must agree to a strike before it can go ahead. The government can ban any strike if it continues beyond 30 days (in which case it is referred to the Labor Court for adjudication), if it involves a public service covered by the Essential Services Ordinance or if it is considered a threat to the national interest. In this last case, the 1974 Special Powers Act can be used to detain trade unionists without charge. The government may ban strikes for renewable periods of three months. Sentences of up to 14 years' forced labor can be passed for offences such as "obstruction of transport".

Strikes are not allowed in new establishments either owned by foreign investors or established as joint-ventures in collaboration with foreign investors for a period of three years from the date the establishment begins commercial production.

Compulsory conciliation and court referral procedures: The labor law requires that parties to an industrial dispute must follow procedures (such as request conciliation, serve notice of a strike or lock-out, or refer the dispute to the Labor Court for settlement) within a specified period or the labor dispute will be considered legally terminated. The issue or subject of an industrial dispute which is terminated in this manner cannot be raised for a calendar year after such termination.

Collective bargaining limited: Only registered unions can engage in collective bargaining, and each union must nominate representatives to a Collective Bargaining Authority committee, which is subject to approval by the Registrar of Trade Unions. The National Pay and Wages Commission, whose recommendations are binding, sets public sector workers' pay levels and other benefits.

EPZ Law—significant restriction continue: The EPZ Trade Union and Industrial Relations Bill 2004 provided for the formation of trade unions in EPZs from 1 November 2006. The ILO Committee on Freedom of Association recommended numerous amendments to the law to bring it into compliance with Conventions no. 87 and 98 which Bangladesh has ratified. The government of Bangladesh has fundamentally failed to take any appreciable steps to comply with the ILO CFA's ruling.

The law foresees the phased introduction of freedom of association, providing for a different type of workers' organization at each stage. However, the law does not go so far as to say that trade unions with full associational rights will be allowed to exist in EPZs after the last stage outlined, which will be after 1 November 2008.

Stage one—worker representation and welfare committees: Until the end of October, workers in Bangladesh's EPZs were still operating under the first stage of the law. They were only allowed to set up Worker Representation and Welfare Committees (WRWC). The law requires all enterprises in the EPZ to have one WRWC, whose elected representatives have the power to negotiate and sign collective agreements on a limited set of topics but not to strike or organize demonstrations. However, workers and labor activists in Bangladesh reported that in 2006 employers generally refused to enter negotiations or sign an agreement with a WRWC.

Under the law, all WRWCs were supposed to cease to exist on 31 October 2006, unless the employer gave an explicit agreement that the WRWC should continue (which they would in practice only do in the case of compliant WRWCs).

Stage two—workers' associations: The second stage of the law provides that a trade union, referred to as a Workers' Association (WA) in the law, can be organized provided over 30 per cent of the workforce requests that the association should be set up. More than 50 per cent of the workers in the factory must vote affirmatively for the WA to be formed.

This was scheduled to start on 1 November 2006 but in practice there were significantly delays, notably because the Bangladesh Export Processing Zone Authority (BEPZA) did not provide the necessary forms for applying to set up WAs. In new enterprises that tart operations after 1 November 2006, workers are not permitted to form an association for the first three months after the commencement of commercial activities.

Only one federation can be formed per EPZ, and over 50 per cent of the registered WA in the zone must vote to affiliate before a federation can be formed.

The BEPZA Executive Chairman also has almost unlimited authority to deregister a Workers' Association, should he determine that the WA has committed an "unfair practice", contravened any part of the WA's own constitution, violated any aspect of the EPZ Law, or failed to submit a report to him. Essentially, the law has made illegal the right of workers to talk about unions in their workplaces or to engage in pressure tactics to persuade recalcitrant employers to sign a collective agreement.

Frequent bans on assembly: The law allows the government to ban any public gathering of more than four people, ostensibly only in cases where "public order" or "public health" is at risk. In fact, the government applied this banning power much more indiscriminately.

Labor appellate tribunal created: The new labor law created an avenue for all the judgments, awards and sentences of the Labor Court to be appealed to a Labor Appellate Tribunal. Previously all such appeals had to be taken up by the Supreme Court, resulting in significant delays in reaching a final legal verdict for labor cases.

Practice of Trade Union Rights in Bangladesh

The trade union movement is relatively weak in Bangladesh. This is partly owing to the multiplicity of trade unions and partly owing to the considerable intimidation imposed in practice, especially workers' fear of losing their jobs should they show any sign of union activity. The right to freedom of association and to collective bargaining at the workplace is not respected in the garment sector or on the tea estates. Where unions do file applications for recognition, their registration is often delayed long beyond the 60 days foreseen by law.

Strike Bans: The government makes regular use of the Essential Services Ordinance in order to ban strikes. The government's use of this order was continuously applied over the past four years to the Power Development Board, the Dhaka Electric Supply Authority, the Chittagong Port Authority, Biman Airlines, and the Bangladesh Petroleum Corporation.

Restrictions on bargaining and union meetings: Since 2003, the government has banned any collective bargaining in jute mills during production time. Only pro-government supporters are allowed to hold meetings during work time and unions not affiliated with the government's labor grouping are not allowed to hold protests even on their day off.

Employers take advantage of legal loopholes: Private sector workers are discouraged from undertaking any union activity. The Industrial Relations Ordinance gives considerable leeway for discrimination against union members and organizers by employers.

Workers who try to create a trade union are not protected before registration and are therefore often persecuted by their employers, sometimes by violent means or with the help of the police. The names of workers who apply for union registration are frequently passed on to employers who promptly transfer or dismiss them, particularly in the textile sector. Even after registration, workers suspected of carrying out trade union activities are regularly harassed. One popular ploy is to dismiss a worker for misconduct, as they are then no longer entitled to become a trade union officer. A complaint to the Labor Court is of little use given the underlying corruption and serious backlog of cases which, in some instances, can stretch back more than several years. **Export processing zones**—anti-union employers: Employers in the EPZs have been consistently hostile towards trade unions, claiming that many of the companies would be ruined and jobs of many workers would be lost if they had to have unions. Some employers in the zones take advantage of the absence of trade unions to commit violations of international labor standards, such as sexual harassment, physical violence, unpaid overtime, child labor, non-compliance with minimum wage regulations and deplorable safety conditions.

Despite protections for WRWC committee members provided by the EPZ Law, discrimination against leaders of active WRWCs was reported in 2006, and an undetermined yet significant number of these leaders and activist members have been terminated with permission from the BEPZA in processes that workers claimed were biased and unfair. Since there is no dispute resolution mechanism or tribunal for workers, except to appeal to the BEPZA, workers in the EPZs had few other options but to protest. After 1 November 2006, those factories with WRWCs turned their attention to frustrating efforts of the workers to form Workers Associations, again including a series of tactics including harassment, intimidation, and termination of leaders.

Failure to set up industrial dispute resolution mechanisms in EPZs: Although the EPZ law provides for the establishment of an EPZ Labor Tribunal and an EPZ Labor Appellate Tribunal, a full two years after the passage of the EPZ law, these two tribunals have yet to be established.

Garment industry anti-union: Textile workers outside the zones fare no better. An estimated two million women workers toil for 3,300 employers to make clothes for export in Bangladesh. Workers are regularly sacked, beaten or subjected to false charges by the police for being active in unions. The General Secretary of the United Federation of Garment Workers (UGFW) has been arrested more than a dozen times. Meanwhile, the country's garment workers are among the lowest paid in the world. They work long hours with very little leave, and face physical, verbal and sexual abuse.

Employer negligence and government indifference kills hundreds of workers: Negligence by employers and the authorities have had appalling consequences that a strong. Vigilant trade union could help to avoid. Based on its analysis of publicly available sources, the respected Bangladesh Institute for Labor Studies found that in 2006 there were 845 workers killed and 3018 injured by occupational accidents. The ready-made garment sector led the way in its toll on workers, with 141 killed, and 1578 hurt or maimed.

Ship recycling industry effectively prohibits unions: The Bangladeshi ship recycling industry is based at Chittagong Port. Workers are employed on an as-needs basis, have no contracts and do not sign any documents which could link them to a specific yard. Thus workers have no legal recourse in the event of a dispute. Largely owing to the fear instilled in them—through violence and the precariousness of their employment situation—workers have no way of standing up for their rights or even claiming their dues. Any claim would provoke instant dismissal. Unions are de facto forbidden on the sites and union organizers find it very difficult to gain access.

CHAPTER XV
Issues in Managing Industrial Relations

Contents

1.0 Issues in Managing Industrial Relations

1.1 Industrial Relations System

A systems approach to industrial relations has been proposed by Professor John T. Dunlop. According to him, industrial relations systems should be viewed as a sub-system of the society. An industrial relations system at any one time in its development is regarded as comprised of certain actors, certain contexts, an ideology which binds the industrial relations system together, and a body of rules created to govern the actors at the work place and work community.

The actors are:

1. A hierarchy of managers and their representatives in supervision,
2. A hierarchy of workers (non-managerial) and any spokesperson, and
3. Specialized government agencies created by the first private agencies (created by the first two actors) concerned with the workers' enterprises and their relationship.

The significant aspects of the environment in which the actors interact are:

1. The technological characteristics of the work place and work community,
2. The market or budgetary constraints which interrupt the actors and
3. The locus and distribution of power in the larger society.

The actors, in given contexts, establish rules for the work place and work community, including those governing the contacts among the actors in an industrial relations system. This web of rules consists of procedures for establishing rules, the substantive rules, and the procedures for deciding their application to particular situations. The establishment of these rules and procedures is the centre of attention in an industrial relations system.

A future element is required to complete the analytical system: an ideology or a set of ideas and beliefs commonly held by the actors, which help to bind the system together as an entity.

Alternative formulations, mostly advanced by behavioral scientists, are more often than not concerned with the attitudinal dimensions of inter-personal and inter-group behavior. While Dunlop favors a multi-disciplinary approach the latter can be characterized as uni-disciplinary. Yet it will be agreed that the problems of industrial relations do not lend themselves to a simple analysis of attitudes and behaviors.

It is necessary to understand the determinants of workers' attitudes and behavior. Again, no simplified explanations can suffice; one would need to explore the procedures of rule-making, the determination of a fair rate of return to capital and an adequate compensation to labor for its contribution to outputs and the organization of the firm including economic, technological and social situations with which a worker is confronted. Thus a "holistic" approach to industrial relations might prove a better strategy for problem solving at the enterprise level.

It may also be emphasized that the micro-environmental variables affect decision making at the enterprise level. Changes in labor laws, government policies with regard to industry and labor, trade union growth and economic and political situations would certainly act as a constraint within which a manager operates. But he or she is primarily concerned with an efficient attainment of the firm's objectives. Consequently, his/her problems are qualitatively different from those of a policy maker at the national level. Employers are now compelled to view industrial relations from a strategic perspective; in other words, not only from the traditional viewpoint of negotiating terms and conditions of employment and performing a personnel and welfare function. Industrial relations are directly relevant to competitiveness, and how they are managed will impact on enterprise performance e.g. its productivity and quality of goods and services, labor costs, quality of the workforce, motivation, prevention of disputes and not only their settlement, and aligning employee aspirations with enterprise objectives.

1.2 Major Issues of Concern

1. **Minimum Wages:** In countries which have a legal minimum wage three concerns are evident. The first is that minimum wage levels sometimes tend to be fixed on extraneous considerations (e.g. political), or on inadequate data needed to define the level of wages. The second concern is that such instances have an adverse effect on competitiveness in the global market and on employment creation where the minimum wage is fixed above a certain level (much of the controversy relates to what that level is).Therefore many employers prefer to see the minimum wage, if there is to be one at all, as a 'safety net' measure to uplift those living below the poverty line. The third concern relates to increases in minimum wages not being matched by productivity gains which help to offset increased labor costs.

2. **Flexible/Performance Pay:** Many employers, and even some governments, have expressed a wish to review traditional criteria to determine pay levels such as the cost of living and seniority. Pay systems which are flexible (i.e. based on profitability or productivity) so as to be able to absorb business downturns and also reward performance, are receiving considerable attention. One major problem in this regard is how employees and their organizations can be persuaded to negotiate on pay reform. The objectives of pay reform will not be achieved unless reforms are the result of consensual agreement and are part of a larger human resource management strategy and change in human resource management systems.

3. **Dispute Prevention:** Although some Bangladeshi organizations have longstanding dispute settlement procedures at the national level (conciliation, arbitration, industrial or labor courts),

they operate only when a dispute arises. Equally important are dispute prevention through communication, consultation and negotiation procedures and mechanisms which operate largely at the enterprise level. Their importance has increased in the current decade when changes in the way organizations are structured and managed have created the potential for workplace conflict. A more positive movement from personnel management to strategic human resource management is called for.

4. **Industrial Relations/Human Resource Management Training:** Not many developing countries, especially Bangladesh, have facilities for training in labor laws and industrial relations—negotiation, wage determination, dispute prevention and settlement, the several aspects of the contract of employment, and other related subjects such as safety and health. Since industrial relations have assumed a particularly important role in the context of globalization, structural adjustment and in the transition to a market economy, employers in each country would need to identify what aspects of industrial relations and human resource management should be accorded priority, how training in them could be delivered, and what concrete role is expected from the employers' organization.

5. **Balancing Efficiency with Equity and Labor Market Flexibility:** During this century industrial relations and the law in industrialized countries have paid considerable attention to the means through which the unequal bargaining position between employees and management can be rectified. The imbalance in their respective positions has been corrected primarily through freedom of association and collective bargaining. Thereafter the focus in some countries has been more on the relationship between management and labor and their organizations rather than on their relationships with the state. This has been due to the fact that the latter has adopted a less interventionist role than in developing countries, based on the premise that regulation of the labor market should to a large extent be left to employers, workers and their organizations.

6. **Freedom of Association, Labor Rights and Changing Patterns of Work:** With the disappearance of major ideological differences with the end of the cold war, unions are moving towards a concentration on their core industrial relations functions and issues. In some Asian countries, like Bangladesh, freedom of association, including labor rights in special economic zones, has arisen as an issue. The need for employees and their representatives to be involved in change and in transition, and the willingness of employers to involve them, is an emerging issue in Bangladesh.

Changing patterns of work (e.g. more homework, part-time work, subcontracting) have created concerns for unions in particular. Job insecurity, social security and minimum conditions of work are some of them. Traditional industrial relations systems based on the concept of a full-time employee working within an enterprise is increasingly inapplicable to the many categories of people working outside the enterprise. In some countries in terms of numbers they are likely in the future to exceed those working within an enterprise. Industrial relations especially in the public sector where negotiation rights, for instance, are less than in the private sector, is also likely to be an issue in the future.

7. Human Resource Management: With increasing reliance by employers in Bangladesh on human resource management as a means of enhancing enterprise performance and competitiveness, important consequences will arise for industrial relations and for unions.

8. Development of Organization in Bangladesh: Organization development is the applied behavioral science discipline dedicated to improving organizations and the people in them through the use of the theory and. practice of planned change. Organizations in Bangladesh face multiple challenges and threats today, threats to effectiveness efficiency, and profitability-challenges from turbulent environments increased competition, and changing customer demands; and the constant challenges to maintain congruence among organizational dimension such as technology strategy, culture, and processes. Keeping organizations healthy and viable in today's world is a daunting task.

The main issue for industrial relations in this regard in the future is not efficiency and equity as antithetic concepts, but how to achieve a balance between the two. This is because while an industrial relations system should facilitate competitiveness, it should also promote equity by ensuring a fair return on labor and a fair sharing of the gains from economic activity, reasonable and safe working conditions, and an environment in which employees can communicate and discuss their concerns and be represented in order to protect and further their interests. Efficiency cannot be achieved through an industrial relations system which is devoid of equity, particularly now when competitiveness depends so much on people, who will withhold efficiency in an environment which is inequitable and de-motivating. Further, political instability is sometimes the result of large sections of the population not being beneficiaries of economic development. This may occur when, for instance, large disparities in wealth continue to grow and there is no significant improvement in the conditions of those living below the poverty line.

It remains to consider some of the basic objectives of IRs, which could be said to include the following:

1. The efficient production of goods and services and, at the same time, determination of adequate terms and conditions of employment, in the interests of the employer, employees and society as a whole, through a consensus achieved through negotiation.
2. The establishment of mechanisms for communication, consultation and cooperation in order to resolve workplace issues at enterprise and industry level, and to achieve through a tripartite process, consensus on labor policy at national level.
3. Avoidance and settlement of disputes and differences between employers, employees and their representatives, where possible through negotiation and dispute settlement mechanisms.
4. To provide social protection where needed e.g. in the areas of social security, safety and health, child labor, etc.
5. Establishment of stable and harmonious relations between employers and employees and their organizations, and between them and the State.

1.3 Classification of Organization in Bangladesh

From the point of view of industrial relations, one could perhaps adopt several criteria for classifying organizations.

One should be able to distinguish organizations on the basis of technological requirements. Thus, an easy classification would be in terms of textiles, engineering, and chemicals. There is no doubt that within each group there will be differences, yet, the technology might be the unifying factor within such groups.

Another method of classification would be in terms of size. One could group the organization along the continuum: large, medium and smell sizes. Usually, the larger the organization is, the greater will be the problems of managing industrial relations. However, there may be several intervening variables more specific to individual organizations, due to which one cannot predict on the basis of this single variable, i.e. size only.

Yet another distinguishing characteristic may be the extent of unionization which differs from industry to industry and also from one organization to another within the same industry. On the other hand, an industry where a representative union does not exist, there is a greater likelihood of inter-union rivalry.

Finally, not all organizations face similar situations with regard to the product and labor markets. An organization, which does not face a stiff competition in the sale of its output, may be in a better position to handle its labor problems. Such an organization has far less budgetary constraints than another organization which has little room to maneuver in economic terms. Likewise, the nature of the labor market the organization faces will have a bearing on that organization's ability to recruit, develop and retrain personnel of various skills.

1.4 Problems of Industrial Relations in Bangladesh

The actual problems faced by managers could thus be traced to the characteristics of their organizations. However, not all organizations would encounter similar problems.

1.4.1 Some Emerging Issues in any Work Situation have been identified

1. **Job Satisfaction:** The extent to which the employees of an organization are satisfied is a function of several subjective and objective factors in a work situation. Technological, economic and cultural factors tend to influence the perception and motivation of individual employees.
2. **Effort-reward correlation:** A related problem is that of fair compensation for efforts put in by the employees. This again is conditioned by many factors: the customary differentials in

wages and salary structure, the motivation to produce more, 'the implementation of' incentive schemes, fixing of appropriate wage rates through job evaluation, etc. and the situation in the labor market.

3. **Absenteeism, indiscipline, and mobility:** These problems could be severe for some occupations and the some organizations. One should look for certain aspects of the organizational life to identify the culture, economics, and politics of the situation. The influence of the labor market might be quite important in the solution of these problems.

4. **Grievance handling and participative management:** In the absence of a well-define grievance procedure, the attitudes on both sides are quite unnecessarily hardened. The evolution of a grievance procedure is related to the style of management. In an authoritarian philosophy, the cooperative tendencies are not likely to develop. On the contrary, an explicit recognition of the "pluralistic" framework for determining the terms and conditions of employment might result in fewer grievances and their speedy redressal.

5. **Industrial disputes:** Industrial disputes should be considered as a form of direct protest. The protest itself arises out of the substantive issues which are complicated on both sides by the rigid attitudes of the management and the trade unions. Some of the disputes might in fact be the outcome of inter union or intra-union rivalry. Even if the latter were true, the managerial responsibility cannot be ruled out. One would need to look into the specific problems of an organization with a view to ascertaining the causes of industrial dispute in that organization. Resort to a legalistic approach only makes the situation still more complicated; but it is not a substitute for sound management.

6. **Cross-Cultural Management:** Bangladesh is a heterogeneous region, characterized by ethnic, cultural, linguistic and religious diversity. Due to substantial increases in investment in Bangladesh from both Asian and Western investors, many employers and unions are dealing with workers and employers from backgrounds and cultures different to their own. Many of the resulting problems and issues (reflected for instance in the proliferation of disputes due to cross cultural 'mismanagement') fall within the concept of cross-cultural management. The problems arise due to differences in industrial relations systems, attitudes to and of unions, work ethics, motivational systems and leadership styles, negotiating techniques, inappropriate communication, consultation and participation procedures and mechanisms, values (the basic beliefs that underpin the way we think, feel and respond), expectations of workers and interpersonal relationships.

7. **Women:** The increasing influx of women into workforces has raised issues relating to gender discrimination, better opportunities for them in relation to training and higher-income jobs and welfare facilities.

8. **Human Resource Development:** As a separate personnel discipline the concept of human relations is based on training groups who effectively identify problems, acquire the skills and also actively collaborate in the problem solving process. Training group leaders, unshackling their traditional role of instructors become facilitators and give focus on how the individual relates to and its influence handling conflicts, expressing feelings, giving and receiving feedback,

competition and cooperation, problem solving, and increasing awareness of oneself and one's impact on others. So, the employers of Bangladesh should take necessary step in the process of developing Training and Organization-Development as a recognized area of professional endeavor, delineating human resource development as a new profession, encompassing the personnel function.

It is necessary to focus the factors which develop the concept of human resource management by replacing the traditional concept of labor welfare and personnel management. These factors are: a. search for competitive advantage, b. model—of excellence, c. failure of personnel management, d. decline in trade union preserve and e. changes in workforce and the nature of work.

1.4.2 Implications for Management

The issues raised here should help in the comprehension of the complexities of the industrial relations system in an organization. Since the problem of industrial relations is multi-faceted, the first step will be to diagnose a situation in terms of the prevailing circumstances in the organization and then to adopt a strategy for effecting changes at crucial points. Yet, conflict in industry cannot be completely eliminated; it can only be contained within reasonable limits. Good industrial relations, while a recognizable and legitimate objective for an organization, are difficult to define since a good system of industrial relations involves complex relationships between:

1. Workers (and their informal and formal groups, i.e. trade union, organizations and their representatives)
2. Employers (and their managers and formal organizations like trade and professional associations)
3. The government and legislation and government agencies.

Oversimplified, work is a matter of managers giving instructions and workers following them—but (and even under slavery we recognize that different 'managing' produces very different results)the variety of 'forms 'which have evolved to regulate the conduct of parties (i.e. laws, custom and practice, observances, agreements) makes the giving and receipt of instructions far from simple.

Two types of 'rule' have evolved:

1. 'Substantive', determining basic pay and conditions of service (what rewards Workers should receive);
2. 'Procedural,' determining how workers should be treated and methods and procedures.

It is necessary to:

1. Protect the weak (hence minimum wage);
2. Outlaw discrimination (race or gender);
3. Determine minimum standards of safety, health, hygiene and even important conditions of service;
4. To try to prevent the abuse of power by either party.

1.5 Benefits of Industrial Relations Planning and Management

The benefits that flow from better planning and management of industrial relations include, but are not limited to:

1. Improvement of the enterprise's 'knowledge bank', industrial relations capability and management focus
2. Improved corporate image through the demonstrated commitment to better management of workplace issues
3. Improved relations with stakeholders (who may include workers, unions, subcontractors, suppliers, industrial tribunals and clients)
4. Efficient project performance from improved communication and knowledge for all stakeholders involved in developing and implementing an industrial relations management focus
5. Less time and effort spent on resolving grievances about compliance with industrial awards and other legal obligations relating to employment
6. Greater control over cost, time, quality and improved project outcomes, and
7. Competitive advantage.
8. Developing an industrial relations management focus will assist contractors and their service providers both in complying with the industrial relations.

1.6 Hr Managers' Responsibilities in Managing the Industrial Relations in Bangladesh

The personnel manager's involvement in the system of industrial relations varies from organization to organization, but normally he or she is required to provide seven identifiable functions, thus:

1. To keep abreast of industrial law (legislation and precedents) and to advise managers about their responsibilities
2. To conduct (or assist in the conduct) of either local negotiations or similarly to act as the employer's representative in national negotiations.
3. To ensure that agreements reached are interpreted so as to make sense to those who must operate them at the appropriate level within the organization
4. To monitor the observance of agreements and to produce policies that ensures that agreements are followed within the organization.
5. To correct the situations which go wrong.
6. To provide the impetus (and often devise the machinery) for the introduction of joint consultation and worker participation in decision-making in the organization.
7. To provide statistics and information about workforce numbers, costs, skills etc. as relevant to negotiations.

1.7 Managing the Industrial Relations: Bangladeshi Context

Changes in labor relations within an organization are often affected by management practices. Therefore attitudes towards industrial relations should be understood in the background of theories and practices relating to the management of enterprises and organizational behavior. The theory, appropriately styled the human relations school, had as one of its earliest and greatest exponents, Douglas McGregor. He gave an impetus to the development of a management theory which focused on the human being as part of an enterprise which, in turn, was viewed as a biological system, rather than as a machine. Human relations, trust, delegation of authority, etc. were some of the features of this theory. They determine also the quality of its successive generations of management of industrial relations.

However, subject to exceptions (such as in Asia, especially in Bangladesh) most large enterprises continued to be dominated by hierarchies. This is reflected in the classic "strategy, structure, systems" of modern corporations. "Structure follows strategy. And systems support structure.

The effectiveness of the procedures and systems which are established for better information flow, understanding and where possible, consensus building, is critical today to the successful management of enterprises and for achieving competitiveness. As such, the basic ingredients of sound enterprise level labor relations are inseparable from some of the essentials for managing an enterprise in today's globalized environment. These developments have had an impact on ways of motivating workers, and on the hierarchy of organizations. They are reducing layers of management 'thus facilitating improved communication.

The present trend in industrial relations and human resource management is to place greater emphasis on employee involvement, harmonious employer—employee relations and mechanisms, and on practices which promote them. One of the important consequences of globalization and intense competition has been the pressure on firms to be flexible. Enterprises have sought to achieve this in two ways. First, through technology and a much wider worker skills base than before in order to enhance capacity to adapt to market changes.

Second, by introducing a range of employee involvement schemes with a view to increasing labor-management cooperation at the shop floor level, necessary to achieve product and process innovation. Achieving flexibility does not depend on the absence of unions. Organization flexibility depends upon trust between labor and management. It implies that workers are willing to forego efforts to establish and enforce individually or through collective action substantive work rules that fix the allocation of work, transfer among jobs, and workloads. Traditional assumptions that efficiency is achieved through managerial control, technology and allocation of resources have given way to the view that efficiency is the result of greater involvement of employees in their jobs, teams and the enterprise. Organizations which have made this shift tend to reflect the following characteristics: few hierarchical levels; wide spans of control; continuous staff development; self managing work teams; job rotation; commitment to quality; information sharing; pay systems which cater to performance rewards and not only payment for the job; generation of high performance expectations; a common corporate vision; and participative leadership styles. It hardly requires emphasis that achieving most of these requires training. In Bangladesh, too, now there is a keen awareness in the business community that radical changes are necessary to sustain dynamic growth. The earlier generation's recipe for success hinged on hard work, smart moves, the right business and political connections, monopolies, protectionist barriers, subsidies, access to cheap funds and, in many cases, autocratic leadership and a docile labor force. The new 'Global-Asian' manager has to exercise greater levels of leadership than before, and balance this with being an entrepreneur, modern manager and deal-maker skilled at public relations. To this has to be added coaching, team-building and motivating the company, the ability to visualize, plan strategically, market and re-engineer products and services, and the belief in a customer driven culture.

A sound industrial relations system is one in which relationships between management and employees (and their representatives) on the one hand, and between them and the State on the other, are more harmonious and cooperative than conflictual and creates an environment conducive to economic efficiency and the motivation, productivity and development of the employee and generates employee loyalty and mutual trust. Industrial relations should seek to balance the economic efficiency of organizations with equity, justice and the development of the individual, to find ways of avoiding, minimizing and resolving disputes and conflict and to promote harmonious relations between and among the actors directly involved, and society as a whole.

Industrial relations operate at different levels—at the national level, at the level of the industry and at the enterprise level. The elements which reflect a sound industrial relations system at all these levels are not necessarily the same. At the national level industrial relations operates so as to formulate labor relations policy. In market economies this is usually done through a tripartite process involving government, employers and workers and their representative organizations. At the industry level industrial relations often takes the form of collective bargaining between employers' organizations and unions. This process may result in determining wages and other terms and conditions of employment for an industry or sector. It may also result in arrangements on issues which are of mutual concern such as training, ways of avoiding or settling disputes, etc. At the enterprise level the relationship between employers and workers is more direct, but the interests of workers may be represented by unions. Employers' organizations, however, are not usually involved (though sometimes they are when negotiations take place between them and unions in respect of enterprise issues) at the enterprise level in representing the employers' interests with workers or their union, but this does not mean that they do not have an important promotional role at this level. Sound industrial relations at the national level build trust and confidence between representatives of workers and employers. Sound relations at the enterprise level build trust and confidence between workers and management, which is the point at which the system must ultimately be effective. Effectiveness at one level would naturally have some impact on the other.

To manage industrial relations system efficiently, a labor management relations policy (LMRP) is required. The following should be some of the objectives:

1. Employment and job security and increased employment opportunities.
2. Raising living standards through improved terms and conditions of employment.
3. Productivity improvement which enables employers to be more competitive and to increase their financial capacity to raise the living standards of the employees.
4. Minimizing conflict, achieving harmonious relations, resolving conflicts through peaceful means and establishing stable social relationships. In Western industrialized societies "harmony" and "harmonious relations" are not explicitly referred to either as an objective or as a means, though basically it represents an important objective in such societies.

A sound industrial relations climate in an enterprise is essential to a number of issues which are critical to employers, employees and the community. The efficient production of goods and services depends to an extent on the existence of a harmonious industrial relations climate. Efficiency and quality depend on a motivated workforce, for which a sound industrial relations climate is necessary. Therefore labor management; relations should be geared to creating the climate appropriate to securing the cooperation necessary for productivity growth. Labor Management Relations (LMR) and Labor Management Cooperation (LMC) are also important to the creation of a culture which is oriented towards innovation, adaptable to and encourages Change, where authority is decentralized and two-way communication, risk-taking and maximizing opportunities are encouraged, and where the output rather than the process is what matters. Changing attitudes, awareness and behavior to move from counter-productivity to a productivity culture requires the appropriate labor management relations climate based on labor management cooperation.

To manage industrial relations system, it is important to remove the main objections of workers and unions to productivity drives by employers. Productivity increases have sometimes been opposed by workers and unions on the grounds that they do not result in equitable sharing of benefits to workers and that increased productivity may lead to redundancy. Developing understanding of basic productivity concepts and of the methods of increasing productivity, as, well as of the formulation of equitable productivity gain-sharing schemes help to dispel such suspicions. This task is easier where there are mechanisms which provide for dialogue and two-way communication between management and workers. Labor management relations therefore play a crucial role in securing acceptance by workers and unions of the need for productivity improvement, and also in obtaining their commitment to achieving it.

Cooperation between management and workers or unions facilitates not only a settlement of disputes or disagreements but also the avoidance of disputes which may otherwise arise. At the industry level the relationship between employers' organizations and representatives of workers is a precondition to collective bargaining. Where collective bargaining takes place at the enterprise level, management workers/union relations determine to a great extent the success or otherwise of collective bargaining.

At the national level a good relationship between representatives of employers and workers enables them to effectively participate in labor-management relations policy formulation and to arrive at a consensus.

In a broad sense, therefore, labor management relations policy formulation (LMRP) should aim at achieving social justice through a process of consensus by negotiation so as to avert adverse political, social and economic consequences. Labor relations reflect the power structure in society, and it emphasizes negotiation and reconciliation by peaceful means of the interests of government, workers and employers who are the main participants in the system. Consensus enables the policy formulated to be implemented with the minimum of conflict as it has the support of all three parties. This is in fact reflected in the ILO's principle of tripartism. In the final analysis, labor management relations policy should seek to achieve development through establishing conditions which are fairer, more stable and more peaceful than they are at any given moment of time. Labor management relations policy also seeks to achieve an acceptable balance between labor and management, necessary for a negotiated development strategy and the establishment or preservation of a society which is essentially pluralist.

At the national level the mechanisms and procedures could be formal and institutionalized, or else informal and ad hoc. Where the labor administration system consults, on an ad hoc basis, workers' and employers' organizations on subjects falling within their purview, it represents a method of policy formulation on labor management relations. Sometimes these consultations may take place between the two social partners and other public authorities. For instance, a finance ministry may consult the social partners on an issue relating to wage policy. National level policy formulation can take place through institutions which provide for periodic tripartite discussion and consultation.

It is important at the outset to separate several issues relating to participation, communication and consultation: the principle of communication; the methods or means to give effect to this principle; and whether the principle and/or means should be enshrined in legislation, or should be the subject of bipartite negotiation, or should be at the employer's initiative.

With increasing acceptance of the fact that the crucial competitive weapon will be the skills and performance of the workforce, emphasis is being placed on greater involvement of employees in matters affecting their work and jobs, through consultation, information sharing and two-way communication procedures. This is all the more necessary in activities requiring the use of skills and knowledge.

Greater worker involvement is likely to occur in the future for the following reasons:

1. Employees at all levels are acquiring higher educational qualifications and skills. As such, they will be less amenable to management through control and commands, and will instead respond better to more participative forms of management.
2. Quality and productivity tend to increase when employees are more involved in arriving at decisions at the point of production.
3. For effective decision making in modern enterprises there should be an information flow and analysis of data and information.
4. Work today requires and involves more interpersonal skills, greater coordination among workers and sharing of information.
5. Enterprises(and economies) which have moved beyond the stage of routine high volume production to more value added and knowledge-based activities need to promote increased innovation, creativity and better application of knowledge, all of which require worker involvement.

Participation is a great motivational tool because it gives people a degree of control, recognizes personal worth, and provides scope for personal growth. Moreover, joint consultation has made a significant contribution to enterprise level labor relations by creating mutual understanding and managing a range of industrial relations issues which impinge on the lives of employees. This in turn has had an impact on collective bargaining, which tends to take place in an atmosphere in which workers have been informed of management objectives, so that the areas for misunderstanding and conflict are considerably reduced.

1.8 Employee employer relationship in context of Bangladesh

Labor management relations have become one of the most delicate and complex issues of modern industrial society. Labor management progress is impossible without cooperation of labors and harmonious relationships. Therefore, it is in the interest of all to create and maintain good relations between employees (labor) and employers (management). The term labor management relations explain the relationship between employees and management which stem directly or indirectly from union-employer relationship.

A labor management relations system consists of the whole gamut of relationships between employers and employees and employers which are managed by the means of conflict and cooperation. A sound labor management relations system is one in which relationships between management and employees (and their representatives) on the one hand, and between them and the state on the other, are more harmonious and cooperative than conflictual and creates an environment conducive to economic efficiency and the motivation, productivity and development of the employee and generates employee loyalty and mutual trust.

Three main parties are directly involved in industrial relations:

1. Employer
2. Employee
3. Government

1.9 Employer

An employer is a person or institution that hires employees or workers. Employers offer wages or a salary in exchange for the worker's labor power, depending upon whether the employee is paid by the hour or a set rate per pay period. Employers include everything from individuals hiring a babysitter to governments and Businesses which may hire many thousands of employees.

1.9.1 Primary Roles of Employer

Employer closely touches the following things:

1. Co-coordinating and controlling a group of people.
2. Management efforts are beyond individual efforts.'

3. The process includes strategic planning, goal setting, managing financial and human resources.
4. Measuring the outcome of the efforts.
5. Its efforts are limited within an enterprise.
6. The process is a regular activity that is carried on consciously, deliberately and prudently.
7. Management success can be attributed to some part to the extent of Responsibility and autonomy associated with the decision making.
8. Professionalism, expert knowledge, etc. are characteristics of management.
9. The process deals with financial, economic issues and the impact could be found in the society.
10. Allocation and distribution of scarce resource is important for management.

Employers operate through various functions, often classified as planning, organizing, leading/motivating and controlling.

1. **Planning** is the ongoing process of developing the business' mission and objectives and determining how they will be accomplished. Planning includes both the broadest view of the organization, e.g., its mission, and the narrowest, e.g., a tactic for accomplishing a specific goal.
    i. The mission of the business is its most obvious purpose—which may be, for example, to make soap.
    ii. The objective of the business refers to the ends or activity at which a certain task is aimed.
    iii. The business's policy is a guide that stipulates rules, regulations and objectives, and may be used in the managers' decision-making. It must be flexible and easily interpreted and understood by all employees.
    iv. The business's strategy refers to the plan of action that it is going to take, as well as the resources that it will be using, to achieve its mission and objectives. It is a guideline to managers, stipulating how they ought to use best the factors of production to the business's advantage. Initially, it could help the managers decide on what type of business they want to form.
2. **Organizing** is establishing the internal organizational structure of the organization. The focus is on division, coordination, and control of tasks and the flow of information within the organization. It is in this function that managers distribute authority to job holders.
3. **Staffing** is filling and keeping filled with qualified people all positions in the business. Recruiting, hiring, training, evaluating and compensating are the specific activities included in the function. In the family business, staffing includes all paid and unpaid positions held by family members including the owner/operators.
4. **Directing** is influencing people's behavior through motivation, communication, group dynamics, leadership and discipline. The purpose of directing is to channel the behavior of all

personnel to accomplish the organization's mission and objectives while simultaneously helping them accomplish their own career objectives.

5. **Controlling** is a four-step process of establishing performance standards based on the firm's objectives, measuring and reporting actual performance, comparing the two, and taking corrective or preventive action as necessary.

6. **Marketing:** Marketing, more than any other business function, deals with customer understanding, creating, communicating and delivering customer value and satisfaction are at the very heart of modem marketing thinking and practice. Not only in Bangladesh, everywhere, marketing is the delivery of customer satisfaction at a profit. In Bangladesh sound marketing is critical to the success of every organization—large or small, for profit or for not-profit, domestic or global.

Employer has a number of responsibilities that accompany his or her role as is mentioned by the Workers Compensation Board (WCB), Alberta.

1. Maintain the account
2. Pay the premiums
3. Work with employees to prevent injuries and illnesses.
4. Record and reporting injuries (see below) and helping injured workers return to work.
5. Inform all workers about the coverage they have and the benefits to which they are entitled under workers' compensation coverage, as detailed in the Worker Handbook.

1.9.2 Employers' Relative Power

An employers' relative level of power over employees is dependent upon numerous factors; the most influential being the nature of the employment relationship. The relationship employers share with employees is affected by three significant factors—interests, control and motivation. It is up to employers to effectively manage and balance these factors to ensure a harmonious and productive working relationship.

1. **Interests:** Interests can be best described as monetary constraints and economic pressures placed on organizations in their pursuit of profits. It covers facets such as labor productivity, wages and the effect of financial markets on businesses.

2. **Control:** Wood et al (2004, p355) describe control can as being either output focused, focusing on desired targets with within managers defining, and using, their own methods for reaching targets, or process controls, which specify the manner in which tasks will be achieved (Ibid, p. 357). Employer and managerial control within an organization rests at many levels and has important implications for staff and productivity alike, with control forming the fundamental link between desired outcomes and actual processes. Thus employers must balance interests

such as decreasing wage constraints with a maximization of labor productivity in order to achieve a prolific employment relationship.

3. **Motivation:** Motivation is the third and most difficult of the factors in the employment relationship for employers to effectively manage. Employee motivation can often be in direct conflict with control mechanisms of employers, and can be broadly defined as that which energizes, directs and sustains human behavior (stone, 2005, p 412). Dubin (1958, P 213) further elaborates on this, noting motivation as "something that moves a person to action, and continues him in the course of action already initiated."

The employment relationship is thus a difficult challenge for employers to manage, as all three facets are often in direct competition with each other, with interests, control and motivation often clashing in the equally important quest for individual employee autonomy, employer command and ultimate profits.

2.0 Employee

Employees (Workers) seek to improve the terms and conditions of their employment. They exchange views with management and voice their grievances. They also want to share decision making powers of management. Workers generally unite to form unions against the management and get support from these unions.

2.0.1 Duties of Employees

1. Being ready and willing to work
2. Rendering personal service to the employer
3. Respecting the employer's trade secrets
4. Taking reasonable care of the employer's property
5. Obeying all reasonable and legitimate duties given by the employer
6. Avoiding the willful disruption of the employer's undertaking
7. Co-Operate with the employer in all possible manners

2.0.2 Employee's Relative Power

Employee's power is basically dependent upon trade union. Previously, there was employer's absolute freedom of the employers. But these were effectively constrained by the growth of trade unionism and collective bargaining, and by the state interventionism in industrial relations. During the second half of the last century, the balance of bargaining power between employers and employees has generally shifted towards the employee's favor. This is wholly due to the increasing number and power of trade unions.

2.1 Relation of Employer—Employee in Bangladesh

2.1.1 History

In Bangladesh the number of the organized working class people is not very big. There are some reasons for that. The history tells that Bangladesh was a British colony for almost 200years. In that period the British authority used this country as a source for the raw materials of different industry. The British authority showed disinclination to set up industrial establishment in this country. Rather they preferred the labor force of this country to produce the raw materials which the British authority shipped to the abroad. So basically in that period almost all the labor force was engaged in the agricultural activities for producing raw materials.

In that period 'Zamindar Protha' was going on. Under this system there was a particular Zamidar or Land-lord for a particular area, who used to take tax from the farmers of that area. Many times farmers were bound to grow the crops that the respective Zamindar wanted. Farmers in those period followed very old way of cultivation. This system got resembles with the Peasant—lord system mentioned in the Interim report on 'Future Industrial Relations' prepared by Robert w. Cox, Jeffrey Harrod & others. Farmers in those period followed very old way of cultivation.

Again even before the colonial period the main activities of our country people were mostly around agriculture. Agrarian structure played the most important role from an earlier period in the making of social stratification what gradually assumed the present shape. The largest bulk of the population lived in the countryside with a small urban counterpart. Those living in the countryside primarily derived subsistence from agriculture, and therefore, one cannot ignore the social relationship grown out of agrarian structure. Zamindars or the revenue collectors were the most powerful class in the agrarian structure since the pre-colonial time in Bengal and the new colonial land policy of 1793 did not disturb the basic equilibrium. There was change of hands in land ownership but the class did not disappear. Below the class of Zamindar there was a vast peasant cultivator class. Subsequent land policy in the colonial period, particularly the sub-infeudation (madhyasvatvas or pattanidari) created intermediate rent collecting interests resulting in the emergence of numerous agrarian layers, known as Jotedar, Gantidar, Howladar, or Talukdar, or Bhuiyan, etc. The aggregate effect of introducing different land tenure measures was the emergence of a highly stratified society based on land interests.

Agrarian society during the colonial time also witnessed the emergence of a rich peasant class who happened to occupy an important position in social stratification. At least one specific development created the pre-condition for the emergence of rich/proto-capitalist peasants: the market integration of Bengal agriculture with the global economy particularly with the onset of indigo and jute cultivation. The rich peasant class enjoyed economic wealth and power in rural society. On the other hand, agrarian society during colonial time also went through the process of proletarianization/pauperization with the consequent emergence of landless class. While different land tenure measures influenced the class composition of the agrarian structure and in turn social stratification, the growing capitalization facilitated the emergence of agricultural wage workers. The social stratification pattern that emerged during the colonial time comprised the superior landed class, landed intermediaries with several layers, rich peasants/proto-capitalists, poor peasants/sharecroppers, and agricultural working class coming from the landless and marginal peasants.

With the introduction of British rule in the urban areas important changes took place at the level of urban social stratification. A pristine 'Bhadralok' or gentlemen class consisted of educated professionals (lawyers, teachers, doctors, engineers, service holders and others) emerged in urban Bengal reaping the benefits from the new educational and occupational opportunities. On the other hand, the size of the newly emerged business class was small and characteristically not comparable with the bourgeois counterpart of the West. Earlier, the social status enjoyed by the traders or 'Banians' was lesser than the higher caste like the Brahmans and it changed during the colonial time. Business class also became educated and the vice versa. Landed aristocracy became the frontrunners among the 'Bhadralok'. In terms of life style and values they presented novel characteristics. In the arenas of art, culture and politics their novelties were prominent.

One of the significant developments immediately after the partition of the subcontinent was the abolition of zamindari land system in Bangladesh. Since historically most Zamindars came from the Hindu community, their migration to India after partition created a sort of vacuum in social structure. The Muslim traditional wealthy class linked to agriculture came to occupy that vacuum, although it was a fact that their size was minuscule.

The following agrarian classes and groups are found to constitute rural society with hierarchical status and prestige: capitalist farmers, rich peasants, middle peasants, marginal peasants and the landless. The capitalist farmers are wealthy, own land and technology, hire outside labor and carry out cultivation for the market. Rich peasants are also wealthy and hire outside labor but they are still engaged in cultivation. Middle peasants are primarily subsistence cultivators with occasional market participation and primarily depending on household labor. Marginal peasants combine cultivation and labor sale to ensure subsistence. The landless people are the wage workers primarily engaged in agriculture. About three/fourths of rural households belong to the categories of marginal peasants and landless.

"The effect of 'pauperization', the process that results in the emergence of landless households without adequate employment, is found quite significant in rural Bangladesh. In rural stratification there are other traditional groups such as kamars (blacksmiths), swarnakars (goldsmiths), sweepers, tantis (weavers), kalus (oil pressers), and others who enjoy minimum status. The roles of some of these groups are now taken over by the professional producers. For example, edible oil comes from the mill.

Long before the partition of India, there was a trade union movement in the cotton textile industry areas. Immediately after the creation of Pakistan, the All India Trade Union Congress (AITUC) initiated a trade union federation in East Pakistan under the leadership of trade unionists. Although Pakistan was one of the first states which ratified the International Labor Organization (ILO) Conventions No. 87 and 98, its workers were deprived of the right to collective bargaining and the right to strike. The Industrial Dispute Act 1947of India was adopted in Pakistan with some amendments until 1959, when worker's rights were further curtailed by the Industrial Dispute Ordinance, promulgated by the martial law authority. Between 1965and 1969, the East Pakistan Labor Dispute Acts was mainly responsible for regulating industrial relations.

2.1.2 Present Situation

Originally, industrial relations were broadly defined to include the relationships and interactions between employers and employees. From this perspective, Labor management relations cover all aspects of the employment relationship, including human resource management, employee relations, and union-management (or labor) relations. Employer—Employment relations pertains to the study and practice of collective bargaining, trade unionism, and labor-management relations, while human resource management is a separate, largely distinct field that deals with nonunion employment relationships and the personnel practices and policies of employers.

The relationships which arise at and out of the workplace generally include the relationships between individual workers, the relationships between workers and their employer, the relationships between employers, the relationships employers and workers have with the organizations formed to promote their respective interests, and the relations between those organizations, at all levels. Labor management relations also includes the processes through which these relationships are expressed (such as, collective bargaining, workers' participation in decision-making, and grievance and dispute settlement), and the management of conflict between employers, workers and trade unions, when it arises.

For the system to work efficiently, both the employer and employee must, to some degree, have a common ideology (acceptance of the economic system and the role of other participants). However, acceptance does not necessarily mean convergence of interests. To the contrary, some degree of worker-management conflict is inevitable as though the interests of the parties overlap, they diverge in key respects (e.g how to divide the profits). So, an effective relations system does not eliminate conflicts, rather it provides with an initiation that minimizes its effect on management, society and employees.

The degree of worker organization is a crucial factor in enhancing worker control over decisions: thus systems in which workers enter the labor market as individuals are to be distinguished from those in which they organize collectively in trade unions.

In Bangladesh, the power relations can be viewed in three different phases. When a daily labor works on hourly basis (say he/she removes soil on the site of building construction), he/she has no power for negotiation. Hence there is no party here.

Again in the case of rickshaw puller or CNG (Auto Rickshaw) driver, they have to give a certain amount of money to their 'Mohajon' but they have the right to work independently and keep the rest of the earned money as their income. They can freely negotiate with their clients. Their 'Mohajon' is only concerned about the certain amount of money they pay him. Hence here is two parties here.

Next comes the labors works in the factories and participate in production. Here comes the interaction of three parties—workers, management and the Government. None of them entirely enjoys power, each of the party share power.

Allegations of opportunism also exist among the trade union leadership of Bangladesh. Trade union leadership can still be observed to be under the control of a certain class of bourgeoisie. They have no real respect for the class struggle of the working class and seek to meet their ends by maintaining liaisons with the employer class in the name of helping the working class. More often than not, basic unions are not much more than pocket unions of the management. Trade union movement has failed to develop to its full form due to the presence of these ailments.

The prime concern of a trade union leader is ideally to protect the best interest of the members of his trade union. However, unions formed in Bangladesh serve as more as labor fronts of political parties, useful for election campaigns and for political agitation than as the representator of worker's rights. Almost all of the 20 registered national trade union federations owe their founding, funding and continued existence to the government's ruling party or to one of that party's factions or to one of the opposition parties. Chances of such unions, the existence itself of which is marked with irregularities, being able to dredge up strong and ethical leaders for the labor population are dubious at best.

The contemporary union scene is pockmarked with conflicts both within the unions itself and between different unions. Leaders are observed to be prone to break away from the mother union because of internal conflict and form unions of their own. This problem stems from the true attitudes of contemporary trade union leaders. Most trade union leaders of Bangladesh are more concerned with the materialistic benefits that their hieratical position has to offer than with the well-being of the union members. It is, thus, not uncommon to find fairly powerful members of a union to start aspiring for the position of the leader and thus resort to low, sometimes destructive, means to oust the current leader from his chair. This generally leads to the Trade union splitting itself into two separate entities. This trend is leading to an increase in the number of unions without any significant increase in total membership. It should be noted that Bangladeshi labor law requires a workplace to have 30-percent union participation before a union can be registered, and a union may be dissolved if membership falls below this level. Prior to official registration, which signifies state recognition of the trade union, a union may not function. Therefore, it is commonly observed that most Trade unions are not even eligible for registration because it is nowhere near to fulfilling its 30% participation quota. Perhaps the most important determinants of the relationship between the parties are the policies adopted by the unions and management, or lack of thereof. The policies adopted by the parties may be identical, different, or amenable to compromise. In any event, these policies and the extent to which to which they exist will influence the general relationship of the union and the management and their specific actions within that relationship.

Our recent history of employer—employee relations is also one of oppression from the owner's/ employers' part. Our industrial relations date back to the 60's of the 18th century when rail lines were established here for the first time. The railway workers had to endure colonial suppression of the most extreme kind. They had to suffer from numerous atrocities inflicted upon them by the colonial rulers. They were underpaid, over-worked and treated like animals. These hapless victims had no platform to voice their issues; nobody was looking out for their interests. Any sort of objection raised on part of the labors could be faced with death in the hands of the owners. The employers main concern was their own profits-not the workers well being. Reflections of this trend are still visible in contemporary Bangladesh.

We only need to look as far as our ship-breaking and garments industries to find strong echoes of the by-gone days. Even in this day and time, when overall awareness about basic human rights has increases many folds since the 60's, it is not uncommon to newspapers reporting deaths of ship-breaking workers in the hands of their cruel taskmasters. These workers are made to work in environments that have become highly toxic from various chemicals, liquid and gaseous, released when ships are manually disbanded. Prolonged presence in such environments can be analogous to being slow poisoned as many life-threatening diseases such as cancer can be triggered by these chemicals. Any 'perceived sloppiness' observed by the ship-yard owners may result in punishment as cruel and barbaric as whippings.

Garments workers are, in a sense, better off, as they have the chance to voice their issues to the owners and sometimes, even to the general public via various news media. However, more often than not, their voices are ignored by the owners. Workers are threatened and coerced by the owners and made to work in unsafe structures and toil in 24 hour shifts.

Bangladeshi Employer—Employee relations must urgently come together across the region. Labor is certainly engaging in substantive alliances with other groups striving for human rights. Such alliances need to be similarly strengthened across the region. This solidarity of labor will obviously strengthen peace efforts in the region, which will in turn help the country to become more economically developed.

2.2 Employee Motivation

2.3 Theoretical Review

The job of a manager in the workplace is to get things done through employees. To do this the manager should be able to motivate employees. But that's easier said than done! Motivation practice and theory are difficult subjects, touching on several disciplines.

In spite of enormous research, basic as well as applied, the subject of motivation is not clearly understood and more often than not poorly practiced. To understand motivation one must understand human nature itself. And there lies the problem.

Human nature can be very simple, yet very complex too. An understanding and appreciation of this is a prerequisite to effective employee motivation in the workplace and therefore effective management and leadership.

Motivation theory and practice concentrate on various theories regarding human nature in general and motivation in particular. Included are articles on the practical aspects of motivation in the workplace and the research that has been undertaken in this field, notably by Douglas McGregor (theory y), Frederick Herzberg (two factor motivation hygiene theory,) Abraham Maslow (theory Z, hierarchy of needs), Elton Mayo (Hawthorne Experiments) Chris Argyris Rensis Likert and David McClelland (achievement motivation.)

2.3.1 Application of Employee Motivation Principles

Quite apart from the benefit and moral value of an altruistic approach to treating colleagues as human beings and respecting human dignity in all its forms, research and observations show that well motivated employees are more productive and creative. The inverse also holds true. The schematic below indicates the potential contribution the practical application of the principles this paper has on reducing work content in the organization.

2.4 Key to Performance Improvement

There is an old saying you can take a horse to the water but you cannot force it to drink; it will drink only if it's thirsty—so with people. They will do what they want to do or otherwise motivated to do. Whether it is to excel on the workshop floor or in the 'ivory tower' they must be motivated or driven to it, either by themselves or through external stimulus.

Are they born with the self-motivation or drive? Yes and no. If no, they can be motivated, for motivation is a skill which can and must be learnt. This is essential for any business to survive and succeed.

Performance is considered to be a function of ability and motivation, thus:

* Job performance = f (ability) (motivation)

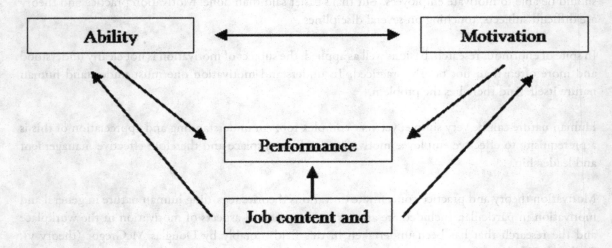

Figure 1 : Factors Influencing Performance Improvement

Ability in turn depends on education, experience and training and its improvement is a slow and long process. On the other hand motivation can be improved quickly. There are many options and an uninitiated manager may not even know where to start. As a guideline, there are broadly seven strategies for motivation.

1. Positive reinforcement / high expectations
2. Effective discipline and punishment
3. Treating people fairly
4. Satisfying employees needs
5. Setting work related goals
6. Restructuring jobs
7. Base rewards on job performance

These are the basic strategies, though the mix in the final 'recipe' will vary from workplace situation to situation. Essentially, there is a gap between an individual's actual state and some desired state and the manager tries to reduce this gap.

Motivation is, in effect, a means to reduce and manipulate this gap. It is inducing others in a specific way towards goals specifically stated by the motivator. Naturally, these goals as also the motivation system must conform to the corporate policy of the organization. The motivational system must be tailored to the situation and to the organization.

In one of the most elaborate studies on employee motivation, involving 31,000 men and 13,000 women, the Minneapolis Gas Company sought to determine what their potential employee's desire most from a job. This study was carried out during a 20 year period from 1945 to 1965 and was quite revealing. The ratings for the various factors differed only slightly between men and women, but both groups considered security as the highest rated factor. The next three factors were:

1. Advancement
2. Type of work
3. Company—proud to work for

Surprisingly, factors such as pay, benefits and working conditions were given a low rating by both groups. So after all, and contrary to common belief, money is not the prime motivator. However, this should not be regarded as a signal to reward employees poorly or unfairly.

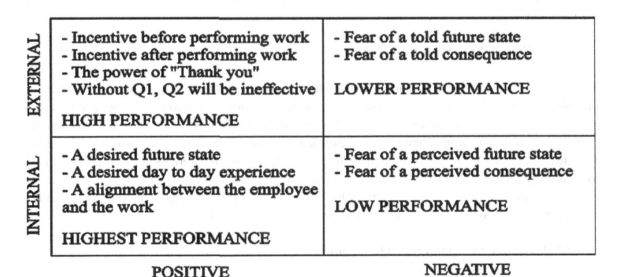

Figure 2 : Employee Motivation and Performance

2.5 Motivation Theorists and Their Theories

Although the process of management is as old as history, scientific management as we know it today is basically a twentieth century phenomenon. Also, as in some other fields, practice has been far ahead of theory.

This is still true in the field of management, contrary to the situation in some of the pure sciences. For instance, Albert Einstein, formulates a theory, which is later proved by decades of intensive research and experimentation. Not so in the field of management.

In fact this field has been so devoid of real fundamental work so far, that Herbert A. Simon is the first management theoretician to win the Nobel Prize for Economics in 1978. His contribution itself gives a clue to the difficulty, bordering on impossibility, of real fundamental work in this field concerned with people. In order to arrive at a correct decision, the manager must have all the information necessary relevant to the various factors and all the time in the world to analyze the same.

This is seldom, if ever, the case. Both the information available and the time at the manager's disposal are limited, but he or she must make a decision. And the decision is, therefore, not the optimum one but a 'satisfying' one—in effect, a satisfactory compromise under the real conditions prevailing in the management 'arena'.

2.5.1 Theory 'X': Sigmund Freud

This can best be ascribed to Sigmund Freud who was no lover of people, and was far from being optimistic. Theory X assumes that people are lazy; they hate work to the extent that they avoid it; they have no ambition, take no initiative and avoid taking any responsibility; all they want is security, and to get them to do any work, they must be rewarded, coerced, intimidated and punished. This is the so-called 'stick and carrot' philosophy of management. If this theory were valid, managers will have to constantly police their staff, which they cannot trust and who will refuse to cooperate. In such an oppressive and frustrating atmosphere, both for the manager and the managed, there is no possibility of any achievement or any creative work. But fortunately, as we know, this is not the case.

2.5.2 Theory 'Y': Douglas Mcgregoi

This is in sharp contrast to theory 'X'. McGregor believed that people want to learn and that work is their natural activity to the extent that they develop self-discipline and self development. They see their reward not so much in cash payments as in the freedom to do difficult and challenging work by them. The manager's job is to 'dovetail' the human wish for self-development into the organizations need for maximum productive efficiency. The basic objectives of both are therefore met and with imagination and sincerity, the enormous potential can be tapped.

Does it sound too good to be true? It could be construed; by some, that Theory 'Y' management is soft and slack. This is not true and the proof is in the 'pudding', for it has already proved its worth in the USA and elsewhere. For best results, the persons must be carefully selected to form a homogeneous group. A good leader of such a group may conveniently 'absent' from group meetings so they can discuss the matters freely and help select and 'groom' a new leader. The leader does no longer hanker after power, lets people develop freely, and may even (it is hoped) enjoy watching the development and actualization of people, as if, by themselves. Everyone, and most of all, the organization, gains as a result.

2.5.3 Theory 'Z': Abraham Maslow

This is a refreshing change from the theory X of Freud, by a fellow psychologist, Abraham Maslow. Maslow totally rejects the dark and dingy Freudian basement and takes us out into the fresh, open, sunny and cheerful atmosphere. He is the main founder of the humanistic school or the third force who holds that all the good qualities are inherent in people, at least, at birth, although later they are gradually lost.

Maslow's central theme revolves around the meaning and significance of human work and seems to epitomize Voltaire's observation in Candide, 'work banishes the three great evils—boredom, vice and poverty'. The great sage Yajnavalkya explains in the Brihadaranyaka Upanishad that by good works a man becomes holy, by evil works evil. A man's personality is the sum total of his works and that only his works survive a man at death. This is perhaps the essence of Maslow's hierarchy of needs theory, as it is more commonly know.

Maslow's major works include the standard textbook (in collaboration with MittlemannJ, Principles of Abnormal Psychology (1941J, a seminal paper, 'A Theory of Human Motivation' (1943) and the book, Eupsychian Management (pronounced yew-sighkeyan) published in 1965. Maslow's theory of human motivation is, in fact, the basis of McGregor's theory 'Y' briefly described above. The basic human needs, according to Maslow, are:

1. Physiological needs (Lowest)
2. Safety needs;
3. Love needs;
4. Esteem needs; and
5. Self-actualization needs (Highest)

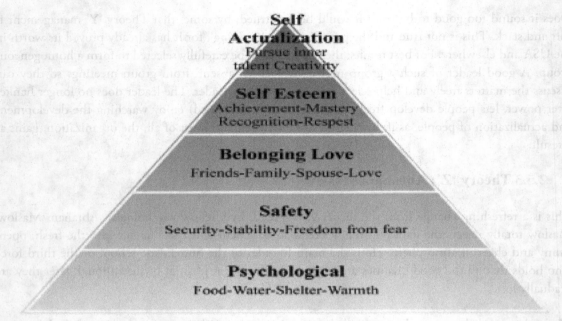

Figure 3 : Maslows's Hierarchy of Need

Mans behavior is seen as dominated by his unsatisfied needs and he is a 'perpetually wanting animal', for when one need is satisfied he aspires for the next higher one. This is, therefore, seen as an ongoing activity, in which the man is totally absorbed in order to attain perfection through self-development.

The highest state of self-actualization is characterized by integrity, responsibility, magnanimity, simplicity and naturalness. Self-actualizers focus on problems external to themselves. His prescription for human salvation is simple, but not easy: 'Hard work and total commitment to doing well the job that fate or personal destiny calls you to do or any important job that "calls for" doing'.

Maslow has had his share of critics, but he has been able to achieve a refreshing

Synthesis of divergent and influential philosophies of:

1. Marx—economic and physical needs;
2. Freud—physical and love needs;
3. Adler—esteem needs;
4. Goldstein—self-actualization.

2.5.4 Frederick Herzberg: Hygiene/Motivation Theory

This is based on analysis of the interviews of 200 engineers and accountants in the Pittsburgh area in the USA. According to this theory, people work first and foremost in their own self-enlightened interest, for they are truly happy and mentally healthy through work accomplishment. Peoples needs are of two types:

1. Animal Needs (hygiene factors)
   - Supervision
   - Interpersonal relations
   - Working conditions
   - Salary
2. Human Needs (motivators)
   - Recognition
   - Work
   - Responsibility
   - Advancement

Unsatisfactory hygiene factors can act as de-motivators, but if satisfactory, their motivational effect is limited. The psychology of motivation is quite complex and Herzberg has exploded several myths about motivators such as:

- Shorter working week;
- Increasing wages;
- Fringe benefits;
- Sensitivity/ human relations training;
- Communication.

As typical examples, saying 'please' to shop-floor workers does not motivate them to work hard, and telling them about the performance of the company may even antagonize them more. Herzberg regards these also as hygiene factors, which, if satisfactory, satisfy animal needs but not human needs.

2.5.5 Chris Argyris

According to Argyris, organization needs to be redesigned for a fuller utilization of the most precious resource, the workers, in particular their psychological energy. The pyramidal structure will be relegated to the background, and decisions will be taken by small groups rather than by a single boss. Satisfaction in work will be more valued than material rewards. Work should be restructured in order to enable individuals to develop to the fullest extent. At the same time work will become more meaningful and challenging through self-motivation.

2.5.6 Rensis Likert

Likert identified four different styles of management:

1. Exploitative-authoritative;
2. Benevolent-authoritative;
3. Consultative;
4. Participative.

The participative system was found to be the most effective in that it satisfies the whole range of human needs. Major decisions are taken by groups themselves and these results in achieving high targets and excellent productivity. There is complete trust within the group and the sense of participation leads to a high degree of motivation.

2.5.7 Fred Lutiians

Luthans advocates the so-called 'contingency approach' on the basis that certain practices work better than others for certain people and certain jobs. As an example, rigid, clearly defined jobs, authoritative leadership and tight controls lead in some cases to high productivity and satisfaction among workers. In some other cases just the opposite seems to work. It is necessary, therefore, to adapt the leadership style to the particular group of workers and the specific job in hand.

2.5.8 Victor Vroom

Vroom's 'expectancy theory' is an extension of the 'contingency approach'. The leadership style should be 'tailored' to the particular situation and to the particular group. In some cases it appears best for the boss to decide and in others the group arrives at a consensus. An individual should also be rewarded with what he or she perceives as important rather than what the manager perceives. For example, one individual may value a salary increase, whereas another may, instead, value promotion. This theory contributes an insight into the study of employee motivation by explaining how individual goals influence individual performance.

We have discussed above only a selection of the motivation theories and thoughts of the various proponents of the human behavior school of management. Not included here are, among others, the thoughts of:

1. Seebohm Rowntree—labor participation in management;
2. EltonMayo—the Hawthorne Experiments;
3. KurtLewin—group dynamics; force field theory;
4. David McClelland—achievement motivation;

5   George Humans—the human group;

6   William Whyte—the organization man.

The overall picture is certainly confusing as the human nature and human mind defy a clear-cut model, mathematical or otherwise.

In some of the theories and thoughts presented, however, one can see some 'glimpses' of the person and how, perhaps, he or she could be motivated. This is rewarding in itself. But, as noted earlier, practice has been ahead of theory in this field, so let us now move to the practical side of management of human behavior and motivation in the workplace.

2.6 Employee Commitment

2.6.1 Building Employee Commitment

The workplace is changing dramatically and demands for the highest quality of product and service is increasing. To remain competitive in the face of these pressures, employee commitment is crucial. This reality is applicable to all organizations but is of particular importance to small and medium sized businesses.

Employee behavior on the job is influenced directly—positively or negatively by his or her immediate supervisor. Positive influences are essential to strengthening employee commitment. Therefore the first step in building commitment is to improve the quality of management. Much has been written recently about the need for improving the education and training of our workforce. As important as this is, at least equal emphasis must be given to improving the quality of management if business is to succeed in achieving greater employee commitment and thereby its profitability.

The benefits of having the best trained workers using the most advanced technology can be nullified by poor people management practices by managers. Management skills which sufficed in the past are not adequate to meet the challenges facing business today.

The two keys to success in today's environment of increasing competition and rapid change are an absolute passion for, and dedication to, excellence in customer service and the effective and enlightened management of our workforce. The latter breed's commitment leads to achieving the desired standards in customer service. Without employee commitment, there can be no improvement in any area of business activity. In the absence of good management, employees will simply treat their work as a job—a 9 to 5 routine without any desire to accomplish any more than is necessary to remain employed. It does not take many uncommitted employees to prevent a business from prospering and thereby ceding a big advantage to its competitors.

In many organizations there is a growing commitment gap—a widening split between the expectations of employers and what workers are prepared to do. There are a number of reasons for this erosion of employee commitment; the most common one being a failure of management in some way or another. To succeed in the face of increasing competition, a business needs improved productivity at all levels. This requires the enthusiastic commitment of all employees which can only be achieved through better management practices. To be effective, the skills of good people management must be installed in an organization so they become part of its culture. In this way there will be consistency and equity with respect to how people are managed from the top down to the most junior employee.

Businesses need good people to succeed. Failure on the part of owners or senior leaders to ensure their managers and supervisors are trained and function effectively can lead to the loss of valued employees because the best employees are attracted to employers who place a premium on good people management.

The second key to success, namely customer service, cannot be achieved without dedicated and committed employees. It is the order clerks, customer service representatives, receptionists, and drivers who interact most with the customers. They relate to them in a manner consistent with how they themselves are managed. Hence the direct link between effective management of employees, their level of commitment to the organization and the standard of customer service.

Properly managed employees can be motivated to achieve excellence in any area of a business. They will contribute willingly, and will do more than expected if they are managed well. Extraordinary results can be achieved by ordinary people if management does its job properly. Managing a business today is difficult enough without forfeiting a competitive advantage by lack of attention to its most valuable asset—its people.

It therefore follows that all organizations should give a high priority to its people management practices if they hope to success and prosper in the face of global competition and consumer demand for the highest quality of product and/or service.

One of the major outcomes of a recent Watson Wyatt Survey, Work USA 2000, was the identification of seven key factors that drive employee commitment. The top rated factors were all quite similar in ranking, but together the list provides a useful list to consider in any company's efforts to improve worker commitment.

2.6.2 Employee Trust and Skills

Employees rated trust in senior leadership and the chance to use their skills on the job as the two most important drivers of employee commitment, followed by job security and receiving a competitive compensation package.

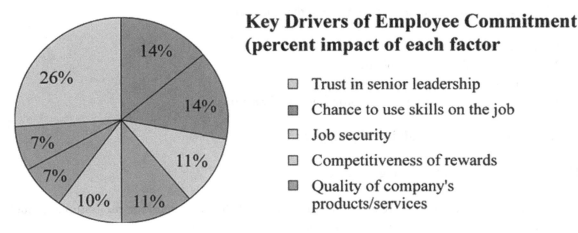

Key Drivers of Employee Commitment (percent impact of each factor

☐ Trust in senior leadership

▨ Chance to use skills on the job

☐ Job security

☐ Competitiveness of rewards

☐ Quality of company's products/services

Figure 4 : Key Drivers of Employee Commitment

Employee commitment used to equate with old-fashioned loyalty to a career employer. But today's mobile workers look for an employer of choice—one they can be proud to work for and whose leadership they trust. This sense of trust in senior leadership is really a key factor in commitment—which is a key factor in creating economic value for the organization.

2.6.3 Trust in Leadership

Companies with employees who had high trust and confidence levels in their senior management had a three-year total return to shareholders of 108 percent, compared with a 66 percent return at companies with low trust and confidence levels. However, only 50 percent of the surveyed workers expressed confidence in the job being done by senior management. Twenty-one percent expressed no confidence, while 29 percent were neutral.

The surveyed employees also identified seven factors that drive their trust in senior leadership, including promoting the most qualified employees, gaining support for the business direction, motivating the workforce to perform at peak levels, and explaining reasons behind major business decisions.

A total of 7,500 workers at all job levels and in all industries were surveyed about their attitudes toward their workplace and employers.

2.7 Employee Involvement

It is a participative style of management and a range of activities that are designed to increase employees' understanding of the organization, utilize their talents, enable them to influence decisions, and encourage their commitment to the goals of the organization.

Few of the benefits of employee involvement are that they can:

1   Improve efficiency
2   Improve quality and competitiveness
3   Increase job satisfaction and motivation
4   Encourage co-operation and improve industrial relations.

2.7.1 Methods of Involving Employees

There are two methods of involving employees:

1   Indirect involvement where a representative acts on behalf of employees, for example through collective bargaining or joint consultation
2   Direct involvement where employees are involved in decisions about how they work, for example through quality circles or autonomous work groups.

Effective communications are essential to the success of employee involvement. It is important to create the right climate and maintain communications systems which aid a free flow of information within an organization. Regular meetings also help to involve employees. For further information see the section on Communications.

2.7.1.1 Employee Representation

Involvement through representatives can take a variety of forms. The most common form of representation is through trade unions and employees have the right to be a member of a trade union, or not to be a member. Employees also have the right not to be excluded or expelled from a trade union except for certain permitted reasons. In some companies representation is through works or office committees or staff associations. Collective bargaining—the principal method of involvement through representatives—is dealt with separately.

2.7.1.2 Joint Consultation

Joint consultation is the process by which management involves employees through their representatives in discussion on relevant matters which affect or concern those they represent. This process allows employees the opportunity to influence the proposal before the final management decision is made.

To effectively make joint consultation work the following measures can be taken:

1   Senior managers should attend regularly
2   There should be a written constitution

3   Make sure there is an agenda for each meeting
4   Establish a procedure for reporting back to managers and employees
5   Provide training for committee members and chair holder
6   See that the committee meets regularly, normally not less than once every two months.

2.7.1.3 Quality Circles

Quality circles are small groups of employees, usually led by a supervisor, who meet regularly to solve problems and to find ways of improving aspects of their work. The circle presents recommendations to management and is normally involved in subsequent implementation and monitoring. A facilitator is usually appointed to arrange training and provide support.

For effective quality circles:

1   Commitment of senior management is crucial
2   Time and money must be allocated for training and meetings
3   Senior managers should be available to attend meetings as appropriate
4   Management must be prepared to support the implementation of the circle's solutions to problems, with resources as necessary
5   Quality circles should operate openly with full recognition given to their achievements
6   The circle should be able to select its own problems to solve, not just those identified by managers and the facilitator
7   Trade unions should be consulted and encouraged to become involved
8   Begin modestly—perhaps with a pilot scheme.

2.7.1.4 Financial Participation

Financial participation through share ownership or periodic sharing of profits can help increase employees' awareness of the financial and market forces affecting a company's performance. This can help employees identify with the progress of their own company and create a more committed workforce.

There are many types of financial participation including:

1   Cash schemes in which cash is distributed to employees from company profits
2   Share option schemes where employees are given an option to buy a certain number of shares at a set price at a particular time
3   Save as you earn share option schemes in which employees save a specified amount over an agreed period with an Inland Revenue approved plan. They have an option to buy shares at the end of the savings period at the market price which prevailed when the option was granted

4 All employee share ownership plans (AESOPs)which aim to involve employees through share ownership—taking advantage of tax concessions—and at the same time providing a new source of capital for the company.

Financial participation is unlikely to be successful if there are weaknesses in existing payment systems. Organizations should therefore examine their wage structure and pay rates to make sure they are fair and are understood by employees. In addition financial participation is more likely to be successful if:

1 Employees and their representatives are consulted before schemes are put into effect
2 Schemes are clearly understood by employees
3 Schemes are reviewed regularly
4 It is part of an overall programme of measures to involve employees.

2.7.1.5 Others Forms of Involvement

Other forms of employee involvement include:

1 Autonomous work groups which have some degree of autonomy or responsibility within a defined area, for example responsibility for work organization, quality and output
2 Job enlargement, job enrichment and job rotation which seek involvement and motivation by improving job satisfaction and effectiveness
3 Joint working parties which involve representatives of management and employees seeking joint solutions to problems. They are non-negotiating forums in which participants work together.

2.8 Bangladesh: Influence of the Motivation Strategies

Use of various motivational strategies and tools are still uncommon practices in the industries of Bangladesh. Hardly any of the local companies feel the need to carry out any of the motivational tools suggested by western intellectuals. They are mainly thought to be of no help irrelevant in the context of our industry structure. This had been the situation of the business world of our country since its inception until recently few of the big companies are showing concern towards different needs and wellbeing of their employees.

Most of the multinational companies do follow few of the modern employee motivation tools. For example, Bangladesh Nokia's core values are respect for the individual, continuous learning, achievement and customer satisfaction. Each Nokia employee is responsible to uphold these values in the workplace, in employee relations, corporate community involvement, health, safety and the environment.

Employees in Bangladesh like other developing countries are deprived of the right of a moderate pay for their work. Employees cannot be effectively motivated, if they are underpaid. Again, if they are well paid but not motivated, the desired services cannot be obtained from them. So, ensuring reasonable pay, the next step has to be employee motivation applying basic tools and techniques of motivation. In the garments sector of Bangladesh this is clearly evident. The pay level of the workers are very poor and with the increasing price of staple food and every day commodities left the workers in no position to carry out their activities neither efficiently nor productively. But recent improvements in the pay level of the garments workers can be seen with effective implementation of the minimum wage rate. Recent unrest of the garment labors and the labor unions brought about the changes in their payroll and created a better healthier work environment.

A study was made to explore the differences and similarities of management philosophies, managerial beliefs and organizational climates about human resources among managers in three manufacturing entities: Japanese companies in Japan, Japanese companies in Bangladesh, and Bangladeshi companies. Managerial samples were drawn from 100 Japanese companies, 50 Japanese companies in Bangladesh, and 50 Bangladeshi companies. In each sample company, five managers were randomly selected as respondents, providing the total number of usable sample for the present analysis (response rate = 32%). Data were analyzed a) to explore the interrelationship between HRM philosophies and managers' beliefs about their companies' human resources, and b) to examine the differences among three groups of managers. The findings indicated that managers in Japanese companies in Japan are the most 'Theory Y oriented", whereas managers in Japanese companies in Bangladesh are the least 'Theory Y oriented." While those in Bangladeshi companies in Bangladesh are the most "Theory X oriented" regarding their beliefs in human resources. Theory Y oriented managers tended to evaluate their companies organizational philosophy and climate to be more democratic and participating than Theory X oriented managers. Managers working for Theory Y oriented companies were found to engage more in self-study and participate more actively in company sponsored learning and training programs.

Although Bangladesh being a developing country had faced many downsides but currently the flow is more towards a positive direction. Most of the motivational theories necessary for the workers to perform more effectively are not practiced in the country. And most importantly, in many of the cases the owners were not even aware of the very existence of these employee motivational practices. The majority of the workers in the industries are treated with contempt and in return the workers perform poorly. It was also seen, as mentioned earlier, they mainly follow Theory 'X' rather than Theory 'Y' of Freud and McGregor. It may be deduced from here the reason why motivational strategies may not work here and therefore lack any such practices. However the current trend does illustrate a move towards the western practices in the businesses of the country. The big and influential companies are becoming aware of the need of such motivational strategies for their future profitability and ultimately their survival. Thus, it can be expected in the near future that the business industries of Bangladesh would develop into a more socially conscious and employee oriented one.

2.9 Employing Agencies of Bangladesh

According to orientation and ownership, enterprises can be divided into 2 categories:

1   Private sector
2   Public sector

3.0 Private Sector

In economics, the private sector is that part of the economy which is both run for private profit and is not controlled by the state. By contrast, enterprises that are part of the state are part of the public sector; private, non-profit organizations are regarded as part of the voluntary sector. Also known as the for-profit sector; organizations and businesses that provide services and products based on market demands for a fee with the intention of producing a profit for owners and shareholders.

The definition is applicable to Bangladesh also. This is the dominating enterprising form active in Bangladesh. Private Sector now represents the global strategy for economic development. It has accelerated at such a pace which one could hardly predict in 1970's. With post-GATT global trade and investment liberalizations global economic and political conditions have undergone unprecedented changes. Democracy at home and globalization externally have now created for Bangladesh vast opportunities for accelerated economic and social development.

To attain its modest objectives, however, Bangladesh will have to meet many challenges, and overcome many hazards and pitfalls. Like time and tide, opportunities do not wait for anyone.

Missed opportunities become inordinately costly. Institutional capacity-building for seizing the opportunities and meeting the challenges will require many changes, some definitely painful, in our administrative and political institutions, economic and financial structures, and also in our social and community ethos and behavior.

Until very recently (1985) Private Sector means few family owned enterprisesdominated the business environment in Bangladesh. The only qualification that mattered at the time was who is whose son or nephew and/or who is connected to whom in politics or in bureaucracy. One's academic background or training, entrepreneurship or potentiality hardly matters, if not irrelevant. However, from 1980's Private Sector has become crucially important to Bangladesh for achieving sustainable and rapid economic growth, alleviating pervasive poverty, enhancing productivity, improving services and ensuring efficient use of its scarce resources. It is encouraging that Private Sector is now continuously featuring prominently in the development strategy of Bangladesh. The Private Sector has been elevated to a dominant role as the engine to spearhead the growth process.

Distribution of ownership type by region

	Reign		
	Rural	Urban	Total
Sole propnetoship	93.77%	92.93%	93.57%
Partnership	5.89%	8.44%	6.20%
Cooperative	05%	07%	06%
Subsidy		08%	01%
Limited Nobility, Publicity trated		00%	00%
Limited Nobility not trated	06%	04%	06%
Joint Venture–Party toreign owned		00%	00%
Franshise		02	01%
Others	23%	44%	28%
Total	100.00%	100.00%	100.00%

Table 1 : Ownership figures segregated by region

Private Sector in Bangladesh has already demonstrated its capability of creating buoyancy in the economy. A new generation of entrepreneurs emerged who are well educated, hard working and eager to face challenges of a globalized competitive market. They have proven their worth in all Sectors where they have had an opportunity to work with freedom and where Government has played the role of facilitator rather than controller, competitor or strangulator. The booming industries in textile, readymade garments, knitwear, ceramics, cement, housing, construction, construction materials, frozen-food, poultry, fishing, light engineering, banking, insurance, micro financing, packaging, cereals and vegetables production, pharmaceuticals, inland shipping, distribution system, road transports, cellular telephone are all clear indicators of the latent capability of the Private Sector. Besides investment in traditional production and service sectors, private entrepreneurs are now ready to play their due role in power, gas, fixed telephone line, Mineral resources, inner-city transport system, education and health service, in fact in every sector of the economy to fulfill its historic role in the 21st Century World Order of nation building process.

Nevertheless there is apathy towards Private Sector among the polity. It is largely due to lack of proper appreciation for the potential and capability of the Private Sector. The Private Sector has struggled for survival during the long period of strangulation between 1970's and 1980's.

However in the recent past it has gradually gained momentum as successive Governments initiated and continued to implement various sectoral reforms and trade liberalization programs to strengthen the free market economy. As free market economic structure taking hold Government's involvement in production related and commercial activities is increasingly becoming limited. Government is being forced to take the position of regulator and/or facilitator.

The Bangladesh Private Sector has traveled a long way within shortest possible time. This is an achievement of historical proportion. The journey thus far has been careless and unsafe. The uncharted; rocky road has been all along full of pitfalls. Nevertheless, by the efforts of a determined group of young, hard working and educated entrepreneurs, a roadmap has been drawn and the Private Sector is now designated as the engine of production and economic growth.

3.1 Public Sector

Public Sector Enterprise often referred to as state sector, government owned undertakings/enterprises or state-owned enterprises. These are formed under the legal proceedings, wholly or partly owned and controlled by the government and produce marketable goods and services, have an explicit or extractable budget, and are supposed to finance their operating costs from their own resources. Public sector enterprises are different from other two sub-sets of public sector, viz. the government and the public sector institutions. In a public sector enterprise, the majority of equity shares is owned by the government directly or indirectly through governmental institutions and the government has decision making control either directly or through its appointed bodies. Public sector enterprise normally has three forms of organizational structure, the departmental undertakings, statutory corporations and joint stock companies.

Departmental undertakings are not formed by or with the consent of the legislative authority. These are set up by the executive actions of government bodies without any capital structure and budget, and charged with the duty of carrying out specially defined functions within the purview of the government bodies that set them up. These undertakings are not independent entities, although they enjoy a fairly high degree of monopoly. They are subject to budgetary, audit and other controls of the government and are managed by civil servants. They are financed by annual appropriation from the Treasury, which also receives their revenues. A departmental undertaking is best suited where the main purpose of the enterprise is to collect revenue for the state and to provide public utilities and services at fair prices in larger public interest. Some examples of departmental undertakings in Bangladesh are the Bangladesh Railway, Postal Department, Telephone and Telegraph Board, Power Development Board, Water Development Board, Customs Department, National Board of Revenue, ordnance factories, overseas communication services, and multipurpose river projects.

Statutory corporations are enterprises normally engaged in economic or manufacturing activities and are set up by act of legislature. These corporations are legal entities separate from the government and also the persons who conduct their affairs. Bangladesh bank, the government owned life and general insurance companies, Biman Bangladesh airlines are examples of statutory corporations. Shares of such corporations are in the name of the government and these are thus owned and controlled by the government. Statutory corporations enjoy extensive legal autonomy, and their rules, objectives, functions and duties are defined and specified in the act. Financing statutory corporations is not part of the Treasury and therefore, they can retain their revenues, and also spend as per the rules laid down by the statute. A statutory corporation set up by an Act cannot be regarded to fit in with the changed circumstances without legislative amendments.

Distribution of enterprises by sector (ISIC-1) and region						
	Region				Total	
	Rural		Urban			
Sector	Total number of MSMEs	% all MSMEs	Total number of MSMEs	% all MSMEs	Total number Of MSMEs	% all MSMEs
Agriculture	1,242.189	27%	71.617	5%	1,313.806	22%
Fishing	208.661	5%	19.897	1%	228.558	4%
Manufacturing	650.875	14%	206.413	15%	857.288	14%
Construction	64.375	1%	12.768	1%	77.143	1%
Whole & retail trade and repairs	1,696.588	38%	684.562	48%	2,381.150	40%
Hotels & restaurants	94.144	2%	183.793	13%	277.937	5%
Transport storage & communications	138.730	3%	27.903	2%	166.633	3%
Financial services			314	0%	314	0%
Real estate, rening & business activities	135.369	3%	43.935	3%	179.304	3%
Education			2510	0%	2510	0%
Health and social work	37.942	1%	15.496	1%	53.438	1%
Other service activities	95.250	2%	59.441	4%	154.591	3%
Unidentified	157.665	3%	83.748	6%	241.414	4%
Total	4,521.789	100%	1,412.397	100%	5,934.186	100%

Table 2 : Sectoral distribution of enterprise numbers

Joint Stock Companies are set up under the provision of the companies act. Establishment of companies is easier and is best suited where the nature of the work is substantially commercial. Most joint stock companies are not public sector enterprises in the strict sense. They are free from day-to-day control by the ministry, and are not subject to government's budgetary discipline. They are managed by the board of directors, and are subject to audit and other provisions of the Companies Act, the distinctive feature of a government controlled joint stock company is that the government. Except when it sets up a mixed enterprise, puts up the entire capital. Such a company is wholly autonomous and makes its own rules and decisions in respect of investment, finance, personnel and commercial audit. Bangladesh Shilpa Bank, Bangladesh Shilpa Rin Sangstha, Bangladesh Krishi Bank, and nationalized commercial banks (NCBs) are examples of joint stock forms of public sector enterprises in Bangladesh.

In Bangladesh public sector enterprises, conceived basically as an instrument of economic development are active in almost all areas of the economy and engage a sizeable volume of resources. The total investment in the industrial sector in 1980-81was estimated at Tk. 43.85 billion, three-fourths of which was in the public sector.

Evidences suggest that the public sector in British India was primarily concerned with the administration and regulation of education, health, broadcasting, posts and telegraph, telephone, roads and railways and defense. Public sector was not very active in areas like transportation and banking. No industry was reserved for public sector in Pakistan, but the role of public sector enterprises in other areas was supportive to the growth and development of the industrial capitalists. Originally, the government created enterprises in the public sector with the objective of transferring them later into private ownership when their profitability was ensured. The Pakistan government accepted the strategy of a laissez-faire economy and promoted the growth of private sector in its five-year plans and banked on private enterprises as the main vehicle of development keeping the public enterprises as their handmaiden.

The government of Pakistan used the state-owned enterprises mainly for the development of the economic condition of West Pakistan during the period between 1958 and 1970. The private sector received little government patronage in East Pakistan, where the public sector investment was, however, relatively larger than in West Pakistan. The public sector of the economy of Pakistan in the early post-partition years between 1947 and 1950 covered communication network, power, irrigation, defense and social service sectors like education and health.

Following the independence of Bangladesh in 1971, major changes were made in the ownership structure of the enterprises of industrial, commercial and financial sectors. Through nationalization, the government gained control over 86%of the total industrial assets in the country. The government took over all the units of the industries abandoned by West Pakistani and other non-Bengali owners and nationalized them. The government also nationalized all industrial units owned by Bangladeshi citizens in the three major sectors, namely cotton textile, jute and jute manufacturing and sugar manufacturing. In July 1972, the government imposed ceiling on private investment. The limit set for private investment in small industrial units was Tk 2.5 million, which was later enhanced to Tk3.5 million including the investment of profits, and simultaneously, the government preserved the right to nationalize any private enterprise whenever felt necessary. The strategy did not work well and within two-three years of nationalization, the state-owned enterprises started experiencing severe deterioration in productivity and profitability largely due to management inefficiency, corruption and an ideological conflict between personal ambitions of the policy makers, managers and employees and the national interest.

In 1974, in an effort to check the accentuating crisis, the government took initiative to revise the investment policy making greater room for private enterprises in the economy. In the revised investment policy of 1974,only 18sectors were reserved for the public sector and the remaining sectors were kept open for private investment and the ceiling for private investment was raised to Tk30 million. The new policy opened scope for foreign private investment in the country. Provisions were made to compensate the owners in the event of nationalization and the moratorium on nationalization was extended from ten to fifteen years.

In 1976, the government brought further changes in the national development strategy and encouraged state-sponsored private industrial development. The industrial policy was again revised and offered concession to both local and foreign private investors. Most reserved sectors for state investments were made open for joint participation of public and private enterprises. The government abolished the provision of moratorium on nationalization, formulated policies to promote private capital and encourage competition between public and private sector enterprises. The public enterprises were restructured through merging some public corporations and creating a few new enterprises. The new goals included revitalization of the private sector, increase in efficiency of the public sector management, organization of efficient import substitution, production of exportable, and restriction on monopoly in production, employment generation, and development of skills and technology. All these were included in the government's industrial policy declared in 1982. This policy clearly demonstrated the intention of the government towards privatization.

The Second Five-year Plan for 1980-85was revised and the allocation for private sector industry was enhanced from 25%in 1980-81to 59.4%in 1981-82.The few sectors kept reserved for state-owned enterprises were air transport, telecommunication, nuclear energy, power, and defense goods. All other sectors and kinds of industries were made open for private investment without any ceiling. The major capital intensive public sectors such as jute and cotton textile, sugar, paper, steel, shipbuilding, heavy electrical, minerals, and oil and gas were also made open for either public or private investment or for partnership of both. To facilitate private investment, the government disinvested more than 390 units of industrial, commercial and financial sectors. To help promote share market and to accumulate required funds, the government unloaded 49%of the shares of some public sector enterprises.

In 1983, in line with the privatization policy, the government returned two nationalized banks, Uttar and Pubali to their former Bangladeshi owners. Simultaneously, the establishment of private banks was allowed, as a consequence of which three private banks namely, the City Bank, the National Bank and the Islami Bank was commissioned in the same year. Later, both military and civil governments encouraged the private sector to flourish in all the areas of the country's economy except (a) arms, ammunitions and other defense equipment and machinery, (b) nuclear energy, (c) forest plantation and mechanized extraction within the bounds of reserved forests, (d) security printing (currency note) and minting, and (e) railways and air transportation (except air cargo and domestic air transportation).

In addition to the provisions made in the investment and industrial policies of different years, the government established the board of investment (BOI) in 1989 for accelerating private investment in the country. BOI is vested with necessary powers to take decisions for speedy implementation of new industrial projects and provide operational support services to the existing ones. Along with other entrusted activities, BOI is now responsible to accelerate the unloading of shares of the public sector enterprises in the light of the government's privatization policies. The industrial policy 1999 was a clear departure from all previous industrial policies in the sense that it showed the least interest of the government in public sector enterprises as a vehicle for economic development.

One of the classifications of public sector enterprises in Bangladesh is that as nonfinancial public enterprises and banking and other financial public enterprises. The number of non-financial public sector enterprise is 40, and according to Bangladesh Standard Industrial Classification (BSIC), these belong to 7 broad sectors. Public sector enterprises in the industrial sector are under 6 public corporations such as Bangladesh Textile Industries Corporation, Bangladesh Steel and Engineering Corporation, Bangladesh Sugar and Food Industries Corporation, Bangladesh Chemical Industries Corporation, Bangladesh Forest Industries Development Corporation and Bangladesh Jute Mills Corporation. Those in the power, gas and utilities sector are Bangladesh Oil, Gas and Mineral Resources Corporation, Bangladesh Power Development Board, Dhaka Electric Supply Authority (DESA), Dhaka Water and Sewerage Authority, and Chittagong Water and Sewerage Authority.

The transportation and communication sector comprises Bangladesh Shipping Corporation, Bangladesh Inland Water Transport Corporation, Bangladesh Biman Corporation, Bangladesh Road Transport Corporation, Chittagong Port Authority, Mongla Port Authority, Chittagong Dockyard Workers Management Board and Mongla Dockyard Workers Management Board. The commerce sector includes Bangladesh Petroleum Corporation, Bangladesh Jute Corporation, and Bangladesh Trading Corporation. The agricultural sector includes Bangladesh Fisheries Development Corporation, and Bangladesh Agricultural Development Corporation. The construction sector includes Chittagong Unnayan Kartippakha, Rajdhani Unnayan Kartippakha, Khulna Unnayan Kartippakha, and Rajshahi Unnayan Kartippakha. Entitiesin the service sector are Bangladesh Freedom Fighter Welfare Trust, Bangladesh Film Development Corporation, Bangladesh Tourism Corporation, Bangladesh Civil Aviation Authority, Bangladesh Small and Cottage industries Corporation, Bangladesh Inland Water Transport Authority, Rural Electrification Board, Bangladesh Export Processing Zone Authority, Bangladesh Handloom Board, Bangladesh Silk Foundation, Bangladesh Water Development Board and Bangladesh Tea Board.

The financial sector includes the 4 nationalized commercial banks viz, Sonali Bank, Janata Bank, Agrani Bank, and Rupali Bank, 6 development financial institutions namely, Bangladesh Shilpa Bank, Bangladesh Shilpa Rin Sangstha, Bangladesh Krishi Bank, Rajshahi Krishi Unnayan Bank, Bank of Small Industries and Commerce Bangladesh and Bangladesh House Building Finance Corporation. The Insurance Sector includes the Life Insurance Corporation and the General Insurance Corporation.

In 1998-99, the non-financial public sector enterprises as a whole suffered operating loss of Tk. 47.56 million while the financial, insurance and other departmental undertakings transferred Tk. 31.58 million from their profit to the treasury. Thirty eight public sector enterprises have been identified as defaulters in repayment of loan of the nationalized commercial banks and development financial institutions and the amount of default on 31 January 2000 stood at Tk. 209.01 million, which was 47% of their total borrowings.

Management of state-owned enterprises in the early days of Pakistan, bureaucratic control and political leadership remained in the hands of Non-Bangalis and the benefits of state policies encouraging the development of a national bourgeoisie were monopolized by immigrants and Punjabi groups. In the 1960s the unpopularity of free enterprise and a market control philosophy of development led to a policy of sponsored capitalism in East Pakistan.

All public sector industrial enterprises in Pakistan were organized as companies. From its very inception Pakistan was committed to a strong private sector, and public sector ventures were to be promotional and supportive in nature. Pakistan Industrial Development Corporation (PIDC) was organized as a statutory corporation, which aimed at developing industries and later divesting them when they would become profitable. The same principle was followed when in early 1970s Pakistan took over many industrial units and places them under holding corporations.

In the post liberation period, private sector industries faced a major setback due to mass exodus of non-bangali owners and managers. The government of Bangladesh (Taking over of Control and Management of Industrial and Commercial Concern) Order, 1972was promulgated to fill in the vacuum. All abandoned properties including 725 industrial units were brought under the government control and management. A management board was—created for each enterprise as provided in the 1972 ordinance.

Later, the government dissolved the management boards and appointed administrators to run these enterprises. On 26 March 1972, the government promulgated Bangladesh Industrial Enterprises (Nationalization) Order, 1972, under which it nationalized all abandoned enterprises of assets valuing at 1.5million and more as well as all industries of the jute, textile and sugar sectors.

Eleven industrial sector corporations were established in pursuance of this order, and all the nationalized units, as well as the enterprises and projects of Bangladesh Industrial Development Corporation (formerly EPIDC) were placed under the control of the respective sector corporations. These measures led to the increase in public ownership of industrial fixed assets from 34% to 92%. Some public corporations of the industrial sector were later merged through an amendment of presidential order 27 in 1976 to form Bangladesh Chemical Industries Corporation (BCIC) (merger of BFCPC, BPBC and BTC), Bangladesh Steel and Engineering Corporation (BSEC) (merger of BESC and BSMC) and Bangladesh Sugar and Food Industries Corporation (BSFIC) (merger of BFAIC and MSMC). These three public corporations along with Bangladesh Jute Mills Corporation (BJMC), Bangladesh Textile Mills Corporation (BTMC) and Bangladesh Forest Industries Development" Corporation (BFIDC) now constitute six manufacturing public corporations with 386 enterprises under them. Of these, 339 are abandoned units, many of which were left with huge liabilities, mostly in the form of mortgages on their assets.

The state-owned enterprises, as indicated in the guidelines of 1976, section 3(3) of the paragraph on 'Relationship between the Corporation/Autonomous bodies and Enterprises under them are;

1 To operate on commercial consideration having due regard to national interest, in the most efficient and economic manner within the policy framework and guidelines prescribed in the rules and regulations;
2 To continuously strive to improve its performance and attain better result; and
3 To earn additional revenue for the government. There is a provision in President's Order 27 for transfer of the government property, assets and liabilities to a corporation. The provision was later amended by the Ordinance No. VII of 1987, which enabled the government, among other things, to sell or transfer shares of the nationalized enterprises to corporations or to any other persons.

The general direction and administration of the officers and business of the corporations were vested in the respective board of directors, which could exercise all powers and do all ads arid things that might be exercised or done by the corporation. The board could delegate its power to the chairman (the chief executive) for the purpose of efficient operation of the corporation. The corporation was authorized to appoint officers, employees and consultants for efficient performance of the corporation on such terms and conditions as it might determine. Under the system, the board operated under the supervision and control of the government and was guided in the discharge of its functions by such general or special instructions as might from time to time be given to it by the government. An annual budget statement for the corporation was to be prepared by the corporation and to be duly approved by the government. The system, however, emphasized more on an appropriate management system than on accountability. The government adopted some corrective measures in the form of directives to the ministries and corporations from improving efficiency in performance by the corporations. These included-

1 Guidelines on the relationship between the government and the autonomous bodies/ corporations and enterprises under them;
2 Recommendations of the committee for reorganization of public statutory corporation;
3 The Public Corporation (Management co-ordination) Ordinance No. 48 of 5 July 1986;
4 Government Order regarding strict observance of the guidelines of 1976 and Resolutions of 1983; the Bangladesh Industrial Enterprise (Nationalization) (Amendment) Ordinance relating to disinvestment and transfer of government shares of nationalized enterprises to the public corporations; and
5 Notification (7 July 1988)of the Ministry of Industry relating to public issue of shares of the government enterprises and holding of 5% share of divested enterprises by the corporations under which they belong (eg, BCIC, BSEC, or BSFIC).

There are many shortcomings and constraints in the structure of control and management of the state-owned enterprises in Bangladesh. Generally speaking, there are four hierarchical levels in the control supervision structure. At the bottom is the enterprise level control involving internal management matters. At the next tier is the corporation control involving supervision, coordination among units, and delegated policy matters. At the third tier is the ministerial control of bureaucratic nature, involving evaluation, coordination amongst ministries and non-delegated policy matters. Finally, at the top is the political control exercised by the minister and the government involving major policy issues. There exists an implied accountability to the Jatiya Sangsad of elected representatives.

At the bottom is the individual enterprise, which is the ultimate object of control and supervision. The enterprises have no policy-making options as they operate within approved budgets, plans, policies and norms. Even when there is an enterprise management board, they limit themselves to routine operational matters and refer everything to the corporation. This resulted from the absence of mutual trust, lack of professionalism and the uncertain and changing state of informal authority and accountability. Above the enterprises are the statutory corporations. The basic function of these juridical bodies as defined in presidential order/ordinances/acts of parliament is to supervise, coordinate and direct the enterprises.

These bodies control and supervise the enterprises directly and contribute towards coordination between enterprises in matters of foreign procurement, personnel, marketing, disposal of surplus, or arrangement of finance. But the statutory corporations are heavily dependent on ministerial decisions. In most matters of policy and in certain matters of operations, they do not enjoy any autonomy. However, the statutory corporation can move on matters of policy on their own behalf and on behalf of the enterprises under them. The third tier is the ministry, which retains all control over the policy matters, which they define in consultations with other ministries, after scrutiny of papers prepared by the corporations. The fourth tier, the minister, who is a people's representative or a guardian of the public interest, often gets involved in small details of day to day administration rather than the policy issues. The minister, however, conducts review meetings, pilot's policy proposals in the cabinet and responds to parliamentary scrutiny on behalf of the enterprises and corporations.

To increase the management skill efficiency, production capacity and marketing network of the state-owned enterprise, an attempt was made in October 1980 to form a forum under the name and style of 'Consultative Committee of Chairman and Managing Directors of Autonomous and Semi-Autonomous Bodies'. It was renamed in 1982 as Consultative Committee of Public Enterprises (CONCOPE). The objective was, among others, to continuously interact with the government for coordinated decision making on administrative and financial management across the public sector corporations and the enterprises under them. CONCOPE regularly holds sittings with the relevant government functionaries including the prime minister and the president for quick decisions administration, financial and related other matters.

3.2 Managerial Approach

Any consideration of 'new' managerial approaches to industrial relations needs to be placed in the context of (a) the major relevant historical literature and (b) the historical development of management structures and strategies. The relevant literature is surveyed and from it a framework of analysis is distilled. It is suggested that labor management must be defined broadly to cover work relations, employment relations and industrial relations, rather than confined to union—management relations and collective bargaining. The paper goes on to discuss the development of management structure and concludes that only through a long-term view of management strategy in the context of the total operations of the firm can we understand 'new' managerial approaches to industrial relations.

A manager's style of managing has been a continuing cause of concern to his organization, his subordinates, and, at times, the manager himself. All have recognized that the manager's style is one of the major contributors to the performance and effectiveness of his unit. The desire to define how a manager should conduct himself while working with others has led to investigations into those variables that may affect levels of managerial performance. This article examines, in summary form, investigations by various management authorities on the subject of managerial styles. These investigations have been developed into three theories of managerial style: trait, behavior, and situation.

Throughout this article, the emphasis will be on the manager's style of leadership. Since there is no single, universally accepted definition of managerial style, the common practice has been to consider the manager's leadership style as his style of managing. Most of the authorities cited in this article use the terms "managerial style" and "leadership style" interchangeably. However, it must be remembered that leadership is only one mechanism that managers may use to motivate others toward organizational goals.

3.3 Trait Theory

From research studies conducted during the 1940sand 1950s, the trait theory of styles focuses on "what the leader is." Leadership is thought of as a function of a finite number of characteristics that differentiate the successful from the unsuccessful leader. Edwin Ghiselli cited the traits of initiative, self-assurance, individuality, supervisory ability, and intelligence. He qualified the trait of intelligence by suggesting that the level of an individual's intelligence was an accurate indication of the probability that he would achieve success as a manager-until a certain intellectual level is reached. Above this level, individuals with higher and higher scores were less and less likely to be successful managers. Other researchers brought in even more traits—personality, height, image, charisma, etc. until at one time ninety traits had been identified.

However, Ralph Stogdill found little or no positive relationship between a manager's traits and his success. Eugene Jennings concluded that fifty years of study had produced nothing to distinguish leaders from non-leaders.

Overall, the trait theory has made a contribution to the study of effective managerial styles, but not as much as was once thought. Seemingly, traits do not consistently distinguish the best leaders, the list of traits keeps growing, many traits are difficult to measure, and the trait theory ignores other important variables in the leadership situation.

3.4 Beha Vioral Theory

Dissatisfaction with the trait theory led to a new theory that focused on the behavior of a leader. The behavioral theory of managerial styles was prominent during the 1950s and 1960s. This theory focused on "what the leader does" by attempting to observe and describe the leader's style of behavior. This theory comprises several approaches: a continuum of styles, independent styles, and two-dimensional models of styles.

3.4.1 Continuum of Style

Robert Tannenbaum and Warren Schmidt developed a continuum of leadership behavior to describe a range of behavioral patterns available to a manager. They related the leader's actions to the degree of authority used by him and the amount of freedom available to his subordinates. The leader's actions described on the left characterize the manager who maintains a high degree of control, while those on the right describe a manager who delegates authority. Tannenbaum and Schmidt felt that a leader should not choose one style and adhere to it strictly but should be flexible and adapt his style to the situation.

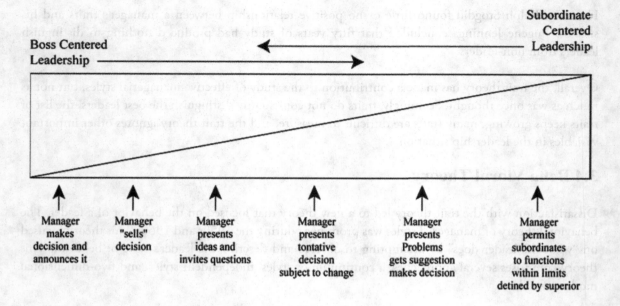

Boss Centered Leadership ← → Subordinate Centered Leadership

| Manager makes decision and announces it | Manager "sells" decision | Manager presents ideas and invites questions | Manager presents tentative decision subject to change | Manager presents Problems gets suggestion makes decision | Manager permits subordinates to functions within limits detined by superior |

3.4.2 Independent Styles

Although flexibility in styles had been stressed, a number of independent leadership styles were analyzed, including the autocratic, the benevolent-autocratic, and the supportive.

Autocratic behavior is usually identified with a leader who commands and has many sanctions at his disposal. He is considered almost totally job-oriented, with little or no concern for the people in his organization. This leader is the one who has all the answers, and people serve only to carry out his instructions. Many times he has been thought of as being dogmatic and arbitrary in his actions.

However, M. E. Shaw discovered that, in problem-solving situations, autocratically supervised persons used less time and made fewer errors than did democratically supervised subjects.

Advanced as a style of behavior by Robert McMurry, the benevolent-autocratic leader is described as powerful and prestigious but one who can be communicated with and is interested in his subordinates' problems. He structures the activities of his subordinates, makes policy decisions affecting them, and enforces discipline. He may encourage participation in planning, but in executing he is the "chief." However, James Gibson, John Ivancevich, and James Donnelly, Jr. say even this style has been weakened by recent changes in attitudes within our society. This may particularly be true for younger generations as they express desires to shift away from any authoritative or paternalistic environment.

The supportive leader is one who is considered as being somewhat democratic and participative in style. He is one who supervises his employees generally, not closely. This type of leader specifies objectives and communicates them but then allows subordinates considerable freedom in accomplishing the tasks. Rensis Likert concluded that employee-centered supervisors tend to have higher producing groups than job-centered supervisors. Stogdill, Coons, Argyle, Blau, Scott, Jennings, and Gibb each had similar findings from their research. However, others do not agree. Spector and Suttle found no significant difference in output between an autocratic and a democratic leadership style. M. Patchen said that close supervision does not necessarily reduce a subordinate's freedom; the subordinate may perceive close supervision as interest in his welfare.

Varying ideas within and between these three independent approaches to leader behavior were never reconciled. However, independent approaches such as these did help to provide the groundwork for the development of subsequent two-dimensional behavioral models.

3.4.3 Two-Dimensional Styles

By developing models to display dual dimensions of a leader's style, researchers were able to consolidate many of the independent thrusts of studies. From group dynamics, Bales founded the Great Man approach: the individual who is both the best idea man and the best-liked member is the best leader. Roger M. Stogdill, Alvin E. Coons, and others at Ohio State University developed a leadership model based on the dimensions of "consideration" and "initiating structure." A leader with a high degree of "consideration" was one who developed a work atmosphere of mutual trust, respect for subordinates' ideas, and consideration of their feelings. A leader with a high degree of "initiating structure" was one who established unit goals, structured his role and those of his subordinates, planned and scheduled work activities, and communicated pertinent information. The most effective manager, it was concluded, was one whose behavior was high in both "consideration" and "initiating structure," with the next-best manager being the one who was high in "consideration" and low in "initiating structure."

Another approach to a two-dimensional theory, the managerial grid, was developed by Robert R. Blake and Jane S. Mouton. Their model was based on the manager's assumptions regarding his "concern for people," the satisfying of their needs, and his "concern for production," the reaching of production objectives. To Blake and Mouton, the best manager would be one who couples the two concerns to provide the highest level of contribution and accomplishment. Their model and its accompanying surveys have possibly been the most widely used instruments to identify managerial styles. However, there is an important caveat associated with this model: it may identify a manager's assumptions and concerns without identifying his actual leadership behavior. The model has had its most informative value when surveys are completed not only by the manager himself but also by his subordinates and superiors concerning him. Blake and Mouton subsequently expanded this model into a three dimensional grid.

Overall, the behavioral theory has made a valuable contribution to the study of managerial styles. It has provided a classification of a number of styles. Much of the research generally supports the idea that styles can be characterized by a combination of two leadership behaviors, one oriented toward the task (initiating structure, concern for production) and one oriented toward interpersonal relations (consideration, concern for people). However, many conflicting opinions within this theory still remain. To some, the' interpersonal-oriented leader is considered more effective; to others, the task-oriented leader; and to still others the leader who is high in both dimensions is the best. Thus there developed a need for research to integrate the various ideas and incorporate the impact of varying situations on leadership styles and their effectiveness.

3.5 Situational Theory

Deficiencies in past theories have provided the stimulus for the most recent of the theories, the situational view of leadership. Leadership is explained in the interaction between the leader and variables in his work situation-his personality, his followers, the task, and the organizational environment. Paul Hersey and Kenneth Blanchard see the manager's leadership process as a function of the leader, the followers, and the situation. D. Katz and R. L. Kahn feel that leadership acts are all different for different organizations, managerial levels, and situations. At high management levels, interpersonal skills are more important, while at lower levels, task approaches are more necessary.

Fred Fiedler's Contingency Theory of Leadership Effectiveness is the principal situational theory. With more than fourteen years of research as a basis, Fiedler concluded that, to be effective, a leader must match his style, whether task—or relationship-oriented, with the demands of the situation. The leader must assess the situation for its degree of favorableness (or unfavorableness) to his style of influence. This favorableness (or unfavorableness) would depend on

1   The level of the leader-member relations,
2   The amount of power inherent in the leader's position, and
3   The degree of structure in the task.

If there were high degrees of value in each of these three variables, the situation would be highly favorable to a leader's influence; if one or two variables are high in degree and the remaining variable(s) low, the situation would be moderately favorable; if low values in the variables, the situation would be highly unfavorable to influence. If, for example, the leader-member relations are good, the leader has the power to fire, promote, or demote, and the task is spelled out step by step, the situation would be highly favorable to the leader and his influence. On the other hand, if the leader member relations are poor, the leader has little inherent power in the position, and the task is nebulous and undefined, the situation would be highly unfavorable to the leader's influence. To Fiedler, it is easier to be the well-esteemed foreman of a construction crew working from a blueprint than it is to be the disliked chairman of a volunteer committee preparing a new policy.

Fiedler concludes that a task-oriented style is more effective in situations in which the leader has very much or very little influence, and a relationship-oriented leader is more effective in situations only moderately favorable to his influence. In Fiedler's words," the appropriateness of the leadership style for maximizing group performance is contingent upon the favorableness of the group-task situations." Although he feels the leader should diagnose the variables in his situation, Fiedler suggests that it may be easier and more effective for the organization to engineer the job to fit the manager than to change a manager's leadership style to fit the job. In other words, the organization should match up a particular manager and his style to the demands of the situation or alter the variables within the situation, i.e., the power that goes with the leadership position, so that the situation becomes more conducive to the manager's style of influence.

Overall, the situational approach to leadership styles has been a valuable contribution. More realistic than previous theories, it shows that there is no "one best" style for all situations. Launching from the early efforts in this theory, greater research efforts are presently being conducted. Fiedler and others suggest that further research is needed to encompass more variables that maybe within the managerial situation.

Attempting to define and determine a proper managerial style is an extremely complex task for any manager. This article has shown that such a task may be just as perplexing for authorities in the field of management. Summarizing some of their ideas, this author has presented the trait, behavioral, and situational theories of leadership styles. Although some leadership traits may still be valid, the trait theory seems to have less importance than in the past. The behavioral theory has formed the basis for many managerial practices of today, but it still has some problems in providing an integrated style of leadership. The situational theory shows promise of integrating a theory of styles, but further clarification is needed. Overall, the evidence is becoming clearer that there is no single, all-purpose style of behavior that is effective in all managerial situations. Someday, experience and research may provide us with "the one best way." Until then, each manager must remain open minded, informed, and adaptable.

"A certain amount of stress is necessary to motivate people".

Management often tries to justify stress in those terms and by doing so they are confusing the issue by mixing terminology. Many things, at home end at work can put someone under pressure—and yes, a certain amount of pressure can be seen as motivational. However, pressures become 'stress', when they reach the level at which people feel they can no longer cope with those pressures. People's ability to deal with pressure and the point at which it becomes harmful to health varies between individuals. For many years, workplace stress was not recognized. Once recognized, it was for a long time badly misunderstood and to suffer or have suffered from it carried an undeserved stigma that was hard to shake off.

However, more recently, stress has slowly been accepted as a mainstream cause of work related ill health. Large amounts of research have emerged to show that there is a clear link between poor work organization and subsequent ill health. Health and Safety Executive (HSE) commissioned research has indicated that:

1 About half a million people in the UK experience work-related stress at a level they believe is making them ill;
2 Up to 5 million people in the UK feel 'very' or extremely' stressed by their work; and
3 Work-related stress costs society about £3.7 billion every year (1995/1996).

3.6 The Role of Management in Enterprises

Management in simple terms means the act of getting people together to accomplish desired goals. Management comprises planning, organizing, resourcing, leading or directing, and controlling an organization (a group of one or more people or entities) or effort for the purpose of accomplishing a goal. Resourcing encompasses the deployment and manipulation of human resources, financial resources, technological resources, and natural resources. Management can also refer to the person or people who perform the act(s) of management.

.Managerial Work: Basic Functions of Management

Management operates through various functions, often classified as planning, organizing, leading/motivating and controlling.

1 **Planning:** deciding what needs to happen in the future (today, next week, next month, next year, over the next 5 years, etc.) and generating plans for action.
2 **Organizing:** making optimum use of the resources required to enable the successful carrying out of plans.
3 **Leading/Motivating:** exhibiting skills in these areas for getting others to play an effective part in achieving plans.
4 **Controlling:** monitoring: checking progress against plans, which may need modification based on feedback.

3.8 Management Structures

One habit of thought regards management as equivalent to "business administration" and thus excludes management in places outside commerce, as for example in charities and in the public sector. More realistically, however, every organization must manage its work, people, processes, technology, etc. in order to maximize its effectiveness.

Although, the traditional view of management is viewed as such, other theorists thinks otherwise. For example, Mintzberg, an internationally renowned academic and author on business and management, classifies managerial behavior into three sets of roles, common to all levels of management. These are:

1   Interpersonal
2   Informational
3   Decisional

In their interpersonal roles, managers act as figureheads, leaders and liaison persons. In informational roles managers act as monitors, disseminators and spokespersons; and in their decisional roles, they act as entrepreneurs, disturbance handlers, resource allocators and negotiators. The importance of Mintzberg's work is that it highlights the uncertainty within which most managers operate. Managers are not normally reflective thinkers, they are "doers", coping with unexpected events and unforeseen circumstances.

Some research also suggests that managers are responsive rather than an analytical activity. Other documental features of managerial work includes verbal nature, managers are talkers and listeners. One study shows that managers have to spend an overwhelming 80% of their time talking. Unless the message is conveyed effectively, no one will be clear of their roles and responsibilities in the organizations. Elements of uncertainty also feature in the above criteria.

The increasing number of managers worldwide is getting a lot of prominence. These professional managers are again employees themselves who have the added bonus to manage other employees and resources in the organizations. They are not a homogeneous group either. It is their task to organize the use of resources including the work of others towards the objective of an enterprise. In short, managers are accountable to those owning the organization's capital assets for its economic viability and success.

3.9 Management, Ownership and Control

In for-profit work, management has as its primary function the satisfaction of a range of stakeholders. This typically involves making a profit (for the shareholders), creating valued products at a reasonable cost (for customers), and providing rewarding employment opportunities (for employees). In nonprofit management, add the importance of keeping the faith of donors. In most models of management/ governance, shareholders vote for the board of directors, and the board then hires senior management. Some organizations have experimented with other methods (such as employee-voting models) of selecting or reviewing managers; but this occurs only very rarely.

For the private sector, control function of ownership is shifting from owners to the top management. The logic behind this "managerialists" approach is that if the largest shareholder or group of shareholders in large companies does not have a sufficient proportion of votes in company affairs, then that particular company is managerially controlled. And since the modern view of management approaches private property differently than its old predecessors, conflict between workers and managers have gone down by a significant extent. However, contrary to this view, other proponents of management differs by believing that the authority to make distributional decisions within industrial, commercial and other enterprises over rides the property factor.

Non-managerialists tend to believe that the lines between ownership and control have not been blurred and are having a negative impact upon them. Managers in general have been favoring the interest of owners than over other groups who have claims on the enterprises' resources. In addition, if management is collectively responsible for business efficiency, then by all means, it cannot be neutral in its contractual relationships with employees either.

In the public sector of countries constituted as representative democracies, voters elect politicians to public office. Such politicians hire many managers and administrators, and in some countries like the United States, political appointees lose their jobs on the election of a new president/governor/mayor. Some 2500 people serve at the pleasure of the United States Chief Executive, including all of the top US government executives.

In the 'old' public sector, the functions of managing, owning and controlling enterprises were generally more clearly delineated than in the private sector. Those managing public enterprises and establishments were appointed to run them in ways likely to achieve the objectives and purposes for which they were created. Ownership rested with the appropriate public authorities, with ultimate control vested in government or other decision taking bodies. This gave rise to policy discrepancies among the political controllers such as secretaries of state, local controllers, or governing bodies and professional managers such as chief executives, heads of institutions etc. But in general, these conflicts are avoided.

Public, private, and voluntary sectors place different demands on managers, but all must retain the faith of those who select them (if they wish to retain their jobs), retain the faith of those people that fund the organization, and retain the faith of those who work for the organization. If they fail to convince employees of the advantages of staying rather than leaving, they may tip the organization into a downward spiral of hiring, training, firing, and recruiting. Management also has the task of innovating and of improving the functioning of organizations.

4.0 Managerial Levels and Hierarchy

Mary Parker Follett (1868-1933), who wrote on the topic in the early twentieth century, defined management as "the art of getting things done through people". One can also think of management functionally, as the action of measuring a quantity on a regular basis and of adjusting some initial plan; or as the actions taken to reach one's intended goal.

Some people, however, find this definition, while useful, far too narrow. The phrase "management is what managers do" occurs widely, suggesting the difficulty of defining management, the shifting nature of definitions, and the connection of managerial practices with the existence of a managerial cadre or class.

Management is a technical function, a political activity and a social cadre. In undertaking its political and technical functions, management is stratified vertically by power and status and horizontally by task and specialism. Vertical jobs are distinguished based on the amount of discretion to decide, whereby management is operating within its own structure and hierarchy of power and authority. Their roles could best be categorized into three main levels of power and influence: corporate, administrative and executive or policy making, programming and interpretive. These terms are more simply used as senior management, middle management and supervisory management respectively. The senior management's main task is to develop and review corporate objectives. Middle management implements the objectives and manages subordinate managers. The last management body takes care of the non-managerial employees. The middle phase is waning out in some industries with the introduction of information technologies into organizations and partly to more decentralized and devolved systems of management.

The management of a large organization may have three levels:

1   Senior management (or "top management" or "upper management")
2   Middle management
3   Low-level management, such as supervisors or team-leaders

Top-level management

1   Require an extensive knowledge of management roles and skills.
2   They have to be very aware of external factors such as markets.
3   Their decisions are generally of a long-term nature.
4   Their decision are made using analytic, directive, conceptual and/or behavioral/participative processes
5   They are responsible for strategic decisions.
6   They have to chalk out the plan and see that plan may be effective in the future.
7   They are executive in nature.

Middle management

1   Mid-level managers have a specialized understanding of certain managerial tasks.
2   They are responsible for carrying out the decisions made by top-level management.

Lower management

1 This level of management ensures that the decisions and plans taken by the other two are carried out.
2 Lower-level managers' decisions are generally short-term ones

Horizontal managerial jobs are differentiated according to their operational, functional or departmental responsibilities, with individual managers heading specific subunits. The major groupings are: production, finance, marketing, research and development, administration and personnel.

4.1 Formation of the Business Policy

1 The mission of the business is its most obvious purpose
2 The vision of the business reflects its aspirations and specifies its intended direction or future destination.
3 The objectives of the business refer to the ends or activity at which a certain task is aimed.
4 The business's policy is a guide that stipulates rules, regulations and objectives, and may be used in the managers' decision-making. It must be flexible and easily interpreted and understood by all employees.
5 The business's strategy refers to the coordinated plan of action that it is going to take, as well as the resources that it will use, to realize its vision and long-term objectives. It is a guideline to managers, stipulating how they ought to allocate and utilize the factors of production to the business's advantage. Initially, it could help the managers decide on what type of business they want to form.

4.1.1 How to Implement Policies and Strategies

1 All policies and strategies must be discussed with all managerial personnel and staff.
2 Managers must understand where and how they can implement their policies and strategies.
3 A plan of action must be devised for each department.
4 Policies and strategies must be reviewed regularly.
5 Contingency plans must be devised in case the environment changes.
6 Assessments of progress ought to be carried out regularly by top-level managers.
7 A good environment is required within the business.

4.1.2 The Development of Policies and Strategies

1 The missions, objectives, strengths and weaknesses of each department must be analyzed to determine their roles in achieving the business's mission.
2 The forecasting method develops a reliable picture of the business's future environment.

3   A planning unit must be created to ensure that all' plans are consistent and that policies and strategies are aimed at achieving the same mission and objectives.

4   Contingency plans must be developed, just in case.

5   All policies must be discussed with all managerial personnel and staff that is required in the execution of any departmental policy.

4.1.3 Where policies and Strategies Fit into the planning process

1   They give mid—and lower-level managers a good idea of the future plans for each department.

2   A framework is created whereby plans and decisions are made.

3   Mid—and lower-level management may add their own plans to the business's strategic ones.

4.2 The Personnel Function

Personnel function mainly deals with the relationship between the management and employees within an enterprise. Non-managerial employees' welfare issues are looked into to bring out the best from them so that they could contribute successfully in the organization's success. The key here is to balance the organizational objectives with the workgroup aspirations.

Personnel management is the responsibility of both the line managers and personnel specialists. The problem arises as to the extent of the responsibility to be borne by each here. Degrees of uncertainty exists. The personnel management also incorporates to varying degrees, both a management-centered control role and an employee centered welfare role. The management control role is rooted in managerial concern for efficiency and effectiveness at work and puts managing people firmly into the mainstream of managerial activity. The welfare role in contrast is concerned with the well-being of individual employees or workgroups and how they are treated by the organizations employing them. Clearly, conflicts of accountabilities can emerge within the personnel function between personnel's concern with efficiency and organizational effectiveness on the one side, and it aims to seek justice, fair terms and satisfying work conditions for employees on the other. One assumes pluralistic work enterprises, the other unitary features.

There are even degrees of role specialization within the specialist personnel function; personnel generalists and personnel subordinates. The former is more likely to be involved in policy determination and industrial relations. The latter's duty incorporates: recruitment, selection, payment administration, record keeping etc.

Since 80s, a new concept came across the organizations, commonly known as Human Resource Management or HRM. Although, it is not a model of personnel function, it is being widely accepted all over with the approach to managing people, aimed at integrating employees and corporate objectives within organizations.

Human resource management (HRM) is the strategic and coherent approach to the management of an organization's most valued assets—the people working there who individually and collectively contribute to the achievement of the objectives of the business. The theoretical discipline is based primarily on the assumption that employees are individuals with varying goals and needs, and as such should not be thought of as basic business resources, such as trucks and filing cabinets. The field takes a positive view of workers, assuming that virtually all wish to contribute to the enterprise productively, and that the main obstacles to their endeavors are lack of knowledge, insufficient training, and failures of process.

Practitioners in the field see HRM as a more innovative view of workplace management than the traditional approach. Its techniques force the managers of an enterprise to express their goals with specificity so that they can be understood and undertaken by the workforce and to provide the resources needed for them to successfully accomplish their assignments. As such, HRM techniques, when properly practiced, are expressive of the goals and operating practices of the enterprise overall. HRM is also seen by many to have a key role in risk reduction within organizations.

4.3 Management into the 21st Century

As the general recognition of managers as a class solidified during the 20th century and gave perceived practitioners of the art/science of management a certain amount of prestige, so the way opened for popularized systems of management ideas to peddle their wares. Towards the end of the 20th century, business management came to consist of six separate branches, namely:

1 Human resource management
2 Operations management or production management
3 Strategic management
4 Marketing management
5 Financial management
6 Information technology management responsible for management information systems

In the 21st century observers, find it increasingly difficult to subdivide management into functional categories in this way. More and more processes simultaneously involve several categories. Instead, one tends to think in terms of the various processes, tasks, and objects subject to management.

Branches of management theory also exist relating to nonprofits and to government: such as public administration, public management, and educational management. Further, management programs related to civil-society organizations have also spawned programs in nonprofit management and social entrepreneurship.

Note that many of the assumptions made by management have come under attack from business ethics viewpoints, critical management studies, and anti-corporate activism.

As one consequence, workplace democracy has become both more common, and more advocated, in some places distributing all management functions among the workers, each of whom takes on a portion of the work. However, these models predate any current political issue, and may occur more naturally than does a command hierarchy. All management to some degree embraces democratic principles in that in the long term workers must give majority support to management; otherwise, they leave to find other work, or go on strike. Hence management has started to become less based on the conceptualization of classical military command-and-control, and more about facilitation and support of collaborative activity, utilizing principles such as those of human interaction management to deal with the complexities of human interaction. Indeed, the concept of Ubiquitous command-and-control posits such a transformation for 21st century military management.

4.4 The Model in Bangladesh Context

If one look at the overall theories and apply the model in the perspective of Bangladesh, one can indeed find many similarities. First, the traditional view of management having to do certain functions such as planning, controlling, leading, motivating is seen over all the industries. Ranging from the local shops to the multinationals, managers basic task comprises of this nature.

It would be a fair statement to say that managers of Bangladesh are more often reactive rather than proactive. Their method to deal with a certain problem is addressed only after the issue is arisen. Generally, the managers are intimidated by what their actions will result in. The element of uncertainty and risk factor hinders them from taking a more proactive role to deal with day-to-day issues. For example, if Grameen Phone (GP) comes up with a management strategy today, Banglalink will immediately come up with another to stay one step ahead of GP and vice versa. The confidence has been left wanting. But having said that, in the era of 2151 century, where increasingly more companies are taking a holistic selling and management approach have started to break the traditional stereotypical notions and incorporating proactive management approaches in its stride.

As far as ownership of control is concerned, very few industries are controlled in the hands of management. Conventionally there are stakeholders for the private sector in particular who are mostly in control of ownership of the corporations. Good examples include garments and pharmaceuticals industries. However, to a large extent, of the overall planning a shaping of these industries are left at the hands of managers. Industries are willing to pay high salaries and benefits to obtain managers with exceptional qualities who are kept in charge of running the enterprises. These managers have a very important role to play whereby they not only have to control the human resources, but also look into other important decision-making aspects set by the owners. For the Garments industry, it is particularly important to take special notice of the workers who can be very sensitive to wage changes. Massive riot and conflicts could be sparked within seconds and that may eventually result in the closure of the enterprises for a prolonged period of time, hampering the business. Such scenarios are common in the context of Bangladesh. Thus, the managers have to be very proactive and emotionally deal with the employee's sensitivities.

In case of public sector, by and large management is apathetic to the ongoing business activities. Because of such indifferent attitudes, many good industries had to borne the brunt like the Adamjee Jute Mill, the biggest in south Asia. Apart from that, jute sector and some service sectors like airlines, railways etc, which are wholly under the public administration, face the adverse impacts.

Management in most of the organizations follows a top-down approach, and is comprised of a top level, mid level and low level process. With an enhancement in performance, suitable and deserving candidates rise upwards. These practices are more common in private industries like banks, telecoms, multinationals etc. Some people can attain the highest level in very short space of time if they can prove their worth by performance. One such example could be found in the like of one HR manager in BAT, Mr. Imtiaz, who has risen to a very high level within one decade. So at the age of 38 only, he is the head of HR department.

The situation is a total far cry in the case of public sectors. Upward promotions have to be dependent upon lobbying and political affiliations. This is one of the main reasons why management is not doing an up to the mark job in the public sector.

The concept of Human Resource Management is coming up in leaps and bounds. Previously not much thought was given to this sector, but the trend is now changing. There is now an increase in the demand for personnel function among the organizations. Many organizations are paying huge sums of money to bring professional HR managers from abroad. HR managers are playing a very decisive role. Employees' concerns are properly addressed and thus a more employee friendly atmosphere can be observed in many organizations today. Although the line managers are eventually responsible for calling the shots, staff managers i.e. HR department does a lot to shape an organizational fit by putting the right persons for the right job at the right time.

Finally, most enterprises in Bangladesh follow a system of horizontal managerial structure, having different managers for different functions. Production managers and marketing managers, or finance managers or human resource managers are not the same. All of them are different and is assigned with different roles. However, they do meet and upon consensus with the CEO stake the final decision as to what changes or policies they might want to implement. But overall, management work is separated from function to function. However, for small corporations or SMEs, sometimes one person can be expected to carry out multiple managerial functions.

In conclusion, in the age of globalization, Bangladesh is following the footsteps of the world is matching up with it. Focus is shifted towards a collaborative approach among the employers and employees. This enhances the overall management structure of the industries, in effect bringing positives for the economy as a whole.

ENDNOTES

References

1   Bangladesh statistical yearbook-2006

2   http://www.asbestos.com/ occupations/industrial-workers.php

3   http://www.nationsencyclopedia.com/economies/Asia-and-the-Pacific/Bangladesh-WORKING CONDITIONS.html

4   Industrial policy of Bangladesh- 2005

5   Annexure 2

6   The Daily Star Web Edition: Vol. 4, Num 22, Thu. June 19, 2003

7   The Daily Star Web Edition: Vol. 4, Num 22, Thu. June 19, 2003

8   BEPZA official website

9   New jobs, investments on wane in EPZs, Retrieved on Saturday April 25, 2009 from The financial Express web edition,
     Dhaka

10   Bangladesh Labor Force Survey 2005-06

11   Annexure 3

12   Bangladesh Labor Force Survey-2005-06, Retrieved from http://www.bbs.gov.bd/dataindex/labor_%20force05-06.pdf
     (Uploaded on 24 September, 07)

13   Bangladesh Labor Force Survey 2005-2006

14   Bangladesh Labor Force Survey 2005-2006

15   Export Promotion Bureau-2005

16   BangladeshNews.com.bd, Retrieved on October6, 2006

17   Institutional Aspects of Ship Breaking Industry in Bangladesh, Working Paper WP044, October 2005

18   Study report on Ship breaking industry of Bangladesh : Status of the Occupational Health and Safety and Worker's Rights at
     Shitakunda. September, 2002

19   Study report on Ship breaking industry of Bangladesh: Status of the Occupational Health and Safety and Worker's Rights at
     Shitakunda. September, 2002

20   Study report on Ship breaking industry of Bangladesh: Status of the Occupational Health and Safety and Worker's Rights at
     Shitakunda. September, 2002

21   Study report on Ship breaking industry of Bangladesh: Status of the Occupational Health and Safety and Worker's Rights at
     Shitakunda. September, 2002

22   Study report on Ship breaking industry of Bangladesh: Status of the Occupational Health and Safety and Worker's Rights at Shitakunda. September, 2002

23   Global Bangladesh: Business News and Lifestyle Magazine, Retrieved on May 25, 2009 from http://www.gbangladesh.com/shipbuilding.html

24   Global Bangladesh: Business News and Lifestyle Magazine, Retrieved on May 25, 2009 from http://www.gbangladesh.com/shipbuilding.html

25   5 pence=10 US cents. 100 US cents =1 Dollar. 1 Dollar= BDT 69 as of July 3, 2009

26   1 Bangladesh Taka(s) = 0.0088 British Pound

27   Decent work means productive work under conditions of freedom equity, security and dignity in which rights are protected and adequate remuneration and social coverage are provided

28   http://banglapedia.search.com.bd/HT/T_0100.htm

29   http://rasheeka.wordpress.com/

30   Khan 1991, BPMI 1997

31   Bangladesh Labor Force Survey-2005-06, Retrieved from http://www.bbs.gov.bd/dataindex/labor_%20force05-06.pdf (Uploaded on 24 September, 07)

32   Bangladesh Labor Force Survey-2005-06, Retrieved from http://www.bbs.gov.bd/dataindex/labor_%20force05-06.pdf (Uploaded on 24 September, 07)

33   Bangladesh Labor Force Survey-2005-06, Retrieved from http://www.bbs.gov.bd/dataindex/labor_%20force05-06.pdf (Uploaded on 24 September, 07)

34   Bangladesh Labor Force Survey-2005-06, Retrieved from http://www.bbs.gov.bd/dataindex/labor_%20force05-06.pdf (Uploaded on 24 September, 07)

35   Bangladesh Labor Force Survey-2005-06, Retrieved from http://www.bbs.gov.bd/dataindex/labor_%20force05-06.pdf (Uploaded on 24 September, 07)

36   Paul-Majumder 2003a: Pratima Paul-Majumder "Health Status of the Garment workers in Bangladesh: Findings from a Survey of employers and Employees," Project report Series 1, BIDS, Dhaka

37   18 year old garment worker, an SSC graduate, who was harassed by supervisor and left her job after one week

38   Based on Interview of workers

39   A factitious name was used for the worker included in the case study to safeguard her identity

40   Based on Interview of workers

41   A factitious name was used for the worker included in the case study to safeguard her identity

42   Annexure 4 : Occupational Wage survey-2007

43   Momen, M.A and Hye, S.A; A. Study Of The Impact O Income-Generating Activities Among Poor Rural Women In Bangladesh on their Income and Employment, ILO/NORAD, 1982 -83

44   Human Migration Guide

45   Siddiqui, Tasneem 1998 'Growth and Sustainability of the NGO Sector in Bangladesh', biiss journal, Vol. 19 No. 3, pp 297-328

46   Siddiqui Tasneem, Chowdhury R. Abrar, September 2003, Migrant Worker Remittances and Micro Finance in Bangladesh, (Refugee and Migratory Movements Research Unit)

47   Paper on "Training workshop for Asia-Pacific Employers Organization in sound Labor Relations Practices", 1992, 2-6 March, Singapore, International Labor Organization (ILO), page 1

48 Paper on "Training workshop for Asia-Pacific Employers Organization in sound Labor Relations Practices", 1992, 2-6 March, Singapore, International Labor Organization (ILO), page 1

49 Official Website of Bangladesh Institute of Labor Studies (BILS).

50 Khan, T.I.M.N.1996, Labor Administration: profile on Bangladesh, International Labor Organization (ILO), p. 25.

51 Ibid. p. 26

52 Ibid. p. 27-30.

53 Khan, T.I.M.N.1996, Labor Administration: profile on Bangladesh, International Labor Organization (ILO), p. 33-39.

54 Khan, T.I.M.N.1996, Labor Administration: profile on Bangladesh, International Labor Organization (ILO), p. 49

55 Ibid p. 50.

56 Khan, T.I.M.N.1996, Labor Administration: profile on Bangladesh, International Labor Organization (ILO), p. 53-56.

57 Khan, T.I.M.N.1996, Labor Administration: profile on Bangladesh, International Labor Organization (ILO), p. 54

58 Khan, T.I.M.N.1996, Labor Administration: profile on Bangladesh, International Labor Organization (ILO), p. 56-58

59 Khan, T.I.M.N.1996, *Labor Administration: profile on Bangladesh,* International Labor Organization (ILO), p. 61

60 Farnham, D. and Pimlott, J., *Understanding Industrial Relations,* London, 5th edition. P. 75

61 Ozaki, M. (1999), *"The role of social partners and the state",* ILO (International Labor Organization), p. 90.

62 *Ibid p. 91.*

63 Industrial Relations and Collective Bargaining in South Asia, International Labor Organization, By- V.C.S Ratnam,. & D.P.A., Naidu, p. 72.

64 Ozaki, M. (1999), *"The role of social partners and the state",* ILO (International Labor Organization), p. 94

65 Khan, T.I.M.N.1996, *Labor Administration: profile on Bangladesh,* International Labor Organization (ILO), p. 64

66 According to available latest official statistics, the poverty has reduced at a slower rate of 0. 0.52 per cent on average per year during 1999-2004 while national output of Bangladesh expanded at an average rate of 5 per cent, with total number of unemployed population witnessing nearly a four-fold increase from 0.6 million in 1989 to 2.2 million in 1999-2000.

67 The neo-liberal paradigm is based on the premise of lesser intervention

68 http://wiki.answers.com/Q/Causes_of_poor_Industrial_Relations_in_Bangladesh

69 Global Bangladesh :: Business News and Lifestyle Magazine, Retrieved on April 11, 2009 from http://www.gbangladesh.com/manufacturing.html

70 Khan, A. A., Labour and Industrial Law

71 Khan, A. A., History of Trade Union

72 Industrial Relations Ordinance 1969, Section 3

73 Privatization Commission Bangladesh Website

74 Trade Union And Labour Rights: Perspective Bangladesh, *Sahal Uddin, Mohammad Abdul Hannan, Nazrul Islam Mondal*

75 The Bangladesh journal of Dhaka, January 7, 2008

76 www.vakilno1.com/saarclaw/bangladesh/arbitrationlaw/arbitration_law_in_bangladesh

77 Guidelines to Fill in the Banking Statistics Returns SBS—1, 2 & 3 (fourth edition)

78 http://en.wikipedia.org/wiki/Public_services

79 http://www.boi-mela.com/banglapedia/ViewArticle.asp?TopicRef=4191

80 http://www.bangladeshgateway.org/ngo.php

81 www.citehr.com

82 http://www.netmba.com/mgmt/ob/motivation/mcgregor/Page 41

83

84   http://en.wikipedia.org/wiki/Goal-setting_theory

85   http://changingminds.org/disciplines/leadership/theories/behavioral_theory.htm

86   http://en.wikipedia.org/wiki/Total_Quality_Management

87   Contact person: Mr.Zaman, General Manager, Sardar Apparels

88   Contact person: Mr. Rakib M. Bhuiyan, Marketing Services Manager, UniMed & UniHealth Manufacturers

89   Contact person: Mr. Asheque al Mahmub, AGM, Structural Engineers Ltd.

90   Ministry of Textile and Jute, Govt. of the People's Republic of Bangladesh

91   http://www.scribd.com/doc/7127363/HRM-Practice-of-Square-Textile-LTD

92   Universal Declaration of Human Rights 1948, Article 23(4).

93   Ahmad, K. (1978). *Labor Movement in Bangladesh*. Dhaka: Inside library

94   Khan, A.A. (2000), *Trade Union Movement*. Banglapedia

95   Hoque, M.M. (2007). Trade Union Movement in Bangladesh. Unpublished researchpaper. IBA, DU

96   Khan, A. A., Labor and Industrial Law

97   Khan, A. A., History of Trade Union.

98   Industrial Relations Ordinance 1969, Section 3.

99   Industrial Relations Ordinance 1969, Section 20.

100 Industrial Relations Ordinance 1969, Section 22.

101 Constitution of the People's Republic of Bangladesh, Article 34(1).

102 Employment of Labor (standing order) Act 1965, Section 9.

103 Employment of Labor (standing order) Act 1965, Section 14.

104 Payment of Wages Act 1936, Section 3.

105 Workmen's Compensation Act 1923, Section 11.

106 Factories Act 1965, Section 58.

107 Constitution of the People's Republic of Bangladesh, Article 38.

108 Employment of Labor (standing order) Act 1965, Section 17 (1) (b).

109 Vaydyanathan. N, ILO Standards for Social Justice and Development of Labour, Deep & Deep Publications, New Delhi, 1992, 29.

110 BILS (2005). Trade Union Memberships (June 2005)

111 Asaduzzaman, M. (2007). Trade union movement of Bangladesh from 1971 to 1990. Unpublished Research Paper, IBA, DU

112 Director of Labor

113 Farnham, D. & Pinlott, J. "Understanding Industrial Relations" Casell, London

114

115 Geen, R. (1994). Human motivation: A psychological approach. Wadsworth Publishing.

116 Oxford English Dictionary, 2nd Edition

117 Maslow, Motivation and Personality, p. 66.

118 Farnham, David and John Pimlott. Understanding Industrial Relations. 5th ed. London: Cassel. p. 45

119 Green, G D. Industrial Relations. 2nd ed. Great Britain: Pitman Publishing, 1987. p. 5.

120 Goodman, John F. Employment Relations in Industrial Society. Oxford: Philip Allan Publishers Ltd., 1984. p. 63.

121 Cox, Robert W., Jeffrey Harrod, et. al. Future Industrial Relations: An Interim Report. Geneva: ILO, 1972. p. 7.

122 Farnham,D. and Pimlott, J., Understanding Industrial Relations, 5th edition, Cassell, London

123 http://en.wikipedia.org/wiki/Conflict_theory

124 http://en.wikipedia.org/wiki/Conflict_theory

125 Farnham,D. and Pimlott, J., Understanding Industrial Relations, 5th edition, Cassell, London

126 www.banglapedia.search.com.bd

127 www.banglapedia.search.com.bd

128 Official Website of Bangladesh Institute of Labour Studies (BILS)

129 Official Website of Bangladesh Institute of Labour Studies (BILS)

130 Department of Labour, Government of Bangladesh, 1997

131 Department of Labor, Government of Bangladesh, 2007. Bangladesh

132 Ratnam, C.S.V. and Naidu. D.P.A. 1999. Industrial Relations and Collective Bargaining in South Asia - Trade Union Perspective. Pp. 2-39

133 Department of Labor, Government of Bangladesh, 1997.

134 Ahmed, S. Country Report - Bangladesh.

135 Sub regional Report on India, Bangladesh, Pakistan, Srilanka and Nepal

136 Official website of Board of Investment, Bangladesh - Investor's Guide - Human Resources & Employment

137 Ibid.

138 Ibid.

139 http://en.wikipedia.org/wiki/Pluralism_%28political_philosophy%29

140 Official website of Ministry of Labor and Employment

141 http://survey07.ituc-csi.org/getcountry.php? IDCountry=BGD&IDLang=EN

142 Official Website of Bangladesh Institute of Labour Studies (BILS)

143 http://www.pinr.com/report.php?ac=view_report&report_id=500&language_id=1

144 Weber, W. 1896. Economy and Society. vol. 1, Bedminister Press, New York. p.4

145 Silverman, D. 1970. The Theory of organizations. Heinemann, London. p. 141

146 Kirkbride, P. 1977. Industrial Relations Theory and Research. Management Decision. vol.17 (4). p. 333.

147 Silverman, op. cit. p.137

148 Understanding Industrial Relations by D. Farnham and J. Pimlott)

149 Ibid. p. 142

150 Hyman, R. 1977. Strikes. Fontana, London. p. 72.

151 Jackson, M.P. 1982. Industrial Relations (2nd ed.). Croom Helm, London, p. 27

152 Ackroyd, S. 1971. Economic Rationality and the relevance of Weberian sociology to Industrial Relations. British Journal of Industrial relations, vol. IX (2). p. 236

153 Goldthorpe, J.H., Lockwood, D., et al. 1968. The Affluent Worker; Industrial Attitudes and Behavior. Cambridge University Press, London. P. 184

154 Ibid, p. 141

155 Silverman, D. 1970. The Theory of organizations. Heinemann, London. P. 141

156 Ibid. p. 141

157 Goldthorpe, J.H., et al., op. cit

158 Ibid. pp. 177-8

159 Bowey, A.M. 1975. Themes in the Industrial society. Industrial relations journal, vol. 6 (2). pp. 57-63

160 Brown, R. 1973. Man and Organization. J. Child (ed.), Allen & Unwin, London

161 Qouted by Bowey, op. cit., p. 58.

162 Silverman, D. and Jones, J. J. Child (ed.), op. cit

163 Eldridge, J.E.T. 1971. Sociology and Industrial Life. Nelson, London. pp. 44-45

164 Bendix, R. 1965. The comparative Analysis of historical change

165 Banks, op. cit

166 Hyman, R. 1972. Strikes. Fontana, London. p. 72

167 See Banks, op. cit.

168 Planning for Industrial Relations Management edited by J.L. Rastogi, et al.

169 Mr. Kabir Ahmed Chowdhury, Deputy Director (Labour), Directorate of Labour. Government of Bangladesh.

170 Burawoy, M. (1985). The Politics of Production. Factory Regimes Under Capitalism and Socialism, Verso, London

171 Kochan, T. H., Katz, H. C., and McKersie, R. B. (1986). The Transformation of American Industrial Relations, Basic Books, New York

172 Archer, M. S. (1995). Realist Social Theory: The Morphogenetic Approach, University Press

173 Coleman, J. S. (1990). Foundations of Social Theory, Harvard University Press, Cambridge, MA.

174 Social Justice Research, Vol. 15, No. 3, September 2002.

175 Eagley, A. H., and Chaiken, S. (1993). The Psychology of Attitudes, Hartcourt Brace College, FortWorth, TX

176 Kluegel, J. R., Mason, D., and Wegener, B. (eds.) (1995). Social Justice and Political

177 Schooler, C. (1996). Cultural and social-structural explanations of cross-national psychological differences

178 Siddique, Shafique Ahmed, and Akkas, M.A., "The Role of State and Industrial Relations System in Banglades", Journal of Business Studies, Vol XXIV, No. 1, June 2003

179 Dunlop, J. D.: Industrial Relations Systems, Carbondale, (Edwardswille, 1958) p. 8

180 Yoder, D.: Personnel Management and Industrial Relations, 3rd Ed., (New York, 1949) p. 6.

181 Fürstenberg, F.: Industrial Relations, Wörterbuch der Soziologie, Bernsdorf, W. (Ed.), (Stuttgart, 1969)

182 T.vlasova. "Marxist-Leninist Philosophy." Progress publisher (1987)

183 T.vlasova. "Marxist-Leninist Philosophy." Progress publisher (1987)

184 T.vlasova.s "Marxist-Leninist Philosophy." Progress publisher (1987)

185 Marxist-Leninist Philosophy, by T.Vlasova, 1987, page 116

186 T.vlasova. "Marxist-Leninist Philosophy." Progress publisher (1987)

187 Marxist-Leninist Philosophy, by T.Vlasova, 1987, (page 122)

188 6 T.vlasova. "Marxist-Leninist Philosophy." Progress publisher (1987)

189 Islam, Nurul. "Development Planning In Bangladesh- a study in political economy". University press limited (1993).

190 Islam, Nurul. "Development Planning In Bangladesh- a study in political economy". University press limited (1993).

191 islam, Nurul. "Development Planning In Bangladesh- a study in political economy". University press limited (1993).

192 Wieler, A. (2004) "Quality in industrial relations: Comparative indicators" European Foundation for the Improvement of Living and Working Conditions

193 Edwards, P. (2004) "The employment relationship and the field of industrial relations

194 Farnham, D. & Pinlott, J. "Understanding Industrial Relations" Casell, London

195   Rose, J B & Chaison, G N (1985) 'The State of the Unions: United States and Canada', Journal of Labor Research, 6(1), Winter, 97-111.

196   Storey, J. 1992: Developments in the Management of Human Resources. Oxford: Blackwell.

197   Redman, T., and Wilkinson, A. (eds) 2001: Contemporary Human Resource Management.London: Financial Times/Prentice Hall.

198   Clegg, H. A. 1979: The Changing System of Industrial Relations in Great Britain. Oxford: Blackwell.

199   Flanders, A. 1970: Management and Unions. London: Faber & Faber.

200   Weber, M. (1930). The Protestant ethic and the spirit of capitalism. New York: Routledge.

201   Edwards, P. (2004) "The employment relationship and the field of industrial relations

202   Hofstede, G. 1984. Culture's consequences: International differences in work-related values, Sage, London.

203   Triandis, H (2001) 'Individualism-collectivism and personality', Journal of Personality, 69(6), December, 908-924.

204   Putnam, R D (1995) 'Bowling alone: America's declining social capital', Journal of Democracy, 6(1), January, 65-78.

205   (2000) Bowling Alone: The Collapse and Revival of American Community, Simon & Schuster, New York.

206   (1996) 'The strange disappearance of Civic America', The American Prospect, 7(24), 1 December.

207   Earley, P C & Gibson, C (1998) 'Taking Stock in our progress on individualism-collectivism: 100 years of solidarity and community', Journal of Management, 24(3), 265-304.

208   Ilmonen, K and Jokivuori, P (2000) 'Post-industrial Society? The Internal Division of the Finnish trade union movement in the 1990s', Work, Employment & Society, 14(1), 137-157,

209   Jarley, P. and N. Johnson (2003) Unions as social capital. Paper presented at the 13th World Congress of the International Industrial Relations Association, Berlin, September.

210   Bailey, J & Brown, K (2004) 'Unions and Social Capital', in M Barry & P Brosnan (eds) New Economies: New Directions, Proceedings of 18th AIRAANZ conference, Volume 1: Refereed Papers, Noosa, http://www.gu.edu.au/school/irl/ airaanz2004/ Papers/Bailey,Brown_018.pdf

211   Isaac, J E (1958) 'The prospects for collective bargaining in Australia', Economic Record, December, 347-61; reprinted in A Flanders (ed) Collective Bargaining: Selected Readings, Penguin, Harmondsworth, 1969, 93-211.

212   Flanders, A (1970) Management and Unions, Faber, London.

213   Webb, S & Webb, B (1920) The History of Trade Unionism, Revised edition, Longmans, London.

214   Brown, W. A., S. Deakin, M. Hudson, C. Pratten, and P. Ryan (1998) The Individualisation of Employment Contracts in Britain, Employment Relations Research Series No 4, Department of Trade and Industry, London.

215   Storey, J & Bacon, N (1993) 'Individualism and collectivism: into the 1990s', International Journal of Human Resource Management, 4(3), September, 665-684.

216   Schein, E H (1996) 'Culture: The Missing Concept in Organisation Studies', Administrative Science Quarterly, 41(2), June, 229-40.

217   Ahmed, S. (2004) "Country report Bangladesh" Jatio Sramik League

218   Ahmed, S. (2004) "Country report Bangladesh" Jatio Sramil League

219   Alauddin and Tisdell, 1987

220   Alauddin and Tisdell, 1991

221   Alauddin and Tisdell, 1991; Hossain, 1989

222   Kabir Ahmed Chowdhury

223   Sen 1975

[224] Tanweer Akram

[225] Policy Paper 0807 (Bangladesh Bank)

[226] Tanweer Akram

[227] Policy Paper 0807 (Bangladesh Bank)

[228] Kabir Ahmed Choudhury, 1979

[229] Islam, 1977; Sobhan and Ahmad, 1980

[230] Kabir Ahmed Choudhury, 1979

[231] http://www.ide-jetro.jp/English/Publish/Periodicals/De/pdf/83_02_03.pdf

[232] http://www.unescap.org/pdd/publications/adpj_11_2/7_kochanek.pdf

[233] http://www.nationsencyclopedia.com/Asia-and-Oceania/Bangladesh-FOREIGN-INVESTMENT.htm

[234] http://www.innovation.cc/peer-reviewed/momen_privatization4e.pdf

[235] http://www.country-data.com/cgi-bin/query/r-1089.html

[236] J. Kelly, Rethinking Industrial Relations: Mobilization, Collectivism and Long Waves, Routledge, London, 1998.

[237] Bassett and Cave 1993; Brown 1990; Cave 1994; Valkenburg and Zoll 1995

[238] Cox. Robert., et. al. Part 1 (Varities of Industrial Relations Systems) - Future Industrial Relations An Interim Report, ILS, Geneva, 1972.

[239] Bangladesh Statistical Yearbook 2007, Labor Force Survey 2005-06

[240] Labor Force Survey 2005-06

[241] http://training.itcilo.it/actrav/courses/2005/A3-00398_web/work/report/Nargis_BJSD.doc

[242] http://www.mole.gov.bd/upload_files/annual%20report/Barsik_Protibedon_2004.doc

[243] http://www.bgw-info.net/DMS/member/files/women%20issue/trade_unions,_gender_issues.pdf

[244] http://www.mole.gov.bd/upload_files/annual%20report/Bangladesh_Labour_Journal_p22.doc

[6] http://banglapedia.search.com.bd/HT/T_0206.htm

[7] The Practice of Industrial Relations By David A. Peach and David Kuechle

[8] http://www.nadir.org/nadir/initiativ/agp/s26/banglad/index.htm#council

[9] Bangladesh Labour Journal, 2006

[11] Bangladesh Labor Journal, 2002

[10] Labor Management in Bangladesh by Kamruddin Ahmad.

[11] Industrial Relations By Dr. M. A. Taher

[245] Annex-A: Ministry of Labor and Employment Charter of Duties (officers)

[246] Asia-Pacific Trade and Investment Review Vol. 1, No. 1, April 2005 Least Developed Countries in Trade Negotiations: Planning Process and Information Needs

[247] Assessment Research of A Trade Union Training Program In Health And Safety. www.interfacehs.sp.senac.br/./translations.asp

[248] www.simpsonmillar.co.uk/./tradeunion/tradeunions.aspx

[249] www.Industrialrelation.com

[250] Constitution of Bangladesh Parishangkhan Bureau Shangsthpan Karmachari Kallyan Shamiti

[251] Constitution of Bangladesh Choturtha Sreni Sharkari Karmachari Shamiti

[252] www.cleanclothes.org/./160-demonstration-for-fair-wage-a-fair-trade-bangladesh -

[253] http://www.fbcci-bd.org/about_fbcci/about.html

[254] http://www.ioe-emp.org/en/members regions/index.html?tx_gsifeuserlist_pi1%5BshowUid%5D=10

255 http://www.dhakachamber.com/aboutUs/index.asp

256 http://www.dhakachamber.com/aboutUs/services.asp

257 http://www.dhakachamber.com/aboutUs/success_stories.asp

258 http://bgmea.com.bd/index.php?option=com_content&task=view&id=12&Itemid=35

259 http://www.lfmeab.org

260   www.industrialreations.com, copyright 2007)

261 Wikpedia: http://en.wikipedia.org/wiki/Strike_action)

262 ILO: http://www.ilo.org/wcmsp5/groups/public/---ed_norm/---normes/documents/publication/ wcms_087987.pdf)

263 Barron's Legal Guides Law Dictionary by Steven H. Gifis, (1996)